NEW TESTAMENT V

D1244496

ACTS

EDITED BY

FRANCIS MARTIN

IN COLLABORATION WITH
EVAN SMITH

GENERAL EDITOR

THOMAS C. ODEN

IVP Academic

An imprint of InterVarsity Press
Downers Grove, Illinois

InterVarsity Press
P.O. Box 1400, Downers Grove, IL 60515-1426
ivpress.com
email@ivpress.com

©2006 by the Institute of Classical Christian Studies (ICCS), Thomas C. Oden and Francis Martin

All rights reserved. No part of this book may be reproduced in any form without written permission from InterVarsity Press.

InterVarsity Press® is the book-publishing division of InterVarsity Christian Fellowship/USA®, a movement of students and faculty active on campus at hundreds of universities, colleges, and schools of nursing in the United States of America, and a member movement of the International Fellowship of Evangelical Students. For information about local and regional activities, visit intervarsity.org.

Scripture quotations, unless otherwise noted, are from the Revised Standard Version of the Bible, copyright 1946, 1952, 1971 by the Division of Christian Education of the National Council of the Churches of Christ in the U.S.A., and are used by permission.

Selected excerpts from Fathers of the Church: A New Translation, ©1947. Used by permission of The Catholic University of America Press, Washington, D.C. Full bibliographic information on volumes of Fathers of the Church may be found in the Bibliography of works in English Translation.

Selected excerpts from The Venerable Bede, Commentary on the Acts of the Apostles, translated by Lawrence Martin and David Hurst, Cistercian Studies Series 117, ©1989. Used by permission of Cistercian Publications, Kalamazoo, Michigan. All rights reserved.

Selected excerpts from Gregory of Nyssa, The Life of Moses, The Classics of Western Spirituality, ©1978. Used by permission of Paulist Press, Mahwah, New Jersey, <www.paulistpress.com>.

Selected excerpts from The Works of Saint Augustine: A Translation for the 21st Century, ©1990-. Used by permission of the Augustinian Heritage Institute, Ardmore, Pennsylvania.

Selected excerpts from Arator's On the Acts of the Apostles, edited by Richard Shrader, ©1987. Used by permission of the American Academy of Religion.

Selected excerpts from Origen, Contra Celsum, translated with an introduction and notes by Henry Chadwick, ©1953. Reprinted with the permission of Cambridge University Press.

Cover design: David Fassett
Images: gold texture background: © Katsumi Murouchi / Getty Images
   stained glass cathedral window: © elzauer / Getty Images
   gold texture: © Katsumi Murouchi / Getty Images
   abstract marble pattern: © NK08gerd / iStock / Getty Images Plus

ISBN 978-0-8308-4357-2 (paperback)
ISBN 978-0-8308-1490-9 (hardcover)
ISBN 978-0-8308-9747-6 (digital)

Printed in the United States of America ∞

InterVarsity Press is committed to ecological stewardship and to the conservation of natural resources in all our operations. This book was printed using sustainably sourced paper.

Library of Congress Cataloging-in-Publication Data
A catalog record for this book is available from the Library of Congress.

P 32 31 30 29 28 27 26 25 24 23 22 21 20 19 18 17 16 15 14 13 12 11 10 9 8 7 6 5 4 3 2 1

Y 47 46 45 44 43 42 41 40 39 38 37 36 35 34 33 32 31 30 29 28 27 26 25 24 23 22 21 20 19

Contents

ANCIENT CHRISTIAN COMMENTARY
PROJECT RESEARCH TEAM

GENERAL EDITOR
Thomas C. Oden

ASSOCIATE EDITOR
Christopher A. Hall

OPERATIONS MANAGER AND
TRANSLATIONS PROJECT COORDINATOR
Joel Elowsky

RESEARCH AND ACQUISITIONS DIRECTOR
Michael Glerup

EDITORIAL SERVICES DIRECTOR
Warren Calhoun Robertson

ORIGINAL LANGUAGE VERSION DIRECTOR
Konstantin Gavrilkin

GRADUATE RESEARCH ASSISTANTS

Steve Finlan	*Alexei Khamine*
Vladimir Kharlamov	*Grant Gieseke*
Kevin M. Lowe	*Baek-Yong Sung*
Jeffery Wittung	

ADMINISTRATIVE ASSISTANT
Judy Cincotta

Introduction to the Acts of the Apostles

The purpose of this introduction is threefold: to provide the reader with a general sense of what is written in the book of Acts, leaving to the modern commentaries the task of providing more detailed information; to give an overview of the patristic material available in regard to Acts and provide some remarks to aid the reader in bridging the gap between these ancient authors and ourselves; and to give an account of how this material was selected and edited. We will begin with some remarks on the book of Acts itself.

The Nature of the Work

That the author begins this volume with a reference to a "first book" and dedicates this book as well to Theophilus makes it clear, if style, theology and other considerations were not enough, that what we call The Acts of the Apostles is intended by the author of the Gospel of Luke to be a sequel. It is significant that these same opening lines speak of the first work as having to do with "all that Jesus *began* to do and to teach." The second volume, then, is a continuation of the story of the activity of Jesus, but now, at least after the ascension (Acts 1:9-12), this activity is from heaven and is part of the divine activity attributed at times also to the Father and the Spirit.

In this light our designation of the work as The Acts of the Apostles can be misleading and make us think of Hellenistic writings of the same period that recount the acts of famous men. We might bear in mind as well that of the four most prominent figures in the book, Peter, Paul, Barnabas and Stephen, Paul and Barnabas are called "apostles" only twice (Acts 14:4, 14), Stephen is never so designated, and Peter, either implicitly or explicitly, is frequently called an apostle as member and leader of the authoritative body ("the Twelve") whose directive role is not mentioned until Acts 16:4, and then the term "apostle" no longer occurs in this book.

The Story of the Church

It is clear that from beginning to end Luke intends to tell the story of the manner in which the church was assembled and grew as a result of divine activity.[1] It is equally clear that the God who forms, guides and empowers the church is the God of Israel. Thus, through the ignorance of the leaders and the people, "what

---

[1] For a more extended account of what follows here see Beverly Roberts Gaventa, *The Acts of the Apostles*, Abingdon New Testament Commentaries (Nashville: Abingdon, 2003).

God foretold by the mouth of all the prophets, that his Christ should suffer, he thus fulfilled" (Acts 3:18). The fact that Jesus is the fulfillment of God's word to Israel is made clear by the number of texts from Israel's Scriptures that are adduced or alluded to throughout Acts, especially in the earlier sections, as well as in the long accounts of Israel's history given in the speeches of Stephen (Acts 7:1-53) and Paul (Acts 13:16-41). Again, Peter tells his audience in Cornelius's house that they doubtless have heard "how God anointed Jesus of Nazareth with the Holy Spirit and with power; how he went about doing good and healing all that were oppressed by the devil, for God was with him." And now this same God "has commanded us to preach to the people, and to testify that he is the one ordained by God to be judge of the living and the dead. To him all the prophets bear witness that every one who believes in him receives forgiveness of sins through his name" (Acts 10:38, 42-43). What is different in Luke's account is that this divine activity is attributed to the Holy Spirit throughout the narrative as well as to Jesus. Significant, for instance, is the interesting double description of the Spirit in Acts 16:6-7 as alternately "the Holy Spirit" and "the Spirit of Jesus" (see Phil 1:19).

Israel and the Gentiles

There is almost universal consensus that, for Luke, the most significant turning point in God's direction of the church occurs with the inclusion of the Gentiles within the call to salvation.[2] This he recounts in his narrative of the action of the Holy Spirit in Acts 10:1—11:18 as a prelude to his description of the "church" already in Antioch (Acts 13:1), the call of the Holy Spirit to separate Barnabas and Saul "for the work to which I have called them" (Acts 13:2), the subsequent mission to the Gentiles and finally the meeting in Jerusalem (Acts 15:1-31). In the account of the preaching at Pisidian Antioch, Paul and Barnabas respond to the opposition of the Jews by announcing, "It was necessary that the word of God should be spoken first to you. Since you thrust it from you, and judge yourselves unworthy of eternal life, behold, we turn to the Gentiles" (Acts 13:46). This seems to refer to a rhythm rather than announce a rejection (see for instance Acts 3:26), since Paul continues to address himself to Jews (Acts 18:4-5) even after repeating this principle for a second time (Acts 18:6; see 18:19; 19:8; 28:17). The criterion for Paul's action is not only Jewish rejection but also Paul's vocation as given to him by the risen Jesus (Acts 9:15), nor can we forget Paul's description of "what the prophets and Moses said would come to pass: that the Christ must suffer, and that, by being the first to rise from the dead, he would proclaim light both to the people and to the Gentiles" (Acts 26:22-23).

In the final scene of the book of Acts (Acts 28:23-31), after calling "the local leaders of the Jews," Paul explains to them that "it is because of the hope of Israel that I am bound with this chain" and proceeds to speak with them "from morning till evening." "Some were convinced by what he said, while others disbelieved." They thus disagreed among themselves and departed after Luke has Paul cite Isaiah 6:9-10 as the words of the Holy Spirit[3] and announce one more time, "Let it be known to you then that this salvation of God has been sent to the Gentiles; they will listen." With a brief notice concerning Paul's ongoing activity,

---

[2]For a good discussion of this event in the early centuries, with attention to modern commentators, see François Bovon, *De Vocatione Gentium: Histoire de L'Intrepretation d'Act 10:1–11:18 dans les Six Premiers Siècles*, Beiträge Zur Geschichte Der Biblischen Exegese 8 (Tübingen: J. C. B. Mohr, 1967).

[3]This text can be found frequently in the New Testament when reflecting on Jewish unbelief: Lk 8:10; Mk 4:12; 8:17-18; Mt 13:14-15; Rom 11:8; Jn 12:39-40.

Luke ends his narrative in a way that shows that the story will continue.

Numerous efforts have been made to assess Luke's final word about God's relation to the Jews. Most reflect the prevailing *Zeitgeist* of the interpreter's own milieu.[4] This is not surprising, since the best that can be said is that Luke, in common with the rest of the New Testament, seems to leave the question unresolved and is thus ambiguous about what Paul calls "this mystery," which includes the fact that "a hardening has come upon part of Israel, until the full number of the Gentiles come in, and so all Israel will be saved; as it is written, 'The Deliverer will come from Zion, he will banish ungodliness from Jacob'" (Rom 11:25-26).[5] Among many Christians the recognition of this ambiguity has been slow in coming; the Shoah finally showed to Christians to what uses their often one-sided interpretation of the New Testament can be put.[6] Number 4 of *Nostra Aetate* began a new life for Christian, especially Catholic, relations with the Jewish people and reestablished the fact that part of the ambiguity is to be found in the impenetrable designs of God: salvation for all is in Christ and his church; yet God still has a special relation to his people Israel. Another way of expressing current understanding of this mystery was uttered by John Paul II in his address in the synagogue at Mainz in November 1980:

"The encounter between the people of God of the Old Covenant, *which has never been revoked by God* (cf. Rom 11:29), and that of the New Covenant is also an *internal* dialogue in our church, similar to that between the first and second part of its Bible."[7]

The Narrative Flow and the Speeches in Acts

Commentators tend most often to view the movement of the narrative either as tracing the apostolic witness "in Jerusalem and in all Judea and Samaria and to the end of the earth" (Acts 1:8) or as successive accounts of the ministry of Peter (Acts 1—12) and Paul (Acts 13—28). Both of these opinions have a basis in the text. However, if we look to Luke's accent on the divine activity we may see the movement as being one that builds and extends the church first among Jews and then among Gentiles. This would explain Luke's threefold account of Paul's abrupt and life-changing meeting with Jesus, who identifies himself in all three accounts with his church and traces out Paul's vocation (Acts 9:1-12 [third person]; 22:3-21; 26:2-23 [both in the first person]) coupled with the twofold narration of the action of the Holy Spirit in bringing Cornelius and his household to faith (Acts 10:1-48 [third person]; 11:3-18 [first person]).

So far, most commentators would agree. However, when one begins to look at the architecture of Acts, that is, its actual parts and their interrelation, there is little agreement. It may be that what Jacques Dupont calls "overlapping" or "interweaving"[8] provides some help, since a work of literature does not have the

---

[4]See Joseph B. Tyson, *Luke, Judaism and the Scholars* (Columbia: University of South Carolina Press, 1999).

[5]For a slightly different translation and a good treatment of this verse, see Joseph Fitzmyer, *Romans: A New Translation with Introduction and Commentary*, Anchor Bible 33 (New York: Doubleday, 1992), 621-25.

[6]In assessing the remarks of the New Testament and the Fathers, some account must be taken of the style of polemics, something affecting both sides, of that day. See Luke Timothy Johnson, "The New Testament's Anti-Jewish Slander and the Convention of Ancient Polemic," *Journal of Biblical Literature* 108 (1989): 419-41.

[7]Eugene J. Fisher and Leon Klenicki, eds., *Spiritual Pilgrimage: Texts on Jews and Judaism 1979-1995: Pope John Paul II* (New York: Crossroad, 1995), 13 (a slightly different translation; first italics added).

[8]"Entrelacemenent." See Jacques Dupont, "La Question du Plan des Actes des Apôtres à la Lumière d'un Texte de Lucien de Samasote," *Novum Testmentum* 21 (1979): 220-31.

clearly delineated parts of a building. In any event, it is clear that the basic flow of the narrative is one in which Luke traces how Jesus Christ changed a Jewish persecutor into a preacher of the gospel and the principal apostle to the Gentiles and how the Holy Spirit presided over the process by which the first Gentiles came into the church.

It is also important in appreciating the nature of Luke's narrative to understand the role of the speeches.[9] In their present form they are Lukan compositions based on sources, one of which may be his own notes. In addition to catechizing the reader, these speeches, as all discourse in ancient times, were considered first and foremost as events and as such were subject to the same laws of interpretive narrative as other actions.[10] Not only in the actual fact of history but also in the world of the narrative, these speeches, especially those by Peter, Paul and Stephen, are events that serve to move along the action of the narrative, and as such they receive a Lukan stamp and interpretive manner of telling them. For the ancients, both speakers and writers, rhetoric "was power and speech was a type of action."[11] This seems to have been taken for granted by the ancient interpreters on Acts with the occasional exception of Chrysostom. While they seem to appreciate the book of Acts as a story of God's activity, they most often comment on the speeches as they find them without attending to their role as part of the narrative.

The Patristic Commentaries on Acts

By a careful combing of the extant patristic literature, Paul Stuehrenberg was able to identify forty authors who had something to say about Acts in the first eight centuries of the church.[12] Unfortunately thirty-seven of these authors are represented only by fragments of lost commentaries or remarks made on incidents in Acts. The only complete commentaries are those by John Chrysostom (d. 407) and the Venerable Bede (d. 735), and there is as well a long Latin epic poem by Arator (d. 550), a subdeacon of Rome, consisting of 2,326 hexameters and covering the whole book.[13] Its relevance to our purposes is minimal. We cite him once in a while to give the reader an idea of the culture of that time as well as examples of a rather consistent anti-Semitism. In order to complete this study, recourse was had to the extant fragments which, for the Greek Fathers, have been conveniently collected by J. A. Cramer[14] and to sermons of the Fathers on the various events recorded in Acts: Pentecost, the martyrdom of Stephen, and so on. In addition to copious material supplied by the editorial board of this series as a result of electronic searches, we also consulted the ever helpful *Biblia Patristica*. Undoubtedly there are omissions and some may question some of our choices,

---

[9]A good precise treatment of this topic can be found in Joseph Fitzmyer, *The Acts of the Apostles: A New Translation with Introduction and Commentary*, Anchor Bible 31 (New York: Doubleday, 1998), 103-8.

[10]For a discussion of this point see Francis Martin, *Narrative Parallels to the New Testament*, SBL Resources for Biblical Study 22 (Atlanta: Scholars Press, 1988). One may also consult Luke's own use of *logos* and *ergon* ("word" and "deed").

[11]Conrad Gempf, "Public Speaking and Published Accounts," in *The Book of Acts in Its Ancient Literary Setting*, ed. Bruce W. Winter and Andrew D. Clarke, vol. 1 of *The Book of Acts in Its First-Century Setting*, 259-304 (Grand Rapids: Eerdmans, 1993). For an extensive treatment of the rhetorical topic of "words and deeds" (often called the *logos-ergon* distinction) in Greek literature from Homer through Thucydides, see the 1957 dissertation of Adam Parry, *Logos and Ergon in Thucydides* (New York: Arno Press, 1981).

[12]Paul F. Stuehrenberg, "The Study of Acts Before the Reformation: A Bibliographic Introduction," *Novum Testamentum* 29, no. 2 (1987): 100-136. The author also consults the unexpanded first edition of Ward Gasque, *A History of the Interpretation of the Acts of the Apostles* (Peabody, Mass.: Hendrickson, 1989).

[13]Arator's *On the Acts of the Apostles (De actibus apostolorum)*, ed. Carl A. Raschke, trans. Richard J. Schrader with Joseph L. Roberts III and John F. Makowski, Arator's, Classics in Religious Studies 6 (Atlanta: Scholars Press, 1987).

[14]J. A. Cramer, *Catena in Acta SS. Apostolorum e Cod. Nov. Coll* (Oxonii: Typographicus Academicus, 1838; reprint, Hildersheim, 1967).

but the collection does give an idea of early thinking about the book of Acts.

The available editions of the principal sources. The principal early source of the collection presented here is, of course, the *Homilies on the Acts of the Apostles* by John Chrysostom. Unfortunately, no critical or even accurate Greek text of the material yet exists. Francis Gignac, S.J., who is preparing a critical edition for the *Corpus Christianorum Series Graeca*, was generous enough to lend us an electronic version of this text. Without him, this volume could not have appeared. Chrysostom's homilies were delivered during Easter season of the year 400. They seem to have been taken down by a stenographer in rough form for eventual polishing by Chrysostom himself, but the tumultuous events of that time in his life probably made this impossible.[15] A smoothed-out version appeared posthumously, and this was eventually combined with the rough version to make still a third rendition. "[A]ll the printed editions of the Greek texts of these homilies provide a mixed text with a preference for the smooth recension."[16] Finally, in the nineteenth century, Henry Browne, entrusted with translating the homilies for the *Oxford Library of the Fathers*, first prepared a Greek text based on the original rough version. The English translation is now found in the NPNF with unfortunate transpositions of sections based on Browne's notion that these were somehow misplaced by the stenographer and later transcribers. There is as well the still further unfortunate fact that Browne never published his Greek text, which is now lost. The result is that, for the sake of reference, we have been obliged to follow the English text in the NPNF with all its warts as the only extant witness to a good Greek text still to make its appearance.

This is the place to mention another challenge facing the collators of commentaries on the book of Acts, namely, that this is the only book in our present Bible for which there are two different and complete textual traditions, known as the Alexandrian and the Western traditions. Commentators are generally agreed that the so-called Western text is a later, probably second-century, expanded version that was known in early Christianity and available to some of the Fathers who thus comment on a text not easily found today. In those rare instances where this makes a difference in the patristic commentaries and remarks cited here, the presence of a Western Text reading is indicated by "WT."[17]

Regarding the other two substantially complete ancient commentaries on Acts we are in a better situation by having a more solid manuscript tradition and modern English translations.[18] As I have already mentioned, many of the fragments of lost commentaries are to be found in the work of Cramer. In regard to patristic passages that are not direct commentaries on Acts, but rather discussions of events or themes recorded there, the textual situation and the available modern translations have already been discussed in this series and will be noted in the course of this collection.

The contribution of the fathers of the church. The primary contribution of the fathers of the church lies in the

---

[15]J. N. D. Kelly, *Golden Mouth: The Story of John Chrysostom, Ascetic, Preacher, Bishop* (Ithaca, N.Y.: Cornell University Press, 1995; reprint, Grand Rapids, Baker, 1998).

[16]Francis T. Gignac, "Evidence for Deliberate Scribal Revision in Chrysostom's *Homilies on the Acts of the Apostles*," in *Nova et Vetera: Patristic Studies in Honor of Thomas Halton*, ed. John Petruccione (Washington, D.C.: Catholic University of America Press, 1998) 209-25.

[17]For an ample discussion of the Western Text problem, see the commentary by Fitzmyer already referred to, as well as that of C. K. Barrett, *A Critical and Exegetical Commentary on the Acts of the Apostles*, vol. 1, International Critical Commentary (Edinburgh: T&T Clark, 1994). For a discussion of the text underlying Chrysostom's homilies see Francis Gignac, "The Text of Acts in Chrysostom's Homilies," *Traditio* 26 (1970): 308-15.

[18]The Venerable Bede, *Commentary on the Acts of the Apostles*, trans. Lawrence T. Martin, CS 117 (Kalamazoo, Mich.: Cistercian Publications, 1989), and Arator's *On the Acts of the Apostles*.

fact that their faith brought them into living and experiential contact with the realities spoken of in the sacred text which they then serve through their often vast learning: thus, they transmit life, they are Fathers.[19] Certain aspects of their thought, which may be termed a biblically enlightened philosophy, facilitated the acquiring and transmitting of this experiential knowledge and promoted what the Vatican II document *Dei Verbum* called "the progress of Tradition," which the document says takes place through study and contemplation, intimate knowledge born of experience and preaching by those entrusted with the task.[20] Many of the Fathers, as bishops, advanced the church's penetration of what had been revealed by and entrusted to the Scriptures in all three of these ways by building on their own contemplation and experience as well as that of many of their faithful. In addition, their manner of speaking, antedating as it does the great controversies in the West in the sixteenth century, can bring us back to a more ecumenical way of speaking and understanding.

Ancient and Modern Approaches

It is important, in a collection of ancient texts in partial form, from a culture different from our own and from *milieux* differing among themselves, that we find a way to enter into this world not only to appreciate it but also in order to integrate this gift from the past into our world. Throughout the course of this commentary we will refer to the opinions and insights of modern scholars. We do this in order to help the reader make an integration of the historically accented modern approach and the theologically accented ancient approach.[21] A few remarks on the weaknesses and strengths of the patristic commentators, as these are found in their commentaries on Acts, will probably prove helpful here.

The shortcomings of the ancient commentators. While the Fathers demonstrate a faith-filled approach to Scripture, a way of reading that is open to it as God's Word both revealing itself to and hiding itself from its readers,[22] their conviction that no historical description is without a moral or mystical meaning can at times look like special pleading.[23] They can use isolated passages of the Scriptures as prooftexts against heresies popular in their day,[24] or in the context of preaching, some, Chrysostom in particular, become more interested in moral exempla to praise or blame, and thus in motivating hearers by pride or shame,[25] than in revealing the mystery for which we all long and which draws us to delight in praising

---

[19]For some recent discussions of the fathers of the church, see Hans Urs von Balthasar, "The Fathers, the Scholastics and Ourselves," *Communio* 24, no. 2 (1997): 347-96; Hans Urs von Balthasar, "Theology and Sanctity," in *Explorations in Theology I: The Word Made Flesh*, 181-210 (San Francisco: Ignatius, 1989); Brian Daley, "Is Patristic Exegesis Still Usable?" *Communio* 29, no. 1 (2000): 185-216.

[20]The text is as follows. "The Tradition which is from the Apostles, makes progress in the church under the guidance of the Holy Spirit. A perception grows of the both the realities and the words which have been handed on, either (1) by the contemplation and study of believers who carry these things in their hearts (see Lk 2:19, 51); or (2) by the intimate understanding of the spiritual realities which they experience; or (3) by the preaching of those who have received through episcopal succession the sure charism of truth. For as the centuries succeed one another, the church constantly moves forward toward the fullness of divine truth until the words of God reach their complete fulfillment in her" (*Dei Verbum*, 8).

[21]A helpful article that traces the need for an integration that includes both approaches is that by Josef Ratzinger [now Pope Benedict XVI], "Biblical Interpretation in Crisis: On the Question of the Foundations and Approaches of Exegesis Today," in *Biblical Interpretation in Crisis: The Ratzinger Conference on Bible and the Church*, ed. Richard John Neuhaus, 1-23, Encounter Series (Grand Rapids: Eerdmans, 1989).

[22]See Origen *Sermon 38, OSF* 106-7.

[23]See, for example, Bede's interpretation of Acts 10:13, "Rise, Peter, kill and eat."

[24]Many of Didymus's comments, though extremely enlightening, come as arguments against a Gnostic group that denied free will and believed in separate classes of humans: a spiritual, saved group and a carnal, damned group. See, for example, his comments at Acts 10:10 and at Acts 20:28a.

[25]For a discussion of shame culture in its classical context, see Bernard Williams, *Shame and Necessity* (Berkeley: University of California Press, 1993).

it.[26] Thus, they sometimes comment on Acts as though it were a Hellenistic biography. In preaching this way, Chrysostom and others were employing techniques of persuasion they had learned in the pagan schools in which history was used to teach morals.[27] In addition—Bede in the eighth century (c. 673-735) is here the primary example—they often adduce these moral lessons by using the expression "the spiritual sense." In the commentary, we tend not to draw attention to an author's rhetoric or to what might annoy a denizen of the twenty-first century; such things are obvious enough. Where clarification of an author's context or of his audience's preoccupations is necessary, we have either given it in the overviews or in a footnote.[28] Our interest has been primarily in showing how the Fathers can help reflect the light of Scripture to us today even though they do belong to and were subject to the horizons of their particular times and places.

The strong points of the Fathers. The most significant strength of the great Fathers, and the reason they continue to give life, is because they were in living and life-giving contact with the divine realities mediated by the sacred text. In addition, their often implicit philosophy shared in the prophetic interpretation of the reality that is inherent in the biblical text. It is about those implicit understandings of reality that we wish to speak now.

Between us and the Fathers, as well as medieval commentators on the Scriptures, stands the towering figure of Immanuel Kant, who summed up and concluded the period known as the Enlightenment and ushered in what is known as modernity. Modernity may be characterized as the search for intelligibility within the confines of a nontranscendent totality. Its successes are with us still, and so are its failures, and these latter are important factors inhibiting the integration we seek. The antitranscendent bias of this period deeply affected three areas of thought that touch directly on biblical studies. The first of these areas may be called foundationalism in the area of knowledge. In epistemology, a foundation is a place to stand; it is a mental acquisition that can form the basis for further thinking, and it is found within the mind, which thus becomes the norm for judging the adequacy of all other reality.[29] In the critical historical study of Scripture this has meant a practical ignoring of the Christian conviction that the sacred text has been authored in some way by God and that it often speaks of realities that are not available to the mind unaided by a special gift of divine light. The modern commentator thus feels the pressure to establish all his conclusions on the basis of what a closed understanding of history can yield to him in much the same way that the positive scientist proceeds within a closed framework established beforehand by principles that he does not question.[30] This latter error was successfully challenged by Michael Polanyi, a

---

[26]See Augustine's famous words, *Confessions* 1.1.1: *tu excitas ut laudare te delectet, quia fecisti nos ad te et inquietum est cor nostrum donec requiescat in te.* "You stir us up so that we delight in praising you, for you have made us for yourself and restless are our hearts until they rest in you" (trans. E. Smith).

[27]As has been said, this is true especially of biography. For more on the nature of ancient historiography and the uses made of history, see the following: Charles W. Fornara, *The Nature of History in Ancient Greece and Rome* (Berkeley: University of California Press, 1983); Jane Chaplin, *Livy's Exemplary History* (Oxford: Oxford University Press, 2000). See also Basil the Great's endorsement of the moral uses of pagan literature in his *Address to Young Men* in *Saint Basil: The Letters*, trans. Roy J. Deferrari, 4 vols. (New York: Putnam and Sons, 1926-1934), 4:363-435; and E. L. Fortin, "Hellenism and Christianity in Basil the Great's Address *Ad Adulescentes*," in *Neoplatonism and Early Christian Thought: Essays in Honor of A. H. Armstrong*, ed. H. J. Blumenthal and R. A. Markus, 189-203 (London: Variorum Publications, 1981).

[28]See, e.g., the discussion of the valuation of manual labor in the overview to Acts 18:1-4.

[29]For an extended discussion of this point I refer the reader to chapter 6 of Francis Martin, *The Feminist Question: Feminist Theology in the Light of Christian Tradition* (Grand Rapids: Eerdmans, 1994).

world-renowned chemist who showed that the error lay not in the undeniable successes of the empirical sciences but in the erroneous way in which scientists attempted to account to themselves for the way the mind functions in acquiring knowledge.[31] In the same way, historians who deal with the biblical text have achieved important advances in our understanding of the context in which the text was composed and thus have added to its intelligibility, but they have unnecessarily closed the world of the text both as a mediator of events and often as a language event itself.[32]

Thus, the second area to be expanded is that of an understanding of temporality.[33] For modern history, time is succession, a dubious and uneven march toward an indeterminate future. The study of history, now capable of genuine reconstruction and insight, records this march. I would propose that we use the term "temporality" rather than "history" or "time" to describe the nature of human existence: temporality includes succession in a vision of eternal presence. I derive this understanding from Augustine, who learned through his conversion and subsequent spiritual experience an understanding of eternity as not being endless changelessness but rather infinite presence. God, the Creator, who is Eternity, is necessarily present in the action of sustaining all that is. Augustine, responding to the opinion that, since God's will to create is eternal, creation itself must be eternal, answers in this manner:

> [If they consider] they would see that in eternity nothing passes, for the whole is present (*sed totum esse praesens*) whereas time cannot be present all at once (*nullum vero tempus totum esse praesens*).[34]

In this deceptively simple presentation we have the way to recover transcendence in regard to human existence. Temporality, the proper mode of creation's existence, is not just succession; it is succession with the dimension of presence. In this sense, *tempus* is intrinsic to creation. "God, in whose eternity there is no change whatsoever, is the creator and director of time . . . the world was not created *in* time but *with time*."[35] To understand, therefore, time as intrinsic to creaturely existence and not an exterior and neutral "container" for the changes of the past and future is to advance toward an understanding of history that includes its mystery. The "mystery" is the eternally present Christological dimension of the events of salvation history as this mystery moves through the succession of "before and after." The meaning is to be found not in the exterior comparison of texts but in the spiritual recognition of the presence of Christ in the Old Testament. Let two patristic texts suffice out of a countless number that could be adduced. "Holy Scripture, in its way of speaking, transcends all other sciences because in one and the same statement while it narrates an

---

[30]Illustrative of this mentality is this text by Rudolf Bultmann, "The historical method includes the presupposition that history is a unity in the sense of a closed continuum of effects in which individual events are connected by the succession of cause and effects. [This continuum] cannot be rent by the interference of supernatural, transcendent powers and that therefore there is no 'miracle' in this sense of the word" (*Existence and Faith: Shorter Writings of Rudolf Bultmann*, ed. Schubert Ogden [New York: Meridian Books, 1960], 291-92. I owe this reference to the more complete discussion in Alvin Plantinga, "Two (or More) Kinds of Scripture Scholarship," *Modern Theology* 14, no. 2 [1998]: 43-77).

[31]For a brief account of Michael Polanyi's thought and its relevance for Christianity, see Avery Dulles, "Faith, Church and God: Insights from Michael Polanyi," *Theological Studies* 45 (1984): 537-50.

[32]"Speeches are not mere commentary on events nor accompaniment to events: they must be seen *as* events in their own right" (Gempf, "Public Speaking and Published Accounts," 261).

[33]The following lines on temporality and history are adapted from a study to be published as part of the Proceedings of the Sacred Heart Seminary Theological Conference held in Washington, D.C., in September 2003 and used here with permission.

[34]Augustine *The Confessions*, ed. John E. Rotelle, trans. Maria Boulding, WSA 1/1 (Hyde Park, N.Y.: New City Press, 1997).

[35]Augustine *De Civitate Dei* 11.6: "*Cum igitur Deus, in cuius aeternitate nulla est omnino mutatio, creator sit temporum et ordinator . . . procul dubio non est mundus factus in tempore sed cum tempore*" (translation is Matthew Lamb's).

event it sets forth the mystery."[36] The two words "event" and "mystery" refer in turn to the literal sense, the event, and then to the same event as it is now seen to have been a participatory anticipation of the mystery of Christ. Augustine has much the same to say; "*In ipso facto* [the event itself], *non solum in dicto* [the text of the Old Testament], *mysterium* [the plan of God revealed in Christ] *requirere debemus.*"[37]

The third area where we are challenged to a retrieval of earlier insights has to do with language itself. One of the most eloquent descriptions of what has gone wrong and what must be recovered comes from George Steiner, who tells us:

> It is this break of the covenant between world and word which constitutes one of the very few genuine revolutions of spirit in Western history and which defines modernity itself.[38]

The covenant between word and world was raised to a unique height in the composing of the sacred Scriptures and then ineffably sealed by the incarnation of the Word himself. Consider this bold statement of Origen, "You are, therefore, to understand the scriptures in this way: as the one perfect body of the Word."[39] The sundering of this covenant has left us ignorant of what Frances Young calls "the sacrament of language," a mode of predication made possible, "[B]ecause the structure of Christian thought revolved around the notion of a transcendent God choosing to accommodate the divine self to the limitations of the human condition in incarnation and Eucharist."[40] The notion that God's mode of relating to us reveals something of the very structure of reality is relevant not only to our understanding of temporality but also to that of language. Words and sentences do not represent reality, they reveal it. The fathers of the church and the medievals (until Ockham) were able to read the Scriptures with their concentration on the realities mediated by the text rather than a "meaning" that can easily become words about words.[41] Their implicit epistemology beckons us to recover their way of receiving a text with courtesy while still respecting the centuries of thought that now intervene.[42]

Finally, we may observe that the Fathers seldom explicitly advert to the "intention of the author" though they are aware of this dimension. In regard to the book of Acts, for instance, we seldom find mention of "Luke" or "Lukan theology" in their writings: they were more aware of what was mediated and paid less attention to the mediating author, and they considered the Scriptures to be a unified whole. Our attention to the author can offer an enrichment if we integrate this with paying attention to what he is talking about and see his work as belonging to the authorship of the people of God as a whole mediated by this one person who shares in the common tradition. Our individualism tends to overlook this aspect of the process of receiving, writing, editing and reception as these were present in the ancient world and particularly in Israel

---

[36]Gregory the Great *Morals on the Book of Job* 20.1 (PL 76:135), *"Sacra Scriptura omnes scientias ipso locutionis suae more transcendit, quia uno eodemque sermone dum narrat gestum, prodit mysterium."*

[37]"We must seek out the mystery, not only in what is said, but in the event itself." *On Psalm 68* (PL 36:858).

[38]George Steiner, *Real Presences* (Chicago: University of Chicago Press, 1989; reprint, paperback, 1991), 93.

[39]Origen Fragment of *A Homily on Jeremiah* (PG 13:544), cited in von Balthasar, *OSF* 88. See also Hugh of St. Victor: "The Word of God comes to man every day, present in the human voice." (*The Word of God* 1.2-3 [SC 155:60]).

[40]Frances Young, *Biblical Exegesis and the Formation of Christian Culture* (Cambridge: Cambridge University Press, 1997), 160.

[41]See once again Steiner, *Real Presences.*

[42]For an excellent example of recovery of the ancient understanding of language that responds to the problems of our own age see Robert Sokolowski, "Semiotics in Husserl's *Logical Investigations,*" in *One Hundred Years of Phenomenology*, ed. D. Zahavi and F. Stjernfelt, 171-83 (Boston: Kluwer Academic Publishers, 2002).

and the church. They were aware of what is called now the analogy of faith, that is, the unity among themselves of the truths revealed in the scriptural tradition.

Acknowledgments

This commentary was composed by me as chief editor and by Evan Smith an invaluable coeditor. The first selections from John Chrysostom, Bede and Arator were made by Ms. Amy Rojek, and the Chrysostom passages finally selected were brought into a more colloquial English on the basis of the Greek text of Chrysostom's homilies supplied to us by Rev. Francis Gignac and Ms. Jie Yuan. Evan Smith's principal task was to complete my initial search for ways of supplying for the lack of commentary material by searching through other patristic material for discussions of the events recorded in Acts and of themes treated therein. His work has been extensive and competent, and it is only just that he be listed as coeditor of this commentary. I am responsible for the final form of the commentary, most of the overviews and the references to modern commentators, as well as this introduction.

It only remains to thank the staff of ACCS for their unfailing help. I would like to mention especially, as many others have done, Michael Glerup and Joel Elowsky along with a hidden battery of graduate students who helped in the collection of texts and their translations. Of course a final word of tribute and thanks goes to Thomas Oden, the originating force behind this important theological, spiritual and ecumenical contribution to Christians everywhere.

THE ACTS
OF THE APOSTLES

1:1-5 THE PROMISE OF THE HOLY SPIRIT

[1]In the first book, O Theophilus, I have dealt with all that Jesus began to do and teach, [2]until the day when he was taken up, after he had given commandment through the Holy Spirit to the apostles whom he had chosen. [3]To them he presented himself alive after his passion by many proofs, appearing to them during forty days, and speaking of the kingdom of God. [4]And while staying[a] with them he charged them not to depart from Jerusalem, but to wait for the promise of the Father, which, he said, "you heard from me, [5]for John baptized with water, but before many days you shall be baptized with the Holy Spirit."

a Or eating

OVERVIEW: In the early chapters of the book of Acts, Luke is intent on demonstrating how those who believe in Jesus form the new people of God. This first chapter is meant to be a preparation for Pentecost, the new formative experience that inaugurates the church. Luke first links the present narrative to his preceding volume (Acts 1:1-2) and then, in five steps, records Jesus' promise of the Holy Spirit (Acts 1:3-5), the discussion about the kingdom and the mission of the apostles (Acts 1:6-8), and Jesus' departure and enthronement (Acts 1:9-11). He follows this with a description of the disciples obeying Jesus and waiting in prayer (Acts 1:12-14) and the reconsti-

tuting of the Twelve with the choice of Matthias (Acts 1:15-26). While the Fathers do not comment at length on the literary approach of Luke, they are sensitive to some of the special functions of this second treatise; for instance, that it narrates the fulfillment of what Christ both did and foretold. They also draw our attention to the rhythm of "doing and saying," mentioned by Luke. They are alert to the significance of Luke's remark that Jesus gave them proofs (*tekmērioi*) of his resurrected reality and are aware that this Lukan account mentions a forty-day period between the resurrection and the ascension not spoken of elsewhere in the Gospels. Finally, they appreciate the fact that Luke mentions the Holy Spirit at the outset of his second book, thus preparing us to see his theology of the church. As Chrysostom observes, Acts tell us what the "other Paraclete" said and did.

1:1 All That Jesus Began to Do and Teach

THE ADVANTAGE OF READING THE SECOND BOOK. CHRYSOSTOM: To many people this book, both its content and its author, is so little known that they are not even aware it exists. I have therefore taken this narrative for my subject, both to initiate those who are ignorant and so that such a treasure shall not remain hidden out of sight. For indeed it will profit us no less than the Gospels themselves, so replete is it with Christian wisdom and sound doctrine, especially in what is said concerning the Holy Spirit. Let us then not pass by it hastily but examine it closely. For here we can see the predictions Christ utters in the Gospels actually come to pass. Truth shines brightly through the facts themselves, and a great change for the better takes place in the disciples now that the Spirit has come upon them. For the words which they heard Christ say—"Anyone who has faith in me will do what I have been doing. He will do even greater things than these"[1]—and the events which he foretold, that they shall be brought before rulers and kings and be scourged in their synagogues, that they shall suffer grievous things and overcome all,[2] that the gospel shall be preached in all the world,[3] all these came to pass in this book exactly as predicted, and many other things which he told them while he was with them. HOMILIES ON THE ACTS OF THE APOSTLES 1.[4]

LOVER OF GOD. BEDE: Theophilus means lover of God or beloved of God. Therefore, anyone who is a lover of God may believe that this work was written for him, because the physician Luke wrote it in order that the reader might find health for his soul. Note also that he says, "all that Jesus began to do and teach," first "do" and then "teach," because Jesus, establishing the pattern of a good teacher, taught nothing except those things which he did. COMMENTARY ON THE ACTS OF THE APOSTLES 1.1.[5]

TEACHING FIRST BY CONDUCT, THEN WORDS. CHRYSOSTOM: Consider how Christ validated his words through actions. "Learn from me," he said, "for I am gentle and humble in heart."[6] He taught us to be poor and demonstrated this through action, for "the Son of man," he says, "has no place to lay his head."[7] Again, he commanded us to love our enemies and taught this lesson on the cross, when he prayed for those who were crucifying him. He said, "If someone wants to sue you and take your tunic, let him have your cloak as well."[8] He gave not only his tunic but also his blood. He bid also the others to teach in this way. Therefore Paul also said, "as you have an example in us."[9] For nothing is more insipid than a teacher who shows his wisdom only in words, since he is then not a teacher but a hypocrite. For this reason, the apostles first taught by their conduct and then by their words. One may even say that they had no need of words, since their deeds spoke loudly. Even Christ's passion may be called action, for in his passion Christ performed that great and wonderful act, by which he destroyed death and effected all else that he did for us. HOMILIES ON THE ACTS OF THE APOSTLES 1.[10]

THE REBUKE OF CONSCIENCE. JEROME: For teaching is put to the blush when a person's conscience rebukes him; and it is in vain that his tongue preaches poverty or teaches almsgiving if he is rolling in the riches of Croesus[11] and if, in spite of his threadbare cloak, he has silken robes at home to save from the moth. LETTER 127.4.[12]

THE SENSE OF ALL. AUGUSTINE: This state-

---

[1]Jn 14:12. [2]Mt 10:18. [3]Mt 24:14. [4]NPNF 1 11:1**. [5]CS 117:9*. [6]Mt 11:29. [7]Mt 8:20. [8]Mt 5:40. [9]Phil 3:17. [10]NPNF 1 11:4**. [11]The final king of Lydia in the west of Asia Minor. He was famous for his wealth. For more, see OCD s.v. "Croesus." [12]NPNF 2 6:254*.

ment teaches us that, previous to this, Luke had written one of those four books of the gospel which are held in the loftiest authority in the church. At the same time, when he tells us that he had composed a treatise of all that Jesus began both to do and teach until the day in which he commissioned the apostles, we are not to take this to mean that he actually has given us a full account in his Gospel of all that Jesus did and said when he lived with his apostles on earth. For that would be contrary to what John affirms when he says that there are also many other things which Jesus did, and if they should all be written down, the world itself could not contain the books.[13] And besides, all agree that many things are narrated by the other Evangelists, which Luke himself does not mention in his history. The sense, therefore, is that he wrote a treatise of all these things to the extent that he made a selection out of the whole mass of materials for his narrative and introduced those facts which he judged fit and suitable to fulfill the duty laid upon him. HARMONY OF THE GOSPELS 4.8.9.[14]

PRACTICE BEFORE YOU PREACH. JOHN CASSIAN: Take care then that you do not rush into teaching before doing, and so be reckoned among the number of those of whom the Lord speaks in the Gospel to the disciples, "So practice and observe whatever they tell you, but not what they do; for they preach but do not practice. They bind heavy burdens, hard to bear, and lay them on men's shoulders; but they themselves will not move them with their finger."[15] CONFERENCE 14.9.[16]

1:2 The Day Christ Was Taken Up

HIS COMMANDMENT. CHRYSOSTOM: What did he command? "Therefore go and make disciples of all nations, baptizing them in the name of the Father and of the Son and of the Holy Spirit, and teaching them to obey everything I have commanded you."[17] Great is the praise of the apostles, when they have been entrusted with such a

charge, that is to say, the salvation of the world. Words full of the Spirit! This he hints at in the expression "through the Holy Spirit." "The words I have spoken to you are spirit,"[18] he said, inducing in the hearer a desire for learning the commandments and establishing the authority of the apostles, since it is the words of the Spirit they are to speak, and the commandments of Christ. HOMILIES ON THE ACTS OF THE APOSTLES 1.[19]

1:3 Appearing During Forty Days

EATING AN EVIDENCE OF HIS HUMANITY. ARATOR: Now, by manifest miracles during forty days in their sight, the Lord confirmed the faith of those whom he bade to be his witnesses to the ends of the earth in its wide boundary. The wonders of creation could not conceal God. What proof [of his real humanity] could the Risen One give so surely as the fact of eating? Human bodies show that they live by this means. About to go to heaven, he went forth to walk round the grove of olive because by its sacred bud it is a place of light and peace. He wished to return [to heaven] from that place, from which the divine fragrance makes agreeable a gleaming person with signed forehead. Since chrism, from the name of Christ, cleanses inwardly those anointed from above, he who will return as victor was raised to the starry firmament and had with him what he had taken on. ON THE ACTS OF THE APOSTLES 1.[20]

HE APPEARED TO THE APOSTLES. CHRYSOSTOM: Why did he not appear to everyone, but only to the apostles? Because he would have seemed a mere apparition to most people, since they did not understand the secret of the mystery. For if even the disciples themselves were at first incredulous and troubled and needed the evidence of actual touch with the hand and of his eating with them, what would have happened to

---

[13]Jn 21:25. [14]NPNF 1 6:230*. [15]Mt 23:3-4. [16]NPNF 2 11:439*. [17]Mt 28:19. [18]Jn 6:63. [19]NPNF 1 11:4**. [20]OAA 26*.

most people? For this reason, it is through the miracles done by the apostles that he renders the evidence of his resurrection unequivocal, so that not only the people of those times, but also all people thereafter, should be certain of the fact that he has risen. For the certainty of the former came from seeing the miracles, while that of everyone else was to be rooted in faith. For this reason, our discussion of the apostles also proceeds from here. For if he did not rise again but remains dead, how did the apostles perform miracles in his name? "They did not perform miracles," some will say. How then was our religion authorized? For certainly they will not disagree with this and argue against what is obvious. Therefore, when they say that no miracles took place, they embarrass themselves more than anyone else. For this would be the greatest miracle of all, if without any miracles the whole world came running to be taken in the nets of twelve poor and illiterate men. For the fishermen prevailed not by wealth of money, nor by cunning of words, nor by any thing else of this kind. Therefore, the unbelievers, though unwilling, will agree that a divine power was present in these men, since no human strength could ever accomplish such great deeds. For this reason then he remained for forty days after the resurrection, giving evidence in this length of time of their seeing him in his own proper person, lest they believe what they saw was a phantom. Indeed, he was not content even with this but added also the evidence of eating at the table. This Luke reveals when he says, "while gathered with them." The apostles themselves also always took this as proof of the resurrection, as when they say, "we who ate and drank with him."[21] HOMILIES ON THE ACTS OF THE APOSTLES 1.[22]

THE FORTY DAYS. BEDE: Now this number [forty] designates this temporal earthly life, either on account of the four seasons of the year or on account of the four winds of the heavens. For after we have been buried in death with Christ through baptism,[23] as though having

passed over the path through the Red Sea, it is necessary for us, in this wilderness, to have the Lord's guidance. May he lead us to the heavenly kingdom and repay us with the denarius of his image. In the presence of the Holy Spirit, may he bless us as by a true jubilee rest.[24] COMMENTARY ON THE ACTS OF THE APOSTLES 1.3.[25]

CONTRARY TO JOHN? AUGUSTINE: It is not meant, however, that they had eaten and drunk with him daily throughout these forty days. For that would be contrary to John's statement, who has interposed the space of eight days, during which he was not seen, and makes his third appearance take place by the sea of Tiberias.[26] At the same time, even although he [should be supposed to have] manifested himself to them with them every day after that period, that would not come into antagonism with anything in the [other] narrative. And, perhaps, this expression, "for the space of forty days," which is equivalent to four times ten and may thus sustain a mystical reference to the whole world or the whole temporal age, has been used just because those first ten days, within which the said eight fall, may not incongruously be reckoned, in accordance with the practice of the Scriptures, on the principle of dealing with the part in general terms as [if it were] the whole. HARMONY OF THE GOSPELS 3.25.84.[27]

1:4 Waiting for the Promise

AN ARMY EQUIPPED. CHRYSOSTOM: "He ordered them not to leave Jerusalem." Why? Just as when soldiers are about to charge a multitude, no one thinks of letting them issue forth until they have armed themselves, or as horses are not allowed to start from the barriers until they have got their charioteer, likewise Christ did not allow

---

[21]Acts 10:41. [22]NPNF 1 11:5**. [23]Rom 6:4. [24]Lev 25:8-19. [25]CS 117:10. [26]For the span of eight days between the first and second appearances, see Jn 20:26-29. For the third appearance, see Jn 21. [27]NPNF 1 6:224**.

them to appear in the field before the descent of the Spirit, so that they would not be easily defeated and taken captive by the many. HOMILIES ON THE ACTS OF THE APOSTLES 1.[28]

THE SPIRIT POURED OUT AFTER THE SON DEPARTED.

CHRYSOSTOM: But why did the Holy Spirit not come to them while Christ was present, rather than immediately after his departure? Instead, although Christ ascended on the fortieth day, the Spirit came to them when the day of Pentecost had come.[29] . . . It was necessary for them to have a longing for the event, and so receive the grace. For this reason Christ himself departed, and then the Spirit came. For if he had been present, they would not have expected the Spirit so earnestly as they did. For this reason he did not come immediately after Christ's ascension, but after eight or nine days. Our desire toward God is most awakened when we stand in need. For this reason, John sent his disciples to Christ at the time when they were to be most in need of Jesus, during his own imprisonment. Besides, it was necessary that our nature should be seen in heaven and that the reconciliation should be perfected, and then the Spirit should come and the joy be unalloyed. For, if Christ had then departed, when the Spirit had already come, and the Spirit remained, the consolation would not have been so great as it was. For indeed they clung to him and could not bear to part with him. To comfort them he said, "It is to your advantage that I go away."[30] For this reason he delayed also for the intervening days, that they, for a while disheartened and standing, as I said, in need of him, might then reap a full and unalloyed joy. . . . For it cannot, it cannot be, that a person should enjoy the benefit of grace unless he is wary. Do you not see what Elijah says to his disciple? "If you see me as I am being taken from you, it will be granted you,"[31] that is, you will have what you ask for. Christ also said everywhere to those who came to him, "Do you believe?" For unless we are made fit for the gift, we do not feel its benefit very much. So it was also in the case of Paul: grace did not

come to him immediately, but three days intervened, during which he was blind, being purified and prepared by fear. For just as the dyers first prepare the cloth that is to receive the dye with other ingredients to prevent the color from fading, likewise in this instance God first prepared the soul so that it was anxiously awaiting and then poured forth his grace. For this reason he did not immediately send the Spirit, but on the fiftieth day. HOMILIES ON THE ACTS OF THE APOSTLES 1.[32]

THE EFFECTS OF THE GIFT OF THE SPIRIT.

HILARY OF POITIERS: He orders them to await the promise of the Father, which has been heard from his mouth. Certainly, the discourse even now[33] is concerned with the promise of his Father. Consequently, the manifestation of the Spirit is through the effects which these powers produce. [Awaiting the promise of the Father,] the gift of the Spirit is not hidden where there is the word of wisdom and where the words of life are heard. The effects of the powers produced by the Spirit are not fully manifest where there is the [rational] perception of the divine knowledge in order that we may not be like the animals, unaware of the author of our life through our ignorance of God, nor even through our faith in God in order that we may not be outside the gospel of God by not believing the gospel of God. The Spirit is not manifested only through the gift of healing in order that by the cure of infirmities we may render testimony to the grace of him who has granted these gifts; or through the performance of miracles in order that the power of God may be recognized in what we are doing; or through prophecy in order that through our knowledge of the doctrine it may be known that we have been taught by God; or through the distinguishing of spirits in order that we may perceive whether anyone speaks through a holy or an evil spirit; or through the various kinds of lan-

---

[28]NPNF 1 11:6**. [29]Acts 2:1-4. [30]Jn 16:7. [31]2 Kings 2:10. [32]NPNF 1 11:6-7**. [33]Acts 1:8.

guages in order that the sermons in these languages may be offered as a sign of the Holy Spirit who has been given; or in the interpretation of the languages in order that the faith of the hearers might not be endangered through ignorance, since the interpreter of a language makes it intelligible for those who are not familiar with the language. Rather it is through all the diversities of these gifts that the effects of the Spirit are poured out for the profit of everyone. ON THE TRINITY 8.30.[34]

1:5 Baptized with the Holy Spirit

THE MANIFOLD WORKINGS OF THE SPIRIT. CHRYSOSTOM: The Gospels, then, are a narrative of what Christ did and said, while the Acts are of what the other[35] Paraclete said and did. Not that the Spirit did not do many things in the Gospels also, just as Christ here in Acts still works in people as he did in the Gospels, but then it was through the temple, while now it is through the apostles. Then the Spirit entered the virgin mother and fashioned the temple, now he enters into the souls of the apostles; then in the likeness of a dove, now in the likeness of fire. Why? There he showed the gentleness of the Lord, but here his also taking vengeance. He reminds them opportunely also of the judgment. For when the need was to forgive sin, there was need of much gentleness; but when we have obtained the gift, it is henceforth a time for judgment and examination. HOMILIES ON THE ACTS OF THE APOSTLES 1.[36]

THE HOLY SPIRIT PRESENT IN THE NAME OF CHRIST. BEDE: When the Lord said, "John indeed baptized with water," he did not continue with "yet you shall baptize" but with "yet you shall be baptized in the Holy Spirit," because neither the apostles nor their followers, who still baptize in the church to this day, had the power to baptize except as John did, that is, with water. However, when the name of Christ is invoked, the interior power of the Holy Spirit is present, which, with the human administration of water, simultaneously purifies the souls and the bodies of those being baptized. This did not happen in the baptism of John—"for the Spirit had not yet been given, since Jesus had not yet been glorified."[37] COMMENTARY ON THE ACTS OF THE APOSTLES 1.5.[38]

PENETRATING GRACE. CYRIL OF JERUSALEM: This grace was not in part, but his power was in full perfection; for as he who plunges into the waters and is baptized is encompassed on all sides by the waters, so were they also baptized completely by the Holy Spirit. The water, however, flows round the outside only, but the Spirit baptizes also the soul within, and that completely. And why do you wonder at this? Take an example from matter, a simple and common example, but one that helps the ordinary person. If the fire passing in through the mass of the iron makes the whole of it fire, so that what was cold becomes burning and what was black is made bright, if fire which is a body thus penetrates and works without hindrance in iron which is also a body, why wonder that the Holy Spirit enters into the very inmost recesses of the soul? CATECHETICAL LECTURE 17.14.[39]

---

[34]FC 25:298-99*. [35]Christ is the first Paraclete: Jn 14:16; 1 Jn 2:1. [36]NPNF 1 11:7**. [37]Jn 7:39. [38]CS 117:11. [39]NPNF 2 7:127-28*.

1:6-11 THE ASCENSION OF JESUS

⁶*So when they had come together, they asked him, "Lord, will you at this time restore the king-dom to Israel?" ⁷He said to them, "It is not for you to know times or seasons which the Father has fixed by his own authority. ⁸But you shall receive power when the Holy Spirit has come upon you; and you shall be my witnesses in Jerusalem and in all Judea and Samaria and to the end of the earth." ⁹And when he had said this, as they were looking on, he was lifted up, and a cloud took him out of their sight. ¹⁰And while they were gazing into heaven as he went, behold, two men stood by them in white robes, ¹¹and said, "Men of Galilee, why do you stand looking into heaven? This Jesus, who was taken up from you into heaven, will come in the same way as you saw him go into heaven."*

OVERVIEW: This passage contains three points: the discussion of the "times and seasons" of the final restoration, the gift of the Holy Spirit with its consequent power to witness and the account of Jesus' ascension. The Fathers examine the fool-ishness of calculating the time of events still to come. They also, like Luke, understand the im-portance of the Holy Spirit's role in empowering the apostles and the whole church to witness. They do not seem, however, to be sensitive to the manner in which Luke announces the structure of his work with the statement that the witness-ing of the apostles will reach "Judea" (Acts 1—7), "Samaria" (Acts 8—12) and the "end of the earth" (Acts 13—28). The teaching that Jesus, in his transformed humanity, is present with the Fa-ther is frequently found in the New Testament.[1] Luke 24:51 and perhaps John 20:17 imply that the ascension took place on Easter day, while the passage in 1 Corinthians 15:3-8 requires a period of time between the resurrection and the ascen-sion. Only Luke, however, specifies the date of the ascension as occurring forty days after the resurrection.[2] The Fathers concentrate more on the fact of the transformed humanity of Christ and his return in that humanity "in the same way" as he went to heaven than on this dilemma, though, as we have seen above, Augustine did note it and applied another method to solve it.

1:6-7 The Time of Restoration

THE FATHER'S AUTHORITY. CHRYSOSTOM: Without saying anything to him of the Holy Spirit, they put this question, "Lord, will you at this time restore the kingdom to Israel?" They did not ask when, but whether it would be at this time, so eager were they to learn the day. But it seems to me they had no clear notion of the nature of that kingdom, for the Spirit had not yet instructed them. . . . For their affections were still formed by sensible objects. They had not yet become better than they were before. Thus from now on they had higher conceptions concerning Christ. Therefore, since their minds were ele-vated, he also speaks to them on a higher level. For he no longer tells them, "Not even the Son knows the day,"[3] but says, "It is not for you to know the times or periods that the Father has set by his own authority." . . . Just as when we see a child crying and stubbornly wishing to take something from us that is not indispensable for him, we hide the thing, show him our empty hands and say, "See, we do not have it." Likewise Christ acted also towards the apostles. And when the child, even after we have shown him our

---

[1]Phil 3:20-21; Eph 4:10; 1 Tim 3:16; Heb 9:11-12; 10:19-21. [2]Acts 1:3. [3]See Mk 13:32.

empty hands, continues to cry, knowing he has been deceived, we leave him with the excuse, "Someone is calling me," and, in our desire to divert him from his first choice, we give him something else, which we tell him is wonderful, and then we hasten away. This is what Christ also did. The disciples asked to have something, and he said he did not have it. And on the first occasion he frightened them. When they asked a second time, again he said he did not have it, except now he did not frighten them, but, after showing his empty hands, he gave them a plausible reason, that "the Father has set it by his own authority." Homilies on the Acts of the Apostles 2.[4]

Respect for the Disciples. Chrysostom: And this he says, because he was very careful to honor them and to conceal nothing from them. Therefore he refers it to his Father, both to make the matter awesome and to dispel further inquiry on what was said. If this were not the reason, but he is ignorant, when will he know? Will he only know at the same time we do? Who would say this? He knows the Father clearly, just as the Father knows the Son.[5] Is he then ignorant of the day? Furthermore, "the Spirit searches everything, even the depth of God."[6] But are we to say that *he* does not even know the time of the judgment? But he knows how he must judge, and he understands the secrets of each. Was he to be ignorant of this, which is much more general? And, if "all things came into being through him, and without him not one thing came into being,"[7] how was he ignorant of the day? For he who made the ages clearly made the times also, and if the times, then also the day. How, then, is he ignorant of what he made? Homilies on the Gospel of Matthew 77.1.[8]

It Is Not for You to Know. Bede: He was telling them that the time of that kingdom is secret, that it is accessible only to the Father's knowledge. And, when he said, "It is not for you to know," he showed them that he himself also

knew (since all things are his which are the Father's), but that it would not be expedient for them, as mortals, to know. Thus, being always uncertain about the coming of the Judge, they should live every day as if the next day they were to be judged.[9] Commentary on the Acts of the Apostles 1.7.[10]

Keeping Watch. Ephrem the Syrian: "It is not for you to know times or seasons." He has hidden that from us so that we might keep watch and that each of us might think that this coming would take place during our life. For, if the time of his coming were to be revealed, his coming would be in vain, and it would not have been desired by the nations and the ages in which it was to take place. He has indeed said that *he will come*, but he did not define when, and thus all generations and ages thirst for him. Commentary on Tatian's Diatessaron.[11]

Why the Son Knows. Hilary of Poitiers: The Son is not lacking in the knowledge of anything that the Father knows, and the Son is not ignorant, because the Father alone knows, since the Father and the Son remain in the unity of the nature. What the Son, in whom all the treasures of wisdom and knowledge are hidden, does not know is in harmony with the divine plan for maintaining silence. The Lord bore testimony to this when he replied to the apostles who had questioned him about the times, "It is not for you to know the times or dates which the Father has fixed by his own authority."

The knowledge is denied them. Not only is it denied, but they are forbidden to be anxious about the knowledge, since it is not for them to know these times. Naturally, after the resurrection, they now interrogate him about the times, since they had been informed previously when they broached the question, that not even the

---

[4]NPNF 1 11:11-12**. [5]Mt 11:27; Jn 10:15. [6]1 Cor 2:10. [7]Jn 1:3. [8]NPNF 1 10:463**. [9]Jerome *Commentary on Matthew* 4.24.36 (CCL 77:232). [10]CS 117:12. [11]ECTD 278**.

Son knows, and they could not believe that the Son did not know in the literal meaning of the term, because they again question him as one who does not know. Since they are aware that the mystery of not knowing is according to the divine plan for maintaining silence, they conclude that now, after the resurrection, the time for speaking has at length arrived, and they bring forth their questions.

And the Son does not tell them that he does not know but that it is not for them to know, because the Father has settled this matter by his own authority. Consequently, if the apostles realize that this statement, that the Son does not know, is in keeping with the plan of salvation and is not a weakness, shall we assert that the Son, therefore, does not know the day because he is not God? God the Father has determined it by his own authority, therefore, in order that it may not come to the knowledge of our human comprehension, and the Son, when previously interrogated, had said that he did not know and now he does not make the same reply that he does not know, but that it is not for them to know, and that the Father, however, has decided upon these times not in his knowledge but in his authority. Since the day and moment are included in the idea of time, it is impossible to believe that the day and moment for restoring the kingdom of Israel is unknown to him who is to restore it. But, to lead us to the knowledge of his birth through the Father's unique power, he answered that it was known to him and, while revealing that the right to acquire this knowledge had not been conferred on them, he declared that this knowledge itself is dependent upon the mystery of the Father's authority. On the Trinity 9.75.[12]

The Unity of the Godhead. Ambrose: But neither is the Father deceived nor does the Son deceive. It is the custom of the holy Scriptures to speak thus, as the examples I have already given, and many others testify, so that God feigns not to know what he does know. In this then a unity of Godhead and a unity of character is proved to

exist in the Father and in the Son; seeing that, as God the Father hides what is known to him, so also the Son, who is the image of God in this respect, hides what is known to him. On the Christian Faith 5.17.218.[13]

Knowledge of the Kingdom. Basil the Great: That is to say, the knowledge of such a kingdom is not for them that are bound in flesh and blood. This contemplation the Father has put away in his own power, meaning by "power" those that are authorized, and by "his own" those who are not held down by the ignorance of things below. Letter 8.7.[14]

The Trinity Possesses Unfailing Knowledge. Cassiodorus: People did not realize what they should not know, and the Son of God was not in any sense unaware of this through weakness of the flesh. But if we were to suspect that the divine Majesty cloaked ignorance (a thing it would be irreverent to say), then that ignorance would be found stronger than the divine nature, and could—to speak foolishness—bring down the providence by which all things were created. But since we are taught that this is quite ridiculous, we must believe that the whole Trinity, whose nature is one and all-powerful, has always an unfailing knowledge of all things. Exposition of the Psalms 9.39.[15]

1:8 Worldwide Witnesses

In the Resurrection and the Ascension. Chrysostom: He had said earlier, "Go nowhere among the Gentiles, and enter no town of the Samaritans."[16] What he did not say then, he added here, "and to the ends of the earth." Having said this, which was more fearful than all the rest, he held his peace. "When he had said this, as they were watching, he was lifted up, and a cloud took him out of their sight." Do you see that they

---

[12]FC 25:397-98*. [13]NPNF 2 10:312*. [14]NPNF 2 8:119*. [15]ACW 51:133-34*. [16]Mt 10:5.

preached and fulfilled the gospel? For great was the gift he had bestowed upon them. In the very place, he says, where you are afraid, that is, in Jerusalem, preach there. And afterwards he added, "and to the ends of the earth." Then again the proof of his words, "as they were watching, he was lifted up." Not "as they were watching," he rose from the dead, but "as they were watching, he was lifted up," since the sight of their eyes was in no way all sufficient then. For they saw in the resurrection the end but not the beginning, and they saw in the ascension the beginning but not the end. HOMILIES ON THE ACTS OF THE APOSTLES 2.[17]

GIFTS ARE FROM THE TRINITY. CHRYSOSTOM: And they did become witnesses by their miracles. This is so, for the grace of the Spirit is ineffable, and innumerable are his gifts. Moreover, this took place that you might learn that the gifts and the power of the Father and of the Son and of the Holy Spirit are one. What appears to be proper to the Father also belongs in reality to the Son and to the Holy Spirit. "How is it, then," you will say, "that no one comes to the Son 'unless the Father draw him'?"[18] But this is shown to be true of the Son also, for he said, "I am the way; no one comes to the Father but through me."[19] And notice that the same thing is true of the Spirit also. For "No one can say, 'Jesus Christ is Lord,' except in the Holy Spirit."[20] And again, we are told that apostles have been given to the church, at one time by the Father, at another by the Son, and at another by the Holy Spirit, so we see that the varieties of gifts belong to the Father and to the Son and to the Holy Spirit.[21] HOMILIES ON THE GOSPEL OF JOHN 86.[22]

THE HOLY SPIRIT IS DIVINE. AMBROSE: And so, when the Lord appointed his servants the apostles, that we might recognize that the creature was one thing and the grace of the Spirit another, he appointed them to different places, because all could not be everywhere at once. But he gave the Holy Spirit to all, to shed upon the apostles though separated the gift of indivisible grace. The persons, then, were different, but the accomplishment of the working was in all one, because the Holy Spirit is one of whom it is said, "You shall receive power, even the Holy Spirit coming upon you, and you shall be witnesses to me in Jerusalem and in all Judea and Samaria, and to the ends of the earth."

The Holy Spirit, then, is uncircumscribed and infinite, who infused himself into the minds of the disciples throughout the separate divisions of distant regions and the remote bounds of the whole world whom nothing is able to escape or to deceive. And therefore holy David says, "Where shall I go from your Spirit, or where shall I flee from your face?"[23] Of what angel does the Scripture say this, of what dominion, of what power, of what angel do we find the power diffused over many? For angels were sent to few, but the Holy Spirit was poured upon whole peoples. Who, then, can doubt that that is divine which is shed upon many at once and is not seen; but that that is corporeal which is seen and held by individuals? ON THE HOLY SPIRIT 1.7.81-82.[24]

1:9 Christ Was Lifted Up

THE ELEMENTS SERVE HIM. ARATOR: [And] let us commend the manner of his rule through the powers that are subject to him: born of a virgin mother, rising again by treading upon death, seeking the scepter of heaven. He announces [such] deeds by these [angelic] servants. Nor do the elements cease to serve their thunderer. In his honor as he is coming, a star does service as a soldier, going before the magi. A cloud waits upon him in obedience as he goes. ON THE ACTS OF THE APOSTLES 1.[25]

THE CLOUD A SYMBOL OF HEAVEN. CHRYSOSTOM: Why "a cloud took him"? This is another

---

[17]NPNF 1 11:13**. [18]Jn 6:44. [19]Jn 14:6. [20]1 Cor 12:3. [21]1 Cor 12:4. [22]FC 41:453-54*. [23]Ps 139:6 (138:7 LXX). [24]NPNF 2 10:104**. [25]OAA 26*.

indication that he ascended to heaven. Not fire, as in the case of Elijah, nor a fiery chariot, but "a cloud took him." This was a symbol of heaven, according to the words of the prophet, "who makes the clouds his chariot,"[26] meaning the Father himself. Because of this he says, "on a cloud," implying, "in the symbol of the divine power," for no other power could dwell upon a cloud. Listen again to what another prophet says: "The Lord is riding upon a swift cloud."[27] Homilies on the Acts of the Apostles 2.[28]

The Obedience of Creation. Bede: Everywhere creation offers obedient service to its Creator. The stars indicated his birth;[29] clouds overshadowed him in his suffering, received him in his ascension, and they will accompany him when he returns for the judgment.[30] Commentary on the Acts of the Apostles 1.9B.[31]

Flesh Can Rise. Pseudo-Justin: And when they were by every kind of proof persuaded that it was himself [resurrected], and in the body, they asked him to eat with them, that they might thus still more accurately ascertain that he had truly risen bodily; and he did eat honeycomb and fish. And when he had thus shown them that there is truly a resurrection of the flesh, he also wished to show them that it is not impossible for flesh to ascend into heaven (as he had said that our dwelling place is in heaven), so "he was taken up into heaven while they beheld," just as he was in the flesh. If, therefore, after all that has been said, any one demand demonstration of the resurrection, he is in no respect different from the Sadducees, since the resurrection of the flesh is the power of God, and, being above all reasoning, is established by faith and seen in works. Fragments of the Lost Work of Justin on the Resurrection 9.[32]

1:11 Taken to Heaven

The Reasons for the Angels' Appearance. Bede: The angels appeared to the disciples

for two reasons, namely, to console them in their sorrow at his ascension by reminding them of his return and to show that he had truly gone to heaven, not merely apparently so, as in the case of Elijah.[33] Commentary on the Acts of the Apostles 1.11A.[34]

He Will Come in the Body. Chrysostom: Now, as they watched, their conceptions were elevated. He gave them not merely a subtle hint of the nature of his second coming. For this phrase—"thus he will come"—means with the body. This is what they desired to hear. And concerning the judgment he said again that he will come in this same way upon a cloud. Homilies on the Acts of the Apostles 2.[35]

Coming in Glory. Bede: He will come to judge in the same form and substance of a body in which he had come to be judged [by Pilate]. To him God truly gave, and did not take away, an immortal nature. His eternal and divine glory, which once was manifested to three of his disciples on a mountain,[36] will be seen by all the saints with the accomplishment of the judgment, when the wicked person will be removed so that he may not see the glory of God. Commentary on the Acts of the Apostles 1.11B.[37]

A Transformed Body. Augustine: How did they see him go? In the flesh which they touched, which they felt, the scars of which they even probed by touching; in that body in which he went in and out with them for forty days, manifesting himself to them in truth, not in any falsity; not as an apparition, not as a shadow, not as a spirit, but as he himself said, not deceiving, "Handle and see, for a spirit does not have flesh and bones, as you see me to have."[38] Now, indeed, that body is worthy of a heavenly dwelling place,

---

[26]Ps 104:3 (103:3 LXX). [27]Is 19:1. [28]NPNF 1 11:13**. [29]Mt 2:2, 9-10. [30]Rev 1:7; 14:14. [31]CS 117:13. [32]ANF 1:298*. [33]2 Kings 2:11. [34]CS 117:13*. [35]NPNF 1 11:14**. [36]Mt 17:1-13. [37]CS 117:13-14*. [38]Lk 24:39.

not subject to death, not changeable through ages. For as he had grown to that age from infancy, so he does not decline to old age from the age which was young adulthood. He remains as he ascended. He is going to come to those to whom, before he comes, he wanted his word to be preached. So, therefore, he will come in a human form. The ungodly, too, will see this. Those placed to the right will see it too; those separated to the left will see it too, as it was written, "They shall see him whom they have pierced."[39] If they will see him whom they have pierced, they will see the same body which they thrust through with a spear; [for] the Word is not struck by a spear. Therefore, the ungodly will be able to see this very one whom they were also able to wound. They will not see the God lying hidden in the body; after the judgment he will be seen by those who will be on the right. This, therefore, is why he said, "The Father judges no one but has given all judgment to the Son,"[40] because the Son will come, clearly visible, to the judgment, appearing in human body to human beings, saying to those on the right, "Come, blessed of my Father, receive the kingdom"; saying to those on the left, "Go into everlasting fire which was prepared for the devil and his angels."[41] TRACTATES ON THE GOSPEL OF JOHN 21.13.2-4.[42]

CHRIST STILL HAS FLESH. CHRYSOSTOM: In us "after the flesh" implies our being in sins; "not after the flesh" implies not being in sins. In Christ, however, "after the flesh" implies his being subject to the affections of nature, such as thirst, hunger, weariness, sleep. (For "he committed no sin, and no deceit was found in his mouth."[43] Therefore he also said, "Which of you convicts me of sin?"[44] and again, "The ruler of this world is coming, and he has no power over me."[45]) For him the phrase "not *after* the flesh," then, means being freed from even these things, not being *without* flesh. For indeed with the flesh he comes to judge the world, with a flesh that is impassible and unmixed. We too will advance toward this, when our body conforms "to the body of his glory."[46] HOMILIES ON 2 CORINTHIANS 11.3.[47]

CHRIST'S HUMAN NATURE IS LIMITED. THEODORET OF CYR: Now they saw his nature as limited. For I have heard the words of the Lord, "You shall see the Son of man coming in the clouds of heaven," and I acknowledge that what is seen by human eyes is limited, for the unlimited nature is invisible. Furthermore to sit upon a throne of glory and to set the lambs upon the right and the kids upon the left indicates limitation.[48] DIALOGUE 2.[49]

---

[39]Zech 12:10. [40]Jn 5:22. [41]Mt 25:34, 41. [42]FC 79:191-92. [43]1 Pet 2:22. [44]Jn 8:46. [45]Jn 14:30. [46]Phil 3:21. [47]NPNF 1 12:332**. [48]Mt 25:31-33. [49]NPNF 2 3:199*.

1:12-14 THE DISCIPLES AT PRAYER

[12]*Then they returned to Jerusalem from the mount called Olivet, which is near Jerusalem, a sabbath day's journey away;* [13]*and when they had entered, they went up to the upper room, where they were staying, Peter and John and James and Andrew, Philip and Thomas, Bartholomew and Matthew, James the son of Alphaeus and Simon the Zealot and Judas the son of James.* [14]*All these with*

one accord devoted themselves to prayer, together with the women and Mary the mother of Jesus, and with his brothers.

Overview: Recent commentators note first how Luke is careful to portray the disciples as still obedient to the law by his reference to the "sabbath day's journey." Again, the mention of Mary here at the beginning of the church recalls her presence at the beginning of Jesus' life and ministry: she is the only one present from beginning to end, at the infancy, in Jesus' public life and at the postresurrection gathering. We also meet here for the first time the notion that this group was of "one accord," an expression that is found five other times in the book of Acts[1] and only once elsewhere. Commentators also point to the number of times the community is described as gathered together for prayer, just as Jesus is recorded to have prayed. The list of apostles is given (minus Judas); "the women" are mentioned, as are Jesus' brothers. Our two patristic witnesses, Bede and Arator, pay little attention to the historical sense of this passage. Both are fascinated by the "sabbath day's journey." That the sabbath referred to life in heaven is not an uncommon interpretation in the Fathers,[2] and here we find Bede transfer the referent of sabbath from a historical day to a possible future state that one reaches through the week, the six days, of work. Arator traces the contradistinctions between Mary and Eve. While his main concern is this distinction between Eve, the mother of humankind, and Mary, the mother of God, the narrative frame hints at how the apostles' return to Mary is, as it were, a return into the womb where the Savior was formed, in order to be reborn in a descent of the Spirit.[3]

1:12 They Returned to Jerusalem

A Sabbath Day's Journey. Bede: According to the historical sense, this indicates that the Mount of Olives was a thousand paces distant from the city of Jerusalem, for the law did not permit one to walk more than a thousand paces

on the sabbath. According to the allegorical sense,[4] however, anyone who becomes worthy of an interior vision of the glory of the Lord as he ascends to the Father, and of enrichment by the promise of the Holy Spirit, here enters the city of everlasting peace by a sabbath journey. There will be for him, in Isaiah's words, "Sabbath after Sabbath,"[5] because, having been free of wicked works here [in this life], he will be at rest there in heavenly recompense. On the other hand, anyone who in this world, as if during the period of the six [week] days, has neglected the working out of his salvation, showing scorn for that text of the Gospel [which says], "pray that your flight may not be in the winter, or on the Sabbath,"[6] will at that time of everlasting rest be shut out from the boundaries of the blessed Jerusalem. Commentary on the Acts of the Apostles 1.12b.[7]

1:14 Devoted to Prayer

Growing Great by Bringing Forth God. Arator: They sought by a swift path, with which it was possible to go a mile on their sabbath, the well-known walls where Mary, the gateway of God, the virgin mother of her Creator, formed by her own son, was sitting at a religious gathering. The second virgin put to flight the woes of Eve's crime; there is no harm done to the sex; she restored what the first took away. Let grief not raise up complaints or vex mourning hearts with groaning over the old law; these very forms of wickedness and crime rather cause delight at this bargain, and a better lot comes to the redeemed world from the fall. The person,

---

[1]Acts 2:46; 4:24; 5:12; 8:6; 15:25. Outside of Acts, Rom 15:6. [2]See, for example, Augustine's *Ennaration* on Ps 37 (38). [3]See Jn 3:4. [4]Bede is using terminology at this point inherited from the patristic era. "Allegory" here is a tropological application of the text; in this instance it is accommodation. See the introduction for a more complete discussion. [5]Is 66:23. [6]Mt 24:20. [7]CS 117:14.

not the nature [of a woman], caused ruin; in those days [of Eve] a pregnant woman [brought forth] peril. In these [of Mary] one grew great to bring forth God, the one begetting mortal things and the other bearing divine—she through

whom the Mediator came forth into the world and carried actual flesh to the heavens. ON THE ACTS OF THE APOSTLES 1.[8]

---

[8]OAA 26-27**.

1:15-26 MATTHIAS CHOSEN TO REPLACE JUDAS

[15]*In those days Peter stood up among the brothers (the company of persons was in all about a hundred and twenty), and said,* [16]*"Brothers, the scripture had to be fulfilled, which the Holy Spirit spoke beforehand by the mouth of David, concerning Judas who was guide to those who arrested Jesus.* [17]*For he was numbered among us, and was allotted his share in this ministry.* [18]*(Now this man bought a field with the reward of his wickedness; and falling headlong[b] he burst open in the middle and all his bowels gushed out.* [19]*And it became known to all the inhabitants of Jerusalem, so that the field was called in their language Akeldama, that is, Field of Blood.)* [20]*For it is written in the book of Psalms,*

"Let his habitation become desolate,
   and let there be no one to live in it";
and
   "His office let another take."

[21]*So one of the men who have accompanied us during all the time that the Lord Jesus went in and out among us,* [22]*beginning from the baptism of John until the day when he was taken up from us— one of these men must become with us a witness to his resurrection."* [23]*And they put forward two, Joseph called Barsabbas, who was surnamed Justus, and Matthias.* [24]*And they prayed and said, "Lord, who knowest the hearts of all men, show which one of these two thou hast chosen* [25]*to take the place in this ministry and apostleship from which Judas turned aside, to go to his own place."* [26]*And they cast lots for them, and the lot fell on Matthias; and he was enrolled with the eleven apostles.*

b Or *swelling up*

OVERVIEW: A salient point noted by commentators is the need to form a group of twelve before they, as the leaders of the reconstituted Israel (see Lk 22:14) meet the twelve tribes of Israel on Pentecost. Matthias is not heard from again, and "the Twelve" are not prominent after Acts

16. The criteria given by Peter for such a replacement are notably different from those mentioned by Paul later on in his letters: Paul and Barnabas are called "apostles" only twice in Acts (14:4, 14), though Paul will often speak of his call to be an apostle as coming from Jesus him-

self.[1] They note the insistence that Judas' treachery and the need to replace him are related to divine necessity ("as a must"). They are aware of the differing descriptions of how Judas died (compare Mt 27:3-10) as well as Luke's notices of other deaths that followed upon departure from God's will (Acts 5:1-11; 12:20-23).

The poet Arator is eager to highlight the prominence of Peter in the first fifteen chapters of Acts. Despite his atrocious mixing of metaphors, he is upholding what would eventually become a stronghold of Catholic dogma on a different level as well, namely, that grace perfects but does not destroy nature. Peter is a symbol of what Christ's coming to the world revealed, that the world's history, and especially that of the chosen people, was a preparation for the coming of Christ; the past is not abnegated but transformed out of the old into the new (see also Bede's comments at Acts 1:26).

Bede offers a glimpse into how seriously these numbers in Scripture would be studied. Both he and Arator, in his comments on the number twelve, show that what often fascinates them are not just corresponding numbers, such as twelve apostles for twelve patriarchs, but how numbers, through arithmetic, can be made to link different typic events or elements in the mystery of God's work in us in Christ (see also Augustine's remarks at Acts 1:26).

Chrysostom keeps matters more practical. He is concerned to find reasons that go beyond numerology for the replacement of Judas, and he uses the description of the early church to motivate his listeners. He employs the rhetorical device of shaming his audience by comparison with the peaceful accord of the early church. We can see that by the early fifth century, Acts was already functioning as a model for comparison and exhortation in the present. Jerome makes similar use of Judas as a warning to clerics of his day. The comments on the selection of Matthias elicit remarks varying from being prooftexts (AMBROSE) to convoluted attempts to explain the casting of lots while maintaining the value of the text (BEDE). Both Bede and Augustine have the narrative of salvation in the background, and so we see Bede using a typological method of reading to explain change as a part of God's constant revelation of the true sacrifice of the body of Christ, while Augustine sees in Judas and his replacement an indication of God's mercy and forbearance that the church, as the body of Christ, signifies to the world.

1:15 Peter Stood Up

THE FISHERMAN'S VOCATION CHANGED. ARATOR: Foremost among the band of apostles, Peter had been called from his small boat; the scaly throng were wont to be caught by this fisher; suddenly, seen from the shore as he drew [his nets], he himself deserved to be drawn; Christ's fishing deigned to seize a disciple who must stretch the nets which are to catch the human race. To the hand that had borne the fishhook was transferred the key. He who had been eager to shift the dripping booty from the depths of the sea to the shore and to fill the craft with spoils, now in another area draws from the better waves [of baptism]; no longer pursuing his profits through the waters, he forsakes his profession. To him the Lamb entrusted the sheep which he saved by his passion; and he enlarges his flock throughout the whole world under this shepherd. ON THE ACTS OF THE APOSTLES 1.[2]

THE SYMBOL OF THE HUNDRED AND TWENTY. BEDE: These hundred and twenty, built up gradually by addition [of the numbers] from one to fifteen yields fifteen as the number of steps [in the calculation]. By reason of the perfection of both laws, this is mystically contained in the psalter, and for this [number of days] the "vessel of election" dwelled with Peter[3] in Jerusalem.[4] COMMEN-

---

[1]Cf. Rom 1:1 and other Pauline salutations. [2]*OAA* 27**. [3]Acts 9:15; Gal 1:18. [4]Bede is dealing with a practice that is traced back to the Pythagoreans, who considered 10 the perfect number and were fond of something called the *tetractus*, the sum of the numbers 1 through 4 (tetra) that equals 10. It seems that the sequence of the sums of bases from 2 to at least 17, but probably higher, was memorized and so the

The Brotherhood of Believers. Chrysostom: "Men, brothers," says Peter. If even the Lord called them brothers, all the more should Peter when they were all present. What dignity of church, what angelic condition! There was no distinction then, neither male nor female.[6] I wish the churches were like that now. No one had his mind full of worldly matter; no one was anxiously thinking about household concerns. In this way even temptations may become a benefit and afflictions an advantage. Homilies on the Acts of the Apostles 3.[7]

1:16 Scripture Fulfilled Regarding Judas

The Former Number of Apostles Regained. Arator: Twelve constellations of the [stellar] choir shine and cast the brilliance of Olympus on the earth. Note what realization this light reveals: The world is divided by the regions of its four sides; a triune faith calls this [world to belief], in whose name [the world] is washed in the font. Therefore, four taken together three times makes up the whole figure which the twelvefold order possesses, and to the devout disciples, to whom this baptism is commanded, a mystic reason gave cause for making up again the former number. On the Acts of the Apostles 1.[8]

Eleven Apostles Would Have Been Absurd. Bede: The apostle Peter was apprehensive about continuing with the number eleven [of apostles], "for every sin is an eleven, because when one does wicked things he goes beyond the commandments of the decalog."[9] Hence, because no righteousness of ours is innocent of itself, the tabernacle which contained the Lord's ark was covered from above by eleven veils of goats' hair.[10] Peter restored the number of apostles to twelve, so that through two parts of six each (for three times four is twelve) they might preserve by an eternal number the grace which they were preaching by word, and so that those who were to

preach the faith of the holy Trinity to the four parts of the world (in line with the Lord's saying, "Go, teach all nations, baptizing them in the name of the Father and of the Son and of the Holy Spirit")[11] might already certify the perfection of the work by the sacramental sign of [their] number as well.[12] According to a deeper sense, however, the evil that the church suffers in false brothers remains grossly uncorrected for the most part. As the fiftieth day drew near the full number of apostles was restored, prefiguring the end of the world when it is believed that the Jews who crucified the Lord are to be reconciled to the church. Commentary on the Acts of the Apostles 1.16.[13]

1:18 The Death of Judas

Judas's Death Was Fitting. Bede: [As an ancient writer says,] "The betrayer, out of his mind, found the punishment that he well deserved, namely, that the knot of the noose slew the throat through which the word of treachery had gone out." He also got the death place that he deserved, for "in hatred of both heaven and earth" (as though he would be associated only with the spirits of the air), he had betrayed the Lord of men and angels to death, and so "he perished in the middle of the air,"[14] following the example of Ahithophel and Absalom, who proceeded against King David.[15] For him death itself surely followed by a well-deserved termination, inasmuch as his bowels, which had conceived the

---

sums (2, 6, 10, 15, 21, 28, etc.) acquired significance. Finding meaning in the tetractus seems to have been an uncommon but respectable practice in the West. See Augustine's elaborate explanation of the catch of 153 fish in John 21 at *Tractate on the Gospel of John* 122.7-8 (FC 92:67-71). 153 is the *tetractus* of 17. Bede here refers to the Psalms of Ascents, 119 (120)—133 (134), one for each step from the Women's Court into the Men's Court in the temple. These psalms came to be interpreted by Christians as an allegory of the soul's progress in virtue and ascent to God; see Cassiodorus *Explanation of the Psalms*, Commentary on Psalm 119 (ACW 53:259-61). [5]CS 117:16. [6]Gal 3:28. [7]NPNF 1 11:18*. [8]OAA 28**. [9]Gregory the Great *Morals on the Book of Job* 32.15.27 (CCL 143c:1650). [10]Ex 26:7. [11]Mt 28:19. [12]See Gregory the Great *Morals on the Book of Job* 1.14.19 (CCL 143a:34). [13]CS 117:17*. [14]Arator *De Actibus Apostolorum* 1 (CSEL 72:15). [15]2 Sam 17:23; 18:9.

evil scheme of treachery, fell torn asunder, and his bodily cavities were exposed to the wind. COMMENTARY ON THE ACTS OF THE APOSTLES 1.18B.[16]

1:19 Field of Blood

A FITTING END. ARATOR: This revenge on Judas is not empty. It denies funeral rites and comes thus as acceptable punishment for an unjust income. He had lately bought fields with the price of his death. He had purchased ground with the name of Blood, reusing tombs for foreign ashes, [appearing to] make the earth fruitful by means of the graves; this wicked one is denied the fertility of his own field and is alone excluded from the lands which bear sepulchers. His cruel trumpet [voice] began the gory wickedness. He is the standard bearer who, by planting a kiss, by a sign of peace, waged war as a wolf on the Lamb. ON THE ACTS OF THE APOSTLES 1.[17]

1:20 Another Will Take His Office

BE ON GUARD. JEROME: Not only does the saying hold true in the time of Judas, but even today. If Judas lost his office of apostle, let priest and bishop be on guard lest they, too, lose their ministry. If an apostle fell, more easily is it possible for a monk to fall. Virtue is not lost, even though man falls and perishes. The Lord continues to lend out his money at interest; if anyone who receives it does not double it, it is taken away and given to another who already has some. The Lord's money cannot lie idle. HOMILIES ON THE PSALMS 35 (PSALM 108).[18]

1:22 A Witness to the Resurrection

THE NECESSITY OF AN EYEWITNESS. CHRYSOSTOM: [Judas must be replaced by] "one of the men who have accompanied us," continues Peter. Note how he requires them to be eyewitnesses, even though the Spirit was about to come. There was still great care concerning this: "One of the men who have accompanied us," he says, "during all the time that the Lord Jesus went in and out among us." He means those who had dwelt with Christ, not simply been present as disciples. . . . "Until the day he was taken up from us—one of these must become a witness with us of his resurrection." He did not say a witness of the rest of his actions but a witness of the resurrection alone. For indeed more trustworthy is the man who can say, "he, who ate, and drank, and was crucified, *he* rose again." Therefore, he must be a witness not only of the time preceding this event or of what followed it and the miracles: the thing required was the resurrection. The other matters were evident and acknowledged, but the resurrection took place in secret and was evident to these only. And they do not say, "Angels told us," but, "*We* have seen." Why is this evident? Because we perform miracles. For this reason they had to be trustworthy, especially then. HOMILIES ON THE ACTS OF THE APOSTLES 3.[19]

1:23 Barsabbas and Matthias Nominated

GOD EXALTS THE HUMBLE. ARATOR: They choose two: Joseph, surnamed the Just, and Matthias—a name, as they say, that means "God's small one" in the Hebrew language, and by calling [him, God] confirms him as humble. Oh, how different are human from heavenly judgments! He who was just according to the praise of humankind is surpassed by the merit of a small one. ON THE ACTS OF THE APOSTLES 1.[20]

1:24 Prayer for the Lord's Choice

GOD KNOWS THE HEARTS OF ALL PEOPLE. AMBROSE: The imperial power is great, but consider . . . how great God is. He sees the hearts of all; he probes their inmost conscience; he knows all things before they come to pass; he knows the innermost secrets of your heart. You do not allow

---

[16]CS 117:18. [17]OAA 27-28**. [18]FC 48:259. [19]NPNF 1 11:21**. [20]OAA 28.

yourself to be deceived; do you expect to hide anything from God? LETTER 11 (57).[21]

THE LORD CHOOSES. CHRYSOSTOM: Why did Peter not ask Christ to give him someone to replace Judas? It is better as it is. For in the first place, they were engaged in other things; second, this was the greatest proof of Christ's presence with them. For just as he chose when he was among them, so he chose now in absence. This was no small consolation. HOMILIES ON THE ACTS OF THE APOSTLES 3.[22]

1:26 Matthias Chosen by Lot

DRAWING LOTS WAS PERMISSIBLE UNTIL THE FULFILLMENT. BEDE: Matthias was chosen by lot so that the choice of the apostle would not appear to be out of harmony with the command of the old law, where it was ordered that the high priest be sought, as was said of Zechariah, "according to the custom of the priest's office, it came about by lot that he offered incense."[23] He [Zechariah] was, as I suppose, selected by lot at that time so that it might be typologically prefigured that they were to continue to seek out a priest until the one came who had replaced him, the one who, not by bloody sacrifices "but by virtue of his own blood, entered once for all into the holy places, having obtained eternal redemption"[24]—his sacrifice was immolated at the time of the Passover but truly brought to perfection by the Holy Spirit in the appearance of fire on the day of Pentecost. For according to old customs, victims acceptable to God were brought to perfection by celestial fire. Therefore until the truth was fulfilled, the practice of the figure was permissible. So it was that Matthias, who was appointed before Pentecost, was chosen by lot, while in the case of the seven deacons, who came later, there was no shaking of lots but only the disciples' choice; and indeed they were appointed by the prayer of the apostles and the imposition of hands.[25] Therefore if there are any who, under the compulsion of some difficult situation think

that because of the example of the apostles they should consult God with lots, they should see that these same apostles needed only the assembly of the brothers gathered together and prayers poured forth to God. COMMENTARY ON THE ACTS OF THE APOSTLES 1.26.[26]

THROUGH THE TWELVE THE TRINITY IS PROCLAIMED EVERYWHERE. AUGUSTINE: This saying, "I have chosen you twelve,"[27] may be understood in this way, that twelve is a sacred number. For the honor of that number was not taken away because one was lost, for another was chosen into the place of the one that perished. The number remained a sacred number, a number containing twelve. These twelve were to make known the Three [the Trinity] throughout the whole world, that is, throughout the four quarters of the world. That is the reason of the three times four. Judas, then, only cut himself off; he did not profane the number twelve. He abandoned his Teacher, but God appointed a successor to take his place. TRACTATES ON THE GOSPEL OF JOHN 27.10.[28]

MATTHIAS PRESERVES THE SACRED NUMBER. AUGUSTINE:[29] He reproved them by saying, "Are there not twelve hours in the day? If any man walks in the day, he does not stumble."[30] Follow me, if you do not wish to stumble: do not give counsel to me, from whom you ought to receive it. To what, then, refer the words "Are there not twelve hours in the day"? So as to point himself out as the day, he chose twelve disciples. If I am the day, he says, and you the hours, is it for the hours to give counsel to the day? The day is followed by the hours, not the hours by the day. If these, then, were the hours, what in such a reckoning was Judas? Was he also among the twelve hours? If he was an hour, he had light; and if he

---

[21]FC 26:64*. [22]NPNF 1 11:18*. [23]Lk 1:9. [24]Heb 9:12. [25]Acts 6:3-6. [26]CS 117:20-21. [27]Jn 6:70. [28]NPNF 1 7:177*. [29]If we compare this text with the preceding text of Augustine we can see an earlier instance of the ancient fascination with numbers, something that we cannot easily understand. See the introduction for the difference between "fact exegesis" and "text exegesis." [30]Jn 11:9.

had light, how was the Day betrayed by him to death? But the Lord, in so speaking, foresaw not Judas himself but his successor. For Judas, when he fell, was succeeded by Matthias, and the twelvefold number preserved. It was not, then, without a purpose that the Lord chose twelve disciples, but to indicate that he himself is the spiritual Day. Let the hours then attend upon the Day, let them preach the Day, be made known and illuminated by the Day, and by the preaching of the hours may the world believe in the Day. And so in a summary way it was just this that he said, "Follow me, if you do not wish to stumble." TRACTATES ON THE GOSPEL OF JOHN 49.8.[31]

THE BLESSING AND RESPONSIBILITY OF COMMUNITY. AUGUSTINE: What lesson then, my brothers, did our Lord Jesus Christ wish to impress on his church, when it pleased him to have one castaway among the twelve, but this, that we should bear with the wicked and refrain from dividing the body of Christ? . . . Such was

this man Judas, and yet he went in and out with the eleven holy disciples. With them he came even to the table of the Lord: he was permitted to converse with them, but he could not contaminate them. Both Peter and Judas partook of one bread, and yet what communion had the believer with the infidel? Peter's partaking was to life, but that of Judas to death. For that good bread was just like the sweet savor. For as the sweet savor, so also does the good bread give life to the good and bring death to the wicked. "For whoever eats unworthily eats and drinks judgment against himself":[32] "judgment against himself," not against you. If, then, it is judgment against him, not against you, bear as one that is good with him that is evil, that you may attain the rewards of the good and not be hurled into the punishment of the wicked. TRACTATES ON THE GOSPEL OF JOHN 50.10.[33]

---

[31]NPNF 1 7:273**. [32]1 Cor 11:29. [33]NPNF 1 7:281-82*.

2:1-4 THE COMING OF THE HOLY SPIRIT

[1]*When the day of Pentecost had come, they were all together in one place.* [2]*And suddenly a sound came from heaven like the rush of a mighty wind, and it filled all the house where they were sitting.* [3]*And there appeared to them tongues as of fire, distributed and resting on each one of them.* [4]*And they were all filled with the Holy Spirit and began to speak in other tongues, as the Spirit gave them utterance.*

OVERVIEW: There are five sections in this chapter: the coming of the Holy Spirit (Acts 2:1-4), the listing of all the nations represented and the amazement of the crowd (Acts 2:5-13), Peter's speech (Acts 2:14-36), the reaction of the hearers (Acts 2:37-41) and a summary description of the restored and new people (Acts 2:42-47). In the

theological presentation of Luke, we first saw the reconstitution of the Twelve, and thus the new Israel (Acts 1:15-26), and the giving of the new law at a new Sinai at Pentecost follows this. Then, in Peter's speech to the old Israel, gathered from the nations in Jerusalem, the new Israel, in the power of the Holy Spirit, addresses the old Israel. The

Fathers are sensitive to Luke's allusive theology of a new Sinai: many remark on the significance of the fifty days, others allude to the "beginnings of the Gospel" (Leo), thus of a new people. They link Christian baptism to this baptism in the Holy Spirit (Chrysostom, Cyril of Jerusalem, Arator). They are aware that Luke is alluding to the undoing of Babel in the gift of tongues (Bede, Cyril) and the significance of the presence of this gift in showing forth the universality of the church (Augustine, Leo, Cyril, Cassiodorus), though they show little curiosity about the precise description of this gift. Finally, Augustine poses the very modern question: what is the relation between the bestowal of the Spirit in John 20:22-23 and that at Pentecost? Typically, he compares the events while modern exegesis, also typically, looks rather to different theological viewpoints in the two authors.

2:1 The Day of Pentecost

THE SAME SPIRIT. LEO THE GREAT: To the Hebrew people, now freed from Egypt, the law was given on Mount Sinai fifty days after the immolation of the paschal lamb. Similarly, after the passion of Christ in which the true Lamb of God was killed, just fifty days after his resurrection, the Holy Spirit fell upon the apostles and the whole group of believers. Thus the earnest Christian may easily perceive that the beginnings of the Old Covenant were at the service of the beginnings of the gospel and that the same Spirit who instituted the first established the Second Covenant. SERMON 75.[1]

THE FIFTIETH DAY. BEDE: It should be noted with respect to the historical sense that among the ancients the day of Pentecost (that is the fiftieth day, on which the law was given) was computed from [the time of] the killing of the [paschal] lamb. In our case, however, it is not from the Lord's passion but from his resurrection, as the blessed Augustine explains it,[2] that we are to calculate the fiftieth day, on which was sent the Holy

Spirit, who, recalling the example of the old sign, most clearly consecrated the Lord's day to himself by his coming. Indeed, by this specific time [of his coming] he also showed that the Passover was to be celebrated on the Lord's day. For here too God appeared in a vision of fire, as he had also in the earlier case, as Exodus says, "For the whole of Mount Sinai was smoking because the Lord had descended upon it in fire."[3] COMMENTARY ON THE ACTS OF THE APOSTLES 2.1.[4]

THE INGATHERING. CHRYSOSTOM: Do you see the type? What is this Pentecost? The time when the sickle was to be put to the harvest and the fruits to be gathered. Look at the reality now, how the time has come to ply the sickle of the Word. The Spirit, keen-edged, came down in place of the sickle. For hear the words of Christ, "Lift up your eyes and see how the fields are ripe for harvesting."[5] And again, "The harvest is plentiful, but the laborers are few."[6] He himself, taking [our nature] as the first fruits, lifted it up high and he was himself the first to ply the sickle. For this reason he calls [the Word] also the Seed. HOMILIES ON THE ACTS OF THE APOSTLES 4.[7]

THE MYSTERY OF THE FIFTY DAYS. AUGUSTINE: Fifty days are reckoned from the celebration of the Passover (which, as Moses ordered, was accomplished by slaying the lamb,[8] a type to signify the future passion of the Lord) to the day on which Moses received the law on tablets written by the finger of God.[9] Likewise, when fifty days had passed from the slaying and resurrection of him who was led as a lamb to the slaughter,[10] the finger of God, that is, the Holy Spirit filled the believers gathered in one place. ON THE SPIRIT AND THE LETTER 16.28.[11]

THE SCENT OF PARADISE. EPHREM THE SYRIAN: When the blessed apostles

---

[1]SC 74:144-45. [2]Augustine Letter 55.1.2 (CSEL 34.2:171). [3]Ex 19:18. [4]CS 117:28*. [5]Jn 4:35. [6]Mt 9:37. [7]NPNF 1 11:25**. [8]Ex 12:3. [9]Ex 31:18. [10]Is 53:7. [11]PL 44:218.

were gathered together
the place shook
and the scent of Paradise,
having recognized its home,
poured forth its perfumes,
delighting the heralds
by whom
the guests are instructed
and come to his banquet;
eagerly he awaits their arrival
for he is the Lover of mankind.
Hymns on Paradise 11.14.[12]

2:2 The Rush of a Mighty Wind

Each Apostle Receives a Spring of Spirit. Chrysostom: Thus Moses was the greatest of the prophets, yet he, when others were to receive the Spirit, suffered diminution himself.[13] But here it is not so. For just as fire kindles as many lamps as it will, so here the abundance of the Spirit was shown. Each one received a spring of Spirit, just as he himself said, that those who believe in him shall have "a spring of water gushing up to eternal life."[14] And it was justly so. For they were not going forth to argue with the pharaoh but to wrestle with the devil. The wonderful thing is this: they made no objections when they were sent; they did not say they were "weak in voice and slow of speech."[15] For Moses had taught them better. They did not say they were too young.[16] Jeremiah had made them wise. And yet they heard many fearful things, much worse than what was in former times, but they were afraid to object. For they were angels of light and the servants of things on high. No one from heaven appeared to people of former times, because they were in pursuit of matters on earth. But when man ascended on high, the Spirit descends from on high, "like the rush of a mighty wind." Through this it is made clear that nothing will be able to stand against them and they will blow away all adversaries like a heap of dust. Homilies on the Acts of the Apostles 4.[17]

Miracles of Sound and Sight. Augustine: But I am surprised that you think it possible for the sound of that voice which said, "You are my Son,"[18] to be produced by the divine will acting on physical nature without the agency of a living being, and you do not think it possible for the physical appearance of any living creature and of movement like that of life to be produced by the divine will in the same way without the agency of any animal life-principle. If created nature obeys God without the actions of a vivifying soul, so that sounds are uttered such as are usually uttered by a living body and the form of articulate speech is brought to the ears, why should it not obey him so that without the agency of a vivifying soul the form and movement of a bird should be presented to the sight by the same power of the Creator? . . . Therefore, there is no need to inquire how the corporeal appearance of the dove was produced, just as we do not inquire how the words of an articulate body produce their sound. For, if it were possible for a soul not to be the medium by which a voice is said to have been made audible and not as a voice usually is, how much more possible was it when the dove was spoken of that this word should signify merely a physical appearance presented to the eyes without the actual nature of a living creature! These words, also, were said in that sense, "And suddenly there came a sound from heaven as of a mighty wind coming, and there appeared to them parted tongues as it were of fire," where a certain phenomenon is said to be "as of a wind" and "as it were" a visible fire, like the natural fire with its customary nature, but it does not seem to mean that natural fire of the customary kind was produced. Letter 169.[19]

Pentecost and Our Baptism. Chrysostom: For in the case of the apostles too, there was a

---

[12]HOP 159. [13]An allusion to Num 11:17, "I will take some of the Spirit that is on you and bestow it on them." [14]Jn 4:14. [15]Ex 4:10. [16]Jer 1:6. [17]NPNF 1 11:27**. [18]Mt 3:16-17; Mk 1:10-11; Lk 3:22. [19]FC 30:58-59*.

"sound of a mighty wind," and visions of fiery tongues appeared, but not for the apostles' sake, but because of the Jews who were then present. Nevertheless, even though no sensible signs take place, we receive the things that have been once manifested by them. Since the dove itself at that time therefore appeared, that as in place of a finger (so to say) it might point out to them that were present, and to John, the Son of God. Not however merely on this account, but to teach you also, that upon you no less at your baptism the Spirit comes. But since then we have no need of sensible vision, faith sufficing instead of all. For signs are "not for them that believe but for them that believe not."[20] HOMILIES ON THE GOSPEL OF MATTHEW 12.3.[21]

THE DISCIPLES' BAPTISM. CYRIL OF JERUSALEM: And lest people should be ignorant of the greatness of the mighty gift coming down to them, there sounded as it were a heavenly trumpet. For suddenly there came from heaven a sound as of the rushing of a mighty wind, signifying the presence of him who was to grant power to people to seize with violence the kingdom of God, that both their eyes might see the fiery tongues and their ears hear the sound. And it filled all the house where they were sitting; for the house became the vessel of the spiritual water; as the disciples sat within, the whole house was filled. Thus they were entirely baptized according to the promise and invested soul and body with a divine garment of salvation. CATECHETICAL LECTURE 17.15.[22]

2:3 Tongues of Fire

WHY WATER AND FIRE. ARATOR: A matter of greatest importance compels [me] not to keep silent long as to why it is that the fostering Spirit is given to *them* as flame [but] at the River Jordan as a dove;[23] I shall fitly sing this [mystery], and I shall fulfill the promises owed if [the Spirit] brings his gifts. These two signs are allegories that there should be simplicity, which very appro-

priately [this] bird loves,[24] [and] that, lest [this simplicity] be sluggish [and] grow lukewarm without the fire of doctrine, there should also be faith that has been kindled. There [in the Jordan] he appointed by means of the waters [that they be] of one mind; here [with fire] he bids that they teach with flaming words. Love presses hard upon their minds; zeal burns in their words. ON THE ACTS OF THE APOSTLES 1.[25]

THE SPIRIT MAKES ONE BURN AND SPEAK. BEDE: Now the Holy Spirit appeared in fire and in tongues because all those whom he fills he makes simultaneously to burn and to speak—to burn because of him and to speak about him. And at the same time he indicated that the holy church, when it had spread to the ends of the earth, was to speak in the languages of all nations. COMMENTARY ON THE ACTS OF THE APOSTLES 2.3A.[26]

UNITY AND DIVERSITY. AUGUSTINE: Therefore, when he sent the Holy Spirit he manifested him visibly in two ways—by a dove and by fire: by a dove upon the Lord when he was baptized, by fire upon the disciples when they were gathered together. . . . The dove shows that those who are sanctified by the Spirit should be without guile. That their simplicity should not continue cold is shown us by the fire. Nor let it trouble you that the tongues were divided; for tongues are diverse, therefore the appearance was that of cloven tongues. "Cloven tongues," it said, "as of fire, and it sat upon each of them." There is a diversity of tongues, but the diversity of tongues does not imply schisms. Do not be afraid of separation in the cloven tongues, but in the dove recognize unity. TRACTATES ON THE GOSPEL OF JOHN 6.3.[27]

PREPARE FOR THE FIRE. CYRIL OF JERUSALEM: They partook of fire, not of burning but of saving fire. This is a fire that consumes the thorns of

---

[20]1 Cor 14:22. [21]NPNF 1 10:77*. [22]NPNF 2 7:128*. [23]Mt 3:16. [24]See Mt 10:16. [25]OAA 29*. [26]CS 117:29*. [27]NPNF 1 7:40*.

sins but gives luster to the soul. This is now coming upon you also in order to strip away and consume your sins, which are like thorns, and to brighten yet more that precious possession of your souls, and to give you grace, the same given then to the apostles. The Spirit descended upon them in the form of fiery tongues, that they might crown themselves with new and spiritual diadems by fiery tongues upon their heads. As a fiery sword had barred of old the gates of paradise, a fiery tongue that brought salvation restored the gift. CATECHETICAL LECTURE 17.15.[28]

2:4 Speaking in Other Tongues

THE CHURCH: A GATHERING OF LANGUAGES.
LEO THE GREAT: O how swift is the speech of wisdom! Where God is the teacher, how quickly is that learned which is being taught! No interpretation is used in order to understand, no practice is needed in order to use it. No time is needed to study, but, with the "Spirit" of truth "blowing wherever he pleases,"[29] the particular voices of each distinct people become familiar in the mouth of the church.

From this day the trumpet of the gospel teaching resounds. From this day showers of graces and streams of benedictions water all the desert and every wasteland, to "renew the face of the earth,"[30] "God's Spirit hovered over the water."[31] To take away the old darkness, beams of new light flash out, when by the splendor of those glowing tongues, the Word of the Lord becomes "clear"[32] and "speech takes fire."[33] Both the force of giving light and the power of burning were present for this reason, to create knowledge and to destroy sin. SERMON 75.2.[34]

TONGUES SIGNIFY A VARIETY OF GRACES.
BEDE: The church's humility recovers the unity of languages that the pride of Babylon had shattered. Spiritually, however, the variety of languages signifies gifts of a variety of graces. Truly therefore, it is not inconsistent to understand that the Holy Spirit first gave to human beings the gift of languages, by which human wisdom is both learned and taught extrinsically, so that he might thereby show how easily he can make people wise through the wisdom of God, which is within them. COMMENTARY ON THE ACTS OF THE APOSTLES 2.4.[35]

SINAI AND PENTECOST: THE CONTRAST.
AUGUSTINE: Now, amid this admirable correspondence, there is at least this very considerable difference in the cases, in that the people in the earlier instance were deterred by a horrible dread from approaching the place where the law was given; whereas in the other case the Holy Spirit came upon them who were gathered together in expectation of his promised gift. *There* it was on tables of stone that the finger of God operated; *here* it was on the hearts of people. *There* the law was given outwardly, so that the unrighteous might be terrified;[36] *here* it was given inwardly, so that they might be justified. For this, "Thou shalt not commit adultery, Thou shalt not kill, Thou shalt not covet; and if there be any other commandment"—such, of course, as was written on those tables—"it is briefly comprehended," says he, "in this saying, namely, Thou shalt love thy neighbor as thyself. Love works no ill to his neighbor: therefore love is the fulfilling of the law."[37] Now this was not written on the tables of stone but "is shed abroad in our hearts by the Holy Spirit, who is given to us."[38] God's law, therefore, is love. "To it the carnal mind is not subject, neither indeed can be;"[39] but when the works of love are written on tables to alarm the carnal mind, there arises the law of works and "the letter which kills" the transgressor; but when love itself is shed abroad in the hearts of believers, then we have the law of faith and the Spirit which gives life to one who loves. ON THE SPIRIT AND THE LETTER 17.29.[40]

---

[28]NPNF 2 7:128*. [29]Jn 3:8. [30]Ps 104:30 (103:30 LXX, Vg). [31]Gen 1:2. [32]Ps 19:9 (18:10 LXX, Vg). [33]Ps 118:140 Vg. [34]FC 93:331*. [35]CS 117:29*. [36]See Ex 19:12, 16. [37]Rom 13:9-10. [38]Rom 5:5. [39]Rom 8:7. [40]NPNF 1 5:95*.

Two Bestowals of the Spirit? AUGUSTINE: For the Lord has transacted even this explicit imparting of the Holy Spirit not once but twice. For later when he arose from the dead, breathing on them, he said, "Receive the Holy Spirit."[41] Then because he gave him at that time, did he therefore not also later send him whom he promised? Or is this not the same Holy Spirit who was both breathed by him then and later sent by him from heaven? Therefore, why his giving, which clearly was done, was done twice is another question. Perhaps this double giving of him was done in manifestation of the two commandments of love, that is of neighbor and of God, in order that love might be shown to belong to the Holy Spirit. And if another reason must be sought, this discourse must not now by an inquiry into it be expanded to greater length than it ought, yet let it be established that without the Holy Spirit we cannot love Christ and keep his commandments. We can and do keep his commandments less as we receive him less, but so much the more as we receive him more.

Accordingly, not only to one who does not have him but also to one who does, he is not promised to no purpose: to the one not having, that he may be had, but to the one having, that he may be had more. For if he were not had less by the one, more by the other, the holy Elisha would not say to the holy Elijah, "May the spirit who is in you be in me in double measure."[42] TRACTATES ON THE GOSPEL OF JOHN 74.2.2-3.[43]

The Speech of Babylon and Pentecost. CYRIL OF JERUSALEM: The Galilean Peter or Andrew spoke Persian or Median. John and the other apostles spoke all the tongues of various nations, for the thronging of multitudes of strangers from all parts is not something new in Jerusalem, but this was true in apostolic times.

What teacher can be found so proficient as to teach people in a moment what they have not learned? So many years are required through grammar and other arts merely to speak Greek well; and all do not speak it equally well. The rhetorician may succeed in speaking it well, the grammarian sometimes less well; and one who is skilled in grammar is ignorant of philosophical studies. But the Spirit taught them at once many languages, which they do not know in a whole lifetime. This is truly lofty wisdom. This is divine power. What a contrast between their long ignorance in the past and this sudden, comprehensive, varied and unaccustomed use of languages. The multitude of those listening was confounded; it was a second confusion, in contrast to the first evil confusion at Babylon. In that former confusion of tongues there was a division of purpose, for the intention was impious. Here there was a restoration and union of minds, since the object of their zeal was righteous. Through what occasioned the fall came the recovery. CATECHETICAL LECTURE 17.16-17.[44]

The Eloquence That Comes from Unity. CASSIODORUS: "He heard a tongue which he knew not."[45] We must interpret tongue here as the precepts of the New Testament, for if you understand it as "language," how did the Jewish people hear a tongue that they did not know, when we are sure that the Lord Christ spoke in Hebrew? So the passage means that in the gospel they heard a tongue or precepts that their earlier knowledge did not embrace; alternatively it refers to the time when the apostles were filled with the Holy Spirit and spoke in unknown and varied tongues. EXPOSITION OF THE PSALMS 80.6.[46]

---

[41]Jn 20:22. [42]2 Kings 2:9. [43]FC 90:90-91*. [44]FC 64:106-7*. [45]Ps 81:5 (80:6 LXX). [46]ACW 52:296.

2:5-13 THE MULTITUDE IS AMAZED

> [5]Now there were dwelling in Jerusalem Jews, devout men from every nation under heaven. [6]And at this sound the multitude came together, and they were bewildered, because each one heard them speaking in his own language. [7]And they were amazed and wondered, saying, "Are not all these who are speaking Galileans? [8]And how is it that we hear, each of us in his own native language? [9]Parthians and Medes and Elamites and residents of Mesopotamia, Judea and Cappadocia, Pontus and Asia, [10]Phrygia and Pamphylia, Egypt and the parts of Libya belonging to Cyrene, and visitors from Rome, both Jews and proselytes, [11]Cretans and Arabians, we hear them telling in our own tongues the mighty works of God." [12]And all were amazed and perplexed, saying to one another, "What does this mean?" [13]But others mocking said, "They are filled with new wine."

OVERVIEW: Luke now recounts how Jews "from every nation under heaven," thus, representatives from all the world, heard the witness of Peter as he proclaimed the new Sinai. The list of nations, perhaps taken from similar lists and then added to, is meant also to show the universality of the proclamation and the unification of those separated by the confusion at Babel. The Fathers generally do not remark on the notion of all Israel representatively present, though they do mention once again the theme of the undoing of Babel (ARATOR) and find different "allegorical" (ARATOR), "mystical" (BEDE) or fulfillment (CYRIL OF JERUSALEM) forms of significance in the reference to new wine. Chrysostom picks up the familiar theme of the power of speech given to uneducated men.

2:6 The Multitude Bewildered

DEVOUT PEOPLE PERPLEXED. CHRYSOSTOM: Notice their piety: they do not pronounce judgment in haste but are perplexed. The reckless ones, on the other hand, pronounce at once, saying, "They are filled with new wine." Now it was in order that they might comply with the law and appear three times each year in the temple that they lived there, the "devout men from all nations." Notice that the writer does not flatter

them: he does not say that they did not pronounce judgment. What does he say? "And at this sound the crowd gathered and was bewildered." This is quite likely, since they thought that things were coming to a head for them because of the outrage committed against Christ. HOMILIES ON THE ACTS OF THE APOSTLES 4.[1]

2:8-11 Hearing of God's Wonderful Works

THE UNCOUTH RUSTIC HAS OVERCOME THEM ALL. CHRYSOSTOM: Even Plato, who talked a great deal, is now silent. His voice was heard everywhere, not only among his own people but also among the Parthians, the Medes, the Elamites, in India, in short, in every part of the earth and to the ends of the world. But where is the arrogance of Greece now? Where the name of Athens? Where the ravings of the philosophers? He of Galilee, he of Bethsaida, he, the uncouth rustic, has overcome them all. Are you not ashamed (confess it!) at the very name of your vanquisher's country? And if you hear his own name as well, that he was called Cephas, you will hide your faces even more. For *this* has utterly defeated you, because you believe it is a disgrace; you believe that glibness of tongue is praisewor-

[1]NPNF 1 11:27**.

thy and lack of glibness a disgrace. You did not travel the road that ought to have been followed. Instead, you left the road to the kingdom, so easy and smooth, and walked the road that was rough, steep and laborious. Therefore, you did not arrive at the kingdom of heaven. HOMILIES ON THE ACTS OF THE APOSTLES 4.[2]

THE CHURCH GATHERS SCATTERED LANGUAGES. ARATOR: Long after the old ark had overcome the waters of the sea, malicious people wished to extend their tower [of Babel] into heaven. In them, irreligious hearts divided the forms of their speech, and the good will in these arrogant confederates perished with their voice. At that time there was a confusion of language for a homogenous race; now there is one [language] for many since [that language] rejoices at the appearance of the coming church, [a language that] will have harmonious sounds; and [the church] brings about a return of eloquence in peace for the obedient [apostles], and the humble order gathers again what arrogant people scattered. ON THE ACTS OF THE APOSTLES 1.[3]

2:13 The Mockery of Others

THE NEW WINE OF THE TRUTH. ARATOR: Also, the error that they are moved by new wine is, by allegorical reasoning, the truth—the intoxicating teaching of heaven has filled them from a fresh spring. New vessels have taken on new liquid and are not spoiled by the bitter [liquid] that filled the old vats,[4] [the new vessels] drinking in from the vine which, with Christ as the cultivator, gave a banquet in words [and] from which

those waters that he transformed are red,[5] and he made the poor flavor of the [old] law boil in the books of the church. ON THE ACTS OF THE APOSTLES 1.[6]

NEW WINE IN NEW SKINS. BEDE: These mockers nevertheless mystically bore witness to truths, for they [the disciples] were not filled with the old wine, which ran short in the marriage of the church, but with the new wine of spiritual grace. For now new wine had come in new skins,[7] since the apostles reechoed the wonderful works of God not "in the oldness of the letter but in the newness of the Spirit."[8] COMMENTARY ON THE ACTS OF THE APOSTLES 2.13.[9]

NEW WINE OF THE NEW COVENANT. CYRIL OF JERUSALEM: For in truth the wine was new, the grace of the New Testament. But this new wine was from a spiritual vine, which already had often borne fruit in the prophets and sprouted forth in the New Testament. For just as in the order of nature the vine, remaining ever the same, brings forth new fruit according to the seasons, so too the same Spirit, remaining what he is, having wrought in the prophets, now manifested something new and marvelous. His grace had indeed been granted to the fathers in times past, but now it came in superabundance; in their case they received a share of the Holy Spirit, now they were baptized in all fullness. CATECHETICAL LECTURE 17.18.[10]

---

[2]NPNF 1 11:29**. [3]OAA 29*. [4]See Lk 5:37-38. The old vats are the scribes and Pharisees. [5]Jn 2:1-11. [6]OAA 29*. [7]Mt 9:17. [8]Rom 7:6. [9]CS 117:31*. [10]FC 64:107*.

2:14-21 PETER ADDRESSES THE MULTITUDE

[14]*But Peter, standing with the eleven, lifted up his voice and addressed them, "Men of Judea and all who dwell in Jerusalem, let this be known to you, and give ear to my words.* [15]*For these men are not drunk, as you suppose, since it is only the third hour of the day;* [16]*but this is what was spoken by the prophet Joel:*

[17]*"And in the last days it shall be, God declares,*
that I will pour out my Spirit upon all flesh,
and your sons and your daughters shall prophesy,
and your young men shall see visions,
and your old men shall dream dreams;
[18]*yea, and on my menservants and my maidservants in those days*
I will pour out my Spirit; and they shall prophesy.
[19]*And I will show wonders in the heaven above*
and signs on the earth beneath,
blood, and fire, and vapor of smoke;
[20]*the sun shall be turned into darkness*
and the moon into blood,
before the day of the Lord comes,
the great and manifest day.
[21]*And it shall be that whoever calls on the name of the Lord shall be saved."*

OVERVIEW: This is the first of the missionary or evangelistic discourses in Acts. It can be divided into two parts. In the first part, after a peroration (remarked upon by BEDE), Peter explains the phenomena the crowd is witnessing by an appeal to the prophecy of Joel in whose last line "the Lord" is considered to be a reference to Jesus.[1] The Fathers are sensitive to the role of the authority of scriptural prophecy (CHRYSOSTOM) and are fascinated with the symbolism of the third hour (ARATOR, BEDE), that the Son who had been crucified on the third hour now sends the Spirit on the third hour (CYRIL OF JERUSALEM). They understand in their own way the eschatological application of Joel's words and their imagery (BEDE, CHRYSOSTOM) though they do not seem to have appreciated Luke's notion that the "Day of the Lord" and "the last days" refer to the age of the church now being inaugurated to be completed at the return of the Lord.

2:14 Peter and the Eleven

ONCE FEARFUL, PETER IS NOW BOLD. CHRYSOSTOM: What is meant by "with the eleven"? They expressed themselves through a common voice, and he spoke for everyone. The eleven stood by as witnesses to what he said. "He raised his voice," that is, he spoke with great confidence, that they might perceive the grace of the Spirit. He, who could not endure the questioning of a poor girl, now discourses with such great confi-

---

[1]See Rom 10:13.

dence in the middle of people all breathing murder upon him. This in itself became an indisputable proof of the resurrection. He spoke [among] people who could deride and make a joke of such sort things! . . . For wherever the Holy Spirit is present, people of clay are changed into people of gold. Look at Peter now, if you would, and scrutinize the timid one, the man without understanding (as Christ said, "Are you also still without understanding?"[2]). This is the man who was called Satan after that marvelous confession.[3] Consider also the unanimity of the apostles. Of their own accord they yielded to him the office of speaking, for there was no need for them all to speak. So "he raised his voice and addressed them" with every confidence. HOMILIES ON THE ACTS OF THE APOSTLES 4.[4]

2:15 The Third Hour of the Day

A TRIUNE SIGNIFICANCE. ARATOR: The third hour became celebrated by the heavenly sayings: the one God has this number, a single Substance distinguished by three Persons; [a Substance] that many proofs demonstrate to us is also at the same time demonstrated by the hour. ON THE ACTS OF THE APOSTLES 1.[5]

THE THIRD HOUR. BEDE: In order to proclaim to the world the glory of the indivisible Trinity, the Holy Spirit descended appropriately at the third hour. And since it was said above, "They were persevering in prayer," they quite rightly received the Holy Spirit at the hour of prayer, so that it might be shown to readers that it is not easy to receive the grace of the Holy Spirit unless the mind is raised from material things by concentration on the things that are above. Now we read that three times a day Daniel bent his knees and prayed,[6] and the church understands these to have been the third, sixth and ninth hours.[7] Also the Lord sent the Holy Spirit at the third hour, he himself ascended the cross at the sixth, and he yielded up his soul at the ninth.[8] He thus saw fit to enjoin these same hours preeminently upon

the rest of us and to sanctify them. COMMENTARY ON THE ACTS OF THE APOSTLES 2.15.[9]

SIGNIFICANT EVENTS AT THE THIRD HOUR. CYRIL OF JERUSALEM: For he who, according to Mark, was crucified at the third hour, has now at the third hour sent his grace. For his grace is not one and the Spirit's another, but he who was then crucified and had promised, fulfilled what he had promised. CATECHETICAL LECTURE 17.19.[10]

2:16 Spoken by the Prophet Joel

THE AUTHORITY OF THE PROPHETS. CHRYSOSTOM: He did not say that it was the Holy Spirit, nor did he mention the words of the prophet, but he brought in the prophecy by itself to fight its own battle. He also said nothing about Judas, although it was clear to everyone what sort of penalty he paid and the punishment he underwent. For nothing was more forceful than to argue with them from prophecy, which was even more forceful than facts. For when Christ performed miracles, they often contradicted him. But when Christ adduced the prophet, saying, "The Lord said to my Lord, Sit at my right hand," they were silent, and "no one was able to give him an answer."[11] HOMILIES ON THE ACTS OF THE APOSTLES 5.[12]

2:17-18 The Lord's Spirit Poured Out

BREATHING FORTH OF SPIRIT. BEDE: The word *effusion* shows the lavishness of the gift, for the grace of the Holy Spirit was not to be granted, as formerly, only to individual prophets and priests, but to everyone in every place, regardless of sex, state of life or position. The prophet subsequently explains what *all flesh* may be, saying, "Your sons and daughters will prophesy"[13] and so

---

[2]Mt 15:16. [3]Mt 16:23. [4]NPNF 1 11:28-29**. [5]*OAA* 29. [6]Dan 6:10. [7]Jerome *Commentary on Daniel* 2.6.10 (CCL 75a:832). [8]Mt 27:45-46. [9]CS 117:31-32*. [10]FC 64:108*. [11]Mt 22:46. [12]NPNF 1 11:33**. [13]Joel 2:28 (3:1 LXX).

forth, and "I will give prodigies in heaven above and signs on the earth beneath."[14] The prodigies in heaven were given when with the Lord's birth a new star appeared, and with his ascending of the cross the sun was dimmed and heaven itself was covered with darkness.[15] The signs on the earth were given when, with the Lord's breathing forth of his spirit, it [the earth] trembled violently, broke open sepulchers, split apart rocks and brought forth alive again the bodies of many of the saints who had fallen asleep.[16] Commentary on the Acts of the Apostles 2.17.[17]

The Spirit on All Flesh. Origen: I see, however, that the special coming of the Holy Spirit to people is declared to have happened after Christ's ascension into heaven rather than before his coming into the world. Before that time the gift of the Holy Spirit was bestowed on prophets only and on a few others among the people who happened to have proved worthy of it. On First Principles 2.7.2.[18]

2:19 Wonders in Heaven

Blood, Fire and Smoke. Bede: [The blood is] of the Lord's side; the fire of the Holy Spirit; the vapor of compunction and tears, because just as smoke is produced from fire, so vapor is produced from the ardor of the Holy Spirit. And as for blood flowing in a vigorous stream from [the Lord's] dead flesh,[19] because this is contrary to the nature of our bodies it remains [for us] to believe that this was done for a sign. A sign of what, to be sure, if not of our salvation and the life that is born from his death? It is also possible to understand the fire as the enlightening of the faithful, and the vapor of smoke as the blindness of the Jews who did not believe. Similarly when about to give the law the Lord descended in fire and smoke[20] because through the brilliance of his manifestation he enlightened the humble, and through the murky smoke of error he dimmed the eyes of the proud. Commentary on the Acts of the Apostles 2.19.[21]

2:20 The Great Day

Do Not Sin with Impunity. Chrysostom: At the same time, the apostle strikes fear into them by reminding them of the darkness that had lately occurred and leading them to expect things to come. "Before that great and glorious day of the Lord come." He means: do not be confident because at present you sin with impunity. . . . Do you see how he shook and shattered their souls and turned laughter into a plea for acquittal? Homilies on the Acts of the Apostles 5.[22]

Day of Judgment. Bede: This is believed partly as something that had been done at the Lord's passion and partly as something to be done in the future, before the great day of the Lord, that is, the day of judgment. For at that earlier time [of the passion], the sun was darkened,[23] but the turning of the moon into blood could not have appeared openly to humankind, for inasmuch as it was then, at Passover, in the fifteenth [day of the lunar month], the moon was hidden by day from the sight of mortals by the interposition of the earth. Commentary on the Acts of the Apostles 2.20.[24]

2:21 Calling on the Name of the Lord

Each According to Deeds. Chrysostom: "Everyone," he says (not yet revealing the meaning), be he priest, slave, free. There is no male, no female in Christ Jesus, no slave, no free, for all these are but shadow. For if in the palaces of kings there is no highborn or lowborn, but each arrives through his deeds, and if in craftsmanship each is shown by his works, all the more so it should be in the pursuit of wisdom. Homilies on the Acts of the Apostles 5.[25]

---

[14]Joel 2:30 (3:3 LXX). [15]Mt 2:2; 27:45. [16]Mt 27:51-52. [17]CS 117:32*. [18]OFP 117*. [19]Jn 19:34. [20]Ex 19:18. [21]CS 117:32-33*. [22]NPNF 1 11:32**. [23]Mt 27:45. [24]CS 117:33*. [25]NPNF 1 11:34**.

2:22-36 PETER DISCOURSES ON THE RESURRECTION

[22]"Men of Israel, hear these words: Jesus of Nazareth, a man attested to you by God with mighty works and wonders and signs which God did through him in your midst, as you yourselves know— [23]this Jesus, delivered up according to the definite plan and foreknowledge of God, you crucified and killed by the hands of lawless men. [24]But God raised him up, having loosed the pangs of death, because it was not possible for him to be held by it. [25]For David says concerning him,

'I saw the Lord always before me,
for he is at my right hand that I may not be shaken;
[26]therefore my heart was glad, and my tongue rejoiced;
moreover my flesh will dwell in hope.
[27]For thou wilt not abandon my soul to Hades,
nor let thy Holy One see corruption.
[28]Thou hast made known to me the ways of life;
thou wilt make me full of gladness with thy presence.'

[29]"Brothers, I may say to you confidently of the patriarch David that he both died and was buried, and his tomb is with us to this day. [30]Being therefore a prophet, and knowing that God had sworn with an oath to him that he would set one of his descendants upon his throne, [31]he foresaw and spoke of the resurrection of the Christ, that he was not abandoned to Hades, nor did his flesh see corruption. [32]This Jesus God raised up, and of that we all are witnesses. [33]Being therefore exalted at the right hand of God, and having received from the Father the promise of the Holy Spirit, he has poured out this which you see and hear. [34]For David did not ascend into the heavens; but he himself says,

'The Lord said to my Lord, Sit at my right hand,
[35]till I make thy enemies a stool for thy feet.'

[36]Let all the house of Israel therefore know assuredly that God has made him both Lord and Christ, this Jesus whom you crucified."

OVERVIEW: After having announced, by his use of the text from Joel, that what his auditors are experiencing proves that a new era of prophecy has been inaugurated, Peter goes on to interpret prophetically the meaning of the event by linking it to the resurrection of Jesus. The event of the resurrection was prophesied by Psalm 16, while the fact that Jesus is now in a position of authority was foretold in Psalm 110 and is verified in his pouring out of the Holy Spirit. Peter concludes with a proclamation of the true identity of the crucified One as revealed by his being made Lord and Christ. The Fathers are sensitive to this important role of Peter (BEDE) and to the constant theme of the apostolic preaching that all that took place was the plan of God (ARATOR). They take a theological stance in dealing with the "pains of death," pointing out that death could not hold Christ (CHRYSOSTOM, AUGUSTINE, BEDE), that his flesh or his humanity died but that the Godhead is immortal (THEODORET, GREGORY OF NYSSA) and that by his risen humanity we are given immortality (GREGORY OF NYSSA). Augustine, typically, comes to grips with the statement that Jesus is the "firstborn of the dead"[1] in the light of the resurrection of the "saints" recorded by Matthew at the moment of Jesus' death.[2] The notion that the humanity of Christ is now the source of the Spirit is highlighted by Chrysostom and Bede, while many Fathers seem to take a contemplative delight in gazing on the transformation of the humanity of Jesus described by Peter's phrase, "God has made him both Lord and Christ."

2:22 People of Israel, Hear

A MAN APPROVED BY GOD. BEDE: As a learned teacher, Peter first admonishes unbelievers for the crime that had been committed, so that once their consciences had been stung by righteous fear, he might afterwards devote [his discourse] more advantageously to the plan of salvation. And because he is speaking to those who know the law, he shows that Christ himself is the one promised by the prophets. Nevertheless, here Peter does not at first give him the name Son of God on his own authority. Rather [he calls him] a man approved, a righteous man, a man raised from the dead—not raised with others in the ordinary and general resurrection (that is, the resurrection that is deferred to the end of the world), but raised in that resurrection celebrated on the third day, so that his assertion of a unique and glorious resurrection might acquire [the value of] a testimonial to his eternal divinity. For when he has proved that the bodies of others underwent corruption after death, he demonstrates that this man, of whom it is said, "I will not give over your holy one to see corruption,"[3] was exempt from human impermanence. Peter also proves that he [Christ] exceeded the merits of the [merely] human condition and that he should therefore be considered to be God rather than [merely] human.

In the history of Cornelius the centurion[4] and in the sermon given by the apostle Paul at Ath-

ens,[5] you will be shown the sort of introduction that the apostles used in preaching among the Gentiles. COMMENTARY ON THE ACTS OF THE APOSTLES 2.22-23.[6]

2:23 Delivered According to God's Plan

THE WOUND BECOMES THE MEDICINE. ARATOR: Also, permitting himself to suffer in accordance with the law of flesh born from the womb of a mother, he himself preferred to die in order that the world might not lose life. But that which was born of a child-bearing virgin, that died. Innocent, he was hung from a tree, and the burden of the tree [of Adam] was removed. Thus the wound of the unrighteous [Adam] became the medicine of God. ON THE ACTS OF THE APOSTLES I.[7]

2:24 God Raised Christ

THE TRAVAIL OF DEATH. CHRYSOSTOM: "But God raised him up, having freed him from the pangs of death, because it was impossible for him to be held in its power." Here he hinted at something great and sublime, for the expression "it was impossible" is in itself that of one assigning something. It shows that even death itself, when it held him, experienced birth pangs and suffered terribly (by pangs of death the Old Testament means danger and disaster[8]). It also shows that he so rose as never again to die. For the words "because it was impossible for him to be held in its power" mean that his resurrection was not common to the rest. HOMILIES ON THE ACTS OF THE APOSTLES 6.[9]

NEVER HELD BY THE PANGS OF DEATH.
AUGUSTINE: And if one is hard put to explain

---

[1]Col 1:18. [2]Mt 27:51-53. [3]Ps 16:10 (15:10 LXX, Vg). [4]Acts 10:34-43. [5]Acts 17:22-31. [6]CS 117:33-34*. [7]OAA 30*. [8]The strange expression "[birth] pangs of death" is found several times in the LXX, notably in 2 Sam 22:6 and Ps 116:3 (114:3 LXX). Luke employs it in Peter's speech, and the Fathers try to deal with it, unaware that it is probably a mistranslation from Hebrew. [9]NPNF 1 11:38-39**.

how the pangs of hell were loosed by him—for he did not stay in them as in bondage and hence did not loose them as if they were chains that bound him—it is easy to understand that they might have been loosed like the snares of hunters, not because they held him, but so that they might not hold him. That is how we can believe that he loosed the pangs that did not bind him but did bind others whom he knew he was to set free.[10] LETTER 164.[11]

HE DIED AND ROSE AS MAN. THEODORET OF CYR: Peter said, "God has made this Jesus both Lord and Christ" and said too, "This Jesus whom you crucified God has raised up." Now it was the humanity, not the Godhead, that became a corpse, and he who raised it was the Word, the power of God, who said in the Gospel, "Destroy this temple, and in three days I will raise it up."[12] So when it is said that God has made him who became a corpse and rose from the dead both Lord and Christ, what is meant is the flesh, and not the Godhead of the Son. DIALOGUE 3.[13]

WE CAN RISE WITH HIM. GREGORY OF NYSSA: But since it was also fitting that he should implant in our nature the power of rising again from the dead, he becomes the "firstfruits of them that slept"[14] and the "firstborn from the dead,"[15] in that he first by his own act loosed the pains of death, so that his new birth from the dead was made a way for us also, since the pains of death, wherein we were held, were loosed by the resurrection of the Lord. REFUTATION OF EUNOMIUS'S "CONFESSION OF FAITH" 2.8.[16]

2:27 The Holy One Will Not See Corruption

HIS HUMANITY GIVES LIFE TO OURS. GREGORY OF NYSSA: Truly the prophet David also, according to the interpretation of the great Peter, said with foresight of him, "You will not leave my soul in hell, neither will you suffer your holy one to see corruption,"[17] while the apostle Peter thus expounds the saying, that "his soul was not left

in hell, neither did his flesh see corruption." For his Godhead, which was the same before taking flesh and in the flesh and after his passion, remains immutably the same, being at all times what it was by nature and so continuing for ever. But in the suffering of his human nature the Godhead fulfilled the dispensation for our benefit by severing the soul for a season from the body, yet without being itself separated from either of those elements to which it was once for all united and by joining again the elements that had been thus parted. [By this was given] to all human nature a beginning and an example that it should follow of the resurrection from the dead, that all the corruptible may put on incorruption, and all the mortal may put on immortality, our firstfruits having been transformed to the divine nature by its union with God, as Peter said, "This same Jesus whom you crucified, God has made both Lord and Christ." And we might cite many passages of Scripture to support such a position, showing how the Lord, reconciling the world to himself by the humanity of Christ, apportioned his work of benevolence to humankind between his soul and his body, willing through his soul and touching them through his body. But it would be superfluous to encumber our argument by entering into every detail. REFUTATION OF EUNOMIUS'S "CONFESSION OF FAITH" 2.13.[18]

2:29 David Died and Was Buried

NO ONE ROSE BEFORE JESUS. AUGUSTINE: I know it seems to some that the death of the Lord brought to certain just souls the same resurrection that is promised to us at the end of time, since it is written that by the earthquake that occurred at his passion the rocks were rent and the graves opened and many bodies of the saints arose and were seen with him in the holy

---

[10]Augustine seems intuitively to sense the meaning of the expression already discussed, which should be translated "the bonds of death." [11]FC 20:383**. [12]Jn 2:19. [13]NPNF 2 3:240*. [14]1 Cor 15:20. [15]Col 1:18. [16]NPNF 2 5:112-13*. [17]Ps 16:10 (15:10 LXX). [18]NPNF 2 5:127*.

city after his resurrection.[19] But, if these did not resume their sleep by the reburial of their bodies, and if so many preceded him in that resurrection, we must certainly examine and find out how Christ is the "firstborn from the dead."[20] The answer to this might be that it was said by anticipation, but it meant that the tombs were opened by the earthquake, while Christ hung on the cross, while the bodies of the just did not rise then, but later, after he had first risen, although it was added to that sentence by anticipation, as I said, so that we should unhesitatingly believe that Christ was the firstborn from the dead, and that it was then granted to the just to rise to eternal incorruption and immortality following his leadership. In that case, there still remains this difficulty, how Peter could say— and he said it with absolute truth, since he asserted that Christ, not David, was foretold by that prophecy—that his flesh did not see corruption, but he added that the tomb of David was still with them. And this would certainly not be a convincing argument, if David's body were no longer there, because, if he had risen at the time of Christ's death, his flesh would not have seen corruption, but his tomb would still be there. It seems hard that David should not have been in that resurrection of the just, when Christ was of his seed, as is so often, so distinctly and so honorably repeated to his praise. Those words also would be made ineffective that were said to the Hebrews concerning the just people of old: that they provided better things for us "that they should not be perfected without us,"[21] which would happen if they were established in that incorrupt resurrection that is promised for our perfection at the end of the world. LETTER 164.[22]

2:31 He Foresaw Christ's Resurrection

NOT ABANDONED TO HELL. BEDE: Christ did indeed descend, with respect to his soul, to those in hell so that he might come to the aid of those for whom it was necessary; but he was not abandoned in hell, because returning immediately he sought his body, which was to rise again. COMMENTARY ON THE ACTS OF THE APOSTLES 2.31.[23]

THE WORD ASSUMED A COMPLETE HUMANITY. THEODORET OF CYR: These and similar passages clearly point out that God the Word assumed not only a body but also a soul. DIALOGUE 2.[24]

2:33 The Promise from the Father

CHRIST RECEIVES AND POURS OUT THE SPIRIT. CHRYSOSTOM: "And having received the promise of the Holy Spirit." This again is important. He speaks of "the promise," because it was made before his passion. Observe how he now makes it all his, quietly making an important point. For if it was he who poured it out, it is of him that the prophet spoke above, "In the last days I will pour out my Spirit upon my servants, both men and women, and I will show portents in the heaven above."[25] Observe what Peter secretly inserted! . . . It also shows that the cross not only did not make him less but rendered him even more illustrious, seeing that formerly God promised it to him but now has given it. Alternatively, "the promise" refers to what he promised to us. He knew beforehand that it will come to pass and gave it to us greater after the resurrection. "He poured it out," that is, not requiring worthiness, and not simply that, but indeed with abundance. HOMILIES ON THE ACTS OF THE APOSTLES 6.[26]

THE PROMISE OF THE HOLY SPIRIT. BEDE: [In reference to the Spirit whom] you see in the tongues of fire; [whom] you hear in our discourse. Indeed, by saying that "he received from the Father the promise of the Holy Spirit, and he poured [the Spirit] forth, both natures of Christ are manifested, for he received [the Spirit] as a

---

[19]Mt 27:51-53. [20]Col 1:18; Rev 1:5. [21]Heb 11:40. [22]FC 20:387-88*. [23]CS 117:35*. [24]NPNF 2 3:196. [25]Acts 2:17. [26]NPNF 1 11:40-41**.

man and poured [him] forth as God."[27] COM-MENTARY ON THE ACTS OF THE APOSTLES 2.33B.[28]

THE LOWLY ONE IS EXALTED. THEODORET OF CYR: Who then was exalted? The lowly or the most high? And what is the lowly if it be not the human? And what is the most high save the divine? But God being most high needs no exaltation, and so the apostle says that the human is exalted, exalted that is in being "made both Lord and Christ." Therefore the apostle does not mean by this term "he made" the everlasting existence of the Lord but the change of the lowly to the exalted that took place on the right hand of God. By this word he declares the mystery of religion, for when he says "by the right hand of God exalted" he plainly reveals the ineffable economy of the mystery that the right hand of God, which created all things, which is the Lord by whom all things were made and without whom nothing consists of things that were made,[29] through the union lifted up to its own exaltation the manhood united to it. DIALOGUE 2.[30]

2:34-35 David Did Not Ascend

SON AND LORD OF DAVID. AUGUSTINE: We know that Christ took his seat at the right hand of the Father after his resurrection from the dead and his ascension into heaven. It is already accomplished. We do not see it, yet we believe it. We have read it in the sacred Books, we have heard it preached, we hold it by faith. And by the very fact that he was the son of David, he has become David's Lord. That which was born of David's seed is so honored that he is also David's Lord. You wonder at this as if such things did not happen in human affairs. For if it should happen that someone became king, though his father was a commoner, would he not be the lord of his father? It is wonderful that it can happen: not only does the son of a commoner become king and thus the lord of his father, but the son of a layman becomes a bishop and thus the father of his father. Therefore, by the very fact that Christ

took on flesh, that in the flesh he died, that in the same flesh he rose again, and in the same flesh he ascended into heaven and sits at the right hand of the Father, and in the same flesh now so honored and glorified, transformed into a heavenly condition, he is still the son of David and also the Lord of David. EXPLANATIONS OF THE PSALMS 109.7.[31]

NOT DIVINITY BUT FLESH. BEDE: For it was not divinity but flesh that was crucified, and this certainly can happen because it was able to be crucified. COMMENTARY ON THE ACTS OF THE APOSTLES 2.34B.[32]

A MAN RECEIVES DIVINE HONORS. THEODORET OF CYR: The words "Sit on my right hand"[33] he speaks as to man, for they are not spoken to him that sits ever on the throne of glory, God the Word after his ascension from earth, but they are said to him who has now been exalted to the heavenly glory as man, as the apostles say, "for David is not ascended into the heavens, but he himself says that the Lord said to my Lord 'Sit on my right hand.'" The order is human, giving a beginning to the sitting; but it is a divine dignity to sit together with God "to whom thousand thousands minister and before whom ten thousand times ten thousand stand."[34] DIALOGUE 2.[35]

2:36 Lord and Christ

THE CRUCIFIED ONE IS EXALTED. IRENAEUS: Thus the apostles did not preach another God or another Fullness or that the Christ who suffered and rose again was one, while he who flew off on high was another and remained impassible; but that there was one and the same God the Father, and Christ Jesus who rose from the dead. They preached faith in him to those who did not believe on the Son of God and exhorted them out of the prophets, that the Christ whom God

---

[27]Augustine *De Trinitate* 15.26 (CCL 50a:527). [28]CS 117:35*. [29]Jn 1:3. [30]NPNF 2 3:208*. [31]CCL 40:1606-7. [32]CS 117:36*. [33]Ps 110:1 (109:1 LXX). [34]Dan 7:10. [35]NPNF 2 3:215-16*.

promised to send, he sent in Jesus, whom they crucified and God raised up. AGAINST HERESIES 3.12.2.[36]

CHRIST'S TRUE IDENTITY REVEALED. GREGORY OF NYSSA: We, learning this from him, say that the whole context of the passage tends one way—the cross itself, the human name, the indicative turn of the phrase. For the word of the Scripture says that in regard to one person two things were wrought—by the Jews, the passion, and by God, honor. It is not as though one person had suffered and another had been honored by exaltation. He further explains this yet more clearly by his words in what follows, "being exalted by the right hand of God." Who then was

"exalted"? He that was lowly, or he that was the highest? and what else is the lowly but the humanity? what else is the highest but the divinity? Surely, God needs not to be exalted, seeing that he is the highest. It follows, then, that the apostle's meaning is that the humanity was exalted: and its exaltation was effected by its becoming Lord and Christ. And this took place after the passion. It is not therefore the pretemporal existence of the Lord that the apostle indicates by the word *made* but that change of the lowly to the lofty that was effected "by the right hand of God." AGAINST EUNOMIUS 5.3.[37]

---

[36]ANF 1:430*.   [37]NPNF 2 5:177-78*.

2:37-41 THE CONVERSION OF THE THREE THOUSAND

[37]*Now when they heard this they were cut to the heart, and said to Peter and the rest of the apostles, "Brothers, what shall we do?"* [38]*And Peter said to them, "Repent, and be baptized every one of you in the name of Jesus Christ for the forgiveness of your sins; and you shall receive the gift of the Holy Spirit.* [39]*For the promise is to you and to your children and to all that are far off, every one whom the Lord our God calls to him."* [40]*And he testified with many other words and exhorted them, saying, "Save yourselves from this crooked generation."* [41]*So those who received his word were baptized, and there were added that day about three thousand souls.* [42]*And they devoted themselves to the apostles' teaching and fellowship, to the breaking of bread and the prayers.*

OVERVIEW: We see here the first instance of a Lukan narrative technique, the interrupted speech (e.g., Acts 7:54; 10:44; 22:22). Peter's response includes four elements: repentance, baptism in the name of Jesus, forgiveness of sins and the reception of the Holy Spirit. Thus, while the question asked by the crowd echoes that asked of John the Baptist (Lk 3:10), the answer is quite different. Luke has a

theology of the name of Jesus that "connotes the real and effective presence of Jesus himself."[1] The expression "were added" once again points to the divine causality governing the life of the church. Chrysostom is, as ever, looking for moral examples to move his audience to put their faith into practice. He is

---

[1]Fitzmyer, *Acts*, 266.

---

keen to point out the temperament of Peter, the character of gentleness that he conveys in order to bring his audience to repentance, but he does not hesitate to shame those who, unlike those recounted here, delay their repentance. Bede pulls the narrative together by setting out an analogy with nature (smoke causing tears) to explain how this repentance was a part of Joel's prophecy that God would pour out his Spirit. He also calls attention to the significance of the time this event occurred, on Pentecost, the day the law was given and the day of the festival of first fruits. Here, the symbol of the fruits comes to light as the souls of the faithful.

2:37 Cut to the Heart

THE GENTLENESS OF PETER. CHRYSOSTOM: Do you see what a great thing gentleness is, how it stings our hearts more than vehemence? It inflicts indeed a keener wound. For in the case of bodies that have become callous, a blow does not affect the sense so powerfully, but if someone first softens them and makes them tender, then a stab is effective. Likewise here one must first soften, and that which softens is not wrath, not vehement accusation, not reproach, but gentleness. . . . For notice how he gently reminded them of the outrages they have committed, adding no comment. He spoke of the gift of God, he brought in the grace that bears witness to the event, and he drew out his discourse to still greater length. They stood in awe of the gentleness of Peter, because he was speaking like a father and caring teacher to them who crucified his master and breathed murder against himself and his companions. They were not merely persuaded; they even condemned themselves. They came to a sense of their past behavior. HOMILIES ON THE ACTS OF THE APOSTLES 7.[2]

FULFILLMENT OF PROPHECY. BEDE: Behold the fulfillment of the prophecy of Joel.[3] Notice that after the fire of the Holy Spirit there followed the vapor of compunction, for smoke tends to cause tears. Those who have laughed in ridicule begin to weep. They beat their breasts. They present their prayer to God as a sacrifice, so that as people who are to be saved they may be able to taste of that blood that before, when they were damned, they had called down upon themselves and their children.[4] COMMENTARY ON THE ACTS OF THE APOSTLES 2.37.[5]

2:38 Repent and Be Baptized

PROVED BY THEIR DEEDS. CHRYSOSTOM: "What shall we do?" They did what must be done, but we the opposite. They condemned themselves and despaired of their salvation. This is what made them such as they were. They knew what a gift they had received. But how will you become like them, when you do everything in an opposite spirit? As soon as they heard, they were baptized. They did not speak these cold words that we do now, nor did they contrive delays, even though they heard all the requirements. For they did not hesitate when they were commanded to "save yourselves from this generation" but welcomed it. They showed their welcome through action and proved through deeds what sort of people they were. HOMILIES ON THE ACTS OF THE APOSTLES 7.[6]

2:41 Three Thousand Souls

FIRSTFRUITS. BEDE: On the fiftieth day of Passover, when the law was given, Moses indeed ordered the festival of firstfruits to be introduced.[7] Now, however, with the coming of the Holy Spirit, it is not sheaves of grain but the firstfruits of souls that are consecrated to the Lord. COMMENTARY ON THE ACTS OF THE APOSTLES 2.41.[8]

---

[2]NPNF 1 11:44**. [3]Joel 2:28. [4]Mt 27:25. Bede reads Matthew's words in a literal sense and thus sees them as an acceptance of condemnation, rather the ironic analogy between these words and the ritual act of being sprinkled with the blood of the lamb at the feast of the atonement and thus a proleptic acceptance of the fruits of Christ's self-surrender. [5]CS 117:36-37*. [6]NPNF 1 11:48-49**. [7]Ex 23:16; 34:22, 26. [8]CS 117:37*.

2:43-47 THE COMMUNITY OF BELIEVERS

[43]*And fear came upon every soul; and many wonders and signs were done through the apostles.* [44]*And all who believed were together and had all things in common;* [45]*and they sold their possessions and goods and distributed them to all, as any had need.* [46]*And day by day, attending the temple together and breaking bread in their homes, they partook of food with glad and generous hearts,* [47]*praising God and having favor with all the people. And the Lord added to their number day by day those who were being saved.*

OVERVIEW: This is the first of what is called the summary statements in Acts. Two others are similar to this one in that they describe the life of the early community, once again showing the work of God in the church (Acts 4:32-37; 5:12-16). The economic dimension of the community is something as important to Luke as is Jesus' teaching on poverty. The mention of having all things in common is probably an allusion to Aristotle's treatise on friendship as it was quoted and implemented in the Pythagorean communities, while the mention in the next statement that there was no one in "need" among them is an allusion to Deuteronomy 15:4, 11 (LXX), implying that now both the biblical and pagan ideals have found their fulfillment in the early community.[1] Of the four characteristics of the early community, the ancients tend to accent detachment from wealth, while the moderns try to determine whether the breaking of the bread is a eucharistic celebration. Most are unclear, while acknowledging a quasi-technical status to the expression in later times. Father Melchior Verheijen has devoted an article to the study of Augustine's use of Acts 4:32-35.[2] There are least fifty occurrences in the writings of Augustine where this text is theologically operative. It will suffice to quote but a few here.

2:44 All Things in Common

DOUBLE ARDOR OF LOVE. BEDE: If the love of God pervades our hearts, without a doubt it will soon engender affection for our neighbor as well. Hence, because of the double ardor of one and the same love, we read that the Holy Spirit was given twice to the apostles, and the possession of everything without [anyone] having anything of his own is a great token of brotherly love. COMMENTARY ON THE ACTS OF THE APOSTLES 2.44.[3]

2:46 Breaking Bread

GLADNESS AND SIMPLICITY OF HEART. CHRYSOSTOM: Do you see that the words of Peter contain this also, namely, the regulation of life? ["And singleness of heart."] For no gladness can exist where there is no simplicity. HOMILIES ON THE ACTS OF THE APOSTLES 7.[4]

REJOICE. AUGUSTINE: One who wishes to make a place for the Lord should rejoice not in private joy but in the joy of all (*gaudio communi*). EXPLANATIONS OF THE PSALMS 131.5.[5]

UNITY OF THE TRINITY. AUGUSTINE: If, as they drew near to God, those many souls became, in the power of love, but one soul and these many hearts but one heart, what must the very source

---

[1]For a discussion of this point, one may consult Francis Martin, "Monastic Community and the Summary Statements in Acts," in *Contemplative Community: An Interdisciplinary Symposium*, ed. Basil Pennington, 13-46, CS 21 (Washington, D.C.: Cistercian Publications, 1972). [2]*Théologie de la Vie Monastique*, 201-12. [3]CS 117:37*. [4]NPNF 1 11:45-46. [5]PL 37:1718.

of love effect between the Father and the Son? Is not the Trinity for even greater reasons, but one God? . . . If the love of God poured forth in our hearts by the Holy Spirit, who is given to us, is able to make of many souls but one soul and of many hearts but one heart, how much more are the Father and the Son and Holy Spirit but one God, one Light, one Principle? Tractates on the Gospel of John 39.5.[6]

All in Common. Augustine: First of all, because you are gathered together in one that you might live harmoniously (*unanimes*) and that there be one soul and one heart toward God. And you should not call anything your own, but let all things be common to you and distributed to each one of you according to need. Letter 211.5.[7]

[6]CCL 36:347-48. [7]CSEL 57:359.

3:1-10 THE HEALING OF THE MAN LAME FROM BIRTH

[1]*Now Peter and John were going up to the temple at the hour of prayer, the ninth hour.* [2]*And a man lame from birth was being carried, whom they laid daily at that gate of the temple which is called Beautiful to ask alms of those who entered the temple.* [3]*Seeing Peter and John about to go into the temple, he asked for alms.* [4]*And Peter directed his gaze at him, with John, and said, "Look at us."* [5]*And he fixed his attention upon them, expecting to receive something from them.* [6]*But Peter said, "I have no silver and gold, but I give you what I have; in the name of Jesus Christ of Nazareth, walk."* [7]*And he took him by the right hand and raised him up; and immediately his feet and ankles were made strong.* [8]*And leaping up he stood and walked and entered the temple with them, walking and leaping and praising God.* [9]*And all the people saw him walking and praising God,* [10]*and recognized him as the one who sat for alms at the Beautiful Gate of the temple; and they were filled with wonder and amazement at what had happened to him.*

Overview: In a rhythm not unlike that of the Fourth Gospel, Acts 3 begins with an account of a miracle followed by a discourse (Acts 3:1-10, 11-26). This healing miracle and the explanation of its significance is the next stage in the witness of the new Israel to the old. There next follows an account of the arrest of Peter and John and another discourse (Acts 4:1-22), and the section concludes with the prayer of the community and the response of the Holy Spirit (Acts 4:23-31). Arator and Bede note Luke's allusive imagery using the helplessness of lameness or paralysis as a symbol for the need for faith.[1] Six of the Fathers draw attention to the relationship between Peter's poverty and his power from Christ, while Chrysostom points us to a common New Testament allusive symbol that employs the verb "to raise" to evoke the notion of healing as a manifestation of the power of Christ's resurrection.[2]

3:1 Peter and John Went to the Temple

[1]See, for example, Acts 14:8-9; Lk 5:20 and par. [2]See, for instance, Mk 1:31 (Mt 8:15; Lk 4:39); Mt 9:25 (Mk 5:41-42; Lk 8:54-55); Jas 5:15.

APOSTOLIC LABOR. BEDE: Then, laboring continuously until evening, they imbued many thousands of people with the word of faith, because the teachers of the church, coming at the end of the world, also preach first to ailing Israel and afterwards to the Gentile world. For they are the laborers whom the householder brought into the vineyard at the ninth and the eleventh hour.[3] COMMENTARY ON THE ACTS OF THE APOSTLES 3.1.[4]

3:2 A Man Lame from Birth

LAME WITHOUT FAITH. BEDE: Because the people of Israel were found rebellious not only after the Lord's incarnation but even from the earliest times when the law was given, they were as if lame from the mother's womb. This was well prefigured by Jacob's being blessed, indeed, but lame when he wrestled with the angel,[5] for this same people, when they prevailed over the Lord in his passion, was in some of [its members] blessed through the faith but in others lame through infidelity.[6] COMMENTARY ON THE ACTS OF THE APOSTLES 3.2A.[7]

THE BEAUTIFUL GATE. BEDE: The beautiful gate of the temple is the Lord. Whoever enters through him will be saved. Enfeebled Israel, being unable to walk to this gate, was brought there by the words of the law and the prophets, so that they might request help from those who were entering into the interior places of the wisdom of the faith which they were to hear. Those who place the prophecies of things to come are, as it were, hearers at the gate. But Peter is the guide into the temple. To him, in virtue of his strong profession of faith, the epithet of "rock" and the keys of heaven were given.[8] COMMENTARY ON THE ACTS OF THE APOSTLES 3.2B.[9]

LAME ISRAEL CARRIED BY THE PROPHETS. ARATOR: The feeble man is laid at the Beautiful Gate. The poor man is not strong enough to go farther or to touch the threshold of the gate. His guilt denies him entrance. Who are those accustomed to carry Israel, lame in its heart, and who strive to bring it to the gate [called] beautiful, which signifies Jesus by its name?[10] Isaiah, Daniel, and those like them who proclaim with prophetic voice in obscure [words] the manifest miracles of Christ; and he who has the name of the gate thus himself warns, "I am the gate for you; he who refuses to enter through me will be a guilty thief."[11] ON THE ACTS OF THE APOSTLES 1.[12]

3:3 The Man Asked for Alms

POVERTY COMPELS US TO PERSEVERE. CHRYSOSTOM: "Peter directed his gaze at him, with John, and said, 'Look at us.'" Yet not even so were the man's thoughts elevated, but he persisted in his insistence. For such is poverty: it compels people to persist even in the face of refusal. Let this put us to shame, we who turn away in our prayers. HOMILIES ON THE ACTS OF THE APOSTLES 8.[13]

3:4 Peter Looked at the Man

THE LAME MAN'S FAITH. CHRYSOSTOM: What then does Peter do? He did not despise him; he did not look about for some rich subject; he did not say, "If the miracle is not done to some great one, nothing great is done." He did not expect any payment from him, nor was it in the presence of others that he healed him. For the man was at the entrance, not inside, where the crowd was. Peter did not look for any of these things, nor did he enter and preach; no, it was his bearing that drew the lame man to ask. And the wonder is that he believed so readily. For those who are set free from diseases of long standing hardly believe their very eyesight. After he was healed he remained with the apostles, giving thanks to

---

[3]Mt 20:5-6. [4]CS 117:43*. [5]Gen 32:24-29. [6]Augustine *City of God* 16.39 (CCL 48:545). [7]CS 117:43*. [8]Mt 16:16-19. [9]CS 117:43-44*. [10]See Ps 45:2 (44:3 LXX). [11]Jn 10:1. [12]*OAA* 33**. [13]NPNF 1 11:50*.

God. "He entered the temple with them, walking and leaping and praising God." Notice how he does not keep quiet. This was both in delight and to shut the mouths of the Jews. And to prevent them from thinking it was an act, he jumped up. This was beyond the possibility of acting. For if previously he was incapable of simply walking, even when oppressed by hunger (indeed, he would not have chosen to share the proceeds of his begging with his litter bearers if he could have fended for himself), this should hold true even more now. And why would he have put on an act for those who had given him no alms? It can only be that the man was grateful, even after his recovery. Both by his thankfulness and by the healing itself his faith is revealed. HOMILIES ON THE ACTS OF THE APOSTLES 8.[14]

3:5 The Man Focused on Them

SURPRISED BY HOPE. ARATOR: Hope disappointed the greedy prayer [for alms], but when [hope] withholds [one thing], it has better things in store. How often things despaired of are helpful to burdened people, and prosperity, born from an inauspicious seed, concealing its joyful nearness by sorrowful beginnings, comes in answer to prayer! The needy man will rejoice to have acquired more from an empty hand; he himself, asking for gifts, has been given to himself. ON THE ACTS OF THE APOSTLES 1.[15]

3:6 No Silver and Gold

SILVER AND GOLD I DO NOT HAVE. BEDE: The ancient tabernacle "indeed had ritual ordinances and a sanctuary, though an earthly one,"[16] embellished with gold and silver. But the blood of the gospel is more precious than the metals of the law. It springs forth because that people, who had been lying enfeebled in mind before the golden doorpost, was saved in the name of him who was crucified and [so now] enters the temple of the heavenly kingdom. In any case, blessed Peter, mindful of the Lord's command which was spo-

ken, "Do not possess gold and silver,"[17] did not hoard for himself the money that was put at the feet of the apostles but was inclined to reserve it for the use of the poor who had lost their birthright. COMMENTARY ON THE ACTS OF THE APOSTLES 3.6.[18]

THE FREEDOM OF POVERTY. CHRYSOSTOM: Let no one then be humiliated on account of his poverty: It is not poverty that humiliates, but wealth, which compels us to have need of many and forces us to be under obligations to many.... So, if poverty had made people wanting in boldness, Christ would not have sent his disciples with poverty to a work requiring great boldness. For the poor person is very strong and has nothing of which he may be wronged or evil to be prayed for. But the rich person is assailable on every side: just in the same way as one would easily catch a person who was dragging many long ropes after him, whereas one could not readily lay hold on a naked person. So here also it does not succeed in the case of the rich person: slaves, gold, lands, affairs innumerable, innumerable cares, difficult circumstances, necessities, make him an easy prey to all. ON THE EPISTLE TO THE HEBREWS 18.4.[19]

POWER IN THE NAME. JOHN CASSIAN: Those men who received power from God never used that power as if it were their own but referred the power to him from whom they received it; for the power itself could never have any force except through the name of him who gave it. And so both the apostles and all the servants of God never did anything in their own name but in the name and invocation of Christ. For the power itself derived its force from the same source as its origin, and it could not be given through the instrumentality of the ministers, unless it had come from the Author. ON THE INCARNATION OF THE LORD AGAINST NESTORIUS 7.19.[20]

---

[14]NPNF 1 11:51**. [15]OAA 32*. [16]Heb 9:1. [17]Mt 10:9. [18]CS 117:44*. [19]NPNF 1 14:453. [20]NPNF 2 11:614*.

SPIRITUAL WEALTH. ORIGEN: Do you see the riches of Christ's ministers? Do you see the greatness and nature of the gifts they bestow when they have nothing? Earthly possession cannot bestow those riches. HOMILIES ON GENESIS 16.5.[21]

GENEROUSLY FOLLOWING THE POOR CHRIST. EUSEBIUS OF CAESAREA: And who would not be astonished at their indifference to money, certified by their not turning from but welcoming a Master who forbade the possession of gold and silver, whose law did not even allow the acquisition of a second coat? Why, anyone only hearing such a law might reject it as too heavy, but these men are shown to have carried out the words in fact. PROOF OF THE GOSPEL 3.5.[22]

3:7 Peter Raised Him Up

THE RIGHT HAND OF EXAMPLE. BEDE: The one whom he encouraged by word he also strengthened by his right hand, because the discourse of a teacher is less efficacious in the hearts of his hearers if it is not also recommended by the example of his own action. COMMENTARY ON THE ACTS OF THE APOSTLES 3.7.[23]

THIS ACT MADE MANIFEST IN THE RESURRECTION. CHRYSOSTOM: "'In the name of Jesus Christ of Nazareth, walk.' And he took him by the right hand and raised him up." Such was also the way of Christ. Often he healed by word, often by an act, often he also held out his hand, when the people were somewhat weak in faith, so that the cure should not seem to occur by itself. "And he took him by the right hand and raised him up." This act made manifest the resurrection, for it was an image of the resurrection. HOMILIES ON THE ACTS OF THE APOSTLES 8.[24]

---

[21]FC 71:222*. [22]POG 1:136*. [23]CS 117:44*. [24]NPNF 1 11:50*.

3:11-16 PETER'S DISCOURSE IN SOLOMON'S PORTICO

[11]*While he clung to Peter and John, all the people ran together to them in the portico called Solomon's, astounded.* [12]*And when Peter saw it he addressed the people, "Men of Israel, why do you wonder at this, or why do you stare at us, as though by our own power or piety we had made him walk?* [13]*The God of Abraham and of Isaac and of Jacob, the God of our fathers, glorified his* servant[c] *Jesus, whom you delivered up and denied in the presence of Pilate, when he had decided to release him.* [14]*But you denied the Holy and Righteous One, and asked for a murderer to be granted to you,* [15]*and killed the Author of life, whom God raised from the dead. To this we are witnesses.* [16]*And his name, by faith in his name, has made this man strong whom you see and know; and the faith which is through Jesus[d] has given the man this perfect health in the presence of you all."*

c Or *child* d Greek *him*

OVERVIEW: The moderns analyze Peter's speech, which consists in an explanation of the healing of the lame man, pointing out how God glorified the very Jesus whom the Jews had denied and killed

(Acts 3:11-15a). He then proclaims that the disciples are witnesses of this resurrection and speaks of how the name of Jesus, and faith in this name, is the source of the man's healing (Acts 3:15b-16). In the second part of the speech Peter acknowledges the ignorance of his audience and, after pointing out the plan of God, calls them to repentance, explaining that this Jesus is the prophet spoken of by Moses (Acts 3:17-26). Chrysostom accents the theme of the apostles' humility and that all power comes from God. Cassian and Cassiodorus join him in this second motif. Ammonius speaks of the twofold faith in God, and Chrysostom points out how sure the apostles were of Jesus' resurrection since they attribute the miracle to him.

3:11 The People Ran Together

PROTECTED BY THE GUIDANCE OF PETER. ARATOR: After the threshold of the temple, the Porch of Solomon, who is rightly called Peacemaker, holds him [the lame man]. In the reign of faith, who will always be Peacemaker in the world except Christ?[1] He protects all who please him under the guidance of Peter, by whose leadership they stand up. ON THE ACTS OF THE APOSTLES 1.[2]

3:12 Why Do You Wonder?

THE APOSTLE'S HUMILITY. CHRYSOSTOM: They increased their glory even more by despising it. They revealed that what had just taken place was not a human act but was divine and that they were worthy of joining the beholders in admiration and not of receiving it from them. Do you see how free of ambition he is and how he rejects the honor paid to him? This is what the ancient fathers also did, as Daniel said, "not because of any wisdom that is in me."[3] HOMILIES ON THE ACTS OF THE APOSTLES 9.[4]

THE GLORY IS GOD'S. CHRYSOSTOM: But what is it that he means? I [Peter] am able, he declares,

to speak of far greater miracles, but I am unwilling, for fear that the greatness of the miracles should raise too high a notion of me among people. For this reason Peter also, when they had restored the lame man and all were wondering at them, in order to restrain the people and persuade them that they had exhibited nothing of this power of themselves or from their native strength, says, "Why do you look so earnestly on us, as though by our own power or holiness we had made this man to walk?" HOMILIES CONCERNING THE STATUES 1.17.[5]

TRUE EXCELLENCE. JOHN CASSIAN: Nor did they think that any one should be renowned for the gifts and marvels of God but rather for the fruits of his own good deeds, which are brought about by the efforts of his mind and the power of his works. For often, as was said above, people of corrupt minds, reprobate concerning the truth, both cast out devils and perform the greatest miracles in the name of the Lord. CONFERENCE 15.6.[6]

THE POWER OF THE KINGDOM. CASSIODORUS: It is through the saints' preaching that God's might and the glory of the kingdom are made known, in case they might be perhaps less sought if people did not know of them. His might was also made known when Peter and John made the man lame from birth walk, and they said, "Men of Israel, why marvel at this, as if by our strength or devotion we had made this man to walk?" And a little later they say that he was made whole in the name of Christ Jesus. The might of the Lord was also made known when the apostles invoked his name and made manifest diverse powers. EXPOSITION OF THE PSALMS 144.12.[7]

THE AUTHOR OF LIFE HAS LIFE FROM HIMSELF. CHRYSOSTOM: Notice again how discreetly he speaks of Christ's power, showing that he

---

[1]According to Jerome, Solomon means *pacificus*, peacemaker (*On Hebrew Names* 93). Cf. Mt 5:9. [2]*OAA* 33*. [3]Dan 2:30. [4]NPNF 1 11:55**. [5]NPNF 1 9:338*. [6]NPNF 2 11:448*. [7]*ACW* 53:427-28*.

raised himself. In his earlier speech he said, "because it was impossible for him to be held in its power;"[8] and here he says that they "killed the Author of life." Thus, it was not from another that he had his life. For the author of evil would be the one who gave birth to evil, the author of murder, the one who gave birth to murder, and likewise the author of life must be the one who has life from himself. HOMILIES ON THE ACTS OF THE APOSTLES 9.[9]

3:16 Made Strong in Jesus' Name

FAITH FOR HEALING. AMMONIUS: "And the faith which is through him." This is said because someone is healed through the faith that is directed to Christ. For it is necessary that the faith of both concur, that is, the faith of the one healed and the faith of the one praying over the sick person. This we see in the case of the paralytic[10] and the woman with the flow of blood.[11] CATENA ON THE ACTS OF THE APOSTLES 3.16.[12]

CERTAINTY OF THE RESURRECTION. CHRYSOSTOM: And yet they did not know it was in his name, but they knew this, that he was lame. Those who had made him stand like a healthy man—they themselves confessed that it was not by their own power but by that of Christ. If this were not so and if they did not truly believe that Christ had risen again, they would not have been willing to establish the honor of a dead man rather than their own, especially while the eyes of the multitude were upon them. HOMILIES ON THE ACTS OF THE APOSTLES 9.[13]

---

[8]Acts 2:24. [9]NPNF 1 11:57**. [10]Mt 9:2 and par. [11]Mt 9:22 and par. [12]CGPNT 3:64. [13]NPNF 1 11:58**.

3:17-26 CHRIST FORETOLD BY THE PROPHETS

[17]"And now, brothers, I know that you acted in ignorance, as did also your rulers. [18]But what God foretold by the mouth of all the prophets, that his Christ should suffer, he thus fulfilled. [19]Repent therefore, and turn again, that your sins may be blotted out, that times of refreshing may come from the presence of the Lord, [20]and that he may send the Christ appointed for you, Jesus, [21]whom heaven must receive until the time for establishing all that God spoke by the mouth of his holy prophets from of old. [22]Moses said, 'The Lord God will raise up for you a prophet from your brothers as he raised me up. You shall listen to him in whatever he tells you. [23]And it shall be that every soul that does not listen to that prophet shall be destroyed from the people.' [24]And all the prophets who have spoken, from Samuel and those who came afterwards, also proclaimed these days. [25]You are the sons of the prophets and of the covenant which God gave to your fathers, saying to Abraham, 'And in your posterity shall all the families of the earth be blessed.' [26]God, having raised up his servant,[c] sent him to you first, to bless you in turning every one of you from your wickedness."

c Or child

43

OVERVIEW: Modern commentators, who since the Middle Ages are more aware of the subjectivity and intentions of the author, see here another instance of Lukan theology and point out the resemblance here to the call to repentance in the speech at Pentecost (Acts 2:38-39). Also intriguing and unique to this passage are the remarks in Acts 3:19-20, which speak of the "times of refreshing," meaning the blessings to flow from repentance and baptism in this time before the Messiah returns from heaven, which is described as "until the time for establishing all." (A more literal and felicitous rendering might be, "until the times for the restoration of all things.") The theme of ignorance of those who were involved in the death of Jesus is a theme that occurs elsewhere in Acts (Acts 13:27; 17:30). Chrysostom states the working out of salvation and forgiveness in a rather unsatisfactory way that makes God appear a manipulator of human ignorance who then coerces through fear of punishment, rather than one who willingly handed himself over in weakness to undo the evil that would come upon him. Here is one of Chrysostom's least astute readings of the mystery of the cross. Didymus's concerns are grammatical but throw light on how the entire Bible, with no attention to the individual style of an author, was seen as a source of comparison for single passages in order to establish the meanings of different words. Origen offers a meditation on the time of restoration.

3:17 Acting in Ignorance

TWO EXCUSING CIRCUMSTANCES. CHRYSOSTOM: As he had been hard on them and had shown that he whom they crucified had risen, he now relaxes, by giving them the power of repentance: "And now, brothers, I know that you acted in ignorance, as did also your rulers." This is one ground of excuse. The second is of a different kind. As Joseph says to his brothers, "God sent me before you."[1] In the earlier speech Peter had briefly said, "This Jesus, delivered up according to the definite plan and foreknowledge of God,

you crucified and killed by the hands of lawless men."[2] He enlarges upon that here: "But what God foretold by the mouth of all the prophets, that his Christ should suffer, he thus fulfilled." HOMILIES ON THE ACTS OF THE APOSTLES 9.[3]

3:18 What God Foretold

GOD USES THE WICKEDNESS OF PEOPLE. CHRYSOSTOM: If indeed it was all the prophets and not only one of them who said this, it follows that, although the event took place through ignorance, it did not take place contrary to God's ordinance. See how great is the wisdom of God, when it uses the wickedness of others to bring about what must be. HOMILIES ON THE ACTS OF THE APOSTLES 9.[4]

3:21 Whom Heaven Must Receive

THE MEANING OF "UNTIL." DIDYMUS THE BLIND: Someone familiar with the way Scripture speaks knows that the words *until* and *then* are not to be taken in the strict sense meaning a specific time, as though when that time passes something else quite different must take place. Thus, what was said by God to some, "I am your God and until you grow old, I am he,"[5] does not imply that, when these addressees grow old, he will no longer be God. He is immortal and eternal. There are thousands of such instances that are contained in the divine teaching, and who can number them? Thus in the present text when it says that "heaven must receive the Lord until the time of restoration," this should be understood to mean that Christ, now received into heaven, will remain there until the consummation of the world. Then he will come in power when everything else is restored as the prophets foretold. Or it can be understood to mean that, when the end

---

[1]Gen 45:5. Joseph here is referring to the fact that his brothers' treachery was used in the plan of God. [2]Acts 2:23. [3]NPNF 1 11 55**. [4]NPNF 1 11:58**. [5]Is 46:4. Didymus has added "your God" to clarify the sense.

is near and sensible things will cease, then Christ will be higher than the heavens, not established in heaven but above heaven with that glory that he had with the Father before the world was.[6] Raised up above every visible creature, he will constitute an end to what is in heaven. CATENA ON THE ACTS OF THE APOSTLES 3.21.[7]

ALL THINGS RESTORED TO RIGHTEOUSNESS. ORIGEN: Everything endowed with reason will come under one law. . . . If we must refer to this subject, it will be with great brevity. The Stoics, indeed, hold that, when the strongest of the elements prevails, all things shall be turned into fire. But our belief is that the Word will prevail over the entire rational creation and change every soul into his own perfection. In this state all, by the mere exercise of his power, will choose what he desires and obtain what he chooses. For although, in the diseases and wounds of the body, there are some which no medical skill can cure, yet we hold that in the mind there is no evil so strong that it may not be overcome by the supreme Word and God. For stronger than all the evils in the soul is the Word and the healing power that dwells in him. This healing he applies, according to the will of God, to everything. The consummation of all things is the destruction of evil, although as to the question whether it shall be so destroyed that it can never anywhere arise again, it is beyond our present purpose to say. Many things are said obscurely in the prophecies on the total destruction of evil and the restoration to righteousness of every soul; but it will be enough for our present purpose to quote the following passage from Zephaniah: "Prepare and rise early; all the gleanings of their vineyards are destroyed. Therefore wait upon me, says the Lord, on the day that I rise up for a testimony. For my determination is to gather the nations, that I may assemble the kings, to pour upon them my indignation, even all my fierce anger. For all the earth shall be devoured with the fire of my jealousy. For then will I bring about a transformation of pure language among the people, that they may all call upon the name of the Lord, to serve him with one consent. From beyond the rivers of Ethiopia my suppliants, even the daughter of my dispersed, shall bring my offering. In that day you will not be ashamed for all your sinful deeds of transgression against me. For then I will take away out of your midst them that rejoice in your pride; and you will be haughty no more because of my holy mountain. I will also leave in your midst an afflicted and poor people, and they will trust in the name of the Lord. The remnant of Israel will not commit iniquity nor speak lies. Neither shall a deceitful tongue be found in their mouth, for they shall feed and lie down, and none shall make them afraid."[8] AGAINST CELSUS 8.72.[9]

3:22 The Lord Will Raise a Prophet

MOSES CONFIDES HIS DISCIPLES TO CHRIST. CHRYSOSTOM: Christ sent the Jews back to Moses so that, through Moses, he might draw them to himself. In the same way, Moses hands over his disciples to his teacher and commands them to believe him in all things. AGAINST THE ANO-MOEANS 12.5.[10]

3:24 All the Prophets Have Spoken

ALL IN ACCORD WITH PROPHECY. CHRYSOSTOM: Then [Peter] takes refuge in what is trustworthy, saying, "The Lord God will raise up for you a prophet from your brothers as he raised me up. You shall listen to him in whatever he tells you." And then the severity of the punishment, "And it shall be that every soul that does not listen to that prophet shall be destroyed from the people. And all the prophets who have spoken, from Samuel and those who came afterwards, also proclaimed these days." . . . It is remarkable that the two stand together, obedience and disobedience, and the punishment. "As I am," he says (why are you alarmed at this?), "You are the sons of the

---

[6]Jn 17:5. [7]CGPNT 3:66-67. [8]Zeph 3:7-13. [9]ANF 4:667*. [10]FC 72:287*.

prophets." It was to you that they spoke, and it was for your sake that all these things have come to pass. They were of the belief that they had alienated themselves through their outrage—for it was illogical that the same one was now crucified and now cherished them as his own. So he proves to them that both the one and the other are in accordance with prophecy. Homilies on the Acts of the Apostles 9.[11]

The Prophetic Movement. Bede: Although the patriarchs and saints of earlier times prophesied many things about Christ by their words and deeds, properly speaking the time of the prophets (I mean those who wrote clearly about the mystery of Christ and the church) had its beginning from Samuel, under whom the period of the kings began in Israel, and it lasted up to the deliverance from the Babylonian captivity. Commentary on the Acts of the Apostles 3.24.[12]

3:25 Sons of the Prophets and of the Covenant

You Are Not to Feel Like Castaways. Chrysostom: "Children of the covenant," that is, heirs. To prevent them from thinking that they are receiving this as a favor from Peter, he reveals that it was owed to them from the beginning, so that they might more readily believe that such is also the will of God. "God, having raised up his servant," he says, "sent him to you first." He did not say simply "he sent his servant to you," but adds that it was after the resurrection and when he had been crucified. Because he did not want them to think that it was he, and not the Father, who granted this favor, he says "to bless you." For if he is your brother and blesses you, it is a matter of promise. That is, so far from your having no share in these blessings, he wishes you to become advocates and authors of them to others. For you are not to feel like castaways. Again the resurrection. "In turning every one of you," he says, "from your wickedness," he blesses you [particularly], not in a general way. What kind of blessing is this? A great

one. For turning from wickedness, of course, does not suffice to destroy it. If it does not suffice to destroy, then what is meant by conferring a blessing? It is certainly not that the transgressor immediately becomes blessed but that he is released from his sins. . . . Then high praise also from the other side, so that for this reason too you are obliged to obey. He calls you "sons of the prophets and of the covenant," that is, heirs. Why then do you feel towards what is your own as if it were another's? True, you have done things worthy of condemnation, but you will be able to obtain pardon. Having spoken this, he is then able to say with truth, "God, having raised up his servant, sent him to you first, to bless you." He does not say, to save you, but what is greater, that the crucified one blesses his crucifiers. Homilies on the Acts of the Apostles 9.[13]

All the Families of the Earth. Bede: Christ indeed is the offspring of Abraham, and through faith in his name a blessing is promised to all the families of the earth, namely, Jews and Gentiles. However, the apostle soothed the minds of the Jews in order to make them more well-disposed to believing by saying that, out of the whole world, the Savior chose to visit and bless them first. Commentary on the Acts of the Apostles 3.25.[14]

3:26 God Sent Him to Bless You

One Person, Two Natures. Bede: Here it must be borne in mind that the one whom he calls the offspring of Abraham is at the same time the Son of God because of the two natures of the one Christ. Thus they should not believe either that Christ is only a man or that there is one son of man and one Son of God. This is the trap of heresy into which the mad Manes and Nestorius were misled. Commentary on the Acts of the Apostles 3.26.[15]

---

[11]NPNF 1 11:56**. [12]CS 117:45*. [13]NPNF 1 11:59-60**. [14]CS 117:45-46*. [15]CS 117:46*.

4:1-4 THE ARREST OF PETER AND JOHN

[1]*And as they were speaking to the people, the priests and the captain of the temple and the Sadducees came upon them,* [2]*annoyed because they were teaching the people and proclaiming in Jesus the resurrection from the dead.* [3]*And they arrested them and put them in custody until the morrow, for it was already evening.* [4]*But many of those who heard the word believed; and the number of the men came to about five thousand.*

OVERVIEW: The first twenty-two verses of Acts 4 recount a further incident in the life of the early community, and these verses are followed by a series of incidents narrated by Luke in order to give an intuitive understanding of how the risen Lord, the prophet like and transcending Moses, continues his work among Israel. Not only is he resurrected, but also the faithful through him (CHRYSOSTOM). The five thousand instructed in the wilderness by Jesus and the same number by apostles designate the people of the nations who would spiritually follow the mysteries of the same law (BEDE).

4:2 Proclaiming the Resurrection

THE POWER OF CHRIST'S RESURRECTION. CHRYSOSTOM: They were annoyed, not only because the apostles were teaching, but because they declared that not only was Jesus Christ himself risen from the dead but that through him we too rise again.... So powerful was his resurrection that he is the cause of resurrection for others as well. HOMILIES ON THE ACTS OF THE APOSTLES 10.[1]

4:3 The Apostles Arrested

SHAMELESSNESS BORN OF SIN. CHRYSOSTOM:

Consider how in the case of Christ they sought out a traitor, but now arrest the apostles with their own hands, having grown more audacious and more impudent since the crucifixion. For sin, while it is yet struggling to the birth, is attended with some sense of shame, but once fully formed, it makes those who practice it more shameless. HOMILIES ON THE ACTS OF THE APOSTLES 10.[2]

4:4 Many Who Heard Believed

FIVE THOUSAND. BEDE: If we take the five thousand men fed by the Lord in the wilderness[3] as [standing for] the people established under the law, but created anew by Christ's favor, they and this five thousand, who were instructed by the teaching of the apostles, can designate the people of the nations who would spiritually follow the mysteries of the same law. Also it was well done that both [groups of five thousand] were granted their heavenly favor in the evening, for when "the fullness of time came God sent his Son."[4] COMMENTARY ON THE ACTS OF THE APOSTLES 4.4.[5]

---

[1]NPNF 1 11:63**. [2]NPNF 1 11:63**. [3]Mt 14:13-21. [4]Gal 4:4. [5]CS 117:49*.

4:5-12 PETER'S DEFENSE

⁵On the morrow their rulers and elders and scribes were gathered together in Jerusalem, ⁶with Annas the high priest and Caiaphas and John and Alexander, and all who were of the high-priestly family. ⁷And when they had set them in the midst, they inquired, "By what power or by what name did you do this?" ⁸Then Peter, filled with the Holy Spirit, said to them, "Rulers of the people and elders, ⁹if we are being examined today concerning a good deed done to a cripple, by what means this man has been healed, ¹⁰be it known to you all, and to all the people of Israel, that by the name of Jesus Christ of Nazareth, whom you crucified, whom God raised from the dead, by him this man is standing before you well. ¹¹This is the stone which was rejected by you builders, but which has become the head of the corner. ¹²And there is salvation in no one else, for there is no other name under heaven given among men by which we must be saved."

OVERVIEW: Peter's speech was directed first to the people and then the leaders. Again the theme is the power of the risen Christ manifest in the healing of the lame man. Jesus had already prepared the apostles for the fact that they would be brought before the authorities (CHRYSOSTOM). By his resurrection he gave life to his own temple (CYRIL OF ALEXANDRIA). The cornerstone joins two walls—the Old and New Testaments (BEDE). Not merely to Israel but to all humanity is the one Mediator given (AUGUSTINE). The faithful of the Old Testament were saved by the incarnation and passion of the same Savior (BEDE).

4:8 Filled with the Holy Spirit

THE PROMISE FULFILLED. CHRYSOSTOM: And now recall what Christ said, "When they bring you before the synagogues, the rulers and the authorities, do not worry about how you are to defend yourselves or what you are to say; for the Holy Spirit will teach you at that very hour what you ought to say."[1] HOMILIES ON THE ACTS OF THE APOSTLES 10.[2]

4:10 Crucified by People, Raised by God

THE WORK OF THE FATHER AND THE SON.
CYRIL OF ALEXANDRIA: That the Father is said to have raised from the dead our Lord Jesus Christ (the effect of the act being on his flesh, clearly) is not in doubt. He, being the life-creating and active power of the Father, gave life to his own temple, as in "Destroy this temple and in three days I will raise it up."[3] What was made alive was not another's body, nor indeed one belonging to a man among us, but his own, the body of the Word. CATENA ON THE ACTS OF THE APOSTLES 4.10.[4]

4:11 The Stone Rejected by the Builders

THE CORNERSTONE EMBRACES TWO WALLS.
BEDE: The builders were the Jews, while all the Gentiles remained in the wasteland of idols. The Jews alone were daily reading the law and the prophets for the building up of the people. As they were building, they came to the cornerstone, which embraces two walls—that is, they found in the prophetic Scriptures that Christ, who would bring together in himself two peoples, was to come in the flesh. And, because they preferred to remain in one wall, that is, to be saved alone, they rejected the stone, which was not one-sided but

---

[1]Lk 12:11-12. [2]NPNF 1 11:64**. [3]Jn 2:19. [4]CGPNT 3:73.

two-sided. Nevertheless, although they were unwilling, God by himself placed this [stone] at the chief position in the corner, so that from two Testaments and two peoples there might rise up a building of one and the same faith. COMMENTARY ON THE ACTS OF THE APOSTLES 4.11.[5]

4:12 Salvation in No One Else

HE EXTENDS THROUGHOUT HISTORY. AUGUSTINE: For "there is one God, and one Mediator between God and men, the man Christ Jesus,"[6] since "there is no other name under heaven given to men, whereby we must be saved," and "in him God has defined to all men their faith, in that he has raised him from the dead."[7] Now without this faith, that is to say, without a belief in the one Mediator between God and humankind, the man Christ Jesus; without faith, I say, in his resurrection by which God has given assurance to all people and which no one could of course truly believe were it not for his incarnation and death; without faith, therefore, in the incarnation and death and resurrection of Christ, the Christian truth unhesitatingly declares that the ancient saints could not possibly have been cleansed from sin so as to have become holy and justified by the grace of God. And this is true both of the saints who are mentioned in holy Scripture and of those also who are not indeed mentioned therein but must yet be supposed to have existed—either before the deluge or in the interval between that event and the giving of the law or in the period of the law itself—not merely among the children of Israel, as the prophets, but even outside that nation, as for instance Job. For cleansing from sin was by the self-same faith. The one Mediator cleansed the hearts of these too, and there also was "shed abroad in them the love of God by the Holy Spirit,"[8] "who blows where he wills,"[9] not following people's merits but even producing these very merits himself. For the grace of God will in no wise exist unless it be wholly free. ON ORIGINAL SIN 2.24.28.[10]

SALVATION IS NOT IN ANY OTHER. BEDE: If the salvation of the world is in no other but in Christ alone, then the fathers of the Old Testament were saved by the incarnation and passion of the same Redeemer, by which we also believe and hope to be saved. For although the sacramental signs differed by reason of the times, nevertheless there was agreement in one and the same faith, because through the prophets they learned as something to come the same dispensation of Christ which we learned through the apostles as something which has been done. For there is no redemption of human captivity [to sinfulness] except in the blood of him who gave himself as a redemption for all. COMMENTARY ON THE ACTS OF THE APOSTLES 4.12.[11]

---

[5]CS 117:49-50*. [6]1 Tim 2:5. [7]Acts 17:31. [8]Rom 5:5. [9]Jn 3:8. [10]NPNF 1 5:247*. [11]CS 117:50*.

4:13-22 PETER AND JOHN ADMONISHED AND RELEASED

[13]*Now when they saw the boldness of Peter and John, and perceived that they were uneducated, common men, they wondered; and they recognized that they had been with Jesus.* [14]*But seeing the man that had been healed standing beside them, they had nothing to say in opposition.* [15]*But when*

they had commanded them to go aside out of the council, they conferred with one another, [16]saying, "What shall we do with these men? For that a notable sign has been performed through them is manifest to all the inhabitants of Jerusalem, and we cannot deny it. [17]But in order that it may spread no further among the people, let us warn them to speak no more to any one in this name." [18]So they called them and charged them not to speak or teach at all in the name of Jesus. [19]But Peter and John answered them, "Whether it is right in the sight of God to listen to you rather than to God, you must judge; [20]for we cannot but speak of what we have seen and heard." [21]And when they had further threatened them, they let them go, finding no way to punish them, because of the people; for all men praised God for what had happened. [22]For the man on whom this sign of healing was performed was more than forty years old.

OVERVIEW: Luke now tells us of what follows from the apostles' address. Modern commentators consider that Luke is working here with a Palestinian source that supplies the narrative material into which Luke inserts the defensive and kerygmatic material. Here as elsewhere in the Lukan writings the accent is placed on the efficacy of God's plan for salvation rather than on, specifically, the death and resurrection of Jesus. Some commentators wish to say that Luke makes no claim about the saving efficacy of Christ's death and resurrection, but this is an exaggeration.[1] Chrysostom, who is the most articulate in commenting on this passage, stresses both the courage of the apostles and the power given to them by which they have been changed and are able to withstand adversity, something he knew by experience. The change in them from crucifixion to resurrection was noted by the authorities. Unlettered men now preached with boldness. Faith and freedom of speech are strengthened through the testing of meekness (CHRYSOSTOM). Bede gives us a historical and a symbolic reading of the forty-year age of the healed man.

4:13 The Apostles Speak Boldly

THE CHANGE IN THE APOSTLES. CHRYSOSTOM: "For there is no other name under heaven given among men by which we must be saved." These words belong to a soul that has renounced the present life. His great outspokenness demon-

strates this. Here he makes it clear that even when he speaks in lowly terms of Christ, he does it not because he is afraid but out of condescension. Now that the time has come, he speaks in lofty terms to amaze all his listeners by this very change. Behold another miracle no less great than the earlier one.

"They recognized that they had been with Jesus." Not without purpose has the Evangelist set down this passage, but so that he might reveal where they were, that is, at the passion. For these men alone were with him then, when indeed they had seen them humble and dejected. It was this that particularly surprised them, namely, the greatness of the change. For in fact Annas, Caiaphas and company were there and had stood by him as well. Now their great outspokenness shocked them. For it was not only by their words that they revealed their lack of concern over the accusations they faced and the extreme danger impending, but also by their bearing, their voice and their gaze—in short, by everything about them they showed the outspokenness with which they confronted the people. HOMILIES ON THE ACTS OF THE APOSTLES 10.[2]

THE POWER OF GOD. BEDE: Unlettered men

---

[1]See, for instance, Alexander Loveday C.A., "The Preface to Acts and the Historians," in *History, Literature and Society in the Book of Acts,* ed. Ben Witherington III, (Cambridge: Cambridge University Press, 1996), 73-103. [2]NPNF 1 11:67**.

were sent to preach, so that the faith of those who believed would not be thought to have come about by eloquence and teaching instead of by God's power. As the apostle says, "not in the wisdom of words, lest the cross of Christ be made void."[3] COMMENTARY ON THE ACTS OF THE APOSTLES 4.13.[4]

4:16 What Shall We Do?

THE POWER OF APOSTLESHIP. CHRYSOSTOM: For what is really marvelous is this, that though they were held in prison and made answerable to charges, though they were imprisoned and beaten, their enemies were still at a loss and in a quandary, since the very things by which they expected to prevail brought about their own downfall. For neither king nor people, neither ranks of demons nor the devil himself had the power to get the better of the apostles, but all were overcome at a very great disadvantage, seeing everything they had planned against them fall on their own heads. Because of this he also says, "we are more than conquerors."[5] For this rule of victory was new: to prevail through their adversaries and never be overcome, but go forth to these struggles as masters of the end. HOMILIES ON ROMANS 15.37.[6]

THE FAITH GAINS GROUND. CHRYSOSTOM: See the difficulty they are in and how human fear again does everything. Just as in the case of Christ they were not able to undo what is done or to hide it in obscurity, and for all their hindering the faith gained ground all the more, so it is now. "What shall we do?" What stupidity to suppose that those who had tasted of the struggle would now take fright! And it would be even greater stupidity if, after their initial failure, they expected to accomplish something after such a specimen of oratory. The more they wished to hinder, the more it prospered. HOMILIES ON ACTS OF THE APOSTLES 10.[7]

4:20 We Must Speak

DELIGHT IN THE MIDST OF DANGERS. CHRYSOSTOM: Already these have borne witness as martyrs. Arrayed in battle against all, they said, "we cannot but speak of what we have seen and heard." If what we say is false, arrest us; but if it is true, why do you stand in the way? Such is philosophy! Those in perplexity, these in gladness; those full of great shame, these with boldness in all actions; those in fear, these in confidence. For who, I ask you, were the frightened? Was it those who said, "in order that it may spread no further among the people," or these who said, "we cannot but speak of what we have seen and heard?" These had a delight, a freedom of speech, a joy surpassing all; those a despondency, a shame, a fear, for they feared the people. While these spoke what they wished to say, those did not do what they wished to do. Which were in chains and dangers? Certainly not these. HOMILIES ON THE ACTS OF THE APOSTLES 10.[8]

THE STRENGTH OF MEEKNESS. CHRYSOSTOM: For better than all others he knows the nature of things. He knows that fierceness is not quenched by fierceness but by meekness. If you wish to see this in action, read the book of the Acts of the apostles and you will see how often, when the people of the Jews was rebelling and sharpening their teeth, these men, imitating the dove and answering with suitable meekness, released their wrath, quenched their madness and dissolved their impetuosity. For when they said, "We gave you strict orders not to teach in this name,"[9] the disciples, although they were able to work countless miracles, neither said nor did anything harsh but answered with all gentleness, saying, "Whether it is right to listen to you rather than to God, you must judge." HOMILIES ON THE GOSPEL OF MATTHEW 33.3.[10]

4:22 The Man Who Was Healed

---

[3]1 Cor 1:17. [4]CS 117:50. [5]Rom 8:37. [6]NPNF 1 11:456**. [7]NPNF 1 11:65*. [8]NPNF 1 11:68**. [9]Acts 5:28. [10]NPNF 1 10:221**.

MORE THAN FORTY YEARS OLD. BEDE: According to the historical sense, this shows that the man's mature age [made him] invincible to detractors. Allegorically, however, [the passage signifies that] that people of Israel not only despised the manna and sought the base things of Egypt[11] for the forty years in the desert, but even in the land of promise they continued always to limp along with the rites of idols together with those of the Lord. Or, if the number forty signifies the fullness of the twofold law (for four times ten makes forty), a transgressor of both, as it were by lying enfeebled, transcends a fortyfold perfection. COMMENTARY ON THE ACTS OF THE APOSTLES 4.22.[12]

---

[11]Num 11:4-6; 21:5. [12]CS 117:51*.

4:23-31 THE DISCIPLES' PRAYER

[23]When they were released they went to their friends and reported what the chief priests and the elders had said to them. [24]And when they heard it, they lifted their voices together to God and said, "Sovereign Lord, who didst make the heaven and the earth and the sea and everything in them, [25]who by the mouth of our father David, thy servant,[c] didst say by the Holy Spirit,

'Why did the Gentiles rage,
and the peoples imagine vain things?
[26]The kings of the earth set themselves in array,
and the rulers were gathered together,
against the Lord and against his Anointed'—[e]

[27]for truly in this city there were gathered together against thy holy servant[c] Jesus, whom thou didst anoint, both Herod and Pontius Pilate, with the Gentiles and the peoples of Israel, [28]to do whatever thy hand and thy plan had predestined to take place. [29]And now, Lord, look upon their threats, and grant to thy servants[f] to speak thy word with all boldness, [30]while thou stretchest out thy hand to heal, and signs and wonders are performed through the name of thy holy servant[c] Jesus." [31]And when they had prayed, the place in which they were gathered together was shaken; and they were all filled with the Holy Spirit and spoke the word of God with boldness.

c Or child   e Or Christ   f Or slaves

OVERVIEW: In the life of Jesus and in the life of Moses and also of the apostles, Luke often portrays a rhythm of withdrawal from rejection and then return in greater power. This section is an example of withdrawal after rejection and subsequent endowment with new strength. The Fathers are most drawn by the description of prayer given by Luke (CHRYSOSTOM, IRENAEUS, ORIGEN) and to the fact that the prayer is addressed to God, the Father, the Creator and Ruler of the world (ORIGEN, DIDYMUS, CHRYSOSTOM). Chrysostom interprets the shaking of the house as a sign from God that the disciples' prayer has been answered, while Bede and Arator link it to the power of the apostolic preaching. Chrysostom's final remark about being filled with grace leads him into the next section.

4:23 The Apostles Reported to Their Friends

NOT AMBITIOUS OF HONOR. CHRYSOSTOM: Let us return to what was said earlier and observe the wisdom of the apostles. They did not go about boasting and say, "How we settled the discussion with the priests!" They were not ambitious for honor but "went to their friends." See how they do not throw themselves upon temptations, but when temptations present themselves endure them with courage. Had it been one of the other disciples, perhaps he might have been emboldened by the crowd's boldness to act with arrogance and speak countless harsh words. But not these, who are true philosophers and do everything with mildness and with gentleness. HOMILIES ON THE ACTS OF THE APOSTLES 11.[1]

4:24 Lifting Voices to God

TRUE PRAYER. CHRYSOSTOM: "And when they heard it, they lifted their voices together to God." That shout arose from joy and great emotion. Such indeed are the prayers that do their work, prayers filled with true philosophy, prayers offered up for such reasons by such persons, on such occasions, in such a manner. All others are abominable and profane. Notice how we hear of nothing that is superfluous, no old wives' talk or fables. No, it is of his power that they speak. HOMILIES ON THE ACTS OF THE APOSTLES 11.[2]

THE PRAYER OF THE SPIRIT. IRENAEUS: These [are the] voices of the church from which every church had its origin; these are the voices of the metropolis of the citizens of the new covenant; these are the voices of the apostles; these are voices of the disciples of the Lord, the truly perfect, who, after the assumption of the Lord, were perfected by the Spirit, and called on the God who made heaven and earth and the sea—who was announced by the prophets—and Jesus Christ his Son, whom God anointed and who knew no other [God]. AGAINST HERESIES 3.12.5.[3]

PRAYING TO THE CREATOR. ORIGEN: Let us, however, touch briefly on the Acts of the Apostles, where Stephen and the apostles direct their prayers to that God "who made heaven and earth" and who "spoke by the mouth of his holy prophets,"[4] calling him "the God of Abraham, Isaac and Jacob,"[5] the God who led his people out of the land of Egypt. These expressions undoubtedly direct our minds to faith in the Creator and implant an affection for him in those who have piously and faithfully accepted this truth in him. ON FIRST PRINCIPLES 2.4.2.[6]

THE ONE TRUE GOD. DIDYMUS THE BLIND: Many of those with heretical views divide the Godhead, saying that the demiurge is one God and the Father of Christ another. From this they go on to divide the Scripture and say that the old covenant is of the demiurge and the new covenant of the Father of Christ. In accordance with their blasphemous view, they say that these gods are in opposition to each other, and their scriptures as well; that those who seek refuge in the Lord are enemies of the demiurge and better people obtain the latter; that people of the demiurge have been accused by Christ and his teaching. The present Scripture passage exposes their impiety by bringing in the apostles. After their release from the plot of the high priests and elders, they went to their friends, that is, to those who shared their faith. Together with them they sent up a hymn of thanks to the Creator of heaven and earth, mentioning that he spoke through the mouth of David (in the Holy Spirit, naturally) what is the second psalm, which begins, "Why do the

---

[1]NPNF 1 11:71-72**. [2]NPNF 1 11:72**. [3]ANF 1:431*. [4]Acts 3:18, 21, 24. [5]Acts 7:2, 32. [6]OFP 96-97*.

nations conspire and the peoples plot in vain?" After all this it is clear that the demiurge and the Father of the Savior is the same God and that both covenants are given by him. CATENA ON THE ACTS OF THE APOSTLES 4.25.[7]

4:27 Your Holy Servant Jesus

CHRIST AS ONE ANOINTED WITH THE SPIRIT. BEDE: They explain the literal meaning of the name of Christ, about whom it was said "and against your Christ,"[8] for "Christ took his name from chrism, that is, from anointing."[9] It is accordingly said, "Therefore God, your God, has anointed you with the oil of gladness,"[10] that is, with the Holy Spirit. COMMENTARY ON THE ACTS OF THE APOSTLES 4.27.[11]

4:28 What God Had Predestined

THEY REFER ALL TO GOD. CHRYSOSTOM: Scripture is accustomed to speak of one as of many. That is, they did not have power to do this, but you did it all, you who gave permission, who called them to account, who brought it to fruition, you the all-skillful and wise, who used your enemies for your own purpose. Here they speak of his exceeding skill and wisdom and of his power. They gathered together as your enemies with murderous intent and in opposition, but in fact they were doing what you wanted them to do, for we read, "to do whatever your hand and your plan had predestined to take place." What is "your hand"? I think here it means the same as power and purpose, that is, for you it is enough simply to will. HOMILIES ON THE ACTS OF THE APOSTLES 11.[12]

4:31 The Place Shaken; Presence of the Spirit

THE EARTH TREMBLED. CHRYSOSTOM: God heard their prayer and manifested this by shaking the place. For "when they had prayed," it is said, "the place was shaken." Why did this happen?

Listen to the words of the prophet: "He looks on the earth and it trembles."[13] For by this he revealed that he is present to their prayers. And again, another prophet says, "The earth was shaken and trembled at the presence of the Lord."[14] And God did this both to make it more fearsome and to lead them to courage. After those threatening conditions, they gained increased boldness. Since it was the beginning of their ministry and they had prayed for a sensible sign for their persuasion (this never happens again afterwards), great was the encouragement they received. In fact, they had no means of proving that he was risen except by miraculous signs. Thus it was not only their own assurance that they sought but also that they might not be put to shame, that they might speak with boldness. "The place was shaken," and that made them all the more unshaken. HOMILIES ON THE ACTS OF THE APOSTLES 11.[15]

THE POWER OF A STOUT HEART. BEDE: Those who sought the power of a stout heart against the deception of their enemies received a token, in the shaking of the earth, that their prayer had already been heard. This was so that they might recognize that earthly hearts would pass away from those under whose feet the earth itself was shaken with dread at the coming of the Holy Spirit. And even the fear of those who, by believing, were to be subject to the apostles, can be understood as joyful, since in shaking off their infirm depression they had learned to rise with Christ and to taste of heavenly things. COMMENTARY ON THE ACTS OF THE APOSTLES 4.31.[16]

THE APOSTLES SHAKE THE EARTH. ARATOR: The power of the apostles' words, which made those created from earth have faith, altered and set in motion the ground; but as to the fact that

---

[7]CGPNT 3:79-80. [8]Ps 2:2. [9]Augustine *The City of God* 16.38 (CCL 48:544). [10]Ps 45:7 (44:8 LXX, Vg). [11]CS 117:51*. [12]NPNF 1 11:72**. [13]Ps 104:32 (103:32 LXX). [14]Ps 18:7 (17:8 LXX). [15]NPNF 1 11:72-73**. [16]CS 117:51-52*.

the one place leaped and was shaken more [than others], Scripture announced that beautiful [are the] feet that bring peace;[17] therefore the joyful earth was moved under the tread of them [the apostles] to whom peace was given by the word of the holy Master. Transported through them, it has gone out into all lands with its swift favor. ON THE ACTS OF THE APOSTLES 1.[18]

COOPERATING WITH GRACE. CHRYSOSTOM: "And when they had prayed, the place in which they were gathered together was shaken." This was the proof that they were heard and of his visitation. "And they were all filled with the Holy Spirit." What is "they were filled"? It means that they were inflamed and the Gift burned within them. "And they spoke the word of God with boldness. And the company of those who believed were of one heart and soul." Do you see that together with the grace of God they also contrib-

uted their part? For it must be observed that everywhere together with the grace of God they also do their part. Just as Peter said above, "I have no silver and gold,"[19] and again, "they were all together," here, having mentioned that they were heard, Luke proceeds to speak also of their virtue. As he is about to embark on the narrative of Sapphira and Ananias, with a view to showing the detestable conduct of that pair he first discusses the noble behavior of the rest. Now tell me, did their love beget their poverty, or the poverty the love? In my opinion, the love begot the poverty, and then the poverty drew tight the cords of love. For notice what he says, they were all "of one heart and soul." Look, heart and soul the same. HOMILIES ON THE ACTS OF THE APOSTLES 11.[20]

---

[17]Is 52:7; Nahum 1:15; Rom 10:15. [18]*OAA* 36. [19]Acts 3:6. [20]NPNF 1 11:71**.

4:32-37 THE COMMUNITY OF CHRISTIANS

[32]*Now the company of those who believed were of one heart and soul, and no one said that any of the things which he possessed was his own, but they had everything in common. [33]And with great power the apostles gave their testimony to the resurrection of the Lord Jesus, and great grace was upon them all. [34]There was not a needy person among them, for as many as were possessors of lands or houses sold them, and brought the proceeds of what was sold [35]and laid it at the apostles' feet; and distribution was made to each as any had need. [36]Thus Joseph who was surnamed by the apostles Barnabas (which means, Son of encouragement), a Levite, a native of Cyprus, [37]sold a field which belonged to him, and brought the money and laid it at the apostles' feet.*

OVERVIEW: This is the second of the three summary statements in the early part of Acts (the others are Acts 2:42-47; 5:11-16), and it is the favorite of the early interpreters, as can be seen by the sudden abundance of available commentary. Modern commentators note how the two con-

trasting accounts of Barnabas on the one hand and Ananias and Sapphira on the other are framed by this summary statement and the one that follows (Acts 5:11-16). Augustine cites this passage more than fifty times in his writings, and it is often, as here, to show the binding power of love among believers as a reflection of the love in the Trinity. Others, such as Basil and Chrysostom, reflect on the peace of mind that comes from seeing nothing as one's own or on how it is simply the truth about this present life. One can catch a glimpse of the enthusiasm of the Fathers as they contemplate Luke's description of what Christian community can be. Those of one heart can be separated in body but not in affection (FULGENTIUS). They are as one born of the same mother (BEDE). What belongs to God belongs to all (CYPRIAN), so they lacked nothing (CHRYSOSTOM). To show that they were willing to trample on covetousness, they laid their possessions at the apostles' feet (JEROME). They laid up treasures where there can be no loss (ARATOR). The spirit of Barnabas, the son of encouragement, was empowered by the Spirit of consolation (BEDE).

4:32 Those Who Believed

THE TRINITY IS UNITED BY LOVE. AUGUSTINE: If love made one soul of so many souls and one heart of so many hearts, how great must be the love between the Father and the Son! Surely it must be greater than that between those people who had one heart. If, then, the heart of many brothers was one by charity, if the soul of many sisters was one by charity, would you say that God the Father and God the Son are two? If they are two Gods, there is not the highest charity between them. For if love is here so great as to make your soul and your friend's soul one soul, how can it be, then, that the Father and the Son are not one God? Let true faith banish the thought. In short, understand from this how excellent that love is: the souls of many people are many, and if they love one another, it is one soul; still, in the case of people, they may be called many souls, because the union is not so strong. But there it is right for you to say one God; two or three Gods it is not right for you to say. From this, the supreme and surpassing excellence of love is shown to you to be such that a greater cannot be. TRACTATES ON THE GOSPEL OF JOHN 14.9.[1]

GOD IS LOVE. AUGUSTINE: For . . . the love that God puts in people makes one heart of many hearts and makes the many souls of people into one soul, as it is written of them that believed and mutually loved one another, in the Acts of the Apostles, "They had one soul and one heart toward God." If, therefore, my soul and your soul become one soul, when we think the same thing and love one another, how much more must God the Father and God the Son be one God in the fountain of love! TRACTATES ON THE GOSPEL OF JOHN 18.4.[2]

THE WEALTH OF NONPOSSESSION. CHRYSOSTOM: Thus they had all things and had nothing: for "they said that none of the things which they possessed was their own"; therefore all things were theirs. For he that considers all things to be common will not only use his own but also the things of others as if they belonged to him. But whoever divides things up and sets himself as master over only his own things will not be master even of these. And this is plain from an example. He who possesses nothing at all, neither house nor table nor garment to spare, but for God's sake is bereft of all, uses the things which are in common as his own; and he shall receive from all whatsoever he may desire, and thus he that has nothing possesses the things of all. But whoever has some things will not be master even of these. For first, no one will give to him who has possessions; and, second, his property shall belong to robbers and thieves and informers and changing events and be anybody's rather than his. HOMILIES ON 1 CORINTHIANS 15.14.[3]

LOVE CALLS FORTH LOVE. CHRYSOSTOM: And not this only, but also because love is increased by the gathering [of ourselves] together; and love being increased, of necessity the things of God must follow also. "And earnest prayer" (it is said) was "made by" the people.[4] "As the manner of

---

[1]NPNF 1 7:97-98**. [2]NPNF 1 7:118*. [3]NPNF 1 12:88*. [4]Acts 12:5.

some is." Here he not only exhorted but also blamed [them].

"And let us consider one another," he says, "to provoke to love and to good works."[5] He knew that this also arises from "gathering together." For as "iron sharpens iron,"[6] so also association increases love. For if a stone rubbed against a stone sends forth fire, how much more soul mingled with soul! But not to emulation (he says), but "to the sharpening of love." What is "to the sharpening of love"? To the loving and being loved more. "And of good works," that so they might acquire zeal. For if doing has greater force for instruction than speaking, you also have in your number many teachers who effect this by their deeds. ON THE EPISTLE TO THE HEBREWS 19.3.[7]

A CHRISTIAN IS NOT HIS OWN. BASIL THE GREAT: The Christian ought to regard all the things that are given him for his use, not as his to hold as his own or to lay up. Moreover, giving careful heed to all things as the Lord's, he should not overlook any of the things that are being thrown aside and disregarded, should this be the case. No Christian should think of himself as his own master, but each should rather so think and act as though given by God to be slave to his fellow brothers and sisters.[8] But "every person in his own order."[9] LETTER 22.1.[10]

THE NEED TO DISCERN. BASIL THE GREAT: For he said that experience was needed in order to distinguish between cases of genuine need and of mere greedy begging. For whoever gives to the afflicted gives to the Lord and from the Lord shall have his reward; but he who gives to every vagabond casts to a dog, a nuisance indeed from his importunity but deserving no pity on the ground of need. LETTER 150.3.[11]

FAITH, THE PRINCIPLE OF UNITY. FULGENTIUS OF RUSPE: Hence it is that any creatures, that is, of the same nature, can be separated from one another because each one individually cannot be everywhere in its entirety; for when, through the

grace of faith it happens that they have "one heart and soul of the multitude of believers," still in their persons they can be separated by being in different places even though they are not separated by the affection of the heart; and some of the faithful can become unbelievers and be severed from the fellowship of that one soul. LETTER 14.5.[12]

IMITATORS OF GOD. CYPRIAN: This is truly to become a son of God by spiritual birth; this is to imitate the equity of God by the heavenly law. For whatever belongs to God belongs to all by our appropriation of it, nor is anyone kept from his benefits and gift, nor does anything prevent the whole human race from equally enjoying God's goodness and generosity. WORKS AND ALMSGIVING 25.[13]

LOVE OF BROTHERHOOD. BEDE: Those who had completely left the world behind by no means pushed themselves forward, one over the other, glorying in the nobility of their birth. Rather, as though born from the womb of one and the same mother, the church, they all rejoiced in one and the same love of brotherhood. COMMENTARY ON THE ACTS OF THE APOSTLES 4.32.[14]

4:33 Great Grace Was on Them

THE GENEROSITY AND HUMILITY OF THE GIVERS. CHRYSOSTOM: This is why the grace [was upon them all,] for that "there was none that lacked." That is, from the exceeding ardor of the givers, none was in want. For they did not give in part and in part reserve: nor yet in giving all, give it as their own. And they lived moreover in great abundance: they removed all inequality from among them and made a goodly order. "For as many as were possessors," etc. And with great respect they did this: for they did not presume to give into their hands, nor did they ostentatiously

---

[5]Heb 10:24. [6]Prov 27:17. [7]NPNF 1 14:455*. [8]1 Cor 9:19. [9]1 Cor 15:23. [10]NPNF 2 8:128*. [11]NPNF 2 8:208*. [12]FC 95:503*. [13]FC 36:251*. [14]CS 117:52*.

present, but they brought to the apostles' feet. To them they left it to be the dispensers, made them the owners, that thenceforth all should be defrayed as from common, not from private, property. This was also a help to them against vainglory. HOMILIES ON THE ACTS OF THE APOSTLES 11.[15]

THAT WEALTH OF GREATER INTEREST. ARATOR: Generous one, you do not do these things as a seller of property, but, ambitious one, as one who wishes to keep his privileges, and you abandon for a short time what you desire to be yours forever. Thus, to scatter the fields was [really] the desire not to be in need; for of what advantage is property that perishes even though it is guarded? Whoever loses it has it to greater advantage laid up in the citadel of heaven. Seek there, creditor, the wealth of greater interest and lay up treasures where they can suffer no loss; there no misfortune wears away perpetual wealth; you will possess everlastingly what you cause the Lord to owe. ON THE ACTS OF THE APOSTLES 1.[16]

4:35 Money Placed at the Apostles' Feet

A SYMBOLIC GESTURE. JEROME: Then, as you know, believers sold their possessions and brought the prices of them and laid them down at the apostles' feet: a symbolic act designed to show that people must trample on covetousness. LETTER 71.4.[17]

4:36 Barnabas, Son of Encouragement

THE HOPE OF THINGS TO COME. BEDE: Wherever the sacred Scriptures give the names of things or persons with an interpretation, it certainly indicates that a more sacred sense is contained in them. Rightly, therefore, is a person called a son of consolation [encouragement], who, despising present things, is consoled by the hope of things to come. And to be sure, the Holy Spirit is given the name Paraclete because through the inner pouring out of his favor he grants the *paraclēsis*, that is, the consolation,[18] of heavenly joys to those who have distress in the world. COMMENTARY ON THE ACTS OF THE APOSTLES 4.36B.[19]

---

[15]NPNF 1 11:73-74*. [16]OAA 36-37. [17]NPNF 2 6:153*. [18]Isidore of Seville *Etymologies* 7.3.10.12. [19]CS 117:53*.

5:1-11 THE SIN OF ANANIAS AND SAPPHIRA

[1]*But a man named Ananias with his wife Sapphira sold a piece of property, [2]and with his wife's knowledge he kept back some of the proceeds, and brought only a part and laid it at the apostles' feet. [3]But Peter said, "Ananias, why has Satan filled your heart to lie to the Holy Spirit and to keep back part of the proceeds of the land? [4]While it remained unsold, did it not remain your own? And after it was sold, was it not at your disposal? How is it that you have contrived this deed in your heart? You have not lied to men but to God." [5]When Ananias heard these words, he fell down and died. And great fear came upon all who heard of it. [6]The young men rose and wrapped him up and carried him out and buried him.*

[7]*After an interval of about three hours his wife came in, not knowing what had happened. [8]And*

Peter said to her, "Tell me whether you sold the land for so much." And she said, "Yes, for so much." [9]*But Peter said to her, "How is it that you have agreed together to tempt the Spirit of the Lord? Hark, the feet of those that have buried your husband are at the door, and they will carry you out."* [10]*Immediately she fell down at his feet and died. When the young men came in they found her dead, and they carried her out and buried her beside her husband.* [11]*And great fear came upon the whole church, and upon all who heard of these things.*

OVERVIEW: In the last two verses of Acts 4, Luke gave the example of Barnabas, who literally enacted the community ideal of unlimited generosity. He now passes to an example of the opposite. Modern commentators point out that the word translated "kept back" often refers to misappropriation or even theft of funds, and that the fault of Ananias and Sapphira was that they declared the money gained from the sale of their property belonged to the community and then kept some of the community's money for themselves. This sin, which is variously described as lying to the Holy Spirit, lying to God and testing the Holy Spirit, serves to show the true nature of the community of believers, just as Jesus' words to Paul reveal another dimension of the same reality: "I am Jesus whom you are persecuting" (Acts 9:5; 22:8; 26:15). The Fathers note especially those aspects of the story that seem most important to Luke. They point out that the sin of Ananias and Sapphira consisted in being false to what they professed to be doing, thus committing a sin against God (CHRYSOSTOM, AMMONIUS, ARATOR, BEDE, BASIL), while also sinning through avarice (CASSIAN). They discuss the interior dynamics of what is meant by Satan entering their heart (CHRYSOSTOM, AMMONIUS, GREGORY OF NYSSA, BEDE[1]). They see this event as a warning for all the faithful (CHRYSOSTOM, JEROME, BEDE).

5:2 Ananias Kept Some of the Proceeds

A SIN OF SACRILEGE. CHRYSOSTOM: If for gathering sticks one could be stoned to death, much more, it may be argued, ought he be stoned for committing sacrilege. This money was sacred. For the person who withdraws his possessions after he has chosen to sell them and distribute them would be guilty of sacrilege. And if this person, who is taking from his own possessions, is sacrilegious, much more so is he who takes from what is not his own. And do not think that because the consequence now is not the same, the crime will go unpunished. Do you see that this is the charge brought against Ananias, that having made the money sacred, he then took it? For were you not able, says Peter, even after the sale to use the proceeds as your own? For you were not forbidden, were you? Why then after you had promised? See how the devil made his attack from the very beginning, how in the midst of such signs and wonders this man became insensible as a rock! . . . For sacrilege is a most grievous crime, insolent and full of contempt. We neither forced you to sell, says the apostle, nor to give the money after you have sold. You chose to do so of your own free will. Why then did you steal from the sacred treasury? HOMILIES ON THE ACTS OF THE APOSTLES 12.[2]

5:3 Why Has Satan Filled Your Heart?

THE ONE WHO COOPERATES WITH SATAN IS CUT OFF. CHRYSOSTOM: "Why has Satan filled your heart?" he says. If it was Satan who did this, why is the man responsible? Because he admitted the influence of Satan and was filled with it. He must be set right, he says. But he could not be set right. For the one who has seen such things and gained nothing from them, neither would he gain

---

[1]As is noted there, and as is his custom, Bede takes some lines from his predecessors in his own explanation (see the introduction). [2]NPNF 1 11:77**.

much by anything else. Therefore the matter could not simply be passed over, but, like gangrene, had to be excised to prevent it from infecting the rest of the body. Homilies on the Acts of the Apostles 12.[3]

The Spirit Reads Our Hearts. Gregory of Nyssa: And of the Holy Spirit also, Peter says to Ananias, "Why has Satan filled your heart, to lie to the Holy Spirit?" showing that the Holy Spirit was a true witness, aware of what Ananias had dared to do in secret, and by whom the secret was made known to Peter. For Ananias became a thief of his own goods, secretly, as he thought, from all people and concealing his sin. But the Holy Spirit at the same moment was in Peter, and detected his intent, dragged down as it was to avarice, and gave to Peter from himself the power of seeing the secret, while it is clear that the Spirit could not have done this had it not been able to behold hidden things. On Not Three Gods.[4]

A Human Soul Drawn to Malice. Bede: "Why has Satan filled your heart?" Here it must be noted that the soul and mind of a person can be filled according to substance by no creature but only by the creating Trinity, because only according to the operation and instigation of the will is the soul filled by those things which are created. Now Satan fills someone's mind and the core of his heart, not, to be sure, by going into him and into his senses—if I may put it this way, entering the doorway of the heart—since this is a power of divinity alone. But like a crafty, wicked, deceitful and fraudulent deceiver, he draws the human soul toward dispositions for malice by thoughts and enticements of vices, of which he is full."[5] Therefore Satan filled the heart of Ananias, not by his own entering in, but by the injection of the venom of his malice. Commentary on the Acts of the Apostles 5.3.[6]

Warning to Others. Jerome: For having made a vow they offered their money to God as if it were their own and not his to whom they had

vowed it; and keeping back for their own use a part of that which belonged to another, through fear of famine which true faith never fears, they drew down on themselves suddenly the avenging stroke, which was meant not in cruelty toward them but as a warning to others. In fact, the apostle Peter by no means called down death upon them, as Porphyry foolishly says. He merely announced God's judgment by the spirit of prophecy, that the doom of two persons might be a lesson to many. Letter 130.14.[7]

5:4 Lying to God

Be Faithful to Your Promises. Arator: But inasmuch as a changed intention bears the crime of deceit, and when there is, moreover, confirmation of a promise, it is proper to stand firm and not wish to violate what was first [promised] by what follows; it is more just to preserve a permanent right than to withdraw it. The punishment of the two established a warning for all, lest anyone should call [back] gifts which a solemn promise requires him to owe. Reflect, you of true faith, and consider the words of Peter, which are bright with blessed teaching, "Whoever persuaded you to be deceitful?" And he concluded by judging, "You do not deceive people by saying such things; you lie to God." The teaching that condemns the wicked strengthens the holy. On the Acts of the Apostles 1.[8]

They Lied to the Holy Spirit. Bede: Peter said above that Ananias had lied to the Holy Spirit. It is therefore clear that the Holy Spirit is God and that the error of Macedonius had been condemned before he was born. Commentary on the Acts of the Apostles 5.4.[9]

A Lie to the Spirit Is a Lie to God. Basil the Great: Peter's words to Sapphira—"How is

---

[3]NPNF 1 11:77**. [4]NPNF 2 5:333*. [5]Didymus *On the Holy Spirit* 60, from Jerome's translation (PL 23:151). [6]CS 117:57*. [7]NPNF 2 6:268*. [8]OAA 37-38. [9]CS 117:57*.

it that you have agreed together to tempt the Spirit of the Lord? You did not lie to men, but to God"—show that sins against the Holy Spirit and against God are the same. And thus you might learn that in every operation the Spirit is closely conjoined with, and inseparable from, the Father and the Son. While God works the differences of operations and the Lord the diversities of administrations, the Holy Spirit is present also, administering in his own power the distribution of the gifts according to each recipient's worth. ON THE SPIRIT 16.37.[10]

5:5 Ananias Fell Down and Died

WE ARE WARNED. BEDE: It was not on account of [this] accusation that Peter gave such a severe sentence to the transgressors, but in the Spirit he foresaw future weeds that would by their deformed character adulterate the simplicity of the church. For from these the worst type of Sarabaits[11] reportedly arose. Although by no means did they give up their possessions, they pretended to preserve apostolic discipline.[12] He did not allow the culprits to be healed by any repentance, but in order to strike fear into the generations to come, he took care to cut the noxious shoot out by its roots. COMMENTARY ON THE ACTS OF THE APOSTLES 5.5.[13]

THE SIN OF ACQUISITIVENESS. JOHN CASSIAN: And so if against those who did not covet other persons' goods but tried to be sparing of their own, and had no desire to acquire but only the wish to retain, there went forth so severe a sentence, what should we think of those who desire to amass wealth, without ever having had any of their own, and, making a show of poverty before people, are before God convicted of being rich, through the passion of avarice? INSTITUTES 7.25.[14]

5:11 Great Fear in the Church

THE NECESSITY OF BEING JOINED TOGETHER. CHRYSOSTOM: None groaned, none lamented, all were terrified. For as their faith increased, the signs also multiplied, and great was the fear among their own company. For things from without do not war against us so much as things within. If we are welded firmly to each other, no war will be difficult to bear; what would be terrible is to be separated and divided. Now they went about in the marketplace, and that with boldness. They even waged an attack and prevailed in the midst of enemies and so fulfilled that saying, "Rule in the midst of your foes."[15] This was a great miracle, that they, arrested and cast into prison, were able to do such things. HOMILIES ON THE ACTS OF THE APOSTLES 12.[16]

---

[10]NPNF 2 8:23*. [11]Characterized as degenerate monks. [12]Cassian *Conference* 18.7 (CSEL 13:513); *The Rule of Benedict* 1.6 (CSEL 75:18). [13]CS 117:57-58*. [14]NPNF 2 11:256*. [15]Ps 110:2 (109:2 LXX). [16]NPNF 1 11:79**.

5:12-16 SIGNS AND WONDERS DONE BY THE APOSTLES

[12]*Now many signs and wonders were done among the people by the hands of the apostles. And they were all together in Solomon's Portico.* [13]*None of the rest dared join them, but the people held them in high honor.* [14]*And more than ever believers were added to the Lord, multitudes both of*

men and women, ¹⁵*so that they even carried out the sick into the streets, and laid them on beds and pallets, that as Peter came by at least his shadow might fall on some of them.* ¹⁶*The people also gathered from the towns around Jerusalem, bringing the sick and those afflicted with unclean spirits, and they were all healed.*

OVERVIEW: This is the third general description or summary statement that Luke gives in regard to the life of the early community in Jerusalem. More than the other two, the accent is on the apostles working "signs and wonders," a phrase often found in the Septuagint to describe God's acts on behalf of his people and used seven times by Luke to convey the same notion, linking it with Jesus and the apostles. In comparison with their remarks on the two previous summaries (Acts 2:42-47; 4:32-35), the Fathers are less abundant in their comments. The most interesting aspect of their teaching is that the healings wrought in the midst of the church reveal its heavenly nature and origin. The signs and wonders made earth look like heaven (CHRYSOSTOM). Peter's intercession is powerful (BEDE). Peter remains the ruling voice for the apostles (ARATOR). Their inner radiance bore a king's image (CHRYSOSTOM).

5:12 Signs and Wonders

EARTH BECAME A HEAVEN. CHRYSOSTOM: Earth was becoming like heaven, for their way of life, boldness of speech, wonders, for all besides. Like angels were they looked upon with wonder. They were unconcerned about ridicule, threats, perils. They were compassionate and beneficent. Some of them they helped with money, and some with words, and some with healing of their bodies and of their souls; they accomplished every kind of healing. HOMILIES ON THE ACTS OF THE APOSTLES 12.[1]

5:15 The Sick Carried into the Streets

RELIEVING THE INFIRM. BEDE: At that time Peter visibly relieved the infirm by the shadow of his body. Now, he does not cease to strengthen the infirm among the faithful by the invisible screen of his intercession. And because Peter is a type of the church, it is beautifully appropriate that he himself walked upright, but by his accompanying shadow he raised up those who were lying down. So the church, concentrating its mind and love on heavenly things, passes like a shadow on the land, and here [on earth], with sacramental signs and temporal figures of heavenly things, it renews those whom there [in heaven] it rewards with everlasting gifts. Some[2] relate to this passage that saying of the Lord in the Gospels: "He who believes in me, the works that I do he also will do, and greater than these he will do."[3] COMMENTARY ON THE ACTS OF THE APOSTLES 5.15.[4]

PETER RULES THE CHURCH AND ITS EARTHLY TYPE. ARATOR: We dwell in the church on earth, which, no one may doubt, signifies a heavenly [church]; but that is more truly [the church] which, at rest above the stars, is called celestial and high. This [earthly church], which is seen in the brief career of an uncertain world, is appointed as the way of life and in this [present] time directs to the eternal [church] those whom it gathers, and to those found acceptable it is the road for going from here to heavenly things. Peter rules both armies, and for their lot he gives the stars to those squadrons led from here, as has been revealed by the words of God, "What you have loosed," he said, "and what you bind on earth thus remain bound or loosed in heaven."[5] This [church] that we see cultivated on soil, therefore, will be a type; what the clouds carry is

---

[1]NPNF 1 11:78-79**. [2]Augustine *Tractates on the Gospel of John* 44.5; 71.3 (CCL 36:384, 506). [3]Jn 14:12. [4]CS 117:58*. [5]Mt 16:19.

firm. Peter, ruling both, designs there the body and here the shadow, in order that those sick people whom he freed from vices and offenses might be led unharmed to it [the church above], which endures in heaven [and] will receive the holy throngs cleansed by this [earthly church]. On the Acts of the Apostles 1.[6]

Manifesting the Inner Radiance. Chrysostom: For had they not borne a king's image and their radiance been unapproachable, their garments and shadows had not wrought so mightily. For the garments of a king are terrible even to robbers. Would you see this beaming even through the body? "Looking steadfastly," he said, "upon the face of Stephen, they saw it as if it were the face of an angel."[7] But this was nothing to the glory flashing within. Homilies on 2 Corinthians 7.6.[8]

---

[6]OAA 39-40*. [7]Acts 6:15. [8]NPNF 1 12:314*.

5:17-26 THE APOSTLES FREED FROM PRISON

[17]*But the high priest rose up and all who were with him, that is, the party of the Sadducees, and filled with jealousy* [18]*they arrested the apostles and put them in the common prison.* [19]*But at night an angel of the Lord opened the prison doors and brought them out and said,* [20]*"Go and stand in the temple and speak to the people all the words of this Life."* [21]*And when they heard this, they entered the temple at daybreak and taught.*

Now the high priest came and those who were with him and called together the council and all the senate of Israel, and sent to the prison to have them brought. [22]*But when the officers came, they did not find them in the prison, and they returned and reported,* [23]*"We found the prison securely locked and the sentries standing at the doors, but when we opened it we found no one inside."* [24]*Now when the captain of the temple and the chief priests heard these words, they were much perplexed about them, wondering what this would come to.* [25]*And some one came and told them, "The men whom you put in prison are standing in the temple and teaching the people."* [26]*Then the captain with the officers went and brought them, but without violence, for they were afraid of being stoned by the people.*

Overview: This incident is meant by Luke to be a prelude to the short speech of Peter in the next section and the longer speech of Gamaliel in the same section. Later, in Acts 12:1-17, there will be another story of Peter's deliverance from prison that is redolent with resurrection allusions. The Fathers are sensitive to these allusions even in the story, as can be seen by their use of resurrection themes in their commentaries.

5:17 The High Priest Rose Up

Dejection and Gladness Interwoven. Chrysostom: Look how their life is woven. First there was dejection because Christ was taken from them; then came joy through the descent of

---

the Spirit; then dejection again because of the scoffers; then joy because of the believers and the sign; then dejection again because of the imprisonment, followed by joy in the result of their defense. And here again both dejection and joy: joy because they were well-known and God made revelations to them, dejection because they made away with some of them. Again, joy from their success and dejection because of the high priest. And the same pattern could be seen throughout. Homilies on the Acts of the Apostles 12.[1]

Who Are the Sadducees? Bede: Therefore "the Sadducees, whose name is interpreted as 'righteous' for they claim to be what they are not" (as we read below), entirely denied the resurrection of the body and said that the soul perishes with the flesh. Indeed, they did not even believe "that there are any angels or spirits, and accepting only the five books of Moses, they scorned the honoring of the prophets."[2] Commentary on the Acts of the Apostles 5.17.[3]

5:19 An Angel of the Lord

For Encouragement and Instruction. Chrysostom: "But at night an angel of the Lord opened the prison doors and brought them out and said, 'Go and stand in the temple and speak to the people all the words of this life.' And when they heard this, they entered the temple at daybreak and taught." This was done for the encouragement of the disciples and for the benefit and instruction of the others. For notice how what Christ once did happened again here: he does not allow them to witness the miracle in action but provides that from which they may learn of it. This is what happened on the occasion of his resurrection: he did not let them see how he rose again. When wine is made from water, the guests do not see it (for they were drunk); the judgment he entrusts to others. Likewise in the present case, they do not see them being led out, but the evidence, from which they might understand what happened, they saw. And it was by night

that the angel put them outside. Why? Because in this way they were more believed than they would have been otherwise. They would not have come to ask questions. They would not have believed otherwise. Homilies on the Acts of the Apostles 13.[4]

An Angel Opened the Prison Doors. Bede: So that Thomas would not doubt that the Lord bore flesh and blood when he had seen him entering with the doors closed,[5] behold, he himself, while he was still clothed in mortal flesh, made his departure with his companions though the doors were closed. Commentary on the Acts of the Apostles 5.19.[6]

His Side Is a Witness. Arator: If anyone in addition considers Thomas, with his feeble heart, let him seek teaching from this: seeing that the closed door, being penetrated, admitted God then,[7] is it astonishing if [Christ], in the flesh, approaches a gate in this manner, [he] whom a virgin bore, whom the unviolated womb of his mother conceived? What reason, I ask, was there to take human flesh unless it was to resurrect it? Returning after that, he presents his side for a witness and teaches that the ashes of our body must be made new by the example of his own, proving they are his limbs by their wounds. On the Acts of the Apostles 1.[8]

5:21 The Apostles Taught in the Temple

Ministers of Light. Arator: This symbol does not lack a voice [to explain] why the holy men left this darkness [of prison]. Endowing them richly, he said that these are the ministers of light and that they shine in the whole house just like lamps set atop a stand.[9] No night holds back those whom the Light himself calls a candle, who have merited the God who bears gifts and is a witness

---

[1]NPNF 1 11:77**. [2]Jerome *Commentary on Matthew* 3.22.23-32 (CCL 77:205-7); Isidore of Seville *Etymologies* 8.4.4. [3]CS 117:59*. [4]NPNF 1 11:81**. [5]Jn 20:26. [6]CS 117:59*. [7]Jn 20:19. [8]OAA 40*. [9]Mt 5:14-16.

[to the question] by what law that place concealed in its caverns so many suns in the [apostolic] order, [suns] by which [that place] had a chance to know the eternal light so that with the expulsion of error the world might conquer darkness. ON THE ACTS OF THE APOSTLES 1.[10]

5:24 The Leaders Perplexed

BLIND TO THE WORK OF GOD. CHRYSOSTOM: And observe, by report of others they are apprised of all the circumstances: they see the prison remaining closed with safety, and the guards standing before the doors. A twofold security is here, as was the case at the sepulcher, having both the seal and the men to watch. See how they fought against God! Say, was this, that befell them, of human doing? Who led them forth when the doors were shut? How did they come out with guards standing before the door? In truth, they must be mad or drunken to talk so. Here are men whom neither prison nor bonds nor closed doors had been able to keep in; and yet they expect to overpower them. Such is their childish folly! Their officers come and confess what has taken place, as if on purpose to debar them from all show of reason. Do you mark how there is miracle upon miracle, differing in kind, some wrought by them, others on them, and these more illustrious than the others? HOMILIES ON THE ACTS OF THE APOSTLES 13.[11]

---

[10]OAA 41*. [11]NPNF 1 11:81**.

5:27-32 QUESTIONED BY THE HIGH PRIEST

[27]*And when they had brought them, they set them before the council. And the high priest questioned them,* [28]*saying, "We strictly charged you not to teach in this name, yet here you have filled Jerusalem with your teaching and you intend to bring this man's blood upon us."* [29]*But Peter and the apostles answered, "We must obey God rather than men.* [30]*The God of our fathers raised Jesus whom you killed by hanging him on a tree.* [31]*God exalted him at his right hand as Leader and Savior, to give repentance to Israel and forgiveness of sins.* [32]*And we are witnesses to these things, and so is the Holy Spirit whom God has given to those who obey him."*

OVERVIEW: The hearing now proceeds in two steps. The leaders of Israel enjoin silence on the leaders of the new community; Peter, once again, answers with a speech. The whole account recorded in this part of Acts 5 has remarkable parallels to the account in Acts 4:1-31: arrest, confrontation between the authorities and Peter, a brief kerygmatic statement and the remark that it is better to obey God than people. Chrysostom once again calls attention to the patience and compassion for their persecutors evinced by the apostles; Bede thinks the high priest must have forgotten that he had already called down upon himself the blood of Jesus.

5:28 Jerusalem Filled with the Apostles' Teaching

BRINGING THIS MAN'S BLOOD ON US. BEDE: The high priest had forgotten the doom that he had called down upon himself and his own when he said, "His blood be on us and on our children."[1] COMMENTARY ON THE ACTS OF THE APOSTLES 5.28.[2]

5:30 God Raised Jesus

NOT DEFIANCE BUT COMPASSION. CHRYSOSTOM: It was not with defiance that the apostles answered them, for they were teachers. And yet who, backed by an entire city and enjoying such grace, would not have spoken and uttered something big? But not these men. For they were not angered, but they pitied and wept over them and looked for a way to free them from their error and anger. No longer did they say to them, "You must judge,"[3] but they declared, "He whom God raised, this man we proclaim." It is by the will of God that these things are done, he says. They did not say, "Did we not say to you even then, that 'we cannot but speak the things which we have seen and heard'?"[4] For they do not lust after honor. He repeats the same things: the cross, the resurrection. And they do not say why he was crucified—that it was for our sakes, but they hint at this, though not yet openly, because they wish to frighten them for a while. And yet what kind of rhetoric is this? No rhetoric at all, but always the passion, the resurrection, the ascension and the wherefore. HOMILIES ON THE ACTS OF THE APOSTLES 13.[5]

5:31 To Give Repentance

FORGIVENESS PROFFERED AS TO BENEFACTORS. CHRYSOSTOM: Notice how every time they mention the crime, they add the mention of forgiveness, showing that what had been done was worthy of death but what was given was offered as if to benefactors. How else could anyone have persuaded them? HOMILIES ON THE ACTS OF THE APOSTLES 13.[6]

---

[1]Mt 27:25. [2]CS 117:60*. [3]Acts 4:19. [4]Acts 4:20. [5]NPNF 1 11:83**. [6]NPNF 1 11:83**.

5:33-42 GAMALIEL'S ADVICE

[33]When they heard this they were enraged and wanted to kill them. [34]But a Pharisee in the council named Gamaliel, a teacher of the law, held in honor by all the people, stood up and ordered the men to be put outside for a while. [35]And he said to them, "Men of Israel, take care what you do with these men. [36]For before these days Theudas arose, giving himself out to be somebody, and a number of men, about four hundred, joined him; but he was slain and all who followed him were dispersed and came to nothing. [37]After him Judas the Galilean arose in the days of the census and drew away some of the people after him; he also perished, and all who followed him were scattered. [38]So in the present case I tell you, keep away from these men and let them alone; for if this plan or this undertaking is of men, it will fail; [39]but if it is of God, you will not be able to overthrow them. You might even be found opposing God!"

[40]So they took his advice, and when they had called in the apostles, they beat them and charged

them not to speak in the name of Jesus, and let them go. ⁴¹Then they left the presence of the council, rejoicing that they were counted worthy to suffer dishonor for the name. ⁴²And every day in the temple and at home they did not cease teaching and preaching Jesus as the Christ.

OVERVIEW: Luke's presentation of Gamaliel's advice is probably intended to portray the possibility of a reasoned tolerance on the part of the old Israel in its relation to the new Israel. Chrysostom once again holds the apostles up as models of joy and equanimity in the face of persecution, a theme also present in Luke's theology. Bede shows himself quite interested in the historical information available to him about Gamaliel, Theudas and Judas. This preoccupation was not new, as the anonymous author(s) cited by Cramer indicate. These, with their recourse to Josephus, or more probably Eusebius or Chrysostom, may have been the source of Bede's information. Modern historians question the chronological discrepancy between Luke's account of Theudas and Judas and that of Josephus.

5:33 Wanting to Kill the Apostles

DO EVIL, SUFFER EVIL. CHRYSOSTOM: "And they wanted to kill them." Behold again these in perplexity and in pain, and those relaxed, in high spirits and joyous. Not only did they suffer pain, but also they were enraged. This then illustrates the proverb, "Do evil, suffer evil." These men were in chains, they had come to be judged in court; but the men who sat in judgment were in danger, in perplexity, in great helplessness. For the person who strikes a blow on steel receives the force of the blow himself. And they saw that not only was [the apostles'] boldness of speech not stopped, but their preaching even increased, and they spoke without a thought of fear and yielded them no advantages. HOMILIES ON THE ACTS OF THE APOSTLES 13.[1]

5:34 Gamaliel Stood

A COMPANION TO THE APOSTLES. BEDE: This Gamaliel, as Clement indicates,[2] was a companion of the apostles in faith, but by their decision he remained among the Jews so that he might be able to calm their fury in such a storm as this. COMMENTARY ON THE ACTS OF THE APOSTLES 5.34.[3]

5:35 Take Care What You Do

FREEDOM FROM PASSION. CHRYSOSTOM: Please note how Gamaliel discourses with gentleness. He speaks briefly to them and relates no ancient stories (though he could have), but he tells of recent events that are powerful in producing belief. He hints at this himself by saying, "For before these days," meaning, not many days ago. If he had opened by saying, "Let these men go," he would have aroused suspicion and his speech would not have been effective. Coming after the examples, however, it acquired its own force.... See how mild his manner is, the speech not long but succinct, and his mention even of those [imposters] without anger. "And all who followed him were scattered," he says. All this without blaspheming Christ.... Again, he checks them by the impossibility and the inexpediency of the thing, saying, "You might even be found opposing God!" HOMILIES ON THE ACTS OF THE APOSTLES 14.[4]

5:36 All Came to Nothing

THEUDAS ROSE UP. BEDE: This Theudas, as Josephus relates,[5] by his power over them persuaded many who were brought out of the city to throng to the banks of the Jordan. And, since he

---

[1]NPNF 1 11:84**. [2]Pseudo-Clement *The Recognitions* 1.65.2 (GCS 51:45). [3]CS 117:60*. [4]NPNF 1 11:88**. [5]Eusebius *Ecclesiastical History* 2.11 (GCS 9.1:131-33); Josephus *Jewish Antiquities* 20.5.1.

was a magician, he said that he was a prophet and that he could provide a way across when the waters of the river were parted by his command. Under the command of the procurator Fadus a throng of horsemen overtook him, and after the slaying and capture of many they brought his head back to Jerusalem. COMMENTARY ON THE ACTS OF THE APOSTLES 5.36.[6]

5:37 *Judas the Galilean*

NO TRIBUTE TO CAESAR. BEDE: Josephus[7] also writes about this Gaulanite of the city Gamala who, when he was drawn into the undertaking by a certain Pharisee called Sadducus, urged the people not to lose their freedom by paying tribute to the Romans, "showing from the law" that the Lord alone was to be served and that they who were bringing tithes to the temple should not pay tribute to Caesar. "This heretical sect grew so large that it even stirred up a large part of the Pharisees and the people, so that" they believed that "the Lord Christ should be asked, 'Is it lawful to give tribute to Caesar or not?'"[8] COMMENTARY ON THE ACTS OF THE APOSTLES 5.37.[9]

5:40 *Taking Gamaliel's Advice*

GAMALIEL ALL BUT PREACHES THE GOSPEL. CHRYSOSTOM: And he did not say, "if Christ is God," but his action makes this clear. He pronounces no judgment on whether it is "of men" or "of God" but entrusts the judgment to the future. "They were persuaded." Then why did you whip them? Such was the incontrovertible justice of his speech that they could not look it in the face; nevertheless, they satisfied their own anger, and again they expected to terrify them in this way. Because the apostles were not present at his speech, he gained a greater hearing, and the sweetness of his words and the justice of his speech persuaded them. In fact, this man all but preached the gospel. HOMILIES ON THE ACTS OF THE APOSTLES 14.[10]

5:41 *Rejoicing in Suffering*

THE ATTRACTIVENESS OF JOY. CHRYSOSTOM: Let us take someone of consular rank, possessed of great wealth and living in the imperial city, who has no business to conduct but is at leisure to live in luxury, seated at the very summit of wealth, honor and power. And let us set against him a Peter, in chains, in evils beyond enumeration, and we will find the latter living in greater luxury. For where there is such an excess of joy, so that one is happy even in chains, imagine how great the joy must be! For just as those in high office, no matter how many terrible things happen, do not perceive them but continue in enjoyment, likewise these men rejoiced all the more precisely because of these circumstances. For it is altogether impossible to put into words the great joy that came to those who suffered something terrible for Christ's sake. For they delighted more in sufferings than in good things. If someone loves Christ, he understands what I am saying. But what about safety? What owner of countless riches, I ask, could escape so many dangers, visiting so many different peoples for the sole purpose of transforming their way of life? For they accomplished everything as if by imperial decree, only more easily. For a decree would not have been so effectual as were the words of those men. An imperial decree compels by necessity, but these men drew followers who came willingly, spontaneously and grateful beyond measure. What imperial decree, I ask, could have persuaded people to part with all their property and their lives, to despise home, country, kindred and even self-preservation? Yet the voices of fishermen and tentmakers accomplished this, so that they were both happy and stronger, more powerful than all others. HOMILIES ON THE ACTS OF THE APOSTLES 13.[11]

---

[6]CS 117:60*. [7]Eusebius *Ecclesiastical History* 1.5 (GCS 9.1:47-49); Josephus *Jewish Antiquities* 18.1.1; Josephus *Jewish War* 2.8.1. [8]Jerome *Commentary on Titus* 3 (PL 26:590-91); Mt 22:17. [9]CS 117:60-61*. [10]NPNF 1 11:88**. [11]NPNF 1 11:84-85**.

PERSEVERANCE IN HOPE. POLYCARP OF SMYRNA: Let us then continually persevere in our hope and the earnest of our righteousness, which is Jesus Christ, "who bore our sins in his own body on the tree," "who did no sin, neither was guile found in his mouth," but who endured all things for us, that we might live in him. Let us then be imitators of his patience; and if we suffer for his name's sake, let us glorify him. For he has set us this example in himself, and we have believed that such is the case. LETTER TO THE PHILIPPIANS 8.[12]

SUPERIORITY OF VIRTUE. CHRYSOSTOM: Of course, the scourging was no cause of satisfaction, to be sure—rather of pain and distress; but scourging for the sake of God and the grounds on which they were scourged gave rise to satisfaction in them. . . . Such a powerful and invincible thing is virtue, proving superior even in the course of suffering such torments. HOMILIES ON GENESIS 23.6.[13]

---

[12]ANF 1:53. [13]FC 82:92.

6:1-7 LAYING HANDS ON THE SEVEN

¹Now in these days when the disciples were increasing in number, the Hellenists murmured against the Hebrews because their widows were neglected in the daily distribution. ²And the twelve summoned the body of the disciples and said, "It is not right that we should give up preaching the word of God to serve tables. ³Therefore, brothers, pick out from among you seven men of good repute, full of the Spirit and of wisdom, whom we may appoint to this duty. ⁴But we will devote ourselves to prayer and to the ministry of the word." ⁵And what they said pleased the whole multitude, and they chose Stephen, a man full of faith and of the Holy Spirit, and Philip, and Prochorus, and Nicanor, and Timon, and Parmenas, and Nicolaus, a proselyte of Antioch. ⁶These they set before the apostles, and they prayed and laid their hands upon them.

⁷And the word of God increased; and the number of the disciples multiplied greatly in Jerusalem, and a great many of the priests were obedient to the faith.

OVERVIEW: This incident, which has its own interest for an understanding of church order (see Ammonius and Chrysostom on the imposition of hands and Chrysostom and Bede on the manner of choice), is intended by Luke to introduce Stephen, whose discourse and martyrdom are a key factor in his narrative. The pastoral implications of the passage are pointed out by Chrysostom, Didymus and Arator: difficulties in the community, the qualities of a leader, the relation between fruitfulness and suffering.

6:1 The Hellenists and the Hebrews

DIFFICULTIES FROM WITHOUT AND WITHIN. CHRYSOSTOM: "And in those days, when the number of the disciples was multiplied, there arose a murmuring of the Hellenists against the Hebrews, because their widows were neglected in the daily ministration." It was not absolutely in those immediate days, for it is the custom of Scripture to speak of things that are about to happen as taking place in immediate succession.

69

But by "Hellenists" I suppose he means those who spoke Greek, for these, being Hebrew, spoke Greek. Behold another trial! Observe how from within and from without there are warrings, from the very first! "Then," it says, "the twelve called the multitude of the disciples to them, and said, It is reasonable that we should leave the word of God, and serve tables." Well said: for the needful must give precedence to the more needful. But see, how they take thought directly for these inferior matters and yet do not neglect the preaching. HOMILIES ON THE ACTS OF THE APOSTLES 14.[1]

UNEQUAL TREATMENT OF WIDOWS. BEDE: The cause of this grumbling was the fact that the Hebrews gave preferential treatment in the ministry to their own widows, inasmuch as they were more fully instructed, over the widows of the Hellenists. COMMENTARY ON THE ACTS OF THE APOSTLES 6.1.[2]

6:2 Continuing to Preach the Word

NOURISHMENT OF THE APOSTLES' WORDS. ARATOR: Oh, rich glory of the apostles' speech, never to permit people to feel a famine of virtues! A distributed sum of money desires increase. The coin of language entrusted [to them] was displeasing when it remained alone. That passage shows that food for the mind is better for an uncultivated people than victuals spread through their limbs and that the richness of the heavenly word nourishes a broadly skilled mind. For of what advantage are the foods of bodily nourishment when the soul is hungry? ON THE ACTS OF THE APOSTLES 1.[3]

6:3 Seven Men of Good Repute

THE PEOPLE CHOOSE. CHRYSOSTOM: Now when Matthias was to be presented, it was said, "It must be someone who has been with us the whole time."[4] But not so here, since this was different. No longer did they put it to the lot, and although they could have made the choice themselves, moved as they were by the Spirit, they wanted the testimony of the people. Determining the number, ordaining the chosen and other such business rested with them, but the choice itself they entrusted to the people, so as not to give the appearance of showing favor. For even God entrusted it to Moses to choose as elders the men he knew.[5] HOMILIES ON THE ACTS OF THE APOSTLES 14.[6]

LIKE COLUMNS OF THE ALTAR. BEDE: For this reason, the apostles or the successors of the apostles throughout all of the churches now decided upon seven deacons who would be of higher rank than the others and who would stand closer around the altar, like the columns of the altar. Their being seven in number is not without some symbolism. COMMENTARY ON THE ACTS OF THE APOSTLES 6.3.[7]

THE DIGNITY OF SERVICE. ARATOR: [L]est, however, the circumstance [waiting on tables] forsaken [by the apostles] be thought more lowly, the handling of it was entrusted to [seven] distinguished deacons, and that precious [service] possessed a heavenly number. ON THE ACTS OF THE APOSTLES 1.[8]

6:5 Full of Faith and of the Holy Spirit

HAVING FAITH AND FULL OF FAITH. DIDYMUS THE BLIND: Of those who have a share in virtue, some possess it perfectly and others imperfectly. Hence it is said of Stephen that he was selected because he was full of faith and the Spirit, as every believer is not full of faith. Someone upon whom Peter looked is said to "have faith" but not to be full of faith.[9] CATENA ON THE ACTS OF THE APOSTLES.[10]

---

[1]NPNF 1 11:89-90**. [2]CS 117:65*. [3]OAA 41*. [4]Acts 1:21. [5]Num 11:16. [6]NPNF 1 11:90**. [7]CS 117:65*. [8]OAA 42. [9]A note in PG 39 at this place points out that Didymus is probably alluding to Acts 14:9, where *Paul* is said to see that some "had faith." [10]PG 39:1663.

WISDOM AS WELL AS FAITH. CHRYSOSTOM: For indeed great wisdom is needed in such ministries. Do not think, just because he was not entrusted with the word, that such a person does not need wisdom; on the contrary, he is in great need of it. HOMILIES ON THE ACTS OF THE APOSTLES 14.[11]

6:6 Prayer and Laying on of Hands

GOD'S HAND ORDAINS. CHRYSOSTOM: They set them apart from the multitude. The people themselves drew them to the ordination, and the apostles did not lead. Notice how he does nothing excessive. He does not say how it was done but only that they were ordained through prayer. For this is the meaning of "ordination" (in Greek, "stretching out the hand"): the hand that is laid upon the head belongs to a person, but God effects it all, and it is his hand that touches the head of the ordained one, if he is duly ordained. HOMILIES ON THE ACTS OF THE APOSTLES 14.[12]

AN ANCIENT CUSTOM. AMMONIUS: It is to be noted that the ordination comes by the word of the leaders through their prayer and the imposition of their hands, and that the rank of deacons was given to deacons from the beginning, and that this custom has been observed until now. CATENA ON THE ACTS OF THE APOSTLES 6.6.[13]

6:7 The Word of God Increased

THE WORD INCREASES AFTER TRIALS. CHRYSOSTOM: In Jerusalem the number increased. It is wonderful that where Christ was slain, there the preaching increased! Not only did it not happen that some people were offended in the case of Ananias, but the awe became even greater; all the while some were flogged, others threatening, others tempting the Spirit and others murmuring. Notice, if you please, under what circumstances the number increased. It was after the trials—not before—that the number increased. And see how great is the mercy of God. The chief priests who were shouting such things, who were indignant, highly vexed, who said, "he saved others. He cannot save himself."[14] It was from the ranks of these that many [priests], it says, "were obedient to the faith." HOMILIES ON THE ACTS OF THE APOSTLES 14.[15]

---

[11]NPNF 1 11:90**. [12]NPNF 1 11:90**. [13]CGPNT 3:101. [14]Mt 27:42. [15]NPNF 1 11:91**.

6:8-15 STEPHEN SEIZED AND BROUGHT BEFORE THE COUNCIL

[8]And Stephen, full of grace and power, did great wonders and signs among the people. [9]Then some of those who belonged to the synagogue of the Freedmen (as it was called), and of the Cyrenians, and of the Alexandrians, and of those from Cilicia and Asia, arose and disputed with Stephen. [10]But they could not withstand the wisdom and the Spirit with which he spoke. [11]Then they secretly instigated men, who said, "We have heard him speak blasphemous words against Moses and God." [12]And they stirred up the people and the elders and the scribes, and they came upon him and seized him and brought him before the council, [13]and set up false witnesses who said,

"This man never ceases to speak words against this holy place and the law; [14]for we have heard him say that this Jesus of Nazareth will destroy this place, and will change the customs which Moses delivered to us." [15]And gazing at him, all who sat in the council saw that his face was like the face of an angel.

OVERVIEW: Stephen is the first nonapostolic major witness in the book of Acts, and his witness (*martyria*) reaches its ultimate goal. Chrysostom points to the increase of power that came with the laying on of hands and to the glory that God bestowed upon Stephen. Bede's use of philology is characteristic of his time, but he is sensitive to the fact that Luke is portraying Stephen as an example of the fulfillment of Jesus' prophecy that he would help those under trial (Lk 21:15).

6:8 Stephen, Full of Grace and Power

THE GIFT OF PREACHING ALONE NOT SUFFICIENT. CHRYSOSTOM: See how even among the seven there was one who was preeminent and who won the first prize. For although the ordination was common to all seven, he drew upon himself greater grace. And notice how he worked no [signs and wonders] before this, but only when he became publicly known. This was to show that the gift of preaching alone is not sufficient and that there is also need of the ordination. Thus was the assistance of the Spirit gained. For if they were full of the Spirit, clearly it came from the bath of baptism. HOMILIES ON THE ACTS OF THE APOSTLES 15.[1]

FULL OF GRACE AND COURAGE. BEDE: The Greek word *Stephen* means "crowned" in Latin.[2] In a very beautiful way he anticipated by the portent in his name what he was about to experience in reality—"abjectly stoned but crowned on high."[3] In Hebrew, however, his name means "your norm."[4] Whose norm, if not that of the subsequent martyrs, for whom, by being the first to suffer, he became the model of dying for Christ? COMMENTARY ON THE ACTS OF THE APOSTLES 6.8.[5]

6:10 The Wisdom and Spirit

TO MARTYRS ELOQUENCE IS GIVEN. BEDE: This is what the Lord himself tells his martyrs: "For I will give you eloquence and wisdom which all your adversaries will not be able to withstand or contradict."[6] It was fitting that in the first martyr he should confirm what he deigned to promise to all those handed over [to martyrdom] for the sake of his name. COMMENTARY ON THE ACTS OF THE APOSTLES 6.10.[7]

6:11 Secret Instigations

THE BATTLE WAS GOD'S. CHRYSOSTOM: What madness! The men who overcame them by works—they expected to overcome these by words! It is just what they did in the case of Christ. And as always they sought refuge in words, because they were ashamed to seize them with no charge against them. And see how those who brought them to trial do not themselves bear witness (for they would have been refuted) but hire others, so that it might not appear to be an act of pure insult and abuse. The same pattern is visible here as in the case of Christ. Look at the power of the preaching. They were not only flogged but also stoned, but it still prevailed. They were not laymen but were persecuted from all sides by enemies who bore witness against them. But not only were their enemies bettered; they did not even have the power to resist, despite their great shamelessness. Thus it obtained by force a conviction against them, even

---

[1]NPNF 1 11:94*. [2]Isidore of Seville *Etymologies* 7.11.3. [3]Augustine *Explanations of the Psalms* 58.1.5 (CCL 39:732). [4]Jerome *On Hebrew Names* (CCL 72:148 MS. H). [5]CS 117:65-66*. [6]Lk 21:15. [7]CS 117:66*.

though they fabricated many unpersuasive arguments, for as the saying goes, "He who casts out devils has a touch of the devil." For the battle was not man's but God's against men. Homilies on the Acts of the Apostles 15.[8]

6:13 False Witnesses

False Accusations Rectified by God. Chrysostom: Where people were not falsely accused, the Scripture mentions nothing of this sort. But in this case since it was false accusation, naturally it is rectified by God. He accomplishes this by the very look of the man. For the apostles were not falsely accused but were forbidden. But this man is falsely accused, and so above all his face pleads for him. This even put the priest to shame. Homilies on the Acts of the Apostles 15.[9]

6:15 Stephen's Face Like That of an Angel

Glory in One of Low Degree. Chrysostom: "And gazing at him, all who sat in the council saw that his face was like the face of an angel." Thus it is possible even for one who is on a lower level to shine. For what did this man have, I ask, that was less than the apostles? He did not lack for miracles, and great was the boldness he showed. "They saw," it says, "that his face was like the face of an angel."[10] This was his grace. This was the glory of Moses. Gracious did God make him, now that he was about to speak, so that immediately by his very look he might strike them with amazement. For indeed there are faces full of spiritual grace, lovely to behold for those who desire them and commanding respect from enemies who hate them. Homilies on the Acts of the Apostles 15.[11]

---

[8]NPNF 1 11:96**. [9]NPNF 1 11:97**. [10]Ex 34:30. [11]NPNF 1 11:95**.

7:1-8 STEPHEN RECOUNTS THE CALL OF ABRAHAM

[1]And the high priest said, "Is this so?" [2]And Stephen said:

"Brothers and fathers, hear me. The God of glory appeared to our father Abraham, when he was in Mesopotamia, before he lived in Haran, [3]and said to him, 'Depart from your land and from your kindred and go into the land which I will show you.' [4]Then he departed from the land of the Chaldeans, and lived in Haran. And after his father died, God removed him from there into this land in which you are now living; [5]yet he gave him no inheritance in it, not even a foot's length, but promised to give it to him in possession and to his posterity after him, though he had no child. [6]And God spoke to this effect, that his posterity would be aliens in a land belonging to others, who would enslave them and ill-treat them four hundred years. [7]'But I will judge the nation which they serve,' said God, 'and after that they shall come out and worship me in this place.' [8]And he gave him the covenant of circumcision. And so Abraham became the father of Isaac, and circumcised him on the eighth day; and Isaac became the father of Jacob, and Jacob of the twelve patriarchs."

OVERVIEW: In Luke's structuring of Acts, Stephen's speech and subsequent martyrdom mark the initial breaking point between the old and the new Israel. Tracing the history of God's people through three of its greatest figures, Stephen gives the story of Abraham (Acts 7:1-8), Joseph (Acts 7:9-19) and Moses (Acts 7:20-40), and then he points to Israel's chronic infidelity (Acts 7:41-50), concluding with a stinging indictment of his hearers, whom he accuses of bringing the rebellion of their ancestors to its culmination (Acts 7:51-53). We see in some of Bede's comments how the Fathers would note or reconcile contradictions between the books of Scripture, as well as how the New Testament was the rule for interpreting the Old. Here, however, the Fathers stress an allegorical reading of the call of Abraham and his descendants. His departure outwardly enacts an inward renunciation (CASSIAN), while God's revelation shows a predilection based on no previous merit, prior to all that the law asked, with a reward obtained through obedience (CHRYSOSTOM). This reward is the resurrection that Abraham and his seed, the God-fearing faithful, will receive (IRENAEUS). The passage of time has proven God true to his word and shown the great faith of Abraham, and it should teach us that we too will suffer trials and testing here before entering the kingdom, and that even in these will God's bounty overflow (CHRYSOSTOM).

7:2 God Appeared to Abraham

GOD APPEARED TO ABRAHAM. BEDE: It must be noted "according to the words of Stephen, that God did not (as appears in Genesis[1]) speak to Abraham after the death of his father, who certainly died in Haran, where his son also lived with him; but [he spoke to him] before he lived in that city, although he was already in the region of Mesopotamia,"[2] of which Haran was a city. COMMENTARY ON THE ACTS OF THE APOSTLES 7.2.[3]

7:3 Leaving Land and Family

DO AS GOD BIDS. CHRYSOSTOM: He shows that these were types, as was Abraham's leaving of his home country, at God's command, not against the law (for home and country is where God shall lead): "Then he departed," he says, "from the land of the Chaldeans." He shows that the Jews, if one looks closely into the matter, are of Persian origin and that, even without miracles, one must do as God says, whatever hardships may result. For even the patriarch left the grave of his father and all that he had in obedience to God's command. If Abraham's father had no part in the migration because he was unworthy, much more unworthy were the children, even though they came much of the way. HOMILIES ON THE ACTS OF THE APOSTLES 15.[4]

MENTAL DEPARTURE. BEDE: Therefore the following words, "Then he went out from the land of the Chaldeans," do not signify a physical but a mental departure, by which he separated himself forever from association with the Chaldeans and their nation. According to the belief of the chronicles, in one and the same year he left Chaldea, entered Mesopotamia, tarried in Haran and was brought into the land of the promise. COMMENTARY ON THE ACTS OF THE APOSTLES 7.3.[5]

THE THREE RENUNCIATIONS. JOHN CASSIAN: [Paphnutius said,] "We read that the Lord commanded Abraham to do these three things all at once when he said to him, 'Leave your country and your kinsfolk and your father's house.'" First he spoke of "your country," namely, of the resources of this world and of earthly wealth; second, of "your kinsfolk," namely, of the former way of life and behavior and vices that have been related to us from our birth by a connection as it were of a certain affinity or consanguinity; third, of "your father's house," namely, of every vestige

---

[1]Gen 11:31—12:1. [2]Augustine *The City of God* 16.15 (CCL 48:519). [3]CS 117:69*. [4]NPNF 1 11:97**. [5]CS 117:69-70*.

of this world which the eyes gaze upon. CONFERENCE 3.6.2.[6]

7:5 Promised to Abraham

THE REWARD OF OBEDIENCE. CHRYSOSTOM: He shows here that the promise had been made before the place, before the circumcision, before sacrifice and before the temple. He also shows that it was not by merit that these people received either circumcision or law, but that obedience alone secured the land as its reward. And even though the circumcision has been given, the promise is not yet fulfilled. HOMILIES ON THE ACTS OF THE APOSTLES 15.[7]

AWAITING THE PROMISE OF GOD. IRENAEUS: Thus did [Abraham] await patiently the promise of God and was unwilling to appear to receive from people what God had promised to give him, when he said again to him as follows, "I will give this land to your seed, from the river of Egypt even to the great river Euphrates." If, then, God promised him the inheritance of the land, yet he did not receive it during all the time of his sojourn there, it must be, that together with his seed, that is, those who fear God and believe in him, he shall receive it at the resurrection of the just. For his seed is the church, which receives the adoption to God through the Lord, as John the Baptist said, "For God is able from the stones to raise up children to Abraham." AGAINST HERESIES 5.32.2.[8]

THE RIGHTEOUS DO NOT STAGGER. CHRYSOSTOM: Do you see how what occurred contradicted the promise? Again he said, "In Isaac will your seed be named,"[9] and Abraham believed. Then he says, "Offer to me as sacrifice this," while this was the one who was to fill all the world from his seed. Did you notice the contradiction between the commands and the promise? He commanded what was in opposition to the promises. Yet not even so did the just man lose his head or say that he had been deceived. ON THE EPISTLE TO THE HEBREWS 25.1.[10]

7:6 His Descendants Would Be Aliens

GOD ALLOWS US TO BE TRIED. CHRYSOSTOM: Notice how many years ago was the promise made and the way in which it was made, and no mention of sacrifice anywhere, or of circumcision. Here he shows how God himself allowed them to suffer terribly, and yet he had no complaint against them. Nevertheless their enemies did act with impunity. "'But I will judge the nation which they serve,' said God." For it was to prevent them from judging people as pious according to the saying, "He puts his trust in God; now let God rescue him"[11] that he, who promised and who gave the land, first permits the sufferings. Likewise also now, even though he had promised a kingdom, he allows us to practice obedience through trial. It was only after four hundred years that the freedom came, so is it any wonder that one has to wait in the case of the kingdom? Nonetheless he did what he promised, and time did not prevail to cast into falsehood his word. HOMILIES ON THE ACTS OF THE APOSTLES 16.[12]

SOJOURNERS IN A STRANGE COUNTRY. BEDE: This is not to be understood as meaning that he said that this offspring was to be mistreated or subjected to slavery for four hundred years. Rather, by hyperbaton it should be read in the sense that his offspring would be wanderers for four hundred years, and during part of that time slavery too would fall to their lot. "Because it is written, 'In Isaac your offspring will be called,'[13] there are counted from the year of Isaac's birth to the year of the departure from Egypt 405 years (which Scripture according to its usual practice calls 400), during which that offspring would be wanderers, either in the land of Canaan or in Egypt."[14] It can thus be understood that the hardship of 400 years may be counted from Isaac's

---

[6]ACW 57:123-24. [7]NPNF 1 11:97**. [8]ANF 1:561. [9]Gen 21:12. [10]NPNF 1 14:477**. [11]Mt 27:43. [12]NPNF 1 11:100**. [13]Gen 21:12; Rom 9:7; Heb 11:18. [14]Augustine *Questions on the Heptateuch* 2.47.6 (CCL 33:92).

fifth year, during which he began to be ill-treated by the son of the slave girl.[15] COMMENTARY ON THE ACTS OF THE APOSTLES 7.6.[16]

7:7 They Shall Worship God

GOD IS RICH IN WAYS TO LIFT US UP. CHRYSOSTOM: It is fitting to say here that God is rich in ways to lift us up, since the resourcefulness of God was especially clear here. For even as it suffered reverses—enslavement, maltreatment, slaughter—the nation increased. HOMILIES ON THE ACTS OF THE APOSTLES 16.[17]

---

[15]Gen 21:9 (Vg). [16]CS 117:70*. [17]NPNF 1 11:101-2**.

7:9-16 GOD PRESERVES JOSEPH

[9]"And the patriarchs, jealous of Joseph, sold him into Egypt; but God was with him, [10]and rescued him out of all his afflictions, and gave him favor and wisdom before Pharaoh, king of Egypt, who made him governor over Egypt and over all his household. [11]Now there came a famine throughout all Egypt and Canaan, and great affliction, and our fathers could find no food. [12]But when Jacob heard that there was grain in Egypt, he sent forth our fathers the first time. [13]And at the second visit Joseph made himself known to his brothers, and Joseph's family became known to Pharaoh. [14]And Joseph sent and called to him Jacob his father and all his kindred, seventy-five souls; [15]and Jacob went down into Egypt. And he died, himself and our fathers, [16]and they were carried back to Shechem and laid in the tomb that Abraham had bought for a sum of silver from the sons of Hamor in Shechem."

OVERVIEW: The God of Abraham works through the process of victimization and makes the victims, those sold into slavery, those persecuted, hated and despised, the ones he exalts and through whom he works to bring about the salvation of all who are willing to repent and be reconciled (CHRYSOSTOM). The many manifestations of this through Israel's history are complex, but the general pattern is what Stephen is attempting to convey to his audience (BEDE).

7:10 God Rescued Joseph

AUTHORS OF SALVATION. CHRYSOSTOM: See how it demonstrates what Gamaliel said, "If it comes from God, you will not be able to destroy it."[1] See how the victims of plots became the authors of salvation to those plotting against them; how the word, plotting against itself and itself plotted against by others, was saved for all this. The famine did not destroy them. And not only that, but they were saved through him who was expected to perish. The royal edict did not destroy them. Their number at that time rather increased, because he died, the one who knew them. Their savior they wished to kill, but for all that, they had not the power to do it. Do you see

---

[1]Acts 5:39.

how by the very means the devil tries to break the promise of God, the promise is increased? Homilies on the Acts of the Apostles 16.[2]

The Slave Reigns As a King. Chrysostom: Thus even the one who was sold as slave, he makes him reign as a king in the place where he was considered a slave. Just as Christ also in death shows his power, so he reigns there, where they sold him. Homilies on the Acts of the Apostles 16.[3]

7:14 Joseph Called Jacob

Seventy-Five Souls. Bede: In his discourse he [Stephen] followed the Septuagint. In the original Hebrew, however, we find only seventy souls. Even if you should wish to count up the same lineage of souls in Genesis, you would find only seventy souls, even with the addition of Jacob himself, and Joseph with his two sons who were in Egypt.[4] Commentary on the Acts of the Apostles 7.14.[5]

7:15 Jacob Went to Egypt

His Bones Were Transferred to Shechem. Bede: In fact, it is only of Joseph that Scripture reports his bones being transferred from Egypt and buried in Shechem.[6] However, from these words of the blessed Stephen and from the writings of Jerome, who was a resident of these very places, it is to be observed that other patriarchs were also buried in the same place, although the memory of Joseph is rightly held more famous, since it was he who commanded that this be done with his bones, and it is to his tribe that this city belonged. Indeed, in his history of the blessed Paula, Jerome reports thus,[7] "She passed through Shechem (not Sychar as many erroneously read), which is now named Neapolis, and she entered the church built on the side of Mount Garizim, in the neighborhood of Jacob's well, upon which the Lord sat."[8] And a little further on he says,[9] "And turning away from there, she saw the tombs of the twelve patriarchs." Likewise, in his [Jerome's] book on the best sort of translating,[10] "But the twelve patriarchs are not buried in Arboc but in Shechem." Commentary on the Acts of the Apostles 7.15.[11]

7:16 Carried Back to Shechem

By the Law He Preached Christ. Bede: Truly when speaking to the populace the blessed Stephen followed the popular opinion in his discourse. In conflating the two accounts he concentrated less on the arrangement of the historical details than on the point with which he was concerned. For this man, who was accused of teaching against the holy place and the law, proceeded to show how it might be demonstrated from the law that Jesus Christ was the promised one and that they [the Jews] had been unwilling to be subject to Moses then, and they were unwilling to be subject to the Lord now. I have given the best explanation that I can, not [intending to] pass judgment in advance on a better opinion, if there should be one. Furthermore, the phrase "from the sons of Hamor, the son of Shechem" in the Greek exemplar is written "from the sons of Hamor, who was in Shechem." This seems to be more in accord with the history in Genesis, although it could have been the case that the same Hamor had both a father and a son named Shechem. Commentary on the Acts of the Apostles 7.16.[12]

---

[2]NPNF 1 11:101**. [3]NPNF 1 11:102**. [4]Gen 46:26-27; Ex 1:5. [5]CS 117:70*. [6]Josh 24:32. [7]Jerome *Letter* 108.13 (CSEL 55:322). [8]Jn 4:5-6. [9]Jerome *Letter* 108.13 (CSEL 55:322). [10]Jerome *Letter* 57.10 (CSEL 54:522). [11]CS 117:70-71*. [12]CS 117:71-72*.

7:17-22 THE BIRTH OF MOSES

[17]"*But as the time of the promise drew near, which God had granted to Abraham, the people grew and multiplied in Egypt* [18]*till there arose over Egypt another king who had not known Joseph.* [19]*He dealt craftily with our race and forced our fathers to expose their infants, that they might not be kept alive.* [20]*At this time Moses was born, and was beautiful before God. And he was brought up for three months in his father's house;* [21]*and when he was exposed, Pharaoh's daughter adopted him and brought him up as her own son.* [22]*And Moses was instructed in all the wisdom of the Egyptians, and he was mighty in his words and deeds.*"

OVERVIEW: We here draw from the Antiochene and Alexandrian traditions concerning Moses' upbringing. Antioch is today known for having produced more historically-minded critics than Alexandria, and yet here we have a comment from Chrysostom, who is unusually terse and figurative, while from Origen and Gregory of Nyssa we see a use of Scripture for a practical purpose: the question of the degree to which Christians should engage themselves in pagan learning. For the Alexandrians, although they are using an allegorical reading technique, Moses was a prime example that the treasures of pagan wisdom could be plundered, as was their gold,[1] provided the student received proper guidance.

7:21 Pharaoh's Daughter Adopted Moses

A FIGURE OF THE RESURRECTION. CHRYSOSTOM: If it was astonishing that Joseph was sold by his brothers, here is something even more astonishing. The king who was to perish nourished the one who was to overthrow his rule. Do you see in all this a figurative enacting, so to speak, of the resurrection of the dead? Yet it is not the same for God himself to do something and for it to come to pass as an act by human choice. For these things indeed came to pass by human choice. HOMILIES ON THE ACTS OF THE APOSTLES 16.[2]

7:22 All the Wisdom of the Egyptians

HUMAN RATIONALITY AND DIVINE WISDOM. ORIGEN: During the time Moses was in Egypt and "was educated in all the wisdom of the Egyptians," he was not "feeble in speech" or "slow in tongue," nor did he profess to be ineloquent.[3] For, so far as concerned the Egyptians, his speech was sonorous and his eloquence incomparable. But when he began to hear the voice of God and recognize divine communications, then he perceived his own voice to be meager and feeble, and he understands his own tongue to be slow and impeded. When he began to recognize that true Word which "was in the beginning with God,"[4] then he announces that he is mute. But let us use an analogy that what we are saying may be more easily understood. If a rational person is compared with the dumb animals, although he may be ignorant and unlearned, he will appear eloquent in comparison with those who are devoid of both reason and speech. But if he is compared with learned and eloquent people who are most excellent in all wisdom, he will appear ineloquent and dumb. But if someone should contemplate the divine Word himself and look at the divine wisdom itself, however learned and wise he be, he will confess that he is a dumb animal in comparison with God to a much greater extent than the cattle are in comparison with us. HOMILIES ON EXODUS 3.1.[5]

---

[1]Ex 12:35. [2]NPNF 1 11:101**. [3]See Ex 4:10. [4]Jn 1:1. [5]FC 71:248*.

The Plunder of the Egyptians. Gregory of Nyssa: Thus Moses led the people out of Egypt, and everyone who follows in the steps of Moses in this way sets free from the Egyptian tyrant[6] all those guided by his word. Those who follow the leader to virtue must, I think, not lack the wealth of Egypt or be deprived of the treasures of the foreigners, but having acquired all the property of their enemies, they must have it for their own use. This is exactly what Moses then commanded the people to do. . . . It commands those participating through virtue in the free life also to equip themselves with the wealth of pagan learning by which foreigners to the faith beautify themselves. Our guide in virtue commands someone who "borrows" from wealthy Egyptians to receive such things as moral and natural philosophy, geometry, astronomy, dialectic, and whatever else is sought by those outside the church, since these things will be useful when in time the divine sanctuary of mystery must be beautified with the riches of reason.

Those who treasured up for themselves such wealth handed it over to Moses as he was working on the tent of mystery, each one making his personal contribution to the construction of the holy places. It is possible to see this happening even now. For many bring to the church of God their profane learning as a kind of gift: Such a man was the great Basil,[7] who acquired the Egyptian wealth in every respect during his youth and dedicated this wealth to God for the adornment of the church, the true tabernacle. Life of Moses 2.112, 115-16.[8]

---

[6]Allegorically understood as the devil. [7]Basil the Great (c. 330-379), bishop of Cappadocia and brother of Gregory of Nyssa. [8]*GNLM* 80-81.

7:30-34 THE BURNING BUSH

[30]"Now when forty years had passed, an angel appeared to him in the wilderness of Mount Sinai, in a flame of fire in a bush. [31]When Moses saw it he wondered at the sight; and as he drew near to look, the voice of the Lord came, [32]'I am the God of your fathers, the God of Abraham and of Isaac and of Jacob.' And Moses trembled and did not dare to look. [33]And the Lord said to him, 'Take off the shoes from your feet, for the place where you are standing is holy ground. [34]I have surely seen the ill-treatment of my people that are in Egypt and heard their groaning, and I have come down to deliver them. And now come, I will send you to Egypt.'"

Overview: Gregory of Nyssa provides us with a wonderful allegorical meditation on Moses before the burning bush as what is required of us as we approach union in prayer and contemplation with the divine. Chrysostom also speaks here of prayer, of its power and the need to be persistent. He speaks of the mystery of God's permissive will that allows evil, and yet his quotation of the "curse" from Genesis 3:19 hints at his frame of mind: it is because we have wandered far from God that God must allow and even inflict sufferings and punishments to bend our wills back to himself.

7:33 Remove the Shoes

The Ineffable and Mysterious Illumination. Gregory of Nyssa: It is upon us who continue in this quiet and peaceful course of life that the truth will shine, illuminating the eyes of our soul with its own rays. This truth, which was then manifested by the ineffable and mysterious illumination that came to Moses, is God. And if the flame by which the soul of the prophet was illuminated was kindled from a thorny bush, even this fact will not be useless for our inquiry. For if truth is God and truth is light . . . such guidance of virtue leads us to know that light that has reached down even to human nature. . . . From this we learn also the mystery of the Virgin: The light of divinity which through birth shone from her into human life did not consume the burning bush, even as the flower of her virginity was not withered by giving birth. That light teaches us what we must do to stand within the rays of the true light: Sandaled feet cannot ascend that height where the light of truth is seen, but the dead and earthly covering skins, which was placed around our nature at the beginning when we were found naked because of disobedience to the divine will, must be removed from the feet of the soul. When we do this, the knowledge of the truth will result and manifest itself. The full knowledge of being comes about by purifying our opinion concerning nonbeing. Life of Moses 2.19-22.[1]

7:34 God Heard Their Groaning

That They Might Give Thanks to God. Chrysostom: Hearing these things, let us in our afflictions flee to him. "And their groans," says he, "I have heard," and not simply, "because of their calamities." But if someone should ask, "Why did he allow them to be mistreated there?" we would answer: above all it was because sufferings are justly the cause of rewards. Then "why did he mistreat them?" To show his power, that he is able; and not only this but also to educate them.

Notice, in fact, that when they were in the desert, they "became fat, grew thick, spread out in girth and kicked."[2] As always, ease was an evil. Therefore in the very beginning he said to Adam, "With sweat on your brow shall you eat your bread."[3] And also that they might give thanks to God after they have come out of much suffering into respite. For affliction is a great good. Listen to what the prophet says: "It is good for me, O Lord, that you have humbled me."[4] Homilies on the Acts of the Apostles 16.[5]

Apply Yourselves to Prayer. Chrysostom: Prayer is a mighty weapon if offered with suitable mind. Learn its strength from the following examples! Continued entreaty has overcome shamelessness, injustice, savagery and effrontery, as when he says, "Listen to what the unjust judge says."[6] On another occasion, continued entreaty also overcame hesitation and accomplished what friendship did not. "Even though he will not give to him because he is his friend, at least because of his persistence he will get up and give to him."[7] Tireless persistence also made her worthy who was unworthy. "It is not fair," he said, "to take the children's food and throw it to the dogs." "Yes, Lord," she replied, "yet even the dogs eat the crumbs that fall from their masters' table."[8] Let us then devote ourselves to prayer. It is a mighty weapon if offered with earnestness, without vainglory and with a sincere mind. Prayer routed enemies and benefited an entire nation, undeserving though it was. "I have heard their groaning," he said, "and I have come down to rescue them." Prayer is a saving medicine and has power to prevent sins and heal misdeeds. It was to prayer that the widow, left all alone, turned her mind.[9] On the Epistle to the Hebrews 27.9.[10]

---

[1]*GNLM* 59-60. [2]Deut 32:15. [3]Gen 3:19. [4]Ps 119:71 (118:71 LXX). [5]NPNF 1 11:103-4**. [6]Lk 18:6. [7]Lk 11:8. [8]Mt 15:26-27. [9]1 Tim 5:5. [10]NPNF 1 14:490**.

7:35-43 THE PEOPLE REJECTED MOSES AND WORSHIPED IDOLS

[35]"This Moses whom they refused, saying, 'Who made you a ruler and a judge?' God sent as both ruler and deliverer by the hand of the angel that appeared to him in the bush. [36]He led them out, having performed wonders and signs in Egypt and at the Red Sea, and in the wilderness for forty years. [37]This is the Moses who said to the Israelites, 'God will raise up for you a prophet from your brothers as he raised me up.' [38]This is he who was in the congregation in the wilderness with the angel who spoke to him at Mount Sinai, and with our fathers; and he received living oracles to give to us. [39]Our fathers refused to obey him, but thrust him aside, and in their hearts they turned to Egypt, [40]saying to Aaron, 'Make for us gods to go before us; as for this Moses who led us out from the land of Egypt, we do not know what has become of him.' [41]And they made a calf in those days, and offered a sacrifice to the idol and rejoiced in the works of their hands. [42]But God turned and gave them over to worship the host of heaven, as it is written in the book of the prophets:

'Did you offer to me slain beasts and sacrifices,
forty years in the wilderness, O house of Israel?
[43]And you took up the tent of Moloch,
and the star of the god Rephan,
the figures which you made to worship;
and I will remove you beyond Babylon.'"

OVERVIEW: Moses prepares the way for Christ as a sign that he will appear in the flesh (BEDE), but it was with Christ that Moses spoke in the wilderness. Christ gave precepts for Moses to give to the people. Sacrifices are of the people's making, not God's (CHRYSOSTOM). It is their attempt to offer their will, even though God is in no need of what they give (BEDE).

7:37 God Will Raise a Prophet

A PROPHET LIKE MYSELF. BEDE: [The prophet will be] like myself in being visible in the flesh, but surpassing me in being terrible in majesty. Stephen says, "Lest the teaching about Christ be said to be new and strange, Moses himself, whom your fathers were unwilling to obey, proclaimed that he would have the form of a man and give precepts of life for all souls."[1] COMMENTARY ON

THE ACTS OF THE APOSTLES 7.37.[2]

7:38 The Congregation in the Wilderness

CHRIST GAVE THE LAW. CHRYSOSTOM: Do not be astonished, he says, if Christ confers benefits on those who decline his kingdom, since it was just the same in the case of Moses. And not only did he deliver them from Egypt, but also he saved them in the wilderness. . . . He shows that the prophecy must by all means be fulfilled and that Moses is not opposed to him. This is the man, he says, "who was in the assembly[3] in the wilderness" and "who spoke to the children of Israel." Do you see that this is where the root[4] comes from and that "salvation is from the Jews"?[5]

---

[1]Deut 18:15-18. [2]CS 117:72-73*. [3]The word also means "church." [4]Rom 11:16. [5]Jn 4:22.

"With the angel," it says, "who had spoken to him." Look, again he affirms that it was he [Christ] who gave the law, since Moses was with him "in the assembly in the wilderness." Homilies on the Acts of the Apostles 17.[6]

7:42 Did You Offer Sacrifices?

Sacrifices Not Necessary. Chrysostom: "But God turned and gave them over to worship the host of heaven." From here come these customs and from here the sacrifices. They themselves were the first to offer sacrifices to the idols. For it is noted that they made a bull calf in Horeb and "offered sacrifices to the idol," since previously "sacrifices" is nowhere mentioned, only "statutes of life" and "words of life." "And they rejoiced," it says, and so the reason for the feasts.[7] "As it is written in the book of the prophets." Notice he does not cite the text without a purpose but shows that there is no need of sacrifices. "Did you offer to me slain beasts and sacrifices? . . ." He speaks emphatically. "You cannot say," he says, "that it was from sacrificing to me that you proceeded to sacrifice to them." And this in the desert, where he had especially shown himself their champion. Homilies on the Acts of the Apostles 17.[8]

God Accepts the Offerer's Will. Bede: Although they may have made offerings to the Lord because of the necessity of offering him service, it is nevertheless true to say that their minds were turned aside to the service of idols "from the time when they had transformed gold into the head of a calf."[9] "For the things we read they afterwards offered to God they did not offer of their own free will, but," as we learn from this passage, "they made them out of fear of punishment and because of the slaying of those who fell on account of the idols."[10] "The Lord, however, does not accept the things offered but the wills of those making the offering. Besides, whenever there was an opportunity they returned in their hearts to Egypt."[11] Commentary on the Acts of the Apostles 7.42.[12]

7:43 The Tent of Moloch

The Tent of Moloch. Bede: Stephen says, "However much you may have been seen bringing victims and sacrifices to the tabernacle of the Lord, nevertheless, with the whole concentration of your minds you clung to the temple of Moloch. Now Moloch, or Melchom as it is often also read, is *the idol of the Ammonites*. It means *your king*."[13] Commentary on the Acts of the Apostles 7.43A.[14]

Your God Remfam. Bede: He says, "You have abandoned the living and true God and taken for your god the star Remfam, that is, 'of your own making.'" It signifies, however, Lucifer, the morning star, to the worship of which the Saracen people were devoted, in connection with the honor paid to Venus.[15] Commentary on the Acts of the Apostles 7.43B.[16]

Led Captive Beyond Babylon. Bede: He says, "On account of these sacrileges you will be led as captives not only into Babylon but even beyond Babylon." "And we should not suppose that the first martyr made a mistake in saying 'beyond Babylon' for what in the prophet is written 'beyond Damascus,'[17] he expressed the idea rather than the word, because they were led beyond Damascus into Babylon, or 'beyond Babylon.'"[18] Commentary on the Acts of the Apostles 7.43D.[19]

---

[6]NPNF 1 11:107**. [7]Ex 32:5-6. [8]NPNF 1 11:108**. [9]Ex 32:1-5. [10]See Ex 32:25-29. [11]Jerome *Commentary on Amos* 2.5.25-27 (CCL 76:296-97). [12]CS 117:73*. [13]Jerome *De Sitibus* (PL 23:912); *Commentary on Isaiah* 16.57.9 (CCL 73A:648); *On Hebrew Names* (CCL 72:147, MSS. BH.). [14]CS 117:73*. [15]Jerome *Commentary on Amos* 2.5.25-27 (CCL 76:296); *Life of Hilarion* 25 (PL 23:41). [16]CS 117:73*. [17]Amos 5:27. [18]Jerome *Commentary on Amos* 2.5.25-27 (CCL 76:297). [19]CS 117:74*.

7:44-50 THE HOUSE OF THE MOST HIGH

⁴⁴*"Our fathers had the tent of witness in the wilderness, even as he who spoke to Moses directed him to make it, according to the pattern that he had seen.* ⁴⁵*Our fathers in turn brought it in with Joshua when they dispossessed the nations which God thrust out before our fathers. So it was until the days of David,* ⁴⁶*who found favor in the sight of God and asked leave to find a habitation for the God of Jacob.* ⁴⁷*But it was Solomon who built a house for him.* ⁴⁸*Yet the Most High does not dwell in houses made with hands; as the prophet says,*

⁴⁹*'Heaven is my throne,*
and earth my footstool.
What house will you build for me, says the Lord,
or what is the place of my rest?
⁵⁰*Did not my hand make all these things?'*

OVERVIEW: The tent of witness bears the testimony of God's work among the Israelites (CHRYSOSTOM). It is not the building that is important but what is symbolized in it, and should a greater truth be revealed, the building shall become a contradiction rather than a preparation for that truth. We must not forget that it is we who need buildings, not God, who is everywhere in everything, but who especially desires us as his abode (BEDE).

7:44 The Tent of Witness in the Wilderness

THEY HAVE GOD FOR A WITNESS. CHRYSOSTOM: But "there was," he says, "a tent of witness." Yes, it was there so that they might have God as witness. This was all. "According to the pattern," he says, "that was shown to you on the mount." Thus on the mount was the original. And this, while in the wilderness, was carried about and not fixed in place. He calls it a tent of witness, that is, a witness of the wonders and of the statutes. That is why both it and they had no temple. Again it was he himself, the angel, who gave the type. HOMILIES ON THE ACTS OF THE APOSTLES 17.[1]

A TENT OF TESTIMONY. BEDE: Since they were

saying that he [Stephen] was acting against the holy place, he showed from this [Old Testament parallel] that the Lord does not place a high value on dressed stone but rather desires the splendor of heavenly souls. From this he wanted them to understand that just as the tent was forsaken when the temple was built, so also they should understand that the temple itself would have to be destroyed when a better dispensation came to take its place, as Jeremiah long before had prophesied saying, "Do not trust in words of falsehood that say, 'This is the temple of the Lord, the temple of the Lord, the temple of the Lord.'"[2] And a little later he says, "I will treat this house in which my name is invoked, and in which you put your trust, just as I treated Shiloh, where my name had its dwelling from the beginning, and I will drive you from my sight."[3] COMMENTARY ON THE ACTS OF THE APOSTLES 7.44.[4]

7:49 What House Will You Build?

WITHIN AND ABOVE ALL THINGS. BEDE: This is not to be understood in a material way, as though God has parts of his body placed in

---

[1]NPNF 1 11:108-9**. [2]Jer 7:4. [3]Jer 7:12-15. [4]CS 117:74*.

heaven and on earth, as we do when we sit down. Rather, to show that he is within and above all things, he [Isaiah] represents heaven as his [God's] throne and earth as a footstool. To demonstrate that he also encompasses all things, in another place he asserts that he measures heaven with his hand and holds the earth in his palm.[5] Spiritually, however, heaven stands for the saints, while the earth stands for sinners, since God watches over the former by dwelling within them; the latter he brings to the ground by condemning them. COMMENTARY ON THE ACTS OF THE APOSTLES 7.49A.[6]

NOT OF MARBLE. BEDE: Not, to be sure, a golden or marble earthly dwelling place. Rather it will be what the prophet adds: "Upon whom does my spirit rest except upon one who is humble and peaceful and who trembles at my words?"[7] COMMENTARY ON THE ACTS OF THE APOSTLES 7.49B.[8]

---

[5]Is 40:12. [6]CS 117:75*. [7]Is 11:2; 66:2. [8]CS 117:75*.

7:51-53 STEPHEN EXCORIATES THE PEOPLE

[51]*"You stiff-necked people, uncircumcised in heart and ears, you always resist the Holy Spirit. As your fathers did, so do you.* [52]*Which of the prophets did not your fathers persecute? And they killed those who announced beforehand the coming of the Righteous One, whom you have now betrayed and murdered,* [53]*you who received the law as delivered by angels and did not keep it."*

OVERVIEW: Stephen's fate is clear as part of the ongoing revelation and offer of God's grace through the wayward actions of people against his chosen ones (CHRYSOSTOM). As befell the prophets, so Christ, and as befell Christ, so those who preach Christ. And those who preach Christ must become both the fire and the gentle dove of the Holy Spirit (AUGUSTINE).

7:51 Resisting the Holy Spirit

A HISTORY OF RESISTANCE. CHRYSOSTOM: "You always resist the Holy Spirit. As your fathers did, so do you." When it was not his will that there should be sacrifices, you sacrificed; and when it is his will, you do not sacrifice. When he would not give you the commandments, you dragged them toward you; when you received them, you neglected them. Again, when the tem-

ple stood, you worshiped idols; and when it is his will to be worshiped without a temple, you do the opposite. HOMILIES ON THE ACTS OF THE APOSTLES 17.[1]

BURNING WORDS, BUT AS A DOVE. AUGUSTINE: Therefore when he sent the Holy Spirit, he manifested him visibly in two ways, as a dove and as fire; as a dove upon the baptized Lord, as fire upon the assembled disciples. . . . Here we saw a dove upon the Lord; there parted tongues upon the assembled disciples; in the one, simplicity is shown, in the other, fervor. For there are those who are said to be simple, and they are indolent; they are called simple, but they are lazy. Not such a one was Stephen, full of the Holy Spirit. He was simple, because he harmed no one; he was

---

[1]NPNF 1 11:109**.

fervent, because he reproached the impious. For he did not keep silence before the Jews; his are those fiery words, "Stiff-necked and uncircumcised in heart and ears, you have always resisted the Holy Spirit." Great vehemence! He rages, but as a dove without bile. For, in order that you may know that he raged without bile, they who were ravens, when they heard these words, immediately ran for stones [to use] against the dove. Stephen began to be stoned; and he, who but a little before was raging and boiling spirit, as if he had attacked his enemies, and as if he had assailed them with violence by those fiery and blazing words as you have heard, "Stiff-necked

and uncircumcised in heart and ears," so that he who heard these words might think that Stephen, if he were allowed, wished them immediately annihilated—when the rocks were coming on him from their hands, on his knees he said, "Lord, lay not this sin to their charge." He adhered to the unity of the dove. For earlier his master, on whom the dove descended, had done that; hanging on the cross, he said, "Father, forgive them, for they know not what they do."[2] TRACTATES ON THE GOSPEL OF JOHN 6.3.1-4.[3]

---

[2]Lk 23:34. [3]FC 78:132.

7:54-60 THE MARTYRDOM OF STEPHEN

[54]*Now when they heard these things they were enraged, and they ground their teeth against him.* [55]*But he, full of the Holy Spirit, gazed into heaven and saw the glory of God, and Jesus standing at the right hand of God;* [56]*and he said, "Behold, I see the heavens opened, and the Son of man standing at the right hand of God."* [57]*But they cried out with a loud voice and stopped their ears and rushed together upon him.* [58]*Then they cast him out of the city and stoned him; and the witnesses laid down their garments at the feet of a young man named Saul.* [59]*And as they were stoning Stephen, he prayed, "Lord Jesus, receive my spirit."* [60]*And he knelt down and cried with a loud voice, "Lord, do not hold this sin against them." And when he had said this, he fell asleep.*

OVERVIEW: Stephen sees Christ in his body standing at God's right hand (THEODORET, BEDE) as an encouragement and as a sign of his reward for his fidelity (ARATOR). Christ stands as one who does battle and gives help (BEDE, AMBROSE), and this vision does not contradict the creed (AUGUSTINE) where he sits as one who judges (BEDE, AMBROSE). Stephen's imitation of the one who paved the way to resurrection is not so much a physical copy but a spiritual one (IRENAEUS), one that teaches what life, in all its paradoxes, is (ARATOR), and what spirit of forgiveness and self-

offering we should express toward those who would kill us (CHRYSOSTOM, AUGUSTINE). Death here is not an end but a beginning of something greater or worse (CHRYSOSTOM, ARATOR).

7:55 Stephen Saw the Glory of God

IN THE FORM OF A BODY. THEODORET OF CYR: The divine nature is invisible, but the thrice blessed Stephen said that he saw the Lord, so even after the resurrection the Lord's body is a body, and it was seen by the victorious Stephen,

since the divine nature cannot be seen. Dialogue (Demonstrations by Syllogisms) 11.[1]

7:56 The Heavens Opened

His Endurance Was Strengthened. Bede:
Since Christ the Lord was the perfect son of both
God and man, why is it that the blessed martyr
preferred to call him the "Son of man" rather
than the Son of God? It would seem that he could
have offered him greater glory if he had chosen to
call him the Son of God rather than the Son of
man—unless by this testimony the infidelity of
the Jews could be confounded, for they remembered that they had crucified a man and that they
had not chosen to believe that he was God.
Therefore, to strengthen the blessed martyr's
endurance the doors of the heavenly kingdom are
opened and, so that the innocent man being
stoned may not stumble to the ground, the crucified God-man appears crowned in heaven.
Hence, because to stand is proper to one who
does battle or to one who gives help, he fittingly
saw standing at God's right hand the one whom
he had as [his] helper among the men who
were persecuting him. And it does not seem
inconsistent that Mark describes him as sitting
at God's right hand, which is the posture of
judging, for "now he judges all things" invisibly,
and "at the end he will come" as the visible
"judge of all."[2] Commentary on the Acts of
the Apostles 7.56.[3]

Christ Was Not Hidden from Him. Arator: Having the light of his heart he sees the
opened heavens, so that what Christ does may
not be hidden. [Christ] rises before the martyr.
[Stephen] then sees him standing, though our
faith is prone rather to honor him as seated. The
very Flesh joined to the Thunderer does honor to
itself in Stephen. The General in his foreknowledge arms those whom he summons to gifts. Lest
anyone here should fight uncertainly, the body is
revealed in the citadel of God as a reward to its
witness. On the Acts of the Apostles 1.[4]

He Followed the Perfect Martyr. Irenaeus: These words [Stephen] said, and he was
stoned. In this way he fulfilled the perfect doctrine, copying in every respect the Leader of martyrdom and praying for those who were slaying
him, in these words, "Lord, lay not this sin to
their charge." Thus were they perfected who
knew one and the same God, who from beginning
to end was present with humankind in the various dispensations, as the prophet Hosea declares:
"I have filled up visions and used similitudes by
the hands of the prophets." Against Heresies
3.12.13.[5]

He Saw with the Eyes of Faith. Augustine: He now sits at the right hand of the Father
in heaven. We ought to give careful consideration
to this fact with the eyes of faith to prevent the
impression that he is immovably fixed in any spot
so as not be permitted to stand or to walk. For,
the fact that St. Stephen said that he saw him
standing does not mean that St. Stephen's vision
was distorted or that his statement is at variance
with the words of the creed. Far be such a
thought, far be such a statement from us! The
Lord's dwelling in lofty and ineffable blessedness
has merely been expressed in this way to indicate
that he dwells there. Sermon 214.8.[6]

Jesus Stood As His Helper. Ambrose: Jesus
stood as a helpmate; he stood as if anxious to help
Stephen, his athlete, in the struggle. He stood as
though ready to crown his martyr. Let him then
stand for you that you may not fear him sitting,
for he sits when he judges. . . . He sits to judge, he
stands to give judgment, and he judges the imperfect but gives judgment among the gods. Letter
59 (63).[7]

7:58 The Death of Stephen

---

[1]NPNF 2 3:248. [2]Gregory the Great *Forty Gospel Homilies* 2.29.7
(PL 76:1217); Mk 16:19. [3]CS 117:75-76*. [4]OAA 43*. [5]ANF 1:435*.
[6]FC 38:138*. [7]FC 26:322-23*.

LIKE CHRIST, HE SUFFERED OUTSIDE THE GATE.

BEDE: The Lord too, who "chose" us "out of the world"[8] for his heavenly kingdom and glory, suffered outside the gate, like Stephen, who, as though he were a stranger to the world, was stoned outside the city. For he had no permanent city here, but with his whole heart he sought the city to come. And, in accordance with the vicissitudes of events, the martyr directed the gaze of his pure heart to heaven, while the stiff-necked persecutor stretched out his hands toward the stones. COMMENTARY ON THE ACTS OF THE APOSTLES 7.58.[9]

OUT OF REBELLION THEY HURLED STONES.

ARATOR: Insane, rebellious Judea, you hurl stones against Stephen, you who will always be stony because of your hard crime. ON THE ACTS OF THE APOSTLES 1.[10]

GOD'S POWER WROUGHT IN PAUL.

CHRYSOSTOM: Notice with what accuracy he narrates all that concerns Paul, to show you that the action was divine. After all this, not only did Paul not believe, but he even sought him with a thousand hands. This is why it says, "And Saul approved of his killing." HOMILIES ON THE ACTS OF THE APOSTLES 18.[11]

A JUST REWARD FOR ALL.

ARATOR: The savage men lay down their garments at the feet of Saul, what the Hebrew calls hell.[12] Both sides now decide to declare what they deserve from this [martyrdom] when the martyr seeks heaven, the executioners "hell." The first circumstance [of martyrdom] reveals and makes as an example what flows from this fountain to one engaged in such a struggle; thus Tartarus quickly comes upon those who commit murder, while heaven lies open for the dying. ON THE ACTS OF THE APOSTLES 1.[13]

7:59 Receive My Spirit

GOD CALLS THE PEOPLE THROUGH SIGNS.

CHRYSOSTOM: This is the reason why his face was also glorified. For God who is merciful wished to make their plots the means of recalling them to himself. And look how many signs there came to be. "Then they cast him out of the city and stoned him," again outside the city, as in the case of Christ. And in death itself, confession and preaching. "And the witnesses laid down their garments at the feet of a young man named Saul. And as they were stoning Stephen, he prayed, 'Lord Jesus, receive my spirit.'" He did this to show them that he is not perishing and also to teach them. HOMILIES ON THE ACTS OF THE APOSTLES 18.[14]

TO FALL IS TO RISE.

ARATOR: O martyr, embark on struggles which will cause happy deaths, where punishment is glory and to fall is a rising, and by slaughter is born immortality embracing the rewards of everlasting life. Lo, to have merited thus to die was the beginning of a blessed life without end. ON THE ACTS OF THE APOSTLES 1.[15]

7:60 Do Not Hold This Sin Against Them

FREEDOM FROM WRATH.

CHRYSOSTOM: This is the boldness of speech that belongs to a man who is carrying the cross. Let us then also imitate this. For although it is not a time for war, it is always the time for boldness. "For I spoke," he says, "in your testimonies before kings, and I was not ashamed."[16] If we happen to be among Gentiles, let us silence them likewise, without anger and without harshness. For if we do this with anger, it is no longer boldness but appears rather as raw passion. If, however, it is done with gentleness, that is true boldness. For in one and the same thing success and failure cannot possibly go together. Boldness of speech is success; anger is failure. Therefore, if we should aspire to boldness,

---

[8]Jn 15:19. [9]CS 117:76*. [10]OAA 42. [11]NPNF 1 11:114**. [12]Wordplay on *Sheol.* [13]OAA 43. [14]NPNF 1 11:113**. [15]OAA 42*. [16]Ps 119:46 (118:46 LXX).

we must be free from anger, in case anyone should attribute our words to the latter. For no matter how just your words may be, when you speak with anger, you ruin everything. This is true no matter how boldly you speak or how fairly you admonish—in short, no matter what you do. See how free from anger this man was when he spoke to them. He did not treat them with any harshness but reminded them of the words of the prophets. Notice that there was no anger, for in his terrible suffering he prayed for them, saying, "Do not hold this sin against them." Thus it was not in anger that he spoke these words but in grief and sorrow for their sakes. As indeed it says of his appearance, "they saw his face that it was the face of an angel," so that they might believe. Let us then be free from anger. The Holy Spirit does not dwell where anger is and cursed is the wrathful. Nothing wholesome can proceed from where anger issued forth. HOMILIES ON THE ACTS OF THE APOSTLES 17.[17]

HE PRAYED FOR HIS PERSECUTORS. AUGUSTINE: And in the Acts of the Apostles, blessed Stephen prays for those by whom he is being stoned, because they had not as yet believed in Christ and were not contending against that universal grace. SERMON ON THE MOUNT 1.22.73.[18]

HE KNELT FOR HIS ENEMIES. BEDE: For himself he prayed standing up; for his enemies he knelt down. Because their iniquity was so great it called out for the greater remedy of falling upon his knees.[19] And marvelous was the virtue of the blessed martyr who was so inflamed with zeal that he openly reproached his captors for their fault in lacking faith and burned so with love that even at his death he prayed for his murderers. COMMENTARY ON THE ACTS OF THE APOSTLES 7.60.[20]

THE PERFECTION OF CHARITY. AUGUSTINE: He showed his love for his murderers, in that he died for them. . . . That is the perfection of love. Love is perfect in him whom it makes ready to die for his brothers; but it is never perfect as soon as it is born. It is born that it may be perfected. Born, it is nourished: nourished, it is strengthened: strengthened, it is made perfect. And when it has reached perfection, how does it speak? "To me to live is Christ, and to die is gain. My desire was to be set free and to be with Christ; for that is by far the best. But to abide in the flesh is needful for your sake."[21] He was willing to live for their sakes, for whom he was ready to die. HOMILIES ON 1 JOHN 5.4.[22]

---

[17]NPNF 1 11:110**. [18]FC 11:100. [19]Augustine *Sermon* 315.3.3; 319.4.4 (PL 38:1433-34, 1441). [20]CS 117:76*. [21]Phil 1:21-24. [22]LCC 8:297*.

8:1-3 THE GREAT PERSECUTION

[1]And Saul was consenting to his death.

And on that day a great persecution arose against the church in Jerusalem; and they were all scattered throughout the region of Judea and Samaria, except the apostles. [2]Devout men buried Stephen, and made great lamentation over him. [3]But Saul was ravaging the church, and entering house after house, he dragged off men and women and committed them to prison.

OVERVIEW: These verses conclude Luke's account of the persecution in Jerusalem, which began with his narrative of what followed from the healing of the lame man at the Beautiful Gate: the hearing before the Sanhedrin,[1] the imprisonment and arraignment before the Sanhedrin[2] and finally, the death of Stephen. Providence is at work in the persecution (CHRYSOSTOM), which becomes the seedbed of the gospel (BEDE). Stephen's body was buried (THEODORET). Even Saul's frenzy was used to an unexpected end (CHRYSOSTOM).

8:1 The Believers Were Scattered

PERSECUTION SPREADS THE SEED OF THE WORD. CHRYSOSTOM: "The persecution," he says, "gained strength." True, but especially then it delivered people who were previously possessed. For it planted miracles like forts among them. Even the death of Stephen did not quench their rage, but rather increased it. It dispersed the teachers, so that the discipleship became greater. There was joy, although there had been great lamentation. Note again the good: the malady lasted long enough, but it was this man who brought them deliverance. HOMILIES ON THE ACTS OF THE APOSTLES 18.[3]

OBEYING THE LORD'S INJUNCTION. BEDE: This is what the Lord himself commanded: "When they persecute you in one city, flee to another."[4] It occurred according to the Lord's will,

"so that the occasion of tribulation might become the seedbed of the gospel."[5] COMMENTARY ON THE ACTS OF THE APOSTLES 8.1.[6]

8:2 The Burial of Stephen

STEPHEN'S BODY WAS BURIED. THEODORET OF CYR: And yet it was the body only which was deemed proper for burial, while the soul was not buried together with the body; nevertheless the body alone was spoken of by the common name. Similarly the blessed Jacob said to his sons, "Bury me with my fathers."[7] He did not say, "Bury my body." LETTER 144.[8]

8:3 Saul Persecuted the Church

EMBOLDENED BY STEPHEN'S MURDER. CHRYSOSTOM: Great was [Saul's] frenzy: that he was alone, that he even entered into houses; for indeed he was ready to give his life for the law. "Arresting," it says, "men and women": mark both the confidence, and the violence and the frenzy. All that fell into his hands, he put to all manner of ill-treatment, for in consequence of the recent murder, he had become more daring. HOMILIES ON THE ACTS OF THE APOSTLES 18.[9]

---

[1]Acts 4:1-22. [2]Acts 5:17-33. [3]NPNF 1 11:114-15**. [4]Mt 10:23.
[5]Jerome *Commentary on Matthew* 1.10.23 (CCL 77:70). [6]CS 117:79*.
[7]Gen 49:29. [8]NPNF 2 3:311. [9]NPNF 1 11:114*.

8:4-13 CHRIST PROCLAIMED IN SAMARIA

[4]Now those who were scattered went about preaching the word. [5]Philip went down to a city of Samaria, and proclaimed to them the Christ. [6]And the multitudes with one accord gave heed to what was said by Philip, when they heard him and saw the signs which he did. [7]For unclean spirits came out of many who were possessed, crying with a loud voice; and many who were paralyzed or

lame were healed. ⁸*So there was much joy in that city.*

⁹*But there was a man named Simon who had previously practiced magic in the city and amazed the nation of Samaria, saying that he himself was somebody great.* ¹⁰*They all gave heed to him, from the least to the greatest, saying, "This man is that power of God which is called Great."* ¹¹*And they gave heed to him, because for a long time he had amazed them with his magic.* ¹²*But when they believed Philip as he preached good news about the kingdom of God and the name of Jesus Christ, they were baptized, both men and women.* ¹³*Even Simon himself believed, and after being baptized he continued with Philip. And seeing signs and great miracles performed, he was amazed.*

OVERVIEW: An outline of Acts is provided by Luke's account of Jesus' prophecy that the apostles would be his witnesses "in Jerusalem and in all Judea and Samaria, and to the end of the earth."[1] With Philip's coming to Samaria, therefore, we reach the next stage in the fulfillment of that prophecy. The Fathers do not comment much on the power of Philip's preaching and his miracles, but they are fascinated by the figure of Simon (CHRYSOSTOM). Justin's account is a good summary of the early notion that Simon was the source of heresies. Either Simon's faith and baptism were sincere and he later reverted to his evil ways, or he was an impostor from the beginning (BEDE). According to Augustine, the exhaustive alternatives are four: When one who is good baptizes one who is good, good comes from good. When one who is evil baptizes one who is evil, evil comes from evil. When one who is evil baptizes one who is good, good may come from evil. When one who is good baptizes one who is evil, evil may come from good.

8:6 The Multitudes Listened

THE CROWDS WERE ATTENTIVE. BEDE: The present chapter and the history of the Samaritan woman[2] prove that these people's souls were ready and willing to believe. COMMENTARY ON THE ACTS OF THE APOSTLES 8.6.[3]

8:9 A Man Named Simon

AN ACCOUNT OF SIMON. JUSTIN MARTYR:

After Christ's ascension into heaven, the devils put forward certain people who said that they themselves were gods; and they were not only not persecuted by you[4] but even deemed worthy of honors. There was a Samaritan, Simon, a native of the village called Gitto, who in the reign of Claudius Caesar, and in your royal city of Rome, did mighty acts of magic, by virtue of the art of the devils operating in him. He was considered a god, and as a god he was honored by you with a statue, which statue was erected on the river Tiber, between the two bridges, and bore this inscription, in the language of Rome, "Simoni Deo Sancto," "To Simon the holy god." And almost all the Samaritans, and a few even of other nations, worship him and acknowledge him as the first god; and a woman, Helena, who went about with him at that time and had formerly been a prostitute, they say fathered this idea. FIRST APOLOGY 26.[5]

8:13 Even Simon Believed

AS CHRIST CHOSE JUDAS. CHRYSOSTOM: How did he come to baptize also Simon? In the same way that Christ also chose Judas. And "seeing" the "signs" that [Philip] worked, since the others did not receive the signs, [Simon] dared not ask for it. How was it then that they did not put him to death, as they did Ananias and Sapphira? The ancient saying is that he who gathered sticks was

---

[1] Acts 1:8. [2] Jn 4:39. [3] CS 117:79. [4] The Roman government. [5] ANF 1:171*.

put to death as a warning to others. No one else suffered this same fate.[6] HOMILIES ON THE ACTS OF THE APOSTLES 18.[7]

FOUR TYPES OF BAPTISM. AUGUSTINE: The good baptized the evil, as Simon Magus was baptized by Philip, a holy man. These four types, therefore, my brothers, are well known. Look, I repeat them again. Hold fast to them, count them, pay attention to them. Beware those types which are evil; hold fast to those which are good. The good are born from the good when holy people are baptized by holy people; the evil from the evil when both they who baptize and they who are baptized live wickedly and impiously; the good from the evil when they who baptize are evil and they who are baptized are good; and the evil from the good when they who baptize are good and they who are baptized are evil. TRACTATES ON THE GOSPEL OF JOHN 11.9.1-2.[8]

STEALING BAPTISM. BEDE: It was either that he too was overcome by the power of the blessed Philip's words so that he truly believed in the Lord, or, as is more believable, that he pretended that he believed until he could receive baptism.[9] For he was so eager for praise that he wished to be believed to be the Christ, as histories tell,[10] and he hoped to learn from him the arts by which he worked miracles. His followers were also taught to do this. "Trained in the evil arts of their founder to enter the church by any sort of deception," they were accustomed to steal baptism.[11] COMMENTARY ON THE ACTS OF THE APOSTLES 8.13.[12]

---

[6]Num 15:32-36. [7]NPNF 1 11:115**. [8]FC 79:19. [9]Eusebius *Ecclesiastical History* 2.1 (GCS 9.1:107-9). [10]Pseudo-Clement *Recognitions* 2.7.1 (GCS 51:55). [11]Eusebius *Ecclesiastical History* 2.1 (GCS 9.1:109). [12]CS 117:79*.

8:14-24 SIMON TRIES TO PURCHASE THE GIFT OF GOD

[14]Now when the apostles at Jerusalem heard that Samaria had received the word of God, they sent to them Peter and John, [15]who came down and prayed for them that they might receive the Holy Spirit; [16]for it had not yet fallen on any of them, but they had only been baptized in the name of the Lord Jesus. [17]Then they laid their hands on them and they received the Holy Spirit. [18]Now when Simon saw that the Spirit was given through the laying on of the apostles' hands, he offered them money, [19]saying, "Give me also this power, that any one on whom I lay my hands may receive the Holy Spirit." [20]But Peter said to him, "Your silver perish with you, because you thought you could obtain the gift of God with money! [21]You have neither part nor lot in this matter, for your heart is not right before God. [22]Repent therefore of this wickedness of yours, and pray to the Lord that, if possible, the intent of your heart may be forgiven you. [23]For I see that you are in the gall of bitterness and in the bond of iniquity." [24]And Simon answered, "Pray for me to the Lord, that nothing of what you have said may come upon me."

Overview: Two aspects in particular of this passage attract an abundance of patristic notice. First is the fact that Peter and John were sent to Samaria and that it was by the laying on of their hands that the Samaritans received the Holy Spirit. Only through the apostles can hands be laid so as to confer the Holy Spirit (Bede). Conversion occurs within the one church to which alone it has been granted to give the grace of baptism and to loose sins (Cyprian). The new converts had not yet received the spirit of miracles (Chrysostom). The Spirit visibly shows himself in his gift of himself (Augustine). Saving baptism is not complete except when performed with the authority of the triune God (Origen). The baptism by Philip did not need to be repeated (Cyprian). Their second focus was upon the person of Simon, his desire for power and his attempt to buy the apostolic power of conferring the Holy Spirit. Simon was washed in the font but not cleansed (Arator). Simon sought power, not grace (Cyril). The simplicity of Peter is contrasted with the malice of Simon (Chrysostom), whose heart was not like the dove (Bede). Peter interiorly perceived God's unerring judgment (Bede, following Gregory the Great). Note that though Peter condemned Simon, he did not exclude him from the hope of forgiveness (Ambrose). But his subsequent career shows his destiny (Eusebius).

The power of the Spirit is not for sale (Cyril of Jerusalem). Those who sell what they have received as a gift will be deprived of its grace (Basil). It is not money that the Spirit seeks but a right heart (Arator), the very center of the person (Cassiodorus). Faith is not acquired by compulsion but received as a gift. It was the power to work signs that the apostles received, not the power arbitrarily to give the Spirit to others. The episode provided a twofold sign—the giving to those whose hearts are ready and the not giving to those who are not (Chrysostom).

8:14 Peter and John Sent to the Samaritans

Only Apostles Can Confer the Holy Spirit. Bede: Arator explains it beautifully,[1] "Peter frequently made John his comrade because a virgin is pleasing to the church." It must be noted that the Philip who preached the gospel to Samaria was one of the seven, for if he had been the apostle [Philip], he would have been able to lay hands on them himself so that they might receive the Holy Spirit. "For this is reserved only to those of pontifical rank. When priests baptize, whether in a bishop's presence or not, they are permitted to anoint those who are baptized with chrism, but because it was consecrated by a bishop, they are not allowed to make the sign of the cross on the forehead with this same oil. This is reserved to the bishops alone when they transmit the Spirit, the Paraclete,"[2] to those who are baptized. Commentary on the Acts of the Apostles 8.14.[3]

8:15 Receiving the Holy Spirit

The Prerogative of the Apostles. Chrysostom: Why were these not in receipt of the Holy Spirit? It may be that Philip kept this honor for the apostles, or that he did not have this gift or that he was one of the seven. The last is most likely. Thus, I take it, this Philip was one of the seven, the one after Stephen, while the Philip in the story of the eunuch was one of the apostles. Notice how the seven did not go forth. It was part of God's plan of salvation for those to go forth and for these to be lacking because of the Holy Spirit. For it was the power to work signs that they received, not the power to give the Spirit to others. This was the prerogative of the apostles. And note [how they sent] not just anyone but the leaders, Peter [and John]. Homilies on the Acts of the Apostles 18.[4]

8:16 The Samaritans Had Not Yet Received the Spirit

---

[1]Arator *De Actibus Apostolorum* 1 (CSEL 72:50). [2]Innocent *Epistula ad Decentium* 25.3.6 (PL 20:554-55). [3]CS 117:79-80. [4]NPNF 1 11:115**.

THE NEW CONVERTS DID NOT RECEIVE THE SPIRIT OF MIRACLES. CHRYSOSTOM: And great signs occurred. How was it then that they did not receive the Spirit? They had received the Spirit of remission of sins but not the Spirit of the signs.... "For it had not yet fallen on any of them, but they had only been baptized in the name of the Lord Jesus. Then they laid their hands on them and they received the Holy Spirit...." To show that this was the case and that it was the Spirit of signs that they had not received, notice how Simon, once he saw the result, came and asked for this. HOMILIES ON THE ACTS OF THE APOSTLES 18.[5]

THE SPIRIT MANIFESTS HIMSELF. AUGUSTINE: For the Holy Spirit was at that time given in such sort, that he even visibly showed himself to have been given. For those who received him spoke with the tongues of all nations, to signify that the church among the nations was to speak in the tongues of all. So then they received the Holy Ghost, and he appeared evidently to be in them. SERMON 49 (99).10.[6]

THE TRIUNE BAPTISMAL FORMULA. ORIGEN: From all of which we learn that the person of the Holy Spirit is of so great authority and dignity that saving baptism is not complete except when performed with the authority of the whole most excellent Trinity, that is, by the naming of Father, Son and Holy Spirit.[7] ON FIRST PRINCIPLES 1.3.2.[8]

8:17 The Apostles Laid Their Hands on Them

THE GIFT RECEIVED BY DEGREES. CHRYSOSTOM: See how many things are brought about by God's providence through the death of Stephen and how by degrees these receive the gift. It was a twofold sign—both the giving to those and the not giving to this man.... This man should have asked to receive the Holy Spirit, but because this was of no concern to him, he asks, on the contrary, for the power to give it to others. But even

those did not receive this power to give, and this man, who was only one of the disciples, wished to be more illustrious than Philip! HOMILIES ON THE ACTS OF THE APOSTLES 18.[9]

THE SPIRIT AND THE LAYING ON OF HANDS. ORIGEN: This is why the passage fitly applies to the Holy Spirit, because he will dwell not in all people or in those who are flesh but in those whose "earth[10] has been renewed." Finally, it was for this reason that the Holy Spirit was bestowed through the laying on of the apostles' hands after the grace and renewal of baptism. ON FIRST PRINCIPLES 1.3.7.[11]

THE BAPTISM BY PHILIP NEED NOT BE REPEATED. CYPRIAN: The Samaritan believers had come to the true faith and had been baptized by Philip the deacon, whom these very apostles had sent, within the one church to which alone it has been granted to give the grace of baptism and to loose sins. Since they had already obtained the lawful baptism of the church, it would have been wrong to baptize them any more. Peter and John supplied only what they lacked. LETTER 73.9.[12]

8:18 Simon Offered Money

SIMON WAS NOT CLEANSED. ARATOR: Simon the magician had been here washed indeed in the fount but not clean in his heart; the subsequent punishment revealed him to the world as ignorant of the faith.[13] He wished to liken the gifts of God to the gathering together of gold and to bring back by means of coin what a merchant buys at a price. ON THE ACTS OF THE APOSTLES 1.[14]

8:19 Give Me Also This Power

SIMON WANTED POWER, NOT GRACE. CYRIL

---

[5]NPNF 1 11:114**. [6]NPNF 1 6:419*. [7]See Mt 28:19. [8]OFP 30. [9]NPNF 1 11:116**. [10]Latin terra. [11]OFP 36*. [12]LCC 5:162*. [13]A reference to Peter's expulsion of Simon from Judea in the Acts of Peter. [14]OAA 43.

OF JERUSALEM: He did not say, "Give me also the participation in the Holy Ghost," but "Give me this power," with a view to selling to others what could not be sold—something he himself did not possess. CATECHETICAL LECTURE 16.10.[15]

8:20 *Seeking to Buy the Gift of God*

A GIFT TO BE RECEIVED WITH SIMPLICITY.

CHRYSOSTOM: Therefore Peter does well to call it a gift. "You thought," he says, "you could obtain the gift of God with money." Do you see how they are always free from money? "For your heart," he says, "is not right before God." Do you see how Simon does everything out of malice? In fact, simplicity was the thing needed. . . . For if it had been done with simplicity, they would even have accepted his eagerness. Do you see how having mean conceptions of great things is to sin doubly? Two things, accordingly, he urges him to do, "Repent and pray that, if possible, the intent of your heart may be forgiven you." HOMILIES ON THE ACTS OF THE APOSTLES 18.[16]

EVEN SIMON WAS OFFERED REPENTANCE.

AMBROSE: Then, when Simon, depraved by long practice of magic, had thought he could gain by money the power of conferring the grace of Christ and the infusion of the Holy Spirit, Peter said, "You have no part in this faith, for your heart is not right with God. Repent therefore of your wickedness, and pray to the Lord, if perhaps this thought of your heart may be forgiven, for I see that you are in the bond of iniquity and in the bitterness of gall." We see that Peter by his apostolic authority condemns him who blasphemes against the Holy Spirit through vain magic, and all the more because he had no clear consciousness of faith. And yet he did not exclude him from the hope of forgiveness, for he called him to repentance. CONCERNING REPENTANCE 2.4.23.[17]

THE POWER OF AN APOSTOLIC SENTENCE.

BEDE: [Gregory says,] "When holy people deliver a curse as a sentence, they pronounce it not out of

a desire for vengeance but out of a just consideration of the case. For they interiorly perceive God's unerring judgment and recognize that they must smite with a curse the evils that arise exteriorly. And in the curse they do not sin insofar as they do not depart from their interior judgment. Since the one who pronounces the curse remains innocent, and at the same time the curse swallows up to the point of destruction the one who is cursed, we conclude from what happens to both parties that the sentence that has been delivered is hurled at the offender by the sole judge of that which is within."[18] So it is that in the present passage Simon, who received a curse from Peter, perished in eternal damnation, and below[19] [we read that] Bar-Jesus, when he had been rebuked by Paul, was presently deprived of the light of day. COMMENTARY ON THE ACTS OF THE APOSTLES 8.20.[20]

SOME OF SIMON'S SUBSEQUENT CAREER.

EUSEBIUS OF CAESAREA: Immediately, the above-mentioned sorcerer, as if struck in the eyes of his mind by a divine and marvelous flash when formerly in Judea he had been detected for his evil deeds by the apostle Peter, set out on a very long journey overseas from east to west and went off in flight, thinking that only in this way could he live according to his wish. And when he came to the city of the Romans, the power that obsessed him cooperated with him greatly, and in short time he was so successful in his undertakings that he was honored as a god by the erection of a statue by those in this city. However, his affairs did not prosper for long. Close on him in the same reign of Claudius, the all-good and kindly providence of the universe guided Peter, the great and mighty one of the apostles, because of his virtue the spokesman for all the others to Rome, as if against a great corrupter of life. And he, like a noble general of God, clad in divine armor, con-

---

[15]FC 64:80. [16]NPNF 1 11:116-17**. [17]NPNF 2 10:348. [18]Gregory the Great *Morals on the Book of Job* 4.1.2 (CCL 143:165). [19]Acts 13:6-12. [20]CS 117:80.

veys the costly merchandise of the light from the east to those in the west, preaching the light itself and the Word that saves souls, the proclamation of the kingdom of heaven. ECCLESIASTICAL HISTORY 2.14.[21]

GREED FOR POWER. CYRIL OF JERUSALEM: He offered money to people without possessions, and that too after seeing people bring the price of what they sold and lay it at the feet of the apostles. He did not realize that they who trod underfoot the wealth offered for the sustenance of the poor would surely never sell him the power of the Holy Spirit for a price. CATECHETICAL LECTURE 16.10.[22]

THE SPIRIT'S POWER IS NOT A BUSINESS TRANSACTION. BASIL THE GREAT: He who through ignorance wishes to buy is less guilty than he who sells the gift of God, making it a business transaction. And, if you sell what you have received as a gift, you will be deprived of its grace, as if you had been sold to Satan. Furthermore, you are introducing into the church, where we have been entrusted with the body and blood of Christ, the bartering of material for spiritual things. LETTER 53.[23]

8:21 Your Heart Is Not Right

A RIGHT HEART OBTAINS THE SPIRIT. ARATOR: Seeing him attempting this, Peter said, "What madness has moved you to this, wretch? Namely, that you think that what the grace of the Lord gives is something for sale. It is not gained by gold but by a [right] disposition [of mind]; nor is it permitted that corrupt money, which the person whose eyes are fixed on the earth loves, should earn heaven. Surely there remains no peace for you in this lot, nor will you, defiled by your tricks, be able to come to these things, you who seek what does not belong to you, swollen as you are with the gall of a bitter heart; for the Spirit enters those halls of the mind which are bright with honesty." ON THE ACTS OF THE APOSTLES 1.[24]

THE CENTER OF A PERSON IS HIS HEART. CASSIODORUS: We must, I think, investigate the fact that often in the divine Scriptures heart stands for understanding. . . . It may be clear to all without doubting that the source of our thoughts is there, and that good and evil are drawn from there. The seat of thought is that tiny part of the body with the appearance of fire, so that it is rightly placed in the position from which good counsel can come to us. EXPOSITION OF THE PSALMS 50.19.[25]

8:23 The Gall of Bitterness

FAITH COMES THROUGH REPENTANCE. CHRYSOSTOM: "For I see that you are in the gall of bitterness and in the bond of iniquity." These are words of strong disapproval, but otherwise he [Peter] did not punish him [Simon], because he did not want faith hereafter to come from compulsion or to appear ruthless in his treatment of the affair, but rather to introduce the subject of repentance. It is sufficient, for the purpose of correction, to convince him, to say what was in his heart. It is sufficient for him to confess he was caught. HOMILIES ON THE ACTS OF THE APOSTLES 18.[26]

SIMON'S HEART WAS NOT LIKE THE DOVE. BEDE: The Holy Spirit descended as a dove in order to teach those who wanted to receive him to be simple. Now one who keeps the gall of bitterness in his heart, although he may appear to be baptized, is not freed from the chains of his iniquity; but as if he was cleansed at one moment, the time of his baptism, he is soon seven times more harried by a fierce demon. In vain, therefore, did this man try to buy the gift of the Spirit, since he did not take care to rid himself of his raven-like mind. COMMENTARY ON THE ACTS OF THE APOSTLES 8.23.[27]

---

[21]FC 19:108-9*. [22]FC 64:80-81. [23]FC 13:140-41. [24]OAA 43-44*. [25]ACW 51:509. [26]NPNF 1 11:117**. [27]CS 117:80-81.

8:25-33 PHILIP MEETS THE ETHIOPIAN EUNUCH

²⁵*Now when they had testified and spoken the word of the Lord, they returned to Jerusalem, preaching the gospel to many villages of the Samaritans.*

²⁶*But an angel of the Lord said to Philip, "Rise and go toward the south^g to the road that goes down from Jerusalem to Gaza." This is a desert road. ²⁷And he rose and went. And behold, an Ethiopian, a eunuch, a minister of the Candace, queen of the Ethiopians, in charge of all her treasure, had come to Jerusalem to worship ²⁸and was returning; seated in his chariot, he was reading the prophet Isaiah. ²⁹And the Spirit said to Philip, "Go up and join this chariot." ³⁰So Philip ran to him, and heard him reading Isaiah the prophet, and asked, "Do you understand what you are reading?" ³¹And he said, "How can I, unless some one guides me?" And he invited Philip to come up and sit with him. ³²Now the passage of the scripture which he was reading was this:*

"As a sheep led to the slaughter
or a lamb before its shearer is dumb,
so he opens not his mouth.
³³*In his humiliation justice was denied him.*
Who can describe his generation?
For his life is taken up from the earth."

g Or *at noon*

OVERVIEW: The two sections that follow form a unity. In commenting on these passages the Fathers do not seem to notice the fact that the Ethiopian is the first Gentile to come to the faith, nor do they develop the key significance of the passage from Isaiah adduced by Luke in telling us what the eunuch was reading. They do, however, appreciate Luke's subtle teaching about the attitudes that lead to faith and baptism. Chrysostom underscores the Ethiopian's zeal in traveling to Jerusalem, in reading the Scriptures even while riding in his chariot and in inviting a poor stranger to join him in order to explain the Scriptures to him. Bede seeks symbolic significance in the various names in the narrative and extols the eunuch's virtue. These two tendencies are present as well in Severus, who speaks of God's desire to save all people, and in Athanasius as well as Augustine, who also draws theological conclusions from the fact that his text included a gloss mentioning that the "Spirit fell" on the eunuch.

8:25 The Apostles Returned to Jerusalem

AS GENERALS DO IN WARS. CHRYSOSTOM: Why do they return to where the tyranny of evil was, where the people were especially thirsty for their blood? This is what generals do in wars: they take control of the part of the battle that is most in distress. Notice again that it is not by choice that they go to Samaria, but driven by persecution, just as it was in the case of Christ, and how the apostles are going to people who are now believers and no longer Samaritans. "Now when the apostles at Jerusalem heard this," it says, "they sent to them Peter and John." They sent them again to free them from magic. And besides, [the Lord] had given them a pattern at the time when the Samaritans believed.

"And in many villages," it says, "of the Samaritans, they preached the gospel." Look how even their journeys were actively employed and how they do nothing without a purpose. HOMILIES ON THE ACTS OF THE APOSTLES 18.[1]

8:26 An Angel of the Lord

ANGELS ASSIST THE PREACHING. CHRYSOSTOM: Look how the angels are assisting the preaching: they themselves do not preach but call these [to the work]. The wonderful nature of the occurrence is also shown by this, that what was rare before and hardly done now takes place, and with what readiness and encouragement to them! HOMILIES ON THE ACTS OF THE APOSTLES 19.[2]

ETHIOPIA IN PROPHECY. BEDE: It is well that it was in the South that this man was sought, found and washed clean. Burning with devotion in his breast he deserved to be consecrated to God as, so to speak, the firstfruits of the Gentiles. In him especially was fulfilled that saying of the psalmist, "Ethiopia will stretch out its hands to God."[3] COMMENTARY ON THE ACTS OF THE APOSTLES 8.26A.[4]

THE WAY TO GAZA. BEDE: It is not the road but Gaza that is referred to as a desert.[5] For the old Gaza, which was formerly "the Canaanites' boundary with Egypt,"[6] was destroyed down to its foundations, and in a different place another [Gaza] was built to replace it. Allegorically this designates the people of the Gentiles, who were once separated from the worship of God, uncultivated by the preaching of the prophets. The road that went down to this same place from Jerusalem and opened the fountain of salvation[7] is the Lord Jesus Christ, who said, "I am the way and the truth and the life."[8] From the Jerusalem above he "came down" to our infirmities, and with the water of baptism he made white the blackness of our guilty condition. COMMENTARY ON THE ACTS OF THE APOSTLES 8.26B.[9]

8:27 An Ethiopian Eunuch

HE FOUND CHRIST WHOM HE WAS SEEKING. BEDE: He is called a man because of his virtue and integrity of mind, and not undeservedly, for he devoted his study solely to the Scriptures, and he did not stop reading them even when he was on the road. Also, he showed so much love in [his] religion that, leaving behind a queen's court, he came from the farthest regions of the world to the Lord's temple. Hence, as a just reward, "while he sought the interpretation of something that he was reading, he found Christ whom he was seeking."[10] Furthermore, as Jerome says, "He found the church's font there in the desert, rather than in the golden temple of the synagogue."[11] For there [in the desert] something happened that Jeremiah declared was to be wondered at, "an Ethiopian changed his skin,"[12] that is, with the stain of his sins washed away by the waters [of baptism], he went up, shining white, to Jesus. COMMENTARY ON THE ACTS OF THE APOSTLES 8.27A.[13]

THE ETHIOPIAN QUEEN AS A FIGURE. BEDE: The sending by the Ethiopian queen of treasures of the nations to Jerusalem signifies that the church would bring gifts of the virtues and of faith to the Lord. The etymology of her name is also appropriate, for in Hebrew Candace means *exchanged*.[14] In the Scriptures (in the psalm "For those who will be exchanged") it is she to whom it was said, "Hear, daughter, and see, and incline your ear. Forget your people and your father's home,"[15] and so forth. COMMENTARY ON THE ACTS OF THE APOSTLES 8.27C.[16]

THE DESCRIPTION SEEN AS AN ALLEGORY. ARATOR: No trifling occasion of hidden allegory

---

[1]NPNF 1 11:117**. [2]NPNF 1 11:121**. [3]Ps 68:31 (67:32 LXX). [4]CS 117:81. [5]This is not the understanding of the RSV, but it is that of the Vg and is a legitimate intepretation of the Greek text. [6]Jerome *De Sitibus* (PL 23:899). [7]Acts 8:36. [8]Jn 14:6. [9]CS 117:81*. [10]Jerome *Commentary on Isaiah* 15.56.3 (CCL 73A:631). [11]Jerome *Letter* 53.5 (CSEL 54:452). [12]Jer 13:23. [13]CS 117:81-82. [14]Jerome *On Hebrew Names* (CCL 72:144). [15]Ps 45:10 (44:11 LXX, Vg). [16]CS 117:82.

shines in the image of [the eunuch's] country: the Almighty gave full approval for Moses to unite the Ethiopian woman to himself in the bond of marriage;[17] Scriptures reveal that he later spoke with the Lord face to face. What is there astonishing if love for the law began to grow at that time when [the law] had been joined [in marriage] to the church? Rather, the Song of Songs does not conceal the fact that the everlasting bride comes from that region: it calls her black and beautiful.[18] She comes from the south, which burns the Ethiopian soil, to praise her Peacemaker in the mouth of Solomon, by which name [Pacificus] what Christ possesses has long been signified. She sends [the eunuch] ahead as guardian of [the church's] riches, by whose protection she might begin to bring forth her wealth. What better treasure is in her than the glory of the font? What richer gold than a wealthy faith in the heart? Finally, how rightly is her herald a eunuch! As [faith] proceeds, lust is driven off, and the chaste capture the heavenly kingdoms. ON THE ACTS OF THE APOSTLES 1.[19]

PRAISE FOR THE EUNUCH. CHRYSOSTOM: Notice also the reason for his journey, sufficient to reveal his God-fearing attitude of mind—I mean, how long a journey he undertakes so as to pay adoration to the Lord. You see, they were still of the mind that worship was conducted in one place only and consequently traveled long distances to offer prayers there. For this reason, of course, he arrived at the place of the temple and Jewish cult so as to [offer] adoration to the Lord. HOMILIES ON GENESIS 35.4.[20]

8:28 Reading the Prophet Isaiah

THE ETHIOPIAN'S FERVOR. CHRYSOSTOM: Consider, I ask you, what a great effort it was not to neglect reading even while on a journey, and especially while seated in a chariot. Let this be heeded by those people who do not even deign to do it at home but rather think reading the Scriptures is a waste of time, claiming as an excuse their living with a wife, conscription in military service, caring

for children, attending to domestics and looking after other concerns, they do not think it necessary for them to show any interest in reading the holy Scriptures. HOMILIES ON GENESIS 35.3.[21]

8:29 Go to His Chariot

THE SPIRIT SPOKE TO PHILIP. BEDE: The Spirit spoke to Philip in his heart. God's Spirit utters certain words to us by a hidden power and tells us what must be done. COMMENTARY ON THE ACTS OF THE APOSTLES 8.29.[22]

8:30 Do You Understand What You Are Reading?

A HUMBLE LEARNER. ATHANASIUS: He was not ashamed to confess his ignorance and implored to be taught. Therefore, to him who became a learner, the grace of the Spirit was given. But as for those Jews who persisted in their ignorance; as the proverb says, "Death came upon them. For the fool dies in his sins."[23] FESTAL LETTER 19.5.[24]

ABLE TO ACKNOWLEDGE IGNORANCE. CHRYSOSTOM: I mean, when the apostle said, "Do you really understand?" and came close in his lowly condition, he was not put off, he made no objection, he did not consider himself disgraced in the way many foolish people react, often preferring to remain in unbroken ignorance through a sense of shame in admitting their ignorance and having to learn from those able to instruct them. HOMILIES ON GENESIS 35.5.[25]

8:31 How Can I, Unless Someone Guides Me?

HE WHO SEEKS, FINDS. CHRYSOSTOM: For it was necessary that he should ask, that he should desire it. Philip showed that he knew that the

---

[17]Num 12:1. [18]Song 1:4-5. [19]OAA 45*. [20]FC 82:306*. [21]FC 82:305. [22]CS 117:83. [23]Prov 24:9 (LXX). [24]NPNF 2 4:546-47*. [25]FC 82:307.

other man knew nothing, when he asks, "Do you understand what you are reading?" At the same time he shows that great indeed is the treasure within. It speaks well of the eunuch that he paid no attention to outward appearance. He did not ask, "Who are you?" He did not find fault with him or make false pretenses; he did not claim to know but confessed his ignorance. Therefore he learns. He shows his wound to the doctor. He saw at a glance that Philip both knows the matter and is willing to teach. Look how free he is from haughtiness! No splendor was presaged by his outward appearance. So desirous was he of learning and so attentive to the teachings that the saying, "He who seeks, finds," was fulfilled in him.[26] Homilies on the Acts of the Apostles 19.[27]

The Ethiopian's Virtue. Chrysostom: Not only did he reply with restraint and continue on as well, but also he showed us the virtue in his own behavior by issuing an invitation in those words—the minister, the barbarian, seated in his chariot, inviting the man of lowly mien, despicable in attire, to mount and ride with him. Homilies on Genesis 35.5.[28]

8:32 As a Sheep Led to the Slaughter

Admit That We Are Straying Sheep. Augustine: See how often it stresses this point and teaches this to those who are proud and contentious: "He was a wounded man," it says, "and one who knew how to endure weaknesses; for this reason his face is turned away, bearing injuries and not much appreciated. He bears our infirmities, and he is amid sorrows on our behalf. And we thought that he was suffering sorrows, wounds and punishment. But he was wounded on account of our sins, and he became weak on account of our iniquities. In him we learned of our peace; by his bruises we were healed. We all went astray like sheep, and the Lord handed him over for our sins. And he did not open his mouth because he was mistreated. He was led off like a sheep for sacrifice, and like a lamb before his shearer, he made not a sound; thus he did not open his mouth. His judgment was removed in humility. Who will tell of his generation? For his life will be taken away from the earth. He was brought to death by the iniquities of my people. I will repay evil people on account of his burial and the rich on account of his death, because he did no wrong and had no deceit upon his lips. The Lord wishes to cleanse him of his wound. If you have given your life on account of your sins, you will see offspring with a long life. The Lord wishes to remove his soul from sorrows, to show him the light and form his mind, to justify the righteous one who serves the many well, and he will bear their sins. For this reason he will have many heirs and share the spoils with the mighty, because his soul was handed over to death and he was reckoned as one of the wicked. And he bore the sins of many and was handed over on account of their iniquities."[29] On the Merits and Forgiveness of Sins and on Infant Baptism 1.54.[30]

Led Like a Sheep to the Slaughter. Bede: Just as a sheep "does not resist when it is led away to be a sacrificial offering, so too he suffered by his *own* will."[31] Or, according to a more profound understanding, just as a lamb was customarily immolated at the Passover, so too "Christ our Passover lamb has been immolated."[32] Commentary on the Acts of the Apostles 8.32a.[33]

Silent Before the Shearer. Bede: He has not only redeemed us with his blood, but he has also clothed us with his wool. This is so that with his clothing he may warm those who are cold with infidelity, and so that we may hear the apostle telling us, "All of you who have been baptized into Christ have put on Christ."[34] He did not open his mouth during his passion when he chose

[26]Mt 7:8. [27]NPNF 1 11:122**. [28]FC 82:307. [29]Is 53:3-12. [30]WSA 1 23:64-65. [31]Jerome Commentary on Isaiah 14.53.8-10 (CCL 73A:592). [32]1 Cor 5:7. [33]CS 117:83. [34]Gal 3:27.

to answer very little to Pilate and the chief priests and nothing at all to Herod.[35] COMMENTARY ON THE ACTS OF THE APOSTLES 8.32B.[36]

THE SHEEP WHO REDEEMS US. CYRIL OF JERU-SALEM: He is called a sheep; not a senseless one, but that which cleanses the world from sin by its precious blood, and when led before its shearer knows when to be silent. CATECHETICAL LEC-TURE 10.3.[37]

8:33 Justice Denied

HIS CONDEMNATION WAS UNJUST. BEDE: "The judge of all did not obtain a true judgment, but, guiltless, he was condemned by the sedition of the Jews and by the voice of Pilate."[38] COM-MENTARY ON THE ACTS OF THE APOSTLES 8.33A.[39]

HIS ORIGINS ARE INEFFABLE. BEDE: With

respect to his divinity, this must be taken to mean that it is impossible to know the mysteries of his divine nativity, about which the Father said, "Before the day star I begot you."[40] Or, with respect to his virgin birth, it means that with difficulty one can explain that [mystery], the plan of which the angel spoke to Mary in answer to her question when he said, "The Holy Spirit will come upon you."[41] Hence, whether by angel or by Evangelist, the mysteries of his nativity are said to be so great that there are very few who can expound them.[42] COMMENTARY ON THE ACTS OF THE APOSTLES 8.33B.[43]

---

[35]Mt 26:62-64; 27:11-14; Lk 23:6-9. [36]CS 117:83. [37]FC 61:196. [38]Jerome *Commentary on Isaiah* 14.53.8-10 (CCL 73A:592). [39]CS 117:83. [40]Ps 110:3 (109:3 LXX, Vg). [41]Lk 1:35. [42]Jerome *Commentary on Isaiah* 14.53.8-10 (CCL 73A:592-93). [43]CS 117:83-84.

8:34-40 THE EUNUCH IS BAPTIZED

[34]*And the eunuch said to Philip, "About whom, pray, does the prophet say this, about himself or about some one else?"* [35]*Then Philip opened his mouth, and beginning with this scripture he told him the good news of Jesus.* [36]*And as they went along the road they came to some water, and the eunuch said, "See, here is water! What is to prevent my being baptized?"*[h] [38]*And he commanded the chariot to stop, and they both went down into the water, Philip and the eunuch, and he baptized him.* [39]*And when they came up out of the water, the Spirit of the Lord caught up Philip; and the eunuch saw him no more, and went on his way rejoicing.* [40]*But Philip was found at Azotus, and passing on he preached the gospel to all the towns till he came to Caesarea.*

[h] Other ancient authorities add all or most of verse 37, *And Philip said, "If you believe with all your heart, you may." And he replied, "I believe that Jesus Christ is the Son of God."*

OVERVIEW: The remarks of the Fathers in regard to this section have already been discussed in the overview to the previous section. In regard to this part of the narrative, modern commentators point to such Lukan themes as joy and the action of the Holy Spirit, themes often present in accounts of a Gentile's conversion. However, some commentators presume that the eunuch was Jewish, arguing that Luke would not relate the first account of the conversion of a pagan to such a small incident. These are not themes to which the patristic commentators devote attention.

8:34 About Whom Does the Prophet Speak?

THE READING OF THE SCRIPTURES. CHRYSOSTOM: But meanwhile, as I was saying, let us be ashamed of ourselves in comparison to the eunuch on account of his baptism and his reading. He lived in wealth and power, but look, he allowed himself no rest even on the road. What must he have been like at home, in his leisure hours, this man who could not bear to be idle even on his travels? What must he have been like at night? Those of you who are in stations of dignity, pay attention! Imitate his modesty and piety! Although he was about to return home, he did not say to himself, "I am going back to my own country; there I shall receive baptism." Such were the cold words spoken by many. But he did not need signs; he did not need miracles. From the prophet alone he believed. . . . But why is it that he sees him not before he goes to Jerusalem but after? It was necessary that he should not see the apostles under persecution, because he was still weak. He was not easily satisfied, for no prophet instructed him. Since even now, if someone should wish to devote himself to the study of the prophets, he does not need miracles. And, if you please, let us take up the prophecy itself. . . . He probably heard that he was crucified, that "his life is taken away from the earth" and everything else about him, "who had done no wrong," that he prevailed to save others as well, and who he is, whose generation is unutterable. He probably saw the riven rocks there and heard how the veil was rent, and how there was darkness, and so on. And all these things Philip said to him, simply taking his text from the prophet. It is a great thing, this reading of the Scriptures! What Moses said was fulfilled, "Sitting, lying down, rising up and walking, remember the Lord your God."[1] HOMILIES ON THE ACTS OF THE APOSTLES 19.[2]

8:35 Telling the Good News of Jesus

PHILIP OPENED HIS MOUTH. BEDE: Philip means "the mouth of a lamp,"[3] and there is a beautiful meaning in "the mouth of a lamp" opening his mouth as he brought the obscurities of prophecy into the light of knowledge. However, according to the historical sense this circumlocution can also designate the considerably longer discourse that he was then about to deliver. COMMENTARY ON THE ACTS OF THE APOSTLES 8.35.[4]

8:36 What Is to Prevent My Being Baptized?

HE HAS THE FAITH PERFECTLY. CHRYSOSTOM: And notice again his modesty. He does not say, "Baptize me," or keep quiet, but he utters something halfway between eagerness and reverent fear, saying, "What is to prevent me?" Do you see that he has learned the doctrines [of faith] perfectly? For the prophet indeed had the entirety: incarnation, passion, resurrection, ascension, judgment to come. If he shows great eagerness, do not wonder. Be ashamed, those of you who are unbaptized! "And he commanded the chariot to stop." He spoke and gave the order before he heard [Philip's answer]. "And when they came up out of the water, the Spirit of the Lord caught up Philip." This was to show that what had happened was divine, that he should not think that it was only a man. HOMILIES ON THE ACTS OF THE APOSTLES 19.[5]

FAITH NECESSARY FOR BAPTISM. BEDE: Here another translation,[6] which follows the Greek

---

[1]Deut 6:7. [2]NPNF 1 11:125-26**. [3]Jerome *On Hebrew Names* (CCL 72:146). [4]CS 117:84. [5]NPNF 1 11:122-23**. [6]Bede here refers to manuscripts of the Vg that follow the WT. Most textual critics consider this text to be a gloss accenting faith in baptism and added under liturgical influence, but it is attested as early as Irenaeus *Against the Heresies* 3.12.8.

model, has a few more verses in which it is written, "Behold, here is water. What is there to prevent my being baptized?" And Philip said to him, "If you believe with all your heart you will be saved." And he answered and said, "I believe in Christ, the Son of God." And he ordered the carriage to stop, and so forth. I believe that these verses were originally inserted in our version too, but through scribal error they were later removed. COMMENTARY ON THE ACTS OF THE APOSTLES 8.36B-38.[7]

8:38 Philip Baptized the Eunuch

WITH OR WITHOUT HUMAN MEDIATION. AUGUSTINE: This same Philip, who had baptized people, and the Holy Spirit had not come upon them until the apostles had come along and laid their hands on them, baptized the eunuch of queen Candace who had been worshiping in Jerusalem, and on his way back from there he was reading the prophet Isaiah in his chariot and not understanding it. Philip was prompted to approach the chariot, and he explained the reading, insinuated the faith, preached Christ. The eunuch believed in Christ and said, when they came to some water, "Look, here is water; who is

to prevent me being baptized? Philip said to him, "Do you believe in Jesus Christ?" He answered, "I believe that Jesus Christ is the Son of God." And immediately he went down with him into the water. Once the mystery and sacrament of baptism had been carried out, since there was no expectation of the apostles coming as on the previous occasion, so that no one should think the gift of the Holy Spirit was at the disposal of mortals, the Holy Spirit came immediately. SERMON 99.11.[8]

8:40 Philip Was Found at Azotus

HE PREACHED UNTIL HE CAME TO CAESAREA. BEDE: This refers to the Caesarea in Palestine, where, as is described below,[9] he [Philip] had a home, which is still shown today, and also a chamber for his four daughters, who were virgins with the gift of prophecy.[10] COMMENTARY ON THE ACTS OF THE APOSTLES 8.40.[11]

---

[7]CS 117:84-85. [8]*WSA* 3 4:57. Augustine seems to have a Vg text deriving from the WT that includes a reference to the Holy Spirit coming upon the eunuch: "The Holy Spirit fell upon the eunuch but the angel [not the Spirit as in our text] of the Lord snatched Philip away." [9]Acts 21:8-9. [10]Jerome *Letter* 108.8 (CSEL 55:313). [11]CS 117:85.

9:1-9 PAUL'S CONVERSION

[1]*But Saul, still breathing threats and murder against the disciples of the Lord, went to the high priest* [2]*and asked him for letters to the synagogues at Damascus, so that if he found any belonging to the Way, men or women, he might bring them bound to Jerusalem.* [3]*Now as he journeyed he approached Damascus, and suddenly a light from heaven flashed about him.* [4]*And he fell to the ground and heard a voice saying to him, "Saul, Saul, why do you persecute me?"* [5]*And he said, "Who are you, Lord?" And he said, "I am Jesus, whom you are persecuting;* [6]*but rise and enter the city, and you will be told what you are to do."* [7]*The men who were traveling with him stood speechless, hearing the voice but seeing no one.* [8]*Saul arose from the ground; and when his eyes were*

opened, he could see nothing; so they led him by the hand and brought him into Damascus. ⁹And for three days he was without sight, and neither ate nor drank.

Overview: Luke begins the major part of his work, which will trace the preaching of the gospel "to the ends of the earth," with two narratives. Both narratives contain the account of two visions, one to Paul and the other to Peter. In Acts 9 we read of the conversion of Paul, an event so important that it is recorded twice more by Luke. The details of the other two narratives, both narrated by Paul in the first person,[1] do not completely agree with this account, but the dialogue between Jesus and Paul in which Jesus identifies himself with the believers is almost identical. Nearly all the ancient commentators (represented here by Ephrem, Augustine and Bede) are sensitive to this Lukan accent, and several are aware of the minor discrepancies in the three accounts.[2] It is clear as well that Luke is showing that the fact of Paul's blindness bespeaks the turning of darkness into faith and baptism. Many of the Fathers are aware of Luke's procedure in this regard (Bede, Arator, Ephrem, Ambrose). All are aware of this act of Christ as being a marvelous manifestation of God's mercy, one that perfectly realizes the heart of Paul's message about justification by grace through faith as well as foreshadowing his teaching on the body of Christ. The wrath of Saul was not permitted to succeed (Cassiodorus). Christ bore the sin of Saul the persecutor (Basil). Saul was converted by the power of the resurrection (Chrysostom).

9:1-2 Saul's Threats and Plans

The Wrath of Saul Was Not Permitted to Succeed. Cassiodorus: Often the merciful Lord does not allow us to perpetrate evil deeds so that pricked by remorse we should prostrate ourselves for our sins, just as Saul was checked when he was sent by the priests to Damascus to ravage the church of Christ with the most savage persecution. He was not permitted to attain great suc-cess, for that could have been the cause of his receiving eternal punishment. Exposition of the Psalms 53.9.[3]

The Humility and Sublimity of the Lord. Ephrem the Syrian: This is why the humble voice accompanied the intense light, so that from the combination of the humble and the sublime, our Lord might produce help for the persecutor, just as all his assistance is produced from a combination of the small and great. For the humility of our Lord prevailed from the womb to the tomb. . . . His nature is not simply humble, nor is it simply sublime; rather they are two natures, lofty and humble, one mixed in the other. Homily on Our Lord 34.[4]

9:4 Why Do You Persecute Me?

The Heavenly Lord on Earth. Augustine: How can we show that he is there and that he is also here? Let Paul answer for us, who was previously Saul. . . . First of all, the Lord's own voice from heaven shows this: "Saul, Saul, why are you persecuting me?" Had Paul climbed up to heaven then? Had Paul even thrown a stone at heaven? It was Christians he was persecuting, them he was tying up, them he was dragging off to be put to death, them he was everywhere hunting out of their hiding places and never sparing when he found them. To him the Lord said, "Saul, Saul." Where is he crying out from? Heaven. So he's up above. "Why are you persecuting me?" So he's down below. Sermon 122.6.[5]

You Did It to Me. Bede: He did not say,

---

[1]Acts 22:3-21; 26:2-18. [2]Didymus (PG 39:1672) like Chrysostom, discussed the discrepancies of detail regarding who heard the voice and what was seen by whom when commenting on Acts 22:9 in Homily 47 (NPNF 1 11:284). [3]ACW 52:17*. [4]FC 91:310*. [5]WSA 3 4:242.

"Why do you persecute my members?" but "Why do you persecute me?" Because he is still suffering from enemies in his body, which is the church. He declared that kindnesses bestowed upon his members are also done to him when he said, "I was hungry and you gave me to eat,"[6] and he added in explanation, "So long as you did it to one of the least of mine, you did it to me."[7] COMMENTARY ON THE ACTS OF THE APOSTLES 9.4.[8]

THE LORD SHARED OUR HUMAN STATE.
BASIL THE GREAT: For it is written, "And when all things are made subject to him, then the Son himself will also be made subject to him who subjected all things to him."[9] Do you not fear, O man, the God who is called unsubjected? For he makes your subjection his own, and, because of your struggle against virtue, he calls himself unsubjected. Thus, he even said at one time that he himself was the one persecuted; for he says, "Saul, Saul, why do you persecute me?" when Saul was hastening to Damascus, desiring to put in bonds the disciples of Christ. Again, he calls himself naked, if anyone of his brothers is naked. "I was naked," he says, "and you covered me."[10] And still again, when another was in prison, he said that he himself was the one imprisoned. For he himself took up our infirmities and bore the burden of our ills.[11] And one of our infirmities is insubordination, and this he bore. Therefore, even the adversities that happen to us the Lord makes his own, taking upon himself our sufferings because of his fellowship with us. LETTER 8.[12]

THE HUMILITY OF JESUS. EPHREM THE SYRIAN: The One who conquered persecutors [here] below and reigns over angels [in heaven] above spoke from above in a humble voice. The One who on earth pronounced ten woes[13] against his crucifiers, above pronounced not a single woe against Saul, his persecutor. Our Lord pronounced woes against his crucifiers to teach his disciples not to flatter their killers. Our Lord spoke humbly from above so that the leaders of his church would speak humbly. HOMILY ON OUR LORD 26.1.[14]

9:5 I Am Jesus, Whom You Are Persecuting

PAUL DRAWN BY CHRIST HIMSELF. CHRYSOSTOM: The eunuch was on the road and Paul was on the road, but the latter was drawn by no other than Christ himself, for this was too great a work for the apostles. It was great indeed that with the apostles at Jerusalem and no one of authority at Damascus, he returned from there converted. And those at Damascus knew that he had not come from Jerusalem converted, for he brought letters that he might place the believers in chains. Like a consummate physician, Christ brought help to him, once the fever reached its height. It was necessary that he should be quelled in the midst of his frenzy, for then especially he would fall and condemn himself as one guilty of dreadful audacity. HOMILIES ON THE ACTS OF THE APOSTLES 19.[15]

9:6 Rise and Enter Damascus

INSTRUCTION FOLLOWS CONVERSION. BEDE: Jesus did not immediately show him what was to be done. Instead, he foretold that he was to hear about it afterwards in the city, "so that later when he arose he would be more firmly established in the good, to the extent that he had first become radically changed and had fallen away from his former error."[16] COMMENTARY ON THE ACTS OF THE APOSTLES 9.6.[17]

CHRIST'S WISE DEALING WITH PAUL.
AMBROSE: Although Paul was struck and taken up and was terrified because blindness had befallen him, still he began to come near when he said, "Lord, what will you have me do?"[18] For that reason he is called the youngest by Christ,[19] so that he who was called to grace could be excused

---

[6]Mt 25:35. [7]Mt 25:40. [8]CS 117:87*. [9]1 Cor 15:28. [10]Mt 25:36. [11]2 Cor 11:5-33. [12]FC 13:33-34. [13]See Mt 18:7; 23:13, 14, 15, 16, 23, 25, 27, 29; 26:24. [14]FC 91:301*. [15]NPNF 1 11:126**. [16]Gregory the Great *Pastoral Care* 3.34 (PL 77:118). [17]CS 117:87*. [18]This question and the ensuing allusion to "the goad" are found in WT, on which Ambrose must in some way be dependent. [19]See Gen 43:29.

from the guilt of his hazardous years. Yes, Christ saw him when the light shone round him; because young people are recalled from sin more by fear than by reason, Christ applied the goad and mercifully admonished him not to kick against it. JOSEPH 10.58.[20]

9:8 Saul Could See Nothing

BLINDNESS LEADS TO SIGHT. BEDE: By no means would he have been able to see well again unless he had first been fully blinded. Also, when he had rejected his own wisdom, which was confusing him, he could commit himself totally to faith. COMMENTARY ON THE ACTS OF THE APOSTLES 9.8.[21]

THE INJURY WAS FOR GOOD. EPHREM THE SYRIAN: [Saul's] impairment did not [result] from our compassionate Lord, who spoke humbly there. Rather, [it was the result] of the intense light that shone intensely here. This light was not a punishment that befell Paul on account of the things he had done. It injured him with the intensity of its rays, as he himself said. HOMILY ON OUR LORD 26.2.[22]

ENCOUNTER WITH CHRIST. AMBROSE: Although he saw nothing when his eyes were opened, still he saw Christ. And it was fitting that he saw Christ present and also heard him speaking. That overshadowing is not the overshadowing of blindness by grace. Indeed, it is said to Mary, "The Holy Spirit shall come upon you, and the power of the Most High shall over-

shadow you."[23] ON THE PATRIARCHS 12.58.[24]

9:9 For Three Days

THE POWER OF THE RESURRECTION. CHRYSOSTOM: "And for three days neither did he eat nor drink, being blinded." What could equal this? To compensate the discouragement in the matter of Stephen, here is encouragement, in the bringing in of Paul. Though that sadness had its consolation in the fact of Stephen's making such an end, yet it also received this further consolation. Moreover, the bringing in of the villages of the Samaritans afforded very great comfort. But why did this take place not at the very first but after these things? That it might be shown that Christ was indeed risen. This furious assailant of Christ, the man who would not believe in his death and resurrection, the persecutor of his disciples, how should this man have become a believer, had not the power of his resurrection been great indeed? HOMILIES ON THE ACTS OF THE APOSTLES 19.[25]

THREE DAYS AND THEN LIGHT. BEDE: Since he had not believed that the Lord had conquered death by rising on the third day, he was now taught by his own experience of the replacement of three days of darkness by the return of the light. COMMENTARY ON THE ACTS OF THE APOSTLES 9.9.[26]

---

[20]FC 65:225. [21]CS 117:88. [22]FC 91:301. [23]Lk 1:35. [24]FC 65:275. [25]NPNF 1 11:124*. [26]CS 117:88.

9:10-19 ANANIAS SENT TO PAUL

[10]*Now there was a disciple at Damascus named Ananias. The Lord said to him in a vision, "Ananias." And he said, "Here I am, Lord."* [11]*And the Lord said to him, "Rise and go to the street*

called Straight, and inquire in the house of Judas for a man of Tarsus named Saul; for behold, he is praying, [12]and he has seen a man named Ananias come in and lay his hands on him so that he might regain his sight." [13]But Ananias answered, "Lord, I have heard from many about this man, how much evil he has done to thy saints at Jerusalem; [14]and here he has authority from the chief priests to bind all who call upon thy name." [15]But the Lord said to him, "Go, for he is a chosen instrument of mine to carry my name before the Gentiles and kings and the sons of Israel; [16]for I will show him how much he must suffer for the sake of my name." [17]So Ananias departed and entered the house. And laying his hands on him he said, "Brother Saul, the Lord Jesus who appeared to you on the road by which you came, has sent me that you may regain your sight and be filled with the Holy Spirit." [18]And immediately something like scales fell from his eyes and he regained his sight. Then he rose and was baptized, [19]and took food and was strengthened.

For several days he was with the disciples at Damascus.

OVERVIEW: In this section Luke shows how Paul is baptized and thus becomes a member of the church, is healed of his blindness (the theme of baptism as "enlightenment" continues), takes food and is strengthened, and becomes a part of a group of believers. Consistent with the incarnation, Saul had to be taught by a lowly man, Ananias (CASSIAN, CHRYSOSTOM), who is portrayed as the sheep that subdues the wolf, Saul (ARATOR). While being taught by a man, he was at the same time being taught by Christ. The Fathers are sensitive to Luke's accent on the Lord's direct guidance of this sequence of events as well as to the relative obscurity of the person sent to minister to Paul, a fact that accents the directness of the Lord's enlightenment. They also remark on Ananias's reluctance to go to Paul (CHRYSOSTOM) as well as on the suffering that the Lord predicts for his chosen instrument (BEDE, OROSIUS). The Holy Spirit fashioned Paul into a vessel of election (CYRIL OF JERUSALEM, JEROME).

9:10 A Disciple Named Ananias

PAUL CONVERTED ONLY BY CHRIST. CHRYSOSTOM: Why was it that he did not draw upon one of the trustworthy and great, or cause one to be forthcoming for the purpose of instructing Paul? Because Paul was not to be brought in by a man but by Christ himself, as in fact this man taught

him nothing but only baptized him. For once baptized, he was to draw upon himself the grace of the Spirit by his zeal and great eagerness. That Ananias was not among the very distinguished is clear. HOMILIES ON THE ACTS OF THE APOSTLES 20.[1]

9:13 I Have Heard About Saul

OBEDIENCE GREATER THAN FEAR. CHRYSOSTOM: Let no one imagine that Ananias speaks in disbelief of what was said or because he imagines that Christ was deceived. Far from it! Rather, afraid and trembling, he did not even pay attention to what was said, once he heard the name Paul. Moreover, the Lord did not say that he has blinded him. Fear had already taken hold of Ananias's soul at the mention of Paul's name. "Look," he says, "to whom you are betraying me. 'Indeed he came here for this very purpose,' to arrest all who invoke your name. I fear he shall take me to Jerusalem. Why do you cast me into the mouth of the lion?" He is terrified even as he speaks these words, so that we may learn from all sides the excellence of the man. For it is not surprising that these things were said by Jews, but that these men should be so terrified shows very great proof of the power of God. Both the fear is shown and the obedience that is greater after the fear. For

---

[1]NPNF 1 11:129**.

there was indeed need of strength. HOMILIES ON THE ACTS OF THE APOSTLES 20.[2]

9:15 A Chosen Instrument

A CHOSEN INSTRUMENT. JEROME: Why is the apostle Paul called a chosen vessel? Assuredly because he is a repertory of the law and of the holy Scriptures. LETTER 53.3.[3]

9:16 He Must Suffer for the Sake of My Name

ONE OF THE SAINTS. BEDE: [The Lord] said that he was not to be feared as a persecutor but rather embraced as a brother, for he was soon to suffer along with the saints the troubles that he had earlier inflicted on them. COMMENTARY ON THE ACTS OF THE APOSTLES 9.16.[4]

AN ACCEPTABLE SACRIFICE. OROSIUS: When Paul was saved there where he had bound Christ by persecuting him, he would be afflicted with suffering for Christ, right up to his own death, but [he would] be glorified in the resurrection. So it is, because "mercy and truth go always before the face of God;"[5] so that if a voluntary sacrifice of an afflicted spirit and a contrite heart is offered in time by the lamenting person, truth arises in mercy, and in the end mercy is exalted over judgment. DEFENSE AGAINST THE PELAGIANS 14.[6]

9:17 Filled with the Holy Spirit

THE ACTION OF THE HOLY SPIRIT. CYRIL OF JERUSALEM: The Holy Spirit worked immediately and not only changed Paul's blindness to sight but also imparted the seal to his soul, making him a vessel of election to carry the name of the Lord who had appeared to him before kings and the children of Israel; and he fashioned his former persecutor into a herald and a good servant who "from Jerusalem round about as far as Illyricum completed the gospel of Christ."[7] CATECHETICAL LECTURE 17.26.[8]

SAUL TAUGHT TO THINK MODESTLY OF HIMSELF. CHRYSOSTOM: It seems to me that both Paul and Cornelius, as soon as the words were spoken, received the Spirit. And yet he who gave it was not great. Thus there was nothing of man [humankind] in what was done, nor was anything done by man, but God was present, the worker of these things. At the same time [the Lord] both teaches him to think modestly of himself, in that he does not bring him to the apostles who were so admired, and shows that there is nothing of man here. He was not filled, however, with the Spirit that works signs, so that in this way as well his faith might be shown. For he worked no wonders. "And immediately," it says, "in the synagogues he proclaimed Jesus, saying, 'He is the Son of God.'" Not that he is risen or that he lives, but immediately and precisely, he expounded the doctrine that he is the Son of God. HOMILIES ON THE ACTS OF THE APOSTLES 20.[9]

THE SHEEP SUBDUES THE WOLF. ARATOR: How much [this] darkness earns! After the loss of his eyesight he sees greater things; fostering faith gives a marvelous example to the ages. Ananias casts out his fury—O strange victory! He whom the Hebrew called Sheep [Ananias] subdues a rapacious wolf. God will be proclaimed to the world by this herald, and pulled from the shadows of the law, under which he was blind, he will bring light into all lands singing about the everlasting Sun. Do not cease, O Saul, to make this day known, in order that the night which is given to you may be filled with the light of many, and you carry your darkness here [in your body] in order that you may be able to purge [the darkness] of the world. ON THE ACTS OF THE APOSTLES 1.[10]

THE RIGHT ORDER OF TEACHING. JOHN CASSIAN: He sent him then to an old man and determined that he must be instructed by his teaching rather than by his own. Otherwise what might

---

[2]NPNF 1 11:131**. [3]NPNF 2 6:98. [4]CS 117:88. [5]Ps 89:14 (88:15 LXX, Vg). [6]FC 99:132-33. [7]Rom 15:19. [8]FC 64:112*. [9]NPNF 1 11:131-32**. [10]OAA 46*.

have been rightly done with regard to Paul would have given a bad example of presumption to those who came after him, since each individual would conclude that he too should be trained in similar fashion under the guidance and by the teaching of God alone rather than by the instruction of his elders. CONFERENCE 2.15.1.[11]

9:18 Sight Restored, Paul Is Baptized

EYES OPEN AND STILL UNSEEING. CHRYSOSTOM: "And there something like scales fell from his eyes." Saying these words [Ananias] laid hands on him. Some say this was a sign of his blindness. Why did he not blind his eyes [entirely]? It was more paradoxical that "when his eyes were opened, he could see nothing." This he suffered in respect to the law, until the name of Jesus was laid on him. "And immediately," it says, "he was baptized and took food and was strengthened." He was weakened then both from his journey and from his fear, both from hunger and from dejection. Wishing therefore to deepen his dejection, he made the man blind until the coming of Ananias; and to prevent him from thinking the blindness imaginary, the scales. Paul needed no other teaching; his experience was his instruction. HOMILIES ON THE ACTS OF THE APOSTLES 20.[12]

THE SCALES OF A DRAGON. BEDE: Every dragon's body is said to be covered with scales. Therefore, because the Jews were called "serpents and a brood of vipers,"[13] this man, who had been an eager follower of their lack of faith, covered over the eyes of his heart, so to speak, with a serpent's skin. With the falling of the scales from his eyes under the hands of Ananias, however, his face showed that he had received the true light in his mind. COMMENTARY ON THE ACTS OF THE APOSTLES 9.18.[14]

PAUL'S CONVERSION WAS NOT COERCED. CHRYSOSTOM: If anyone should call this the effect of compulsion, [let him note that] the same thing happened to Elymas. How was it then that he was not changed? What could be more compelling than the earthquake at the resurrection, the report of the soldiers, the other miracles and the sight of him risen? These things, however, do not compel belief but are apt to teach it. HOMILIES ON THE ACTS OF THE APOSTLES 19.[15]

---

[11]ACW 57:99*. [12]NPNF 1 11:130**. [13]Mt 23:33. [14]CS 117:88. It is likely that Bede got the image of "snake scales" from Arator (OAA 46*). [15]NPNF 1 11:125**.

9:20-25 PAUL BEGINS TO PREACH

[20]And in the synagogues immediately he proclaimed Jesus, saying, "He is the Son of God." [21]And all who heard him were amazed, and said, "Is not this the man who made havoc in Jerusalem of those who called on this name? And he has come here for this purpose, to bring them bound before the chief priests." [22]But Saul increased all the more in strength, and confounded the Jews who lived in Damascus by proving that Jesus was the Christ.

[23]When many days had passed, the Jews plotted to kill him, [24]but their plot became known to Saul. They were watching the gates day and night, to kill him; [25]but his disciples took him by night and let him down over the wall, lowering him in a basket.

OVERVIEW: The moderns note that Saul begins his preaching by proclaiming that Jesus is the Son of God (the only time the title occurs in Acts, though it occurs five times in Luke's Gospel). Very soon after that the prophecy concerning his suffering begins to be fulfilled. His escape described here may allude to Joshua and his companions (Josh 2:15) and is referred to by Paul in 1 Corinthians 11:32-33. Chrysostom also notes that Paul's proclamation had to do with the divine sonship of Jesus. Chrysostom, whose love and admiration for Paul are remarkable, comments that Paul's spiritual strength and courage are greater miracles than the more common form of miracle wrought in confirmation of the gospel. From the beginning Paul was preaching the full gospel with the zeal of one who had been forgiven much (CHRYSOSTOM). Regarding Paul's escape by night from Damascus, nearly all the ancient commentators, represented here by Chrysostom and Augustine, make some allusion to Paul's words in writing to the Philippians that he would rather "set out and be with Christ" but that he is willing, as an act of prudence for the sake of preaching (CHRYSOSTOM), to stay in order to be of use to the church (AUGUSTINE).[1] Both Arator and after him Bede elaborate an accommodated sense of Luke's words in describing Paul's escape. The basket of rushes and palm leaves designates the conjunction of faith and hope (BEDE), or in a more elaborate extension, baptism and martyrdom (ARATOR).

9:20 *Immediately Paul Proclaimed Jesus*

PAUL PREACHES THE FULL GOSPEL FROM THE BEGINNING. CHRYSOSTOM: "And immediately," it says, "in the synagogues he preached Jesus." Not that he is risen—not this. No, nor that he lives. What then? Immediately he strictly expounded the doctrine that this "is the Son of God." HOMILIES ON THE ACTS OF THE APOSTLES 20.[2]

9:24 *Their Plot Known to Saul*

THEY SOUGHT TO KILL HIM WITHOUT A TRIAL. CHRYSOSTOM: When they saw that it was spreading, they did not even use the form of a trial. "But their plot became known to Saul. They were watching the gates day and night, to kill him." For this, more than anything, was intolerable to them—more than the miracles that had already taken place, more than the five thousand, more than the three thousand, in short, more than everything. HOMILIES ON THE ACTS OF THE APOSTLES 20.[3]

9:25 *Escape by Night*

PRUDENCE FOR THE SAKE OF THE PREACHING. CHRYSOSTOM: Let us imitate this man. Let us take our souls in our hands, ready to confront all dangers. His flight was not an act of cowardice; he was saving himself for the preaching. Had he been a coward, he would not have gone to Jerusalem. He would not have immediately resumed teaching. He would have compromised his vehemence. He would have learned a lesson from Stephen's suffering. No, on the contrary, he was being prudent. He considered it no great thing to die for the gospel, unless one could do this to great advantage. He was even willing not to see Christ, whom [more than anything] he was most eager to see, while the work of his stewardship among people was not yet complete.[4] Such must be the soul of a Christian. From the beginning and at the very outset, the character of Paul declared itself. No, even before this, even in what he did "not according to knowledge,"[5] it was not by human reasoning that he was moved to act as he did. For if after such a long time he was unwilling to weigh anchor, much more unwilling was he at the start of his trading voyage, when he had just left the harbor. Many things Christ leaves to be done by human wisdom, so that we may learn that his disciples were human beings and that it was not all [a direct act of divine inter-

---

[1]See Phil 1:23-24. [2]NPNF 1 11:132*. [3]NPNF 1 11:132**. [4]Phil 1:23-24. [5]Rom 10:2.

vention] at every turn, since otherwise they would have been merely motionless logs. But in fact they often managed matters themselves. It is not less than martyrdom to decline no suffering for the sake of the salvation of the many. Nothing so delights God. HOMILIES ON THE ACTS OF THE APOSTLES 20.[6]

THE ZEAL OF HIM WHO HAS BEEN FORGIVEN MUCH. CHRYSOSTOM: "But his disciples took him by night and let him down over the wall, lowering him in a basket."... For they sent him out alone, and no one was with him. This was fortunate, because it resulted in him showing himself to the apostles in Jerusalem. Now his disciples sent him out on the assumption that he ought to procure safety by flight, but he himself did just the opposite: he leaped into the midst of those raging against him. This is what it means to be on fire, to be fervent! From that day on he knew all the commands that the apostles had heard, "Anyone who does not take up his cross and follow me."[7] The very fact that he had been slower to come than the rest made him more zealous (for "to whom much is forgiven, he will show more love"[8]), so that the later he came, the more he loved. But an ambush [against Christians] he had made in his former life, and thinking he had done ten thousand wrongs, he believed he could never do enough to efface his previous deeds. HOMILIES ON THE ACTS OF THE APOSTLES 20.[9]

PAUL PRESERVED HIMSELF FOR THE SAKE OF THE CHURCH. AUGUSTINE: He would not have fled from the snares laid for him by the prince, his persecutor,[10] except that he wished to save himself for others who needed him, and that is why he said, "But I am pulled between the two: having a desire to be dissolved and to be with Christ, a thing by far the better; but to abide still in the flesh is needful for you."[11] LETTER 228.[12]

THE DISCIPLES ARE CHRIST'S. BEDE: That is, Christ's disciples, for in the Greek the "his" is not stated, but only "disciples," so that we may under-

stand it in general, as the disciples of Christ or of the church. For we do not read of Paul as having yet made disciples but only of having confounded the Jews who were living in Damascus. COMMENTARY ON THE ACTS OF THE APOSTLES 9.25A.[13]

LOWERED OVER THE WALL IN A BASKET. BEDE: Even today this sort of escape is preserved in the church whenever someone who has been enveloped in the snares of the ancient enemy or in the traps of this world is saved through the defenses of his hope and faith. For the wall of Damascus (which means *drinking blood*[14]) is the adversity of the world. King Aretas (which means *a descent*[15]) is understood to be the devil. The basket, which is usually constructed of rushes and palm leaves, designates the conjunction of faith and hope, for the rush signifies the freshness of faith, and the palm signifies the hope of eternal life. Therefore, anyone who sees himself encircled by a wall of adversity should be quick to climb into the basket of the virtues, in which he may make his escape. COMMENTARY ON THE ACTS OF THE APOSTLES 9.25B.[16]

AN ACCOMMODATED APPLICATION OF THE INCIDENT. ARATOR: Since he had risen above the wicked, he deserves to escape their ambush while the gates are closed. A basket, which is customarily woven with bulrushes and palms in turn, gives covering to Saul, in glory retaining an allegory of the church, for there is always contained in it the bulrush, by the waters [of baptism], and the palm, by the crowns [of martyrdom]. The wave of baptism and the blood of martyrdom promote the church. Not long since, the food produced beneath the tooth began to swell the insides of seven baskets while the multitude was feeding;[17] Scripture truly proclaims *that* number of

---

[6]NPNF 1 11:133**. [7]Mt 10:38. [8]Lk 7:47. [9]NPNF 1 11:132-33**. [10]See 1 Cor 11:32-33. [11]Phil 1:23-24. [12]FC 32:147. This same observation is made by Gregory the Great in his Second Dialogue (FC 39:65). [13]CS 117:88. [14]Jerome *On Hebrew Names* (CCL 72:110). [15]2 Cor 11:32-33; Jerome *On Hebrew Names* (CCL 72:154). [16]CS 117:89. [17]Mt 15:36-37.

churches in the world,[18] inasmuch as the Spirit is the working force thus present in them and virtue marks their names, although we, however, sing the praises of one church in them all. Therefore the visible form [the basket] protects the man; he himself serves it as a soldier [and] as a vessel [of election] remaining in the Vessel [Christ], and with him as General he escapes safely from the enemy, a commander who conquers for him in all battles. ON THE ACTS OF THE APOSTLES 1.[19]

---

[18]See Rev 1:4, 11. [19]OAA 46-47*.

9:26-31 PAUL JOINS THE DISCIPLES

[26]And when he had come to Jerusalem he attempted to join the disciples; and they were all afraid of him, for they did not believe that he was a disciple. [27]But Barnabas took him, and brought him to the apostles, and declared to them how on the road he had seen the Lord, who spoke to him, and how at Damascus he had preached boldly in the name of Jesus. [28]So he went in and out among them at Jerusalem, [29]preaching boldly in the name of the Lord. And he spoke and disputed against the Hellenists; but they were seeking to kill him. [30]And when the brothers knew it, they brought him down to Caesarea, and sent him off to Tarsus.

[31]So the church throughout all Judea and Galilee and Samaria had peace and was built up; and walking in the fear of the Lord and in the comfort of the Holy Spirit it was multiplied.

OVERVIEW: Both Chrysostom and Bede reflect the same problem that besets modern commentators in comparing the accounts Paul gives of his movements to and from Jerusalem and those given by Luke. Their solutions are moderate, as are most of the more attentive moderns.[1] The account makes it clear that the apostle was not exempt from the ordinary course of risk-laden human life. While Chrysostom sets forth many attempts to reconcile Acts and Galatians, Bede proposes a particular order accounting for Paul's presence in Jerusalem. It is ironic that Paul disputed with Greeks in Jerusalem and Jews in Damascus. With the short summary statement concerning the peace and consolation enjoyed by the Jerusalem community Luke brings this part of his narrative about Paul to a close, and he goes on in the next section to tell of Peter's activity and of his call to minister to the Gentiles.

9:26 When Paul Came to Jerusalem

RECONCILING ACTS AND THE LETTER TO THE GALATIANS. CHRYSOSTOM: One may well be much at a loss here to understand how it is that, whereas in the epistle to the Galatians Paul says, "I went, not to Jerusalem" but "into Arabia" and "to Damascus," and, "After three years I went up to Jerusalem," and "to see Peter,"[2] here [in Acts] the writer says the contrary. There, Paul says, "And I saw none of the apostles," but here, it is said that Barnabas "brought him to the apostles."

---

[1]See for instance, Fitzmyer, *Acts*, 136-38. [2]Gal 1:17-18.

Well, [among several alternatives] either Paul means, "I went up," not with the intent to refer or attach myself to them—for what does he say? "I did not refer myself, nor did I go to Jerusalem to those who were apostles before me"—or else, that the laying await for him in Damascus was after his return from Arabia. Or another alternative is that the visit to Jerusalem was after he came from Arabia. Certainly of his own accord he went not to the apostles but "sought to join himself to the disciples" as a teacher, not a disciple. "I went," he says, "not for this purpose, that I should go to those who were apostles before me. Certainly, I learned nothing from them." Or he does not speak of this visit but passes it by, so that the order is, "I went into Arabia, then I came to Damascus, then to Jerusalem, then to Syria." Or else, again, that he went up to Jerusalem, then was sent to Damascus, then to Arabia, then again to Damascus, then to Caesarea. Also, the visit "after fourteen years" probably was when he brought up the alms to the brothers together with Barnabas.[3] Or else he means a different occasion.[4] For the historian, for conciseness, often omits incidents and condenses the times. Observe how unambitious the writer is, and how he does not even relate that vision[5] but passes it by. "He sought," it says, "to join himself to the disciples. And they were afraid of him." By this again is shown the ardor of Paul's character, for not only from the mouth of Ananias and of those who wondered at him there but also of those in Jerusalem came the statement that "they did not believe that he was a disciple." For truly that was beyond all human expectation. HOMILIES ON THE ACTS OF THE APOSTLES 21.[6]

COMPARING DIFFERENT ACCOUNTS. BEDE: We are not to believe that he came to the apostles in Jerusalem immediately after he was baptized. Rather, as he himself wrote to the Galatians,[7] he first went away to Arabia and again returned to Damascus. Then, after three years, he came to Jerusalem and saw Peter and remained with him for fifteen days, but he saw none of the other apostles except for James, the brother of the Lord. And then, as Luke also tells, he came to the regions of Syria and Cilicia.[8] It is not, however, readily apparent whether it was during the first or the second visit to Damascus that he survived the snares [of the Jews]. Support for taking it as the second time can be found in the statement that after many days had passed the Jews made a plan about killing him. Therefore Luke seems to have disregarded Arabia because he [Paul] preached very little there, as he himself said later, when he was speaking to King Agrippa, "I preached first to the people of Damascus and Jerusalem, and in every region of Judea, and to the Gentiles."[9] COMMENTARY ON THE ACTS OF THE APOSTLES 9.26.[10]

9:27 Barnabas Took Him

A KIND MAN. CHRYSOSTOM: Barnabas was called "son of encouragement"; accordingly, he was accessible to Paul. His exceeding kindness[11] is revealed both in the present instance and in the case of John (Mark).[12] Why was Barnabas not afraid? (For Paul was a man whose very look inspired fear.) It is likely that Barnabas, also at Damascus, had heard all about him. HOMILIES ON THE ACTS OF THE APOSTLES 21.[13]

9:29 Preaching Boldly

CONTENDING WITH GREEKS IN JERUSALEM AND JEWS IN DAMASCUS. BEDE: Note that he taught Greeks in Jerusalem and Jews in Damascus, which is a Gentile city, even though this should signify that Gentiles were to be included in the city of God and Jews were to fall into the faithlessness of the Gentiles, in accordance with what Isaiah said: "Lebanon shall be changed into Carmel, and Carmel shall be regarded as a waste-

---

[3]Gal 2:1. [4]Cf. Acts 11:30. [5]See Acts 22:17-21. [6]NPNF 1 11:134-35**. [7]Gal 1:17-21; Jerome *Commentary on the Epistle to the Galatians* 1.1.17 (PL 26:328). [8]Acts 15:41. [9]Acts 26:20. [10]CS 117:89-90. [11]Acts 11:24. [12]See Acts 15:36-40. [13]NPNF 1 11:135**.

land."[14] COMMENTARY ON THE ACTS OF THE APOSTLES 9.29.[15]

MAKING NO EXCUSES. CHRYSOSTOM: "But they," it says, "went about to slay him." This is a sign of his energy and triumphant victory and of their exceeding annoyance at what had happened. Fearing that the issue should be the same as in the case of Stephen, they sent him to Caesarea. For it says, "When the brothers were aware of this, they brought him down to Caesarea and sent him forth to Tarsus,"[16] at the same time to preach, and likely to be more in safety, as being in his own country. But observe, I pray you, how far it is from being the case that everything is done by grace [particular acts of providence]. Note how, on the contrary, God does in many things leave them to manage for themselves by their own wisdom and in a human way, so to cut off the excuse of idle people, for if it was so in the case of Paul, much more in theirs. HOMILIES ON THE ACTS OF THE APOSTLES 21.[17]

9:31 *The Church Had Peace*

UNAFRAID, PETER LEAVES JERUSALEM. CHRYSOSTOM: He is about to relate that Peter goes down [from Jerusalem]. Therefore, that you may not impute this to fear, he first says this. For while there was persecution, he was in Jerusalem, but when the affairs of the church are everywhere in security, then it is that he leaves Jerusalem. HOMILIES ON THE ACTS OF THE APOSTLES 21.[18]

---

[14]Is 29:17 (Vg). [15]CS 117:90*. [16]Acts 11:30. [17]NPNF 1 11:135-36*. [18]NPNF 1 11:136*.

9:32-43 THE HEALING OF AENEAS AND TABITHA RAISED FROM THE DEAD

[32]Now as Peter went here and there among them all, he came down also to the saints that lived at Lydda. [33]There he found a man named Aeneas, who had been bedridden for eight years and was paralyzed. [34]And Peter said to him, "Aeneas, Jesus Christ heals you; rise and make your bed." And immediately he rose. [35]And all the residents of Lydda and Sharon saw him, and they turned to the Lord.

[36]Now there was at Joppa a disciple named Tabitha, which means Dorcas.[x] She was full of good works and acts of charity. [37]In those days she fell sick and died; and when they had washed her, they laid her in an upper room. [38]Since Lydda was near Joppa, the disciples, hearing that Peter was there, sent two men to him entreating him, "Please come to us without delay." [39]So Peter rose and went with them. And when he had come, they took him to the upper room. All the widows stood beside him weeping, and showing tunics and other garments which Dorcas made while she was with them. [40]But Peter put them all outside and knelt down and prayed; then turning to the body he said, "Tabitha, rise." And she opened her eyes, and when she saw Peter she sat up. [41]And he gave her his hand and lifted her up. Then calling the saints and widows he presented her alive.

⁴²And it became known throughout all Joppa, and many believed in the Lord. ⁴³And he stayed in Joppa for many days with one Simon, a tanner.

x The name Tabitha in Aramaic and the name Dorcas in Greek mean *gazelle*

OVERVIEW: Luke begins with two miracle stories and continues with the account of Peter's vision and subsequent visit to Cornelius, who also had a vision. Luke shows us the importance of the events in Cornelius's house, in which we see the call of the Gentiles, by narrating it once, as in the case of Paul's conversion, and then on two occasions reporting Peter's account of the event, again as he does for Paul.[1] It is difficult to know whether the patristic commentators were aware of this literary procedure on the part of Luke. They do not mention it. It is possible that their concentration on event rather than text and their familiarity with such procedures made explicit commentary otiose. A feature of Luke's narrative, which will become more apparent, is that he subtly draws parallels between Jesus and the apostles. Didymus sees the parallels between the healing of Aeneas and the healing of the lame man at the pool of Bethesda. This narrative is itself drawing on terminology in the Synoptic account of the healing of a paralytic, and Luke's vocabulary reflects both sets of narratives.[2] Though Bede tends to derive moral applications from these miracles, he is not far from the New Testament symbolic understanding of paralysis and sin. Nearly all the seven accounts in the New Testament of the healing of a paralytic contain an allusion to sin.[3] Finally, the account of the raising of Tabitha has, in addition to the sound evocation (TALITHA) in Mark's account of Jesus' raising of a dead child,[4] multiple allusions to both Mark's narrative and the stories of the raising of the dead by Elijah and Elisha.[5] The Fathers are sensitive to parts at least of Luke's manner of showing us the life and ministry of Jesus continued in the church. Like a general leading troops, Peter's place as foremost among the apostles is clear everywhere he went (CHRYSOSTOM). Bedridden for eight years, Aeneas was symbolic of the persistent frailty of humanity

and the power of the risen Christ (CHRYSOSTOM, BEDE). Healing preceded faith to draw people to trust in God (CHRYSOSTOM). To shake off torpor Aeneas is commanded to make his bed (BEDE). In the narrative of Tabitha, providence has already hidden meaning in the naming of Tabitha, suggesting Dorcas, a fallow gazelle in the high mountains, living by its wits among predators, analogous to the saints (BEDE, CHRYSOSTOM). The intercession of the widows was not by means of words only but of acts of mercy and alms for the poor (BEDE). The gathering of widows to give alms and perform good deeds constitutes a monument greater than any physical memorial (CHRYSOSTOM). Touched by Peter's hand, Tabitha arose (BEDE) from death to life, recalling the transition from law to gospel (ARATOR). Praying, Peter commanded her to rise, and she was first brought back to consciousness, then to activity (CHRYSOSTOM, BEDE) as an act of God's mercy to one who was merciful (CYPRIAN). Peter's stay of many days with the poor tanner of Joppa shows his identification with the humble poor (CHRYSOSTOM).

9:32 As Peter Went About

THE APOSTLES SOUGHT PETER FIRST AS THEIR LEADER. CHRYSOSTOM: Like a general [Peter] went around inspecting the ranks— which part was well-trained, which in good order and which needed his presence. See how on all occasions he goes about first. When an apostle

---

[1]See Acts 11:4-18; 15:7-11. [2]Lk 5:17-26 and par. [3]In addition to accounts mentioned in the previous note see Acts 3:1-10; 9:32-35; 14:8-10. [4]Mk 5:21-24, 35-42. [5]Thus, Peter sends everyone out of the room (Acts 9:40; Mk 5:40) and prays (1 Kings 17:20; 2 Kings 4:33). Tabitha opens her eyes (2 Kings 4:35) and sits up (Lk 7:15). Peter takes her by the hand (Mk 5:41) and presents her to the "saints and widows" (1 Kings 17:23; 2 Kings 4:36).

had to be chosen, he was first; when the Jews had to be told that these were not drunk, he was first; when the lame man had to be healed, he was first; when the crowd had to be addressed, he was before the rest; when the rulers had to be addressed, he was the man; when Ananias had to be addressed, when healings were worked by the shadow, still it was he.[6] And look, where there was danger, he was the man; where the situation is calm, all of them act in common. He did not seek a greater honor. When there was need to work miracles, he leaps forward, and here again he is the man to labor and toil. HOMILIES ON THE ACTS OF THE APOSTLES 21.[7]

9:33 Bedridden for Eight Years

AENEAS AS A SYMBOL. BEDE: This Aeneas signifies the ailing human race, at first weakened by pleasure but healed by the work and words of the apostles. Since the world itself is raised up in four territories, and in this world the course of the year is divided into four seasons, anyone who embraces the unstable joys of the present is as though flattened upon his bed, devoid of energy for twice times four years. For the bed is that sluggishness in which the sick and weak soul takes its rest in the delights of the body, that is, and in all worldly pleasures. COMMENTARY ON THE ACTS OF THE APOSTLES 9.33.[8]

9:34 Jesus Christ Heals You

FIRST HEALING, THEN FAITH. CHRYSOSTOM: Peter does well to give a proof of the miracle. For they not only released people from their diseases but also provided health, as well as strength. Moreover, at that time they had not yet offered proof of their own power, and so it was unreasonable to demand faith from the man (nor had they done so in the earlier case of the lame man[9]). Therefore, just as Christ in the beginning of his miracles did not demand faith, neither did these. For it was in Jerusalem, naturally, that their faith was first shown, "at least the shadow

of Peter," it says, "might fall across some of them as he went past."[10] Many miracles had been performed there, but here in Lydda and Sharon this is the first. For some of the miracles were performed to draw people to faith, and others to comfort the believers. HOMILIES ON THE ACTS OF THE APOSTLES 21.[11]

ARISE AND MAKE YOUR BED. BEDE: When Peter had cured him of paralysis, he commanded him to rise at once and make his bed. Spiritually this informs us that whoever has received into his heart the firm foundation of faith will not only shake off the torpor in which he has been lying idle but will also produce the good works in which he will be able to rest after his toil. COMMENTARY ON THE ACTS OF THE APOSTLES 9.34.[12]

9:36 Tabitha, Which Means Dorcas

PROVIDENCE IN NAMING. CHRYSOSTOM: It was not without purpose that the writer informed us of the woman's name, but to show that her character matched her name—she was active and wakeful as a gazelle. For many names are bestowed by providence, as we have often said to you. "She was full," it says, "of good works." Not only of alms but also "of good works," both in general and of this good work in particular, "which Dorcas made while she was with them." What humility! Unlike us, all of them were together, and she worked and made clothes. HOMILIES ON THE ACTS OF THE APOSTLES 21.[13]

THE MEANING OF DORCAS. BEDE: Now at Jaffa there was a woman disciple by the name of Tabitha, which means Dorcas, that is, "deer," or "fallow deer," signifying souls exalted by the practice of virtues although contemptible in the eyes of people. For the blessed Luke would not have provided the meaning of the name if he had not

---

[6]See Acts 1:15; 2:15; 3:4-12; 4:8; 5:3-15. [7]NPNF 1 11:136**. [8]CS 117:90. [9]See Acts 3:6. [10]Acts 5:15. [11]NPNF 1 11:136**. [12]CS 117:90-91. [13]NPNF 1 11:137**.

known there was strong symbolism in it. The deer and the fallow deer are animals that are similar in nature, though different in size. They dwell on high mountains, and they see all who approach, no matter how far away they may be. Hence in Greek they are called *dorcades* from the sharpness of their vision.[14]

So it is with the saints. As they dwell on high by the merits of their works, through mental contemplation they simultaneously direct their attention with wisdom toward things above, while always watching out for themselves with prudent discretion. Moreover, these animals are clean according to the law[15] but timid and unwarlike according to their nature, as Martial depicts it: "The boar is feared because of his tusk; the stag's horns defend him. What are we unwarlike fallow deer except prey?"[16] Does not this clearly describe those who are content to live simply and with discretion in their course of action, as it were walking with split hooves and ruminating in continual meditation on the Word of God? A person who has met with spiritual death, if it was out of ignorance or infirmity, may nevertheless deserve to be revived for the integrity of his right intention, just as is shown to have happened through Peter to that woman to whom we can very rightly apply what is written [above] concerning the deer. COMMENTARY ON THE ACTS OF THE APOSTLES 9.36.[17]

TRUE FAME. CHRYSOSTOM: If you want to be remembered and are anxious for true repute, imitate her, and build edifices like that, not going to expense on lifeless matter but displaying great generosity in regard to your fellow human beings. This is the remembrance that is worth admiring and brings great benefit. HOMILIES ON GENESIS 30.8.[18]

9:38 Please Come to Us

SO AS NOT TO TAKE AWAY FROM THE PREACHING. CHRYSOSTOM: Why did they wait until she was dead? Why was Peter not troubled

before? They considered it unworthy, true believers as they were, to trouble the disciples about such matters and to take them away from their preaching. Indeed, this is why it mentions that the place was nearby. If what they were asking was of somewhat secondary importance, it was not then by way of going first. For she was a woman disciple. HOMILIES ON THE ACTS OF THE APOSTLES 21.[19]

9:39 The Widows Wept

ALMS DONE ON BEHALF OF THE DEAD. CHRYSOSTOM: Let us not concern ourselves with grave monuments or memorials. This is the greatest memorial: gather the widows around; tell them his name; ask them all to offer prayers and supplications on his behalf. This will overcome God; for although it was not done by the [dead] man himself, it is through him that another is responsible for the almsgiving. This too is of the mercy of God. "Widows standing around and weeping" know how to rescue people not from the present death but from the death that is to come. Many have enjoyed the benefit of these alms performed by others on their behalf. For they found, if not perfect deliverance, at least some consolation. HOMILIES ON THE ACTS OF THE APOSTLES 21.[20]

THE WIDOWS STOOD WEEPING. BEDE: The widows are the repentant soul's holy thoughts, which for a long time had lost the vigor of their original purpose, as though they had lost for a time the guidance of a husband. They must humbly pray for the soul that has done wrong. COMMENTARY ON THE ACTS OF THE APOSTLES 9.39A.[21]

TUNICS AND CLOAKS THAT DORCAS HAD MADE. BEDE: They interceded for the dead

---

[14]Isidore of Seville *Etymologies* 12.1.15. [15]Lev 11:3; Deut 14:6. [16]Isidore of Seville *Etymologies* 12.1.22, which includes the epigram of Martial (13.94). [17]CS 117:91. [18]FC 82:226. [19]NPNF 1 11:137**. [20]NPNF 1 11:140**. [21]CS 117:92.

woman, not with their voices but by means of her own works, for almsdeeds free one not only from the second death but also from the first. COMMENTARY ON THE ACTS OF THE APOSTLES 9.39B.[22]

9:40 Tabitha, Rise

GOD TAKES THOUGHT FOR THEIR SALVATION. CHRYSOSTOM: They did not perform all their miracles with the same ease. This helped them. For truly God took thought not only for the salvation of others but also of their own. He who healed so many by his very shadow, how is it that now he has to do so much first? There are cases in which the faith of the applicants also assisted. This is the first dead person he has raised. Notice how he awakens her as if out of sleep. First, she opened her eyes; then, at the sight of Peter, she sat up; then, from his hand she received strength again. Look at the gain, look at the harvest, but note that it was not for display. That is why he sent them all outside, imitating his teacher also in this. HOMILIES ON THE ACTS OF THE APOSTLES 21.[23]

OPENING EYES AND SITTING UP. BEDE: A most perfect order in her rising from death, that she would first open the eyes of her mind, and then, on recognizing Peter's voice, that she would sit up and receive the light of her discretion, which she had lost, and that she would live according to the teaching of those who had come to her aid. COMMENTARY ON THE ACTS OF THE APOSTLES 9.40.[24]

AN ALLEGORY OF LAW AND GOSPEL. ARATOR: If we are rightly inspired, the renewed day of her soul is clearly suitable for allegory, [a soul,] turned back to the voice of Peter, which the darkness of exceedingly ancient peril had pressed down: the life burdened previously in the bosom of the dark law, rising just like a second [soul], stands up in the church's presence, and the light of works, the companion of faith, drives away the shadows, a salvation that had not been promised by the voice of the law, because grace undertakes to give gifts of eternal life to those reborn in the font. ON THE ACTS OF THE APOSTLES 1.[25]

THE MERITS OF MERCY. CYPRIAN: So powerful were the merits of mercy, so much did just works avail! She who had conferred upon suffering widows the assistance for living deserved to be recalled to life by the petition of widows. WORKS AND ALMSGIVING 6.[26]

9:41 Peter Presented Tabitha Alive

HE RAISED HER UP. BEDE: When she was touched by Peter's hand, Tabitha rose again, since there is no better way for the soul that has become weak because of its sins to regain its strength than the example of the saints. COMMENTARY ON THE ACTS OF THE APOSTLES 9.41.[27]

9:43 Peter Stayed in Joppa

LEADING PEOPLE TO HUMILITY. CHRYSOSTOM: "And he stayed in Joppa for many days with one Simon, a tanner." Look at Peter's unassuming conduct, look at his moderation, how he does not stay with this lady or with someone of prominence but with a tanner. By all his actions he leads people to humility. He allows neither the poor to be ashamed nor the great to be elated. For they needed his instruction, those who believed through the miracles. HOMILIES ON THE ACTS OF THE APOSTLES 21.[28]

---

[22]CS 117:92. [23]NPNF 1 11:138**. [24]CS 117:92. [25]OAA 49*. [26]FC 36:233. [27]CS 117:92-93. [28]NPNF 1 11:137*.

10:1-8 CORNELIUS SEES A VISION

¹At Caesarea there was a man named Cornelius, a centurion of what was known as the Italian Cohort, ²a devout man who feared God with all his household, gave alms liberally to the people, and prayed constantly to God. ³About the ninth hour of the day he saw clearly in a vision an angel of God coming in and saying to him, "Cornelius." ⁴And he stared at him in terror, and said, "What is it, Lord?" And he said to him, "Your prayers and your alms have ascended as a memorial before God. ⁵And now send men to Joppa, and bring one Simon who is called Peter; ⁶he is lodging with Simon, a tanner, whose house is by the seaside." ⁷When the angel who spoke to him had departed, he called two of his servants and a devout soldier from among those that waited on him, ⁸and having related everything to them, he sent them to Joppa.

OVERVIEW: In the following selections from the early Christian authors on the first verses (Acts 10:1-8) of this episode, we see a notable division between the concerns of eastern (CHRYSOSTOM) and western authors (AUGUSTINE, BEDE) over the role of Cornelius's good deeds and piety, and yet there prevails a similar use of the character of Cornelius as an exemplum for either the audience's beliefs (AUGUSTINE) or their behavior (CHRYSOSTOM). Chrysostom engages in a detailed laudatory construction of Cornelius's moral character in order to motivate his audience to better behavior and dispositions in very specific matters that concern primarily those in positions of power. Augustine and Bede are concerned to foster a humble disposition that the apparent Pelagianism in God's blessing of Cornelius's actions could undermine, and so the specificity, which begets a multitude of different perspectives in Chrysostom, narrows to a radical concern over the question of merit in Latin authors. Three other eastern authors (BASIL, AMMONIUS, ORIGEN) illustrate different uses of Cornelius's vision. Basil makes a distinction that Chrysostom at times misses, that between inchoate and perfect faith, and yet like Chrysostom he is concerned to acknowledge God's love of a sincere heart earnestly desirous of the truth. It is the difficulty in achieving this purity of intention that breeds heresy (AMMONIUS). While there is evident in all these authors a concern to give a description of how God not only has worked but also continues to work—a conviction that through the story of Cornelius, or of all Scripture, one can glean principles applicable to today—two selections from Bede (Acts 10:3, 7) do not look at this particular historical event to gain a universal understanding of God's actions in history but see therein evocations of other particular historical events or a prophetic hint of the future structure of the church (BEDE).

Among modern exegetes, the conversion of Cornelius and the justification of this event by Peter (see Acts 11:1-18) are the turning point in Luke's account of the spread of the gospel beyond the Jewish people. Modern exegesis emphasizes how Luke portrays the event as one under heavenly guidance, not initiated by people. There is, however, a typically western concern among some (e.g., Barrett, 503) that a works theology lingers beneath (something that is somewhat evident in Chrysostom's interpretations), while others (e.g., Fitzmyer, 448) insist that there is no evidence in the episode itself that Cornelius has "merited" this from God.

10:1 A Man Named Cornelius

NOT BECAUSE OF HIGH RANK. CHRYSOSTOM: This man is not a Jew, nor of those under the law, but he had already anticipated our manner of life. Observe, thus far, two persons, both of high rank, receiving the faith, the eunuch at Gaza and this man; and the pains taken on behalf of these men. But do not imagine that this was because of their high rank: God forbid! It was because of their piety. The Scripture mentions their dignified stations to show the greatness of their piety, since it is more wonderful when a person in a position of wealth and power is such as these were. HOMILIES ON THE ACTS OF THE APOSTLES 22.[1]

10:2 A Devout Man

ALL GLORY TO GOD. AUGUSTINE: For it is often said, "He deserved to believe, because he was a good man even before he believed." This may be said of Cornelius since his alms were accepted and his prayers heard before he had believed on Christ; and yet without some faith he neither gave alms nor prayed. For how did he call on him on whom he had not believed? But if he could have been saved without the faith of Christ, the apostle Peter would not have been sent as an architect to build him up. For, "Except the Lord build the house, they labor in vain who build it."[2] And we are told, faith is of ourselves; other things that pertain to works of righteousness are of the Lord; as if faith did not belong to the building— as if, I say, the foundation did not belong to the building. But if the foundation primarily and especially belongs to the building, he labors in vain who seeks to build up the faith by preaching, unless the Lord in his mercy builds it up from within. Whatever, therefore, of good works Cornelius performed, whether before he believed in Christ or when he believed or after he had believed, all to be ascribed to God. Otherwise, it might be assumed that human initiative is being lifted up. PREDESTINATION OF THE SAINTS 1.7.12.[3]

HE DID NOT NEGLECT HIS OWN HOUSE. CHRYSOSTOM: But here again is a high commen-

dation of alms, just as was there given by means of Tabitha. "A devout man," it says, "and one that feared God with all his house." Let us hear this, lest we neglect those of our own house. This man was also concerned for his soldiers. "And who gave alms," it says, "to all the people." Both his doctrines and his life were right. HOMILIES ON THE ACTS OF THE APOSTLES 22.[4]

VIRTUES RECEIVED BY FAITH. BEDE: "One does not attain faith by virtues, but rather one attains virtues by faith," as the blessed Pope Gregory explains.[5] Cornelius, he says, "whose alms-deeds before his baptism were praised by an angelic witness, did not come to faith by works but came to works by faith. For if he had not believed in the true God even before his baptism, to whom was he praying? Or how had almighty God heard this man, if it was not that he had been asking to be perfected in the good by this very God? Therefore he knew God as the creator of all things, but he did not know that the all-powerful Son had become flesh. He had faith, this man whose prayers and alms were able to please [God], and by his good deeds he earned the right to know God perfectly and to believe in the mystery of the incarnation of his only begotten, so that he might approach the sacrament of baptism. Therefore, through faith he came to works, yet through works he was strengthened in faith." COMMENTARY ON THE ACTS OF THE APOSTLES 10.1.[6]

10:3 An Angel of God

A MESSAGE CONCERNING BAPTISM. BEDE: It is fitting that it was at the ninth hour that [Cornelius] received the divine message concerning the baptism he was to ask for, since he was to be baptized in the death of the one who sent forth his spirit at the ninth hour.[7] COMMENTARY ON THE ACTS OF THE APOSTLES 10.3.[8]

---

[1]NPNF 1 11:141-42**. [2]Ps 127:1 (126:1 LXX, Vg). [3]NPNF 1 5:504**. [4]NPNF 1 11:142**. [5]Gregory the Great *Homilies on Ezekiel* 2.7.9 (CCL 142:322-23). [6]CS 117:95. [7]Mt 27:46. [8]CS 117:95.

10:4 *Prayers and Alms*

THE VIRTUE OF ALMS. CHRYSOSTOM: See how great the virtue of alms, both in the former discourse and here! There, it delivered from temporal death; here, from eternal death, and opened the gates of heaven. Such are the pains taken for the bringing of Cornelius to the faith, that both an angel is sent, and the Spirit works, and the chief of the apostles is fetched to him, and such a vision is shown, and, in short, nothing is left undone. How many centurions were there besides, and tribunes and kings, and yet none of them obtained what this man did! Hear, all you that are in military commands, all you that stand beside kings. "A just man," it says, "fearing God"; "devout"; and what is more than all, with all his house. Not as we who do everything that our servants may be afraid of us, do everything, but not that they may be devout. . . . Not so this man; but he was "one that feared God with all his house," for he was as the common father of those with him and of all the others [under his command.] But observe what [the soldier] says himself. . . . He adds this also, "well reported of by all the nation." So what if he was uncircumcised? No, the alms give him a good report. There is nothing like alms. Great is the virtue of this practice, when the almsgiving is poured forth from pure stores; for it is like a fountain discharging mud when it issues from unjust stores, but when from just gains, it is as a limpid and pure stream in a paradise, sweet to the sight, sweet to the touch, both light and cool, when given in the noonday heat. Such is alms. HOMILIES ON THE ACTS OF THE APOSTLES 22.[9]

SANCTIFIED THROUGH GIVING. ARATOR: Cornelius, born of Gentile stock, was highly respected in the city of Caesarea; his life, given over to godly works, sanctified him for the waters, and he, who did whatever faith was inclined to perform in those washed by baptism, . . . began to believe through his actions. For an angel, sent from the stars, drawing near to [Cornelius] said, "The wealth that you distribute, the words that you pray, stand [pleasing] in the sight of the highest Lord. Rewards for your virtue will not be lacking. Accept the certain Way when Peter comes here." Thus the glistening messenger implanted with his word the commands for eternal washings. ON THE ACTS OF THE APOSTLES 1.[10]

CORNELIUS: A WORKER CALLED AT THE ELEVENTH HOUR. BASIL THE GREAT: Are there even now some who work from the first hour and others from the eleventh, and who are they? Perhaps [the answer to this] is most evident to anyone from the events recounted in the divinely inspired Scripture that while there are many, in the words of the apostle, who have learned the holy Scriptures from childhood,[11] many still, such as Cornelius, although making good use of natural movements, are slow in coming to perfection of knowledge because of a lack of teachers. "For how," he says, "do they believe, if they do not hear?"[12] If, therefore, it happens that some, like Cornelius, are engaged in nothing evil but rather are desirous of perfection and genuinely demonstrate the good that they can and that comes to their knowledge, to these God gives the same blessings as he did to Cornelius by not holding them culpable for the period of idleness, since it was not their fault, as I said, and he is content with their desire that was previously made manifest through their eager actions and what has been more diligently set right in relation to perfection. THE SHORT RULES 2.224.[13]

SOBER AND OF GOOD WILL. CHRYSOSTOM: Did you see what assurance came from prayers and almsgiving to this man, whose whole life was spent in the cloak and belt of the soldier? Let them hear this who have enlisted in the army and let them learn that military service presents no hindrance to virtue for the one who is willing to be sober. Let them learn that one can take great

---

[9]NPNF 1 11:146-47**. [10]*OAA* 50*. [11]See 2 Tim 3:15. [12]Rom 10:14. [13]PG 31:1229-32.

care of virtue, even though he wears the soldier's cloak and belt, even though he has a wife, the care of children, the management of a household, and even though he has undertaken a public duty. Look at this admirable man, who wore the soldier's cloak and belt, who commanded troops, for he was a centurion! Of what care did heaven deem him worthy because of his good will, his sobriety and his vigilance?

And that you may know clearly that grace wings its way down to us from on high only after we have first done our fair share, hear the story itself. After Cornelius had taken the first step by his frequent and generous almsgiving, he was devoting himself earnestly to prayer. About the ninth hour, the Scripture says, an angel stood beside him as he prayed and said, "Cornelius, your prayers and your alms have gone up and been remembered in the sight of God."

Let us not simply pass these words by, but let us carefully consider the virtue of the man. Then let us learn how loving and kind the Master is and how he overlooks no one. But where he sees a soul that is sober, there he lavishes his grace upon him. Here is a soldier who has had benefit of no instruction, who was tangled up in the affairs of this life, who has each day a thousand things to distract and bother him. Yet he did not waste his life in banquets and drinking and gluttony but spent his time in prayer and almsgiving. He showed such eagerness on his own initiative, he attended so constantly to prayer, he was so generous in his almsgiving, that he showed himself deserving of such a vision. BAPTISMAL INSTRUCTIONS 7.28-29.[14]

PRAY TO KNOW THE TRUTH. AMMONIUS: It must be noted that whoever, with pure conscience, earnestly prays to God and gives alms, does not remain in the same condition, but God makes known, through the vision of an angel or through a pious person, the true faith through which we are saved. In the case where one does not know whether this or that action is pleasing to God, it is best earnestly to pray to God so that

the truth may be revealed. This is essential especially if one is at a loss concerning the faith, what it is necessary to think or in whom one must believe. For this reason there are many heresies among those who seem to be Christians. CATENA ON THE ACTS OF THE APOSTLES 10.4.[15]

ALL EFFORTS IN VAIN WITHOUT CHARITY. CHRYSOSTOM: We seek those virtues that are most salutary for our salvation and for our neighbor. Such is almsgiving and such is prayer, or rather the latter becomes efficacious and capable of flight as a result of the former. "Your prayers," the text says, "and your alms have ascended for a memorial before God." This is true not only of prayer, but fasting has its strength from this as well. If you fast without giving alms, your fasting is not considered to be valid. Rather, such a person is worse than a glutton and a drunkard, and so much worse as cruelty is harder to bear than luxury. And why do I speak about fasting? Even though you are chaste, even though you observe virginity, if you do not cultivate charity you are out of the bridal chamber. HOMILIES ON THE GOSPEL OF MATTHEW 77 (78).6.[16]

10:5 Bring Peter

THROUGH THE MINISTRY OF PEOPLE. AUGUSTINE: Let us beware of such dangerous temptations of pride, and let us rather consider the fact that the apostle Paul himself, although stricken down and admonished by the voice of God from heaven, was yet sent to a man to receive the sacraments and be admitted into the church. Cornelius the centurion, although an angel announced to him that his prayers were heard and that his alms were remembered, was yet handed over to Peter for instruction, and not only received the sacraments from the apostle's hands but was also instructed by him as to the proper objects of faith, hope and love. And without doubt it was possible to have done everything through the

---

[14]ACW 31:116-17*. [15]CGPNT 3:173. [16]PG 58:710.

instrumentality of angels, but the condition of our race would have been much more degraded if God had not chosen to make use of people as the ministers of his word to [other people]. For how could that be true which is written, "The temple of God is holy, and that temple you are,"[17] if God gave forth no oracles from his human temple but communicated everything that he wished to be taught to people by voices from heaven or through the ministration of angels? Moreover, love itself, which binds people together in the bond of unity, would have no means of pouring soul into soul, and, as it were, mingling them one with another, if people never learned anything from [others]. CHRISTIAN INSTRUCTION, PREFACE 6.[18]

10:7 Cornelius Called Two Servants

ZEAL OF PREACHING. BEDE: Cornelius sent three people to Peter because the Gentile world, which was to come to believe in the faith of the apostles, had subjugated Europe, Asia and Africa, which were to be taken over partly by militant zeal (that is, by urgent preaching) and partly by domestic business dealings. Note also that one soldier and two domestic servants were sent, for among the members of the church, the greater their strength, the fewer you will find. There are more who know how to hear the word than those who know how to speak it. COMMENTARY ON THE ACTS OF THE APOSTLES 10.7.[19]

10:8 Sent to Joppa

NOT BY WORLDLY AUTHORITY. CHRYSOSTOM: "And when the angel that spoke to Cornelius had left, he called two of his household servants and a devout soldier of them that waited on him continually; and when he had declared all these things to them, he sent them to Joppa." Do you see that it is not without purpose that the writer says this? [It shows] that those also "who waited on him continually" were such as he. "And when he had declared the whole matter to them," observe the unassuming character of the man: for he does not say, "Call Peter to me," but in order also to induce him to come, he declared the whole matter. This was so ordered by Providence, for he did not choose to use the authority of his rank to fetch Peter to him; therefore "he declared the matter;" such was the moderation of the man. And yet no great notion was to be formed of one lodging with a tanner. HOMILIES ON THE ACTS OF THE APOSTLES 22.[20]

---

[17]1 Cor 3:17. [18]NPNF 1 2:520. [19]CS 117:96. [20]NPNF 1 11:142**.

10:9-16 THE VISION OF THE UNCLEAN ANIMALS MADE CLEAN

[9]*The next day, as they were on their journey and coming near the city, Peter went up on the housetop to pray, about the sixth hour. *[10]*And he became hungry and desired something to eat; but while they were preparing it, he fell into a trance *[11]*and saw the heaven opened, and something descending, like a great sheet, let down by four corners upon the earth. *[12]*In it were all kinds of animals and reptiles and birds of the air. *[13]*And there came a voice to him, "Rise, Peter; kill and eat."*

14But Peter said, "No, Lord; for I have never eaten anything that is common or unclean." 15And the voice came to him again a second time, "What God has cleansed, you must not call common." 16This happened three times, and the thing was taken up at once to heaven.

OVERVIEW: The early Christian authors delight in finding the universal in the particular, be it historical or spiritual. Following the pattern of rabbinic exegesis, they search for spiritual meaning in every word of the sacred text, and most particularly in sacred numbers. Peter's place of prayer teaches not merely about a suitable physical location of prayer (CHRYSOSTOM), but even about the transformative nature of prayer (GREGORY OF NYSSA), and that when we pray, we are in the house of the divine tanner (ORIGEN). The cloth is viewed as the whole world (ARATOR, GREGORY OF NYSSA) or evokes a covering for a banquet table and the baptismal garment (GREGORY OF NYSSA) or symbolizes the church (BEDE), while the animals are all the races of people who are acceptable to God (DIDYMUS, CYRIL OF ALEXANDRIA). The triple command and rebuke evokes the Trinity that cleanses through the trinitarian baptismal formula (GREGORY OF NYSSA, ORIGEN) or both the cloth and the triple rebuke together can express the call of all the nations (AUGUSTINE), whom Christ has cleansed by his blood (IRENAEUS). The time of this event, the sixth hour, likewise illustrates the universal call to faith in Christ, for we see in Peter the hunger and thirst of Christ breaking through (ARATOR). It is difficult at times to know whether the Fathers are allegorizing ("this stands for that") or whether they are merely making explicit what we intuitively understand to be the message of the vision and its role in preparing Peter to enter a Gentile's house and ultimately to baptize them. The primary concerns of modern interpreters are to determine the exact nature of the vision as something appropriate to the admission of the Gentiles to the church and to avoid typology or allegory in understanding Peter's vision. To secure that this vision was as Luke portrays it, they resort to theories that find it emerging out of Peter's physical (he is hungry, so he thinks of food) or local (he is looking out into the Mediterranean and sees the sails of passing ships) condition, or that the vision is suggestive and his response hints at his rejection of the Gentiles.

10:9 *Peter Went to the Housetop to Pray*

LEAVING BEHIND EARTHLY DESIRES. BEDE: This signifies that when the church has left behind earthly desires, it will have its way of life in heaven. COMMENTARY ON THE ACTS OF THE APOSTLES 10.9A.[1]

SEEKING THINGS ABOVE. ORIGEN: But the apostle Peter, when he was in Joppa and "wanted to pray, ascended into the upper part"[2] [of the house]. Immediately, I take these words to be not in vain, that he did not pray in lower places but "ascended to the higher." For the reason that so great an apostle chose to pray "in a higher place" is not superfluous, but rather, I believe, to show that Peter, because "he had died with Christ, was seeking the things that are above, where Christ is sitting at the right hand of God" and "not the things upon the earth."[3] "He ascended" there, to that "roof," to those heights about which the Lord also says, "Let the one who is on the roof not go down to remove anything from the house."[4] Then, so that you may know that we do not say these things suspiciously about Peter because "he ascends to the higher," you will confirm it from the following. It says, "He went up to the higher place to pray, and he saw the heavens open." Does it not yet appear to you that Peter had gone up "to the higher," not only in the body but also in mind and spirit? . . .

It is appropriate that Peter stays "at the house of a tanner," that one, perhaps, about whom Job

---

[1]CS 117:96. [2]Acts 10:9. [3]See Rom 6:8; Col 3:1-2. [4]Mt 24:17.

says, "you clothed me with skin and flesh."[5] Homilies on Leviticus 7.4.4-6.[6]

For the Salvation of the World. Bede: At the sixth hour, in the midst of his prayer, Peter became hungry—hungry indeed for the salvation of the world, which in the sixth age the Lord had come to seek and to save.[7] Christ himself also wished to indicate this when, at the same hour of the day, he became thirsty at the Samaritan well.[8] Commentary on the Acts of the Apostles 10.9b.[9]

The Hunger and Thirst of God. Arator: Peter proceeds to go to the high upper story as it is now the blazing middle of the day: the high place looking down upon the earth teaches Peter always to follow heavenly, not earthly things; the circuit of the sixth hour also discloses the [number of the] age in which Christ came into the world to dispense the wealth of him who saves. The number, with respect to days, manifests the pattern by which he earlier established the world which the Redeemer, coming in this very age, forbids to be crushed under the sway of sin. Finally it is said that these things also took place at the sixth [hour]; when the Master, weary from his journey [and] sitting at the mouth of the well, asks for a cup of water by means of the maid's vessel, he is about to provide his church's rest everywhere from the font.[10] In the [same] hour that Peter was hungry, his godly Master thirsted, always loving to add to his gifts. He who increased the honor of [Peter's] name enabled him at the same time to nourish faith. The earth will rejoice, filled by this hunger [of Peter's] which, richer than any gift, flows deliciously and, as it brings eternal feasts, leaves no one empty. On the Acts of the Apostles 1.[11]

10:10 Peter Fell into a Trance

A Spiritual View. Chrysostom: Observe how the Spirit connects the times: no sooner than this, and no later, he causes this to take place: "Peter about the sixth hour went up upon the housetop to pray"; that is, privately and quietly, as in an upper chamber. "And he became very hungry and would have eaten; but while they made ready, there fell upon him a trance." What does this expression, "trance," mean? There was presented to him in the ecstatic vision a kind of spiritual view; the soul, so to speak, was caused to be out of the body. Homilies on the Acts of the Apostles 22.[12]

Fasting and Prayer. Ambrose: And what is the purpose of Scripture in teaching us that Peter fasted and that the mystery regarding the baptism of the Gentiles was revealed to him when he was fasting and praying if not to show that the saints themselves, when they fast, become more illustrious? Moses received the law when he was fasting,[13] and so Peter, when he was fasting, was taught the grace of the New Testament. Daniel, too, by virtue of his fasting, stopped the jaws of the lions and saw the events of future times.[14] Or what salvation can we have unless by fasting we wipe out our sins, since Scripture says fasting and almsgiving purge away sin![15] Letter 59 (63).[16]

The Unity of Humanity. Didymus the Blind: Those[17] heretics who introduce [different] natures [into the argument that some are evil by nature] claim that those people who are called, because of their depravity, "dogs" and "pigs," are unable to have a share of salvation, and that it is to these that the Savior forbade the giving of what is holy, the divine pearls. They also say that these people, who are called ravenous wolves and foxes along with the names of all the other brute animals, are evil by nature. Their claim is to be refuted from the vision in this passage that none of them is evil by nature but by his intentions. For when God wanted to teach Peter

---

[5]Job 10:11. [6]FC 83:143-44. [7]Arator *De Actibus Apostolorum* 1 (CSEL 72:65). [8]Jn 4:5-7. [9]CS 117:96. [10]Jn 4:6-14. [11]OAA 51*. [12]NPNF 1 11:143**. [13]Ex 34:28. [14]Dan 6:10-8:27; 9:2-3. [15]Tob 12:8-9. [16]FC 26:326-27. [17]The Manichaeans or some Gnostic sect.

that no one must be rejected as impure and polluting, he sent down from heaven to earth by its four corners a certain vessel similar to a linen cloth, in which were all the species of brute animals, from which Peter was ordered to sacrifice and eat. And, since he still observed the Jewish laws and thought that what he was seeing was physical, he refused to eat, saying that he had never eaten anything impure and unclean. When he had spoken these words, he heard the divine oracle: "What God has purified do not call unclean." Drawing from this the conclusion that these things were said about the character of people, he said that God had shown him that no one is unclean by his nature. He therefore went without objection to the house of Cornelius, who desired to receive the fruit of the gospel teaching together with all his family. Thus it has been shown that four-footed animals, reptiles and birds, in reference to the different characters of human beings, are acceptable to God. And therefore, not because of an opposing nature has it been forbidden to throw pearls or what is holy to dogs and pigs, but because of the extremely evil character that can be left behind until no dog or pig exists anymore. Thus the Syrophoenician woman[18] was made from a dog into a human being, so that Jesus also granted her the bread of the children.

"He fell into a trance," Scripture says, "and saw the heavens opened." Those who love to be the disciples of delirious women—those from Phrygia[19]—claiming to be prophets, inspired by the Holy Spirit, do not understand their own utterances at the moment of prophecy. They believe they have proof for their error from this passage of Scripture that Peter fell into a trance. But let the foolish and truly insane know that this word[20] means many different things. For it indicates both the awe at something wondrous, and the action of going out of the tangible world to the spiritual, as well as the delirium of senses, which cannot be applied to Peter or the prophets, but the other meanings of this word can be. For without a doubt, Peter, in a trance, followed along

so as to proclaim what he saw and heard and what the signs, which he received, revealed. And you can certainly say the same about all the prophets who followed along with and saw the things that they reported to have seen. Indeed they were wise and learned from the same mouth what they proffered, for the Lord openly commanded them, after his resurrection, to instruct all the nations in his doctrine. So why did the apostles in Jerusalem, after hearing what had been done at the house of Cornelius, argue with Peter?

Clearly Peter, the all-holy leader of the apostles, needed the divine revelation concerning the nations. He did not know that there is no distinction between circumcised and uncircumcised with respect to the faith. Furthermore, he did not clearly know that the Lord called for the nations to be made into disciples apart from the visible worship according to the law until he revealed the mystery of God's unspoken will and revelation. And through the figure shown by the linen cloth and through the granting of the grace of the Holy Spirit in like manner to the nations according to faith, he made the case that in Christ there is no distinction between Jew and Gentile. CATENA ON THE ACTS OF THE APOSTLES 10.10.[21]

PETER INSTRUCTED TO BAPTIZE THE NATIONS. GREGORY OF NYSSA: I also know that the blessed Peter was both hungry and at the same time drunk in such a type of drunkenness as this.[22] Before his bodily meal was brought to him, when "he became hungry and wanted to take food," while his own were preparing the table for him, there came upon him a divine and sober drunkenness. Through this drunkenness he stood outside himself and saw the gospel linen sent down from above by four corners and holding the whole human race within itself in the myriad forms of birds and quadripeds and creeping things and beasts formed according to the cults, whose beastly

---

[18]Mk 7:25-30. [19]That is, the followers of Montanus. [20]That is, "trance," *ekstasis* in the Greek text. [21]CGPNT 3:175-77. [22]Song 5:1.

and irrational form the Word commanded Peter to sacrifice, in order that by being cleansed what was left would become edible. This cleansing is clear from the word of piety not being handed over naked, for the divine voice says not once that what God has made clean is not unclean, but this proclamation happens thrice, so that we may learn from the first voice that God the Father purifies and from the second that in the same way the God purifying is the only-begotten God and from the third that equally the God purifying all that is unclean is the Holy Spirit. HOMILIES ON THE SONG OF SONGS 10.[23]

10:11 *Like a Great Sheet*

A SYMBOL OF THE WHOLE WORLD. CHRYSOSTOM: What is this? It is a symbol of the whole world. The man was uncircumcised. He had nothing in common with the Jews—they would all accuse him as a transgressor: "You went into the house of uncircumcised men, and ate with them";[24] this was a thing altogether offensive to them. Observe then what is providentially managed. [Peter] himself also says, "I have never eaten," not being himself afraid—far be the thought from us—but it is so ordered by the Spirit, in order that he may have it to say in answer to those accusing him, that he did object: for it was altogether necessary for them to observe the law. He was in the act of being sent to the Gentiles: therefore that these also may not accuse him, see how many things are shaped [by the providence of God]. For, that it may not seem to be a mere fancy, "this was done three times." He said, "Not so, Lord, for I have never eaten anything common or unclean. And the voice came to him, 'What God has cleansed, you must not call common.'"[25] It seems indeed to be spoken to him, but the entire message is meant for the Jews. For if the teacher is rebuked, much more these also. This is what the linen sheet denotes. The earth, then, and the wild beasts in it, are the Gentiles. The command, "Kill and eat," denotes that he must go to them also; and that this is

done three times denotes triune baptism. HOMILIES ON THE ACTS OF THE APOSTLES 22.[26]

THE CHURCH INCORRUPTIBLE. BEDE: "This vessel signifies the church," endowed with an incorruptible faith, "for a moth, which corrupts other cloth, does not consume linen." Therefore, whoever wishes to be part of the mystery of the Catholic church "should root out from his heart the corruption of evil" thoughts, "and in this way he may be incorruptibly strengthened in faith, so that he will not be consumed by perverse thoughts, like moths, in his mind."[27] Alternatively, the moth is a heretic, wishing to corrupt the Lord's robe but unable to do so because the Lord does not permit it. This is also prefigured by the Lord's tunic, which the soldiers did not presume to tear.[28] COMMENTARY ON THE ACTS OF THE APOSTLES 10.11A.[29]

LOWERED BY ITS FOUR CORNERS. BEDE: The four corners by which the linen sheet hangs down designate the four regions of the world to which the church extends,[30] for it is "the city of our God on his holy mountain,"[31] spreading sounds of joy to every land. [That the sheet] is lowered from heaven indicates that [the church] will be preserved as well as increased only by the grace of the Holy Spirit coming upon it. Hence John says in the Apocalypse, "I saw the holy city, the new Jerusalem, coming down out of heaven from God."[32] Also, the four corners may be figures of the Evangelists, through whom the church is nourished and exalted with heavenly gifts. COMMENTARY ON THE ACTS OF THE APOSTLES 10.11B.[33]

THE UNITY OF THE EVANGELISTS. ARATOR: Enjoying his office, the celestial keeper of the keys sees heaven opened. From there an image of a ves-

---

[23]GNO 6:309. [24]Acts 11:3. [25]Cf. Acts 11:8. [26]NPNF 1 11:143-44**. [27]Augustine *Sermon* 149.5-6, 8-9 (PL 38:802-3). [28]Jn 19:23-24. [29]CS 117:96-97. [30]Augustine *Sermon* 149.5-6 (PL 38:802); Arator *De Actibus Apostolorum* 1 (CSEL 72:66). [31]Ps 48:1-2 (47:2 LXX, Vg). [32]Rev 21:2. [33]CS 117:97.

sel is let down, so that there might be a vision on earth that all things can be taken by the body of Peter, who makes into food for the church whatever he takes to be eaten. The vision is brought before him, let down by its four sides: it is one image of the church, which rises from the four parts of the world and spreads the eloquence of the same number of heralds [evangelists], keeping together every kind of bird and domestic beast, of wild animal and reptile: these [animals] are connected to humans on account of their merits and vices. It is therefore clear that the Creator bids the Gentiles to be poured into the bowels of the church, as he instructs [Peter], "Kill and eat, take away what they are and make them like yourself." He who is turned about is considered changed. Saul perished at length because Paul began to live. On the Acts of the Apostles 1.[34]

Called to the Corners of the Earth. Augustine: So, by the grace of the blessed Trinity, the whole earth from its four corners is called to the faith. According to this reckoning, when four is taken three times, the apostolic number, twelve, is consecrated as symbolizing the salvation of the whole world from its four corners in the grace of the Trinity. This number was also indicated by the vessel full of all kinds of animals, as it were of all nations, shown to Peter. For this vessel, let down from the heavens by the four corners, was lowered and taken up three different times, so that the four became twelve. On that account, perhaps, when twelve days had elapsed after the birth of Christ, the magi, the firstfruits of the Gentiles, came to see and to adore Christ and thus merited, not only to insure their own salvation, but also to prefigure that of all Gentiles. Sermon 203.3.[35]

10:12 Containing All Kinds of Animals

All the Animals Symbolize All the Nations. Bede: These animals are all the nations, unclean in their error but cleansed by a threefold lowering, that is, by the mystery of the holy Trinity in baptism. Leaving behind the form of humans, they take on the shapes of beasts and serpents. Hence, because of his treacherous and wicked character, it is said of Herod, "Go and say to that fox";[36] and the Pharisees are referred to as "a brood of vipers."[37] Of the lustful it is said, "Horses made mad for their mares";[38] of the shameless, "Do not give what is holy to dogs,"[39] and of the voluptuous, "Do not cast your pearls before swine."[40] Of those who are proud and at the same time treacherous it is said, "The foxes have dens and the birds of the air have nests."[41] And of all people in general it is said, "And man, when he was held in esteem" (that is, made in the image of God), "did not understand; he was like foolish cattle."[42] Solomon, however, shows man [humankind] as he truly is, that is, uncorrupted, when he says, "Fear God and keep his commandments, for this is all there is to man."[43] Commentary on the Acts of the Apostles 10.12.[44]

10:13 Kill and Eat

An Invitation to Christ. Bede: It [the voice that Peter heard] told him: Arise to make ready to preach the gospel. Kill in the Gentiles what they had been, and make [them] what you are; for whoever eats food lying outside of himself turns it into his own body. Therefore it [the voice] taught that the nations, which had formerly lain outside through their lack of belief, would, once their former life had been put to death, be incorporated within the society of the church. This Peter indicates, just as the apostle Paul had said of himself, "Through the law I have died to the law that I may live to God in Christ."[45] And again, "It is no longer I who live, but Christ lives in me."[46] Indeed, those who are taken in by heretics are as though devoured by death while they are still alive. Commentary on the Acts of the Apostles 10.13.[47]

---

[34]OAA 51*. [35]FC 38:77. [36]Lk 13:32. [37]Mt 3:7. [38]Jer 5:8. [39]Mt 7:6. [40]Mt 7:6. [41]Mt 8:20. [42]Ps 49:12 (48:13 LXX, Vg). [43]Eccles 12:13. [44]CS 117:97-98. [45]Gal 2:19. [46]Gal 2:20. [47]CS 117:98.

10:14 Not Eating Anything That Is Common

THE TIME OF CORRECTION. CYRIL OF ALEXANDRIA: The law is spiritual and does not provide an explanation that stops at physical meanings. For while the holy Peter still desired to follow the customs of the Jews, and since he was trying to advance towards better things, yet because he was terribly overcome by his reverence for these figures, God sent down from heaven the linen filled with animals, which . . . were condemned figuratively by the decrees of the law as impure. He then ordered Peter to kill and, if he should choose, to eat. But the disciple was reluctant and spoke as a Jew: "Absolutely not, Lord, because I have never eaten anything that is common and unclean, and no impure meat has entered my mouth." So the voice of the Lord came down, not only because God was rebuking him but also he was saying clearly, "What God has cleansed, you must not call common." Then [Peter] immediately understood that the time had come when the shadows had to be transformed into truth. And so the passage of the figures into truth fulfilled them and should not show, as some people think, that they were placed there without a reason. Doubtless, the lawgiver does not consider a pig, or the other animals, now clean, now unclean. No, for he knows that they are well-made, for it is written, "And God saw all that he had made, and behold all was very good, and he blessed it."[48] For to the extent that each thing of creation has come to be and to the extent that it has been made, it will only have, so I suppose, in itself what is good. So even though the pig cannot chew the cud, it is not unclean, but rather is perfectly edible, and what is proper to something's nature does not pollute it. As I have said, the law was figures and shadows that remained "until the time of correction."[49] AGAINST JULIAN 9.318-19.[50]

10:15 What God Has Cleansed

CLEANSED THROUGH THE BLOOD OF CHRIST. IRENAEUS: At that time Peter saw a vision in which a heavenly voice answered him, "What God has cleansed, you must not call common." For the God who had distinguished through the law the pure food from the impure, that same God had cleansed the nations through the blood of his Son, and that is the God whom Cornelius worshiped. CATENA ON THE ACTS OF THE APOSTLES 10.15.[51]

10:16 Three Times

A SYMBOL OF THE TRINITY. BEDE: For the mystery of the holy Trinity was to be preached throughout the four regions of the world by the twelve apostles.[52] It is for this reason that four linen cords were let down from heaven three times. Or, as it is interpreted by the blessed Ambrose,[53] "The third repetition of the figure expressed the operation of the Trinity. And so in the mysteries a threefold question is put and a threefold confirmation is proclaimed. Nor can anyone be purified except by a threefold confession. Hence in the gospel Peter himself was asked three times whether he loved the Lord,[54] so that his threefold response might loose the bonds with which he had bound himself by denying the Lord." These things shown to Peter were very appropriate to the situation, since the Gentile Cornelius appealed to him to show him that he should not hesitate to entrust the Christian faith to the uncircumcised. For he was from among those living things that were manifested in the evangelical vessel. Hence it was confirmed by the Holy Spirit that he should act in the same way. COMMENTARY ON THE ACTS OF THE APOSTLES 10.16A.[55]

THE CHURCH AS PILGRIM. BEDE: After the threefold lowering the vessel was taken up to heaven, since after the affairs of this world, through which the church travels as a pilgrim

---

[48]Gen 1:31. [49]Heb 9:10. [50]PG 76:989-92. [51]CGPNT 3:180. [52]Augustine Sermon 149.9-10 (PL 38:803). [53]Ambrose On the Holy Spirit 2.10.105 (CSEL 79:127). [54]Jn 21:15-17. [55]CS 117:99.

who has been cleansed by faith and baptism, there then follows a happy and everlasting heavenly dwelling. COMMENTARY ON THE ACTS OF THE APOSTLES 10.16B.[56]

A THREEFOLD REMINDER OF SALVATION. ARATOR: Three times the voice of the Lord resounds. This is repeated for [our] salvation: the Father and the Son and the Holy Spirit do this together. Arius, contentious against this faith, fell by denying that the One is in three Persons; Sabellius admitted the One, but [it is] the Father, he said, who then in turn is called Son and Holy Spirit, being the same, but so that the whole is the Father himself; and what the One greatest contains in its threefold order the former divides and the latter abandons. Both lie vanquished; for

the threefold command of the [Lord's] bidding indicates a single number in [three] Persons, with their own qualities, [and] by this command he calls the Gentiles: to believe this is right, if we wish to believe perfectly. ON THE ACTS OF THE APOSTLES I.[57]

CLEANSED THROUGH BAPTISM. ORIGEN: For the things made clean are made clean not by a single invocation nor by a second, but unless a third invocation is pronounced, no one is cleansed. For unless you were cleansed in the Father and the Son and the Holy Spirit, you could not be clean. HOMILIES ON LEVITICUS 7.4.5.[58]

---

[56]CS 117:99. [57]OAA 51-52. [58]FC 83:144.

10:17-23 PETER IS SUMMONED

[17]*Now while Peter was inwardly perplexed as to what the vision which he had seen might mean, behold, the men that were sent by Cornelius, having made inquiry for Simon's house, stood before the gate* [18]*and called out to ask whether Simon who was called Peter was lodging there.* [19]*And while Peter was pondering the vision, the Spirit said to him, "Behold, three men are looking for you.* [20]*Rise and go down, and accompany them without hesitation; for I have sent them."* [21]*And Peter went down to the men and said, "I am the one you are looking for; what is the reason for your coming?"* [22]*And they said, "Cornelius, a centurion, an upright and God-fearing man, who is well spoken of by the whole Jewish nation, was directed by a holy angel to send for you to come to his house, and to hear what you have to say."* [23]*So he called them in to be his guests.*

The next day he rose and went off with them, and some of the brothers from Joppa accompanied him.

OVERVIEW: That this event be understood as having a divine, and not a human initiative, demands that Peter, though he was not averse to Gentile converts, remain confused by the vision until the visitors should come. Peter's initial con-

fusion makes him a more credible witness before those who will object (CHRYSOSTOM), while his being called forth to a world as tumultuous as the sea, mirrors the call of the church to preach to a world in need of the gospel (BEDE). Here we see a difference in tone between the approach of Chrysostom, staying close to the events and making sense of what will happen later in the text, and Bede, drawing on the events as paradigms for understanding the nature of the church. Modern commentators see Peter's invitation to the guests as a significant shift from his recently expressed adherence to Jewish purity laws to a willingness to dine with Gentiles.

10:17 Peter Was Perplexed

GOD'S USE OF CONFUSION. CHRYSOSTOM: At the right time, the men come who resolve his confusion. When Christ allowed Joseph to be thrown into confusion, then too, he sent an archangel to him.[1] Here Peter's soul, having been confused, calmly accepts the resolution . . . when they inquire whether he is staying there. CATENA ON THE ACTS OF THE APOSTLES 10.17.[2]

10:19 The Spirit Speaks to Peter

THE AUTHORITY OF THE SPIRIT. CHRYSOSTOM: While Peter thought on the vision, the Spirit said to him, "Behold, three men are looking for you. Rise and go down, and accompany them without hesitation; for I have sent them." And this again is a plea for Peter not to doubt in response to the visitors. He was instructed to doubt nothing. "For I," he says, "have sent them." Great is the authority of the Spirit! What God does is what the Spirit is said to do. Not so the angel, but having first said, "Your prayers and your alms have ascended as a memorial before God," to show that he is sent from God. Then the angel adds, "And now send men," etc.; the Spirit, however, says, "For I have sent them." HOMILIES ON THE ACTS OF THE APOSTLES 22.[3]

10:20 Go Without Hesitation

RETURN TO THE ACTIVE LIFE. BEDE: He was ordered to descend from the roof and to go to preach in order to show that the church should not only watch for the Lord by climbing to the heights, but, returning to the active life as if rising from its bed, it should preach this same Lord to all the lowliest and to those still situated outside, as it were, but [who are] nevertheless knocking at the door of Simon, that is, at the door of obedience.[4] As the Lord said, "You will see heaven opened and the angels of God ascending and descending upon the Son of man."[5] It is well that it is mentioned that Peter's house was situated by the seashore,[6] for the sea designates the wave-tossed tumults and frenzies of the world, where greedy people pursue and devour each other like voracious fish. The saints' "way of life is in heaven,"[7] and although "the earthly house in which they dwell may be destroyed, they have a building from God, an eternal house in heaven not made by human hands."[8] COMMENTARY ON THE ACTS OF THE APOSTLES 10.20.[9]

10:21 Peter Went to the Men

PARTIAL PROPHECY OF THE SPIRIT. BEDE: "The Spirit told the soldiers to visit [Peter], and concerning the cause of their coming he [the Spirit] was silent," because in order to preserve the humility of the human mind, "at times the spirit of prophecy partly touches the soul and partly does not."[10] COMMENTARY ON THE ACTS OF THE APOSTLES 10.21.[11]

---

[1]See Mt 2:13. [2]CGPNT 3:180. [3]NPNF 1 11:144**. [4]Jerome *On Hebrew Names* (CCL 72:148). [5]Jn 1:51. [6]Acts 10:6. [7]Phil 3:20. [8]2 Cor 5:1. [9]CS 117:99-100. [10]Gregory the Great *Homilies on Ezekiel* 1.1.11-12 (CCL 142:10). [11]CS 117:100.

10:24-29 PETER MEETS CORNELIUS

[24]*And on the following day they entered Caesarea. Cornelius was expecting them and had called together his kinsmen and close friends.* [25]*When Peter entered, Cornelius met him and fell down at his feet and worshiped him.* [26]*But Peter lifted him up, saying, "Stand up; I too am a man."* [27]*And as he talked with him, he went in and found many persons gathered;* [28]*and he said to them, "You yourselves know how unlawful it is for a Jew to associate with or to visit any one of another nation; but God has shown me that I should not call any man common or unclean.* [29]*So when I was sent for, I came without objection. I ask then why you sent for me."*

OVERVIEW: The meeting of Cornelius and Peter displays the generosity and persuasive goodness of the former among his family and friends (CHRYSOSTOM). His homage to Peter makes known the humility of his heart (BEDE), and Peter's raising of him foreshadows his and everyone's equality in the faith (BEDE, ARATOR), especially those the world has cast out (AMMONIUS).

10:24 Cornelius Called His Kinsmen

THE PART OF A GOOD FRIEND. CHRYSOSTOM: This is the part of a friend, this the part of a devout person, that where such blessings are concerned, he takes care that his near friends shall be made partakers of all. Of course [his "near" friends], those in whom he had ever full confidence; fearing, with such an interest at stake, to entrust the matter to others. In my opinion, it was by Cornelius himself that both friends and kinsmen had been brought to a better mind. HOMILIES ON THE ACTS OF THE APOSTLES 23.[1]

10:25 Cornelius Worshiped Peter

THE HUMILITY OF FAITH MAKES US EQUALS. BEDE: By the posture of his body Cornelius demonstrated what devotion he had within his heart. He came as a pupil to meet his teacher, and full of zeal, with pure heart, attentive ears and eager

desire, he received the word of faith. Now one who is slowly dragged to belief is as though raised up from a prone position by his teacher. However, one who, out of shame for the stains of life, shows signs of humility and of shame at once by falling prostrate on his face justly deserves to be raised up by his master. COMMENTARY ON THE ACTS OF THE APOSTLES 10.25.[2]

10:26 I Too Am a Man

AS IN BAPTISM, A FREE GIFT. ARATOR: [Peter] does not permit [Cornelius] to throw himself at his feet with bent knee; accustomed to giving gifts freely, he prevents a gesture of respect. Hence you, a new world, raise your head, you who had been struck down by the tooth of your ancient parent, and the font gives back a birthday to you; born again, do not press down your necks with your own sins, now that they are free from another's. ON THE ACTS OF THE APOSTLES 1.[3]

A GOSPEL OF EQUALITY. AMMONIUS: If such a man as Peter did not allow him to kneel down before him but rather made himself an equal of Cornelius, and he said these things to one who was still a Gentile, what must we say about all other people? CATENA ON THE ACTS OF THE APOSTLES 10.26-27.[4]

---

[1]NPNF 1 11:148**. [2]CS 117:100-101. [3]OAA 52. [4]CGPNT 3:183.

10:28 Calling No One Common or Unclean

SENT TO THE OUTCASTS. AMMONIUS: We must note that God himself ordered the Christian people not to call anyone common or unclean but to associate with them[5] as those who hope most of

all for faith in Christ. CATENA ON THE ACTS OF THE APOSTLES 10.28.[6]

---

[5]Those so-called unclean ones. [6]CGPNT 3:184. The syntax of this passage is unclear; in the Greek the antecedent of the final appositional clause ("as ones hoping…") is unclear, but the only plural antecedent is "them."

10:30-33 CORNELIUS RECOUNTS HIS VISION

[30]*And Cornelius said, "Four days ago, about this hour, I was keeping the ninth hour of prayer in my house; and behold, a man stood before me in bright apparel,* [31]*saying, 'Cornelius, your prayer has been heard and your alms have been remembered before God.* [32]*Send therefore to Joppa and ask for Simon who is called Peter; he is lodging in the house of Simon, a tanner, by the seaside.'* [33]*So I sent to you at once, and you have been kind enough to come. Now therefore we are all here present in the sight of God, to hear all that you have been commanded by the Lord."*

OVERVIEW: All grace flows from the cross, and inasmuch as Cornelius symbolizes the nations, so too does the time of his prayer show the efficacy of Christ's intercessory prayer upon the cross (BEDE). This message of salvation, however, comes through men and women in time, so in receiving God's messengers, we receive God (CHRYSOSTOM).

10:30 A Man in Bright Clothing

HE PERSEVERED IN PRAYER. BEDE: In the Greek, and in some Latin manuscripts, it is written thus: "Three days ago at this very hour I was fasting and worshiping from the sixth hour to the ninth, and behold, a man," and so forth. And it was very fitting that his prayer was heard, since he persevered in the earnestness of his prayer for three hours, extending it from the sixth hour to

the ninth—the time at which the Lord himself, whom he entreated, was praying, with his hands stretched out upon the cross, for the salvation of the whole world.[1] COMMENTARY ON THE ACTS OF THE APOSTLES 10.30.[2]

10:33 Present in the Sight of God

LISTEN TO GOD'S SERVANTS. CHRYSOSTOM: But Cornelius says, "We are present before God to hear all things that are commanded you of the Lord"; not "before man" but "before God." This is the way one ought to attend to God's servants. Do you see his awakened mind? Do you see how worthy he was of all these things? HOMILIES ON THE ACTS OF THE APOSTLES 23.[3]

---

[1]Mt 27:45-46. [2]CS 117:101. [3]NPNF 1 11:150**.

10:34-43 PETER PREACHES TO CORNELIUS AND HIS HOUSEHOLD

³⁴And Peter opened his mouth and said: "Truly I perceive that God shows no partiality, ³⁵but in every nation any one who fears him and does what is right is acceptable to him. ³⁶You know the word which he sent to Israel, preaching good news of peace by Jesus Christ (he is Lord of all), ³⁷the word which was proclaimed throughout all Judea, beginning from Galilee after the baptism which John preached: ³⁸how God anointed Jesus of Nazareth with the Holy Spirit and with power; how he went about doing good and healing all that were oppressed by the devil, for God was with him. ³⁹And we are witnesses to all that he did both in the country of the Jews and in Jerusalem. They put him to death by hanging him on a tree; ⁴⁰but God raised him on the third day and made him manifest; ⁴¹not to all the people but to us who were chosen by God as witnesses, who ate and drank with him after he rose from the dead. ⁴²And he commanded us to preach to the people, and to testify that he is the one ordained by God to be judge of the living and the dead. ⁴³To him all the prophets bear witness that every one who believes in him receives forgiveness of sins through his name."

OVERVIEW: That God is no respecter of persons does not mean that all prayers are answered as we would like (AMBROSE). Nonetheless, God in an abundance of mercy calls even sinners, and so there is no surprise that he pours out greater blessings on those who strive to live justly and to know the truth. God answers our ultimate desires for this truth, even when our passion for it, like Saul's, leads us astray (CHRYSOSTOM). By coming to a full and complete comprehension of the truth of God in Christ, Cornelius, in living as a God-fearer, stands as testimony to the truth of the Old Covenant (IRENAEUS), and God's invitation through Peter to the Gentiles only affirms the Jews' position of primacy in the order of salvation (CHRYSOSTOM). But this reconciliation of peace between God and creation in the Spirit is for all, and Christ prefigured our access to it in his humble submission to baptism at the hands of John (BEDE), a baptism that shows forth the unity of the Trinity (GREGORY OF NYSSA, BASIL) and teaches us the truth of who God is and who we are in Christ (BASIL). Our access to this salvation comes

through his sin-and-death-destroying incarnation, crucifixion, death and resurrection in which our souls participate through a faith in Christ, the anointed One (GREGORY OF NYSSA),[1] a faith that is called forth by the various proofs that he gave to the apostles (THEODORET, SEVERUS) and to which all the prophets bear witness (DIDYMUS). Modern commentators are puzzled by Peter's words that imply knowledge of Jesus to some degree. Chrysostom makes a distinction between knowing about Jesus (which is how he understands Peter's words) and knowing Jesus. For the moderns, the assumption that those in Caesarea would have known something of Jesus is a saying hard to bear. Fitzmyer claims these words "are to be understood as addressed to the Christian reader of Acts, not to Cornelius" (464). The contrast with the Fathers shows up the oddity of this statement in that they have the confidence to take everything as addressed to their current situation, even someone as

---

[1]For Gregory of Nyssa, our bodies participate by receiving the eucharist. See his *Great Catechetical Oration* 37.

historically grounded as Chrysostom. Another enlightening point of contrast with the Fathers occurs at verse 40. Fitzmyer makes a distinction between when Jesus was raised and when he was known to have risen: "Peter dates the resurrection of Christ on the 'third day' after his death. Actually no one knows when the 'resurrection' [sic] occurred. The tomb in which Jesus was buried was discovered on the 'third day' after his death, when one counts both ends (day of death, sabbath, day after sabbath)" (465). Fitzmyer finds proof for this distinction in Luke 23:43, where Jesus says to the penitent thief, "Today you shall be with me in paradise," and he concludes " 'today' must refer to the day of Jesus' death" (ibid). By use of the familiar dichotomy of body and soul, however, Gregory of Nyssa is able to take account of both passages without denying what is here stated so plainly: God raised him on the third day.[2] Other commentators ponder the gradual transformation of Peter: did his vision or God's association, through his angel, with Cornelius, lead Peter to perceive that God shows no partiality? They conclude that Luke may well have both factors in mind. This attempt, as it were, to inhabit the text, is not found much among the ancients, except for Chrysostom. Other commentators see Peter here coming to a full realization of the import of having been called from Caesarea.

10:34 No Partiality

GOD ANSWERS OUR PRAYERS FREELY. AMBROSE: Even if God is merciful, were he always granting the prayers of all he would seem no longer to act freely, but, as it were, like someone under compulsion. Then, since all ask, if he were to hear all, no one would die. How many things do you not ask for daily? Must God's design be destroyed because of you? When you know that a petition cannot always be granted, why do you grieve that sometimes your petition is not obtained? ON HIS BROTHER SATYRUS 1.65.[3]

THOSE WHO CHOOSE THE WAY OF VIRTUE.

CHRYSOSTOM: "God [you remember] is no respecter of person." Rather, if he finds even one person in such a multitude doing what pleases him, far from scorning him he regales him with his particular providence and shows the greater care for him the more closely he has chosen the way of virtue at a time when there are others who are bent on evil. HOMILIES ON GENESIS 22.18.[4]

10:35 Anyone Who Does What Is Right

GOD DOES NOT OVERLOOK THE RIGHTEOUS. CHRYSOSTOM: What then? Was he "a respecter of persons" beforetime? God forbid! For beforetime likewise it was just the same: "anyone who fears him and does what is right is acceptable to him." As when Paul says, "When Gentiles who have not the law do by nature what the law requires,"[5] and "who fears him and does what is right," he assumes both doctrine and manner of life "is acceptable to him." For, if he did not overlook the magi, nor the Ethiopian, nor the thief nor the harlot, much more shall he not overlook those who do what is right. "What say you then to this, that there are reasonable and civilized people, and yet they are not willing to believe?" There you yourself have named the cause: they do not want to believe. But besides the reasonable person that he speaks of here, is not this sort of person the one "that works righteousness," that is, the one who in all points is virtuous and irreproachable when he has the fear of God as he ought to have it? But whether a person is such, God only knows. See how this man was acceptable. See how, as soon as he heard, he was persuaded. "And now," you say, "if an angel were to come, anyone, no matter who he may be, would believe." But the signs of today are much greater than these here, and many still do not believe. HOMILIES ON THE ACTS OF THE APOSTLES 23.[6]

---

[2]For further comparison between this passage from Gregory and Fitzmyer's position, see Joseph Fitzmyer, *Luke the Theologian: Aspects of His Teaching* (Mahwah, N.J.: Paulist Press, 1989), 203-33. [3]FC 22:188. [4]FC 82:82. [5]Rom 2:14. [6]NPNF 1 11:151**.

GOD REWARDS THE PASSIONATE HEART.

CHRYSOSTOM: That is, God calls and attracts him to the truth. Can you see Paul? He was more vehement than any one in warring and persecuting. Yet because he led an irreproachable life and did these things not through human passion, he was both received and reached a mark beyond all. HOMILIES ON 1 CORINTHIANS 8.4.[7]

CORNELIUS FEARED GOD.

IRENAEUS: He thus clearly indicates, that he whom Cornelius had previously feared as God, of whom he had heard through the law and the prophets, for whose sake also he used to give alms, is, in truth, God. The knowledge of the Son was, however, lacking to him. AGAINST HERESIES 3.12.7.[8]

10:36 The Word Sent to Israel: Peace

THE JEWS NOT CAST OFF. CHRYSOSTOM: That [the Jews] may not seem to be in the condition of persons cast off he adds, "You know the word that he sent to Israel, preaching good news of peace by Jesus Christ (he is Lord of all)." He says this for the sake of the Jews, that he may persuade them also. This is why he forces Cornelius to speak. He says that he "is Lord of all." But observe at the very outset, "The word," he says, "which he sent to Israel"; he gives them the preeminence. Then [Peter] adduces these Gentiles themselves as witnesses, "You know," says he, "the word which was proclaimed throughout all Judea, beginning from Galilee after the baptism which John preached, how God anointed Jesus of Nazareth with the Holy Spirit and with power; how he went about doing good and healing all that were oppressed by the devil, for God was with him." He does not mean, You know Jesus, for they did not know him, but he speaks of the things done by him. HOMILIES ON THE ACTS OF THE APOSTLES 23.[9]

ALL MAY RECEIVE FORGIVENESS OF SINS.

BEDE: He says, "It is clear that God is no respecter of persons, for he sent his only begotten Son, who is the Lord and creator of all, to make peace with the human race. In his name, as the prophets bore witness, not only the Jews, but all who believe, may receive forgiveness of sins." COMMENTARY ON THE ACTS OF THE APOSTLES 10.36.[10]

10:38 God Anointed Jesus of Nazareth

PROOF FROM THE GOOD THAT HE DID. CHRYSOSTOM: First he discourses of Jesus' being Lord and in exceeding elevated terms, seeing he had to deal with a soul more than commonly elevated and that took all in with ardor. Then he proves how he was Lord of all, from the things that he achieved "throughout all Judea." For, he says, you know "the word that was proclaimed throughout all Judea," and, what is the wonderful part of it, "beginning from Galilee after the baptism that John preached: how God anointed Jesus of Nazareth with the Holy Spirit and with power; how he went about doing good and healing all who were oppressed by the devil, for God was with him. First he speaks of his success, and then again [Peter] says concerning him, "Jesus of Nazareth." Why, what a stumbling block, this birthplace! "How God anointed him with the Holy Spirit and with power." Then again the proof—how does that appear?—from the good that he did. "Who went about doing good, and healing all who were oppressed of the devil," and the greatness of the power shown when he overcomes the devil; and the cause, "Because God was with him." HOMILIES ON THE ACTS OF THE APOSTLES 23.[11]

ANOINTED WITH THE SPIRIT AND WITH POWER. BEDE: Another text says, "Inasmuch as God anointed him." John preached Jesus inasmuch as God anointed him with the Holy Spirit at the time when he said, "He will baptize you with the Holy Spirit";[12] and again, "I saw the

---

[7]NPNF 1 12:45**. [8]ANF 1:432. [9]NPNF 1 11:150**. [10]CS 117:101. [11]NPNF 1 11:151-52**. [12]Mt 3:11.

Spirit descending as a dove upon him."[13] Jesus was anointed "not with oil but with the gift of grace, which is signified by the visible oil with which the church anoints those who are baptized. Yet, Christ was not anointed with the Holy Spirit at the time when it descended as a dove upon him at his baptism, for at that time he condescended to prefigure his body, that is, his church, in which the baptized principally receive the Holy Spirit. Rather, he must be understood to have been anointed with a mystical and invisible anointing when the Word of God was made flesh, that is, when human nature, without any preceding merits from good works, was joined to God the Word in the womb of the Virgin, so as to become one person with him. Because of this we confess that he was born of the Holy Spirit and of the Virgin Mary."[14] Commentary on the Acts of the Apostles 10.38a.[15]

The Holy Spirit Shares in His Kingship.

Gregory of Nyssa: But the Son, having all things which are the Father's, is himself proclaimed a king by holy Scripture. Now the divine Scripture says that the Holy Spirit is the unction of the Only Begotten, interpreting the dignity of the Spirit by a transference of the terms commonly used in this world. For as, in ancient days, in those who were advanced to kingship, the token of this dignity was the unction that was applied to them, and when this took place there was thenceforth a change from private and humble estate to the superiority of rule, and he who was deemed worthy of this grace received after his anointing another name, being called, instead of an ordinary man, the Anointed of the Lord. For this reason, that the dignity of the Holy Spirit might be more clearly shown to humankind, he was called by the Scripture "the sign of the kingdom" and "Unction," whereby we are taught that the Holy Spirit shares in the glory and kingdom of the only begotten Son of God. For as in Israel it was not permitted to enter upon the kingdom without the unction being previously given, so the word, by a transference of the

terms in use among ourselves, indicates the equality of power, showing that not even the kingdom of the Son is received without the dignity of the Holy Spirit. And for this reason he is properly called Christ, since this name gives the proof of his inseparable and indivisible conjunction with the Holy Spirit. If, then, the only-begotten God is the Anointed, and the Holy Spirit is his Unction, and the appellation of Anointed points to the kingly authority, and the anointing is the token of his kingship, then the Holy Spirit shares also in his dignity. If, therefore, they say that the attribute of Godhead signifies dignity and the Holy Spirit is shown to share in this last quality, it follows that he who partakes in the dignity will also partake in the name that represents it. On the Holy Trinity.[16]

Baptized in the Name of the Trinity.

Basil the Great: Do not be misled because the apostle frequently omits the names of the Father and the Holy Spirit when he speaks of baptism. Do not imagine because of this that the invocation of their names has been omitted. St. Paul says, "As many of you as were baptized into Christ have put on Christ"[17] and . . . "all of us who have been baptized into Christ Jesus were baptized into his death."[18] To address Christ in this way is a complete profession of faith, because it clearly reveals that God anoints the Son (the anointed One) with the unction of the Spirit. We can learn this from Peter's words in Acts, "God anointed Jesus of Nazareth with the Holy Spirit,"[19] or from Isaiah, "The Spirit of the Lord God is upon me, because the Lord has anointed me,"[20] or from the Psalms, "Therefore God, your God has anointed you with the oil of gladness above your fellows."[21] But the Scripture also speaks of baptism in the context of the Spirit alone, for example, "For by one Spirit we are all baptized into one body."[22] There are other pas-

---

[13]Jn 1:32. [14]Augustine On the Trinity 15.26 (CCL 50A:526-27). [15]CS 117:102. [16]NPNF 2 5:329-30. [17]Gal 3:27. [18]Rom 6:3. [19]Acts 10.38. [20]Is 61:1. [21]Ps 45:7 (44:8 LXX). [22]1 Cor 12:13.

sages that agree with this: "You shall be baptized with the Holy Spirit,"[23] and "He will baptize you with the Holy Spirit."[24] No one would claim that on the basis of these passages the invocation of the Spirit's name alone makes baptism complete and perfect. ON THE SPIRIT 12.28.[25]

SANCTIFIED BY THE SPIRIT. PSEUDO-BASIL: He is Christ [Anointed] because of the Spirit and the anointing that is in the Spirit. Therefore, the anointing of the Lord is not of something foreign to the divinity, nor is the name Christ nor those called Christian after him. For, in truth, someone would lament if the name of our salvation both had its source in a creature and were derived from a creature and if we had our adoption through a slave. A creature does not make a creature holy, but all creation[26] is made holy by the sole holy one who says concerning himself, "I sanctify myself."[27] But through the Spirit he sanctifies. . . . The Spirit, of course, is not a creature but the mark of the sanctity of God and the fountain of holiness for all. In the holiness of the Spirit were we called, as the apostle teaches.[28] This renews us and shows us once again to be the images of God, and through the bath of rebirth and renewal of the Holy Spirit we are made adopted sons [children] of God. AGAINST EUNOMIUS 5.[29]

10:40 Raised on the Third Day

BY DEATH HE CONQUERED THE DEATH OF HUMANITY. GREGORY OF NYSSA: Therefore, since it was necessary that the good Shepherd lay down his life on behalf of the sheep, so that through his own death he might destroy death, the captain of our salvation, by bringing death to pass, becomes a composite in his human nature, both as a priest[30] and a lamb in the ability to receive a share of suffering. For since death is nothing but the dissolution of both soul and body, the one who united himself to both, I mean to both soul and to body, is separated from neither—"incapable of repentance," as the apostle says, "are the graces of God."[31] So having distrib-

uted himself to both body and soul, on the one hand he opens paradise to the thief through his soul, and through his body he establishes the work of destruction. Now this is death's obliteration, that the destruction annihilated in the life-giving nature is made impotent, and this, which happens in regard to these [body and soul] becomes a shared benefit and grace of our nature. In this way, he who is in both, through his resurrection fits together all that was separate, he who, according to his power, gives his body to the heart of the earth, as it has been written,[32] while he puts his soul away from himself, saying, on the one hand, to his father, "Into your hands I hand over my spirit,"[33] and on the other, to the thief, "Today you will be with me in paradise."[34] . . . So in this way he comes both to be in death and not to be mastered by death. . . . The proof . . . is the operation that worked incorruption with regard to the body and a passing over into paradise with regard to the soul. . . . He[35] demonstrates this who says that "God raised him from the dead."[36] For not as Lazarus or anyone else of those who have returned to life by the power of another is he brought back to life—so clear is it how the resurrection of the Lord is to be conceived. Rather the Only Begotten himself raises up the person who was mixed together with himself, having both separated the soul from the body and having reunited both, and in this way a common salvation of human nature is effected. AGAINST APOLLINARIS.[37]

10:41 Those Who Were Chosen

PROOF OF THE RESURRECTION. THEODORET OF CYR: For since eating is proper to them that live this present life, of necessity the Lord by means of eating and drinking proved the resurrection of the flesh to those who did not acknowledge it to

---

[23]Acts 1:5. [24]Lk 3:16. [25]*OHS* 48-49**. [26]See Col 1:16. [27]Jn 17:19. [28]2 Thess 2:13. [29]PG 29:725-27. [30]He brings about his own death and so is both priest and victim. [31]Rom 11:29 (all translations from Scripture are the editor's). [32]Mt 12:40. [33]Lk 23:46. [34]Lk 23:43. [35]Paul. [36]Acts 13:30. [37]GNO 3.1.152.30-154.14.

be real. This same course he pursued in the case of Lazarus and of Jairus's daughter. For when he had raised up the latter he ordered that something should be given her to eat,[38] and he made Lazarus sit with him at the table[39] and so showed the reality of the rising again. DIALOGUE 2.[40]

BELIEVING IN CHRIST IS EATING WITH CHRIST. SEVERUS OF ANTIOCH: Now, certainly, he shared a new food, one not in accord with the prior order in which he had eaten and drunk with them before the resurrection. For at that time, having been made similar to us in everything except for sin, he ate and drank just as we do. Moreover, clothing himself in the flesh, he willingly sought the benefit of nourishment, and so he willingly assimilated himself to the experience of hunger. After the resurrection he did not need to eat or drink anymore, but only as one believed in by and as one giving evidence to his intimate disciples. Another reason [he ate and drank was that] those who later on were to believe in the true nature of the body—that body that suffered voluntarily and arose in a divine way (totally driv-

ing away the idea of an accursed apparition and phantasm)—needed these actions. After the resurrection, he named food and drink for himself together with his disciples, not according to his previous practice but something new. CATENA ON THE ACTS OF THE APOSTLES 10.42.[41]

10:43 All the Prophets Bear Witness

THE PROPHETS BEAR WITNESS TO FORGIVENESS IN CHRIST. DIDYMUS THE BLIND: If one repents from the evil things he has done and believes in the name of the Lord, he receives absolution from the sins that he has sincerely recognized. All the prophets, whose teaching is brought to the people of the Jews, have spoken according to their trust and faith in their Father. Therefore it will be universally admitted that all the prophets testify that the absolution from sin is given to those who believe in the Lord. CATENA ON THE ACTS OF THE APOSTLES 10.43.[42]

---

[38]Mk 5:43. [39]Jn 12:2. [40]NPNF 2 3:198*. [41]CGPNT 3:188. [42]CGPNT 3:189.

10:44-48 THE HOLY SPIRIT POURED OUT ON THE GENTILES

[44]*While Peter was still saying this, the Holy Spirit fell on all who heard the word.* [45]*And the believers from among the circumcised who came with Peter were amazed, because the gift of the Holy Spirit had been poured out even on the Gentiles.* [46]*For they heard them speaking in tongues and extolling God. Then Peter declared,* [47]*"Can any one forbid water for baptizing these people who have received the Holy Spirit just as we have?"* [48]*And he commanded them to be baptized in the name of Jesus Christ. Then they asked him to remain for some days.*

OVERVIEW: The Spirit takes the initiative in bringing the Gentiles into the church in order to give Peter, who was open to their admission, the

ground of obedience on which to defend himself (CHRYSOSTOM, BEDE, IRENAEUS). The apparent singularity of this action is only a more clearly divine intervention that occurs in the preaching of the gospel as a whole (ORIGEN). In this event, we see how our barriers can become obstacles to the spread of the gospel and how God knocks these down as dramatically as might be necessary (SEVERUS). Peter's actions show that there is a mysterious necessity to baptism by water (CHRYSOSTOM, CYRIL OF JERUSALEM). Modern commentators often point out that asking how they received the Spirit without having been baptized is to miss the point of the Lukan story. Though they have already received the Spirit, Gentiles are still baptized because that is part of the process by which one becomes a Christian. Other commentators stress that Luke wants to emphasize that, from beginning to end in this story, God takes the initiative. They discuss how Luke portrays and perhaps would have understood baptism and the event here since the relation between baptism and the Holy Spirit is portrayed differently. Here, baptism is ordered after the coming of the Spirit. In Acts 2:38 the Spirit seems called down as a consequence of baptism. In Acts 8:16 the baptism is not followed by the Spirit's descent, which happens only when Peter and John lay their hands on the baptized. Baptism and the laying on of hands precede the gift of the Spirit in Acts 19:5-6. So while the event's order in Caesarea is sometimes said to be exceptional, in fact Luke may not have considered that there was a fixed order.[1]

10:44 The Holy Spirit Descends on All

PETER PRESENT TO BE TAUGHT. CHRYSOSTOM: Observe God's providential management. He does not suffer the speech to be finished or the baptism to take place upon a command of Peter, but, when he has made it evident how admirable their state of mind is, and a beginning is made of the work of teaching and they have believed that assuredly baptism is the remission of sins, then the Spirit immediately comes upon them. Now this is done by God's so disposing it as to provide for Peter a mighty ground of justification.

And it is not simply that the Spirit came upon them, but "they spoke with tongues," which was the thing that astonished those who had come together. They altogether disliked the matter, wherefore it is that the whole is of God; and as for Peter, it may almost be said, that he is present only to be taught (with them) the lesson, that they must take the Gentiles in hand and that they themselves are the persons by whom this must be done. HOMILIES ON THE ACTS OF THE APOSTLES 24.[2]

THE HOLY SPIRIT TESTIFIED. BEDE: Lest there might be any hesitation about conferring baptism upon the Gentiles, support was supplied by the testimony of the Holy Spirit, who in an unexpected sequence of events acted in advance of the waters of the baptismal bath, which are ordinarily the means of sanctification. This is reported to have happened once in testimony to the faith of the Gentiles but never in the case of the Jews. COMMENTARY ON THE ACTS OF THE APOSTLES 10.44.[3]

THE OUTPOURING OF THE HOLY SPIRIT. ORIGEN: Do you want to know that it is not just Jesus alone in his speaking who transmits the Holy Spirit to his hearers, but that everyone who speaks God's word in his name actually hands on the Spirit of God to those who listen? See then, how in the Acts of the Apostles, when Peter is speaking to Cornelius, Cornelius himself and those with him were filled with the Holy Spirit. Hence, if you speak God's word and do so faithfully with a pure conscience, it can come about that while you are speaking the fire of the Holy Spirit will inflame the hearts of your hearers and immediately make them warm and eager to carry out all you are teaching in order to implement what they have learned. COMMENTARY ON ROMANS 6.13.[4]

---

[1]Three commentators who could be consulted on these points are Fitzmyer, Barrett and Gaventa. [2]NPNF 1 11:155**. [3]CS 117:103. [4]OSF 154.

10:45 Even on the Gentiles

DESTROYING THE DIVIDING WALL. CHRYSOSTOM: Gentiles? What Gentiles now? They were no longer Gentiles, the Truth having come. It is nothing wonderful, he says, if before the act of baptism they received the Spirit: in our own case this same happened. Peter shows that not as the rest were they baptized, but in a much better way. This is the reason why the event takes place in this manner, that they [his opponents] may have nothing to say but even in this way may account them [the Gentiles] equal with themselves [the Jews]. HOMILIES ON THE ACTS OF THE APOSTLES 24.[5]

10:46 Speaking in Tongues

GOD SURPRISES US TO THE DEGREE NECESSARY. SEVERUS OF ANTIOCH: At the beginning of the preaching, when the apostles announced the gospel, those who received holy baptism both spoke with tongues and prophesied in order to prove that they had received the Holy Spirit. When unbelief was at its climax, then, as was necessary, the miracles flourished. Yet, with the faith spread far and wide, there is no need of signs, for what comes from God is not for show but for the salvation, healing and benefit of those who receive. CATENA ON THE ACTS OF THE APOSTLES 10.44.[6]

10:47 Can Anyone Forbid Water?

PETER SHOWS HIS HAND. CHRYSOSTOM: Peter seizes his advantage, and notice the argument he makes of it: "Can anyone forbid water for baptizing these people who have received the Holy Spirit just as we have?" Mark the conclusion to which he brings it; how he has been travailing to bring this forth. So entirely was he of this mind! "Can anyone," he asks, "forbid water?" It is the language, we may almost say, of one triumphantly pressing his advantage against such as would forbid, such as should say that this ought not to be.

The whole thing, he says, is complete, the most essential part of the business, the baptism with which we were baptized. "And he commanded them to be baptized in the name of Jesus Christ." After he has cleared himself, then, and not before, he commands them to be baptized: teaching them by the facts themselves. HOMILIES ON THE ACTS OF THE APOSTLES 24.[7]

PETER OBEDIENT TO THE SPIRIT. IRENAEUS: Through these words[8] he shows that he would have never gone to them if he had not been ordered to do so. Likewise, he would have never baptized them so unscrupulously if he had not heard them prophesy when the Holy Spirit rested on them. And that is why he said, "Can anyone forbid water that these, who have received the Holy Spirit as well as we, should not be baptized?" He wanted to show and teach those who were with him that if the Holy Spirit had not come to rest upon them, there would have been someone who would have kept them from baptism. CATENA ON THE ACTS OF THE APOSTLES 10.28.[9]

THE NECESSITY OF WATER. CHRYSOSTOM: That the need of water is absolute and indispensable, you may learn in this way. On one occasion, when the Spirit had been poured out before the water was applied, the apostle did not stay at this point, but, as though the water were necessary and not superfluous, observe what he says: "Can any one forbid water for baptizing these people who have received the Holy Spirit just as we have?" HOMILIES ON THE GOSPEL OF JOHN 25.2.[10]

A TWOFOLD PURIFICATION. CYRIL OF JERUSALEM: For since a person is of twofold nature, soul and body, the purification also is twofold, the one incorporeal for the incorporeal part, and the

---

[5]NPNF 1 11:157**. [6]CGPNT 3:190. [7]NPNF 1 11:155-56**. [8]Irenaeus is referring to the words from verse 28, "God showed me that I should not call anyone common or unclean." [9]CGPNT 3:183-84. [10]NPNF 1 14:89**.

other bodily for the body. The water cleanses the body, and the Spirit seals the soul, that we may draw near to God, "having our heart sprinkled" by the Spirit "and our body washed with pure water."[11] . . . Neither does he who is baptized with water, but not found worthy of the Spirit, receive the grace in perfection; nor if a person is virtuous in his deeds, but receives not the seal by water, shall he enter into the kingdom of heaven. A bold saying, but not mine, for it is Jesus who has declared it, and here is the proof of the statement from holy Scripture. Cornelius was a just man who was honored with a vision of angels and had set up his prayers and alms deeds as a good memorial before God in heaven. Peter came, and the Spirit was poured out on them that believed, and they spoke with other tongues and prophesied. And after the grace of the Spirit the Scripture says that Peter commanded them to be baptized in the name of Jesus Christ; in order that, the soul having been born again by faith, the body also might by the water partake of the grace. CATECHETICAL LECTURE 3.4.[12]

10:48 Peter Commanded Them to Be Baptized

BAPTIZED IN THE UNITY OF THE NAME. BEDE: Since the rule of the church is that the faithful are baptized in the name of the holy Trinity, a question arises as to how it is that in the whole text of this book Luke bears witness to the giving of baptism only in the name of Jesus Christ. The blessed Ambrose resolves this question as follows.[13] "Through the unity of the name the mystery is completed. If you say 'Christ,' you have designated at the same time God the Father, by whom the Son was anointed, and the Son who was himself anointed, and the Spirit with whom he was anointed, for it is written, 'Jesus of Nazareth, how God anointed him with the Holy Spirit.' If you say, 'the Father,' you also indicated at the same time his Son and the Spirit of his mouth (if, moreover, you also comprehend this in your heart). And if you say, 'the Spirit,' you have also named God the Father, from whom the Spirit proceeds, and also the Son, because the Spirit is also the Son's. Hence, as authority may be joined to reason, Scripture indicates that we can also properly be baptized in the Spirit when it says, 'But you will be baptized in the Holy Spirit.'"[14] And the apostle says, "For in one body we were all baptized into one Spirit."[15] According to another way of looking at the question, it is particularly appropriate for us to be baptized in the name of the Lord Jesus Christ, since, as the apostle says, "All of us who have been baptized in Christ Jesus have been baptized in his death,"[16] and so forth. COMMENTARY ON THE ACTS OF THE APOSTLES 10.48.[17]

---

[11]Heb 10:22. [12]NPNF 2 7:15**. [13]Ambrose On the Holy Spirit 1.3.43-45 (CSEL 79:32-33). [14]Acts 1:5. [15]1 Cor 12:13. [16]Rom 6:3. [17]CS 117:103-4. One may note the similarity of the argument here to that of Basil given above in his treatise On the Holy Spirit.

11:1-12 PETER RECOUNTS HIS VISION

[1]Now the apostles and the brothers who were in Judea heard that the Gentiles also had received the word of God. [2]So when Peter went up to Jerusalem, the circumcision party criticized him, [3]saying, "Why did you go to uncircumcised men and eat with them?" [4]But Peter began and

explained to them in order: [5]*"I was in the city of Joppa praying; and in a trance I saw a vision, something descending, like a great sheet, let down from heaven by four corners; and it came down to me.* [6]*Looking at it closely I observed animals and beasts of prey and reptiles and birds of the air.* [7]*And I heard a voice saying to me, 'Rise, Peter; kill and eat.'* [8]*But I said, 'No, Lord; for nothing common or unclean has ever entered my mouth.'* [9]*But the voice answered a second time from heaven, 'What God has cleansed you must not call common.'* [10]*This happened three times, and all was drawn up again into heaven.* [11]*At that very moment three men arrived at the house in which we were, sent to me from Caesarea.* [12]*And the Spirit told me to go with them, making no distinction. These six brothers also accompanied me, and we entered the man's house.*

OVERVIEW: This passage is another example of Luke's repetition technique, accenting important events in the story of the church. Peter retells in the first person the turning point narrative recounted by Luke in the first person in the previous chapter and twice (Acts 11:7, 12) announces the fact that the preaching to the Gentiles occurred at the specific direction of the Holy Spirit. Peter's need to recount and defend his actions introduces a dynamic to the events of Acts 11, and the early Christian authors locate this dynamic in different ways, but much of what they say renders various portraits of Peter. Chrysostom sees the controversy in this chapter as something that Peter would not have entered into had he not been forced. In Chrysostom's view the problem is not in the belief of the Jewish Christians of Jerusalem that the Gentiles could not be baptized but that Peter should not have eaten with Cornelius and his friend, and so the dispute arises providentially because of the concerns of the Jerusalem Christians and not by Peter's initiative. Gregory the Great finds Peter's way of responding to demonstrate humble dialogue proper to one in a position of authority, while Chrysostom shows how Peter's true authority and persuasiveness comes from his reluctant obedience to God's initiative, which is a call to holiness that cannot be confined (BEDE). Bede sees the universal nature of this call to perfection reflected in the number of Peter and his companions being seven to recall the sevenfold gifts of the Spirit.

11:3 Why Did You Go to the Uncircumcised?

PETER ACCUSED SO THAT THEY MIGHT LEARN. CHRYSOSTOM: The question was not "Why did you preach to them?" but "Why did you eat with them?" But Peter does not respond to this frigid (yes, frigid) objection; he relies on this profound argument: if they had received the Spirit, how could one refuse to give them baptism? But why did they not object in the case of the Samaritans? For on the contrary, neither before nor after their baptism was there any controversy, and they did not become angry on that occasion but, on hearing the news, sent the apostles for this very purpose. As a matter of fact, even here they are not complaining of this, for they knew it was of divine grace. What they ask is, "Why did you eat with them?" Besides, the difference between Samaritans and Gentiles is not so great. Surely it was part of the divine plan for Peter to be accused, so that they too might learn. For Peter would not have spoken without cause. HOMILIES ON THE ACTS OF THE APOSTLES 24.[1]

PETER WAS A HUMBLE SHEPHERD. GREGORY THE GREAT: For if, when he was blamed by the believers, he had paid regard to the authority that he had received in holy church, he might have replied that the sheep should not dare to find fault with the shepherd to whom they had been

---

[1]NPNF 1 11:156**.

committed. But, had he said anything of his own power in answer to the complaint of the believers, he would not have been truly a teacher of gentleness. He pacified them, therefore, by giving a reason humbly, and he even produced witnesses to defend him from blame, saying, "Moreover these six brothers accompanied me." If, then, the pastor of the church, the prince of the apostles, who singularly did signs and miracles, did not disdain humbly to give a reason in defending himself from blame, how much more ought we sinners, when we are blamed for anything, to pacify those who blame us by giving a reason humbly! LETTER 45.[2]

11:4 Peter Explained

GOD INITIATED THIS. CHRYSOSTOM: The words were not those of the prudent Peter but of the Spirit. And in his defense he showed God as the absolute author and himself as the author of nothing. He said what he did in his ecstasy, "I was in the city of Joppa, and he showed the vessel, as I have said before; and again he said and I did not hear. The Spirit ordered me to leave, and so, after leaving, I did not run. I said that God had sent me, and so I did not baptize after these things, but again God did everything. God himself baptized, not I." CATENA ON THE ACTS OF THE APOSTLES 11.4.[3]

11:6 Animals and Beasts of Prey

ALL ARE CALLED TO THE GOSPEL OF CHRIST. BEDE: I am amazed at how some people interpret this as having to do with certain foods that were prohibited by the old law but that are now to be consumed, since neither serpents nor reptiles can be eaten. Nor did Peter himself understand it in this way. Rather [he understood it as meaning that] all people are equally called to the gospel of Christ and nothing is naturally defiled. For when he was reproached,[4] he explained the symbolism of this vision, not [as giving the reason] why he ate beasts but why he associated with Gentiles. COMMENTARY ON THE ACTS OF THE APOSTLES 11.6.[5]

11:12 The Spirit Told Me to Go

AN APPROPRIATE NUMBER. BEDE: It is beautifully appropriate that when the sevenfold gifts of the Holy Spirit[6] were poured out, the witnesses were brothers who were seven in number. Alternatively, because this world was formed in six days, the works accomplished [by Peter] were demonstrated through the six brothers who fittingly accompanied the teacher when, among the words of his exhortation, he described to his hearers the exemplary work that he had accomplished. COMMENTARY ON THE ACTS OF THE APOSTLES 11.12.[7]

---

[2]NPNF 2 13:65*. [3]CGPNT 3:193. [4]Acts 11:2-3. [5]CS 117:107. [6]Here, Bede is refering to Is 11:2-3. For an extended treatment of the development of the seven gifts of the Holy Spirit in the Fathers see Gustave Bardy, "Dons du Saint-Esprit. I. Chez les Pères," in Dictionnaire de Spiritualité Ascétique et Mystique (Paris: Beauchesnes, 1957), book 3, col. 1579-87. The first clear instance of understanding Is 11:2-3 as referring to the gifts of the Spirit working in the faithful is in Justin Martyr's Dialogue with Trypho 39.2; 87.2. [7]CS 117:107.

11:13-18 THE CIRCUMCISION PARTY PERSUADED

¹³And he told us how he had seen the angel standing in his house and saying, 'Send to Joppa and bring Simon called Peter; ¹⁴he will declare to you a message by which you will be saved, you and all your household.' ¹⁵As I began to speak, the Holy Spirit fell on them just as on us at the beginning. ¹⁶And I remembered the word of the Lord, how he said, 'John baptized with water, but you shall be baptized with the Holy Spirit.' ¹⁷If then God gave the same gift to them as he gave to us when we believed in the Lord Jesus Christ, who was I that I could withstand God?" ¹⁸When they heard this they were silenced. And they glorified God, saying, "Then to the Gentiles also God has granted repentance to life."

OVERVIEW: Acts 11:13 moves the debate beyond ritual purity to that of salvation, and Acts 11:16 ties in Jesus' prophetic words about baptism in the Spirit repeated from Acts 1:5 and found in all four Gospels.[1] Luke thus has Peter portray this as an extension of the ministry of Jesus. Luke shows us how the gradual inclusion of the non-Jews (the Samaritans, the Ethiopian) and of a persecutor culminates in this action by which a group of Gentiles share the blessing brought by Christ. This revelation, that God's salvific will is universal, brought great joy in Jerusalem as had been foretold (AUGUSTINE, BEDE), and the Jerusalem community recognizes this work as leading to life. The inclusion of the Gentiles in the church as they were, apart from observing the Mosaic law, required an action, beyond dispute, that affirmed them as belonging on the basis of upright belief and lives (CHRYSOSTOM). This event, in the midst of life, does not dispense with a future judgment (a baptism by fire) and hence with the need to live out a life in the Spirit (ORIGEN), of which one consequence is a constant openness to being corrected and moved to repentance, a humility that recognizes the temptation to establish one's holiness by the exclusion of others (CHRYSOSTOM).

11:15 *The Holy Spirit Descends*

TO SHOW THAT ALL WAS OF GOD. CHRYSOS-

TOM: It was out of superabundance that this [sending of the Holy Spirit] takes place, to show that even the beginning did not come from the apostle. For if Peter had set out of his own accord and [the Holy Spirit had not come first], they would have been completely thunder-struck. Consequently, from the start he tries to bring their thoughts around to his side by saying, "who have received the Holy Spirit just as we have." HOMILIES ON THE ACTS OF THE APOSTLES 24.[2]

11:16 *Remembering God's Word*

THE ESCHATOLOGICAL NATURE OF BAPTISM. ORIGEN: The people received John, who was less than Christ. They reflected and thought, "Perhaps he is the Christ." But they did not receive him who had come, who was greater than John. Do you want to know the reason? Recognize this: John's baptism could be seen; the baptism of Christ was invisible. John said, "For I baptize you in water, but he who comes after me is greater than I. He will baptize you in the Holy Spirit and in fire."[3] When does Jesus baptize "with the Holy Spirit"? And again, when does he baptize "with fire"? Does he baptize at one and the same time "with Spirit and fire," or at distinct and different

---

[1] Mt 3:11-12; Mk 1:7-8; Lk 3:15-18; Jn 1:24-28. [2] NPNF 1 11:157**. [3] Lk 3:16.

times? He says, "But you will be baptized with the Holy Spirit not many days hence."[4] After his ascension into heaven, the apostles were baptized "with the Holy Spirit." But Scripture does not record that they were baptized "with fire."[5]

At the Jordan River, John awaited those who came for baptism. Some he rejected, saying, "generation of vipers," and so on.[6] But those who confessed their faults and sins he received. In the same way, the Lord Jesus Christ will stand in the river of fire near the "flaming sword."[7] If anyone desires to pass over to paradise after departing this life and needs cleansing, Christ will baptize him in this river and send him across to the place he longs for. But whoever does not have the sign of earlier baptisms, him Christ will not baptize in the fiery bath. For it is fitting that one should be baptized in "water and the Spirit."[8] Then, when he comes to the fiery river, he can show that he preserved the bathing in water and the Spirit. Then he will deserve to receive in addition the baptism in Christ Jesus, to whom be glory and power for ages of ages. Amen. Homilies on the Gospel of Luke 24.[9]

11:17 God Gave the Same Gift

Dismantling a Holiness Based on Exclusion. Chrysostom: [Peter] shows that he did nothing himself. "For it was the very thing that we obtained," he says, "that those men received." "If then God gave the same gift to them as he gave to us when we believed in the Lord Jesus, who was I that I could withstand God?" To silence them more effectively, he added "the same gift." Do you see how he does not allow them to have less? "When they believed," he says, "God gave the same gift to them as he gave to us when we believed in the Lord Jesus." He makes them clean, and he does not say "to you" but "to us." That is, why do you feel aggrieved when we call them partners? "When they heard this they were silenced. And they glorified God, saying, 'Then to the Gentiles also God has granted repentance to life.'" Do you see how it all came about

through the oratory of Peter, who did well to report the events? They glorified God because he had given them repentance. They were humbled by these words. From this point on the door of faith was open to the Gentiles. Homilies on the Acts of the Apostles 24.[10]

11:18 Glorifying God

Their Praise Was Foretold. Augustine: "Zion heard and was glad."[11] What did Zion hear? That all God's angels worship him? Yes, to be sure; but what else did Zion hear? This is what it heard: "The heavens have proclaimed his justice, and all nations have seen his glory. Let all who worship graven images be put to shame, those who boast of their idols."[12] The church had not yet extended to the Gentiles, you see. Some of the Jews in Judea had come to believe, but these Jews imagined that they alone belonged to Christ. Then the apostles were sent to the Gentiles, and the word was preached to Cornelius. He believed and was baptized, and his companions were baptized with him. You know what happened to lead them to baptism. . . . An angel was sent to Cornelius; the angel sent Cornelius to Peter, and Peter came to Cornelius's house. But Cornelius was from the Gentiles, so he and his friends were uncircumcised. In order, therefore, that Peter and his companions might have no hesitation about delivering the gospel to uncircumcised persons, the Holy Spirit came upon Cornelius and the others even before they were baptized; the Spirit filled them, and they began to speak in tongues. Until this time the Holy Spirit had never fallen upon any unbaptized person; but he fell on these before their baptism. Peter might well have hesitated over whether to baptize the uncircumcised, but the Holy Spirit came, and they began to speak in tongues. The invisible gift

---

[4]Acts 1:5. [5]Origen apparently does not consider the tongues of fire to have constituted a baptism of fire. [6]Lk 3:7. [7]Gn 3:24. [8]Jn 3:5. [9]FC 94:103-4. [10]NPNF 1 11:157**. [11]Ps 97:8 (96:8 LXX, Vg). [12]Ps 97:6-7 (96:6-7 LXX, Vg).

was conferred and removed any doubt about the visible sacrament, so they were all baptized.

Now you find it recorded in Scripture that "the apostles and the brothers in Judea heard that the Gentiles too had accepted the word of God, and they glorified God." It is this thanksgiving on their part that is mentioned in our psalm: "Zion heard and was glad, and the daughters of Judea leaped for joy."[13] EXPLANATIONS OF THE PSALMS 96.13.[14]

AND THEY GLORIFIED GOD. BEDE: Here is

what we read in the book of the blessed Job: "Gold will come from the north, and fearful praise to God,"[15] since the splendor of faith first sprang to life in the cold heart of the Gentile world, and in virtue of this same unexpected faith, the Jewish world, trembling with fear, glorified God.[16] COMMENTARY ON THE ACTS OF THE APOSTLES 11.18.[17]

---

[13]Ps 97:8 (96:8 LXX, Vg). [14]*WSA* 3 18:451-52. [15]Job 37:22 (Vg). [16]Gregory the Great *Morals on the Book of Job* 27.43.71 (PL 76:440). [17]CS 117:107-8.

11:19-26 BARNABAS SENT TO ANTIOCH

[19]*Now those who were scattered because of the persecution that arose over Stephen traveled as far as Phoenicia and Cyprus and Antioch, speaking the word to none except Jews.* [20]*But there were some of them, men of Cyprus and Cyrene, who on coming to Antioch spoke to the Greeks[i] also, preaching the Lord Jesus.* [21]*And the hand of the Lord was with them, and a great number that believed turned to the Lord.* [22]*News of this came to the ears of the church in Jerusalem, and they sent Barnabas to Antioch.* [23]*When he came and saw the grace of God, he was glad; and he exhorted them all to remain faithful to the Lord with steadfast purpose;* [24]*for he was a good man, full of the Holy Spirit and of faith. And a large company was added to the Lord.* [25]*So Barnabas went to Tarsus to look for Saul;* [26]*and when he had found him, he brought him to Antioch. For a whole year they met with[j] the church, and taught a large company of people; and in Antioch the disciples were for the first time called Christians.*

i Other ancient authorities read *Hellenists* j Or *were guests of*

OVERVIEW: Modern commentators note that Luke now moves on to narrate how the principle established by the dramatic event relating to Cornelius is now given substantial existence through some Greek-speaking Jews. He is also careful to describe Barnabas in words reminiscent of Stephen.[1] He shows us Paul's resumption of activity as being commissioned from Jerusalem and declares the decidedly non-Jewish nature of this

activity by mentioning his Greek name. The specter of human violence can be daunting to us, but its often beneficial place in the spread of the gospel is undisputed, almost as if it were a spur to move us beyond what had seemed to be the places most likely to receive the word. We know, however, from history that great reputations can ob-

---

[1]Acts 6:5.

scure God's message (CHRYSOSTOM) and familiarity can engender disbelief and even hatred (ORIGEN). Paul, who himself had exercised such violence against Christ and provoked such a scattering, now with Barnabas, fosters and sees the abundant harvest in Antioch (CHRYSOSTOM) of many Christs, a share in the anointing of the one Mediator that had so recently seen extension beyond Judea (GREGORY OF NYSSA).

11:19 Those Believers Who Were Scattered

THE FAITH IS SPREAD BY PERSECUTION.
CHRYSOSTOM: The persecution brought a not inconsiderable success. "For by turning everything to their good, God cooperates with those who love him."[2] Had their purpose been to work zealously to establish the church, they would not have done anything different. They dispersed the teachers, and look how the preaching spread. HOMILIES ON THE ACTS OF THE APOSTLES 25.[3]

11:20 Some Spoke to the Greeks

TRUSTING IN THE GRACE OF GOD. CHRYSOSTOM: Look! Not even in tribulation did they succumb to lamentations and tears, as we do, but dedicated themselves to a great and good work and preached the word even more undaunted. They did not ask, "Should we, who are Cyrenians and Cyprians, attack so splendid and great a city?" Instead, trusting in the grace of God, they applied themselves to the work of teaching, and the Gentiles themselves did not disdain to learn from them. Notice how all these things were accomplished through small means; how the preaching grew; and how, similar to those in Jerusalem, they bestowed their care on everyone, treating the entire world as a single household. HOMILIES ON THE ACTS OF THE APOSTLES 25.[4]

11:22 Barnabas Sent to Antioch

THAT THE GOSPEL MAY SPREAD. CHRYSOSTOM: "News of this came to the ears of the church

in Jerusalem, and they sent Barnabas to Antioch." When such a great city was receiving the word, why did they not go themselves? Because of the Jews. But they sent Barnabas. Only it was no small part, and so it was providentially arranged for Paul to go there as well. It was both natural and providential that they turned him [toward Antioch] and that he was not shut up in Jerusalem, that voice of the gospel, that trumpet of heaven. Do you see how on all occasions Christ uses their faults to serve a need for the benefit of the church? HOMILIES ON THE ACTS OF THE APOSTLES 25.[5]

11:24 A Good Man

GREAT GRACE THROUGH SMALL MEANS.
CHRYSOSTOM: The more insignificant they were, the brighter the grace working great results by small means. "And he exhorted them all to remain faithful to the Lord, for he was a good man." I think by "good" here he means a kind, unaffected person, very much eager for the salvation of his neighbors. "For he was a good man, full of the Holy Spirit and of faith." "With steadfast purpose," he says. With encomium and praise, for, like rich land, this city received the word and brought forth much fruit. HOMILIES ON THE ACTS OF THE APOSTLES 25.[6]

11:25 Barnabas Looked for Saul

PERSECUTION TO BE EXPECTED FROM THOSE WE KNOW BEST. ORIGEN: Now it is good to read through the history what Jeremiah suffered among the people, in reference to whom he said, "I said: No more shall I speak or name the name of the Lord,"[7] and again elsewhere, "I have unceasingly been an object of derision."[8] But whatever he also suffered at the hand of the reigning king of Israel[9] has been written in his prophecy. But that those from among the people came frequently to stone even Moses has also

---

[2]Rom 8:28. [3]NPNF 1 11:162**. [4]NPNF 1 11:164**. [5]NPNF 1 11:162**. [6]NPNF 1 11:164**. [7]Jer 20:9. [8]Jer 20:7. [9]Joachim.

been written, and the stones of that place were not his homeland, but those following him were, that is, the people, by whom he too was dishonored. And Isaiah is reported to have been cut up by the people. Now, if someone does not accept this report because it is found in the apocryphal Isaiah, let him believe in what is written in the letter to the Hebrews: "They were stoned, cut up, put to the test."[10] The "cut up" is referred to Isaiah, just as the verse "they were murdered by the sword"[11] applies to Zechariah, who was murdered "between the temple and the altar,"[12] as the Savior taught bearing witness, I believe, to a writing not contained in the shared and publicly accepted books but to one that is probably apocryphal. But they were dishonored by the Jews and went about "in sheepskins, in goatskins, impoverished, suffering tribulation" and the following.[13] For "all who desire to live uprightly in Christ Jesus will suffer persecution."[14] Now it is probably because he learned that a prophet cannot have honor "in his homeland," that Paul, having proclaimed the word in many other places, did not preach in Tarsus. COMMENTARY ON MATTHEW 10.18.[15]

11:26 Called Christians

BECAUSE OF PAUL, THEY WERE WORTHY OF THE NAME. CHRYSOSTOM: Surely they were called Christians because Paul spent such a long time among them. "For a whole year," it says, "they met with the church and taught a large company of people; and in Antioch the disciples were for the first time called Christians." This is no small praise for the city, but enough to match it against all cities. For Antioch was the first city, before all the others, to have the benefit of listening to Paul for so long, and because of this the people there were the first to be deemed worthy of the name. Look at the success of Paul, to what heights it raised, like a standard, that name! Elsewhere, three thousand or five thousand or so great a number believed, but nothing like this. Elsewhere, the believers were called "they of the way"; here, they were given the name Christians. HOMILIES ON THE ACTS OF THE APOSTLES 25.[16]

WHAT DOES THE NAME MEAN? GREGORY OF NYSSA: Our good Master, Jesus Christ, bestowed on us a partnership in his revered name, so that we get our name from no other person connected with us, and if one happens to be rich and well-born or of lowly origin and poor, or if one has some distinction from his business or position, all such conditions are of no avail because the one authoritative name for those believing in him is that of Christian. Now, since this grace was ordained for us from above, it is necessary, first of all, for us to understand the greatness of the gift so that we can worthily thank the God who has given it to us. Then, it is necessary to show through our life that we ourselves are what the power of this great name requires us to be. The greatness of the gift of which we are deemed worthy through the partnership with the Master becomes clear to us if we recognize the true significance of the name of Christ, so that, when in our prayers we call upon the Lord of all by this name, we may comprehend the concept that we are taking into our soul. . . . Paul, most of all, knew what Christ is, and he indicated, by what he did, the kind of person named for him, imitating him so brilliantly that he revealed his own Master in himself, his own soul being transformed through his accurate imitation of his prototype, so that Paul no longer seemed to be living and speaking, but Christ himself seemed to be living in him. As this astute perceiver of particular goods says, "Do you seek a proof of the Christ who speaks in me?"[17] and, "It is now no longer I that live but Christ lives in me."[18]

This man knew the significance of the name of Christ for us, saying that Christ is the "power of God and the wisdom of God."[19] And he called him "peace,"[20] and "light inaccessible"[21] in whom

---

[10]Heb 11:37. [11]Heb 11:37. [12]Mt 23:35; cf. 2 Chron 24:20-22. [13]Heb 11:37. [14]2 Tim 3:12. [15]GCS 40:24. [16]NPNF 1 11:163**. [17]2 Cor 13:3. [18]Gal 2:20. [19]1 Cor 1:24. [20]Eph 2:14. [21]1 Tim 6:16.

God dwells, and "sanctification and redemption,"[22] and "great high priest,"[23] and "passover,"[24] and "a propitiation" of souls,[25] "the brightness of glory and image of substance,"[26] and "maker of the world,"[27] and "spiritual food,"[28] and "spiritual drink and spiritual rock,"[29] "water,"[30] "foundation" of faith,[31] and "cornerstone,"[32] and "image of the invisible God,"[33] and "great God,"[34] and "head of the body of the church,"[35] and "the firstborn of every creature,"[36] "firstfruits of those who have fallen asleep,"[37] "firstborn from the dead,"[38] "firstborn among many brothers,"[39] and "mediator between God and humanity,"[40] and "only begotten Son,"[41] and "crowned with glory and honor,"[42] and "lord of glory"[43] and "beginning" of being,[44] speaking thus of him who is the beginning, "king of justice and king of peace,"[45] and "ineffable king of all, having the power of the kingdom,"[46] and many other such things that are not easily enumerated. When all of these phrases are put next to each other, each one of the terms makes its own contribution to a revelation of what is signified by being named after Christ, and each provides for us a certain emphasis. To the extent that we take these concepts into our souls, they are all indications of the unspeakable greatness of the gift for us. However, since the rank of kingship underlies all worth and power and rule, by this

title the royal power of Christ is authoritatively and primarily indicated (for the anointing of kingship, as we learn in the historical books, comes first[47]), and all the force of the other titles depends on that of royalty. For this reason, the person who knows the separate elements included under it also knows the power encompassing these elements. But it is the kingship itself that declares what the title of Christ means. Therefore, since, thanks to our good Master, we are sharers of the greatest and the most divine and the first of names, those honored by the name of Christ being called Christians, it is necessary that there be seen in us also all of the connotations of this name, so that the title be not a misnomer in our case but that our life be a testimony of it. Being something does not result from being called something. The underlying nature, whatever it happens to be, is discovered through the meaning attached to the name. ON PERFECTION.[48]

---

[22]1 Cor 1:30. [23]Heb 4:14. [24]1 Cor 5:7. [25]Rom 3:25. [26]Heb 1:3. [27]Heb 1:2. [28]1 Cor 10:3. [29]1 Cor 10:4. [30]Jn 4:13-14. [31]1 Cor 3:11. [32]Mt 21:42; Mk 12:10; Lk 20:17. [33]Col 1:15. [34]Tit 2:13. [35]Col 1:18. [36]Col 1:15. [37]1 Cor 15:20. [38]Col 1:18. [39]Rom 8:29. [40]1 Tim 2:5. [41]Jn 3:16. [42]Heb 2:7; cf. Ps 8:6 (8:7 LXX). [43]1 Cor 2:8. [44]Col 1:18. [45]Heb 7:2. [46]See Lk 1:33. [47]1 Kings 9:16; 10:1ff.,12ff. [48]FC 58:95-98.

11:27-30 RELIEF SENT DURING FAMINE

[27]Now in these days prophets came down from Jerusalem to Antioch. [28]And one of them named Agabus stood up and foretold by the Spirit that there would be a great famine over all the world; and this took place in the days of Claudius. [29]And the disciples determined, every one according to his ability, to send relief to the brothers who lived in Judea; [30]and they did so, sending it to the elders by the hand of Barnabas and Saul.

OVERVIEW: Modern commentators accent the connection between Jerusalem, as mother

church, and Antioch through Barnabas. They also raise the vexing historical question as to how this account of Paul's visit to Jerusalem, his second since his conversion (see Acts 9:26), accords with Galatians 2:1. There is no clear answer. The "worldwide" famine mentioned also draws historical attention, though the term Luke uses (*oikoumenē*) could mean the empire. The ancient commentators concentrate rather on the moral and spiritual lessons that these events as recounted by Luke can teach us. The famine that was suffered by the Jerusalem church and borne in common by the church in Antioch causes us to examine how we respond to the needs not just of our near neighbors but even of those upon whom we depend for hearing the gospel. Our failure to hear, in the cry of the poor, the call of the gospel, is in itself a spiritual famine for us much as it is a physical one for those we ignore (CHRYSOSTOM). Some in our midst are supposed to call us to greater awareness of how God's blessings come to us through one another in times of trial, whether we be the ones who suffer need or the ones called to give (BEDE, CHRYSOSTOM). Those in Antioch, aware of the poverty and tribulations of those in Jerusalem, were prepared to meet these needs (BEDE).

11:28 A Great Famine

A TWOFOLD FAMINE AND A TWOFOLD ABUNDANCE. CHRYSOSTOM: But no one does this now, even though the famine is more severe than the one then. For it is not the same when misfortune is borne in common and when everyone else has plenty, but the poor one is famishing. Back then, even those who gave were poor. "Everyone according to his ability," it says. The famine is twofold, just as the abundance is twofold. Back then, this was a severe famine—a famine not only of hearing the word of the Lord but also of being nourished by alms. Back then, both the poor in Judea enjoyed the benefit and those in Antioch who gave their money, and the latter more than the former. Now, both we and the poor are famishing: they from a lack of necessary sustenance and we because we, in our luxury, lack the mercy of God. HOMILIES ON THE ACTS OF THE APOSTLES 25.[1]

REVELATION THROUGH THE SPIRIT. BEDE: Agabus can be said to mean *herald of tribulation*.[2] In accordance with his name he also here prophesied a general famine, and [as we learn] below, he prophesied chains for Paul the apostle.[3] COMMENTARY ON THE ACTS OF THE APOSTLES 11.28.[4]

11:29 The Disciples Determine to Send Relief

THE FAMINE AN OCCASION OF SALVATION. CHRYSOSTOM: Do you see how for them the famine was an encouragement to salvation, an opportunity to give alms and a harbinger of many blessings? And so it could have been for you, if you were so inclined. But you were not. The famine was foretold so that they might prepare themselves beforehand for almsgiving. For they were enduring terrible hardships, but before this they were not suffering from famine. And they sent it to the elders by the hand of Barnabas and Saul. "The disciples," it says, "each according to his ability." Do you see that as soon as they believed, they bore fruit not only for their own people, but also for those far away? HOMILIES ON THE ACTS OF THE APOSTLES 25.[5]

THE SAINTS IN JERUSALEM HAD HELPED THE APOSTLES. BEDE: They knew that the famine would rage most severely in Judea, and especially in Jerusalem, where among the saints there were poor people who had sold their goods, homes and fields, and had brought the proceeds to the apostles, so that they had no way left to obtain much more money. And some were punished by the unbelieving Jews for their confession of the faith by having their own property taken away. To

---

[1]NPNF 1 11:165**. [2]Jerome *On Hebrew Names* (CCL 72:143). [3]Acts 21:10-11. [4]CS 117:108. [5]NPNF 1 11:163-64**.

them the apostle said, "You joyfully accepted the plundering of your goods."[6] Among these givers of alms we are told of the pious deed of Helen, queen of the Adiabeni, who purchased grain from Egypt and most generously provided for the needs of those dwelling in Jerusalem. She thus merited a sepulcher to honor her before the gates of the same city.[7] COMMENTARY ON THE ACTS OF THE APOSTLES 11.29.[8]

---

[6]Heb 10:34. [7]Eusebius/Rufinus *Ecclesiastical History* 2.12 (GCS 9.1:133). [8]CS 117:108-9.

12:1-5 PETER ARRESTED AND PUT IN PRISON

[1]*About that time Herod the king laid violent hands upon some who belonged to the church.* [2]*He killed James the brother of John with the sword;* [3]*and when he saw that it pleased the Jews, he proceeded to arrest Peter also. This was during the days of Unleavened Bread.* [4]*And when he had seized him, he put him in prison, and delivered him to four squads of soldiers to guard him, intending after the Passover to bring him out to the people.* [5]*So Peter was kept in prison; but earnest prayer for him was made to God by the church.*

OVERVIEW: These verses set the stage for the narrative of Peter's deliverance from certain death. They recall Jesus' prophecy about the persecution the disciples can expect and which, in fact, befell him.[1] There are other allusive parallels established between Jesus and Peter: this takes place "during the days of Unleavened Bread," with accompanying allusions to the exodus. The questions that intrigue modern commentators, Herod's motive for killing James, the reason for placing this self-enclosed narrative at this point, and so on are not reflected upon by the Fathers, though Chrysostom is sensitive to Luke's laconic style in recounting James's death and sees it as mediating a "random" act of violence. On the whole, however, the Fathers' line of thought differs: the continued suffering that Acts recounts is not in vain but in line with God's purpose, which is to demonstrate the futility of fighting against him. Although the Jews are no longer directly working against the Jerusalem church, they are its benefactors in that they are the ones God is trying to convince of the truth of the gospel, both by these ultimately failing persecutions and the fulfillment of Gamaliel's words (CHRYSOSTOM). Gregory of Nyssa imagines what might have happened at James's trial: an attempt at forcing him to deny Christ, something that Acts does not recount, but a process, familiar from martyrdom accounts, to those who lived in the fourth century. Gregory's point, while nonhistorical, is worthy of note: a threat to physical integrity, even one that brings death, is nothing compared with what comes with being separated from Christ, the head of a great body. The connections in this body are most evident in the mutual support that its members give to and receive from one another, regardless of relative status, through prayer (CHRYSOSTOM, SEVERUS).

12:2 Herod Killed James

---

[1]See Lk 21:12-13.

WHY GOD PERMITS THIS DEATH. CHRYSOS-
TOM: "And," it says, "he killed James the brother
of John with the sword"; simply that, as if it happened by chance. If someone should ask why God
permitted this, we would answer that it was for
the sake of the Jews themselves. First of all,
[God] thereby persuades them that even when
being put to death, the apostles triumph, which
also happened in the case of Stephen. Second,
[God] gives them an opportunity, after satiating
their anger, to return from their madness. Third,
he shows that it was with his consent that this
happened. HOMILIES ON THE ACTS OF THE
APOSTLES 26.[2]

EVERY CHRISTIAN'S TRUE HEAD. GREGORY OF
NYSSA: James, under pressure to cut off Christ,
his true head, was [physically] decapitated, yet
the [true] head of every person is Christ according to the apostle[3] and at the same time
the head of the entire church. HOMILY 2 ON
ST. STEPHEN.[4]

12:3 James's Death Pleased the Jews

**GAMALIEL'S ADVICE, THEIR CONDEMNA-
TION.** CHRYSOSTOM: How was it that he did not
kill Peter immediately? It mentions the reason, "it
was the day of unleavened bread." The more likely
reason is that he wanted to make a spectacle of
the slaughter. For their part, the Jews, following
the advice of Gamaliel, now abstained from
bloodshedding (besides, they did not even try to
invent accusations), but by the hands of others
they achieved the same results. . . . This, in particular, was their condemnation; for the preaching was shown to be no longer a thing of
humankind. HOMILIES ON THE ACTS OF THE
APOSTLES 26.[5]

12:5 Earnest Prayer Offered for Peter

PRAYER ARISING FROM LOVE FOR A FATHER.
CHRYSOSTOM: The stricter the watch, the more
wonderful the demonstration. This was done on
behalf of Peter, who became more esteemed as a
result, and to demonstrate his innate virtue.
"Prayer was earnestly made," it says. It was the
prayer of heartfelt love. They all sought a father, a
gentle father. "Earnest prayer," it says. Listen as
to how they were disposed toward their teachers.
They did not divide into factions or make an
uproar but turned to prayer, that true alliance
which is invincible. In this they sought refuge.
They did not say, "Am I, a lowly good-for-noth-
ing, to pray for him?" For since they acted out of
love, they did not give these things any thought.
HOMILIES ON THE ACTS OF THE APOSTLES 26.[6]

THE GROANING BODY. SEVERUS OF ANTIOCH:
This we urge you, by both supplications and
tears, to contribute to us—insignificant ones. For
the shared sufferings of the church call for shared
prayers, just as when Peter, the head of the apostles, was bound in prison by two chains and
watched over by guards . . . "there was made constant prayer by the church to God for him."
When this is the case for an apostle, who needs
help, and prayers are offered up by the church,
how would we, the uninitiated and brood of sin,[7]
not all the more beg these prayers to be offered
for us by the faithful, those noble limbs of the
church and educated to groan[8] with godly and
spiritual perception? CATENA ON THE ACTS OF
THE APOSTLES 12.5.[9]

---

[2]NPNF 1 11:168**. [3]1 Cor 11:3; Eph 5:23. [4]GNO 10 1:102. [5]NPNF
1 11:169-70**. [6]NPNF 1 11:170**. [7]Severus was addressing those
preparing for baptism. [8]See Rom 8:23. [9]CGPNT 3:202-3.

12:6-11 PETER RESCUED BY AN ANGEL

[6]*The very night when Herod was about to bring him out, Peter was sleeping between two soldiers, bound with two chains, and sentries before the door were guarding the prison;* [7]*and behold, an angel of the Lord appeared, and a light shone in the cell; and he struck Peter on the side and woke him, saying, "Get up quickly." And the chains fell off his hands.* [8]*And the angel said to him, "Dress yourself and put on your sandals." And he did so. And he said to him, "Wrap your mantle around you and follow me."* [9]*And he went out and followed him; he did not know that what was done by the angel was real, but thought he was seeing a vision.* [10]*When they had passed the first and the second guard, they came to the iron gate leading into the city. It opened to them of its own accord, and they went out and passed on through one street; and immediately the angel left him.* [11]*And Peter came to himself, and said, "Now I am sure that the Lord has sent his angel and rescued me from the hand of Herod and from all that the Jewish people were expecting."*

OVERVIEW: The image portrayed here—rescue, angel, light—is meant to evoke the resurrection of Jesus and, as Chrysostom notes, contrasts the power of God, who enables his servants to carry out his will through a power that establishes peace and is kept in a virtuous life, which had become lost through sin. Here, this power results in a miracle unbelievable even to the one experiencing it, and from it we can see how God honors his people with the ministry of his angels (CHRYSOSTOM).

12:6 Peter Asleep Between Two Soldiers

SHARING IN CHRIST'S POWER. CHRYSOSTOM: See how Peter slept and was not in anguish or fear. In the very night when he was about to be brought before the court he slept, leaving everything to God. Indeed the multitude becomes powerful when virtue is present. And it had such a power that even though the doors were closed, chains bound the apostle and the jailers slept at both his sides, virtue delivered him and saved him from all those difficulties. So if virtue is present the multitude has great strength, but if vice is present it makes no benefit. CATENA ON THE ACTS OF THE APOSTLES 12.6-7.[1]

12:9 Seeing a Vision?

THE EXCESSIVE GREATNESS OF THE MIRACLE. CHRYSOSTOM: [Peter] thought he was seeing a vision. Well might he think that, considering the excessive greatness of the things taking place. Do you see what it means for a miracle to be excessive? How it strikes the onlooker dumb, how it does not permit him to disbelieve? If Peter thought he was seeing a vision throughout such a long period of time, even though he had put on his belt and shoes, what would have happened to another person? "And passing," it says, "the first guard and the second, they came to the iron gate. And they went out and passed on through one street, and immediately the angel departed from him." What happened within was more marvelous; from here on it is more human. When there was no hindrance, the angel departed. For Peter would not have gotten away otherwise, with so many hindrances in place. It was truly mind-boggling. HOMILIES ON THE ACTS OF THE APOSTLES 26.[2]

12:11 The Lord Sent an Angel

---

[1]CGPNT 3:203. [2]NPNF 1 11:170**.

THE LORD HONORS PETER BY SENDING AN ANGEL. CHRYSOSTOM: Why was this not done through themselves? In this way God honors them, rescuing them through his angels. Why did it not happen like this in the case of Paul? With good reason, because there the prison guard was to be converted,[3] while here only the apostle was to be released. In different ways God disposes different things. There, it is well for Paul to sing hymns; here, for Peter to sleep. HOMILIES ON THE ACTS OF THE APOSTLES 26.[4]

---

[3]Acts 16:25-33. [4]NPNF 1 11:171-72**.

12:12-19 PETER GOES TO THE HOUSE OF MARY

[12]*When he realized this, he went to the house of Mary, the mother of John whose other name was Mark, where many were gathered together and were praying.* [13]*And when he knocked at the door of the gateway, a maid named Rhoda came to answer.* [14]*Recognizing Peter's voice, in her joy she did not open the gate but ran in and told that Peter was standing at the gate.* [15]*They said to her, "You are mad." But she insisted that it was so. They said, "It is his angel!"* [16]*But Peter continued knocking; and when they opened, they saw him and were amazed.* [17]*But motioning to them with his hand to be silent, he described to them how the Lord had brought him out of the prison. And he said, "Tell this to James and to the brothers." Then he departed and went to another place.*

[18]*Now when day came, there was no small stir among the soldiers over what had become of Peter.* [19]*And when Herod had sought for him and could not find him, he examined the sentries and ordered that they should be put to death. Then he went down from Judea to Caesarea, and remained there.*

OVERVIEW: In Peter's actions we see a care for the Jerusalem church, one that extends even to those that others would consider insignificant. These become messengers of the good news of Peter's release, but before they do so, they must be convinced that Peter, and not his guardian angel, has come to them in the midst of affliction to reveal God's marvels (CHRYSOSTOM). As Chrysostom and Arator point out, both the course of events and the reactions to Peter are similar to what occurred at Christ's resurrection, even the need to receive some sort of testimony from those who were on guard. In this instance, the guards are put to death, and yet this attempt to hide the facts only makes the truth more evident. Chrysostom's remark that the special mention of James shows affection for a fellow apostle is closer to the mark than modern conjectures about transfer of authority.

12:12 The House of Mary

DO NOT HIDE GOD'S MARVELS. CHRYSOSTOM: Therefore, let us not conceal the wonders of God, but to our own advantage, let us parade them with zeal, for the edification of others. He is to be admired for choosing to be imprisoned but even more for not withdrawing before he had reported everything to his friends. And he said, "Tell this to James and to the brothers,"[1] so that they might rejoice and not worry about him. And it is through these that those find out, not those through this. Thus did he take thought for the humbler part! HOMILIES ON THE ACTS OF THE APOSTLES 26.[2]

AFFLICTION MAKES THEM VIGILANT. CHRYSOSTOM: Look how much they achieved by praying at night. How great a good is affliction. How much it awakened them. Did you notice the gain from Stephen's death? Or how great a benefit this prison conferred? For it is not by taking vengeance on those who wronged them that God shows the greatness of the gospel. Rather, it is in the wrongdoers themselves, without their suffering anything terrible, that he shows the greatness of afflictions in themselves by themselves, so that we would in no way seek deliverance from them, not even vengeance for the wrongs done us. HOMILIES ON THE ACTS OF THE APOSTLES 26.[3]

12:13 A Maid Named Rhoda

THE SERVANT EQUAL TO THE REST. CHRYSOSTOM: Consider how even their servant girls had an equal share of honor as they did. "For joy," it says, "she did not open the gate." This too happens for a good reason, that they might not be dumbfounded, seeing him at once and so disbelieve, but that their thoughts might be prepared. She does what we would all do: she runs in so that she might be the one bringing the good news. For truly it was good news. HOMILIES ON THE ACTS OF THE APOSTLES 26.[4]

12:15 It Is His Angel

THEY LEARN ALL CLEARLY. CHRYSOSTOM: "And they said to her:'You are mad!' But she confidently affirmed that it was so. And they said,'It is his angel.'" This is true because everyone has an angel. And what does the angel want? From the time of the night this is what they expected. "But

Peter continued knocking; and when they had opened, they saw him and were amazed. But he motioned them with his hand" and produced a great silence, so that they might hear what had happened to him. He was now much more sought after by the disciples, not only because he was saved but also on account of his arrival and immediate departure. His friends heard about everything clearly, and strangers would have too, if indeed they had wished to, but they did not. This also happened in the case of Christ. "Tell these things," he said, "to James and to the brothers." Is he not free from vainglory? He did not even say, "Make these things known to people everywhere" but "to the brothers." . . . It was to prevent them from saying, "It was his angel," after his departure, that they say this first and then see the man himself, who controverts that idea. Had it been the angel, he would not have knocked at the door or withdrawn to another place. They were assured of this by what happened the next day. HOMILIES ON THE ACTS OF THE APOSTLES 26.[5]

12:16 The Believers Were Amazed

PETER SHOWS FORTH THE RESURRECTION. ARATOR: Immediately, free from the enemy, he sings the praises of God's work. The first girl demonstrates that he has come back from the darkness because the grace of Christ allowed a similar thing to be, inasmuch as the Lord himself, rising [from the dead], approached the sight of women; the glory of his returning flesh spoke to the sex that his mother has. It is clear from this also that the church, which must carry unrestrained gladness to every flock, recognized its prophet [Peter]. ON THE ACTS OF THE APOSTLES I.[6]

12:17 Peter Went to Another Place

HE DID NOT TEMPT GOD. CHRYSOSTOM: And [Peter] withdrew to another place. He did not

---

[1]Acts 12:17. [2]NPNF 1 11:172**. [3]NPNF 1 11:171**. [4]NPNF 1 11:171**. [5]NPNF 1 11:171**. [6]OAA 55-56.

tempt God or even throw himself into temptation. When they were commanded to do something, they did it. "Go," the angel said, "and speak in the temple to the people."[7] The angel did not say this here, but, by silently removing him and bringing him out by night, he gave him the power to withdraw. And this is done to teach us that matters are often providentially arranged in human terms, in this case, to prevent him from falling into danger again. HOMILIES ON THE ACTS OF THE APOSTLES 26.[8]

12:19 Herod Orders the Death of the Soldiers

NOT YET THE TIME OF JUDGMENT. CHRYSOSTOM: Some people may be at a loss to explain how God allowed his champions to be put to death. And why did the soldiers die on account of Peter, although it was possible for God, after he had saved Peter, to rescue them as well? But it was not

yet the time of judgment, to render to each according to his deserts. Besides, it was not Peter who put them into his hands. For what most annoyed Herod was being mocked. Just as when his grandfather was deceived by the wise men,[9] it cut him to the heart being made a laughingstock. "He examined the sentries," it says, "and ordered that they should be put to death." And yet he had heard from them (for he examined them) that the chains had been discarded, that Peter had taken his sandals and that until that night he was with them. But what did the sentries conceal? Why didn't they also flee? Surely, Herod ought to have been amazed and astonished at this. This becomes clear to everyone through these men's death. The wickedness of Herod is discovered, and that the wonder is of God. HOMILIES ON THE ACTS OF THE APOSTLES 27.[10]

---

[7]Acts 5:20. [8]NPNF 1 11:171**. [9]Mt 2:16. [10]NPNF 1 11:173-74**.

12:20-25 HEROD'S DEATH

[20]Now Herod was angry with the people of Tyre and Sidon; and they came to him in a body, and having persuaded Blastus, the king's chamberlain, they asked for peace, because their country depended on the king's country for food. [21]On an appointed day Herod put on his royal robes, took his seat upon the throne, and made an oration to them. [22]And the people shouted, "The voice of a god, and not of man!" [23]Immediately an angel of the Lord smote him, because he did not give God the glory; and he was eaten by worms and died.

[24]But the word of God grew and multiplied.

[25]And Barnabas and Saul returned from[k] Jerusalem when they had fulfilled their mission, bringing with them John whose other name was Mark.

k Other ancient authorities read to

OVERVIEW: This is another instance of Luke's theocentric understanding of the events that concern the church. We have little indication of how the Fathers understood Acts 12:25, which, as modern authors note, should read, "When they had finished their service to Jerusalem, Barnabas and Saul returned." As in the last entry above, so too here, the source of the violence and suffering as recounted in Acts is a concern. Herod's actions against the soldiers were permitted by God, who can right unjust actions when the end comes (CHRYSOSTOM, at Acts 12:19 above). Chrysostom, however, brings out an irony in Herod's death. The assumption of divinity, the claim to be beyond death and worthy of worship, calls for punishment when it is false. So Herod's acceptance of the people's declaration, one implying immortality, is met with the onset of death that has no human agent. Christ's death, however, despite the import of his words, was inflicted by people whose judgment was as equally meaningless as in the case of Herod. Herod's death also serves the people as a divine correction of their hyperbolic flattery.

12:22 The Voice of a God

HEROD'S DEATH PROCLAIMS CHRIST'S DIVINITY. CHRYSOSTOM: If this man, because he heard himself called "the voice of a god, and not of man!" suffered such a fate, even though he said nothing, much more would Christ have suffered, were he not God. For he was always saying such things as "these words of mine are not mine," "angels minister to me,"[1] etc. That man, then, ended his life in shame and misery, and no more was seen of him. HOMILIES ON THE ACTS OF THE APOSTLES 27.[2]

12:23 An Angel Struck Herod

OTHERS LEARN FROM HEROD'S PUNISHMENT. CHRYSOSTOM: Notice how the writer does not conceal this. Why does he mention this story? Tell me, what does it have to do with the gospel that Herod is incensed with the Tyrians and Sidonians? . . . But it is of no small importance how immediately justice overtook him, even though it was not on account of Peter but because of his own haughtiness. And yet, one may ask, if it was those people who shouted, what does it have to do with him? But he accepted the acclamation, he deemed himself worthy of the adoration. Through him a lesson is taught, especially to those who flattered him without cause. Do you see how both parties deserved punishment, but only he was chastised? For this is not the time of judgment. He punishes the one who had most to answer for and leaves the rest to benefit by this man's example. "But the word of God," it says, "grew and multiplied" after this had happened. HOMILIES ON THE ACTS OF THE APOSTLES 27.[3]

---

[1]Jn 14:10; 18:36. [2]NPNF 1 11:175**. [3]NPNF 1 11:174**.

13:1-5 BARNABAS AND SAUL SET APART

[1]Now in the church at Antioch there were prophets and teachers, Barnabas, Simeon who was called Niger, Lucius of Cyrene, Mana-en a member of the court of Herod the tetrarch, and Saul. [2]While they were worshiping the Lord and fasting, the Holy Spirit said, "Set apart for me Barnabas and Saul for the work to which I have called them." [3]Then after fasting and praying they laid their hands on them and sent them off.

[4]So, being sent out by the Holy Spirit, they went down to Seleucia; and from there they sailed to

Cyprus. *⁵When they arrived at Salamis, they proclaimed the word of God in the synagogues of the Jews. And they had John to assist them.*

OVERVIEW: These verses set the explicit missionary activity of the church under the direct command of the Holy Spirit which was given prophetically at a liturgy of prayer and fasting followed by the laying on of hands. Modern commentators see three blocks in Paul's missions and this, the first, encompasses Acts 13:1 to Acts 14:28. This first mission does not seem to be reflected in Paul's letters, and this has led commentators to question its occurrence. Not all commentators are so skeptical and see glimpses of it in Galatians 1:21-23 and Philippians 4:15.[1] As Acts 13:1-3 is preparatory for the first mission, so the first mission is preparatory for the council of Acts 15. The Fathers' focus is twofold: the nature of the Spirit and the mission of the church. The action of the Holy Spirit in people's lives can be unpredictable, but it requires cooperation to be effective (AMMONIUS). The Fathers cite this obedience to the Spirit's actions for their own debates over the divine nature (CHRYSOSTOM, PSEUDO-BASIL). In their remarks, there is also an attentiveness to how the story of Acts is important for the continuing story of Christianity, not just in its debates over the Godhead, but in its self-understanding as well. It is not coincidental that these insights into the mission of the church occur within the context of an account of the mission of the Spirit. First, there is seen the initiative of the Spirit to keep scattering messengers of the gospel; second, how servants of the Word do not need to be great by human standards; and third, that human cooperation with God does not deprive God of the initiative and efficacy in the work of salvation (CHRYSOSTOM).

13:1 Prophets and Teachers

COOPERATING WITH THE SPIRIT. AMMONIUS: "And Manaean, who had been brought up with Herod the tetrarch." Behold the customs of each

of them: not even the fact of being brought up together saves them both. See how absolutely evil Herod was, for he did not want to be converted. But his foster brother Manaean certainly changed a great deal, because he was considered worthy of the gift of prophecy. CATENA ON THE ACTS OF THE APOSTLES 13.1.[2]

13:2 Set Apart Barnabas and Saul

THEY COULD BE SUFFICIENT FOR MANY. CHRYSOSTOM: But consider the authority of the Holy Ghost. "While they were worshiping the Lord and fasting, the Holy Spirit said, 'Set apart for me Barnabas and Saul.'" What being, unless of the same authority, would have dared to say this? And this happened so that they should not remain together among themselves. The Spirit saw that they had greater power and could be sufficient for many. HOMILIES ON THE ACTS OF THE APOSTLES 27.[3]

REMAINING ATTENTIVE. AMMONIUS: It must be noticed that the Holy Spirit does not speak to those who happen to be there by chance but to those who serve him and observe fasting. And it must be noticed again that they did not lay hands on the deacons at random but on those who were previously fasting and praying. CATENA ON THE ACTS OF THE APOSTLES 13.2.[4]

13:3 Ordained and Sent Off

ORDAINED THROUGH THE GRACE OF THE SPIRIT. CHRYSOSTOM: "While they were worshiping the Lord and fasting, the Holy Spirit said, 'Set apart for me Barnabas and Saul for the work to which I have called them.' Then after

---

[1]For a detailed discussion, see Fitzmyer, *Acts*, 136-37. [2]CGPNT 3:212. [3]NPNF 1 11:175-76**. [4]CGPNT 3:212.

fasting and praying they laid their hands on them and sent them off." What does "worshiping" mean? It means preaching. "Set apart Barnabas and Saul." What does "set apart for me" mean? It means for the work, for the apostleship. Remember who ordained him? Lucius the Cyrenean and Manaen, or rather, one should say, the Spirit. For the more lowly the personages involved, the more palpable the grace of God. Paul is ordained henceforth to apostleship, to preach with authority. How is it then that he himself says, "Not from men nor by men"?[5] Because it was not humankind that called him or brought him over. This is what "or by men" means. For this reason he says that he was not sent by this man but by the Spirit. HOMILIES ON THE ACTS OF THE APOSTLES 27.[6]

THE THREE PERSONS PERFORMING ONE ACTION. PSEUDO-BASIL: The Lord, upon appearing to Paul from heaven, said, "Go to Damascus, and you shall be told that you are my chosen vessel,"[7] because [the Lord] had established him as the herald of the gospel to all the world. Then Ananias said to him, when he arrived in Damascus, "Brother Saul, see once more: the God of the fathers has preordained you."[8] And lest you think this word [i.e., God] refers to Christ, he adds, "to do his will and to know his just one Jesus."[9] [Paul], making this calling and preordaining a title, says, "Paul a slave of Jesus Christ, called apostle."[10] Then he says something else regarding this calling, "Set aside for the gospel of God."[11] The Acts of the Apostles

taught that the Spirit directed the setting aside, for it says, "While the apostles were fasting and praying, the Holy Spirit said, 'Set aside for me Paul and Barnabas for the work to which I have called them.'" If the Lord, the God of the fathers, chose him whom he had preordained, while the Son called him forth, and the Spirit, using the operation of [the divine] nature, set the same one aside, how is there a difference of nature in the Trinity in which an identity of operation is found? AGAINST EUNOMIUS 5.[12]

13:4 Sent by the Holy Spirit

THE SPIRIT DIRECTS THEIR MOVEMENTS. CHRYSOSTOM: As soon as they were ordained they went forth and hastened to Cyprus, seeing that no plot was being hatched against them there and the Word had already been sown. In Antioch there were enough [teachers]. As to Phoenice, it was near Palestine, but not so Cyprus. However, do not ask why, when it is the Spirit that directs their movements. For they were not only ordained by the Spirit but also sent forth by him. HOMILIES ON THE ACTS OF THE APOSTLES 28.[13]

---

[5]Gal 1:1. [6]NPNF 1 11:174-75**. [7]Acts 9:15; 22:10. [8]Acts 22:13-14. [9]Cf. Acts 22:14. The author of *Against Eunomius* has significantly altered this verse of Acts, which reads, "The God of our fathers has preordained you to know his will and to see his just one and to hear a voice from his mouth." The author's point, however, stands. [10]Rom 1:1. [11]Rom 1:1. [12]PG 29:720-21. [13]NPNF 1 11:178**.

13:6-12 THE CONVERSION OF SERGIUS PAULUS

[6]*When they had gone through the whole island as far as Paphos, they came upon a certain magician, a Jewish false prophet, named Bar-Jesus.* [7]*He was with the proconsul, Sergius Paulus, a man of intelligence, who summoned Barnabas and Saul and sought to hear the word of God.* [8]*But Ely-*

mas the magician (for that is the meaning of his name) withstood them, seeking to turn away the proconsul from the faith. ⁹But Saul, who is also called Paul, filled with the Holy Spirit, looked intently at him ¹⁰and said, "You son of the devil, you enemy of all righteousness, full of all deceit and villainy, will you not stop making crooked the straight paths of the Lord? ¹¹And now, behold, the hand of the Lord is upon you, and you shall be blind and unable to see the sun for a time." Immediately mist and darkness fell upon him and he went about seeking people to lead him by the hand. ¹²Then the proconsul believed, when he saw what had occurred, for he was astonished at the teaching of the Lord.

OVERVIEW: Luke's sudden attention to Saul/Paul's Semitic and Greek names probably reflects the "Europeanizing" of Paul's center of attention from now on. Jerome's mention that Sergius Paulus was Paul's first convert, and so Paul changed his own name from Saul to Paul, is not as fanciful as Augustine's connection of Paulus with small (*parvulus*). Even though their readings are not without influence in later ages, today neither holds favor. Modern and ancient commentators disagree on why Sergius Paulus converted, and no one of the latter comments directly on the proconsul's wonder at the gospel message. Clear, however, is their understanding of what Paul, or rather God through Paul, was doing in this miracle. Overcoming evil is elsewhere as here referred to as "teaching."[1] The topos of a change of name is very familiar in biblical literature (Abram to Abraham, Jacob to Israel, Simon to Cephas). The connection of the name, however, is only the beginning, as we see Paul doing to Bar-Jesus what Jesus had done to Paul (CHRYSOSTOM) so that Sergius Paulus and others, as well as the magician himself, might not be hindered from coming to the faith (ISIDORE OF PELUSIUM). Chrysostom is once again sensitive to Luke's accent on the divine action.

13:7 A Man of Intelligence

A BADGE OF HONOR. JEROME: As Sergius Paulus, proconsul of Cyprus, was the first to believe in his preaching, he took his name from him because he had subdued him to faith in Christ. ON ILLUSTRIOUS MEN 5.4.[2]

13:9 Paul Filled with the Spirit

THE LEAST OF THE APOSTLES. AUGUSTINE: The apostle Paul, who was previously called Saul, had no other reason, it seems to me, for choosing this name but to point out his own smallness as the least of the apostles. Hence, in order to praise this grace of God, he frequently fought courageously and vigorously against the proud and the arrogant and those who relied on their own works. After all, the grace of God was really seen more clearly and more obviously in him. ON THE SPIRIT AND THE LETTER 7.12.[3]

13:10 Making Crooked the Straight Paths

REPROOF, BUT NOT VENGEANCE. CHRYSOSTOM: Why didn't Paul perform another miracle? Because there was none equal to this—the capture of the enemy. And notice how he first makes his indictment and shows that the man suffers justly by saying, "O full of all deceit." Nothing [Paul] said was lacking, and he said it well. "Of all deceit," because the man was playing the part of a hypocrite. "Son of the devil," because he was doing his work. "Enemy of righteousness," because this [which they preached] was the whole of righteousness. It seems to me that he is also reproving his manner of life. It was not out of anger that he spoke, and to show this, the writer begins with, "filled with the Holy Spirit," that is, with his operation.

---

[1]See Mk 1:27; Lk 4:36. [2]FC 100:12. [3]WSA 1 23:156.

"And now behold the hand of the Lord is upon you." It was not vengeance, then, but healing. For it is as though he had said, "It is not I but the hand of God." Look how unassuming it is! No "light," as in the case of Paul, "shone round about him."[4] "Thou shall be blind," he says, "not seeing the sun for a season," so that he may give him a chance for repentance. Never did they wish to become conspicuous by their sternness, even in the case of enemies. But in respect to their own people, they were stern; in the case of others, no, lest [the obedience of faith] be thought a matter of compulsion and fear. HOMILIES ON THE ACTS OF THE APOSTLES 28.[5]

13:11 Blinded

BLINDNESS MEANT FOR HIS CONVERSION.
CHRYSOSTOM: "And now, behold, the hand of the Lord is upon you, and you shall be blind." It was the sign by which [Paul] was himself converted, and by this he wished to convert this man. And the words "for a season" were spoken by one who seeks not to punish but to convert. For if he had wanted to punish, he would have made him blind forever. This is not what happens here, but only "for a season," so that he may gain the proconsul. For the man was prepossessed by sorcery, and he

had to teach him a lesson by this punishment, just as the magicians [in Egypt] were taught by the boils.[6] HOMILIES ON THE ACTS OF THE APOSTLES 28.[7]

BLINDED SO THAT HE MIGHT SEE. ISIDORE OF PELUSIUM: Be reasonable now. What happened to the magician through the intervention of the apostle is not contrary to the divine commandment that commands us to love our enemies. But since that man distorted the ways of preaching and drove the proconsul away from the faith through which the entire multitude could easily have been admitted to salvation, Paul punished that blasphemer on the basis of his own way of working things out. After he was warned by being blinded he was then led to knowledge. Indeed he was taught through Paul to cure his infidelity with a remedy, just as Paul cured the contradictions of the law. After he set the limit "until the right time" for judgment so that it might cause in itself the recuperation of the man, he changed his ways for the better. CATENA ON THE ACTS OF THE APOSTLES 13.10.[8]

---

[4]Acts 9:3. [5]NPNF 1 11:179-80**. [6]Ex 9:11. [7]NPNF 1 11:179**. [8]CGPNT 3:216.

13:13-15 PAUL ARRIVES IN ANTIOCH OF PISIDIA

[13]Now Paul and his company set sail from Paphos, and came to Perga in Pamphylia. And John left them and returned to Jerusalem; [14]but they passed on from Perga and came to Antioch of Pisidia. And on the sabbath day they went into the synagogue and sat down. [15]After the reading of the law and the prophets, the rulers of the synagogue sent to them, saying, "Brothers, if you have any word of exhortation for the people, say it."

OVERVIEW: Again, Luke accents the new position of Paul ("Paul and his company") and shows them

following a pattern of going to the Jews first as at Cyprus. It is interesting that none of the Fathers make much comment about John Mark's leaving the missionary band. Paul shows patience, prudence and courage in his conduct (CHRYSOSTOM).

13:14 Going into the Synagogue

THEY PREPARE THE WAY FOR THE WORD.
CHRYSOSTOM: "They sat down in the synagogue," he says, "and on the sabbath day," to prepare the way beforehand for the Word. And they did not speak first but when invited, seeing that they summoned them as strangers. Had they not waited, there would have been no discourse. Here for the first time we have Paul preaching. And

notice his wisdom: where the word was already sown, he passes on; but where there was none, he makes a stay. It is as he himself writes, "Yes, so have I strived to preach the gospel, not where Christ was named."[1] Great courage was also embodied in this. Truly from the very outset a wonderful man! Crucified, drawn up in the line of battle, he knew how great was the grace he obtained, and he brought in an equal zeal. HOMILIES ON THE ACTS OF THE APOSTLES 28.[2]

---

[1] Rom 15:20. [2] NPNF 1 11:180**.

13:16-25 PAUL RECOUNTS THE HISTORY OF ISRAEL

[16]So Paul stood up, and motioning with his hand said:

"Men of Israel, and you that fear God, listen. [17]The God of this people Israel chose our fathers and made the people great during their stay in the land of Egypt, and with uplifted arm he led them out of it. [18]And for about forty years he bore with[m] them in the wilderness. [19]And when he had destroyed seven nations in the land of Canaan, he gave them their land as an inheritance, for about four hundred and fifty years. [20]And after that he gave them judges until Samuel the prophet. [21]Then they asked for a king; and God gave them Saul the son of Kish, a man of the tribe of Benjamin, for forty years. [22]And when he had removed him, he raised up David to be their king; of whom he testified and said, 'I have found in David the son of Jesse a man after my heart, who will do all my will.' [23]Of this man's posterity God has brought to Israel a Savior, Jesus, as he promised. [24]Before his coming John had preached a baptism of repentance to all the people of Israel. [25]And as John was finishing his course, he said, 'What do you suppose that I am? I am not he. No, but after me one is coming, the sandals of whose feet I am not worthy to untie.'

m Other ancient authorities read cared for (Deut 1.31)

OVERVIEW: This is the first time that Luke gives us a discourse of Paul. Modern commentators note that the discourse emphasizes a continuity between the history of Israel, how God took care of it through various leaders and what God has

done in Jesus. Unlike the earlier speeches, which build to a climax intended to bring repentance, this speech builds the case that Jesus was foreshadowed in the history of the chosen people. Chrysostom notes how Luke shows Paul beginning to take precedence in the missionary activity over Barnabas. He also notes how Paul's speech witnesses to the abundance of God's love toward the people of Israel. Further, Paul's use of prophecy and the fulfillment of it in Christ shows how neither the Old Testament nor the New stands alone but they unlock each other's potentials (CHRYSOSTOM, ORIGEN). Even John the Baptist's proclamation, which Paul cites, only hints at the great mysteries that the full revelation of the gospel holds (ORIGEN).

13:16 Paul Stood

BARNABAS GIVES WAY TO PAUL. CHRYSOSTOM: Look how Barnabas gives way to Paul—how should it be otherwise?—to him whom he brought from Tarsus, just as John gives way to Peter on all occasions, even though he commands more respect. Indeed, it was to the common advantage that they both looked. HOMILIES ON THE ACTS OF THE APOSTLES 29.[1]

13:18 God Bore with Israel in the Wilderness

PAUL EMPHASIZES GOD'S KINDNESS. CHRYSOSTOM: And notice how he passes over the times of their misfortunes and nowhere brings forward their faults but only God's kindness, leaving the rest for them to think over. . . . "And afterward they desired a king." Again [Paul] does not speak of their ingratitude but always the kindness of God. HOMILIES ON THE ACTS OF THE APOSTLES 29.[2]

13:23 A Savior for Israel

THE OLD TESTAMENT AND THE GOSPEL CONFIRM EACH OTHER. CHRYSOSTOM: Notice how [Paul] weaves his discourse from things present and from the prophets. Thus he says, "from [this man's] seed according to the promise," and then adduces John again, saying, "By condemning they fulfilled all that was written." Both the apostles as witnesses of the resurrection, and David bearing

witness. For neither do the Old Testament proofs seem so cogent when taken by themselves, nor the later testimonies apart from the former. Therefore it is through both that he makes his discourse trustworthy. HOMILIES ON THE ACTS OF THE APOSTLES 29.[3]

13:24 John Preached a Baptism of Repentance

JOHN BEGINS THE GOSPEL. ORIGEN: It must be said, on the one hand, that the Old [Testament] is not a Gospel since it did not show "the one coming"[4] but announced him beforehand, and on the other that the entire New [Testament] is the gospel, speaking not just in a way similar to the beginning of the Gospel, "Behold, the lamb of God that takes away the sin of the world,"[5] but encompassing manifold praises and teachings of the one on whose account the Gospel is the gospel. COMMENTARY ON THE GOSPEL OF JOHN 1.17.[6]

13:25b John Unworthy to Untie Jesus' Sandals

BEING WORTHY TO UNTIE JESUS' SANDALS. ORIGEN: If the passage about the sandals has a mystic meaning we should not reject an investigation of it. Now I consider that the full humanization, when the Son of God assumes flesh and bones, is seen in one of his shoes. The other humbling is the descent to Hades, whatever that Hades might be, and the journey with the Spirit to the prison. As to the descent into Hades, we read in the sixteenth psalm, "You will not abandon my soul to Hades."[7] As for the journey in prison with the Spirit, we read in Peter in his Catholic epistle, "Put to death," he says, "in the flesh but quickened in the Spirit, in which also he went and preached to the spirits in prison, which at one time were disobedient, when the long-suffering of God once waited in the days of Noah

---

[1]NPNF 1 11:182**. [2]NPNF 1 11:182**. [3]NPNF 1 11:183**. [4]Jn 1:9. [5]Jn 1:29. [6]GCS 10:7. [7]Ps 16:10 (15:10 LXX).

while the ark was in preparation."[8] He, then, who is able worthily to set forth the meaning of these two journeys is able to untie the strap of the sandals of Jesus. Such a one is whoever bends down in his mind and goes with Jesus as he goes down into hades, and whoever descends from heaven and the mysteries of Christ's divinity to the advent that he had to spend with us when he took on humanity (as his sandals). Now he who put on humanity also put on the dead, since "for this end Jesus both died and revived, that he might be Lord both of the dead and the living."[9] This is why he put on both the living and the dead, that is, the inhabitants of the earth and those of hades, that he might be the Lord of both the dead and the living. Who, then, is able to stoop down and untie the latchet of such sandals, and having untied them not to let them drop, but by the second faculty he has received[10] to take them up and bear them, by bearing the meaning of them in his memory? COMMENTARY ON THE GOSPEL OF JOHN 6.18.[11]

---

[8]1 Pet 3:18-20. [9]Rom 14:9. [10]Memory. [11]ANF 9:367-68*.

13:26-33 THE PROPHETS FULFILLED IN JESUS

[26]"Brothers, sons of the family of Abraham, and those among you that fear God, to us has been sent the message of this salvation. [27]For those who live in Jerusalem and their rulers, because they did not recognize him nor understand the utterances of the prophets which are read every sabbath, fulfilled these by condemning him. [28]Though they could charge him with nothing deserving death, yet they asked Pilate to have him killed. [29]And when they had fulfilled all that was written of him, they took him down from the tree, and laid him in a tomb. [30]But God raised him from the dead; [31]and for many days he appeared to those who came up with him from Galilee to Jerusalem, who are now his witnesses to the people. [32]And we bring you the good news that what God promised to the fathers, [33]this he has fulfilled to us their children by raising Jesus; as also it is written in the second psalm,*

    'Thou art my Son,

      today I have begotten thee.'

OVERVIEW: Paul's preaching aims to persuade his audience to accept the fulfillment of God's blessings and not, as Peter's preaching in Jerusalem, to move the Jerusalemites to repentance. Yet, among this Jewish audience, such acceptance requires an acknowledgment that leaders of the Jewish people were wrong in their understanding of how God was fulfilling the covenant. The Jewish leaders were not wicked but acted out of ignorance (CHRYSOSTOM). The resurrection reveals the told power and wisdom of God at work in history (SEVERUS). The undreamed of happened and in many, both Jews as here and later pagans, an incredulity demanded evidence that, as Origen shows, lay in God's sustenance of his people through the prophecies of which Paul speaks and in their fulfillment as attested by upright and sincere eyewitnesses, of whom Paul was one. Two passages present the patristic commentators with a problem: Acts 13:30 and 33. The subsequent patristic debates about the nature of the Son, whether and how he was divine or a creature, focused on passages of this sort that can be read by misguided interpreters as contradicting either the eternity or divinity of the Son. Bede reads Psalm 2:7 as a reference to the incarnation. As modern study has shown, the use of Psalm 2:7 is a common New Testament theme. The "begetting" of the king took place when he entered upon his royal authority. Jesus did so at his resurrection when his humanity was transformed by the divine action and he became king/Son.[1]

13:26 The Message of This Salvation

They May Sever Themselves from Those Who Crucified Christ. Chrysostom: Here the words "to you" do not mean "to the Jews," and he himself gave them a right to separate themselves from those who committed the murder. What follows makes this clear, "for those who live in Jerusalem," he says, "because they did not recognize him." Homilies on the Acts of the Apostles 29.[2]

13:30 God Raised Jesus from the Dead[3]

He Raised the Body. Theodoret of Cyr: So it is clear to them that pay attention that at the raising of the body the Son is said by Paul to have been raised from the dead, for he refers what concerns the body to the Son's person. Similarly when he says "the Father gave life to the Son,"[4] it must be understood that the life [the Father gave the Son] was given to the flesh. For if he himself is life, how can the life receive life? Dialogue 3.[5]

The Son Raised Himself. Severus of Antioch: Do not be troubled by the fact that Jesus is said to have been raised by God. Indeed, if Jesus is none other than the incarnate Word, he is also the power of the Father through whom everything occurs. This is according to the words,

"Christ is the power of God and the wisdom of God."[6] He himself will be considered to have raised himself while he is also said to have been raised by the Father to whom all things are referred as the eternal source and cause. Christ himself, in fact, says,[7] "Destroy this temple, and in three days I will raise it up." Catena on the Acts of the Apostles 13.30-31.[8]

13:31 For Many Days He Appeared

Pagan Myths Compared with the Gospel Witness. Origen: By comparing what the prophetic Scriptures tell us of Jesus with what his history tells us, we find nothing dissolute about him recorded. For even those who conspired against him and looked for false witnesses to aid them did not find any plausible grounds for advancing a false charge of licentiousness against him. His death was indeed the result of a conspiracy and bore no resemblance to the death of Asclepius by lightning.[9] And what is venerable about the madman Dionysus, clothed in female garments, that he should be worshiped as a god? If those who defend such beings resort to allegorical interpretations, we must examine each individual allegory to ascertain whether it is well founded and whether those beings who were torn down by the Titans[10] and cast from their heavenly throne[11] can have a real existence and deserve respect and worship. But when our Jesus "appeared to the members of his own troop"—for I will take the word that Celsus employs—he *really* did appear. But Celsus makes a false accusation against the gospel, saying that what appeared was a shadow. Let their histories and that of Jesus be carefully compared. Will Celsus hold that the former are true, but the latter are

---

[1]See Rom 1:1-4 and commentaries. [2]NPNF 1 11:184**. [3]See also the entry from Gregory of Nyssa at Acts 10:40. [4]Jn 5:26. [5]NPNF 2 3:237*. [6]1 Cor 1:24. [7]Jn 2:19. [8]CGPNT 3:223. [9]Origen is referring to the healing god Asclepius, whose tale is told by Pindar in *Pythian* 3. Asclepius raises some people from the dead and incites Zeus to jealousy, which leads the latter to kill Asclepius with a thunderbolt. For more on Origen's sources, see the notes in Chadwick (OCC 142-43). [10]Dionysus. [11]Asclepius.

inventions, even though the histories of Jesus were recorded by eyewitnesses who showed that they clearly understood the nature of what they had seen by their actions and who manifested their state of mind by what they cheerfully underwent for the sake of his gospel? Now who, desiring to act in conformity with right reason, would yield assent at random to what is related in their histories and without examination refuse to believe what is recorded of Jesus?

Again, when it is said of Asclepius that a great multitude both of Greeks and Barbarians acknowledge that they have frequently seen and still see no mere phantom but Asclepius himself healing and doing good and foretelling the future, Celsus expects us to believe this; and he finds no fault with believers in Jesus, when they express their belief in such stories. But when we give our assent to the disciples who were eyewitnesses of the miracles of Jesus and who clearly manifested the honesty of their convictions (because we see their guilelessness, as far as it is possible to see the conscience revealed in writing), we are called by him a set of "silly" individuals. AGAINST CELSUS 3.23-24.[12]

13:32b *What God Promised*

THE PROPHETS OF ISRAEL NOT FRAUDS. ORIGEN: Let Celsus, and those who agree with him, tell us whether it is at all like "an ass's shadow" that the Jewish prophets predicted the birth place of him who became the ruler of those who had lived righteous lives and are called the "heritage" of God,[13] that Emmanuel was conceived by a virgin, that such signs and wonders were performed by him who was the subject of prophecy, that his word spread so speedily that the voice of his apostles went forth into all the earth, that he suffered after his condemnation by the Jews, and that he rose again from the dead.[14] For was it by chance that the prophets made these announcements with no conviction of the truth in their minds, moving them not only to speak but to believe their announcements should be committed to writing? And did so great a nation as that of the Jews, who had long ago received a country of their own to dwell in, recognize certain men as prophets and reject others as false prophets, without any conviction of the soundness of the distinction? And was there no motive that induced them to class the words of those persons who were later deemed to be prophets with the books of Moses, which were held as sacred? And can those who charge the Jews and Christians with folly show us how the Jewish nation could have continued to exist had there not been among them a promise of the knowledge of future events? And how, while each of the surrounding nations believed in agreement with their ancient institutions that they received oracles and predictions from those whom they accounted gods, this people alone—who were taught to view with contempt all those who were considered gods by the heathen as not being gods, but demons, according to the declaration of the prophets, "For all the gods of the nations are demons"[15]—had among them no one who professed to be a prophet and who could dissuade those with a desire to know the future from deserting to the demons of other nations? Judge, then, whether it was necessary that the whole nation that had been taught to despise the deities of other lands should have an abundance of prophets, who made known events that were of far greater importance in themselves and that surpassed the oracles of all other countries. AGAINST CELSUS 3.2.[16]

13:33 *Fulfilled to Us Their Children*

THEY RECEIVE THE REALITY BEHIND THE PROMISE. CHRYSOSTOM: But let us look back to what was said. The promise then, he says, was what the fathers received, but you the reality. . . . And notice how nowhere does he mention their right deeds but only benefits on God's part: "he

---

[12]ANF 4:472-73**. [13]Deut 32:9. [14]Mic 5:2; Ps 19:5 (18:4 LXX); Is 53:5; Ps 16:10 (15:10 LXX). [15]Ps 96:5 (95:5 LXX). The LXX reads *daimones* (demons). The Hebrew word is usually translated *idols*, but its etymology is uncertain. See Mitchell Dahood, *Psalms II: 51-100* (Garden City, N.Y.: Doubleday, 1968), 358. [16]ANF 4:465-66**.

chose, he exalted, he bore with them." These words are not praises of them. "They asked, he gave." But David he does praise, and him alone, because it is from him that Christ was to come. Homilies on the Acts of the Apostles 29.[17]

You Are My Son. Cyril of Alexandria: The only one who knows the Father and who is only known by the Father as his Wisdom and Word and as "the Angel of great counsel" according to the prophet,[18] perfectly explains to us the mystery of the incarnation. Since he was Son by nature and by truth and had shone forth from the very essence of God the Father, he was made flesh, that is, man, according to John.[19] He desired to be called the brother of those who are in the world and to be born according to flesh like us. However, he was before time and sat with his parent even though he was made flesh. The Father knew him also as Son and said to him, "You are my Son; today I have begotten you."[20] Observe the explicit confession, nay rather, the proclamation! Indeed, he said, "you are" in order to point out that he existed before time. Actually, he was never in time but was always the same, to be sure, the Son. And he added, "today I have begotten you," in order to indicate his final generation according to the flesh that he voluntarily under-

went in the womb of the holy Virgin so that he was also called "begotten of God."[21] Catena on the Acts of the Apostles 13.33.[22]

The Second Psalm. Bede: It should not be supposed that this example of the psalm pertains to Christ's resurrection, even though he [Paul] mentions it next to [his reference to] that event. Instead, it pertains to his incarnation, about which he spoke above. Moreover, the following verse very clearly bears witness to the resurrection. Since in the preceding verses he [Paul] concerned himself with his [Christ's] incarnation, passion and resurrection, he wished to provide each [of these events] equally with testimonies furnished by a psalm. You then, he says, are eternal, Son before the ages. Now will you appear, born in time. Some manuscripts have, "just as is written in the first psalm." This is explained as follows, "Among the Hebrews the first and second psalms" are conflated "in one psalm, which begins with blessedness and comes to a close in blessedness."[23] Commentary on the Acts of the Apostles 13.33.[24]

---

[17]NPNF 1 11:184**. [18]Is 9:6 (9:5 LXX). [19]Jn 1:14. [20]Ps 2:7. [21]Jn 1:18. [22]CGPNT 3:224. [23]Jerome *Commentary on Psalm* 1.1 (CCL 72:178-79). [24]CS 117:119-20.

13:34-41 PAUL PROCLAIMS THE RESURRECTION

[34]*And as for the fact that he raised him from the dead, no more to return to corruption, he spoke in this way,*

'I will give you the holy and sure blessings of David.'

[35]*Therefore he says also in another psalm,*

'Thou wilt not let thy Holy One see corruption.'

[36]*For David, after he had served the counsel of God in his own generation, fell asleep, and was laid with his fathers, and saw corruption;* [37]*but he whom God raised up saw no corruption.* [38]*Let it*

be known to you therefore, brothers, that through this man forgiveness of sins is proclaimed to you, ³⁹*and by him every one that believes is freed from everything from which you could not be freed by the law of Moses.* ⁴⁰*Beware, therefore, lest there come upon you what is said in the prophets:*

⁴¹*'Behold, you scoffers, and wonder, and perish;*

for I do a deed in your days,

a deed you will never believe, if one declares it to you.' "

OVERVIEW: Here we reach the climax of Paul's speech that outlines the effects of the resurrection: forgiveness of sins and justification apart from the Mosaic law. This is the only time in Acts where justification by faith is mentioned. Luke's manner of describing justification is another way of speaking of the forgiveness of sins, a view that is not assumed in Paul's undisputed letters. The resurrection, as Paul says above at Acts 13:33, is the fulfillment to the people of Israel of God's promises and shows to us the incorruptibility that is also in store for those who believe and live beyond death (SEVERUS), the death from which the law was unable to set people free. The forgiveness that is in Christ, however, is precisely this freedom. This freedom empowers Christ's witnesses to spread his forgiveness, in the face of hatred, even to the ones who called for his execution (CHRYSOSTOM), the very means of which (hanging on a tree) had proclaimed him cursed by the Mosaic law.[1] To those who were familiar with the law, the action, by someone whose death had marked him cursed by God's law, of returning to life would be an undoing of the curse of death that had come by the transgression of the law and therefore would stand as a proclamation of forgiveness to all who believe in him (CHRYSOSTOM, AMMONIUS). Paul's interest is in making the latter known by stressing the forgiveness that comes from the resurrection rather than that the law had served its purpose and would soon pass, since to do so might have roused them to anger. Instead, Paul tried to rouse his audience to fear God's judgment (CHRYSOSTOM).

13:35 God's Holy One Will Not See Corruption

THE HOPE OF THOSE IN CHRIST. SEVERUS OF ANTIOCH: From [the tomb] Christ was raised for us and rose as the true lord of incorruptibility, so that we also, by rising up from our tombs to the anticipated resurrection, may run toward heaven and to the clouds in which he returns in his divine glory. CATENA ON THE ACTS OF THE APOSTLES 13.35-36.[2]

13:38 Forgiveness of Sins Proclaimed Through Jesus

PERSUADED BY THE FORGIVENESS OF SINS. CHRYSOSTOM: Look what they said to persuade people—"he was crucified." What could be less persuasive than this? That he was buried by those to whom it was promised that he should be the salvation, that he who was buried forgives sins, even more than the law? And he does not say, "from which you would not," but "from which you could not be freed by the law of Moses." "Everyone," that is, whoever he is. For those [ordinances] are of no use, unless some benefit comes from them. This is why he brings in forgiveness later and shows it to be greater, when that which is impossible comes about. "Who are his witnesses," he says, "to the people"—the people that killed him. They would not have been his witnesses had they not been strengthened by a divine power. They would not have borne such witness to bloodthirsty people, the very people who killed him. "Today I have begotten you," he said. It is on this that the rest follows. Why didn't

---

[1]Cf. Gal 3:10-14 and Paul's citations of Deut 21:23; 27:26. [2]CGPNT 3:225.

[Paul] adduce some text, through which they would be persuaded that forgiveness of sins is through him? Because this was what he was trying to do: first to show he was risen; when this is acknowledged, the other becomes indisputable. And indeed *"by him"* is the remission of sins. Moreover, he wanted to make them yearn after this great thing. HOMILIES ON THE ACTS OF THE APOSTLES 29.[3]

13:39 Everyone Who Believes Is Freed

THE LAW COULD NOT JUSTIFY. AMMONIUS: It should be noticed that those who believe in Christ are justified and obtain absolution from their sin. In fact, the law of Moses was not unjust. Rather, it was difficult and able to justify only those who had followed the entire law perfectly. Therefore it was clearly incapable of correcting people because the one who had fallen into a single crime was made guilty of all. Thus the law was not able to justify. And, since the law itself was incapable of justifying anyone, its inability to correct made people incapable of being justified by the precepts of the law. CATENA ON THE ACTS OF THE APOSTLES 13.39.[4]

13:40 Beware

WHAT IS FOR ISRAEL'S GOOD. CHRYSOSTOM: And he does not spend a long time on these [ingratitudes of the ancestors], taking it for granted that the word is of course believed. But he expands on the punishment and goes after that which they love, showing that the law is being cast out, and he dwells on what is for their good, [telling them] that great shall be the blessings for those who obey and great the evils for those who do not.... Paul loved them exceedingly. And notice how he does not dwell on the ingratitude of the fathers but puts before *them* what they must fear. For Stephen indeed does this with good reason, seeing that he was about to be put to death, and was not teaching them but showing them that the law is even now on the point of being abolished.[5] But not so Paul; he only threatens and puts fear in them. HOMILIES ON THE ACTS OF THE APOSTLES 29.[6]

---

[3]NPNF 1 11:185**. [4]CGPNT 3:226. [5]See Acts 7. [6]NPNF 1 11:184**.

13:42-48 PAUL IS CONTRADICTED AND TURNS TO THE GENTILES

[42]*As they went out, the people begged that these things might be told them the next sabbath.* [43]*And when the meeting of the synagogue broke up, many Jews and devout converts to Judaism followed Paul and Barnabas, who spoke to them and urged them to continue in the grace of God.*

[44]*The next sabbath almost the whole city gathered together to hear the word of God.* [45]*But when the Jews saw the multitudes, they were filled with jealousy, and contradicted what was spoken by Paul, and reviled him.* [46]*And Paul and Barnabas spoke out boldly, saying, "It was necessary that the word of God should be spoken first to you. Since you thrust it from you, and judge yourselves unworthy of eternal life, behold, we turn to the Gentiles.* [47]*For so the Lord has commanded us, saying,*

'I have set you to be a light for the Gentiles,

that you may bring salvation to the uttermost parts of the earth.'"

[48]*And when the Gentiles heard this, they were glad and glorified the word of God; and as many as were ordained to eternal life believed.*

Overview: Modern observations take note that at Acts 13:43, Luke finally has Paul mention grace, an important part of Paul's teaching in his letters. They also call attention to Paul's words in Acts 13:46, "we now turn to the Gentiles," and note they are neither a definitive abandonment of the Jewish people nor a turning point in Paul's mission, as Acts 9:15 makes clear. This narrative is less about the move in the mission from Jew to Gentile and more about the consequences of rejecting the message of salvation. Another insight is that the way Paul quotes Isaiah 49:6 (LXX), on first reading, directs the words to himself and Barnabas, but since the "you" is singular, it seems that he is making Barnabas and himself instruments that show forth Christ, the light to the nations. For other Lukan uses of this Isaiah verse, see Luke 2:32 and Acts 26:18. Many of these points were anticipated by the older commentators. In the passages from the Fathers, we see Paul's proclamation of Jesus, the crucified and resurrected one, as the fulfillment of the hope of Israel. The preaching scatters seeds that begin to bear fruit yet require a longer period of instruction. The envy that the success of Paul and Barnabas raises, however, does not stop the gospel from spreading (Chrysostom) and in fact serves to demonstrate that the nature of this message is universal as it comes from God who wills all who repent to be saved. It is we who freely judge ourselves to be unworthy of eternal life (Ammonius).[1] Paul and Barnabas do not here reject the Jews and will continue to approach them, but they cannot keep themselves from preaching to the rest of the world (Chrysostom) as they have been called to extend Christ's light (Bede).

13:42 The People Begged to Hear Paul

Paul Plants the Seed of the Word. Chry-

sostom: Did you notice Paul's wisdom? Not only did he win admiration at the time, but also put in them a second longing for listening, sowing as it were seeds in his speech and not resolving the issues at hand or following the subject to its conclusion, so as to ready them and accustom them to himself and not to make them flaccid by hurling everything at their souls at once. He said, "Through this man forgiveness of sins is proclaimed to you," but he did not reveal how. After this point, he puts Paul first. Do you see their great eagerness? "They followed them," he says. Why didn't he baptize them immediately? It was not the proper time; there was need to persuade them so that they might remain steadfast. Homilies on the Acts of the Apostles 30.[2]

13:45 Filled with Jealousy

This Envy Extends the Preaching. Chrysostom: Do you see how by their contentious behavior they extended the preaching further and [how the apostles] gave themselves the more to the Gentiles, having made their defense and cleared themselves of indictments from their own people? . . . Through their jealousy they brought it about that the apostles spoke out boldly and went to the Gentiles. For this is why he said, "Paul and Barnabas spoke out boldly, saying, 'It was necessary that the word of God should be spoken first to you. Since you thrust it from you and judge yourselves unworthy of eternal life, behold, we turn to the Gentiles.'" They were about to go out to the Gentiles. But notice how the boldness is accompanied with measure. For if Peter defended himself, much more are these in need of a defense, since no one had called them

---

[1]See 1 Tim 2:3-6. [2]NPNF 1 11:188**.

there.[3] And by saying "first," he showed that to those as well it was their duty [to preach], and by saying "necessary," he showed that it was necessary to preach to them as well. "Since you turn away," he does not say, "woe to you" and "you are punished," but "we turn to the Gentiles." The boldness is full of much gentleness. Homilies on the Acts of the Apostles 30.[4]

13:46 Turning to the Gentiles

God Desires the Salvation of All. Ammonius: Therefore God declares that nothing is unworthy of salvation or of entering the kingdom, nor, on the contrary, does he judge that humankind deserves damnation. Rather, we judge ourselves, through our freely committed malice, to be unworthy of eternal life and worthy of eternal damnation. Therefore the judgment is in ourselves as well as the lot of our future state. Catena on the Acts of the Apostles 13.46.[5]

13:47 A Light for the Gentiles

Israel Not Abandoned. Chrysostom: "It was necessary," he says, "that the word should be spoken first to you. Since you thrust it from you." Not an affront, but the same thing they had also done in the case of the prophets, "Speak not to us," said they, "with talk."[6] "Since you thrust it from you," he says, not "us." For the affront from you was not against us. To prevent anyone from thinking "you judge yourselves unworthy" was an expression of their piety, [Paul] says first, "you thrust it from you," and then "we turn to the Gentiles." Full of great gentleness are these words. He did not say, "we abandon you," but so that it is possible, he says, that we may turn to here again. And this was not the result of your affront, "for so the Lord has commanded us." Then why have you not done this? There was indeed need that the Gentiles should hear. But the "before you" came about not from us but from you. "For so the Lord has commanded us. 'I have set you to be a light for the Gentiles, that you may bring salvation.'" That is, to be the knowledge to salvation. And not only for the Gentiles but for all who were ordained to eternal life. This is also a proof that it was in accordance with the mind of God that they received the Gentiles. Homilies on the Acts of the Apostles 30.[7]

Light for the Gentiles. Bede: What was said with specific reference to Christ the Lord[8] is here taken by the apostles as referring to themselves, as they call to mind that they are his members; just as he himself said, because of the oneness of his body, "Saul, Saul, why do you persecute me?"[9] Commentary on the Acts of the Apostles 13.47.[10]

---

[3]Acts 11:4-18. [4]NPNF 1 11:189**. [5]CGPNT 3:229. [6]Is 30:10. [7]NPNF 1 11:191**. [8]Lk 2:32; Acts 26:32. [9]Acts 9:4. [10]CS 117:120.

13:49-52 PAUL AND BARNABAS DRIVEN OUT OF THE DISTRICT

[49]And the word of the Lord spread throughout all the region. [50]But the Jews incited the devout women of high standing and the leading men of the city, and stirred up persecution against Paul and Barnabas, and drove them out of their district. [51]But they shook off the dust from their feet

against them, and went to Iconium. [52]And the disciples were filled with joy and with the Holy Spirit.

OVERVIEW: Here, Ammonius sees in these rich women a seduction of women akin to the devil's seduction of Eve and thus a closing of the doors of life, the doors of salvation, the doors of paradise through those who should be doors to life, salvation and paradise. As women are seen as holding a place in the service of a male-defined world, they are not the source of evil but its instrument: Paul's opponents are using their women to cut themselves off from life and their inheritance. To symbolize their response to those in Pisidian Antioch to those who rejected the labor of Paul and Barnabas, the latter shook the dust, out of which humankind is made, from their feet. Here, as the Fathers point out, the preachers are obeying a gospel injunction. This difficulty, however, does not curtail their joy in the Spirit (BEDE).[1]

13:50 Driven Out of the District

CLOSING PARADISE. AMMONIUS: "Honest rich women," the text says, "and pious," but not faithful. They certainly were Greek-Jewish women. In fact they, being most evil and imitators of the archevil demon and transgressor, endeavor through women to close to men the way of salvation, just as that one closed paradise to men through Eve until the proper time. But the divine Jesus opens it again for those who believe in his name and also allowed them to enter there, the first of whom entered with him as a thief. CATENA ON THE ACTS OF THE APOSTLES 13.50.[2]

13:51 Shaking the Dust from Their Feet

NO HURT TO THE DISCIPLES. CHRYSOSTOM: "But they shook off the dust from their feet against them," he says, "and went to Iconium." Here they used that terrible sign, which Christ enjoined, "If any do not receive you, shake off the dust from your feet."[3] But these did not do it lightly but because they were driven away by them. In no way did this hurt the disciples; on the contrary, all the more did they continue in the word, "And the disciples were filled with joy and with the Holy Spirit." For the suffering of the teacher does not check his boldness but makes the disciple more courageous. HOMILIES ON THE ACTS OF THE APOSTLES 30.[4]

DUST OF THEIR FEET. BEDE: According to the commandment in the Gospel, dust was shaken off from their feet in testimony of their labor,[5] because they entered into their city, and the apostolic preaching reached all the way to them [the Antiochenes]. Alternatively, the dust was shaken off so that they would take nothing, not even a thing so basic to life, from those who had rejected the gospel. COMMENTARY ON THE ACTS OF THE APOSTLES 13.51.[6]

13:52 The Disciples Filled with Joy

FILLED WITH JOY AND WITH THE HOLY SPIRIT. BEDE: The Greek has, "But the disciples," so that we may understand that although the Jews persecuted the faith, the disciples on the contrary were endowed with spiritual joy. COMMENTARY ON THE ACTS OF THE APOSTLES 13.52.[7]

---

[1]This act of shaking dust from their feet was expected of Jews returning to Israel from pagan lands, so that they would not carry what is impure into the land. [2]CGPNT 3:231. [3]Mt 10:14; Mk 6:11. [4]NPNF 1 11:189**. [5]Mt 10:14. [6]CS 117:121. [7]CS 117:121.

14:1-7 ICONIUM DIVIDED OVER THE APOSTLES

¹Now at Iconium they entered together into the Jewish synagogue, and so spoke that a great company believed, both of Jews and of Greeks. ²But the unbelieving Jews stirred up the Gentiles and poisoned their minds against the brothers. ³So they remained for a long time, speaking boldly for the Lord, who bore witness to the word of his grace, granting signs and wonders to be done by their hands. ⁴But the people of the city were divided; some sided with the Jews, and some with the apostles. ⁵When an attempt was made by both Gentiles and Jews, with their rulers, to molest them and to stone them, ⁶they learned of it and fled to Lystra and Derbe, cities of Lycaonia, and to the surrounding country; ⁷and there they preached the gospel.

OVERVIEW: Modern commentators see Paul and Barnabas here as good examples of the church under stress. There is a division of opinion over the use of the title *apostolos* being applied to Paul and Barnabas only at Acts 14:4 and 14 and nowhere else in Acts: did Luke consider them among the apostles or, less likely, did he fail to edit his source here? The actions of Paul and Barnabas, being extensions of the prophesied actions of Christ, meet with the same response that their master experienced from their fellow Jews (AMMONIUS). The eagerness of Paul and Barnabas for the gospel serves them well as God uses them to extend the kingdom (CHRYSOSTOM). The environment, however, grew too hostile so that it was prudent to flee (AMMONIUS).

14:2 Unbelieving Jews Incited the Gentiles

THE NATIONS CLAMOR. AMMONIUS: They caused an uprising against the faithful. The Jews joined forces with the Greeks so that what was said in the psalm might be fulfilled: "Why do the nations clamor and peoples devise plans in vain?"[1] when, all the while, the faithful, throughout all their exhortations, kept calling them brothers when they said, "My brothers."[2] And in the same manner, the psalm, speaking for Christ, also prophesied about the Lord as doing and saying

this very thing, "I will declare your name to my brothers."[3] CATENA ON THE ACTS OF THE APOSTLES 14.2.[4]

14:3 The Lord Bore Witness

GOOD WILL AND MIRACLES CAUSE SUCH BOLDNESS. CHRYSOSTOM: Why didn't the apostles go forth from there? Because they were not driven away, only attacked. "So they remained for a long time, speaking boldly for the Lord, who bore witness to the word of his grace, granting signs and wonders to be done by their hands." This caused their boldness; or rather, what caused their boldness was their own good will. It is for this reason that for a long time they worked no miracles. The conversion of the hearers was [the effect] of the signs, though their boldness also contributed somewhat. HOMILIES ON THE ACTS OF THE APOSTLES 30.[5]

14:6 Paul and Barnabas Fled

WHEN THEY PERSECUTE YOU.[6] AMMONIUS: It

---

[1]Ps 2:1. [2]The phrase is literally "men brothers." It occurs in earlier speeches of Peter and Stephen at Acts 2:29; 3:17; 7:2, 26. Paul has already used this phrase in addressing his fellow Jews at Acts 13:26, 38. He will continue to do so: Acts 23:1, 5, 6; 28:17. [3]Ps 22:22 (21:23 LXX). [4]CGPNT 3:232. [5]NPNF 1 11:190**. [6]Mt 10:23.

is not odd that the saints flee from those intending to attack them. Nor, because of this, do they
appear to flee from the martyr's battle. CATENA

ON THE ACTS OF THE APOSTLES 14.5-7.[7]

[7]CGPNT 3:233.

14:8-20 PAUL AND BARNABAS MISTAKEN FOR GODS

[8]Now at Lystra there was a man sitting, who could not use his feet; he was a cripple from birth,
who had never walked. [9]He listened to Paul speaking; and Paul, looking intently at him and seeing
that he had faith to be made well, [10]said in a loud voice, "Stand upright on your feet." And he
sprang up and walked. [11]And when the crowds saw what Paul had done, they lifted up their voices,
saying in Lycaonian, "The gods have come down to us in the likeness of men!" [12]Barnabas they
called Zeus, and Paul, because he was the chief speaker, they called Hermes. [13]And the priest of
Zeus, whose temple was in front of the city, brought oxen and garlands to the gates and wanted to
offer sacrifice with the people. [14]But when the apostles Barnabas and Paul heard of it, they tore
their garments and rushed out among the multitude, crying, [15]"Men, why are you doing this? We
also are men, of like nature with you, and bring you good news, that you should turn from these
vain things to a living God who made the heaven and the earth and the sea and all that is in them.
[16]In past generations he allowed all the nations to walk in their own ways; [17]yet he did not leave
himself without witness, for he did good and gave you from heaven rains and fruitful seasons, satis-
fying your hearts with food and gladness." [18]With these words they scarcely restrained the people
from offering sacrifice to them.

[19]But Jews came there from Antioch and Iconium; and having persuaded the people, they stoned
Paul and dragged him out of the city, supposing that he was dead. [20]But when the disciples gath-
ered about him, he rose up and entered the city; and on the next day he went on with Barnabas to
Derbe.

OVERVIEW: This is Paul's first speech to pagans.
He makes no mention of Jesus but only tries to
convert them to monotheism: a first step in the
rhythm of preaching summed up in his account
of the ministry in Thessalonica.[1] Commentators
observe a progression of events similar to those
in Pisidian Antioch and Iconium: initial success
followed by controversy provoked by Jews, persecution and flight. Here, the persecution goes
further than before: Paul is stoned, but he sur-

vives. There is an irony in these events. On the
one hand, Paul, doing good, is deified by pagans
and declared immortal, an appellation Paul rejects in his preaching, while, on the other, in his
preaching of a Jewish message, the Jews try to

[1]1 Thess 1:9-10: "For they themselves report concerning us what a welcome we had among you, and how you turned to God from idols, to
serve a living and true God, and to wait for his Son from heaven, whom
he raised from the dead, Jesus who delivers us from the wrath to come."

kill him but fail. The Fathers focus closely on particular elements of the story and use these events to demonstrate larger truths about the faith. Bede sees Paul, like Peter and John with the lame Jewish man, demonstrating in the lame Gentile man's physical body the spiritual effects of the gospel that God intends for the whole of humanity. Just as the lame man whom Peter and John cured prefigured the salvation of the Jews, so did this sick Lycaonian prefigured the salvation of the Gentiles (BEDE). Chrysostom too sees a spiritual truth in this physical healing: Paul could see that the man's spirit had not been debilitated by his physical condition but that he had faith to be made well because he was already predisposed in his resolution. While the bodies of some were healed before their souls, the soul of the crippled man of Lystra was already predisposed to the hearing of the Word. The Fathers also pay close attention to the premature conclusion that Paul and Barnabas were divine (BEDE, AMMONIUS). The danger of such a conclusion among those being evangelized was part of the reason that God allowed his apostles to suffer illness (BASIL). It was not so much for the benefit of the apostles who were well aware of their humanity and outraged at this behavior (CHRYSOSTOM). Rather it was for those who did not know the creating and living God, who needs no sacrifice (LETTER TO DIOGNETUS) but who has in fact been the one who has redeemed us by entrusting himself into our hands first on the cross. Likewise he became for us the Bread of life, thus making it possible for our lives to be a return to him as self-sacrifices to him (ORIGEN). Paul begins to turn the Lycaonians from their idolatry by teaching them of God's love as first apparent in his creation and especially in his forebearance of their ingratitude. The Lycaonians' insistence on offering sacrifice attests, in an uninformed way, to the source of his message, while Paul's actions after he is stoned are indeed imitations of the abundance of God's goodness toward humanity, for the resurrection victory of Christ is one that demonstrates and brings for-

giveness in action in response not just to ignorance but even to hatred and violence. This spirit of love and forgiveness lifts up Paul in his weakness in a way more marvelously than the healing of the lame man (CHRYSOSTOM).

14:8 A Man Crippled from Birth

PREFIGURING THE GENTILES. BEDE: Just as that lame man whom Peter and John cured at the door of the temple[2] prefigured the salvation of the Jews, so too this sick Lycaonian prefigured the people of the Gentiles, who were for a long time remote from the religion of the law and the temple. [The Lycaonians] who were brought in by the preaching of the apostle Paul, who said, "They [Peter, James and John] gave to Barnabas and me the right hand of fellowship, so that we might go to the Gentiles, but they to the circumcised."[3] The times [when the two cures occurred] are appropriate to the exposition, for the former [i.e., the lame man cured by Peter and John] was cured in the earliest days of the faith, when the word was not yet believed by Gentiles. The latter [i.e., the lame Lycaonian] was cured in the midst of the new joys of the converted Gentile world, when the Jews had been excluded for their lack of faith and sprinkled with the dust of damnation.[4] COMMENTARY ON THE ACTS OF THE APOSTLES 14.8.[5]

14:9 Faith to Be Made Well

HIS SOUL NEEDED NO HEALING. CHRYSOSTOM: Look, he paid attention, it says, to Paul's words. Do you see the elevation of his mind? In no way did his lameness hinder his eagerness to listen. "Paul, looking intently at him and seeing," it says, "that he had faith to be made well." He was already predisposed in his purpose and resolution. And yet in the case of the others it was the opposite. Their bodies were healed before their

---

[2]Acts 3:1-11. [3]Gal 2:9. [4]Acts 13:50-51. [5]CS 117:125-26.

souls. Not so with this man. It seems to me that Paul saw into his soul. HOMILIES ON THE ACTS OF THE APOSTLES 30.[6]

14:11 The Apostles Considered Gods

DECEPTIVE APPEARANCES. BEDE: This was a stupid error on the part of Gentiles, who thought that everything which they saw above themselves was a god. COMMENTARY ON THE ACTS OF THE APOSTLES 14.11.[7]

14:12 Barnabas Called Zeus

NO ONE HAS EVER SEEN GOD. AMMONIUS: In the writers of ancient stories you can find that Jove, even though he was a man, made himself a god and said that he was a god, just as many Roman and Macedonian kings styled themselves gods. There one ought to believe in what was said long ago about this, namely, that some were misled and called certain persons gods.[8] Consequently these too were misled in regard to Barnabas and Paul. . . . Barnabas's followers, in order to close their mouths and to instruct them gently, kept saying, "No one has ever seen God."[9] We are what we look like, not gods but human. In Jesus alone it happened that he was God and man at the same time for the principle of union. But in this case, these were only men who performed miracles through the Holy Spirit. CATENA ON THE ACTS OF THE APOSTLES 14.12.[10]

14:14 Tearing Their Garments

THE APOSTLES FREE OF THE LUST OF GLORY. CHRYSOSTOM: Look! On all occasions they are free of the lust of glory, not only not coveting but even repudiating it when offered, as Peter too said, "Why do you gaze upon us, as though by our own power or holiness we had made him to walk?"[11] These men say the same. And Joseph also said of his dreams, "Is not their interpretation of God?"[12] And Daniel likewise, "And to me also, not through the wisdom that is in me was it revealed."[13] And

Paul always says this, as when he says, "And for these things who is sufficient?"[14] And again, "Not that we are sufficient of ourselves to think [aught] as of ourselves, but our sufficiency is of God."[15] HOMILIES ON THE ACTS OF THE APOSTLES 30.[16]

THE DEVIL DID NOT PREVAIL. CHRYSOSTOM: Notice the vehemence with which all this is done by the apostles: "They tore their garments and rushed out among the multitude, crying." All because their very beings were turning away in horror from what had happened. For truly it was grief, a grief inconsolable—they were about to be called gods and so introduce idolatry, the very thing they came to destroy! This was the devil's contrivance, but they did not keep quiet. For what do they say? "We are men, of like nature with you." Immediately, from the very outset, they overthrew the evil. They did not simply say "men" but "with you." And then, so that they should not seem to honor the gods, "we bring you good news, that you should turn from these vain things to a living God who made the heaven and the earth and the sea and all that is in them." Notice how they do not mention the prophets at all. . . . This is because they had learned that one should strive not so much to say something worthy concerning God as something that is of use to one's listeners. HOMILIES ON THE ACTS OF THE APOSTLES 31.[17]

14:15 Turn from Vain Things

CORRECTING A WONDER WORKER. BASIL THE GREAT: We find a reason for some illnesses in the saints, such as in the apostle, for, lest he appear to go beyond the bounds of nature and lest anyone consider him to possess, in his nature, something greater and more excellent than is fitting—which was the case among the Lycaonians, who offered him crowns and bulls—he was struck with ill-

---

[6]NPNF 1 11:190**. [7]CS 117:126. [8]On this theory, see OCD s.v. "Euhemerus." [9]Jn 1:18. [10]CGPNT 3:235. [11]Acts 3:12. [12]Gen 40:8. [13]Dan 2:30. [14]2 Cor 2:16. [15]2 Cor 3:5. [16]NPNF 1 11:190-91**. [17]NPNF 1 11:195**.

ness in order to show his nature was human. THE LONG RULES 55.4.[18]

THE USELESSNESS OF SACRIFICES. ANONYMOUS: Now he who made heaven and earth and all that is in them and gave to us all what we need would himself have no need of any of these things he offers to those who believe that he has given them. But as for those who believe that they offer to him sacrifices through blood and incense and holocausts and that they revere him with such honors, they seem to me to be no different from those who display the same lavish munificence to deaf idols that are incapable of receiving honor. To think that they offer anything to one in need of nothing! LETTER TO DIOGNETUS 3.4-5.[19]

MY FLESH FOR THE LIFE OF THE WORLD.[20] ORIGEN: To sacrifice son or daughter, beast or booty is something completely foreign to us; to offer one's very self to God and to be pleasing not by another's work but by one's own is something more perfect and more illustrious than all vows. Whoever does the latter is an imitator of Christ,[21] who gave to us the earth, the sea and all that is in them, and to serve our needs he gave the sky above and the ground below, the moon and the stars. The rains, the winds and all in the world he gave to us. But after all this, he gave his very self. "So much did God love the world that he gave his only begotten Son,"[22] "for the life of the world."[23] What then shall a human do of any greatness when he sacrifices himself to God after God has already sacrificed himself to him? HOMILIES ON NUMBERS 24.2.6.[24]

14:17 Not Without Witness

THE FREELY OFFERED BENEFITS OF CREATION. CHRYSOSTOM: Notice that [Paul's] wish was not to increase the accusation against them but rather that they themselves should refer everything to God. . . . Notice how covertly he phrases the accusation. And yet if he did this, he would not have allowed them [to walk in their own ways]. He would have had to punish them for having enjoyed so many goods without acknowledging him as their provider. But he does not say this clearly. "He gave you rain from heaven." Thus also David, "From the fruit of their corn and wine and oil were they made to abound";[25] and in many places when he is speaking of creation, he brings forward these benefits. Jeremiah also mentions first the creation, then the providence that is shown by the rains. Taught by those Scriptures, the apostle says, they were satisfied "with food and gladness." With liberality is the food given, not only for sufficiency or even according to need. "With these words they scarcely restrained the people from offering sacrifice to them." Indeed, it was especially with this that they gained admiration. Do you see that their point was to put an end to that madness? HOMILIES ON THE ACTS OF THE APOSTLES 31.[26]

14:19 They Stoned Paul

PAUL DID NOT HATE. CHRYSOSTOM: Believe me, it is possible to suffer things now worse than what Paul suffered. Those enemies pelted him with stones, but it is now possible to pelt with words that are worse than stone. What then must one do? The same that he did. He did not hate those who cast the stones. After they dragged him out, he entered their city again, to be a benefactor to those who had done him such wrongs. If you too had endured the one who harshly insulted you and done you wrongs, you too would have been stoned. For do not say "I have done him no wrong." For what wrong had Paul done to be stoned? He was announcing a kingdom, he was leading them away from error and bringing them to God. Such things are worthy of crowns, worthy of proclamations by heralds, worthy of ten thousand good things, *not* worthy of stones. And yet having suffered the opposite, he did the opposite to

---

[18]PG 31:1049-52.   [19]SC 33.2:58.   [20]Jn 6:51.   [21]See 1 Cor 11:1.   [22]Jn 3:16.   [23]Jn 6:51.   [24]SC 461:172-74.   [25]Ps 4:7 (4:8 LXX).   [26]NPNF 1 11:195-96**.

what was expected. For this is the splendid victory. HOMILIES ON THE ACTS OF THE APOSTLES 31.[27]

14:20 *Paul Rose and Entered the City*

STRENGTH MADE PERFECT IN WEAKNESS.
CHRYSOSTOM: "But when the disciples gathered about him, he rose up and entered the city." . . . Here the saying is fulfilled, "My grace is sufficient for you, for my strength is made perfect in weak-

ness."[28] This is greater than the raising of the lame man! . . . "He entered the city." Do you see his zeal? Do you see how fervent he is, how set on fire? He entered the city itself again, to show that if he should ever withdraw, it is because he had sown the word and did not wish to inflame their anger. HOMILIES ON THE ACTS OF THE APOSTLES 31.[29]

---

[27]NPNF 1 11:198** [28]2 Cor 12:9. [29]NPNF 1 11:196**.

14:21-28 PAUL AND BARNABAS STRENGTHEN THE DISCIPLES

[21]*When they had preached the gospel to that city and had made many disciples, they returned to Lystra and to Iconium and to Antioch,* [22]*strengthening the souls of the disciples, exhorting them to continue in the faith, and saying that through many tribulations we must enter the kingdom of God.* [23]*And when they had appointed elders for them in every church, with prayer and fasting, they committed them to the Lord in whom they believed.*

[24]*Then they passed through Pisidia, and came to Pamphylia.* [25]*And when they had spoken the word in Perga, they went down to Attalia;* [26]*and from there they sailed to Antioch, where they had been commended to the grace of God for the work which they had fulfilled.* [27]*And when they arrived, they gathered the church together and declared all that God had done with them, and how he had opened a door of faith to the Gentiles.* [28]*And they remained no little time with the disciples.*

OVERVIEW: This is the end of the first missionary journey. Commentators note the number of times Luke mentions the fact that Paul spends time with people and does not merely preach and move on.[1] There is a problem with the mention of the appointment of *presbyteroi* ("elders"), since Paul nowhere, neither in the uncontested nor in the contested letters, mentions them, neither as addressees nor as people he appointed. The Fathers do not mention this unique occurrence of the term. This mission is summarized in Acts 14:27 and is seen to prepare for the council of Acts 15. The Fathers' comments turn the events toward

their moral application in the life of the reader. The followers of Jesus do not go looking to be persecuted and do not want to play the victim, but they know to expect trials, hatred and perhaps even persecution to the death from those who will think they are doing good.[2] Jesus spoke of this,[3] and he also promised a heavenly joy, a beatitude, as belonging to such.[4] Jesus' words are here fulfilled in Paul and Barnabas, not just in their own words to the disciples but even in their

---

[1]Acts 9:43; 10:48; 11:26; 15:33, 35; etc. See Gaventa, *Acts*, 210. [2]Jn 16:2. [3]Jn 15:18-25. [4]Mt 5:11-12.

actions (Chrysostom). We are fallible, we have concupiscence, a desire for prestige,[5] and so we will always need correction especially in trying to serve the gospel (Basil). Yet, these difficulties are never crushing but strengthen us and show forth God's grace working in our weakness (Basil, Chrysostom).

14:22 Entering the Kingdom of God

Rejoicing in Tribulations. Chrysostom: This [the apostles] said, this they showed. But it is purposely so done, not only by the apostles but by the disciples also, that they may learn from the very outset both the power of the preaching and that they must themselves also suffer such things, that they may stand nobly, not idly gaping for the miracles but much more ready for the trials. Therefore also the apostle himself said, "Having the same conflict which you saw in me and heard."[6] ... And they were taught this by Christ when he said, "Rejoice not that the devils obey you."[7] For the joy indeed and without alloy is this, to suffer anything for Christ's sake. Homilies on the Acts of the Apostles 31.[8]

The Desire for Vainglory. Basil the Great: We must receive rebuke and castigation as a medicine that destroys disordered passion[9] and restores health. From this it is clear that those who feign goodness out of a disordered desire[10] to please people lose all profit and plot against the true life itself. The Morals 72.5.[11]

Approval Through Tribulation. Basil the Great: "And he snatched me from all my tribulations."[12] The just person's entire life is tribulation,[13] "both straight and narrow the way,"[14] and "many are the tribulations of the just ones."[15] Therefore the apostle elsewhere says that he has been "afflicted in every way,"[16] and here, that "we must enter the kingdom of God through many afflictions." God does rescue the holy from affliction, but he does so not by rendering them untested but by blessing them with endurance. For if "affliction brings about endurance, then endurance brings about an approved character."[17] Whoever rejects affliction deprives himself of approval. Just as none is crowned who has no rival, so none can be pronounced worthy except through tribulations. Therefore, "he snatched me from all my tribulations," not by allowing me not to be afflicted but by granting with the test a way out, in order to be able to endure.[18] Homily on Psalm 33.4.[19]

14:27 Declaring What God Had Done

That the Mission Be Firmly Established. Chrysostom: They did not say what they themselves had done but "what God had done with them." It seems to me that they mean through their trials. It was not for nothing that they went there, nor to rest. They were providentially guided by the Spirit, so that the preaching to the Gentiles might be firmly established. ... And note Paul's ardor. He does not ask if there is need to speak to Gentiles; he speaks at once. This is why he says, "I did not refer myself to flesh and blood."[20] Homilies on the Acts of the Apostles 31.[21]

---

[5]See Jn 5:44. [6]Phil 1:30. [7]Lk 10:20. [8]NPNF 1 11:196**. [9]Basil writes pathos. [10]Again, pathos. [11]PG 31:849. [12]Ps 34:4 (33:5 LXX). [13]See Job 7:1. [14]Mt 7:14. [15]Ps 34:19 (33:20 LXX). [16]2 Cor 4:8. [17]Rom 5:3-4. [18]See 1 Cor 10:13. [19]PG 29:360. [20]Gal 1:16. [21]NPNF 1 11:197-98**.

15:1-5 CONTENTION ARISES
REGARDING CIRCUMCISION

[1]*But some men came down from Judea and were teaching the brothers, "Unless you are circumcised according to the custom of Moses, you cannot be saved."* [2]*And when Paul and Barnabas had no small dissension and debate with them, Paul and Barnabas and some of the others were appointed to go up to Jerusalem to the apostles and the elders about this question.* [3]*So, being sent on their way by the church, they passed through both Phoenicia and Samaria, reporting the conversion of the Gentiles, and they gave great joy to all the brothers.* [4]*When they came to Jerusalem, they were welcomed by the church and the apostles and the elders, and they declared all that God had done with them.* [5]*But some believers who belonged to the party of the Pharisees rose up, and said, "It is necessary to circumcise them, and to charge them to keep the law of Moses."*

OVERVIEW: Commentators usually consider this chapter to be the center of Luke's story and its turning point. There are problems in that this is not the only account of this event. Paul, in Galatians 2:1-10, gives another version that lays the initiative with himself (due to a revelation), whereas Luke's version makes it a decision of the Antiochene church to consult the apostles and elders in Jerusalem. Paul's account seems to say that the controversy arose not in Antioch but first in Jerusalem. Over who started the controversy ("some from Judea" in Acts, "false brothers" in Paul) there is disagreement. Some interpreters see none of these discrepancies as great enough to establish these as accounts of separate events, while others think that Luke and Paul speak of different events. Luke's account of the great event of Acts 15 raised many questions for the early Christians. Origen and Chrysostom handle historical questions, while others, such as Ammonius, raise questions about the need for a discerning authority that weighs matters of law and custom. Chrysostom even attempts to solve the problems, much discussed among modern commentators, about the congruity of this chapter and Paul's letter to the Galatians, though he approaches the problem differently. The early days of the church were not innocent of disputes

and disagreement. While it is not uncommon for Christians to hold a romantic view of the church as small and settled in uniformity, for the pagan Celsus these disputes became an argument against the sincerity of the Christian faith (ORIGEN). Origen's response implies a process of development and a need for a living authority guided by the Spirit. Ammonius notes how the Antiochians turned to Jerusalem as their source of authority. Ammonius's comments on Jerusalem as the center of authority give a different view of Paul than does Chrysostom, who sees Paul as in no way confused or seeking enlightenment from Jerusalem.

15:1 Teaching the Believers

THE EARLY CHURCH NO STRANGER TO DOCTRINAL DISPUTES. ORIGEN: Observe what he alleges as a proof of his statement:[1] "Christians at first were few in number and held the same opinions, but when they grew to be a great multitude, they were divided and separated, each wishing to have his own individual party. This was their object

---

[1]Origen is referring to the claim of Celsus that "if all men wanted to be Christians, the Christians would no longer want them" (*Against Celsus* 3.9).

from the beginning." That Christians at first were few in number, in comparison with the multitudes who subsequently became Christian, is no doubt true. . . .

He also says that "all the Christians were of one mind," not noticing, even in this particular, that from the beginning there were differences of opinion among believers regarding the meaning of the books held to be divine. At all events, while the apostles were still preaching and eyewitnesses of Jesus were still teaching his doctrine, there was no small discussion among the converts from Judaism regarding Gentile believers and whether they ought to observe Jewish customs or reject the burden of clean and unclean meats as not being obligatory on those who had abandoned their ancestral Gentile customs and had become believers in Jesus. AGAINST CELSUS 3.10-11.[2]

15:2 Paul and Barnabas Go to Jerusalem

RECONCILING ACTS AND GALATIANS. CHRYSOSTOM: How can he say in his letter to the Galatians, "I did not go up to Jerusalem to see those who were apostles before me, nor did I move"?[3] We suggest this: in the first place because he had not gone up spontaneously but had been sent by others; and in the second place because he did not come in order to learn something[4] but to persuade others. Indeed, from the beginning he held that opinion that the apostles approved later, namely, that it was not necessary to circumcise. Until that day, however, it had seemed to them that [Paul] was not worthy of faith, but they rather listened more to those who lived in Jerusalem. So [Paul] went up, not in order to gain what he had been ignorant of before but in order to persuade his opponents because those who were in Jerusalem agreed with them. He had recog-

nized from the start what had to be done and needed no teacher. And he had a clear and sure idea, beyond any discussion, of what the apostles would have decreed after a long discussion. Since it had seemed opportune to the brothers that he might learn something about them, he went up not for himself but for them. Even though he says, "I did not go up," we can explain that. He did not go up at the beginning of his preaching or in order to learn. And he means both these things when he says, "I did not go immediately in flesh and blood." He did not simply say, "I did not go" but "I did not go immediately." CATENA ON THE ACTS OF THE APOSTLES 15.2-4.[5]

THE SIGNIFICANCE OF THE LAW. AMMONIUS: It is to be noted that the early believers, with much searching and great eagerness, discussed dogmas, and that they benefited to such an extent through their discussions and that the Antiochians did not hesitate to send [someone] to Jerusalem to inquire about the controversy. And yet their inquiry was not, in the first place, about the Godhead, or the providential incarnation of the Son, or the Holy Spirit, or angels, or powers, or heaven, or anything like this, but about circumcision, about the least part of a man's genitals. They were aware of the fact that the words "a single iota and a single point of the law"[6] were full of a great spiritual meaning. The Antiochian disciples were afraid to take authority, but they took so much thought even for questions that seemed to be trifling, seeing that those from Antioch sent Paul and Barnabas to consult those in Jerusalem, while the disciples from Jerusalem sent Judah and Silas back to Antioch with their letters. CATENA ON THE ACTS OF THE APOSTLES 15.7-8.[7]

---

[2]ANF 4:468-69**. [3]Gal 1:17. [4]Gal 1:18. [5]CGPNT 3:242-43. [6]Mt 5:18. [7]CGPNT 3:244-45.

15:6-12 PETER ARGUES AGAINST
GENTILE CIRCUMCISION

⁶*The apostles and the elders were gathered together to consider this matter. ⁷And after there had been much debate, Peter rose and said to them, "Brothers, you know that in the early days God made choice among you, that by my mouth the Gentiles should hear the word of the gospel and believe. ⁸And God who knows the heart bore witness to them, giving them the Holy Spirit just as he did to us; ⁹and he made no distinction between us and them, but cleansed their hearts by faith. ¹⁰Now therefore why do you make trial of God by putting a yoke upon the neck of the disciples which neither our fathers nor we have been able to bear? ¹¹But we believe that we shall be saved through the grace of the Lord Jesus, just as they will."*

¹²*And all the assembly kept silence; and they listened to Barnabas and Paul as they related what signs and wonders God had done through them among the Gentiles.*

OVERVIEW: As modern commentators view this speech by Peter, it is neither missionary nor kerygmatic but judicial or constitutive, one that moves the assembly to come to a doctrinal decision.[1] This decision, that Gentiles need not undergo circumcision, was the single issue of one gathering, and James's subsequent speech is from another occasion but is added here because it too was from the church in Jerusalem. Peter here is the representative of the Jerusalem church in that he is the only one from among its officials who has had experience with the Gentiles, to which he refers. Chrysostom's analysis of Peter's speech is that it has two parts: events detailed, conclusions drawn. Peter's speech comes at the end of the debate. Chrysostom sees Peter as being persuasive precisely because he still lived as a Jew and as a Jew was chosen as God's instrument to proclaim the gospel to the Gentiles. God, through him, has shown three things to his chosen people: first, that salvation is a gift; second, that goodness lies in the heart; and third, that Christ unmasks fleshly distinctions to reveal, in himself, the unity of humanity. Peter's speech stresses the power of faith and shows to the Jews their own failure to live by the Mosaic law (CHRYSOSTOM). This faith, however, is not a mere acknowledgment of the one God or of Jesus as his

Son, as Augustine is eager to show: the goodness that lies in the heart comes from a faith that overflows in love today and hopes one day to see God face to face. The insistence on the part of certain Jewish Christians that they are the standard implies a questioning of God's actions among the Gentiles and is a dangerous attitude (CHRYSOSTOM). Augustine insists that God, in revealing in Christ his saving grace, has made known that this same grace was always present among the Jewish people and to it the law and prophets bore witness, though these were not that grace's Mediator.

15:7 The Gentiles Hear the Gospel

GOD'S CHOSEN INSTRUMENT. CHRYSOSTOM: See how Peter was, from the beginning, removed from the debate and how he was following the ways of the Jews even still.[2] "You know," he says.

---

[1]In other words, this is directed to members of one's own group, not to outsiders, yet with the aim of persuading. In this type of discourse, the speaker looks to the nature of the group, its constitution, for the principles of his argument.   [2]Chrysostom seems to draw this conclusion from the time at which Peter began to speak. Since there had been "much debate," he thinks that Peter, being the head of the apostles, would have spoken sooner had he not been reluctant because he was judaizing. Although Chrysostom does not use the same words, he evokes Paul's account of his rebuke of Peter in Gal 2:11-15, where Peter is said not to be living as a Jew.

Perhaps some of those who had once accused him with regard to Cornelius were present and had entered with him, so that he brings them as witnesses. "From the ancient days God chose among you." What does "among you" mean? It means either "in Palestine" or the "you" is those who were present. "Through my mouth." See how [Peter] shows that God spoke through him and there was nothing human. "And God, who knows human hearts, testified to them"—he refers them to the testimony of the Spirit—"by giving them the Holy Spirit just as he did to us." CATENA ON THE ACTS OF THE APOSTLES 15.7-8.[3]

15:8 God Gave Witness to Them

TESTIMONY TO THEIR VIRTUE. CHRYSOSTOM: Then he shows that it was not simply because of grace but on account of their virtue that the testimony was given to them and that what was offered to them was in no way less [than what was offered to us]. "For he made no distinction," he says, "between us and them." It is the heart then that one must always look to, and it is very aptly said, "God who knows the heart bore witness to them"; and likewise in an earlier instance, "Thou, Lord, that knows the hearts of all people."[4] Notice what he adds to show that this is the meaning, "he made no distinction between us and them." When he mentioned the testimony borne to them, he uttered that great word, which Paul speaks, "Neither circumcision avails anything, nor uncircumcision."[5] "That he may make the two one in himself."[6] HOMILIES ON THE ACTS OF THE APOSTLES 32.[7]

15:9 Cleansed by Faith

GIFTS OBTAINED THROUGH FAITH ALONE. CHRYSOSTOM: "And God who knows the heart bore witness to them." He refers them to the spiritual testimony, "giving them the Holy Spirit just as he did to us." Everywhere he places the Gentiles on an equal footing. "And he made no distinction between us and them but cleansed their hearts by faith." From faith alone, he says, they obtained the same gifts. This is also meant as a lesson to those [objectors]; this is able to teach even them that faith alone is necessary, and not works or circumcision. For indeed they do not say all this only as an apology for the Gentiles, but also to teach [the Jewish believers] to abandon the law. For the moment, however, this is not said. "Now therefore why do you make trial of God by putting a yoke upon the neck of the disciples which neither our fathers nor we have been able to bear? But we believe that we shall be saved through the grace of the Lord Jesus, just as they will." What does "make trial of God" mean? As if he were not strong enough, he means, to save by faith, that is, "why do you disbelieve God?" Thus it is from a want of faith that the law is brought in. . . . "But we believe that we shall be saved through the grace of the Lord Jesus, just as they will." How powerful are these words! Likewise Paul says in the epistle to the Romans, "For if Abraham was justified by works, he has something to glory in, but not before God."[8] Do you see that all this is more a lesson for them than an apology for the Gentiles? HOMILIES ON THE ACTS OF THE APOSTLES 32.[9]

FAITH THAT PURIFIES. AUGUSTINE: Faith in God purifies the heart, the pure heart sees God. But faith is sometimes defined as followed by people who wish to deceive themselves; as if it were enough merely to believe—some people, you see, promise themselves the vision of God and the kingdom of heaven for believing while living bad lives. Against these the apostle James indignantly took umbrage out of spiritual charity, so he says in his letter, "You believe that God is one." You pat yourself on your back for your faith; you observe that many godless people assume there are many gods, and you congratulate yourself for believing that there is only one God. "You do well. The demons also believe—and shud-

---

[3]CGPNT 3:244. [4]Acts 1:24. [5]1 Cor 7:19. [6]Eph 2:15. [7]NPNF 1 11:202-3**. [8]Rom 4:2. [9]NPNF 1 11:201-2**.

der."[10] Shall they too see God? Those who are pure of heart shall see him. Whoever would say that the unclean spirits are pure of heart? And yet, "they believe—and shudder."

So our faith must be distinguished from the faith of demons. Our faith, you see, purifies the heart, their faith makes them guilty. . . . So let us distinguish our faith and see that believing is not enough. That is not the sort of faith that purifies the heart. "Purifying their hearts," it says, "by faith." But which faith, what sort of faith? The one, surely, which the apostle Paul defines when he says "faith that works through love."[11] This faith is different from the faith of demons, different from the morals of dissolute and desperate people. "Faith," he says. "Which faith?" The one "that works through love," hopes for what God promises. You could not have a more perfect, a more carefully thought-out definition than that. SERMON 53.10-11.[12]

FAITH PREPARES US FOR THE HOLY SPIRIT.
BEDE: Therefore there is no need of circumcision of the flesh to cleanse those whose hearts were purified by so much faith that even before baptism they deserved to receive the Holy Spirit. COMMENTARY ON THE ACTS OF THE APOSTLES 15.9.[13]

15:10 Trying God

WHAT THE LAW CANNOT DO, FAITH CAN.
CHRYSOSTOM: Notice how he concludes with something frightening. He does not discourse to them from the prophets but from things present, of which they themselves were witnesses. Of course the prophets also add their testimony and make the reason stronger by what has now come to pass. And notice how [Peter] first allows the question to be debated in the church and then speaks. And he did not say "those of the circumcision" but "the Gentiles." For this [gradual advance] little by little is stronger. For this is the action of one trying to see if he is able to save even after the law. Look what he does. He shows

that they are in danger. For what the law could not do faith had power to do, but if faith falls off, see how they themselves are in perdition. And he did not say, "Why do you disbelieve?" which is more harsh, even when the fact had been demonstrated. HOMILIES ON THE ACTS OF THE APOSTLES 32.[14]

THE NEW LAW OF FAITH. AUGUSTINE: Why did he say this, unless they were saved through the grace of our Lord, Jesus Christ, not through the law of Moses? Through the law there came not healing but the knowledge of sin, as the apostle teaches when he says, "For knowledge of sin came through the law. But now the righteousness of God has been revealed apart from the law, though the law and the prophets have borne witness to it."[15] Therefore, if it has been revealed, it existed at that time but was hidden. The veil of the temple signified its being hidden, and that veil was torn at Christ's death to signify its revelation.[16] At that time the grace of the one mediator between God and human beings, the man Christ Jesus, existed in the people of God, but it was hidden as rain upon fleece—a rain that God bestows on his heritage,[17] not as something due but as gratuitous. But now, with the fleece squeezed dry, that is, with the Jewish people rejected, it lies revealed in all the nations as upon the threshing floor.[18] ON ORIGINAL SIN 2.29.[19]

15:11 Saved Through the Grace of Jesus

ALL SALVATION COMES THROUGH THE GRACE OF CHRIST. AUGUSTINE: You, who are enemies of this grace, reject the idea that we should believe that the people of old were saved by the same grace of Jesus Christ. Rather, you distinguish the different times in the manner of Pelagius in whose books this is found. You say that prior to the law they were saved by nature,

---

[10]Jas 2:19. [11]Gal 5:6. [12]WSA 3 3:71. [13]CS 117:130. [14]NPNF 1 11:203**. [15]Rom 3:20-21. [16]Mt 27:51. [17]Ps 68:9 (67:10 LXX). [18]Judg 6:36-40. [19]WSA 1 23:449.

then through the law and finally through Christ, as if for the human beings of the two earlier periods, namely, prior to the law and under the law, the blood of Christ was not necessary. In that way, you destroy the statement, "For there is one God and one mediator between God and humankind, the man Christ Jesus."[20] AGAINST TWO LETTERS OF THE PELAGIANS 1.39.[21]

THE UNITY OF FAITH. BEDE: "If therefore they also, that is, the fathers who were unable to bear the yoke of the old law, believed that they were

saved through the grace of the Lord Jesus, it is clear that this grace made even the just people of old to live, for 'The just person lives by faith.'"[22] Therefore, on account of the diversity of the times the sacramental signs could be diverse, though nevertheless reverting most harmoniously to the unity of the same faith. COMMENTARY ON THE ACTS OF THE APOSTLES 15.11.[23]

---

[20]1 Tim 2:5. [21]WSA 1 24:137. [22]Augustine *Letter* 190.2.6 (CSEL 57:142); Rom 1:17; Gal 3:11. [23]CS 117:130.

15:13-21 JAMES ALSO ARGUES FOR THE GENTILES

[13]After they finished speaking, James replied, "Brothers, listen to me. [14]Simeon has related how God first visited the Gentiles, to take out of them a people for his name. [15]And with this the words of the prophets agree, as it is written,

[16]'After this I will return,
    and I will rebuild the dwelling of David, which has fallen;
I will rebuild its ruins,
    and I will set it up,
[17]that the rest of men may seek the Lord,
    and all the Gentiles who are called by my name,
[18]says the Lord, who has made these things known from of old.'
[19]Therefore my judgment is that we should not trouble those of the Gentiles who turn to God, [20]but should write to them to abstain from the pollutions of idols and from unchastity and from what is strangled[n] and from blood. [21]For from early generations Moses has had in every city those who preach him, for he is read every sabbath in the synagogues."

n Other early authorities omit *and from what is strangled*

OVERVIEW: In modern times there is much debate over the sources for the speeches in Acts. The discrepancies between the matters dealt with by Peter, the circumcision of Gentiles and whether they are subject to the Mosaic law, and

the matters in James's speech, some dietary and other norms, raise the problem. Most modern commentators distinguish between at least two events, each of which is seen reflected in the two speeches given, and Luke's use of them to explain the eventual separation of the church from Judaism. "In this chapter one has to distinguish the historical background of what is recounted from the Lukan literary presentation of it and what seems to have been the Lukan telescoping of materials, and to reckon also with the relation of what is recounted here, not only to other things yet to come in Acts, but also to Galatians 2."[1] The Fathers' focus is primarily on the significance of this process as an example to the church in its deliberations and on the message about the nature of salvation in Christ as seen in relation to the law. The momentous nature of the events, the refusal to see the law as intended for the Gentiles, could have made for tumultuous proceedings, jockeying over who would speak and whose will would win out. That this was not so illustrates how these men lacked arrogance and conceit (CHRYSOSTOM). Chrysostom discerns an orderliness in the sequence of speakers, one that begins with actors outside Jerusalem and ends in Jerusalem with the one in authority there giving a final and practical conclusion to the events. The order of speakers follows the order of action, authority and geography. The prior speeches gave historical evidence, while James teaches from the Scriptures and shows the consistency of these events with the calling of Israel from among the Gentiles in order that they may become a beginning of the extension of salvation to all nations (CHRYSOSTOM). The Fathers do not seem to be aware that the enactments legislated for the Gentiles pertain to the Noachic laws. James's use of the prophets makes two important points: the history of Israel is an argument to the nations that they convert to God, but more importantly, according to Cyril of Alexandria, when this history is interpreted in Christ, we see how God's rebuilding of David's dwelling is not a call to observe the law but to a new creation in Christ. Bede, understanding David's dwelling as the law, interprets the prophecy as Christ's fulfillment and extension of it throughout the world. While Peter's experience demonstrated this, James's reasoning from what was written in the prophets and from the resur-

rection affirms what was not written, that the law had become a scandal to the Gentiles. To refuse to acknowledge God's work in this was to fight against God (CHRYSOSTOM). Only those things in the Old Testament that God asked of both Jews and the Gentiles who dwelled among them remain binding on Christians, according to Origen, whereas Bede sees a pastoral concession to the Gentiles who, as they came to know more of the law, would advance in knowledge of perfection.[2]

15:12 All Were Silent

NO ARROGANCE IN THE CHURCH. CHRYSOSTOM: There was no arrogance in the church. After Peter, Paul speaks, and no one silences him. James waits patiently and does not jump up. Great is the orderliness [of the proceedings]. No word from John here, and nothing from the other apostles. They hold their peace. For James was invested with the chief rule, and they did not begrudge him, so free was their soul from love of glory. HOMILIES ON THE ACTS OF THE APOSTLES 33.[3]

15:13 James Replied

THE BISHOP SPEAKS. CHRYSOSTOM: This James was bishop, as they say, and therefore he speaks last. Here is fulfilled that saying, "In the mouth of two or three witnesses shall every word be established."[4] But notice his wisdom, how he bases his argument on the prophets of old. For he had no acts of his own to declare, as had Peter and Paul. And indeed it is wisely ordered that this part is assigned to those two, who are not intended to stay in Jerusalem, but James, who is to teach them, is not responsible and so is not separated from them in opinion. . . . "Brothers," he says, "listen to me." Great is his moderation, and more complete is this speech, as indeed it

[1]For a thorough discussion of the problems, see Fitzmyer, *Acts*, p. 552. See also the overview at Acts 15:22-29. [2]For more on this question, see also the selections below at Acts 21:21. [3]NPNF 1 11:207**. [4]Deut 19:15; Mt 18:16.

puts an end to the matter under discussion. Homilies on the Acts of the Apostles 33.[5]

15:14 A People for God's Name

Chosen from the Nations. Chrysostom: "To take out of the Gentiles," he says, "a people for his name"—not simply "he chose" but "for his name." That is, for his glory. His name is not shamed by taking the Gentiles; indeed, all the greater is his glory. Here something truly great is hinted at, that these are chosen before all. Homilies on the Acts of the Apostles 33.[6]

15:16 Rebuilding the Dwelling of David

A New Creation in Christ. Cyril of Alexandria: The tabernacle of David means the race of the Jews. It must be known that after Cyrus had freed Israel from captivity, they returned to Judea and built the temple of God. Then, after they had again fortified the cities that had been destroyed before, they lived in security day by day for a long time, that is, for many days and long periods. They became an example and an assurance for all the other nations that it was necessary thereafter to turn to God. . . . This is an explanation of the history of these things, but a more hidden and truer interpretation would be in Christ. Indeed after he came back to life from the dead in his tabernacle that had fallen into death, that is, after God had raised his earthly flesh, then at that very moment he brought all human things back to their original ordering and all our things that had been overthrown have been brought to a new dignity. For if, as Scripture states,[7] anyone in Christ is a new creation, we have then been raised together with him. So whereas death demolished the tabernacles of all, God the Father rebuilt them in Christ. Catena on the Acts of the Apostles 15.16-17.[8]

The Law Refashioned. Bede: The tabernacle of David signifies a trace of the law, which was corrupted and torn to pieces by the betrayals of the Pharisees. However, with the Lord's return, that is, his appearance in the flesh, it was built up by God with spiritual grace, so that not only the Jews but also all the Gentile nations would seek after his name. Commentary on the Acts of the Apostles 15.16.[9]

15:19 The Gentiles Who Turn to God

Not Necessary to Keep the Old Law. Chrysostom: The objectors did not say that the Gentiles must not be received upon believing but that it must be done in accordance with the law. On this subject Peter spoke forcefully. But when this aroused his listeners above all else, on this point too he soothed them. And notice how Peter brought forward what had to be enacted as a rule, that it is not necessary to keep the law. But what was ours and had been received of old, this is what James says, and he dwells on that concerning which nothing is written, so that he might sooth their minds by what is acknowledged and, at an opportune time, introduce this as well. "Therefore my judgment," he says, "is that we should not trouble those of the Gentiles who turn to God," that is, not upset them. For, if God called them, and these observances upset them, we are fighting against God. Homilies on the Acts of the Apostles 33.[10]

15:20 Abstain from Idolatry and Unchastity

Laws for All. Origen: "Speak to Aaron and his sons and to all the sons of Israel, and tell them: If anyone who is from among the sons of Israel or from among foreigners, who happens to be among you, eats any blood, I shall place my spirit over the spirit which shall have eaten the blood, and I shall abolish it from among the people, since the spirit of every flesh is its blood. To you I have also given the blood so that by it upon the altar there might be propitiations for your

---

[5]NPNF 1 11:205**. [6]NPNF 1 11:207**. [7]2 Cor 5:17. [8]CGPNT 3:249-50. [9]CS 117:130. [10]NPNF 1 11:208**.

spirits, since the blood will make expiation for the spirit. Therefore, I have said to the sons of Israel: Every spirit among you shall not eat blood, and any foreigner among you shall not eat blood."[11] You see, therefore, that this law regarding blood, given equally to both the sons of Israel and to foreigners, is even observed by us from among the Gentiles who believe in God through Jesus Christ. Scripture tends to call proselytes foreigners, as when it says, "The foreigner who is among you will rise up above you, while you descend below. He shall be your head, and you shall be his tail."[12] Therefore, even the church of the Gentiles took in common with the people of Israel the law regarding blood, for that blessed council of the apostles, understanding that these things had been so written in the law, then ordered and decreed in writing the teachings for the Gentiles that they abstain not only from what had been sacrificed to idols and from fornication, but also from blood and from what had been suffocated. Now perhaps you will ask, "If Scripture was so clear with regard to blood, should it not also teach clearly about what has been suffocated, whether a law was given as common to the people of Israel and to foreigners, since the teachings of the apostles decree that Gentiles also observe this law?" Listen how observantly even this is guarded against in the laws of God: "If a man, any man," it says, "from the sons of Israel and from the foreigners among you, hunts a beast or a bird, let him pour out its blood and cover it with earth, for the spirit of every flesh is its blood."[13] COMMENTARY ON ROMANS 2.13.[14]

A PRUDENT COMPROMISE. BEDE: These concessions were made to those who came from a Gentile life, in view of their rudimentary faith and the long-standing custom of the Gentile world. However, lest these same things be thought to be sufficient even for the more perfect, James watchfully added: ["But we should write to them to abstain only from things polluted by idols and from fornication and from whatever has been strangled and from blood."] COMMENTARY

ON THE ACTS OF THE APOSTLES 15.20.[15]

15:21 Those Who Preach Moses

THE PRIMITIVE CHURCH RETAINED SOME JEWISH PRACTICES. BEDE: Although they are not now weighed down by us with the full rigor of the precepts, nevertheless, as time goes on, in coming together very often for the reading of the law and the prophets, little by little they will receive the principles of life and the rules requiring the keeping of mutual love. For it is very certain that the primitive church, still practicing Jewish ways, continued to use these [readings] in their sabbath celebrations. COMMENTARY ON THE ACTS OF THE APOSTLES 15.21.[16]

JAMES UNBINDS THE LAW. CHRYSOSTOM: Moses discourses to them. Look how great is the condescension [to their weakness]! Where it did no harm, he set him up as teacher and indulged them with a gratification that hindered nothing, permitting Jews to listen to him in regard to these matters while leading away the Gentiles. Look at his wisdom! He seemed to honor him and to set him up as the authority for his own people, but at the same time he led the Gentiles away from him. Why shouldn't they learn from him? Because of the strangeness of these things. He shows that even the Jews need observe no more [than these necessary things]. And if we do not write to them, it is not because they are bound to observe anything more but because they have one to tell them. And he does not say, "do not offend them" or "do not turn them back," which is what Paul said to the Galatians, but "do not trouble them." He shows that success in this case would bring nothing but nuisance. Thus he made an end of the whole matter. And while he seems to preserve the law by adopting these rules from it, he unbinds it by taking these alone. HOMILIES ON THE ACTS OF THE APOSTLES 33.[17]

---

[11]Lev 17:10-12. [12]Deut 28:43-44. [13]Lev 17:13-14. [14]PG 14:905. [15]CS 117:130**. [16]CS 117:131. [17]NPNF 1 11:208-9**.

15:22-29 THE APOSTLES WRITE TO THE BELIEVERS AT ANTIOCH

[22]*Then it seemed good to the apostles and the elders, with the whole church, to choose men from among them and send them to Antioch with Paul and Barnabas. They sent Judas called Barsabbas, and Silas, leading men among the brothers,* [23]*with the following letter: "The brothers, both the apostles and the elders, to the brothers who are of the Gentiles in Antioch and Syria and Cilicia, greeting.* [24]*Since we have heard that some persons from us have troubled you with words, unsettling your minds, although we gave them no instructions,* [25]*it has seemed good to us, having come to one accord, to choose men and send them to you with our beloved Barnabas and Paul,* [26]*men who have risked their lives for the sake of our Lord Jesus Christ.* [27]*We have therefore sent Judas and Silas, who themselves will tell you the same things by word of mouth.* [28]*For it has seemed good to the Holy Spirit and to us to lay upon you no greater burden than these necessary things:* [29]*that you abstain from what has been sacrificed to idols and from blood and from what is strangled[n] and from unchastity. If you keep yourselves from these, you will do well. Farewell."*

n Other early authorities omit *and from what is strangled*

OVERVIEW: Many of our contemporary preoccupations with the text are also those of the ancients, though the way of approaching them is different. We give here some lines from Joseph Fitzmyer's commentary so that the reader can get an idea of the different mindsets. Noteworthy about the letter is the mention of the guidance of the Holy Spirit and the decision of the assembly is said also to be that of the Holy Spirit. "The letter offers a solution to the problem in the Antiochene church that rose out of the incident of Paul's public rebuke of Peter there (Gal 2:11-14). In other words, after the departure of Peter and Paul from Antioch subsequent to that rebuke, a problem developed about Gentile Christians living and eating with Jewish Christians. So the church in Antioch eventually sent emissaries (among them Simeon Niger, 13:1) to Jerusalem and sought advice about it from James and the church there. The Jerusalem church responded in the letter sent. Luke, however, because he found the letter in an Antiochene source, as he had also learned about the Jerusalem 'Council' joined the

two accounts and presented the two (originally independent) Jerusalem decisions as events of the 'Council.' . . . He has joined them in order to explain how the Christian church eventually achieves its own independent status and mode of living as it emancipates itself from its Jewish matrix."[1] The Letter to the Churches of Antioch, Syria, and Cilicia affords the early Christian writers opportunity to reflect on several historical matters: the Holy Spirit's role in this event, the content of what the letter proscribes, as well as the matter of its credibility among the recipients. The Spirit is the source of inspiration for the council's decision (CHRYSOSTOM, CYRIL, BEDE). Origen sees in the contents of the letter proof that revelation does not supplant human reason that has guided civilizations in making laws, but rather that revelation completes and fulfills reason. Chrysostom's comments on the last of these elements, that of credibility, are very perceptive: a piece of writing in and of itself was no more a

[1]Fitzmyer, *Acts*, pp. 562-63.

guarantee of authenticity in the ancient world than it is today, and so trustworthy messengers were needed to confirm the truth of its words.[2] He also notes how controversy breeds distrust, and so, even though it was enough that their decision had as its source the Holy Spirit, he sees in the apostles' self-reference, "and to us," an eagerness to show to the Gentiles their goodwill toward them. Controversy, however, has also often been an occasion of growing deeper in faith, and Acts 15 became a model in the early church of the ecumenical council. This is a clarifying process and has had a large role in what has come to be called the development of doctrine: as time proceeds, the Holy Spirit grants to the Bride of Christ a deeper understanding into the content of the one faith. Development of doctrine was not the predominant way of speaking among the early Christians. We can see this in the words of Chrysostom to a congregation in Antioch whom he is exhorting to be on guard against those who teach that Christ is not divine. He uses a model common in the ancient world that the origins are pure, but later generations fall from this height just as a pure stream, flowing from its source and growing larger, becomes a muddy river.[3] Although Chrysostom's perspective on the past is not ours, his point has a relevance: it reminds us that we have been given a great responsibility in cooperating with the Holy Spirit to preserve, grow in and pass on this great gift of the faith.

15:24 Troubled with Words

The Responsibility to Defend the Faith. Chrysostom: You[4] have received as your patrimony the desire never to allow the teachings of our faith to degenerate into heresy. What makes this clear? In the time of your ancestors, people came here from Judea who were muddying the clear waters of the doctrine taught by the apostles. They were exhorting your ancestors to practice circumcision and to observe the Mosaic law. Those who then lived in your city did not remain silent, nor did they put up with this innovation.

They were like courageous hounds who saw wolves attacking and destroying the entire flock. They sprang after the wolves and did not let up chasing them and driving them away. They saw to it that the apostles from every corner of the world sent them their decision in the form of a letter that would protect them from any attack launched against the faithful by those innovators and all such as might come thereafter. Against the Anomoeans 2.4-5.[5]

15:26 Risking Their Lives for the Sake of Christ

These Have a Right to Be Believed. Chrysostom: As they are "beloved," they will not be dismissed. As they "have risked their lives," they have a right to be believed. "We have sent" them as well, it says, to announce the same things by word of mouth. For it was necessary that there be more than the letter alone, lest they should say that they said one thing instead of another. The praise bestowed on Paul stopped their mouths. For Paul came neither by himself nor with Barnabas alone but was accompanied by others from the church (and not only by those from Jerusalem), so that he should not be suspected. It shows that they have a right to be believed. Homilies on the Acts of the Apostles 33.[6]

15:28 It Seemed Good

Of the Spirit, but Also Spoken by People. Chrysostom: "For it has seemed good to the Holy Spirit and to us." Why did they add "and to us," when "to the Holy Spirit" was enough? The latter prevents them from thinking

---

[2]For a comic glimpse of the importance of letter carriers, see Jerome's *Letter* 105 to Augustine (*Letter* 72 in Augustine's *Letters*). [3]See the prologue to Livy's *History of Rome* 1.9 as well as Hesiod's *Works and Days* 106-201, and for the contrast between the pure stream and the muddy river, see Callimachus *Hymn to Apollo* 2.105-12. [4]Chrysostom delivered this homily in Antioch when a heresy called Anomoeism, which taught that the Son was completely unlike (*anomoios*) the Father, had arisen. [5]FC 72:72-73. [6]NPNF 1 11:209**.

it came of people, while the former teaches them that they too welcome [the Gentiles], even though they [as Jewish Christians] are circumcised. They have to speak to people who are still weak and afraid of them. This is the reason why this is added as well. HOMILIES ON THE ACTS OF THE APOSTLES 33.[7]

FROM THE HOLY SPIRIT. CYRIL OF JERUSALEM: They indicated clearly by what they wrote that though the decree had been written by men who were apostles, it was from the Holy Spirit and universal. Barnabas and Paul took this decree and confirmed it to the whole world. CATECHETICAL LECTURE 17.29.[8]

RIGHT TO THE HOLY SPIRIT AND TO US. BEDE: That is, it has pleased the Holy Spirit, who, appearing as the arbiter of his own powers, "breathes where he wills"[9] and speaks the things which he wishes. And it has pleased us, not in accordance with our own will alone but by virtue of the prompting of the same Spirit. COMMENTARY ON THE ACTS OF THE APOSTLES 15.28.[10]

15:29 *Abstain from Sacrifices to Idols*

DIVINE LAW COMPLETES HUMAN LAW. ORIGEN: Now in these precepts where it says that no other burden ought to be imposed on Gentile believers except abstinence from the sacrifices of idols, from blood, from what has been suffocated and from fornication, homicide is not forbidden, nor adultery, nor theft, nor homosexual acts, nor other crimes that are punished by divine and human laws. But if it is saying that Christians must observe only that which it has recounted, it will appear to some that it granted license concerning the rest. But consider how the Holy Spirit manages affairs: since other crimes are avenged by laws of the world, it seemed superfluous for those things, which are sufficiently covered by human law, also to have been forbidden by divine law. It only decreed those things about which human law had said nothing and which seemed proper to religion. COMMENTARY ON ROMANS 9.28.[11]

---

[7]NPNF 1 11:209**. [8]FC 64:114. [9]Jn 3:8. [10]CS 117:131. [11]PG 14:1228.

15:30-35 ANTIOCH RECEIVES THE EXHORTATION

[30]*So when they were sent off, they went down to Antioch; and having gathered the congregation together, they delivered the letter.* [31]*And when they read it, they rejoiced at the exhortation.* [32]*And Judas and Silas, who were themselves prophets, exhorted the brothers with many words and strengthened them.* [33]*And after they had spent some time, they were sent off in peace by the brothers to those who had sent them.*[o] [35]*But Paul and Barnabas remained in Antioch, teaching and preaching the word of the Lord, with many others also.*

o Other ancient authorities insert verse 34, *But it seemed good to Silas to remain there*

OVERVIEW: In these events are evident the later means whereby the church would settle its internal disputes: appeals to those in authority to answer the question, a faith in the Scripture that it offered guidance, and in the promise of Christ never to leave us orphaned but to guide us by his Spirit, both through events and through convening. The normal state of the church, however, is peace where charity reigns, not strife. That reason alone was sufficient to see the way through this crisis (CHRYSOSTOM), many would dispute, but the principle is clear: those who cause controversy over superfluous matters and disturb the peace of the church sin.

15:33 Sent in Peace

HUMAN REASON CAN ARRIVE AT PAUL'S VIEW. CHRYSOSTOM: No more strife. On that occasion it seems to me that they received the right hand, as [Paul] himself says, "They gave to me and Barnabas right hands of fellowship."[1] There he says, "They added nothing to me."[2] For they confirmed his view; they praised and admired it. It shows that even with human reason—that is, not only by the Holy Spirit—it is possible to see that they[3] have committed a sin not easily rectified. For such things do not require the Spirit. It shows that the rest[4] are not necessary but superfluous. These things, however, are necessary. "If you keep yourselves from these," it says, "you will do well." It shows that they lack nothing, that this is sufficient. For it would have been possible even without the letter, but they sent the epistle so that there may be a law in writing, that they may obey the law and speak to them. And they did this, in peace no less. HOMILIES ON THE ACTS OF THE APOSTLES 33.[5]

---

[1]Gal 2:9. [2]Gal 2:6. [3]Those who stirred up the controversy. [4]Here Chrysostom seems to mean the rest of the precepts of the law. [5]NPNF 1 11:210**.

15:36-41 PAUL AND BARNABAS SEPARATE

[36]And after some days Paul said to Barnabas, "Come, let us return and visit the brothers in every city where we proclaimed the word of the Lord, and see how they are." [37]And Barnabas wanted to take with them John called Mark. [38]But Paul thought best not to take with them one who had withdrawn from them in Pamphylia, and had not gone with them to the work. [39]And there arose a sharp contention, so that they separated from each other; Barnabas took Mark with him and sailed away to Cyprus, [40]but Paul chose Silas and departed, being commended by the brothers to the grace of the Lord. [41]And he went through Syria and Cilicia, strengthening the churches.

OVERVIEW: A major division of the book of Acts begins after this pivotal event of the council and ends at Acts 22:21. This section narrates what is known as the second missionary journey. Unlike the first missionary journey, however, the two principal missionaries are not together. The pastoral implications of this division coming right af- ter a council and decree that looked radically to the unity of the church are not lost to modern commentators who interpret its placement as showing how there can be legitimate disputes and divisions within the greater unity of the body. Here, the mission of spreading the gospel is seen as hindered by an insistence on refusing to separate. For the Fathers, the pastoral implications are primary. The continuous efforts of Paul and Barnabas offer us an example of great dedication to the gospel. Although our calling to spread the Word may take a different form, every believer has this responsibility for which God will require an account (SEVERUS). We see here also that despite our common responsibility of bearing fruit for Christ, we have different talents that answer different needs in the church, and so we will bear fruit in different ways: some will serve the church in leadership while others will receive that service to the profit of themselves and their neighbors, and sometimes the best thing might be to work separately for the greater good (CHRYSOSTOM, BEDE).

15:36 Returning to Visit the Believers

THE CHRISTIAN'S RESPONSIBILITY. SEVERUS OF ANTIOCH: If it seemed necessary to the apostles to travel around, and to return often to the same cities where they had preached the gospel, and to visit the believers and to examine closely how they were, what justification will we have before God if we do not fulfill through our writings what they fulfilled by traveling with great toil on their feet and going spontaneously to those who were in need and teaching what is useful for salvation? CATENA ON THE ACTS OF THE APOSTLES 15.36-38.[1]

15:38 Not Including One Who Had Withdrawn

DIVERSE GIFTS AND CHARACTERS. CHRYSOSTOM: Luke has already described the apostles' character to us, showing that one was more tender and forgiving and the other more strict and austere. For the gifts bestowed on them were different. That this is indeed a gift is clear. One befits one set and the other another set of characters. And if they should make an exchange, harm would result. . . . Likewise in the prophets we find different opinions and different characters.

Elias, for example, is austere, while Moses is meek. Thus here Paul is more vehement. But notice even so his gentleness. "He thought best," it says, "not to take with them one who had withdrawn from them in Pamphylia." . . . Although there appears to be a sharp contention, in fact it was part of the divine plan that each man should receive his proper place. Besides, it was necessary that not everyone have the same honor but that one should lead and the other be led. HOMILIES ON THE ACTS OF THE APOSTLES 34.[2]

THE NEED FOR STRENGTH AND CONSISTENCY. BEDE: When he [John Mark] placed himself in the very front line of the fray, he had been too lukewarm about taking a stand.[3] Therefore Paul rightly rejected him, lest the strength of others might be corrupted by the contagious influence, so to speak, of this man. COMMENTARY ON THE ACTS OF THE APOSTLES 15.38.[4]

15:39 Sharp Contention

THEY YIELD TO ONE ANOTHER. CHRYSOSTOM: The point is not that they differed in their opinions but that they accommodated themselves to each other. Thus a greater good resulted from their parting, for which this provided an excuse. What then? Did they withdraw in enmity? God forbid! Recall how after this Barnabas received much praise from Paul in his epistles. "There arose," it says, "a sharp contention," not hatred or rivalry. The contention grew so great that it parted them. For what each supposed was advantageous, this he did not admit after this because of his association with the other. I think that the parting took place advisedly and that they said to each other, "Since I wish to, but you do not, let us distribute the places so that we should not fight." Therefore it was because they yielded to each other that they parted. For Barnabas wanted Paul to prevail and so withdrew. Likewise Paul

---

[1]CGPNT 3:255-56. [2]NPNF 1 11:212-13**. [3]Acts 13:13. [4]CS 117:131.

wanted Barnabas to prevail and he, too, withdrew. Would that we should part such partings to go forth for preaching. "Paul," it says, "chose Silas and departed, being commended by the brothers to the grace of the Lord." A wonderful man is he, and very great! HOMILIES ON THE ACTS OF THE APOSTLES 34.[5]

A QUARREL OCCURRED. BEDE: Do not think this a moral fault, for it is not evil to be agitated. Rather it is evil to be agitated unreasonably, when no just reason demands it. COMMENTARY ON THE ACTS OF THE APOSTLES 15.39A.[6]

15:40 Paul Chose Silas

FOR MARK'S INSTRUCTION. CHRYSOSTOM: The sharp contention took place with good reason, to teach Mark a lesson and so that the matter should not look like stage playing. For would he, who had always yielded, not yield on this occasion? He who loved Paul so much that he sought him in Tarsus, brought him to the apostles, undertook the alms in common with him and received the business relating to the decree together with him? [Barnabas] would not have become angry for something like this. No, they parted from each other so that they might educate and bring to perfection those who needed their teaching. HOMILIES ON THE ACTS OF THE APOSTLES 34.[7]

15:41 Syria and Cilicia

GREAT GOOD COMES OF THIS CONTENTION. CHRYSOSTOM: "And he went through Syria and Cilicia, confirming the churches." This too is part of the divine plan. For the Cyprians had shown nothing of the kind as was shown by those in Antioch and elsewhere. Those needed the softer character, but these needed such a character as Paul's. . . . For just as a general would not choose to always have a lowly baggage carrier, neither did the apostle. This both taught the others and instructed [Mark] himself. Did Barnabas act badly then? Not at all. It is out of place to even think such a thing. For how is it not out of place to say because of such a small thing that he acted badly? Look, in the first place, nothing bad happened if they, each sufficient for entire nations, separated from one another. Rather, a great good took place. Second, if this had not happened, they would not easily have chosen to leave each other. Please appreciate how the writer does not conceal this at all. But if they had to separate, could it not be done without sharp contention? But it is through this especially that he shows what was human [in the preaching of the gospel]. For if this had to happen in the case of Christ, then all the more so here. Besides, the sharp contention was not trivial, since each argued on behalf of such things and with just reason. Had one of them been looking after himself and seeking his own glory, well then! But on the contrary, each wishing to educate and to teach, one went one way and the other another. What is there to find fault with? In many things, indeed, they acted with human judgment; for they were not made of stone or wood. HOMILIES ON THE ACTS OF THE APOSTLES 34.[8]

---

[5]NPNF 1 11:213-14**. [6]CS 117:131. [7]NPNF 1 11:215**. [8]NPNF 1 11:213**.

16:1-5 TIMOTHY ACCOMPANIES PAUL

¹And he came also to Derbe and to Lystra. A disciple was there, named Timothy, the son of a Jewish woman who was a believer; but his father was a Greek. ²He was well spoken of by the brothers at Lystra and Iconium. ³Paul wanted Timothy to accompany him; and he took him and circumcised him because of the Jews that were in those places, for they all knew that his father was a Greek. ⁴As they went on their way through the cities, they delivered to them for observance the decisions which had been reached by the apostles and elders who were at Jerusalem. ⁵So the churches were strengthened in the faith, and they increased in numbers daily.

OVERVIEW: Here begins the second missionary journey, a major journey that takes Paul into Europe and that begins from and ends in Antioch at Acts 18:22. Modern commentators, as well as the ancients, see in the circumcision of Timothy a reflection of 1 Corinthians 9:20 ("to Jews I became as a Jew in order to win Jews"). Paul's choice of Timothy is surprising, since Paul knew that his continued preaching among the Jews could be hindered by having an uncircumcised companion (CHRYSOSTOM). Paul wisely does what is needed and circumcises Timothy (CHRYSOSTOM). From this it is clear that although he in no way saw the observance of the law as salvific, Paul did not condemn the customs of the Jews, which prepared the way for Christ (AUGUSTINE). Paul's actions are in conformity with God's gradual revelation to us of the fullness of truth in Christ (GREGORY OF NAZIANZUS). So even though Paul, and the church as well, had come to see the law as a figure that prepared for Christ, he acted according to the figure as needed for the benefit of those who had yet to see this (ORIGEN, CLEMENT OF ALEXANDRIA). For there was the possibility that too abrupt a change would drive away the Jews (BEDE). In this event Clement of Alexandria sees that whoever takes on the responsibility to teach others the truth about God realizes that he must eventually pass on to others truths they might not be ready for and thus accommodates himself to his listeners, even to the extent of deceiving

another for his own good. Paul not only acted in this way himself but even taught Timothy to live in this way, and so to appear to the Jews to be preserving the law when in fact they were loosening it (CHRYSOSTOM).[1] The various opinions of the Fathers show the same ambiguity regarding Jewish observance that we wrestle with today: is it still lawful and profitable for Jews to continue their ancient practices once they have become Christian?

16:3 Paul Circumcised Timothy

NOT ACCORDING TO HIS OWN PREFERENCES. CHRYSOSTOM: The wisdom of Paul is indeed amazing. He, who fought so many battles against circumcision, who moved everything for this, who did not give up until he had carried his point, once the decision was confirmed, he circumcised his disciple. Not only did he not forbid others, but he himself did this. "Timothy," it says, "he wanted as his companion." It is surprising that he even brought him along. "Because of the Jews," it says, "that were in those places." This is the reason for the circumcision. For they would not have endured to hear the Word from one

---

[1]Elsewhere Augustine has another opinion, namely, that the observances of the law could be observed until the new law was widely known; in this he disagrees with Jerome. See the discussion in Thomas Aquinas *Summa Theologiae* 1-2, 103, ad primum.

uncircumcised. Nothing could be wiser. So in all things he looked to what was advantageous. He did nothing at all according to his own preference. And what was the result? Look at his success. He circumcised to take away circumcision. For he preached the decisions of the apostles. Homilies on the Acts of the Apostles 34.[2]

Paul Did Not Forsake Moses. Augustine: As to Paul's circumcising of Timothy, performing a vow at Cenchrea[3] and undertaking on the suggestion of James at Jerusalem to share the performance of the appointed rites with some who had made a vow,[4] it is manifest that Paul's design in these things was not to give to others the impression that he thought that by these observances salvation is given under the Christian dispensation. [His intent was] to prevent people from believing that he condemned, as no better than heathen idolatrous worship, those rites that God had appointed in the former dispensation as suitable to it and as shadows of things to come. For this is what James said to him, that the report had gone abroad concerning him that he taught people "to forsake Moses." This would be by all means wrong for those who believe in Christ, to forsake him who prophesied of Christ, as if they detested and condemned the teaching of him of whom Christ said, "If you had believed Moses, you would have believed me, for he wrote of me." Letter 82.8 to Jerome.[5]

A Gradual Following of the Gospel. Gregory of Nazianzus: There have been in the whole period of the duration of the world two conspicuous changes of people's lives, which are also called two Testaments, or, on account of the wide fame of the matter, two earthquakes; the one from idols to the law, the other from the law to the gospel. And we are taught in the Gospel of a third earthquake, namely, from this earth to that which cannot be shaken or moved. Now the two Testaments are alike in this respect, that the change was not made on a sudden or at the first movement of the endeavor. Why not (for this is a

point on which we must have information)? That no violence might be done to us but that we might be moved by persuasion. For nothing that is involuntary is durable; like streams or trees that are kept back by force. But that which is voluntary is more durable and safe. The former is due to one who uses force, the latter is ours; the one is due to the gentleness of God, the other to a tyrannical authority. Therefore God did not think it behooved him to benefit the unwilling but to do good to the willing. And therefore like a tutor or physician he partly removes and partly condones ancestral habits, conceding some little of what tended to pleasure, just as doctors do with their patients, that their medicine may be taken, being artfully blended with what is nice. For it is no very easy matter to change from those habits that custom and use have made honorable. For instance, the first cut off the idol but left the sacrifices; the second, while it destroyed the sacrifices did not forbid circumcision. Then, when once men had submitted to the curtailment, they also yielded that which had been conceded to them; in the first instance the sacrifices, in the second circumcision; and became instead of Gentiles, Jews, and instead of Jews, Christians, being beguiled into the gospel by gradual changes. Paul is a proof of this; for having at one time administered circumcision and submitted to legal purification, he advanced till he could say, and I, brothers, if I yet preach circumcision, why do I yet suffer persecution?[6] His former conduct belonged to the temporary dispensation, his latter to maturity. On the Holy Spirit, Theological Oration 5 (31).25.[7]

He Accommodated the Symbol. Origen: [But] perhaps it has been recorded at some time or other with good reason that even the true worshiper who worships in spirit and truth[8] performs certain symbolic acts so that, by acting in a most accommodating manner, he might free those who

---

[2]NPNF 1 11:214**. [3]Acts 18:18. [4]Acts 21:23-24. [5]NPNF 1 1:352**. [6]Gal 5:11. [7]NPNF 2 7:325-26*. [8]Jn 4:23.

are enslaved to the symbol and bring them to the truth that the symbols represent. Paul appears to have done this in the case of Timothy, and perhaps also in Cenchrea and Jerusalem, as it is written in the Acts of the Apostles.[9] COMMENTARY ON THE GOSPEL OF JOHN 13.III.[10]

ON ACCOUNT OF THE JEWS. BEDE: [It was] not because he believed that the symbolic actions of the law could provide anything of use now that the truth of the gospel was shining forth. [Paul did this] instead so that the Jewish [Christians] would not fall away from the faith because of the pretext of the Gentiles. Nevertheless, the old trace [of the law of circumcision] was to be gradually removed for them, just as the depravity of their ancient ways was to be removed in the case of the Gentiles, as has been said above. For these traces of the law were used from time to time by the apostles, as if they were at one time established by the Lord, in order to avert lack of belief on the part of the Jewish [Christians]. The saints, however, never had anything to do with the practices of the Gentiles, inasmuch as they were acquired from Satan. COMMENTARY ON THE ACTS OF THE APOSTLES 16.3.[11]

ACCOMMODATING ONESELF FOR ANOTHER'S GOOD. CLEMENT OF ALEXANDRIA: Whatever . . . [the gnostic][12] has in his mind, he bears on his tongue, to those who are worthy to hear, speaking as well as living from assent and inclination. For he both thinks and speaks the truth; unless at any time, medicinally, as a physician for the safety of the sick, he may deceive or tell an untruth, according to the Sophists. To illustrate: the noble apostle circumcised Timothy, though loudly declaring and writing that circumcision made with hands profits nothing.[13] But that he might not, by dragging all at once away from the law to the circumcision of the heart through faith those of the Hebrews who were reluctant listeners, compel them to break away from the synagogue, he, "accommodating himself to the Jews, became a Jew that he might gain all."[14] He, then, who sub-mits to accommodate himself merely for the benefit of his neighbors, for the salvation of those for whose sake he accommodates himself, not partaking in any dissimulation through the peril impending over the just from those who envy them, such a one by no means acts with compulsion. But for the benefit of his neighbors alone, he will do things that would not have been done by him primarily, if he did not do them on their account. Such a one gives himself: for the church; for the disciples whom he has begotten in faith; for an example to those who are capable of receiving the supreme economy of the philanthropic and God-loving instructor, for confirmation of the truth of his words, for the exercise of love to the Lord. Such a one is unenslaved by fear, true in word, enduring in labor, never willing to lie by uttered word and in it always securing sinlessness; since falsehood, being spoken with a certain deceit, is not an inert word but operates to mischief. STROMATEIS 7.9.[15]

CIRCUMCISING TO END CIRCUMCISION. CHRYSOSTOM: Before blessed Paul, who himself had received circumcision, sent Timothy to teach the Jews, he first circumcised him in order that Timothy, as teacher, might be more acceptable to his audience. So Paul [actually] engaged in circumcision in order to abolish it. He knew why he had circumcised Timothy but chose not to disclose his reasons to the disciples. In fact, if they had known that he had circumcised him with the intention of abolishing circumcision, they would have not listened to anything Timothy had to say, and all the progress he had achieved would have been lost. Indeed, their ignorance was quite useful. As long as they believed that he circumcised Timothy in order to preserve the law, they generously received him and his doctrine. Therefore, by receiving [that doctrine] little by little, and by being taught, they abandoned their old customs.

---

[9]Acts 18:18-22; 21:23-24. [10]FC 89:91. [11]CS 117:135. [12]As is clear from this passage, Paul was, in Clement's words, a gnostic (i.e., one who truly knows God). [13]Rom 2:25. [14]1 Cor 9:20. [15]ANF 2:538.

However, this would never have happened if they had known the reason from the beginning. In fact, if they had known, they would have opposed the circumcision and by opposing it they would have remained in their previous error. CATENA ON THE ACTS OF THE APOSTLES 16.1-3.[16]

---

[16]CGPNT 3:262.

16:6-10 PAUL CALLED TO MACEDONIA

[6]And they went through the region of Phrygia and Galatia, having been forbidden by the Holy Spirit to speak the word in Asia. [7]And when they had come opposite Mysia, they attempted to go into Bithynia, but the Spirit of Jesus did not allow them; [8]so, passing by Mysia, they went down to Troas. [9]And a vision appeared to Paul in the night: a man of Macedonia was standing beseeching him and saying, "Come over to Macedonia and help us." [10]And when he had seen the vision, immediately we sought to go on into Macedonia, concluding that God had called us to preach the gospel to them.

OVERVIEW: In Acts 16:10 we have the first occurrence of what modern commentators term the "we source." Luke is probably drawing on his own travel journal. The episode's message is that the Christian disciple must wait patiently on the guidance of the Spirit, or perhaps this is another instance of showing how the Holy Spirit has this work of the body of Christ under his authority. For some undisclosed reason Paul is prevented from preaching in the province of Asia (CHRYSOSTOM), though Bede surmises the reason to be God's mercy, since Asia was not ready and would have rejected the gospel. Chrysostom sees this event of Paul being turned away from Asia as evidence that he was largely proceeding as he thought best, in what Chrysostom likes to term a human manner. Ammonius, however, provides an example of a very different mentality, one foreign not only to us but even to those who preceded and followed him. He sees here evidence that Paul was always led by the Spirit and avoids the sort of confident speculations into reasons that we see in Bede. Our commentators are also in-trigued by the manner of direction given to Paul. Chrysostom sees this dream as more human than divine and thus as showing a growing docility and obedience in Paul to what the Spirit wanted. Bede understands the Macedonian man to be the guardian angel of Macedonia. In this line, Origen, whose comments are taken from a homily on the angels' appearance to the shepherds at Christ's birth, reflects on how God ministers to us through various types of shepherds, one of which was the angel-shepherd responsible for Macedonia.

16:6 Phrygia and Galatia

THE LORD WITHDREW HIS SERVANT FROM ASIA. BEDE: Truly "terrible" is the Lord "in his councils upon the sons of men."[1] The one who promised that he would follow the master through everything was not granted permission,[2] and another man who had been ordered to follow

---

[1]Ps 66:5 (65:5 LXX, Vg). [2]Mt 8:19-20.

did not receive the delay he asked for in order to bury his father.[3] Paul, who was fighting against [Christ], was attracted in spite of himself.[4] Cornelius, who devoted himself to prayers and almsgiving, was shown the way of salvation as his reward.[5] And God, who knows hearts, on account of his kindness, withdrew [his] teacher from Asia lest, if what is holy were given to dogs,[6] the error of their wicked hearts "might be judged more reprehensible on account of their disregard of his preaching."[7] On the other hand the Macedonian legate, whom we believe to have been the angel of that people, asked the apostles, who were concerned with other matters, that crumbs of the Lord's bread might be offered to them.[8] Commentary on the Acts of the Apostles 16.6-9.[9]

16:7 The Spirit of Jesus

The Apostles Followed Human Customs. Chrysostom: The text does not say why they were prevented but only that they were prevented. It teaches us that we only have to obey and not to enquire about the reasons, and it shows us that they did many things according to human customs. Catena on the Acts of the Apostles 16.7.[10]

Unquestioning Obedience. Ammonius: It should be noted that the apostle did nothing according to his own will. Rather, whatever he did or did not do, it was under the impulse of the Spirit. Therefore it is dangerous to despise what was done by Paul or investigate what was directed by the Spirit. Consequently, we ought not to ask why the Spirit did not allow Paul to preach in Asia. Catena on the Acts of the Apostles 16.8.[11]

16:9 Paul Sees a Vision

Not a Vision of Angels. Chrysostom: "When he had seen the vision, immediately we sought to go on into Macedonia, concluding that God had called us." Look, no longer through an angel, as it was with Philip[12] and Cornelius.[13] But how? Through a vision it appears to him, in a manner now more human, no longer as divine. For where obedience came more easily, revelation was of a more human sort; where much force was needed, of a more divine sort. Thus when he was only urged to preach, a dream appeared to him; but when he could not bear not to preach, it was the Holy Spirit who revealed it to him. So it was with Peter. "Arise, go down."[14] For the Holy Spirit did not work what was easy; a dream was enough in his case. Also for Joseph, who obeyed readily, it was in a dream, but for others,[15] including Cornelius and Paul himself, it was in a vision. And notice how it says "a man of Macedonia was standing beseeching him and saying." Not "ordering" but "beseeching," that is, on behalf of the very people in need of caring. What does "concluding" mean? It means they made an inference. From the fact that Paul saw him and not someone else, that Paul was "forbidden by the Holy Spirit" and that they were at the borders—from all this they reached their conclusion. Homilies on the Acts of the Apostles 34.[16]

God's Shepherds. Origen: Listen, shepherds of the churches! Listen, God's shepherds! His angel always comes down from heaven and proclaims to you, "Today a Savior is born for you, who is Christ the Lord."[17] For, unless that Shepherd comes, the shepherd of the churches will be unable to guard the flock well. Their custody is weak, unless Christ pastures and guards it along with them. We just read in the apostle, "We are coworkers with God."[18] A good shepherd, who imitates the good Shepherd, is a coworker with God and Christ. He is a good shepherd precisely because he has the best Shepherd with him, pasturing his sheep along with him. For, "God established in his church apostles,

[3]Mt 8:21-22. [4]Acts 9:1-9. [5]Acts 10. [6]Mt 7:6. [7]Gregory the Great Forty Gospel Homilies 1.4.1 (PL 76:1089). [8]Mt 15:21-27. [9]CS 117:135-36. [10]CGPNT 3:264. [11]CGPNT 3:264. [12]Acts 8:26. [13]Acts 10:3. [14]Acts 10:20. [15]Mt 1:20; 2:13, 19. [16]NPNF 1 11:216**. [17]Lk 2:11. [18]1 Cor 3:9.

prophets, evangelists, shepherds and teachers. He established everything for the perfection of the saints."[19] Let this suffice for a simpler explanation.

But we should ascend to a more hidden understanding. Some shepherds were angels that governed human affairs.[20] Each of these kept his watch. They were vigilant day and night. But, at some point, they were unable to bear the labor of governing the peoples who had been entrusted to them and accomplish it diligently. When the Lord was born, an angel came and announced to the shepherds that the true Shepherd had appeared.

Let me give an example. There was a certain shepherd-angel in Macedonia who needed the Lord's help. Consequently, he appeared to Paul in his dreams as a Macedonian man "and said, 'Cross over to Macedonia and help us.'" Why do I speak of Paul, since the angel said this not to Paul but to Jesus who was in Paul? So shepherds need the presence of Christ. Homilies on the Gospel of Luke 12.2-3.[21]

---

[19]Eph 4:11-12; 1 Cor 12:28. [20]See Dan 10:13. [21]FC 94:48-49.

16:11-15 THE CONVERSION OF LYDIA

[11]Setting sail therefore from Troas, we made a direct voyage to Samothrace, and the following day to Ne-apolis, [12]and from there to Philippi, which is the leading city of the district[x] of Macedonia, and a Roman colony. We remained in this city some days; [13]and on the sabbath day we went outside the gate to the riverside, where we supposed there was a place of prayer; and we sat down and spoke to the women who had come together. [14]One who heard us was a woman named Lydia, from the city of Thyatira, a seller of purple goods, who was a worshiper of God. The Lord opened her heart to give heed to what was said by Paul. [15]And when she was baptized, with her household, she besought us, saying, "If you have judged me to be faithful to the Lord, come to my house and stay." And she prevailed upon us.

x The Greek text is uncertain

Overview: Recent commentators note that this is the first place in Europe to be evangelized by Paul. The first convert is somewhat similar to Cornelius: she is probably a God-fearer, not a Jew, and they end up staying with her as Peter did with Cornelius. The fruit that comes of Paul's voyage to Macedonia, being so rapid, shows that the separation from Barnabas was part of the divine plan (Chrysostom). God works through Paul and his companions to open Lydia's heart, but he does not

work against her will (Chrysostom, Ammonius). She immediately shows her fidelity by her hospitality to the apostles (Chrysostom).

16:11 A Direct Voyage to Samothrace

The Rapid Progress of the Word. Chrysostom: Therefore the "sharp contention"[1] was

---

[1]Acts 15:39.

brought to pass as part of the divine plan. For otherwise it would not have been the work of the Holy Spirit, and Macedonia would not have accepted the Word. Such a rapid progress of the Word is a sign that what happened was more than human. HOMILIES ON THE ACTS OF THE APOSTLES 34.[2]

16:14 The Lord Opened Lydia's Heart

ATTENTIVENESS OF HEART. CHRYSOSTOM: Therefore we need God, who can open the heart. (God, however, opens hearts that are willing. For there are also hearts that are crippled, incapable of seeing.) . . . "To give heed to what was said by Paul." The opening, then, was God's work, the "give heed," hers. Therefore it was both God's doing and Paul's. "And when she was baptized," it says, "she sought us, saying, 'If you have judged me . . .'" Look, as soon as she is baptized, she receives the apostles with an entreaty more earnest than Abraham's.[3] And she mentions no other proof but that by which she was saved. She did not say, "if you have judged me a great woman" or "if you have judged me a devout woman." What does she say? "If you have judged me to be faithful to the Lord"—if faithful to the Lord, all the more so to you, unless you dispute it. And she did not say "stay with me" but "come to my house and stay," thus showing the great eagerness with which she was doing this. Truly a faithful woman! HOMILIES ON THE ACTS OF THE APOSTLES 35.[4]

16:15 Stay in My House

GOD WANTS THE WILLING. CHRYSOSTOM: Notice again the absence of pride. She was a woman, and she was lowly and a manual laborer. Note, however, that the woman was a lover of wisdom.[5] The first evidence of this is her testimony that God called her. See how the writer of the story was not ashamed to report the habits of life. . . . And as for us, let us not be ashamed of these students or of any student of these

things. Peter stays with the tanner, and Paul with the dealer in purple and a foreign one for that matter. Where is their pride? Therefore let us pray to God that he may open our heart. In fact God opens those hearts that want to be opened, as he can see those that are hardened. The opening is God's part, being attentive hers: this is something that is, in fact, both human and divine. CATENA ON THE ACTS OF THE APOSTLES 16.13.[6]

GOD VIOLATES THE FREEDOM OF NONE. AMMONIUS: Observe that instruction came first, and then, after the disciples heard the word, baptism followed. But if someone dares to say, "Behold! God saves only those whom he wants to save, he has compassion on and opens only the hearts of those he wants," as if he were seeking to assign to God the reason why we are either saved or not saved, so that he can say that God is responsible—if he says, "Look, see how he opened the heart of Lydia," we must reply to him, "Search the Scripture,"[7] for he who does not search does not find what he requires. How do we say that what is said about Cornelius is by the grace of God? We answer that God opens the door to those who live a righteous life but err about faith because of the error transmitted to them by their fathers. And so Lydia too worshiped God but did not know the way in which she had to be saved, which God revealed to her through the true teaching. Therefore the text says "she was a worshiper of God." On the other hand, if God does not open the heart of someone, he does not open it because that person is impious and receives his words in vain. For even if someone should establish the word of God through manifest proofs, just as the apostles did through signs and wonders, while he, still desiring to be a slave to his passions and wickedness, rejects the word, he is responsible for himself. In fact, God never aids someone in evil, but

---

[2]NPNF 1 11:217**. [3]Gen 18:2-3. [4]NPNF 1 11:220-21**. [5]Or *a philosopher.* [6]CGPNT 3:266. [7]Jn 5:39.

because of his love of goodness he joins anyone in approving what is noble. But as for what is evil, he allows each to walk in his desires:[8] each may live for whatever he wishes. CATENA

---

[8]See Is 56:11 (LXX). [9]CGPNT 3:266-67.

16:16-18 A SPIRIT EXPELLED FROM A SLAVE GIRL

[16]As we were going to the place of prayer, we were met by a slave girl who had a spirit of divination and brought her owners much gain by soothsaying. [17]She followed Paul and us, crying, "These men are servants of the Most High God, who proclaim to you the way of salvation." [18]And this she did for many days. But Paul was annoyed, and turned and said to the spirit, "I charge you in the name of Jesus Christ to come out of her." And it came out that very hour.

OVERVIEW: Modern commentators explain Paul's actions here as Luke's way of showing the triumph of the faith over pagan ways in that even through a pagan medium, a demonic voice in the world of humankind, comes the profession that salvation comes from the most high God of Christianity. The Fathers see parallels to Christ's ministry before his passion. Just as Christ was proclaimed by demons, so is the truth of Paul's testimony. Paul also shows that those who believe in Christ are more powerful than demons by releasing the girl from its power (AMMONIUS). Also as Christ did, Paul does not accept witness from demons (ORIGEN). The true witness to Paul and his companions comes from the presence of the Spirit that forces the demon to give true witness, while Paul is unwilling to accept what is true from a deceptive source (BEDE). Had he done so, he would have contradicted his message that proclaimed freedom from such things (CHRYSOSTOM).

16:16 A Spirit of Divination

HOW POWERFUL THE WORDS OF CHRIST'S SERVANTS. AMMONIUS: It should be noted that

Christ was announced through demons, in which the Gentiles were believing. It was also these that gave witness and said that the apostles were servants of God, that their preaching was saving and that Jesus was God and not a mere man. That was the proclamation of the ones concerning Paul and Silas. . . . After the demon had repeatedly testified that the message of the apostles was saving, Paul ordered him to come out in order to demonstrate to those who believed him, that every believer was stronger than the demon, and to show that each had power both to allow the demon to stay as one subject to the believer and to release him. See how powerful the words of the servants of Christ were: as soon as they gave a command, the demons came out. CATENA ON THE ACTS OF THE APOSTLES 16.17.[1]

16:17 Servants of the Most High God

AS JESUS DID. ORIGEN: Jesus our Lord does not accept witness from demons, as he said, "Be silent and come out of him."[2] So, in imitation of

---

[1]CGPNT 3:270-71.   [2]Mk 1:25; Lk 4:35.

him, his apostle Paul "grieving" it says, "turned and addressed the spirit of Python, 'I command you in the name of Jesus Christ, depart from her.'" Perhaps you may ask why Paul is grieving when he rebukes the spirit of Python. It had spoken no blasphemy, had it, for it says, "A woman with the spirit of Python was following Paul and his companions and kept shouting, 'These men are servants of God the most high, and they proclaim to you the way of salvation.' And she kept doing this for many days." It is clear that Paul was not grieving because of blasphemy but because he considered testimony given by the spirit of Python unworthy of his message. Homilies on Numbers 16.7.10.[3]

Compelled by the Holy Spirit, She Spoke.

Bede: That confession is not voluntary that is followed by a reward for confessing, but under the compulsion of fear of the Holy Spirit, the deceitful spirit spoke the truth, not daring any longer to hide its darkness in the presence of the light. "But to the sinner God says, 'Why do you recite my judgments?'"[4] As Arator says, "If she who was a servant of falsehood prophesies what is true, let us not be corrupted by the bitter honey of deceit."[5] Commentary on the Acts of the Apostles 16.17.[6]

16:18 In the Name of Jesus Christ

Paul's Wisdom in Rebuking the Demon.

Chrysostom: Why did the demon utter these words, and why did Paul forbid him? The one acted maliciously, the other wisely. For [Paul] did not want to make him believable. If Paul had admitted his testimony, the demon would have deceived many of the believers, since he was accepted by Paul. For this reason he allows him to say things against them, in order to establish things for him, and the demon uses agreement for the purpose of destruction. At first then, Paul did not admit him but spat upon him, not wishing to cast himself entirely upon miracles. But when the demon continued to do this for many days and pointed to their work, "These men are servants of the most high God, who proclaim to you the way of salvation," he commanded it to come out. Homilies on the Acts of the Apostles 35.[7]

Silencing False Preachers of the Truth.

Chrysostom: In imitation of his teacher; for so too did Christ rebuke. For he did not wish to have testimony from them. And why did the demon do this? Because he wanted to confound the order of things, to snatch away the apostles' dignity and to persuade many to pay attention to him. If that had happened, they would have appeared trustworthy from then on and introduced their own designs. To prevent this and to forestall deceit, [Paul] silences them even though they speak the truth, so that no one should pay any attention to their lies but stop listening altogether to what they say. Homilies on 1 Corinthians 29.3.[8]

---

[3]SC 442:254-56. [4]Ps 50:16 (49:16 LXX, Vg). [5]Arator De Actibus Apostolorum 2 (CSEL 72:102). [6]CS 117:136-37. [7]NPNF 1 11:220**. [8]NPNF 1 12:170**.

16:19-24 PAUL AND SILAS THROWN INTO PRISON

[19]*But when her owners saw that their hope of gain was gone, they seized Paul and Silas and dragged them into the market place before the rulers;* [20]*and when they had brought them to the magistrates they said, "These men are Jews and they are disturbing our city.* [21]*They advocate customs which it is not lawful for us Romans to accept or practice."* [22]*The crowd joined in attacking them; and the magistrates tore the garments off them and gave orders to beat them with rods.* [23]*And when they had inflicted many blows upon them, they threw them into prison, charging the jailer to keep them safely.* [24]*Having received this charge, he put them into the inner prison and fastened their feet in the stocks.*

OVERVIEW: Modern commentators are intrigued by the second charge of Acts 16:21. They see it as a point easily rebutted in that the Roman magistrates would hardly be able to tell the difference between Judaism, a religion the Romans tolerated, and nascent Christianity, which was emerging from Judaism and could be construed as a new religion. In Paul's imprisonment, the Fathers see much irony. By having Paul and Silas thrown into prison, the owners of the possessed girl show that they did not care about what the demon prophesied but only about their profits (CHRYSOSTOM). The command that the guards hold the prisoners securely is a witness to the power of Paul and Silas (AMMONIUS). Locking them up in chains, in which they will remain, will only show the power of Christ all the more (CHRYSOSTOM).

16:21 Advocating Unlawful Customs

CONTRADICTORY BEHAVIOR. CHRYSOSTOM: What do you say? Do you believe the demon? Does not he say here, "servants of the most high God"? You say, "They are disturbing our city." He says that they proclaim to you a way of salvation. You say, "They are advocating customs that are not lawful for us to adopt"; see how they do not even listen to the demon but are influenced by greed. CATENA ON THE ACTS OF THE APOSTLES 16.20-21.[1]

16:23 Charging the Jailer

THE JAILER'S IDENTITY. AMMONIUS: This is Stephen whom Paul mentions in the first letter to the Corinthians. CATENA ON THE ACTS OF THE APOSTLES 16.31-32.[2]

CONVICTED BY THEIR OWN WORDS. AMMONIUS: "They ordered the jailer to keep them securely." Since they knew their virtue, they deceived themselves by saying, "Keep them securely." But by doing so they testified that they were not ordinary but great men who had the power to do, through the Lord, whatever they wanted. CATENA ON THE ACTS OF THE APOSTLES 16.23.[3]

16:24 In the Inner Prison

PAUL'S POWER SHOWN IN WEAKNESS. CHRYSOSTOM: Do you see how his power was perfected in weakness? If Paul had been freed and had shaken that building, the event would not have been so wonderful. "Therefore," he says, "remain in chains! Let the walls be shaken from every side, and let the prisoners be freed!—so that my power may appear all the greater, when through you, the one confined and in fetters, all who are in

---

[1]CGPNT 3:272. [2]CGPNT 3:277. [3]CGPNT 3:273.

chains are freed." This is what amazed the jailer, that Paul, held in such constraints, was able, through prayer alone, to shake the foundations, open the doors of the prison and free all who were in chains. HOMILIES CONCERNING THE STATUES 1.16.[4]

[4]NPNF 1 9:337*.

16:25-34 THE CONVERSION OF THE JAILER

[25]But about midnight Paul and Silas were praying and singing hymns to God, and the prisoners were listening to them, [26]and suddenly there was a great earthquake, so that the foundations of the prison were shaken; and immediately all the doors were opened and every one's fetters were unfastened. [27]When the jailer woke and saw that the prison doors were open, he drew his sword and was about to kill himself, supposing that the prisoners had escaped. [28]But Paul cried with a loud voice, "Do not harm yourself, for we are all here." [29]And he called for lights and rushed in, and trembling with fear he fell down before Paul and Silas, [30]and brought them out and said, "Men, what must I do to be saved?" [31]And they said, "Believe in the Lord Jesus, and you will be saved, you and your household." [32]And they spoke the word of the Lord to him and to all that were in his house. [33]And he took them the same hour of the night, and washed their wounds, and he was baptized at once, with all his family. [34]Then he brought them up into his house, and set food before them; and he rejoiced with all his household that he had believed in God.

OVERVIEW: Modern commentators draw attention to a shift in language here, and some imply that since it is idyllic and akin to folklore, its historicity is questionable. Others note, however, that the way a story is told is not a measure of its truth. Nearly all highlight the parallels between Peter and Paul: As an angel set Peter free (Acts 12:6-11), so now an earthquake delivers Paul. Where Peter confounded a Samaritan magician (Acts 8:9-24), Paul rebukes a Greco-Roman soothsayer. The imprisonment of Paul and Silas offers the Fathers an example for exhorting and inspiring their listeners. Being in prison does not lead the apostles to despair, but they use God's word to praise God and give us an example for our own trials (AMMONIUS, SEVERUS, BEDE). Chrysostom shines a light on the difference between the experience of the apostles, their sufferings and pain, and that of most people in order to prompt his audience to a greater awareness of the formers' virtue. At the same time, Chrysostom pays close attention to the nature of the event. He sees God's providential hand in their vigil, which he contrasts with Peter's sleep in Acts 12: Paul and Silas needed to be awake, not just to exhort us to keep vigil but to prevent the jailer's suicide. The power of Christ in weakness is evident in this event in its transformation of the powerful into the powerless, of the powerless into the powerful, of the prisoners into liberators, of the means of imprisonment into means of salvation (CHRYSOSTOM). Chrysostom, however, sees the event as narrowly focused and only benefiting the jailer, and he makes much of the time of the event to support this perspective. Ammonius reflects on the unconverted fellow prisoners of Paul and Silas, and on the event as a whole, quite differently. For Ammonius, the unconverted had the opportunity to come to faith but, for whatever reason, chose not to. He draws parallels between the apostles' imprisonment, with its display of power intended to free all, both jailer and prisoners, to Christ's imprisonment in hell that was intended to free its captives, only some of whom came to Christ, while others, for whatever reason, stayed away. Chrysostom notes how some, in his day, would see in this passage a reason for staying away from Christ, namely, that those here converted are of the lower classes. Using this prejudice, Chrysostom argues for these as a source of credibility for the faith and, in a twist on Paul's idea that God chose the weak of this world to shame the strong, makes their believing a greater means of persuasion than the belief of the upper classes.

16:25 Praying and Singing

AS THE PSALMIST DID. AMMONIUS: They followed the psalmist, who says, "At midnight I will rise to confess to you."[1] CATENA ON THE ACTS OF THE APOSTLES 16.25.[2]

OFFERING THE SACRIFICES OF PRAISE. SEVERUS OF ANTIOCH: You see, the holy Scripture clearly states that they sang hymns, not only in their hearts but also in order to be heard, as is written in the Psalms: "With my voice I cried to the Lord, with my voice I was in need before God." After the great fame of their actions it was necessary to offer the sacrifices of praise for everything to God, that is, "the fruit of the lips, which confess his name," as Paul says. David expresses the same saying, "By praising I invoke the Lord, and I will be saved from my enemies." CATENA ON THE ACTS OF THE APOSTLES 16.25.[3]

FROM THE DEPTHS THEY SANG OUT. BEDE: The devotion of the apostles' hearts and the

power of prayer are expressed [here] together, since in the depths of the prison they sang hymns, and their praise moved the earth of the prison, shook the foundation, opened the doors and finally loosened the very chains of those who had been bound. In other words, anyone of the faithful "considers it all joy when he falls into various trials."[4] "And he gladly glories in his infirmities, so that the power of Christ may dwell in him."[5] Such a one undoubtedly sings hymns with Paul and Silas within the darkness of the prison, and with the psalmist he recites to the Lord, "You are my refuge from the distress which surrounds me, my exaltation."[6] COMMENTARY ON THE ACTS OF THE APOSTLES 16.25.[7]

SPURRED BY ADVERSITY. CHRYSOSTOM: Who is equal to these souls? After being whipped they received numerous blows and underwent insults and extreme dangers. While fastened in stocks in the innermost cell, they stayed awake not wanting to fall asleep. Do you see how great the affliction of the righteous is? We sleep in soft beds without any fear throughout the night. Maybe they stayed awake because they were in this state. The tyrant sleep did not catch them, pain did not bend them, fear did not make them dispirited, but these things spurred them on even more. CATENA ON THE ACTS OF THE APOSTLES 16.25.[8]

A SAVING VIGIL. CHRYSOSTOM: Let us set against that night these nights of revelry, drunkenness and wanton excesses, when sleep is no different from death and sleeplessness worse than sleep. For while some people sleep without sense or feeling, others lie awake to pitiful and wretched purpose, weaving treacherous plots, scheming for money, struggling to ward off those who wrong them, nursing hatred, counting up words of abuse spoken during the day. Thus they stoke the fire of their wrath, working up unbear-

---

[1]Ps 119:62 (118:62 LXX). [2]CGPNT 3:274. [3]CGPNT 3:274-75. [4]Jas 1:2. [5]2 Cor 12:9. [6]Ps 32:7 (31:7 LXX, Vg). [7]CS 117:137-38. [8]CGPNT 3:273-74.

able things. Look how Peter slept.[9] It was part of the divine plan. For the angel came to him and it was necessary that no one should see what happened. Likewise here, it was well that Paul was awake: he prevented the jailer from killing himself. HOMILIES ON THE ACTS OF THE APOSTLES 36.[10]

16:26 All the Doors Were Opened

ONLY MIRACLES THAT ARE NECESSARY FOR SALVATION. CHRYSOSTOM: And why did no other miracle take place? Because this especially was enough to convert him and make him believe, since he himself would have been in danger, if this had not happened. For it is not so much miracles that convince us as things that come to our salvation.[11] Lest the earthquake should seem to have occurred of its own accord, this[12] follows and bears witness to it. And it appeared at night; for the apostles did not work for display but for people's salvation. HOMILIES ON THE ACTS OF THE APOSTLES 36.[13]

A GOD OF REVERSALS. CHRYSOSTOM: The prison shook to disrupt the mindset of the faithless, to set the prison guard free and to proclaim the word of God. . . . You see how the nature of shackles destroys the shackles, for just as the death of the Lord put death to death, so also the shackles of Paul set the captives free, shook the prison, opened the doors. And yet this is not the nature of shackles, but they do the opposite— they hold the prisoner in security, they do not open up the walls for him. But while the simple nature of shackles is not this, the nature of these shackles is such because of Christ. CATENA ON THE ACTS OF THE APOSTLES 16.26-28.[14]

16:28 Do Not Harm Yourself

A REASONABLE TIME. CHRYSOSTOM: For whom did that event happen at midnight? And for whom was it accompanied by an earthquake? Listen to God's dispensation and be filled with won-

der! The chains were loosed and the doors opened. But this event happened for the jailer alone. It was not for show but salvation. That the prisoners did not know they were freed is clear from what Paul says . . . , "He cried out with a loud voice and said, 'Do not harm yourself, for we are all here.'" They would not have stayed within if they had known that the doors had been opened and they had been freed. Those who break through walls, leap over roofs and eaves and dare anything even when they are bound would have not tolerated staying when their chains had been loosed and the doors had been opened and the jailer sleeping. . . . And the imprisoned are usually bound during the night, and not during the day. With much care, therefore, he was able to see them carefully bound again and sleeping. If these things had been done during the day, there would have been a big riot. Why was the prison shaken by the earthquake? In order that the jailer might get up to see that spectacle: only he was worthy of salvation. CATENA ON THE ACTS OF THE APOSTLES 16.25.[15]

16:29 The Jailer Fell Down Before Paul and Silas

THE REFUSAL TO BELIEVE. AMMONIUS: From this event it can be established that the faith of people is something in their power. See how, after such a fright, only the jailer believed. And yet, most of all, those imprisoned should have been moved to believe, since they had experienced a greater wonder when they saw their iron chains suddenly broken. Being foolish, they were frightened at the moment when the foundations of the prison were shaken and the doors were opened. But being despisers of God, after such a sign,

---

[9]Acts 12:6. [10]NPNF 1 11:224**. [11]Chrysostom is using the word *salvation* in a broader sense than the gift of eternal life. He can intend by it both a physical and spiritual safety in this life as well as the next. So he can speak of the salvation of the jailer and mean the prevention of his suicide to the exclusion of salvation in Christ, or he can speak of salvation in its fullness. [12]The opening of the doors. [13]NPNF 1 11:224**. [14]CGPNT 3:275-76. [15]CGPNT 3:274.

they forgot what had happened, so that they did not speak to the jailer or to anyone about the terror that had happened. For, no doubt, had they heard from the jailer or from the followers of Paul the reason for such a wonder, they would perhaps have been converted. I think that a similar event happened in hell, when our Lord Jesus Christ, the Word of God, descended there tasting death for a brief time. The foundations of the earth were shaken and the chains of all were loosed. Whoever went to meet the Savior and believed in him was saved like the jailer and his house. Whoever rejected him and did not endeavor to investigate the strange miracle stayed in hell. Just as those who followed Paul, after the chains were loosed, came out of the prison in the morning, so Christ, coming back from hell in the dark of earliest morning and having been freed—as it was not fitting for him, being God, to be held by death—arose, and in the first place appeared to his faithful disciples and the women around Mary, and comforted them and confirmed them in faith by saying, "Take heart." He was then assumed into heaven, where he remains with God his Father. Likewise, the followers of Silas, who came out of the prison, visited Lydia and the brothers and departed. CATENA ON THE ACTS OF THE APOSTLES 16.29-30.[16]

16:30 What Must I Do to Be Saved?

THEY OPEN THE DOORS OF HIS HEART. CHRYSOSTOM: Observe, he did not respond because he had been saved,[17] but because he was astonished by their virtue. Do you see what happened in the earlier case and what happened here? Earlier a girl was released from a spirit and they threw them in jail, because they had freed her from the demon. Here they only showed him the doors opened, and it opened the doors of his heart, loosened the double chains and kindled the light. For the light in his heart was bright. "And he rushed in and fell before them," and he did not ask, "How did this happen? What happened?" Instead, right away he says, "What must I do to

be saved?" And what does Paul answer? "Believe in the Lord Jesus, and you will be saved," he says, "you and your household." This especially draws men, that their household too will be saved. "And they spoke the word to him and to all that were in his house." He washed them and was washed. He washed their wounds; he himself was washed of his sins. He fed and was fed. "And he rejoiced," it says. And yet it was nothing but words alone and good hope. This was a sign of his having believed, that he was released from all. What is worse than a jailer? What more savage, more ruthless? Nevertheless it was with great honor that [the jailer] received them. It was not when he was saved that he rejoiced but when "he had believed in God." HOMILIES ON THE ACTS OF THE APOSTLES 36.[18]

16:33 Baptized at Once

NOT THE POWERFUL. CHRYSOSTOM: Let us remember the jailer throughout, not the miracle. What do the Gentiles say? How did he, a prisoner, persuade his jailer? And the man who had to be persuaded, what was he but defiled, wretched, of no understanding, full of ten thousand ills and easily led? Still more, the Gentiles claim this as well. For who, except a tanner, a seller of purple, a eunuch, a jailer, slaves and women, believed? What will they be able to say when we produce also men of rank and station, the centurion, the proconsul, those from that time to the present, the rulers themselves, the emperors? But for my part, I speak of something else, something greater than this. Let us take a look at these lowly people. "And what is the wonder?" you ask. It is this. For if someone is persuaded of any old thing, it is no wonder. But when he speaks to lowly people about resurrection, about the kingdom of heaven and about a life of devotion, and he persuades them, it is more wonderful than if he persuades wise people. For if there is no danger and someone persuades them,

---

[16]CGPNT 3:276-77. [17]Kept from committing suicide because he had failed in his duty. [18]NPNF 1 11:225**.

it is justifiable to point to a lack of understanding. But when he speaks to the slave, "If you are persuaded by me, you do so at your own peril. You will have all people for enemies; you must die and suffer ten thousand wrongs," if even so he wins that person's soul, it is no longer due to a lack of understanding. For if the doctrines had contained pleasure, it would be possible to say so. But if, what the philosophers would not have chosen to learn, this the slave learns, greater is the wonder. If you please, let us bring before us the tanner himself and review the words Peter spoke to him. Or, if you would rather, let us look at this jailer. What did Paul say to him? "Christ is risen," "there is a resurrection of the dead," "there is a kingdom." And he easily persuaded one who was easily led. What then? Did he speak nothing of life, that he must be temperate, that he must be superior to money, that he must not be cruel, that

he must give his goods to others? Indeed, being persuaded of these things was not indicative of a deficit in understanding but of a truly great soul. Let it be that, as far as the doctrines are concerned, it is because of their lack of understanding that they are more apt to accept them. But to accept such a life of true devotion, what sort of a deficit in understanding is that? HOMILIES ON THE ACTS OF THE APOSTLES 36.[19]

HIS SINS WERE WASHED AWAY. BEDE: A beautiful exchange—for them he washed the wounds from their blows, and through them he was relieved of the wounds of his own guilty acts. COMMENTARY ON THE ACTS OF THE APOSTLES 16.33.[20]

---

[19]NPNF 1 11:225-26**. [20]CS 117:138.

16:35-40 PAUL AND SILAS RELEASED FROM PRISON

[35]*But when it was day, the magistrates sent the police, saying, "Let those men go."* [36]*And the jailer reported the words to Paul, saying, "The magistrates have sent to let you go; now therefore come out and go in peace."* [37]*But Paul said to them, "They have beaten us publicly, uncondemned, men who are Roman citizens, and have thrown us into prison; and do they now cast us out secretly? No! let them come themselves and take us out."* [38]*The police reported these words to the magistrates, and they were afraid when they heard that they were Roman citizens;* [39]*so they came and apologized to them. And they took them out and asked them to leave the city.* [40]*So they went out of the prison, and visited Lydia; and when they had seen the brothers, they exhorted them and departed.*

OVERVIEW: Modern commentators draw out the legal implication of this passage and note that it makes no reference to the miraculous event in the night. Paul makes his case from his position as a Roman citizen; his citizenship protected him from flogging and guaranteed him a right to trial.

They see Paul as implying to these authorities that he could press charges. The action of the magistrates indicates that Paul and Silas had done nothing against the law. The Fathers do not comment on the legal nature of this event. Their focus is on the latter part of the passage. Paul and

Silas depart, albeit reluctantly, because they must continue their preaching elsewhere, while those they have brought into Christ, despite their worldly lowliness (AMMONIUS), are able to continue spreading the gospel in Philippi (CHRYSOSTOM).

16:40 They Left the Prison and Visited Lydia

THE APOSTLES' HUMILITY. AMMONIUS: How great was their modesty and charity! Paul and Silas would not have put up with leaving, even though they had been dismissed by the magistrates, if they had not been able to go to the poor woman and the others, whom they called brothers, and made themselves their equals. CATENA ON THE ACTS OF THE APOSTLES 16.40.[1]

WORKS OF SUPERNATURAL GRACE. CHRYSOSTOM: They departed, not in obedience to the magistrates, but hastening to the work of preaching. For the city had been sufficiently benefited by the miracle. It was necessary that they remain no longer. For the miracle seems greater in the absence of those who worked it; it speaks louder by itself. The faith of the jailer was a voice in itself. What can equal this? He is put in chains and he loosens, though in chains, a twofold bond. He who put him in chains he releases by being in chains. Truly these are works of grace. HOMILIES ON THE ACTS OF THE APOSTLES 36.[2]

---

[1]CGPNT 3:279. [2]NPNF 1 11:225**.

17:1-4 PAUL ARGUES IN THE SYNAGOGUE OF THESSALONICA

[1]*Now when they had passed through Amphipolis and Apollonia, they came to Thessalonica, where there was a synagogue of the Jews.* [2]*And Paul went in, as was his custom, and for three weeks[p] he argued with them from the scriptures,* [3]*explaining and proving that it was necessary for the Christ to suffer and to rise from the dead, and saying, "This Jesus, whom I proclaim to you, is the Christ."* [4]*And some of them were persuaded, and joined Paul and Silas; as did a great many of the devout Greeks and not a few of the leading women.*

p Or sabbaths

OVERVIEW: Commentators note two familiar patterns: Paul has evangelized Philippi and left Luke behind there; and the familiar pattern of initial success followed by persecution and then flight. The phrase "it was necessary for the Christ to suffer and to rise from the dead," bears a close resemblance to Luke 24:26, where in both cases the "necessity" (dei) is derived from the will of God expressed in the whole of Scripture, not necessarily one passage. The apostles understand how knowledge spreads more quickly from larger places to smaller places and so focus on those cities with greater populations. Paul's love of his people and his refusal to give the Gentiles an excuse to turn from the Jews is evident here, and he refrains from miracles, as did Christ, since too great a reliance on them can breed suspicion (CHRYSOSTOM). Instead, he aimed at convincing his audience not only of the content of the prophecies of the Old Testament, but also of their fulfillment in the person of Jesus of Nazareth (BEDE).

17:1 Thessalonica, Where There Was a Synagogue

LARGE CITIES SOURCES OF INFORMATION. CHRYSOSTOM: Again they pass through the small towns and hurry to the biggest, since the word was to flow to nearby cities as from a source. CATENA ON THE ACTS OF THE APOSTLES 17.1.[1]

PAUL'S AFFECTION FOR ISRAEL NOT FORGOTTEN. CHRYSOSTOM: "And as was his custom, Paul went into the synagogue of the Jews." Although he had said, "We turn to the Gentiles,"[2] he did not abandon these people, for great was his desire toward them. Listen to what he says, "Brothers, my heart's desire and prayer to God for Israel is, that they might be saved,"[3] and, "I wished myself accursed from Christ for my brothers."[4] He did this because of the promise and the glory of God and because he did not wish to offend the Gentiles. HOMILIES ON THE ACTS OF THE APOSTLES 37.[5]

17:2 Arguing from the Scriptures

REFRAINING FROM MIRACLES. CHRYSOSTOM: "For three weeks," it says, "he argued with them from the Scriptures." That is, when they were not at work. For this is what Christ, too, did; he often made his argument from the Scriptures and not by miracles. For his listeners were hostile and accused him of being a deceiving sorcerer. For it is natural for him who tries to persuade people by miracles alone to be suspected, but one who persuades by the Scriptures does not arouse this suspicion. Indeed, we often see Paul persuading people by his teaching. In Antioch, for example, "the whole city gathered together"[6] to hear his teaching. This is something so great: it is not a small but an exceedingly great miracle. HOMILIES ON THE ACTS OF THE APOSTLES 37.[7]

17:3 Christ Suffered and Rose from the Dead

SUFFER AND RISE FROM THE DEAD. BEDE: He made both things known from the Scriptures at the same time, that the Christ had to suffer and to rise and that this suffering and resurrection pertained to none other than Jesus of Nazareth. For there were certain ones among the Jews, just as there are today, who were so lacking in faith that, although they could not deny that the suffering and resurrection of the Christ were present in the Scriptures, they nevertheless entirely denied that these things pertained to Jesus, and they preferred to look forward to the antichrist rather than to believe in Jesus Christ. And therefore Paul not only preached the mysteries of the Christ, but he also taught that these mysteries were accomplished in Christ Jesus. COMMENTARY ON THE ACTS OF THE APOSTLES 17.3.[8]

---

[1]CGPNT 3:280. [2]Acts 13:46. [3]Rom 10:1. [4]Rom 9:3. [5]NPNF 1 11:228**. [6]Acts 13:44. [7]NPNF 1 11:229**. [8]CS 117:141.

17:5-9 THE CITY SET IN UPROAR

⁵But the Jews were jealous, and taking some wicked fellows of the rabble, they gathered a crowd, set the city in an uproar, and attacked the house of Jason, seeking to bring them out to the people. ⁶And when they could not find them, they dragged Jason and some of the brothers before the city authorities, crying, "These men who have turned the world upside down have come here also, ⁷and Jason has received them; and they are all acting against the decrees of Caesar, saying that there is another king, Jesus." ⁸And the people and the city authorities were disturbed when they heard this. ⁹And when they had taken security from Jason and the rest, they let them go.

OVERVIEW: Some commentators have wondered why the prominent women of Thessalonica were not able to stop this persecution. Of the three charges (disturbance of world order, actions against some unspecified decrees of Caesar and the heralding of Jesus as king) the last comes from calling Jesus the Messiah. There are disputes about how to translate the Greek *basileus* ("king") and thus over the depth of this political charge. Some think "emperor" is intended, which would have amounted to charging Paul and his followers with sedition. Others claim it anachronistic.[1] If it does mean "emperor," then Luke would be portraying the charge that Paul and his companions were proclaiming Jesus the head of the imperial forces. Such a process, undertaken by the army, became the standard means of elevating someone to this position. As for the question of anachronism, there is an instance in the Palatine Anthology, 10.25 by Antipater of Thessalonica of the late first century B.C. and early first century A.D., where *basileus* is understood to refer to the emperor.[2] The whole question turns on the meaning of *basileus*, and by Ammonius's day, it was the common title of the emperor. Jesus is a king, but his kingdom, while it exists within the confines of history, vastly exceeds them and is eternal.[3]

17:7 Acting Against the Decrees of Caesar

A KING UNSEEN. AMMONIUS: In the same manner, their fathers accused Jesus by saying that he called himself king. The former, however, even though they had a kind of charge that was, on the surface, likely to deceive because the one charged was living, how could these latter hide their lying when they were saying that they, the apostles, were proclaiming Jesus a king, who, according to these accusers, was dead? That is, unless he was alive but was not visible. Concerning such a one, the kings of the earth never had need to fear, unless they should see him when entirely visible. But, as it seems from their proclamation of the truth, they knew that even though he was not visible, he was still truly king, and of his kingdom there shall be no end. CATENA ON THE ACTS OF THE APOSTLES 17.8.[4]

---

[1]For more on these terms and the political roles they denote, see OCD s.v. "imperator" and "rex." [2]LCL 85, *The Greek Anthology* 4.10.25, dates the epigram to A.D. 11. [3]Lk 1:32; Jn 18:36-37. [4]CGPNT 3:281.

17:10-15 THE WORD PREACHED
AT THE SYNAGOGUE OF BEROEA

[10]*The brothers immediately sent Paul and Silas away by night to Beroea; and when they arrived they went into the Jewish synagogue.* [11]*Now these Jews were more noble than those in Thessalonica, for they received the word with all eagerness, examining the scriptures daily to see if these things were so.* [12]*Many of them therefore believed, with not a few Greek women of high standing as well as men.* [13]*But when the Jews of Thessalonica learned that the word of God was proclaimed by Paul at Beroea also, they came there too, stirring up and inciting the crowds.* [14]*Then the brothers immediately sent Paul off on his way to the sea, but Silas and Timothy remained there.* [15]*Those who conducted Paul brought him as far as Athens; and receiving a command for Silas and Timothy to come to him as soon as possible, they departed.*

OVERVIEW: Chrysostom, always being eager to examine the nature of persuasion, notes the absence of miracles at Thessalonica and in Beroea. As Chrysostom has noted before, he does not consider miracles of themselves persuasive,[1] as he makes clear here: Paul preaches Christ crucified and wins followers, something that often does not happen even with miracles. The great miracle that God works is faith in the heart of the believer, and at times God so prevails with and at other times without miracles. Ammonius approaches the new believers with a different concern, that of preventing them from becoming an example of skepticism toward the Scripture for people of his day. Their investigation is one filled with and guided by their new faith as it has been handed on to them by their teachers. Among these, Paul is forced to leave, but he cannot fulfill his task alone, in the face of such a great harvest. Paul shows here the body of Christ working in harmony, the head in need of the feet (CHRYSOSTOM).

17:10 Paul and Silas Sent Away by Night

GOD PREVAILS WITHOUT SIGNS. CHRYSOSTOM: Why didn't they stay? Why didn't they perform miracles? For if he stayed a long time where

he was stoned (i.e., at Lystra), all the more could he have stayed here. What was the reason then? Because God did not always want them to perform miracles. For it is no less a miracle for them, persecuted as they are, to prevail without performing miracles. Therefore, just as now he prevails without miracles, often then he wished to prevail in the same way. And so the apostles did not chase after miracles either, as he himself says, "We preach Christ crucified."[2] To those who seek miracles, to those who seek wisdom, we offer this,[3] which is not able to persuade even with miracles, and we persuade them. This is a great miracle. HOMILIES ON THE ACTS OF THE APOSTLES 37.[4]

17:12 Many People Believed

FAITH SEEKING UNDERSTANDING. AMMONIUS: They did not investigate like skeptical people, because they had already believed, but like people who were unaware of the prophets' ancient doctrine. Or rather, they believed more because, after examining the Scriptures, they saw that the circumstances of the incarnation of the Lord agreed

---

[1]Cf. his comments above at Acts 16:26. [2]1 Cor 1:23. [3]The crucified Lord. [4]NPNF 1 11:230**.

with the words of the ancient prophets. CATENA ON THE ACTS OF THE APOSTLES 17.12-13.[5]

17:15 Silas and Timothy to Come to Paul

EVEN PAUL IS IN NEED OF OTHERS. CHRYSOSTOM: "And receiving," it says, "a command for Silas and Timothy to come to him as soon as possible, they departed." For even though he was Paul, he still needed them. So with good reason they were urged to go to Macedonia by God; for Greece lay there bright[6] before them.... Notice how much eagerness was shown by the disciples toward their teachers. It is not so among us, separated and divided into great and small. Some of us are exalted, others are envious. They are envious because we are puffed up and cannot bear to be equals with them. The reason why there is harmony in the body is because nothing is puffed up, and there is nothing puffed up because the limbs are by necessity in a state of mutual need. The head needs the feet, and the feet the head. HOMILIES ON THE ACTS OF THE APOSTLES 37.[7]

---

[5]CGPNT 3:282. [6]See Jn 4:35. [7]NPNF 1 11:230-31**.

17:16-21 THE PHILOSOPHERS OF ATHENS CONFRONT PAUL

[16]*Now while Paul was waiting for them at Athens, his spirit was provoked within him as he saw that the city was full of idols.* [17]*So he argued in the synagogue with the Jews and the devout persons, and in the market place every day with those who chanced to be there.* [18]*Some also of the Epicurean and Stoic philosophers met him. And some said, "What would this babbler say?" Others said, "He seems to be a preacher of foreign divinities"—because he preached Jesus and the resurrection.* [19]*And they took hold of him and brought him to the Areopagus, saying, "May we know what this new teaching is which you present?* [20]*For you bring some strange things to our ears; we wish to know therefore what these things mean."* [21]*Now all the Athenians and the foreigners who lived there spent their time in nothing except telling or hearing something new.*

OVERVIEW: Most commentators consider this speech at Athens, which Luke still regards, despite its faded glory, as the center of the pagan world's self-understanding, as a model of the confrontation of two outlooks on reality. They are the biblical understanding of reality, as this biblical understanding has been raised to a new level by the reality of Jesus Christ, especially his resurrection, and that of the surrounding culture, with its sophisticated but nontranscendent understanding of the universe. Commentators enquire about background (such as Is 45:18-25, Wis 13-14) and point to similar modes of thought in the Pauline writings. It must be borne in mind, moreover, that for the ancients a speech was an event every bit as much as a battle or any other action and was to be interpretatively presented in the same way as any other action. Thus questions regarding sources and other matters have a different significance. The Fathers instinctively knew the literary world within which Luke and Paul are moving and their attention is elsewhere. The schools of philosophy that Paul encountered in Athens, the Epicureans and the Stoics, contemplated the means to human happiness in this life. Bede provides a caricature of what these schools taught, and he shows that his knowledge of them is secondhand. The Epicureans were materialists and aimed at an undisturbed existence that was erroneously labeled by some as hedonism. The Stoics aimed at becoming a sage, the ideal wise person who saw the greatest human good to be in a virtuous soul. Bede's simplifications aside, his point that Christianity looks beyond a dualism of body and soul to a perfection never achievable here, but found only by God's grace in a resurrection from the dead, marks a major shift in how human wholeness and happiness can be conceived of as only beginning here. This revelation opens up human contemplation to the hope of a new world and radically transforms leisure by lifting it out of idle curiosity to a constant state of preparation for God's gifts (BASIL). Here, the oddity of the resurrection to these people comes out most clearly in that they misunderstand it to be a new divinity along with Jesus. Despite these miscommunications, Paul's conversations, though slow to bear fruit, begin a process of cleansing a city possessed by demons (CHRYSOSTOM).[1]

17:18 Some Philosophers Met Paul

CERTAIN EPICUREAN AND STOIC PHILOSOPHERS. BEDE: The Epicureans, following the stupidity of their teacher, put the happiness of humanity in the pleasure of the body alone, while the Stoics placed it solely in the virtue of the mind. Although indeed they disagreed with each other, they nevertheless were united in opposition to the apostle with respect to [his belief that] a human being subsists in soul and body. Thus he taught that [one] ought to be happy in both [body and soul][2] but that this will not be achieved in the present time or by human power

but by the grace of God through Jesus Christ in the glory of the resurrection. COMMENTARY ON THE ACTS OF THE APOSTLES 17.18A.[3]

A NEW GOD. CHRYSOSTOM: By the term *resurrection* the Athenians understood a god, for they were accustomed even to worship females. . . . They called their gods *daimones*, for their cities were full of daimones.[4] CATENA ON THE ACTS OF THE APOSTLES 17.18.[5]

17:21 Telling or Hearing Something New

GOOD AND BAD LEISURE. BASIL THE GREAT: "Be at leisure and know that I am God."[6] To the extent that we take our leisure in matters apart from God, we cannot attain knowledge of God. For who, concerned over the things of the world and immersed in fleshly distractions, can pay attention to discourses concerning God and measure up to the rigid discipline of contemplations so long and great? Don't you see that the Word that falls among thorns is choked by the thorns?[7] Now the thorns are fleshly pleasures and wealth and glory and cares of this life. The one who seeks knowledge of God must become separated from all these things, and, being at leisure apart from passions, thus receive the knowledge of God. For how can contemplation about God enter a mind crowded by thoughts that preoccupy it? Even Pharaoh knew that being at leisure is proper to the search for God, and for this reason he mocked the Israelites, "You are idling about, you men of leisure, and you say, 'We will pray to

---

[1]Christians in Chrysostom's day believed that their presence in the cities purified them. This cleansing was most successful where martyrdom occurred. See Prudentius *Peristephanon* II, especially the end of Lawrence's prayer, lines 469-72, and Chrysostom's second *Homily on Babylas* 8-9. [2]Augustine *Sermon* 150.4.5-5.6 (PL 38:810-11). [3]CS 117:141-42. [4]The Greek *daimones*, "divinities" in the translation, had by Chrysostom's day gone through peioration, the process whereby a once acceptable word comes to have only a negative meaning. *Daimones*, among Christians in his day, were demons. This understanding of the Greek word *daimones*, however, is evident already in the LXX: see Ps 96:5 (95:5 LXX). [5]CGPNT 3:285. [6]Ps 46:10 (45:11 LXX). [7]Mt 13:22.

the Lord our God.'"[8] While this leisure is good and profitable for the one in leisure as it brings peace for the reception of the Savior's teachings, the leisure of the Athenians was evil, since "they devoted their leisure to nothing more than saying or listening to something new." HOMILY ON PSALM 45.[9]

---

[8]Ex 5:17. [9]PG 29:428-29.

17:22-28 PAUL PREACHES AT THE AREOPAGUS

[22]So Paul, standing in the middle of the Are-opagus, said: "Men of Athens, I perceive that in every way you are very religious. [23]For as I passed along, and observed the objects of your worship, I found also an altar with this inscription, 'To an unknown god.' What therefore you worship as unknown, this I proclaim to you. [24]The God who made the world and everything in it, being Lord of heaven and earth, does not live in shrines made by man, [25]nor is he served by human hands, as though he needed anything, since he himself gives to all men life and breath and everything. [26]And he made from one every nation of men to live on all the face of the earth, having determined allotted periods and the boundaries of their habitation, [27]that they should seek God, in the hope that they might feel after him and find him. Yet he is not far from each one of us, [28]for

'In him we live and move and have our being';

as even some of your poets have said,

'For we are indeed his offspring.'

OVERVIEW: Rather than seek to identify the possible sources employed in the speech, many commentators point to a common Jewish mode of challenging the surrounding pagan culture, with the accent on the uniqueness of God the Creator. The monotheistic tone with a mention of Jesus coming late in the discourse (and effectively terminating it) is not that different from the type of preaching that lies behind the rhythm of conversion described in 1 Thessalonians mentioned before.[1] The Fathers use the occasion to discuss what it means to know and recognize God and his authority as this had been revealed. To conclude that there is a divine being, to whom we ourselves give various names based on our insufficient reasoning, is not to know the divine being so much as attempts to know things about the divine being: such a one remains personally unknown. The God of Jesus Christ is one whom we can know only through revelation, the grace of Jesus Christ (CLEMENT OF ALEXANDRIA). But Paul, so that he cannot be accused of introducing a new god, turns to what the Greeks themselves have provided, an altar to this unknown God, in order to show that they have anticipated what he proclaims (CHRYSOSTOM). His teaching, then, follows a logical progression from creation as a mark

---

[1]1 Thess 1:9-10: "For they themselves report concerning us what a welcome we had among you, and how you turned to God from idols, to serve a living and true God, and to wait for his Son from heaven, whom he raised from the dead, Jesus who delivers us from the wrath to come."

of divinity to its more important consequences about the Godhead (CHRYSOSTOM, BEDE). Paul gives the Athenians the basics so that they will not be overwhelmed by the newness of what he teaches (BEDE). Most importantly, however, he imparts to them, using their own writers, the truth that they have reversed the order of things by fashioning dwellings for the uncontainable divine who has come among us to make us into his dwelling (CLEMENT OF ALEXANDRIA), so that we would live in complete gratitude and not think that God is so meager as to depend upon our sacrifices. God has offered everything to his creatures: both a time of searching for him—a time we wasted—as well as now the revelation that fulfills the hope of that search (CHRYSOSTOM); he offers even himself in his constant presence, even when we are far from him (AUGUSTINE, ORIGEN). Not all of the Greeks failed in perceiving this presence, the all-encompassing power of God, as Paul shows by quoting Aratus. They still, however, worshiped him indirectly and as one unknown, and yet this nearness of God is reflected in Paul, who comes quoting their writers, as one bound by the law of Christ to unbind the lawless and to give sight to the blind (ORIGEN, CLEMENT OF ALEXANDRIA). So while they perceived the ordering power of God (AUGUSTINE cited by BEDE), they were unaware that God wanted a deeper, more intimate relationship with them through adoption, by the Spirit, in Christ (BEDE).

17:22 Very Religious

THEIR SUPERSTITION. CHRYSOSTOM: Paul found an altar, on which the words "to an unknown god" were engraved: who was that unknown god but Christ? Do you see the wisdom in changing the name? Do you see the reason he released the inscription from captivity? . . . To save and benefit them. What else? Perhaps one might say that the Athenians wrote these words for Christ? . . . They certainly wrote that with a different meaning, but he was, nevertheless, able to change it. . . . Why did they write it? They had

many gods, or rather many demons, "All the gods of the Gentiles are demons,"[2] and some of them were native, others were foreign. . . . They had received some of their gods from their fathers, others from the neighboring nations, such as the Scythians, the Thracians and the Egyptians. . . . What did they do then? They erected an altar and inscribed it with the words "to an unknown god" in order to signify through the inscription: If by any chance there is another god who is still unknown to us, we will worship him too. See their immoderate superstition! For this reason Paul said from the beginning, "I see how extremely religious you are in every way . . . you not only worship the gods who are known to you, but also those who are still unknown to you." Therefore they had written, "To an unknown god." . . . The unknown God is none other than Christ. CATENA ON THE ACTS OF THE APOSTLES 17.23.[3]

17:23 "This I Proclaim to You"

OUR GREAT NEED OF REVELATION. CLEMENT OF ALEXANDRIA: To talk about God is most difficult. . . . For how can that be expressed which is neither genus, nor difference, nor species, nor individual nor number; moreover is neither an event nor that to which an event happens? No one can rightly express him wholly. For on account of his greatness he is ranked as the All and is the Father of the universe. Nor are any parts to be predicated of him. For the One is indivisible and therefore also is infinite, not considered with reference to inscrutability but with reference to its being without dimensions and not having a limit. And therefore it is without form and name. And if we name it, we do not do so properly, terming it either the One, or the Good, or Mind, or Absolute Being, or Father, or God, or Creator or Lord. We speak not as supplying his name, but for need, we use good names, in order that the mind may have these as points of sup-

---

[2]Ps 96:5 (95:5 LXX). [3]CGPNT 3:288-89.

port, so as not to err in other respects. For each one by itself does not express God, but all together are indicative of the power of the Omnipotent. . . . Nor any more is he apprehended by logic. For that depends on primary and better known principles. But there is nothing antecedent to the Unbegotten. It remains that we understand, then, the Unknown, by divine grace and by the Word alone that proceeds from him; as Luke in the Acts of the Apostles relates that Paul said, "Men of Athens, I perceive that in all things you are too superstitious. For in walking about, and beholding the objects of your worship, I found an altar on which was inscribed 'To the Unknown God.' Therefore, the one you ignorantly worship, I declare to you." STROMATEIS 5.12.[4]

USING THEIR OWN WITNESSES. CHRYSOSTOM: He did not find in the city a holy book but an altar to an idol with the inscription "To an unknown god." The holy Paul, who had the grace of the Spirit, did not pass by but turned the altar with its inscription on its head. . . . He did not omit what the idolatrous Athenians had written. . . . We see what great value that inscription produced. . . . Paul entered the town, found an altar on which the words "to an unknown god" were engraved. What did he have to do? . . . Did the words of the Gospels need to be declared? They would have mocked them. Or maybe the words from the books of the prophets or from the precepts of the law should have been talked about? But they would not have believed. What did he do then? He rushed to the altar and defeated them with the weapons of the enemies themselves. And that was what he said, "I became everything to everyone: to the Jews a Jew, to those outside the law as if I were outside the law."[5] CATENA ON THE ACTS OF THE APOSTLES 17.23.[6]

17:24 God Made the World

CREATION A DIVINE PREROGATIVE. CHRYSOSTOM: He says that "the world and everything in it" is the work of God. Do you notice the conciseness

and, in the conciseness, the clearness? And what was strange to them? The fact that God made the world. These things, now known to anyone, the Athenians did not know, not even the wise among them. For if he made them, it is clear that he is Lord. Notice what [Paul] affirms as the mark of divinity: creation, which the Son also has. HOMILIES ON THE ACTS OF THE APOSTLES 38.[7]

A LOGICAL ARGUMENT. BEDE: The order of the apostle's argument deserves careful examination. Among Gentiles the treatment of the apostle's subject takes the form of a series of steps. First, he teaches that the one God is the originator of the world and of all things, and in him we live and move and are, and we are his offspring. Thus he demonstrates that God is to be loved not only because of his gifts of light and life but also because of a certain affinity of kind. Next, he disposes of the opinion that is the explicit reason for idols [by saying] that the founder and Lord of the entire world cannot be enclosed in temples of stone, that the granter of all favors has no need of the blood of victims, that the creator and governor of all people cannot be created by human hands, and finally that God, in whose image humankind was made, should not be appraised in terms of the value of metals. He teaches that the remedy for such errors is the practice of repentance. Now if he had chosen to begin by destroying the idolatrous rites, the ears of the Gentiles would have rejected [him].

When he had persuaded them that there is one God, then he added that by his judgment salvation was given to us through Christ. To him, however, he applied the term *man* rather than God, and he began with those things which he [Christ] did in the body, describing them as divine, so that it might seem that he was more than a man. [He taught that] death was conquered by the power of one man, and that one who was dead was raised up again from hell (for

---

[4]ANF 2:463-64**. [5]1 Cor 9:19-21. [6]CGPNT 3:287. [7]NPNF 1 11:235**.

faith grows little by little), so that when it appeared that he was more than a man, they might believe that he was God. For what difference does it make in what order anyone believes? Perfected things are not sought at the start, but from beginnings one comes to the things that are perfect. COMMENTARY ON THE ACTS OF THE APOSTLES 17.24.[8]

GOD'S TRUE TEMPLE AND ITS HOLINESS. CLEMENT OF ALEXANDRIA: Is it not the case that rightly and truly we do not circumscribe in any place that which cannot be circumscribed; nor do we shut up in temples made with hands that which contains all things? . . . It would indeed be ridiculous, as the philosophers themselves say, for a person, the plaything[9] of God, to make God, and for God to be the plaything of art. . . . Works of art cannot . . . be sacred and divine. . . . And if the word *sacred* has a twofold application, designating both God himself and the structure raised to his honor, how shall we not, through knowledge, properly call the church "holy," "made for the honor of God," "sacred to God," "of great value," not being constructed by mechanical art . . . but by the will of God fashioned into a temple? For it is not now the place but the assembly of the elect that I call the church. STROMATEIS 7.5.[10]

17:25 Giving to All Life and Breath and Everything

THE SELF-SUFFICIENCY AND GENEROSITY OF GOD. CHRYSOSTOM: How was he served by human hands when he was among the Jews? No, it was not by their hands but by their thoughts, since he did not seek those things, as though he were in need. "Shall I eat," he says, "the flesh of bulls or drink the blood of goats?"[11] Then Paul says, "Nor is he served by human hands, as though he needed anything." Even this affirmation by Paul, that he is in need of nothing, is not enough. For although this is a mark of divinity, something else must be added. Paul adds, "He himself gives to all people life and breath and

everything." These are the two proofs of divinity Paul points to, that he is in need of nothing and that he gives to all people everything. HOMILIES ON THE ACTS OF THE APOSTLES 38.[12]

17:27 Seeking God

GOD ENABLES THE SEARCH. CHRYSOSTOM: "Having determined allotted periods and the boundaries of their habitation, that they should seek God, in the hope that they might feel after him and find him." He means that they are not forced to go about and seek God or that God determines their seeking of God, not continuously but in "allotted periods." With this Paul shows that even if they sought him they would not find him, although he was as conspicuous for discovery as something tangible in their midst. . . . "Yet he is not far from each one of us" but close to all people. What Paul means is this. Not only did he give "life and breath and everything," but also the sum and total of everything: he led people to the knowledge of himself, giving us the means through which we can find him and understand him. But we did not wish to seek him, even though he was close at hand. "Not far," Paul says, "from each of us." He means that he is close to all people all over the world. What can be greater than this? HOMILIES ON THE ACTS OF THE APOSTLES 38.[13]

CLOSE EVEN WHEN WE ARE FAR AWAY. AUGUSTINE: If this were spoken in a material sense, it could be understood of our material world: for in it too, so far as our body is concerned, we lie and move and are. We must take the text, then, as spoken of the mind, which is made in his image, and of a manner of being more excellent, not visible but spiritual. What is there indeed that is not "in him," of whom holy Scripture says, "for from him and through him and in

---

[8]CS 117:142-43*. [9]*Paignion theou* is a phrase used by Plato. [10]ANF 2:530. [11]Ps 50:13 (49:13 LXX). [12]NPNF 1 11:235**. [13]NPNF 1 11:235-36**.

him are all things"?[14] If in him are all things, in whom, save in him in whom they are, can the living live or the moving move? Yet all people are not with him after the manner of the saying "I am always with you."[15] Nor is he with all after the manner of our own saying, "the Lord be with you." It is a person's great misery not to be with him without whom people cannot be. Certainly, people are never without him, in whom he is; yet if a person does not remember him, does not understand him or love him, he is not with him. On the Trinity 16.[16]

God's Nearness. Origen: "You are near, Lord, and all your commandments are truth."[17] God says elsewhere, "I am a God who is near and not a God who is far away, says the Lord."[18] For the power of God is everywhere according to the word of creation and providence. Knowing this, Paul, addressing the Greeks as recorded in the Acts of the Apostles, says, "We do not seek God far from us, for in him we live and move and are," and "the Spirit of the Lord has filled the earth."[19] He is thus, for his part, close, but if we ourselves make no effort, though he be close, to draw near to him, we will not enjoy his nearness. For this reason, sinners are far from God: "Behold, those who distance themselves from you perish."[20] But the just ones strive to approach God, for he is not present to them just as a creator, but he even shares himself with them: "And Moses alone draws near to God, but the rest do not draw near."[21] According to the degree of will and perfection, the one who approaches God is that one about whom Paul says, "The one joined to the Lord is one spirit."[22] Palestinian Catena on Psalm 118.151.[23]

17:28 Offspring of God

Bound by the Law of Christ. Origen: "Being as one outside the law to those outside the law."[24] He came to Athens, he found philosophers, and he did not use the words of the prophets or from the law, but as one perhaps recalling

this pagan teaching from a school of rhetoric he spoke to the men of Athens. For [Paul] said, "Just as some of your poets have said, 'For we are his offspring too.'"[25] In this place, he was as one outside the law to those outside the law, in order to gain the lawless. It is as if he were to say "I was doing nothing contrary to the law in making this concession to them, but I was keeping myself bound by the law of Christ, in order to gain the lawless." Commentary on 1 Corinthians 43.[26]

Sight to the Blind. Clement of Alexandria: It is clear that by using poetic examples from the *Phaenomena* of Aratus [Paul] approves the best statements of the Greeks. Besides, he refers to the fact that in the person of the unknown god the Greeks are indirectly honoring God the Creator and need to receive him and learn about him with full knowledge through the Son. "I sent you to the gentiles for this purpose," says Scripture, "to open their eyes, for them to turn from darkness to light and from the power of Satan to God, for them to receive release from sins and an inheritance among those who are sanctified by faith in me."[27] So these are the "opened eyes of the blind," which means the clear knowledge of the Father through the Son, the direct grasp of the thing to which the Greeks indirectly allude. Stromateis 1.19.[28]

All Creation Is in God. Bede: Since this verse is difficult to understand, it should be explained in the words of the blessed Augustine, who says, "The apostle shows that God is ceaselessly at work in the things which he has created. It is not with respect to his substance that we are in him. For instance, it has been said that he has life in himself,[29] but since we are certainly different from him, we are not 'in him' in any other way except that he brings it [our existence] about; and

---

[14]Rom 11:36. [15]Ps 73:23 (72:23 LXX). [16]LCC 8:114*. [17]Ps 119:151 (118:151 LXX). [18]Jer 23:23. [19]Wis 1:7. [20]Ps 73:27 (72:27 LXX). [21]Ex 24:2. [22]1 Cor 6:17. [23]SC 189:426. [24]1 Cor 9:21. [25]From Aratus's *Phaenomena*. [26]JTS 9:513*. [27]Acts 26:17-18. [28]FC 85:92-93. [29]Jn 5:26.

this is his work, whereby he contains all things. And it has been said that his wisdom reaches 'mightily from one end of the earth to the other and orders all things well.'[30] It is through this 'ordering' that 'in him we live and move and are.' Hence we infer that if he withdrew this work of his from things, we would neither live nor move nor be."[31] COMMENTARY ON THE ACTS OF THE APOSTLES 17.28A.[32]

CREATION AND RE-CREATION. BEDE: "We are" very rightly "called the offspring of God, not in the sense that we were brought forth out of his nature but in the sense that through his Spirit we are both created by his will and re-created by his adoption."[33] COMMENTARY ON THE ACTS OF THE APOSTLES 17.28C.[34]

---

[30]Wis 8:1. [31]Augustine *Literal Interpretation of Genesis* 4.12 (CSEL 28:109). [32]CS 117:143-44. [33]Gregory the Great *Morals on the Book of Job* 20.16.41 (CCL 143A:1033). [34]CS 117:145.

17:29-34 PAUL PROCLAIMS THE RESURRECTION FROM THE DEAD

[29]*"Being then God's offspring, we ought not to think that the Deity is like gold, or silver, or stone, a representation by the art and imagination of man.* [30]*The times of ignorance God overlooked, but now he commands all men everywhere to repent,* [31]*because he has fixed a day on which he will judge the world in righteousness by a man whom he has appointed, and of this he has given assurance to all men by raising him from the dead."*

[32]*Now when they heard of the resurrection of the dead, some mocked; but others said, "We will hear you again about this."* [33]*So Paul went out from among them.* [34]*But some men joined him and believed, among them Dionysius the Are-opagite and a woman named Damaris and others with them.*

OVERVIEW: God, coming to us as the man Jesus of Nazareth and through the apostolic preaching, refashions our understanding of God as not dependent on our human fashionings. He corrects our misunderstanding by offering in the resurrection his love and forgiveness to our rejections of him based in ignorance (AMMONIUS). Chrysostom affirms that this error of the Athenians is not culpable but that they are being invited, through the risen Christ, into the abundant mercy of God through this change of mind and heart from their previous conceptions of divinity. This offer, how-ever, points to a day awaiting all, a day of resurrection when Christ will pass judgment on all. Paul teaches as did Christ, gradually revealing the deeper truths that lie behind these actions, namely, that Jesus is not just a man but even God (CHRYSOSTOM). It is worth noting that Luke makes a distinction between those who "mock" and those who seem genuinely interested in hearing more ("but others said"). This is not often adverted to either in antiquity or now.

17:29 *The Deity Is Not Like Gold*

Unlike Any Human Fashioning. Ammonius: He teaches that the human mind cannot comprehend God as he is according to nature. Their mouths, which say the deity is of human form, are closed with these words. Indeed, one can mold or sculpt or draw people and images of people, or one can paint the likeness of any earthly thing. God, however, is similar to no human work. According to the word of the apostle, the deity is absolutely undetermined, incomprehensible, without image, incorporeal, not similar to human form or any other thing. Catena on the Acts of the Apostles 17.29.[1]

17:31 The Resurrection Gives Assurance

The Resurrection: An Offer of Forgiveness. Ammonius: Surely if God overlooked from the foundation of the world the transgressions committed by people out of ignorance, and he gives to each the forgiveness of transgressions, fittingly did he come among us at the end of the ages, in order that his boundless love of humankind might be received in accord with the measure that he reveals his presence. Catena on the Acts of the Apostles 17.30.[2]

The Resurrection: Universal Call to Repentance. Chrysostom: What? Is none of these to be punished? No, not if they are willing to repent. [Paul] says this not of the departed but of those whom he is addressing. He does not [yet] call you to account, Paul says. He does not say, "He neglected" or "He permitted," but "You were ignorant. He overlooked." That is, he does not exact punishment from you as from people deserving punishment. You were ignorant. And he does not say, "You willfully did wrong," which is what he showed above when he said, "everywhere to repent." Here he hints at the whole

world. See how he leads them away from the partial deities. "Because he has fixed a day," he says, "on which he will judge the world in righteousness." Look, again he uses the expression *world*, referring thus to humans. "By a man whom he has appointed, by raising him from the dead." See how he again declares the passion by pointing to the resurrection. That the judgment is true is clear from the resurrection, for the latter helps to establish the former. That everything he said was spoken with truth is clear from the fact that he rose again. That they gave to all people this assurance, that he rose from the dead, this is clear hereafter. Homilies on the Acts of the Apostles 38.[3]

The Resurrection of the Body. Chrysostom: Look, he even introduced the subject of the resurrection of all. For in no other way can the world be judged. The words "by raising him from the dead" are spoken in regard to the body. For this is what was dead, what had fallen. Homilies on the Acts of the Apostles 38.[4]

Teaching As Christ Taught. Chrysostom: What do you do, Paul? You say nothing about the form of God nor that he is equal to God or anything concerning the splendor of his glory. Indeed the time to say these things had not yet come, but it was enough that they admitted that he was a man. And Christ did the same, and Paul actually learned these things from him. In fact, Christ did not reveal his divinity immediately, but first Christ was believed to be simply a man and a prophet; then he appeared to be what he really was. Catena on the Acts of the Apostles 17.31.[5]

---

[1]CGPNT 3:295-96. [2]CGPNT 3:296-97. [3]NPNF 1 11:237**. [4]NPNF 1 11:237**. [5]CGPNT 3:299.

18:1-4 PAUL STAYS WITH AQUILA AND PRISCILLA

[1]*After this he left Athens and went to Corinth.* [2]*And he found a Jew named Aquila, a native of Pontus, lately come from Italy with his wife Priscilla, because Claudius had commanded all the Jews to leave Rome. And he went to see them;* [3]*and because he was of the same trade he stayed with them, and they worked, for by trade they were tentmakers.* [4]*And he argued in the synagogue every sabbath, and persuaded Jews and Greeks.*

Overview: Modern commentators locate the probable date of Claudius's edict at A.D. 49; it would thus have lapsed some five years later at his death. The ancients were more interested in this passage for the light it shows on a Christian understanding of manual labor, which, regardless of the level of skill, was proper to the lower classes of the Greco-Roman world. In Greek, words denoting manual labor had long carried negative connotations.[1] Although the social status and mobility of manual laborers varied at different times and in different places, such a view was common throughout most of antiquity.[2] Some pagan philosophers whose lives functioned as criticisms of the dominant social mores had, in Chrysostom's view, discovered the benefits to their souls of good and honest work. Christianity, with its focus on the hereafter, infuses into human toil a different perspective, one that early urban and monastic Christians sometimes overlooked. In the monastic tradition work, in addition to being the fundamental means of self-support, takes on a use of pulling the person out of himself, orienting him to a communal life and keeping him from sloth.[3] Augustine, who had to censure some idle monks, wrote a letter extolling work's utility in the Christian life, and he drew his argument primarily from Paul's writings.[4] Chrysostom faces an urban audience among whom Paul's manual labor and the home of an artisan carry not honor but amusement. He too makes Paul a goad to their idleness. Among the early Christians, Paul is often the prime example for them that a life aimed at idleness and luxury is amiss: Paul was practical not to give scandal by seeking luxury and set an example of an honest though hard life that can keep us focused on our true goal (Chrysostom). He did not do this out of greed but for the sake of the kingdom (Augustine). Moreover, these apparently earthly actions that answered to people's physical needs were not cut off from his vocation as an apostle, but they pointed to the spiritual benefits that Paul was bequeathing to his audience, his churches and to us (Origen).

18:3 Of the Same Trade

The Value of a Life of Work. Chrysostom: Let no one who is a craftsman be ashamed, but rather those who are reared for no purpose and do nothing, the ones who employ many servants and enjoy an immense court. For being raised as an unceasing worker is the nature of philosophy. The minds of such people are purer, more vigorous. The one who does nothing is really one who does much in vain and, full of indolence, in an entire day accomplishes nothing. The one

---

[1]See the entries *banausia, banausos,* and *phortikos* in H. G. Liddell, R. Scott and H. S. Jones, *A Greek Lexicon,* 9th ed. (Oxford: Oxford University Press, 1996). [2]For a discussion of the rise of the modern valuation of labor in America, see Gordon Wood, *The Americanization of Benjamin Franklin* (New York: Penguin, 2004). On manual labor and laborers in antiquity, see *OCD,* s.v. "labor," "artisans and craftsmen" and "art, ancient attitudes to." [3]See *The Rule of the Master 50,* and *The Rule of St. Benedict* 48 along with the commentary of Adalbert de Vogüé, *The Rule of Saint Benedict: A Doctrinal and Spiritual Commentary* (Kalamazoo, Mich.: Cistercian Publications, 1983), chap. 15. [4]*On the Work of Monks,* which can be found in FC 16:331-94.

engaged in work will take on nothing superfluous in haste, neither in deeds nor words nor thoughts. For such a person's entire soul, throughout the day, has been set on a painful means of existence. We, therefore, ought not to scorn those who support themselves by the work of their hands, but we should really count them blessed because of this. . . . Paul, after countless journeys, despite such great wonders, stayed with a tentmaker and sewed skins. Angels honored him and demons trembled at him, and still he was not ashamed to say, "These same hands served my needs and those who were with me."[5] CATENA ON THE ACTS OF THE APOSTLES 18.3-5.[6]

PAUL DOES NOT LIVE IN IDLENESS. CHRYSOSTOM: It was with them that [Paul] stayed, and he was not ashamed to do so; on the contrary, he stayed precisely because he had found a suitable lodging place. For it was much more suitable for him than royal palaces. And do not laugh as you listen. . . . For just as to an athlete the gym is more useful than soft cushions, likewise to a warrior an iron sword is useful and not a golden one. And he worked while preaching.[7] Let us be ashamed, we who live idle lives even though we are not occupied with preaching. HOMILIES ON THE ACTS OF THE APOSTLES 39.[8]

EARNING AN HONEST LIVING. AUGUSTINE: [Paul] has repeatedly said of himself that he was working with his own hands so as not to burden anyone,[9] and it is written of him that he joined with Aquila because of the similarity of their handicraft, so that they might work together to maintain a livelihood. From these and other such passages of the Scripture it is clear enough that our Lord does not reprove a person for procuring these things in the usual manner, but that he reproves a person who would serve in the army of God for the sake of these things, one who in his works has his eye fixed not on the kingdom of God but on the acquisition of these things. This entire precept is reduced, therefore, to the following rule: namely, that even in the procuring of

these things we should keep our mind on the kingdom of God and that in the service of the kingdom of God we should give no thought to these things. In this way, even if these things be lacking at times (and God permits this usually for the purpose of exercising us), not only do they not weaken our resolve, but they even strengthen it for trial and approval. SERMON ON THE MOUNT 2.17.57-58.[10]

MAKING HEAVENLY TENTS—THE SPIRITUAL SENSE OF PAUL'S LABOR. ORIGEN: Tents can refer to perfect souls, which also is true of the name Israel derived from "seeing God."[11] Now these "tents," says Scripture, are "just like shady groves, like paradises beside streams and like tents that the Lord has pitched."[12] It thus shows that there are other tents that the Lord has pitched, which the tents of Israel resemble. I have to go forth beyond this world in order to see those that are "the tents the Lord has pitched." They, no wonder, are those he showed to Moses when he was building the tent in the desert. The Lord said to him, "Behold, you shall make all according to the model that has been shown to you on the mountain."[13] In imitation of these tents, therefore, Israel must make its tents, and each of us must prepare and build our own tent. In light of this, I do not believe it happened by chance that Peter and Andrew and the sons of Zebedee were fishermen and that Paul was a tentmaker. And as they, summoned from their trade of catching fish, are changed and become fishers of people when the Lord says, "Come, follow me, and I shall make you fishers of men,"[14] so too Paul—for he too was called "apostle" through my Lord Jesus Christ—was changed by a similar transformation of his trade so that, just as they were turned from fishermen into fishers of men,

---

[5]Acts 20:34. [6]CGPNT 3:302. [7]Chrysostom here implies that this is remarkable, and he uses it to shame his audience. Paul, in 1 Cor 9, argues that those who preach the word are entitled to being supported by those who hear their preaching. [8]NPNF 1 11:241**. [9]1 Cor 4:12; 1 Thess 2:9; 2 Thess 3:8. [10]FC 11:167-68. [11]This is not a correct etymology. [12]Num 24:6. [13]Ex 25:40. [14]Mt 4:19.

so he was moved from making earthly tents to building heavenly tents. He made heavenly tents by teaching each path of salvation and showing the way of the blessed dwellings in the heavens. Paul made tents also by establishing churches when "he proclaimed, in its fullness, the gospel of God from Jerusalem all the way around to Illyri-cum."[15] In this way he too made tents in the likeness of the heavenly tents, "which God showed to Moses on the mountain."[16] Homilies on Numbers 17.4.6-7.[17]

---

[15]Rom 15:19. [16]Ex 25:40. [17]SC 442:294-96.

18:5-11 THE JEWS OF CORINTH OPPOSE PAUL

[5]*When Silas and Timothy arrived from Macedonia, Paul was occupied with preaching, testifying to the Jews that the Christ was Jesus. [6]And when they opposed and reviled him, he shook out his garments and said to them, "Your blood be upon your heads! I am innocent. From now on I will go to the Gentiles." [7]And he left there and went to the house of a man named Titius[q] Justus, a worshiper of God; his house was next door to the synagogue. [8]Crispus, the ruler of the synagogue, believed in the Lord, together with all his household; and many of the Corinthians hearing Paul believed and were baptized. [9]And the Lord said to Paul one night in a vision, "Do not be afraid, but speak and do not be silent; [10]for I am with you, and no man shall attack you to harm you; for I have many people in this city." [11]And he stayed a year and six months, teaching the word of God among them.*

q Other early authorities read *Titus*

Overview: Paul continues to try to spread the gospel among his fellow Jews, and he thus gives an example that, even where the gospel is not welcome, we cannot neglect to pass it on to those for whom we bear responsibility. Declaring his innocence, he tries to bring home to them the frightening nature of their choice (Chrysostom), something akin to taking their own lives (Ammonius). Didymus finds in Paul's subsequent actions some evidence of his fear of the pagan city, a fear perhaps of suffering or of an incredulous audience. God upbraids him for this fear (Chrysostom) and encourages him, since God knew of the many there who would believe (Didymus, Chrysostom).

18:6 Your Blood Is on Your Heads

Accountable for Those Entrusted to Us. Chrysostom: "He argued in the synagogue every sabbath and persuaded Jews and Greeks." But "when they opposed and reviled him," he withdrew. By this [Paul] expected to draw them all the more. For why did he leave that house and go to one near the synagogue? Was it not for this? For it was not danger that he saw there. "Testifying to them," it says. He did not yet teach, but he testified. "When they opposed," it says, "and reviled him, he shook out his garments and said, 'Your blood be upon your heads!'" He does this to frighten them not only with words but also with action. And he argues rather vehemently inasmuch as he has already persuaded many of them. "I am innocent," he says, "from now on I will go to the Gentiles." So we too are accountable for the blood of those entrusted to us, if we neglect them. HOMILIES ON THE ACTS OF THE APOSTLES 39.[1]

REJECTION OF THE GOSPEL AS SUICIDE.

AMMONIUS: "Your blood be on your own heads." These words are obscure, but I think they mean this: Whoever does not believe in Christ, who is life, seems to kill himself by passing from life to death and shedding, as it were, his own blood through his self-inflicted death. Therefore he means that when you kill yourselves through disbelief, you receive the punishment of murder, so I am innocent. Following this train of thought it may be also said that he who kills himself is punished by God as a murderer. Similarly if a person is the reason why someone kills himself, he will be guilty in the same way. CATENA ON THE ACTS OF THE APOSTLES 18.6.[2]

18:9 Do Not Be Afraid

STRENGTHENING FOR WITNESS. DIDYMUS THE BLIND: In Corinth, God appeared in a vision to the apostle and urged him not to be afraid to teach, and he made clear to him the reason why he should speak and not be silent, namely that, in that town, there were many that God knew would receive the proclamation of the gospel. For since it was natural that Paul, being human, was afraid of some attack against himself, seeing that then nearly everyone there was still pagan, God encourages and rouses the teacher to be brave by saying, "I am with you and will prevent anybody from attempting to harm you, so that nobody lays a hand on you."[3] CATENA ON THE ACTS OF THE APOSTLES 18.9-11.[4]

18:10 I Am with You

ALLAYING APPREHENSION. CHRYSOSTOM: "Do not be afraid," he says. This was enough to rouse him, either because he was reproved as being afraid or because he was not reproved but encouraged that he would not suffer this. (For he did not always allow them to suffer terribly, so that they might not become too weak.) For nothing pained Paul so much as those who disbelieved and gave opposition. This was more difficult for him to bear than dangers. "And do not be silent," he says, "for I have many people in this city." It was probably for this reason that Christ appeared to him. HOMILIES ON THE ACTS OF THE APOSTLES 39.[5]

---

[1]NPNF 1 11:241**. [2]CGPNT 3:303. [3]The special presence of God to his chosen ones is often the source of their strength: see Deut 31:6; Josh 1:6-7; *The Martyrdom of Polycarp* 9; *The Third Life of Daniel the Stylite* 13. [4]CGPNT 3:304. [5]NPNF 1 11:242**.

18:12-17 PAUL BROUGHT BEFORE THE TRIBUNAL

[12]*But when Gallio was proconsul of Achaia, the Jews made a united attack upon Paul and brought him before the tribunal,* [13]*saying, "This man is persuading men to worship God contrary to the law."* [14]*But when Paul was about to open his mouth, Gallio said to the Jews, "If it were a matter of wrongdoing or vicious crime, I should have reason to bear with you, O Jews;* [15]*but since it is a matter of*

*questions about words and names and your own law, see to it yourselves; I refuse to be a judge of these things." *[16]*And he drove them from the tribunal.* *[17]*And they all seized Sosthenes, the ruler of the synagogue, and beat him in front of the tribunal. But Gallio paid no attention to this.*

OVERVIEW: Modern historical study has been able to use this passage as a valuable fixed point in dating the life of Paul. Gallio's proconsulship should be dated to 52-53 and most probably was cut short in the fall of 52 because of his health. Thus Paul was brought before Gallio sometime between the spring and early fall of 52. The charge brought by the Jews echoes that brought against Stephen (Acts 6:1), but there is a difference: they accuse Paul of breaking Roman law by influencing "the people" (Acts 18:13) and not just the Jews. It is likely that the Jews were trying to show Paul's religion as so different ("contrary to the law") from Judaism in order to bring up the question of Paul's legal status. If they could show that Paul was not practicing Judaism, then his activity would have to count as a new religion and be deprived of legal status. Gallio's speech shows that he considers the differences between Christianity and Judaism minor and internal such that Christianity does not stand as a new religion. Such a judgment sets a precedent in Roman law, portrayed here as the first of its kind, that Christianity is not a crime. The actions of some of the Jews of Corinth against Paul are similar to the actions of the Jewish leaders against Jesus before Pilate, and yet here, Gallio's actions stand as a condemnation of Pilate's, which contradicted his declaration of Jesus' innocence (CHRYSOSTOM). Chrysostom portrays Gallio as a prudent governor who sees through the pretext of the Jews and as one who presents himself as having no concern for the matters at hand in order to keep the Jews out of his court. Such shame reveals the nature of these people as violent when they pounce upon Sosthenes, whom Chrysostom sees as Paul's later companion and who, he believes, is also called Gaius in 1 Corinthians. In his being beaten, Chrysostom sees evidence of his faith in that he is drawn into an imitation of Christ, a sharing with God, who endures, and does not give, insult and injury.

18:14 No Wrongdoing

THE IMPLICATIONS OF GALLIO'S ACTIONS. CHRYSOSTOM: He condemns Pilate, who did not find any proven accusation against Jesus, the Word of God, yet had him flogged and handed him over to death, saying, "I find no pretext for the death of this man." CATENA ON THE ACTS OF THE APOSTLES 18.14.[1]

18:17 Gallio Paid No Attention

SHAME LEADING TO VIOLENCE. CHRYSOSTOM: He taught them that such matters do not demand a judicial sentence, but they were doing everything out of order. And he does not say, "It is not my duty," but "I do not choose," so that they may not trouble him again. Thus Pilate said in the case of Christ, "Take him, and judge him according to your law."[2] But they were just like drunkards and madmen. "And he drove them from the judgment seat"—he effectively closed the tribunal against them. "Then all seized Sosthenes the ruler of the synagogue and beat him before the judgment seat. And Gallio cared for none of these things." This thing, of all others, set them on to this violence: their persuasion that the governor would not even let himself become aware of it. It was a splendid victory. O the shame they were put to! For it is one thing to have come off victorious from a controversy and another for those to learn that he cared nothing for the affair. HOMILIES ON ACTS OF THE APOSTLES 39.[3]

---

[1]CGPNT 3:305. [2]Jn 18:31. [3]NPNF 1 11:242*. The English text differs from TLG 2062.154 (see NPNF 1 11:242 n. 2).

SOSTHENES. CHRYSOSTOM: "Crispus the ruler of the synagogue believed in the Lord, with his whole house: and many of the Corinthians hearing believed and were baptized."[4] "With his whole house": observe the converts in those times doing this with their entire household. [Paul] refers to this Crispus where he writes, "I baptized none save Crispus and Gaius."[5] This [same] I take to be called Sosthenes—evidently a believer, insomuch that he is beaten and is always present with Paul. HOMILIES ON THE ACTS OF THE APOSTLES 39.[6]

IMITATING SOSTHENES. CHRYSOSTOM: This man let us also imitate: to them that beat us, let us return blow for blow, by meekness, by silence, by long-suffering. More grievous these wounds, greater this blow and more heavy. . . . You, a human being, insult your fellow man? You, a servant, your fellow servant? But why do I wonder at this, when many even insult God? Let this be a consolation to you when suffering insult. Are you insulted? God also is insulted. Are you reviled? God also was reviled. Are you treated with scorn? Why, so was our Master also. In these things he shares with us but not so in the contrary things. For he never insulted another unjustly: God forbid! He never reviled, never did a wrong. So that we are those who share with him, not you.[7] For to endure when insulted is God's part; to be merely abusive is the part of the devil. HOMILIES ON THE ACTS OF THE APOSTLES 39.[8]

---

[4] Acts 18:8. [5] 1 Cor 1:14. [6] NPNF 1 11:241*. [7] The ones who insult. [8] NPNF 1 11:243.

18:18-22 PAUL LEAVES CORINTH

[18] *After this Paul stayed many days longer, and then took leave of the brothers and sailed for Syria, and with him Priscilla and Aquila. At Cenchre-ae he cut his hair, for he had a vow.* [19] *And they came to Ephesus, and he left them there; but he himself went into the synagogue and argued with the Jews.* [20] *When they asked him to stay for a longer period, he declined;* [21] *but on taking leave of them he said, "I will return to you if God wills," and he set sail from Ephesus.*

[22] *When he had landed at Caesarea, he went up and greeted the church, and then went down to Antioch.*

OVERVIEW: Paul continues to carry out things proper to Jews, such as the Nazarite vow, in order to convey to Jews who he was, to avoid giving them scandal and not to appear to them as having rejected what he had not rejected but saw as fulfilled (JEROME, BEDE, DIDYMUS, CHRYSOSTOM).

18:18 Paul Cut His Hair

PAUL HAD A VOW. JEROME: Granted that he did what he did not wish to do, through the compelled fear of the Jews: why did he let his hair grow in consequence of a vow and afterward cut it at Cenchrea in obedience to the law. Because the Nazarites who vowed themselves to God were accustomed to do this according to the commands of Moses?[1] LETTER 75.[2]

HE HAD A VOW. BEDE: Now according to the law of Moses, those who vowed themselves to God were ordered to let their hair grow for as long as they wished to be Nazarites and afterwards to have it cut and to consign it to the fire.[3] Paul did these things, not indeed because he had forgotten what he, along with the other apostles, had settled at Jerusalem concerning the abolition of the law,[4] but so that those among the Jews who had come to believe might not be scandalized, he played the part of a Jew himself in order to win over the Jews. COMMENTARY ON THE ACTS OF THE APOSTLES 18.18.[5]

A JEW TO JEWS. DIDYMUS THE BLIND: After his resurrection the Savior said to his disciples, "Go and make disciples of all nations."[6] They to whom the command had been given knew that "God wants all people to be saved and to attain knowledge of the truth."[7] Since the human race had been divided into two religious groups, Jews and pagans, a division of the heralds of the gospel was also made so that some were assigned to teach the Jews, while others to be apostles of the nations.

But since all the teachers had the single aim of leading all to the knowledge of the one God and to the teaching of the gospel, Paul, though an apostle of the nations, if he happened to be able to benefit the Jews would, without a doubt, become a Jew to the Jews[8] so that they might not be estranged from him as if he had departed from the law, although he had already crossed over and beyond the Jewish shadow. In this way, therefore, according to the customs of his homeland, he shaved his head at Cenchrea, since he was under a vow according to the prescription of the old law. CATENA ON THE ACTS OF THE APOSTLES 18.18.[9]

18:19 *Paul Went into the Synagogue*

NO HINDRANCE TO TEACHING THE GOSPEL. CHRYSOSTOM: [Paul] left them in Ephesus so that they might teach. Indeed those who had stayed with him for such a long time had learned many things; he had not, however, completely detached them from the Jewish customs. CATENA ON THE ACTS OF THE APOSTLES 18.19.[10]

---

[1]Num 6:1-8. [2]FC 12:352*. [3]Num 6:1-8, 18. [4]Acts 15. [5]CS 117:150. [6]Mt 28:19. [7]1 Tim 2:4. [8]1 Cor 9:20. [9]CGPNT 3:307. [10]CGPNT 3:308.

18:23-28 APOLLOS SPEAKS OF JESUS

[23]*After spending some time there he departed and went from place to place through the region of Galatia and Phrygia, strengthening all the disciples.*

[24]*Now a Jew named Apollos, a native of Alexandria, came to Ephesus. He was an eloquent man, well versed in the scriptures.* [25]*He had been instructed in the way of the Lord; and being fervent in spirit, he spoke and taught accurately the things concerning Jesus, though he knew only the baptism of John.* [26]*He began to speak boldly in the synagogue; but when Priscilla and Aquila heard him, they took him and expounded to him the way of God more accurately.* [27]*And when he wished to cross to Achaia, the brothers encouraged him, and wrote to the disciples to receive him. When he*

arrived, he greatly helped those who through grace had believed, [28]*for he powerfully confuted the Jews in public, showing by the scriptures that the Christ was Jesus.*

OVERVIEW: Here begins the third missionary journey, which will end at Acts 20:38 and covers the years 54 to 58. Luke introduces Apollos, known from 1 Corinthians, but there are some discrepancies between Luke's account and what can be gleaned from Paul's letter. Paul's Apollos seems to have come to Ephesus after he arrived in Corinth after Paul, whereas Luke never has them meet and describes Apollos as beginning in Ephesus and continuing on to Achaia. Luke does not answer the question as to how one so eloquent about Jesus as Messiah did not know about baptism after twenty years of the Christian movement. The Fathers find Apollos mysterious for reasons different from those of the modern commentators. The spirit in Acts 18:25, understood today as referring to Apollos's spirit, is the Holy Spirit in the Fathers, which presented them with a dilemma: how did Apollos have the Holy Spirit when he had not received baptism in Christ?[1] For Ammonius, Apollos's knowledge of the Scriptures enabled him to show his opponents how Jesus was the prophesied Messiah, but for Didymus, it is his knowledge of the Scriptures that makes him speak in the Spirit. Chrysostom sees Apollos as similar to Cornelius, a man whose eagerness and goodness has drawn the Holy Spirit to him and thus emboldened him in his limited knowledge. Chrysostom and Didymus explain the Spirit's role as concomitant with his limited knowledge and not as fulfilling it. Only Ammonius sees Apollos's possession of the Spirit as something that imparts knowledge to him, and yet he does not realize that this raises the question of why Apollos was not directly given full knowledge about Jesus by the Spirit. Chrysostom, however, sees divine providence in Priscilla and Aquila, who have been left there to supplement what Apollos is lacking and thus to prepare him for his work in Corinth. This schooling is odd in that here is a man, well-educated in the Scriptures, a scholar of sorts, sitting not only at the feet of tentmakers but of a woman (AMMONIUS). In the Greco-Roman world women, if educated at all, would only very rarely receive the same level of education that men of their families did, and so to be taught by a woman could constitute a disgrace in general, but even more so for one known for his learning.

18:24 An Eloquent Man

APOLLOS'S SKILLS. AMMONIUS: He was learned in the Scriptures, able to dispute with those who questioned him and able to demonstrate that the recent events were in agreement with the Old Testament. CATENA ON THE ACTS OF THE APOSTLES 18.24.[2]

18:25 He Taught Accurately About Jesus

THE NATURE OF APOLLOS'S IGNORANCE. DIDYMUS THE BLIND: Speaking somewhat accurately the things concerning Jesus is not different from laying out somewhat accurately the things concerning the way, the teaching of Christ, for it is possible that someone, having a generally precise knowledge about the things of Christ, needs a most nuanced explanation of them. Apollos, being a Jew, had the opportunity to know the Old Testament that gives witness concerning Jesus. Therefore, being learned, he was speaking in the Spirit, and he was teaching in the synagogues what he knew about Jesus. Being students of the apostle Paul, Priscilla and Aquila take him, being full of eagerness, aside in order to pass on to him the entire way of the gospel. It is probable that Apollos knew that Jesus had lived among human-

---

[1]For one opinion of how the word *spirit* in the Scriptures always means Holy Spirit, and how the Spirit dwells only in the saints, see Origen *On First Principles* 1.3.4-8. [2]CGPNT 3:310.

kind and had commanded these things of the way, but it is unlikely that he knew why he had come among us. CATENA ON THE ACTS OF THE APOSTLES 18.28.[3]

18:26 Priscilla and Aquila Heard Him

JUST AS CORNELIUS. CHRYSOSTOM: The boldness of the man was great: he spoke precisely about Jesus, but he was in need of precision, of other further teaching. And still, in this way, even though [Apollos] did not know all, he had, because of his eagerness, drawn to himself the Holy Spirit, just as those at the house of Cornelius. CATENA ON THE ACTS OF THE APOSTLES 18.26-27.[4]

BOILING WITH THE SPIRIT. AMMONIUS: How did this man, who had only been baptized according to John's baptism, have the Holy Spirit, but his followers did not? To this it must be said that for this reason was he boiling with the Spirit: being enlightened by the grace of God, he knew precisely and taught from the Scriptures that Jesus is the Christ. And this very knowledge did not allow him to keep quiet, but he himself, doing the work of an evangelist, taught, as did his disciples, about Jesus. CATENA ON THE ACTS OF THE APOSTLES 18.25.[5]

NO SHAME TO BE TAUGHT BY A WOMAN. AMMONIUS: It must be noted that we must believe that women passed on the faith: see how completely desirous of salvation Apollos was, for even though he was an educated man and was well versed in the Scripture's secrets, he did not consider it worthless to learn the fullness of the faith from a woman. He did not become conceited as if he were receiving a rebuke from a woman that "you should learn more fully the things concerning God the Word's ordaining." Therefore [Priscilla] explained to him in her teaching the things of faith, and Apollos listened and received them, for while he knew that Jesus was the Christ and the servant of God and concluded so from the Scriptures, his knowledge was imperfect, since he did not know what had been spoken and prophesied to the apostles through the Holy Spirit. And so the circle of Aquila, being followers of Paul, laid out more clearly to him the way of God, such as worship in the Spirit and the circumcision not by hands and whatever else had been spoken for the perfection of the church. CATENA ON THE ACTS OF THE APOSTLES 18.25.[6]

THE COUPLE LEFT AT EPHESUS FOR APOLLOS'S SAKE. CHRYSOSTOM: It was not for nothing that [Paul] left them at Ephesus. For Apollos's sake the Spirit planned this, so that he might advance upon Corinth with greater force. HOMILIES ON THE ACTS OF THE APOSTLES 40.[7]

---

[3]CGPNT 3:312. [4]CGPNT 3:311. [5]CGPNT 3:310-11. [6]CGPNT 3:311. [7]NPNF 1 11:247**.

19:1-7 THE HOLY SPIRIT COMES UPON THE TWELVE AT EPHESUS

---

[1]While Apollos was at Corinth, Paul passed through the upper country and came to Ephesus. There he found some disciples. [2]And he said to them, "Did you receive the Holy Spirit when you believed?" And they said, "No, we have never even heard that there is a Holy Spirit." [3]And he

said, "Into what then were you baptized?" They said, "Into John's baptism." [4]And Paul said, "John baptized with the baptism of repentance, telling the people to believe in the one who was to come after him, that is, Jesus." [5]On hearing this, they were baptized in the name of the Lord Jesus. [6]And when Paul had laid his hands upon them, the Holy Spirit came on them; and they spoke with tongues and prophesied. [7]There were about twelve of them in all.

OVERVIEW: Commentators today see in this second incident at Ephesus Luke's way of saying that even after Jesus had died and risen there were still those who were followers of John. It is not clear whether or not the whole incident took place in Ephesus or whether it is a composite narrative drawn from various reports. Nearly all commentators discuss how and in what sense Luke can already call the men "disciples." There is no consensus. Most of the attention of the Fathers is centered on the relation of John's baptism and that conferred by Jesus through those he sends. The interest, as for Luke, concentrates on the role of the Holy Spirit (CHRYSOSTOM, BEDE, TERTULLIAN, AUGUSTINE, AMMONIUS). Sometimes there is protracted consideration of the activity of the Holy Spirit (ORIGEN). Bede, in contrast to ancient and modern commentators, sees a symbolic significance in the number twelve.

19:2 Did You Receive the Holy Spirit?

JOHN'S BAPTISM INCOMPLETE. CHRYSOSTOM: And [Paul] does not ask them, "Do you believe in Jesus?" but "Did you receive the Holy Spirit?" For he knew that they had not. And he wished them to acknowledge this, so that they might learn what they lacked and ask for it. "And when Paul had laid his hands upon them," it says, "the Holy Spirit came on them; and they spoke with tongues and prophesied." The baptism itself led to their giving prophecies. John's baptism did not have this effect and was therefore incomplete. Rather, it prepared them beforehand so that they would be deemed worthy of such things. So this was the intent of John's baptism, that they should believe in the one who was to come after him. Here is shown an important doctrine, that the baptized are completely cleansed of their sins. For if they were not cleansed, they could not have received the Spirit and be immediately deemed worthy of such gifts. And look, the gift was twofold: tongues and the ability to prophesy. Paul spoke well when he said John's baptism was of repentance and not of forgiveness. He led them forward, persuading them that John's baptism lacked the latter. For forgiveness was the work of the one who was given afterwards. And how is it that they who received the Spirit did not teach, but Apollos did when he had not yet received the Spirit? Because they were not so fervent or even so instructed. He, on the other hand, was instructed and very fervent. It seems to me that great was the man's boldness. But even if he taught the things concerning Jesus accurately, [Apollos] still needed more accurate teaching. So, though he did not know everything, by his enthusiasm he drew to himself the Holy Spirit, as did Cornelius and his companions. HOMILIES ON THE ACTS OF THE APOSTLES 40.[1]

CHRIST GIVES BAPTISM ITS POWER. CHRYSOSTOM: Christ, then, did not need baptism—not John's or any other's; rather, baptism was needful of the power of Christ. In fact, that which was lacking was the chief of all blessings, namely, for the baptized to be deemed worthy of the Spirit. Therefore, [Paul] added this valuable gift of the Spirit when he came. HOMILIES ON THE GOSPEL OF JOHN 17.[2]

DID YOU RECEIVE THE HOLY SPIRIT? BEDE: That is: After baptism did you receive the imposition of hands, by which the Holy Spirit is ordi-

---

[1]NPNF 1 11:247**. [2]FC 33:166*.

narily given? COMMENTARY ON THE ACTS OF THE APOSTLES 19.2.[3]

19:4 John's Baptism of Repentance

BAPTISM OF REPENTANCE. BEDE: This baptism, he says, could not grant the remission of sins but only teach repentance. For just as the sign of circumcision among the patriarchs had been a mark of the faith that they lived by, so also repentant people received this washing as a singular mark of their devotion. Nevertheless, it also figuratively pointed to Christ's baptism, by which remission of sins would be given. COMMENTARY ON THE ACTS OF THE APOSTLES 19.4.[4]

HEAVENLY AND NOT HEAVENLY. TERTULLIAN: John's baptism had already raised the question, which our Lord himself posed for the Pharisees, whether it was something heavenly or just from earth.[5] They, clearly not understanding because of their unbelief, could not come to a definite answer. We, however, having only a slight understanding that accords with our slight faith, can still judge that John's baptism was, on the one hand, divine in that God commanded it, but on the other, it was not divine in its power. We read that John had been sent by the Lord for this purpose, which was still human in nature, for he, established as a preacher of repentance, which is a question of a person's will, was offering nothing heavenly but was making way for the heavenly. Therefore, the scribes and the Pharisees who were unwilling to believe were also unwilling to undergo repentance. But if repentance is something human, then it must be that the baptism was of the very same nature, for had it been heavenly it would have given both the Holy Spirit and remission from sins. But no one forgives sins or grants the Holy Spirit but God alone. Besides, the Lord himself said that the Spirit would otherwise not descend unless he first should ascend to the Father. And so what the master would not yet give, the slave would surely not be able to offer. And again, later, in the Acts of the Apostles we find that those who had received John's baptism had not received the Holy Spirit of whom they had never even been told. Therefore, it was not of heaven because it offered nothing heavenly. ON BAPTISM 10.1-5.[6]

19:5 Baptized in Jesus' Name

THE TRUE BAPTISM IS CHRIST'S. AUGUSTINE: Did he baptize after a heretic had baptized? Or, if perhaps you dare to say that the friend of the bridegroom[7] was a heretic and was not in the unity of the church, I wish you would write that also. But, if it is complete madness either to think or to say that, then it is the duty of your prudence to reflect on the reason why the apostle Paul baptized after John. If he baptized after an equal, all of you ought to baptize after yourselves; if after a superior, you ought to baptize after Rogatus;[8] if after an inferior, Rogatus should have baptized after you, because you baptized as a priest. On the other hand, if the baptism that is now given is equally valid to those who receive it in spite of the unequal merit of those who give it, because it is the baptism of Christ, not of those by whom it is administered, I think you now understand that Paul gave to some the baptism of Christ for the reason that they had received the baptism of John but not that of Christ. LETTER 93.[9]

BAPTIZED IN THE NAME OF THE LORD JESUS. BEDE: A question is often put forward as to whether those should be rebaptized who, perhaps through ignorance, were baptized by others who, though correct in faith, were not baptized. I think this is explained in the chapters under discussion. For what difference does it make whether one was baptized at that time, before the inauguration of Christ's baptism, or at this time, apart from the succession [of those baptized with

---

[3]CS 117:153. [4]CS 117:153. [5]Mt 21:25. [6]CCL 1:284-85. [7]Jn 3:29. [8]This letter was written to a bishop, Vincent, who succeeded Rogatus as bishop of Cartenna in the Roman province of Mauretania. [9]FC 18:99-100*.

Christ's baptism], since even John himself proclaimed that those should be rebaptized whom he had baptized in faith and in the name of the Christ who was to come. He said, "I baptize you in water; he will baptize you in the Holy Spirit."[10] Now if, as some have taught, at the present time a sharing in the body and blood of Christ can, by itself, suffice as a remedy for such as these, so also at that time those whom John had baptized with water could have been confirmed by participation in his blood alone, and it would not have been necessary for them to be baptized by Christ's disciples. COMMENTARY ON THE ACTS OF THE APOSTLES 19.5.[11]

IN THE SPIRIT AND HAVING THE SPIRIT.
AMMONIUS: Therefore the baptism of John was an exhortation to repentance only, but it did not provide a purification from sins. This, then, is the difference between the baptism of John and that of the faithful: the baptism of the faithful gives the gift of the remission of sins. While baptizing, John said, "I baptize you for the one coming after me, and I ask you to believe in him, because he is the Lamb of God."[12] Now the one who faithfully baptizes says, "I baptize you in the name of the Father and of the Son and of the Holy Spirit," so that you may believe in the consubstantial Trinity. He washes the baptized thoroughly, strips away his previously existing superstition, and reclothes him with Christ, as he purely proclaims the true faith. Furthermore, it must be noted first that after baptism into Christ, the Holy Spirit descends upon those baptized when the one baptizing lays his hands on them, and second that those baptized with the baptism of John did not possess the Holy Spirit. How then did Apollos, who had only been baptized with John's baptism, burn with the Spirit? Even if Apollos burned with the Spirit, it is not said that he possessed the Holy Spirit. In fact, he neither was speaking in tongues nor prophesying. Therefore, it is one thing to burn with the Spirit and another to possess the Holy Spirit. Whoever possessed the Holy Spirit had it dwelling within him, and the

Spirit itself spoke from within. Many of these things are referred to previously, as when the Spirit spoke to Philip, to Peter, to the apostles and to Paul and his companions, when he ordered them either to speak or not speak the word in certain cities. Whoever burned with the Spirit did this or that through an external illumination and impulse, as one led by the Spirit, just as someone might be led or protected by an angel. Now, do not say to me, "How is it possible for one who does not share in the Spirit to burn with the Spirit?" For it is necessary to establish what is unseen on the basis of what is seen. If the sun and fire, being outside of us, by drawing near to our bodies or also to be at a small distance, as is the case with fire, warm our bodies, what should we say about the divine Spirit that is truly hot and sets our interior person on fire, even if the Spirit does not live within but is without? It is possible, in the way that everything is possible to God, that someone be set on fire, even if the heat is not dwelling within. CATENA ON THE ACTS OF THE APOSTLES 19.5.[13]

INVOKING THE SPIRIT. ORIGEN: Of the existence of the Holy Spirit . . . we are taught in many passages of Scripture. For instance, David says in the fiftieth psalm, "And take not your Holy Spirit from me,"[14] and in Daniel it is said, "The Holy Spirit, who is in you."[15] But in the New Testament we have proofs in abundance, as when the Holy Spirit is related to have descended upon Christ,[16] and when the Lord breathed on his apostles after the resurrection and said, "Receive the Holy Spirit,"[17] and the angel said to Mary, "The Holy Spirit shall come upon you,"[18] and Paul teaches us that "no one can say that Jesus is the Lord except in the Holy Spirit,"[19] and in the Acts of the Apostles "through the laying on of the apostles' hands the Holy Spirit was given"[20] in baptism. From all of which we learn that the per-

---

[10]Mt 3:11. [11]CS 117:153-54. [12]Jn 1:26-27, 29. [13]CGPNT 3:313-14. [14]Ps 51:11 (50:13 LXX). [15]Dan 4:6 (in Theodotion's translation). See 4:9. [16]Mt 3:16. [17]Jn 20:22. [18]Lk 1:35. [19]1 Cor 12:3. [20]Acts 8:18.

son of the Holy Spirit is of so great authority and dignity that saving baptism is not complete except when performed with the authority of the whole most excellent Trinity, that is, by naming the Father, Son and Holy Spirit.[21] ON FIRST PRINCIPLES 1.3.2.[22]

19:6 The Holy Spirit Came on Them

THE SUPERIORITY OF CHRISTIAN BAPTISM. ANONYMOUS: See here is fulfilled the saying "the least in the kingdom of heaven is greater than he."[23] Look, he is the last of the apostles, in respect to his calling, and that very thing John did not give in his baptism, those being baptized receive through the hands of Paul. CATENA ON THE ACTS OF THE APOSTLES 19.6-7.[24]

19:7 About Twelve in All

TWELVE MEN. BEDE: Truly, "the judgments of

God [are like] mighty depths."[25] Behold, Asia, which not long before was unworthy to be visited by the apostles,[26] now consecrated by the apostolic number [i.e., twelve] and exalted by a prophetic gift! And it should be noted that the Holy Spirit showed signs of his coming, both here in the twelve disciples, and earlier in the hundred and twenty[27] (which is the number twelve multiplied ten times). I believe that the former [manifestation occurred] in Jerusalem, and this one in Ephesus, which is a Greek city, to show that whether the one who believes is from the Jews or the Gentiles, he [the Spirit] fills only those who share in the unity of the catholic and apostolic church. COMMENTARY ON THE ACTS OF THE APOSTLES 19.7.[28]

---

[21]See Mt 28:19. [22]OFP 29-30*. [23]Lk 7:28. [24]CGPNT 3:315. [25]Ps 36:6 (35:7 LXX, Vg). [26]Acts 16:6. [27]Acts 1:16; 2:1-4. [28]CS 117:154.

19:8-10 PAUL ARGUES AT EPHESUS

[8]*And he entered the synagogue and for three months spoke boldly, arguing and pleading about the kingdom of God;* [9]*but when some were stubborn and disbelieved, speaking evil of the Way before the congregation, he withdrew from them, taking the disciples with him, and argued daily in the hall of Tyrannus.*[r] [10]*This continued for two years, so that all the residents of Asia heard the word of the Lord, both Jews and Greeks.*

r Other ancient authorities add *from the fifth hour to the tenth*

OVERVIEW: The Fathers did not consider this description of Paul's ministry in Ephesus important enough to comment upon at length. Chrysostom draws a conclusion about the necessity of withdrawing from opposition using Paul's gesture as valuable teaching for his own generation. The modern commentators consider these verses to be

a summary statement introducing accounts of Paul's God-given power to work healings and exorcisms and the effect on the Ephesians. In the summary statement they consider terms such as "kingdom of God" and "the Way."

19:9 Paul Withdrew

DEPART FROM EVIL-SPEAKING PEOPLE. CHRYSOSTOM: "He withdrew from them, taking the disciples with him." That is, [Paul] put a stop to their evil speaking. This he did and withdrew, since he did not wish to kindle their envy or to lead them to greater strife. . . . From this let us learn not to meet the evil-speaking people but to withdraw from them. He did not speak evil, though he himself was spoken ill of. Instead, "he argued daily" and gained many friends especially because of this, that he neither turned away nor separated himself though he was spoken ill of. . . . Thus by withdrawing from them, he defeats those who maligned and spoke evil of the doctrine (for this is what he called the Way). He himself withdrew so as not to force the disciples to go back or to rouse their anger, thereby revealing his opponents to be pushing away salvation on every occasion. Here he does not even defend his actions before them, since the Gentiles everywhere have believed. HOMILIES ON THE ACTS OF THE APOSTLES 41.[1]

THE WAY. CHRYSOSTOM: Fittingly do they call this "the way," as it truly was the way that leads to the kingdom of heaven. Or the Scripture is saying that Christ is the way, as he is called the way, or it is speaking of the true faith, that which is proclaimed through Paul, by which any wayfarer arrives at the kingdom of heaven. CATENA ON THE ACTS OF THE APOSTLES 19.9.[2]

19:10 *All Asia Heard the Word*

THE FRUITS OF SEPARATION. CHRYSOSTOM: See how much separating oneself accomplishes: both the Jews and Hellenes came to listen. He teaches those who believe in the Son of God to separate themselves from those who blaspheme him. CATENA ON THE ACTS OF THE APOSTLES 19.10.[3]

---

[1]NPNF 1 11:251-52**. [2]CGPNT 3:315. [3]CGPNT 3:315-16.

19:11-17 THE SONS OF SCEVA OVERCOME BY EVIL SPIRITS

[11]*And God did extraordinary miracles by the hands of Paul,* [12]*so that handkerchiefs or aprons were carried away from his body to the sick, and diseases left them and the evil spirits came out of them.* [13]*Then some of the itinerant Jewish exorcists undertook to pronounce the name of the Lord Jesus over those who had evil spirits, saying, "I adjure you by the Jesus whom Paul preaches."* [14]*Seven sons of a Jewish high priest named Sceva were doing this.* [15]*But the evil spirit answered them, "Jesus I know, and Paul I know; but who are you?"* [16]*And the man in whom the evil spirit was leaped on them, mastered all of them, and overpowered them, so that they fled out of that house naked and wounded.* [17]*And this became known to all residents of Ephesus, both Jews and Greeks; and fear fell upon them all; and the name of the Lord Jesus was extolled.*

OVERVIEW: Some modern commentators see this episode as legend and suggest that its source is folklore. A good number however, see this as a narrative of an actual event. Many see the inability of Sceva's sons to cast out the spirit, even after adding Paul's name to that of Jesus, as an insistence by Luke that Christianity has nothing to do with magic. The ancients comment on the event as showing the need for faith (CHRYSOSTOM, DIDYMUS). Chrysostom also discusses how the life of Christ is manifest through the body of believers as well as how exorcism proves the resurrection of Jesus. Bede discusses exorcisms before Christ and seeks to discern the meaning of numbers in the sacred text.

19:12 Aprons Carried from Paul's Body to the Sick

THE GREATEST PROOF OF THE RESURRECTION. CHRYSOSTOM: What Christ is saying is this, "Whoever believes in me will, in my name, do greater signs than I have done."[1] And these are the greater signs that they did: their shadows raised the dead. Thus was the power of Christ especially proclaimed, since it was not so marvelous that he performed miracles while living, as it was that, when he had died, others were able to do greater than [Christ] in his own name. This itself was the most irrefutable demonstration of the resurrection. He would not, even had he been seen, have been believed to such an extent, since they could have said that he was a phantasm, but should someone see greater signs occur from the mere mention of his name—even when he was among humankind in the flesh—that one, unless terribly shameless, would not have refused to believe. CATENA ON THE ACTS OF THE APOSTLES 19.11-12.[2]

19:13 Pronouncing the Name of Jesus

THE NAME HAS POWER ONLY WHEN SPOKEN BY FAITH. CHRYSOSTOM: Look, they had no intention to believe but wished to cast out demons by the name. . . . Therefore in secret they did this, but their weakness was then paraded in public. . . . So the name has no power unless it is spoken by faith. . . . Look how they

turned their weapons against themselves. . . . So far were they from thinking of Jesus as something great that they added Paul as well, because they thought that he was something great here. One may justly wonder at this point why the demon did not cooperate with the exorcists' deception but refuted them completely and exposed their stage act. It seems to me that he was very angry, just as if he were someone in the gravest danger, who is being refuted by a pitiful wretch and wants to vent all his rage against him. For, to prevent any slight on the name of Jesus, he first acknowledges him and takes this acknowledgment as permission. HOMILIES ON THE ACTS OF THE APOSTLES 41.[3]

EXORCISM BY PERSONS UNFIT. BEDE: Josephus reports that King Solomon devised and taught to his people methods of exorcism by which unclean spirits which were driven out of a person would not dare to return anymore.[4] This happens sometimes, even through the agency of those who are reprehensible, either for the condemnation of those who do it or for the benefit of those who see and hear, so that although people may despise those performing the signs, they may nevertheless honor God, through whose invocation such great miracles are done. COMMENTARY ON THE ACTS OF THE APOSTLES 19.13.[5]

THE DEMON IS MORE RIGHT-MINDED THAN THE EXORCISTS. CHRYSOSTOM: But here, as if the demon did not know him, the exorcists added, "I adjure you by the Jesus whom Paul preaches." For the reply he gave shows that he knew. The exorcists said simply "Jesus," when they should have said, "the savior of the world, he who rose again." They did not wish to acknowledge his glory. For this reason, the demon censures them. He leaps on them and says, "Jesus I know, and Paul I know." It is as if he had said,

---

[1]Jn 14:12 [2]CGPNT 3:316. [3]NPNF 1 11:251**. [4]The Jews were considered to have special powers of exorcism: Josephus *Jewish Antiquities* 8.2.5. [5]CS 117:154.

"You do not believe, but you abuse the name when you say this. Therefore the temple is desolate, the vessel easy to overcome. You are not preachers, but you are mine." Great was the demon's anger. The apostles had the power to do this to them, but they did not do it as of yet. For the apostles, who had power over the demons who did this to people, had even greater power over the people themselves. HOMILIES ON THE ACTS OF THE APOSTLES 41.[6]

19:14 Seven Sons of Sceva

THE SEVEN SONS OF SCEVA. BEDE: Therefore, since "Satan himself disguises himself as an angel of light,"[7] [Satan] has no fear of covering his ministers as well with the same false appearance. It is customary to represent the gifts of the Holy Spirit by the number seven. As a figure of this, the Lord after his resurrection took food with seven disciples,[8] and seven of the brothers came to preach the gospel to Cornelius, who was to be baptized with the Holy Spirit.[9] Hence the sons of Sceva, as men who would drive out evil spirits, are reckoned as seven in number. Because they called upon the name of Christ and the apostles not out of belief in them but to put them to the test, they were rightly condemned for the cunning deceitfulness, not only by God but also by the demons themselves. Thus they were called sons of Sceva, which means "a yelping little fox."[10] This animal, which is very shrewd with respect to deceit and craftiness, represents one, whether Jew, Gentile or heretic, who is always plotting against the church of God, and, as it were, continuously making a racket with their babbling voices. Concerning them the command is given to the guardians of the church, "Catch for us the tiny foxes that are wrecking the vineyards."[11] COMMENTARY ON THE ACTS OF THE APOSTLES 19.14.[12]

19:15 Who Are You?

THERE IS A GREATER POWER THAN POWER

OVER DEMONS. CHRYSOSTOM: There may be someone among you who, on hearing this, wishes he were in possession of this power, so that the demons should not be able to look him in the face, and he considers those holy men fortunate because they had such power. But let him listen to Christ, who says, "Do not rejoice because the demons are subject to you."[13] He knew that all people especially rejoice in this because of vainglory. For if you seek what pleases God and what is for the common good, another road is greater. For to free people from a demon is not so great as to rescue them from sin. It is not demons that prevent one from attaining to the kingdom of heaven. On the contrary, they assist, albeit unwillingly, by making him who has the demon more sensible. Sin, on the other hand, expels him. But perhaps someone will say, "God forbid it should befall me to be sensible in this way!" I, too, do not wish this for you, but rather that you should do everything because of something else, namely, the love of Christ. But if, God forbid, this should happen, I would comfort you with this. If the demon does not leave, but sin does, to free one of the latter is a greater good deed. HOMILIES ON THE ACTS OF THE APOSTLES 41.[14]

19:16 The Evil Spirit Leaped on Them

KNOWING JESUS. DIDYMUS THE BLIND: As one confessing God in word alone, he denies him with his deeds. This is "knowing Jesus" according to mere opinion. Therefore, it is no paradox if the evil spirit says to the Jewish exorcists, "I know Jesus" and the following, just as other demons used to say, with a loud cry, to Jesus himself, "I know who you are, the Holy One of God."[15] To these you can add the passage, "even demons believe and they tremble,"[16] for it provides no evidence that evil spirits have faith accounted as righteousness. We must also say with regard to

---

[6]NPNF 1 11:254**. [7]2 Cor 11:14. [8]Jn 21:1-2, 12-13. [9]Acts 11:12. [10]Jerome *On Hebrew Names* (CCL 72:149). [11]Song 2:15. [12]CS 117:155. [13]Lk 10:20. [14]NPNF 1 11:254**. [15]Mk 1:24. [16]Jas 2:19.

our current passage that just as those who receive cures from Jesus do so according to their faith, so those calling on Jesus for the expulsion of a demon or for another cure accomplish this in accord with the faith they have. Here, however, the evil spirit says, "Who are you that call on

Jesus, for I do not perceive the power that I have often experienced when his name is called." CATENA ON THE ACTS OF THE APOSTLES 19.13.[17]

---

[17]CGPNT 3:317-18.

19:18-22 THE BOOKS OF MAGIC BURNED

[18]*Many also of those who were now believers came, confessing and divulging their practices.* [19]*And a number of those who practiced magic arts brought their books together and burned them in the sight of all; and they counted the value of them and found it came to fifty thousand pieces of silver.* [20]*So the word of the Lord grew and prevailed mightily.*

[21]*Now after these events Paul resolved in the Spirit to pass through Macedonia and Achaia and go to Jerusalem, saying, "After I have been there, I must also see Rome."* [22]*And having sent into Macedonia two of his helpers, Timothy and Erastus, he himself stayed in Asia for a while.*

OVERVIEW: The effect of Paul's preaching here is quantified in economic terms, and thus this episode lays the foundation for Demetrius's speech that follows. This passage presents problems to modern commentators inasmuch as scholars today are still struggling to come to a clearer picture of the ancient economy. What fifty thousand denarii, the standard silver coin, would have amounted to in terms of wages is a confusing subject in itself.[1] The point, however, is clear that conversion to Christianity from magic requires the renouncing of all profit from the latter in order to reap the benefits of the faith. The jury is also out on Paul's resolution "in the S/spirit" as to whether the spirit here is the Holy Spirit. The ancient commentators note the power of an honest confession of sins (AMMONIUS) or the power of Christian preaching to effect such a confession (EUSEBIUS). Didymus uses the incident to defend Christians against the charge of being magicians while Bede is fascinated by the symbolic potential

of the fifty thousand pieces of silver.

19:19 Those Who Practiced Magic

A FRUITFUL CONFESSION OF SINS. AMMONIUS: Every sinner must confess his sins and, through his self-conviction, turn away from continuing to commit them, so that he may become just according to the passage, "Confess your sins first so that you may be justified,"[2] and the passage, "Just is the man who accuses himself."[3] The idolaters and magicians were so many in Ephesus that they prepared magicians' books at a high price, as if these books held the most noble things in life. Upon believing in Christ, they did not sell them, even though there were many who wanted to obtain them, but they burned them. And they did this first so that no one could take part in their soul-destroying ruin, and second so that

---

[1]See OCD s.v. "wages." [2]Is 43:26 (LXX). [3]Prov 18:17 (LXX).

they could have no profit from it. For just as it is forbidden to offer to God the value of a dog[4] or profit from impurity, so also did they judge it an injustice to lay at the apostles' feet money from such a source. CATENA ON THE ACTS OF THE APOSTLES 19.18.[5]

BRINGING FORBIDDEN THINGS TO LIGHT.
EUSEBIUS OF CAESAREA: It shows what our Savior's disciples were; it shows the extraordinary influence of their words when they addressed their audience, that people so touched the depths of their souls, caught hold of and pierced the individual conscience, that men no longer hid anything away in concealment but brought forth their forbidden things to light and themselves completed the indictment of themselves and their own former wickedness. It shows what their pupils were like, how pure and honorable in disposition, determined that nothing evil in them should lurk below the surface, and how boldly they prided themselves on their change from the worse to the better. Yes, they who gave their magic books to the flames and voted for their complete destruction left no one in any doubt that they would never again have anything to do with sorcery, and from that day forth they were pure from the slightest suspicion of it. PROOF OF THE GOSPEL 3.6.[6]

DISCERNING MEANING IN FIFTY. BEDE: In the Gospel, too, debtors are forgiven debts that number fifty and five hundred denarii[7] because, I believe, while we are subsisting with the five senses of the body in this life, we transgress the commandments of the Decalogue. Here, however, because of the enormity of the crime of magic, the number [fifty] is increased a thousand-fold. Alternatively, "the number fifty is" often "related to repentance"[8] and to the pardon of sins. Hence also the fiftieth psalm[9] is the psalm of repentance, and the fiftieth year is the year of pardon.[10] COMMENTARY ON THE ACTS OF THE APOSTLES 19.19B.[11]

CHRIST'S DISCIPLES ARE NOT MAGICIANS.
DIDYMUS THE BLIND: Let those who accuse Christ's disciples of being magicians be refuted by this reading, since it shows clearly that all magic is destroyed by the power of their teaching. See these people, not being incompetent but having great ability in this art, after being purified of the magical arts or of their customary demons, how they gathered together all the books of magic and burned them before all present at that time, even though they were of great value. CATENA ON THE ACTS OF THE APOSTLES 19.19-20.[12]

19:22 Two Helpers Sent to Macedonia

SUPERSTITION AND PHILOSOPHY. CHRYSOSTOM: He sends them ahead to announce his coming and thus to rouse their expectations, but most of all to stay a while in Asia. And for good reason, since there ruled the tyranny of philosophers. He went and spoke with them more, since there was much superstition. CATENA ON THE ACTS OF THE APOSTLES 19.21.[13]

---

[4]Deut 23:18: "You shall not allow a common prostitute's fee, or the pay of a male prostitute [Hebrew = "dog"], to be brought into the house of the Lord your God in fulfillment of any vow, for both of them are an abomination to the Lord your God" (NEB). [5]CGPNT 3:319. [6]POG 1:148*. [7]Lk 7:41-42. [8]Jerome Commentary on Isaiah 2.3.3 (CCL 73:44). [9]Ps 51 in the MT. [10]Lev 25:8-19. [11]CS 117:156. [12]CGPNT 3:320. [13]CGPNT 3:320.

19:23-29 DEMETRIUS AND
THE SILVERSMITHS BEGIN A RIOT

²³*About that time there arose no little stir concerning the Way.* ²⁴*For a man named Demetrius, a silversmith, who made silver shrines of Artemis, brought no little business to the craftsmen.* ²⁵*These he gathered together, with the workmen of like occupation, and said, "Men, you know that from this business we have our wealth.* ²⁶*And you see and hear that not only at Ephesus but almost throughout all Asia this Paul has persuaded and turned away a considerable company of people, saying that gods made with hands are not gods.* ²⁷*And there is danger not only that this trade of ours may come into disrepute but also that the temple of the great goddess Artemis may count for nothing, and that she may even be deposed from her magnificence, she whom all Asia and the world worship."*

²⁸*When they heard this they were enraged, and cried out, "Great is Artemis of the Ephesians!"* ²⁹*So the city was filled with the confusion; and they rushed together into the theater, dragging with them Gaius and Aristarchus, Macedonians who were Paul's companions in travel.*

OVERVIEW: For the sake of clarity we have divided this incident into two parts: an account of Demetrius's successful attempt to stir up the silversmiths and others of Ephesus (Acts 19:23-29) and the continued story of the riot and its quelling by the city clerk (Acts 19:30-41). In regard to the first part, the modern commentators provide valuable information concerning the cult of Artemis. They also remind us of how closely religion, finance, politics and the crafts can be intertwined in ancient culture, though they are not in agreement as to how important a role the religious aspect of the Artemis cult played in this event. Among the Fathers, Bede picks up on the economic implications of the events and extends them to the very materials of Demetrius's craft; for Bede, everything about Demetrius points to an inward emptiness of worth, regardless of how rich his words or his metals are. Chrysostom, too, focuses on the worldly thrust of Demetrius's concerns, but he, unlike Bede, notes how the silversmith's words are an unwitting witness to Paul's truthfulness and his imitation of Christ. Ammonius concludes that Demetrius is afraid that his deception would be exposed through Paul's teaching.

19:24 Demetrius, a Silversmith

A SILVERSMITH NAMED DEMETRIUS. BEDE: This Demetrius, who strove to make trouble for the way of the Lord, acted in accord with his own name, for it means "persecuting greatly."[1] Hence it is appropriate that the shrines of Diana that he made were constructed of no other metal than silver, for in the Scriptures eloquence is customarily indicated by silver,[2] just as true knowledge is indicated by gold, and the craftiness of the Gentiles customarily constructed its religion not out of any consideration of meaning but out of the empty brilliance of discourse.[3] COMMENTARY ON THE ACTS OF THE APOSTLES 19.24.[4]

19:25 Wealth from the Making of Shrines

---

[1]Jerome *On Hebrew Names* (CCL 72:145). [2]Ps 12:6 (11:7 LXX, Vg).
[3]Arator *De Actibus Apostolorum* 2 (CSEL 72:118-19). [4]CS 117:156-57.

MONEY IS ALWAYS BEHIND IDOLATRY. CHRYSOSTOM: Notice how in every case idolatry arises from money. With those people it was because of money, and likewise here. They did not fear that their religion was in danger but that their skills might no longer have a market. And look at the man's evil. He was well-off and to him this would have been no great loss. But to them it would have been a great loss, since they were poor and subsisted on their daily earnings. Nevertheless, it was not these men who said anything, but he. HOMILIES ON THE ACTS OF THE APOSTLES 42.[5]

19:26 A Large Number of People

DEMETRIUS BEARS WITNESS TO PAUL. CHRYSOSTOM: Do you see how he demonstrated that Paul's power was the greater and revealed all their gods to be miserable wretches, since a mere human, persecuted and only a tentmaker, had so much power? See how the enemies bore witness to the apostles. Earlier they said, "You have filled Jerusalem with your teaching."[6] Here, "Artemis may be deposed from her magnificence." Earlier, the men "who had turned the world upside down" heard, "They have come here also."[7] Here, "There is danger that this trade of ours may come into disrepute." So said the Jews with regard to Christ, "You see how the world is going after him,"[8] and, "The Romans shall come and take away our city."[9] HOMILIES ON THE ACTS OF THE APOSTLES 42.[10]

19:27 Artemis Deposed from Her Magnificence

THEIR RELIGION IS RIGHTLY THREATENED. BEDE: That is: Not only will our work be discredited as vain and not deserving of payment but indeed our religion too will be brought into disgrace, if Paul prevails with his teaching that idols are not gods and that it is an extraordinary stupidity on the part of the Gentiles not to be ashamed to worship those whom they acknowledge can be constructed or destroyed. COMMENTARY ON THE ACTS OF THE APOSTLES 19.27.[11]

DEMETRIUS KNEW BETTER. AMMONIUS: Demetrius knew that he was deceiving people by making temples and gods of silver for them. So he was afraid that his roguery and deception would be exposed through Paul's true teaching. It must be noted that the true faith shined forth to such an extent, even though it had not yet conquered the world, that Demetrius was afraid that ultimately the temple of Artemis in Ephesus would be destroyed. He thus prophesied the temple's destruction, which has come to pass. CATENA ON THE ACTS OF THE APOSTLES 19.25.[12]

---

[5]NPNF 1 11:258**. [6]Acts 5:28. [7]Acts 17:6. [8]Jn 12:19. [9]Jn 11:48. [10]NPNF 1 11:258**. [11]CS 117:157. [12]CGPNT 3:321.

19:30-41 QUELLING THE RIOT

[30]Paul wished to go in among the crowd, but the disciples would not let him; [31]some of the Asiarchs also, who were friends of his, sent to him and begged him not to venture into the theater. [32]Now some cried one thing, some another; for the assembly was in confusion, and most of them did not know why they had come together. [33]Some of the crowd prompted Alexander, whom the Jews had put forward. And Alexander motioned with his hand, wishing to make a defense to the people.

³⁴*But when they recognized that he was a Jew, for about two hours they all with one voice cried out, "Great is Artemis of the Ephesians!"* ³⁵*And when the town clerk had quieted the crowd, he said, "Men of Ephesus, what man is there who does not know that the city of the Ephesians is temple keeper of the great Artemis, and of the sacred stone that fell from the sky?*ˢ ³⁶*Seeing then that these things cannot be contradicted, you ought to be quiet and do nothing rash.* ³⁷*For you have brought these men here who are neither sacrilegious nor blasphemers of our goddess.* ³⁸*If therefore Demetrius and the craftsmen with him have a complaint against any one, the courts are open, and there are proconsuls; let them bring charges against one another.* ³⁹*But if you seek anything further,*ᵗ *it shall be settled in the regular assembly.* ⁴⁰*For we are in danger of being charged with rioting today, there being no cause that we can give to justify this commotion."* ⁴¹*And when he had said this, he dismissed the assembly.*

s The meaning of the Greek is uncertain   t Other ancient authorities read *about other matters*

OVERVIEW: Alexander the Jew and Paul, the Jew who is a Christian, might reasonably be expected to oppose idolatry. Neither ancients nor moderns attempt to explain how the Asiarchs became friends of Paul or why the city clerk can declare that Paul and his companions "are neither sacrilegious nor blasphemers of our goddess." It is interesting to observe that by this speech the Way is given *droits de cité* in a city of the empire. The Fathers do not comment much on this incident, with the exception of three different texts of Chrysostom that draw different moral lessons from Luke's narrative: The faithful act with restraint. Do nothing without orderly consideration. Do not make religion a pretext for greed.

19:31 Believers Beg Paul Not to Go into the Theater

THE FAITHFUL SOUGHT RESTRAINT. CHRYSOSTOM: "They urged him not to hand himself over" to the disorderly mob and the violence in the theatre, and Paul was persuaded, since he was neither vainglorious nor ostentatious.... Knowing his eagerness, they begged him, since all these faithful loved him so much. CATENA ON THE ACTS OF THE APOSTLES 19.30-31.[1]

19:32 The Crowd in Confusion

ONE OUGHT DO NOTHING WITHOUT STRICT EXAMINATION. CHRYSOSTOM: Such is the way with the vulgar, to jump to conclusions and become enraged on any pretext. That is why one must do everything after careful consideration. But see how contemptible they are, how exposed to all excitements.... "Some cried one thing, some another; for the assembly was in confusion." For such is the behavior of a crowd. It simply follows, as when fire alights on wood. "And most of them did not know why they had come together." HOMILIES ON THE ACTS OF THE APOSTLES 42.[2]

19:35 The Temple Keeper of Artemis

THEIR RELIGION A PRETEXT FOR GREED. CHRYSOSTOM: Rightly does the grammarian say, "Who is ignorant of the city of the Ephesians?"... He does not say "Who does not know Artemis?" but "Who does not know your city?" which is what they were worshiping: ... they were trying to make their faith a pretext for making money. CATENA ON THE ACTS OF THE APOSTLES 19.35.[3]

¹CGPNT 3:323. ²NPNF 1 11:258-59**. ³CGPNT 3:325.

20:1-6 PAUL TRAVELS TO TROAS

¹*After the uproar ceased, Paul sent for the disciples and having exhorted them took leave of them and departed for Macedonia. ²When he had gone through these parts and had given them much encouragement, he came to Greece. ³There he spent three months, and when a plot was made against him by the Jews as he was about to set sail for Syria, he determined to return through Macedonia. ⁴Sopater of Beroea, the son of Pyrrhus, accompanied him; and of the Thessalonians, Aristarchus and Secundus; and Gaius of Derbe, and Timothy; and the Asians, Tychicus and Trophimus. ⁵These went on and were waiting for us at Troas, ⁶but we sailed away from Philippi after the days of Unleavened Bread, and in five days we came to them at Troas, where we stayed for seven days.*

OVERVIEW: Modern commentators frequently make note that in Acts 20:5 we find once again a "we section," which picks up in Philippi, where the first such section ended (Acts 16:17). Many of them also hold that it was during these three winter months of 57 to 58 in Corinth that Paul wrote his letter to the Romans. Some of them also point out that with the decision reached to go to Jerusalem (Acts 19:21) there is a successive rhythm to the journey of travel and discourse and that the travel descriptions are the most detailed to date in Acts. The Fathers do not attach much importance to these verses and have little to say about them.

20:7-12 EUTYCHUS IS RAISED FROM THE DEAD

⁷*On the first day of the week, when we were gathered together to break bread, Paul talked with them, intending to depart on the morrow; and he prolonged his speech until midnight. ⁸There were many lights in the upper chamber where we were gathered. ⁹And a young man named Eutychus was sitting in the window. He sank into a deep sleep as Paul talked still longer; and being overcome by sleep, he fell down from the third story and was taken up dead. ¹⁰But Paul went down and bent over him, and embracing him said, "Do not be alarmed, for his life is in him." ¹¹And when Paul had gone up and had broken bread and eaten, he conversed with them a long while, until daybreak, and so departed. ¹²And they took the lad away alive, and were not a little comforted.*

OVERVIEW: Let this commentary by Joseph Fitzmyer serve as an example of a good close modern reading of the text: "This Lucan story about Paul parallels Peter's resurrection of Tabitha in 9:36-41. Eutychus (whose Greek name means 'lucky one') is aptly named by Luke who depicts him restored to 'life' in the context of a eucharistic 'breaking of the bread.' To be noted is that Luke depicts Paul celebrating the Eucharist, even though no mention is made of the distribution of the 'broken bread'...; he is thus the only individual Christian so depicted in the NT.... This Lucan episode depicts Paul celebrating the liturgy of the word and the breaking of bread on a Sunday, the Christian equivalent of keeping holy the Sabbath day. Such a celebration was the liturgical recollection of the Lord's resurrection, his triumph over death. So it becomes a fitting context for the event in which Paul resuscitates Eutychus."[1] Chrysostom notes the ironies of this memorable situation: Paul is leaving, but the hearers are unaware of it. The young man's life appears gone but is spared. In allegorizing the text, Bede urges plain language that does not put the hearer to sleep. Arator uses the occasion to condemn sloth. Bede compares the negligence of Eutychus with the weakness of Tabitha. Augustine understands the eucharistic context of the incident.

20:7 Gathered Together to Break Bread

A Memorable Gathering. Chrysostom: "When we were gathered together," it says, "to break bread." At the opportune time, when they showed they were hungry (and this not untimely), his speech began and was prolonged. So it was not primarily to hear his teaching that they came together but to break bread; however, once [Paul] began speaking, he prolonged the teaching. See how at Paul's table all partook. It seems to me that even while seated at the table he was speaking, thus teaching us to consider all the rest secondary. Picture to yourself, please, that house with the lights, with the crowd, with Paul in the middle, speaking, with even the windows occupied by many people, and to hear that trumpet, to behold that gracious countenance! ... But why did he speak at night? Because [Paul] was about to depart and never see them again. This he does not tell them, since they are too

weak, but he did tell the others. At the same time, the miracle that took place made them remember that evening forever. Great was the pleasure experienced by his audience; though interrupted, it was further extended. So the fall took place to the benefit of the teacher. Besides, all who were indifferent were about to be censured by that young man who underwent death to hear Paul. Homilies on the Acts of the Apostles 43.[2]

An Allegorical Reading of the Text. Bede: We can speak allegorically here, for the upper room is the loftiness of spiritual gifts; night is the obscurity of the Scriptures; the abundance of lamps is the explanation of the more enigmatic sayings;[3] the Lord's day is the remembrance of either the Lord's resurrection or our own. And [this passage serves] to warn the spiritual teacher that if he is ever attracted by the sweetness of the resurrection and the joys of the life to come, and he arouses his listeners to the heights of virtue, and if in a lengthy discussion he touches upon any enigmas of the Scriptures, he should very soon, for the sake of weak listeners, shed light on those same [enigmas] by the lamp of plain explanation, just as the apostle did. When he said, "Abraham had two sons, the one by a slave girl and the other by a free woman,"[4] he soon added by way of explanation, "These are the two covenants," and so forth.[5] Commentary on the Acts of the Apostles 20.7-8.[6]

20:9 Eutychus Sitting in the Window

The Fervor of Paul's Audience. Chrysostom: Observe, if you please, how crowded the audience was—for the disciples, it says, had gathered together, and what sort of miracle it was. For it was in the window, it says, that [Eutychus] sat, and this at the dead of night. So great was his desire to listen! Let us be ashamed, we who

[1]Fitzmyer, *Acts*, 67-68. [2]NPNF 1 11:265**. [3]Arator *De Actibus Apostolorum* 2 (CSEL 72:120). [4]Gal 4:22. [5]Gal 4:24. [6]CS 117:159-60.

would not do this even during the day. But it was Paul who spoke then, you say. What do you mean? Paul speaks now as well, or rather, it was not Paul either then or now, but Christ, and no one listens. There is no window now, and neither hunger nor sleep troubles us, and still we do not listen. No crowding in a tight place or any other similar discomforts. And the wonderful thing is this: though a young man, he was not indifferent, and though he was being overtaken by sleep, he did not leave, nor was he afraid of the danger of falling. Do not be amazed that [Eutychus] nodded off and fell. For it was not out of indifference that he fell asleep but from necessity of nature. But notice, if you please, that so fervent was their zeal that they were even on the third floor. For not yet did they have a church. HOMILIES ON THE ACTS OF THE APOSTLES 43.[7]

EUTYCHUS. BEDE: In Hebrew "Eutychus means senseless, while in Greek it means fortunate."[8] One of these [meanings] fits a person who, through the pleasures of youth, has fallen from the peak of virtues. The other fits a person who, through the loving help of a preacher, has returned to the heights of virtue. COMMENTARY ON THE ACTS OF THE APOSTLES 20.9A.[9]

EUTYCHUS'S SLOTHFULNESS. ARATOR: Eutychus, alone, banished from the wakeful ones keeping watch, entrusted to a window with limbs sunk in heavy sleep. O rest wrongly won! O hearts always given over to sleep, unprotected by good! How great the disasters he lies open to, whom night alone guards and who never raises his troubled head to better things! He who allows [himself] to fall asleep from God does not know how to be wakeful for danger. Why do you seek the empty chaos of the window, young man, or why are you restful in that place where you will come to disaster? It is a matter harmful for well-being to seek high, hanging [places] and to wish to snatch furtive dreams on a steep couch. ON THE ACTS OF THE APOSTLES 2.[10]

20:10 His Life Is in Him

THE TWO WHO WERE RAISED FROM THE DEAD. BEDE: Then [Paul] goes down, lies down on him and embraces him; this is what he [Paul] himself said, "My little children, again I am in labor with you until Christ is formed in you."[11] It is harder to revive those who sin through negligence than it is to revive those who do so through weakness. The former is represented by Eutychus, the latter by Tabitha, whom Peter restored to life.[12] She fell ill and died in the daytime; he fell and died at midnight. After her death she was washed and placed in an upper room; he dropped from the third story and was mourned as dead below. In the latter case the teacher [Paul] was present and teaching; in the earlier case the teacher [Peter] was absent. Paul went down to him; Peter went up to restore life to her. She sat up as soon as she saw Peter; [Eutychus] died at midnight, and finally in the morning he rose again, and, revived by the inspiring son of righteousness, was led away. COMMENTARY ON THE ACTS OF THE APOSTLES 20.10.[13]

20:11 Paul Conversed a Long Time

CELEBRATING THE EUCHARIST ON THE LORD'S DAY. AUGUSTINE: Far be it from us to accept this as affirming that the apostles were accustomed to fast habitually on the Lord's day. For the day now known as the Lord's day was then called the first day of the week, as is more plainly seen in the Gospels; for the day of the Lord's resurrection is called by Matthew "first day of the week"[14] and by the other three Evangelists "the first day of the week,"[15] and it is well ascertained that the same is the day which is now called the Lord's day. Either, therefore, it was after the close of the seventh day that they had assembled—namely, in the beginning of the night

---

[7]NPNF 1 11:264**. [8]Jerome On Hebrew Names (CSEL 72:145). [9]CS 117:160. [10]OAA 81. [11]Gal 4:19. [12]Acts 9:36-42. [13]CS 117:160-61. [14]Mt 28:1. [15]Mk 16:2; Lk 24:1; Jn 20:1.

that followed and that belonged to the Lord's day or the first day of the week—and in this case the apostle, before proceeding to break bread with them, as is done in the sacrament of the body of Christ, continued his discourse until midnight, and also, after celebrating the sacrament, continued still speaking again to those who were assembled, being much pressed for time in order that he might set out at dawn upon the Lord's day. Or if it was on the first day of the week, at an hour before sunset on the Lord's day, that they had assembled, the words of the text, "Paul preached to them, ready to depart the next day," themselves expressly state the reason for his prolonging his discourse—namely, that he was about to leave them and wished to give them ample instruction.

The passage does not therefore prove that they habitually fasted on the Lord's day but only that it did not seem proper to the apostle to interrupt, for the sake of taking refreshment, an important discourse that was listened to with the ardor of most lively interest by persons whom he was about to leave, and whom, on account of his many other journeys, he visited but seldom, and perhaps on no other occasion than this, especially because, as subsequent events prove, he was then leaving them without expectation of seeing them again in this life. LETTER 36.12.28.[16]

---

[16]NPNF 1 1:268-69*.

20:13-16 PAUL HASTENS TOWARD JERUSALEM

[13]*But going ahead to the ship, we set sail for Assos, intending to take Paul aboard there; for so he had arranged, intending himself to go by land.* [14]*And when he met us at Assos, we took him on board and came to Mitylene.* [15]*And sailing from there we came the following day opposite Chios; the next day we touched at Samos; and*[u] *the day after that we came to Miletus.* [16]*For Paul had decided to sail past Ephesus, so that he might not have to spend time in Asia; for he was hastening to be at Jerusalem, if possible, on the day of Pentecost.*

u Other ancient authorities add *after remaining at Trogyllium*

OVERVIEW: This section has not elicited much comment from either modern or ancient interpreters. Some of the moderns think that another reason for passing by Ephesus may have been Paul's memory of the recent silversmiths' riot. Others point to the resemblance that Luke seems to establish between Jesus' determined journey to Jerusalem (Lk 9:51; 13:22; 17:11) and that of Paul. The earlier commentators speak of Luke as a devoted and observant companion of Paul (IRE-NAEUS), of Paul, the saint, as sharing our human nature and limitations (CHRYSOSTOM), and that Paul did not want to delay appearing in Jerusalem at the feast of Pentecost (BEDE).

20:13 Intending to Board a Ship

LUKE AS ACCURATE REPORTER OF PAUL. IRE-NAEUS: That this Luke was inseparable from Paul and his fellow laborer in the gospel, he himself clearly evinces, not as a matter of boasting but as bound to do so by the truth itself. For he says that when Barnabas, and John who was called Mark, had parted company from Paul and sailed to Cyprus, "we came to Troas";[1] and when Paul had beheld in a dream a man of Macedonia, saying, "Come into Macedonia, Paul, and help us," "immediately," he says, "we endeavored to go into Macedonia, understanding that the Lord had called us to preach the gospel to them. Therefore, sailing from Troas, we directed our ship's course towards Samothracia." And then he carefully indicates all the rest of their journey as far as Philippi, and how they delivered their first address, "for, sitting down," he says, "we spoke to the women who had assembled,"[2] and certain ones believed, even a great many. Again [Luke] says, "But we sailed from Philippi after the days of unleavened bread and came to Troas, where we stayed for seven days."[3] And all the remaining details of his course with Paul he recounts, indicating with all diligence both places and cities and number of days, until they went up to Jerusalem; and what happened to Paul there, how he was sent to Rome in bonds; the name of the centurion who took him in charge; and the signs of the ships, and how they made shipwreck; and the island on which they escaped, and how they received kindness there, Paul healing the chief man of that island; and how they sailed from there to Puteoli, and from there arrived at Rome; and for what period they sojourned at Rome.[4] As Luke was present at all these occurrences, he carefully noted them down in writing, so that he cannot be convicted of falsehood or boastfulness, because all these particulars proved both that he was senior to all those who now teach otherwise and that he was not ignorant of the truth. AGAINST HERESIES 3.14.1.[5]

20:16 Hastening to Jerusalem

SAINTS SHARE IN THE SAME NATURE AS WE DO. CHRYSOSTOM: "For he was hastening," it says, "to be at Jerusalem, if possible, on the day of Pentecost." So it was for this reason that [Paul] could not stay. Look at him moved like other people, desiring, hastening and often not obtaining his object. These things take place to prevent us from thinking that he was above human nature. For those great and holy men partake of the same nature as we do, but not of the same will. This is why they attract great grace to themselves. See how many things they dispense on their own. For this reason he said, "So that we put no obstacle in the way of the willing," and again, "so that no fault may be found with our ministry."[6] Look, both an irreproachable life and much condescension. This is called planning, to arrive at the summit of both sublime virtue and humble condescension. And hear how he, who went beyond the commandments of Christ, was in turn the humblest of all, "I am made all things to all people," he says, "that I might gain all."[7] HOMILIES ON THE ACTS OF THE APOSTLES 43.[8]

HURRYING TO BE IN JERUSALEM. BEDE: There was a certain commandment of the law that all Jews should gather in Jerusalem three times a year—that is, at the times of Passover, Pentecost and the Feast of Tabernacles. The apostle, however, since he had broken the ties to his people, was hurrying to celebrate the fiftieth day, that is, the day of pardon and of the Holy Spirit. COMMENTARY ON THE ACTS OF THE APOSTLES 20.16.[9]

---

[1]Acts 16:8. [2]Acts 16:13. [3]Acts 20:6. [4]Acts 27—28. [5]ANF 1:437*. [6]2 Cor 6:3. [7]1 Cor 9:22. [8]NPNF 1 11:265**. [9]CS 117:161.

20:17-24 PAUL SPEAKS TO THE ELDERS OF EPHESUS

[17]*And from Miletus he sent to Ephesus and called to him the elders of the church.* [18]*And when they came to him, he said to them:*

"You yourselves know how I lived among you all the time from the first day that I set foot in Asia, [19]*serving the Lord with all humility and with tears and with trials which befell me through the plots of the Jews;* [20]*how I did not shrink from declaring to you anything that was profitable, and teaching you in public and from house to house,* [21]*testifying both to Jews and to Greeks of repentance to God and of faith in our Lord Jesus Christ.* [22]*And now, behold, I am going to Jerusalem, bound in the Spirit, not knowing what shall befall me there;* [23]*except that the Holy Spirit testifies to me in every city that imprisonment and afflictions await me.* [24]*But I do not account my life of any value nor as precious to myself, if only I may accomplish my course and the ministry which I received from the Lord Jesus, to testify to the gospel of the grace of God.*

OVERVIEW: The modern commentators point to this third important Pauline speech as the only one addressed to Christians and as containing more Pauline vocabulary than any other speech. As Paul's last will and testament, a speech that belongs to a well-known genre known as farewell speeches, Luke intends this speech to be the way in which people should remember Paul. It is also another example of Luke's artistry. The speech to the Areopagus (Acts 17) fits with the sophisticated philosophical audience of Athens, while this speech clearly echoes Paul's letters to Christians. In the patristic selections given here we see the Fathers analyze and praise the speech (IRENAEUS, CHRYSOSTOM), speak of Paul's generous ministry and courage (CHRYSOSTOM) and remark on the prophecies that have been made in his regard (BEDE). The disposition of Paul is that of one bound in the Spirit and ready to suffer freely as a captive of Christ whose Spirit he has (DIDYMUS) and not under compulsion (CHRYSOSTOM). Unknown challenges await (AMMONIUS) as Paul, the former persecutor, contends for the peace of the church, aware that his temporal life is not to be valued more highly than his eternal life (BEDE).

20:17 The Elders of the Church in Ephesus

DIRECT AND HONEST SPEECH. IRENAEUS: That Paul taught with simplicity what he knew, not only to those who were with him but those that heard him, he does himself make manifest. For when the bishops and presbyters who came from Ephesus and the other cities adjoining had assembled in Miletus, since he was himself hastening to Jerusalem to observe Pentecost, after testifying many things to them and declaring what must happen to him at Jerusalem, he added, "I know that all you among whom I have gone preaching the kingdom will see my face no more. Therefore I testify to you this day that I am innocent of the blood of all of you, for I did not shrink from declaring to you the whole counsel of God. Take heed to yourselves and to all the flock, in which the Holy Spirit has made you overseers, to care for the church of God that he obtained through his own blood."[1] Then, referring to the evil teachers who should arise, he said, "I know that after my departure shall grievous wolves come to you, not sparing the flock. Also of your own selves shall people arise, speaking perverse things, to draw away disciples after them."[2] "I have not shunned," he says, "to declare to you all

---

[1]Acts 20:25-28. [2]Acts 20:29-30.

the counsel of God."[3] Thus did the apostles simply, and without respect of persons, deliver to all what they themselves had learned from the Lord. Thus also does Luke, without respect of persons, deliver to us what he had learned from them, as he has himself testified, saying, "Even as they delivered them to us, who from the beginning were eyewitnesses and ministers of the Word."[4] AGAINST HERESIES 3.14.2.[5]

20:18 How I Lived Among You

PAUL SPEAKS OF HIMSELF ONLY WHEN NECESSARY. CHRYSOSTOM: Look, although [Paul] was in a hurry to sail past, he did not overlook them but planned everything. He sent for the leaders and broadcast his words through them. It is worthy of admiration how finding himself under compulsion to say something great about himself, he tries to make the least of it. For just as Samuel, about to hand over the rule to Saul, said in their presence, "Have I taken anything from you? You are witnesses and God also."[6] . . . Likewise Paul himself says to the Corinthians, "I have been a fool! You forced me."[7] Even God does this: he speaks of himself not for no reason but when he is disbelieved, and then he offers his benefits. Observe, then, what Paul does here. First he brings up their testimony, so that you should not think he is boasting, and calls the listeners themselves to be witnesses of his words, since he was not likely to lie in their presence. HOMILIES ON THE ACTS OF THE APOSTLES 44.[8]

20:20 Declaring What Was Profitable

THE CHARACTER OF GOOD TEACHING. CHRYSOSTOM: This is success for a teacher, to educate his disciples by his own accomplishments. . . . Notice, if you please, the character of the teaching here. He lays down love and bravery. "I kept back nothing," he says, thereby showing both generosity and resoluteness. "Of what was profitable." Well said! For there were things that they did not need to learn. For just as it is envy not to say

some things, so it is folly to say everything. For this reason he adds, "of what was profitable," that is, "I not only spoke but also taught." He means he was not doing this merely for form's sake. What follows shows that this is what [Paul] means, for he adds, "in public and from house to house." This shows his long toil, great earnestness and endurance. HOMILIES ON THE ACTS OF THE APOSTLES 44.[9]

20:22 Not Knowing What Will Happen

A SLAVE OF CHRIST. DIDYMUS THE BLIND: The one who has been united to the Holy Spirit has been bound in him so that he does not separate from the Spirit in any way. The person of such a disposition is a captive of Christ whose Spirit he has. For if whoever does not have the Spirit of Christ is not of Christ,[10] who has the Spirit, it is clear that whoever has Christ is in the Spirit. Whoever is bound and decorated with these chains begets, by both the gospel's and his own chains, those he teaches. . . . This verse must be read in respect to the following, which says that the apostle is ready to be clothed with chains because of his beliefs. When it is said to him that he must not go up to Jerusalem, since there he will certainly be covered with chains and afflictions, he says that he is bound in the Spirit now to make his way to Jerusalem in full knowledge of what would befall him there. His words, "Daily I die,"[11] are a manifestation of this determination of his, as are his words, "Ever are we, while living, handed over to death because of Christ Jesus."[12] To this you can add the words of the psalmist, "I am ready to be scourged."[13] CATENA ON THE ACTS OF THE APOSTLES 20.22.[14]

20:23 Imprisonment and Afflictions

---

[3]Acts 20:27. [4]Lk 1:2. [5]ANF 1:438**. [6]1 Sam 12:3, 5. [7]2 Cor 12:11. [8]NPNF 1 11:267**. [9]NPNF 1 11:268**. [10]Rom 8:9. [11]1 Cor 15:31. [12]2 Cor 4:11. [13]Ps 38:17 (37:18 LXX). The MT reads "I am about to fall." [14]CGPNT 3:333.

PAUL TEACHES THEM BOLDNESS AND OBEDI-ENCE. CHRYSOSTOM: Why do you say this? Why do you mention this? What has happened? Have you nothing to accuse them of? He first alarms them, then adds, "And now, behold, I am going to Jerusalem, bound in the Spirit, not knowing what shall befall me there; except that the Holy Spirit testifies to me in every city that imprisonment and afflictions await me. But I do not account my life of any value or as precious to myself, if only I may accomplish my course and the ministry that I received from the Lord Jesus, to testify to the gospel of the grace of God." Why does [Paul] say this? He is preparing them to be always ready for dangers both seen and unseen and to obey the Spirit in everything. He shows that he is led away for great things. "Except that the Holy Spirit testifies to me in every city." He shows that he is led away willingly, and[15] so that you should not imagine him forced by compulsion or necessity, he says, "in every city." Then he adds, "I do not account my life as precious to myself, if only I may accomplish my course and the ministry that I received from the Lord Jesus." Do you see that these are not the words of one lamenting but of one who is in control, teaching and sympathizing with them in what has happened? He did not say, "We grieve, but it is necessary to bear it," but "I do not account...." He repeats this, not to extol himself but to teach them, through the earlier words, humility, and through these, bravery and boldness. HOMILIES ON THE ACTS OF THE APOSTLES 44.[16]

EXCEPT THAT IN ALL THE CITIES THE HOLY SPIRIT ASSURES ME. BEDE: When [Paul] says "in the cities," he clearly shows that the things that were going to happen to him had not been revealed to him directly but to others concerning him. Among them were the prophet Agabus,[17] and also those disciples who, when he was staying in Tyre, admonished him "through the Spirit not to go up to Jerusalem."[18] COMMENTARY ON THE ACTS OF THE APOSTLES 20.23A.[19]

CONTENDING FOR THE PEACE OF THE

CHURCH. BEDE: So that he might now contend for the peace of the church in the place where he once persecuted the church.[20] COMMENTARY ON THE ACTS OF THE APOSTLES 20.23B.[21]

UNKNOWN CHALLENGES AWAIT. AMMONIUS: It must be noted that the prophets do not know everything but only what the Holy Spirit reveals to them. So see how Paul, like a prophet, foretells "that chains and afflictions await me," and that the Ephesians will never see him again[22] and that there will arise among them heretics and some of bad faith, and yet about the first of these he confesses not to know what exactly their end shall be.[23] So although the Lord revealed to him everything else, this one thing he hid from him, namely, what would happen to him after the chains and afflictions, lest, being puffed up and knowing that everything would arrive at such a point, [Paul] fail out of negligence. Instead, so that he, dreading the weakness of the flesh, would beg God to deliver him from trials,[24] the Spirit left this end unclear for him. CATENA ON THE ACTS OF THE APOSTLES 20.22.[25]

20:24 Paul's Ministry

DIFFICULTIES ENDURED FOR THE LORD. CHRYSOSTOM: Do not think that I am lamenting as I say this. "I do not consider my life so precious." He says this to elevate their mind and to persuade them not only not to flee but to bear it nobly. For this reason he calls it "course" and "ministry": "course," or "race," because of the glory; "ministry," because of the obligation. I am a minister, he says; I have nothing more. HOMILIES ON THE ACTS OF THE APOSTLES 44.[26]

I DO NOT VALUE MY LIFE AS MORE PRECIOUS THAN MYSELF. BEDE: By life, he means

---

[15]Cf. NPNF 1 11:273. [16]NPNF 1 11:268-69**. [17]Acts 21:11. [18]Acts 21:4. [19]CS 117:161-62. [20]Acts 9:21. [21]CS 117:162. [22]Acts 20:25. [23]See Acts 20:22. [24]See Mt 6:13. [25]CGPNT 3:332-33. [26]NPNF 1 11:270**.

that temporal life in the body that he reckoned as least in value, since he looked forward to eternal joy in another life. COMMENTARY ON THE ACTS OF THE APOSTLES 20.24.[27]

[27]CS 117:162.

20:25-38 PAUL BIDS FAREWELL TO THE EPHESIANS

[25]And now, behold, I know that all you among whom I have gone preaching the kingdom will see my face no more. [26]Therefore I testify to you this day that I am innocent of the blood of all of you, [27]for I did not shrink from declaring to you the whole counsel of God. [28]Take heed to yourselves and to all the flock, in which the Holy Spirit has made you overseers, to care for the church of God[v] which he obtained with the blood of his own Son.[w] [29]I know that after my departure fierce wolves will come in among you, not sparing the flock; [30]and from among your own selves will arise men speaking perverse things, to draw away the disciples after them. [31]Therefore be alert, remembering that for three years I did not cease night or day to admonish every one with tears. [32]And now I commend you to God and to the word of his grace, which is able to build you up and to give you the inheritance among all those who are sanctified. [33]I coveted no one's silver or gold or apparel. [34]You yourselves know that these hands ministered to my necessities, and to those who were with me. [35]In all things I have shown you that by so toiling one must help the weak, remembering the words of the Lord Jesus, how he said, 'It is more blessed to give than to receive.'"

[36]And when he had spoken thus, he knelt down and prayed with them all. [37]And they all wept and embraced Paul and kissed him, [38]sorrowing most of all because of the word he had spoken, that they should see his face no more. And they brought him to the ship.

v Other ancient authorities read of the Lord   w Greek with the blood of his Own or with his own blood

OVERVIEW: Both moderns and ancients see in Paul's description of his missionary activity an ideal for leaders in the church. Most intriguing to the moderns is the expression in Acts 20:28, translated above, "to care for the church of God that he obtained with the blood of his own Son." The word *church* here must refer to a single group, to the worldwide company of the redeemed. Paul did not hesitate to say "the blood of God," because of the oneness of person in two natures of the same Jesus Christ (BEDE). The false teacher is guilty of the souls that receive his teaching, as if he had poured out their blood, which is their life (AMMONIUS). The Fathers, nearly all of whom were preachers, warmed to this section. Chrysostom analyzes and admires the progression in the speech, and he, along with Gregory, speaks of the need for the bishop or preacher to speak the truth and thus be innocent of the blood of the people. Paul's self-description is seen as an example of care for his people (CHRYSOSTOM), of attention to his own salvation (DIDYMUS, CASSIAN, BEDE) and of poverty and detachment (BEDE, JEROME, CHRYSOSTOM, AUGUSTINE). The teacher does no harm

(DIDYMUS, AMMONIUS, GREGORY). The church must be protected against the wolves of false teaching (DIDYMUS, ORIGEN, CHRYSOSTOM). Arator allegorizes the metaphor of Paul's teaching "night and day." When Paul is most torn between contemplation and service (CASSIAN) he finds that the level of grace rises to meet the level of temptation (CHRYSOSTOM). More will come from less (JEROME). Readiness to abandon earthly goods is characteristic of the Christian teacher (BEDE).

20:26 *Innocent of Your Blood*

HE WHO DOES NOT SPEAK HAS BLOOD TO ANSWER FOR. CHRYSOSTOM: [Paul] is about to say something more burdensome, that is, "I am innocent of the blood of all of you." With this he prepares them and shows that nothing is lacking. Since he was about to place upon them the entire burden with all its weight, he first appeases their feelings by saying, "And now, behold, I know that you will see my face no more." He then adds, "I am innocent of the blood of all of you." The pain is twofold: one, to see his face no more; two, that this applies to all of them. For he says, "All you among whom I have gone preaching the kingdom will see my face no more." Therefore it is natural that "I testify to you," since I will no longer be here, "that I am innocent of the blood of all of you, for I did not shrink from declaring to you the whole counsel of God." Do you see how he frightens them and crushes their souls, troubled and afflicted as they are? But this was necessary. "For I did not shrink," he says, "from declaring to you the whole counsel of God." So it is he who does not speak who is responsible for the blood, that is, for the murder. Nothing could be more terrifying than this. He shows that they too, if they do not act, are responsible for the blood. So although he seems to be justifying his own actions, he is, in fact, putting fear into them. HOMILIES ON THE ACTS OF THE APOSTLES 44.[1]

INNOCENT BECAUSE HE SPOKE HONESTLY.

GREGORY THE GREAT (quoted by BEDE): "Paul believed that he was innocent of the blood of his neighbor, inasmuch as he did not spare their vices, which demanded to be castigated."[2] COMMENTARY ON THE ACTS OF THE APOSTLES 20.26.[3]

PAUL'S INNOCENCE. AMMONIUS: "I am clean of the blood of all." . . . The false teacher is guilty of the souls that receive his teaching, as if he had poured out their blood, which is our life.[4] By saying "I am clean," he means, "I give witness that my teaching has deprived none of life everlasting but that it sets forth a heavenly kingdom. Anyone, therefore, not persuaded by me should consider himself as his own murderer, for I am innocent of the blood of all who hear me and do not believe." CATENA ON THE ACTS OF THE APOSTLES 20.26.[5]

20:27 *Declaring All of God's Counsel*

THE WHOLE COUNSEL. DIDYMUS THE BLIND: If a teacher, in educating those who are able to profit, harms none of these students, even in this does he imitate Paul. He will say that he is clean of the blood of all his students, meaning that by his teaching he has not slaughtered any through error, as if he had poured out the vital force of his soul, which is allegorically called blood. In addition to this he declares openly that he has set out and announced to them the entire counsel of God. But understood simply the entire counsel of God is incomprehensible to creatures, "for who knows the mind of the Lord?"[6] So we must find out what meaning this passage bears. Now, since we have here the phrase "I announced to you," it means something different, namely, that [Paul] calls that "entire counsel" what it was possible for humans to say and hear. This interpretation is in agreement with his sentiment that "we know in part," and this very knowledge is, in relation to

---

[1]NPNF 1 11:269**. [2]Gregory the Great *Pastoral Care* 3.25 (PL 77:96). [3]CS 117:162. [4]See Lev 17:11-14; Deut 12:23. [5]CGPNT 3:335. [6]Rom 11:34; 1 Cor 2:16.

the coming age, partial in itself, be it of any sort and of the greatest fullness. It is possible that "the entire counsel of God" means the plan concerning the giving of the law and the prophets and the gospel. CATENA ON THE ACTS OF THE APOSTLES 20.26.[7]

20:28 Heeding Yourselves and the Church

CARE FOR SELF AND FLOCK. CHRYSOSTOM: "Take heed to yourselves and to all the flock, in which the Holy Spirit has made you overseers, to care for the church of God that he obtained with his own blood." Do you see how [Paul] gives two orders here? Success with others alone does not bring any benefit—for I fear, he says, "lest after preaching to others I myself should be disqualified."[8] Equally, caring only for oneself brings no benefit. For such a one is selfish and seeks only his own good, like the man who has buried his gold. He says this not because our own salvation is more precious than that of the flock but because when we attend to ourselves, the flock also benefits. HOMILIES ON THE ACTS OF THE APOSTLES 44.[9]

BISHOPS AND PRESBYTERS. BEDE: He had said previously that the presbyters of Ephesus had been summoned to Miletus. Now he calls them bishops, that is, overseers. One city could not have several bishops, but under the name bishops [Paul] indicates these presbyters as being in fact priests, for the order was connected, and in many it was practically the same. COMMENTARY ON THE ACTS OF THE APOSTLES 20.28A.[10]

THE CHURCH IS PRECIOUS TO THE LORD. CHRYSOSTOM: Do you see how many compelling necessities there are? "You were ordained by the Spirit," he says, for this is what "the Holy Spirit has made you overseers" means. This is one. Then, "to care for the church of God." This is another. And the third, "which he obtained with his own blood." Through his words [Paul] shows that a great deal hinges on this and that matters

of no small value are at risk, if, with the master not sparing even his own blood on behalf of his church, we look down upon our brothers' salvation. For it was to reconcile enemies that he poured out his blood. . . . Look, not only does he mention "wolves" but adds "fierce," thereby hinting at their excess and recklessness. Even worse, he says that these wolves will arise from among themselves. This is exceedingly difficult to bear, since it is also a civil war. He is right when he says, "Take heed . . . ," thereby showing that the matter is exceedingly serious (for it is the church), the venture great (for he redeemed it with blood) and the battle mighty and twofold. HOMILIES ON THE ACTS OF THE APOSTLES 44.[11]

THE BLOOD OF GOD. BEDE: He did not hesitate to say "the blood of God," because of the oneness of person in two natures of the same Jesus Christ. On account of this it has also been said, "the Son of man, who is in heaven."[12] Therefore let Nestorius stop separating the Son of man from the Son of God and making for himself two Christs. COMMENTARY ON THE ACTS OF THE APOSTLES 20.28B.[13]

THE ROLE OF THE SHEPHERD. DIDYMUS THE BLIND: "Take care for yourselves and for the entire flock," and the following. Since it is not according to nature but according to an appropriation of the power that comes from the Spirit that a person is ordained to the episcopacy by the Holy Spirit for our sake, it is possible for one holding such a position to fall from it, without due care. For if someone were established as a shepherd of the church because of the state of his being, that person would hold whatever office without possibility of change. But it not only says that bishops must pay heed to themselves but also to the flock that the Savior acquired by his blood. And just as he will not fall if he is attentive to himself by taking care for both the requisite

---

[7]CGPNT 3:335-36. [8]1 Cor 9:27. [9]NPNF 1 11:269**. [10]CS 117:162. [11]NPNF 1 11:269-70**. [12]Jn 3:13. [13]CS 117:162.

virtues and his faith—that is, he will neither start speaking the perverse things of heresies nor follow selfish ambition by attempting to lure Christ's disciples away in order to imitate himself and follow him—so also he must take care for the flock by turning away from it the wolves who are falsely called apostles and who, being ravenous, live on the ruin of the flock. . . . Now he turns away these wolves, if he, established by the Holy Spirit to oversee the church, is a good shepherd. A hired man, not being a shepherd, flees when a wolf comes to scatter and kill the sheep. Furthermore, a hired man is no shepherd, since he takes charge of the community for profit and pay, and not come what may. So it is to be realized that the Holy Spirit establishes shepherds and bishops for the church just as God establishes in the church "first apostles,"[14] and the following. Catena on the Acts of the Apostles 20.28.[15]

20:29 Fierce Wolves

Stay Away from Contamination. Origen: If you touch "what is seized by a wild beast," you will be unclean.[16] Which wild beast? Is it a lion or a wolf that ravishes persons or animals? I believe that beast is the one about whom the apostle Peter says, "your adversary, the devil, goes around like a roaring lion seeking whom he can devour. Resist him, strong in the faith."[17] And again, the apostle Paul says concerning these, "For after my departure, fierce wolves will come in, not sparing the flock." If you see one made captive by these beasts, do not follow him, do not touch him, lest you also be made unclean. Furthermore, there are also other unclean animals whose carcass it is forbidden to touch.[18] Unclean animals are people who are without Christ, in whom there is neither reason nor anything religious. Therefore, if you see the "carcasses," that is, the sins of all these, the lawgiver tells you not to take hold, not to touch, not to handle. Homilies on Leviticus 3.3.5.[19]

20:30 Arising from Among You

The Character of Heretics. Ammonius: "In order to draw away the disciples after them." Heretics strive to make the people their own instead of the Lord's, so that they might boast in themselves, when the name of the heretics is attached to these people, and so that they can profit from the name. For example, from Mani comes Manichaean, from Arius, Arian, and from Nestorius, Nestorian, and the other types of heresies. Paul himself checked this beforehand when he silenced and censured those who were saying, "I'm Paul's; I'm Apollos's; I'm Cephas's,"[20] since he did not want their faith to be explained by the name of a person but by Christ's name; he wanted them all to be called Christians, even though they had been taught by different teachers. Accordingly, whenever all the teachers strive for the same goal of proclaiming the true faith, of profiting the students while suppressing their own names, they are called, by the same name, Christians. If, however, the teachers pervert any of the teachings of the church, then the title of Catholic is denied, and they are called after the name of the teacher. Catena on the Acts of the Apostles 20.29-30.[21]

20:31 Admonishing Everyone with Tears

He Would Have Done This for a Single Soul. Chrysostom: Notice how many strong expressions [Paul] uses, "with tears," "night and day" and "everyone." It is not that when he saw more than one, he refrained, but that he knew he did everything even for one soul. It was thus that he welded them together. Homilies on the Acts of the Apostles 44.[22]

An Allegory on Paul's Words. Arator: But because [Paul] said, "Night and day for three years I gave these teachings for your salvation," an allegory is revealed by this reckoning [of his]: he who utters three doctrines of the church rather

---

[14]1 Cor 12:28. [15]CGPNT 3:337-38. [16]See Lev 5:2. [17]1 Pet 5:8-9. [18]See Lev 5:2. [19]FC 83:58. [20]1 Cor 1:12. [21]CGPNT 3:339-40. [22]NPNF 1 11:270.

often brings forth the historical and allegorical Book, proclaiming [also] a moral [sense]. For thus the six pots reddened with the new liquid out of the old law took three measures apiece.[23] The ancient form of the perfect sacrifice commanded that one offer three loaves from the basket;[24] to these [mysteries] is added what Christ said to his disciples, that three loaves ought to be given to one asking when it was already night;[25] that night surely is the world, so that, if anyone here desires the food of the word, you should produce a banquet, you who are asked, and teach the willing one that the Father and the Son [and] the Holy Spirit are one God and that a single Substance trebles the number. ON THE ACTS OF THE APOSTLES 2.[26]

20:32 Commended to God

CONFIDENCE IN GRACE. CHRYSOSTOM: When [Paul] speaks in council, he follows what he does in writing an epistle. He begins with exhortation and ends with prayer. For since he has alarmed them greatly by saying, "Fierce wolves will come in among you," look at the consolation he gives so that they should not be panic-stricken and lose all hope. "And now," as always, "I commend you, brothers, to God and to the word of his grace." That is, to his grace. For it is grace that saves. He reminds them of grace constantly, making them more earnest because they are debtors and persuading them to be of good courage. "Which is able to build you up." He did not say "build" but "build up," thereby showing that they were already built. Then he reminds them of the hope to come, "to give you the inheritance among all those who are sanctified." HOMILIES ON THE ACTS OF THE APOSTLES 45.[27]

THE UNITY OF FATHER AND SON. AMMONIUS: He demonstrates obscurely and secretly that the Father, who is God, and his Son Jesus, the God-Word, are one. He does not speak in the plural "to those capable," but with a unifying name he indicates the singular being of both by saying "to

the one capable." Thus we know, from what Paul says in preparing the churches of Asia, that there is one being of both Father and Son and that they are and subsist as two, not according to mere names but in truth. CATENA ON THE ACTS OF THE APOSTLES 20.32.[28]

20:33 Coveting No One's Wealth

SELF-SUFFICIENCY REQUISITE FOR PREACHERS. ANONYMOUS: He establishes a law for teachers on how they ought to manage their possessions. For preachers of the gospel, a mark of the greatest and purest boldness is to be dependent on the earthly goods of none. CATENA ON THE ACTS OF THE APOSTLES 20.33.[29]

20:34 Ministering to His Own and Others' Necessities

A POVERTY BETTER EVEN THAN FOREGOING POSSESSIONS. CHRYSOSTOM: For indeed he has demonstrated boldness in the face of danger, sympathy with those over whom he ruled, teaching with boldness, humility and poverty. But this is even greater than poverty. For he says in the Gospel, "If you wish to be perfect, sell what you have."[30] But when, in addition to taking nothing, [Paul] also feeds others, what can equal this? The first step is to cast off one's own possessions; the second, to be sufficient for oneself; the third, to provide for others as well; the fourth, for him who is preaching and therefore has a right to take or not to take. Therefore, Paul is far better than those who have merely given up their possessions. HOMILIES ON THE ACTS OF THE APOSTLES 45.[31]

EAT TO PREACH OR PREACH TO EAT. AUGUSTINE: For neither ought we, for example, to preach the gospel with this object, that we may

---

[23]Jn 2:6. [24]See 1 Sam 10:3. [25]Lk 11:5. [26]OAA 84. [27]NPNF 1 11:272**. [28]CGPNT 3:340. [29]CGPNT 3:341. [30]Mt 19:21. [31]NPNF 1 11:274**.

eat; but to eat with this object, that we may preach the gospel: for if we preach the gospel for this cause, that we may eat, we reckon the gospel of less value than food; and in that case our good will be in eating, but that which is necessary for us is preaching the gospel. And this the apostle also forbids, when he says it is lawful for himself even, and permitted by the Lord, that they who preach the gospel should live of the gospel, that is, should have from the gospel the necessaries of this life; but yet that he has not made use of this power. SERMON ON THE MOUNT 2.16.54.[32]

TORN BETWEEN CONTEMPLATION AND SERVICE. JOHN CASSIAN: And although for this there were great rewards for his merits prepared, yet [Paul's] mind, however holy and sublime it might be, could not help being sometimes drawn away from that heavenly contemplation by its attention to earthly labors. Further, . . . he saw himself enriched with such practical fruits, and on the other hand considered in his heart the good of meditation and weighed as it were in one scale the profit of all these labors and in the other the delights of divine contemplation. For a long time he had corrected the balance in his breast, while the vast rewards for his labors delighted him on one side, and on the other the desire for unity with and the inseparable companionship of Christ inclined him to depart this life. At last in his perplexity [Paul] cries out and says, "What I shall choose I know not. For I am in a strait between two, having a desire to depart and to be with Christ, for it were much better: but to abide in the flesh is more necessary for your sakes."[33] Though then in many ways he preferred this excellent good to all the fruits of his preaching, yet he submits himself in consideration of love, without which none can gain the Lord; and for their sakes, whom hitherto he had soothed with milk as nourishment from the breasts of the gospel, does not refuse to be parted from Christ, which is bad for himself though useful for others. For he is driven to choose this the rather by that excessive goodness of his whereby for the salva-tion of his brothers he is ready, were it possible, to incur even the last evil of an anathema. CONFERENCE 23.5.4-6.[34]

THE GENEROSITY OF A LEADER OF THE CHURCH. DIDYMUS THE BLIND: These words are spoken to the leaders of the church so that, in addition to the other things, they might judge themselves imitators of Paul by refusing to accept money. This is quite obvious from the words that follow: "I have given you example in all things that those who toil must come to the help of the weak" and provide for them. If the words of the Lord should be remembered, they will provide the principle: "It is better to give than to receive." Let giving be preferred by bishops. CATENA ON THE ACTS OF THE APOSTLES 20.34.[35]

20:35 More Blessed to Give Than to Receive

THE WISDOM OF DETACHMENT. JEROME: Somehow or other the very one who begs leave to offer you a gift holds you the cheaper for your acceptance of it; while, if you refuse it, it is wonderful how much more he will come to respect you. LETTER 52.16.[36]

I HAVE SHOWN YOU ALL THINGS. BEDE: That is, not only that devotion to teaching is necessary amid oppression and tears, but also that manual labor is demanded so that none of the weak may be burdened.[37] This is, however, what was said: "And whatever you spend in addition I will repay you when I return,"[38] which means to preach the gospel and not to see one's support from the gospel.[39] COMMENTARY ON THE ACTS OF THE APOSTLES 20.35A.[40]

IT IS MORE BLESSED TO GIVE THAN TO RECEIVE. BEDE: He does not value the rich, even if they give alms, more highly than those who

---

[32]NPNF 1 6:51. [33]Phil 1:22-24. [34]ACW 57:795**. [35]CGPNT 3:341-42. [36]NPNF 2 6:96. [37]2 Thess 3:2-9. [38]Lk 10:35. [39]1 Cor 9:14-15. [40]CS 117:163.

have left all things and followed the Lord. Rather, he extols most highly those who have given up at once everything they had and who nevertheless labor, "working with their hands at what is good in order to have something to give to one who is suffering need."[41] COMMENTARY ON THE ACTS OF THE APOSTLES 20.35B.[42]

---

[41]Eph 4:28. [42]CS 117:163.

21:1-6 PAUL VISITS TYRE

[1]*And when we had parted from them and set sail, we came by a straight course to Cos, and the next day to Rhodes, and from there to Patara.*[x] [2]*And having found a ship crossing to Phoenicia, we went aboard, and set sail.* [3]*When we had come in sight of Cyprus, leaving it on the left we sailed to Syria, and landed at Tyre; for there the ship was to unload its cargo.* [4]*And having sought out the disciples, we stayed there for seven days. Through the Spirit they told Paul not to go on to Jerusalem.* [5]*And when our days there were ended, we departed and went on our journey; and they all, with wives and children, brought us on our way till we were outside the city; and kneeling down on the beach we prayed and bade one another farewell.* [6]*Then we went on board the ship, and they returned home.*

x Other ancient authorities add *and Myra*

OVERVIEW: There is little to comment upon in this short passage. Modern commentators point to the guidance of the Spirit and Paul's determination to go to Jerusalem. Bede finds it prefigured in Psalm 45.

21:5 Praying on the Beach

A PROPHECY FULFILLED. BEDE: That prophecy was fulfilled that says, proclaiming about the church, "The daughters of Tyre offer you gifts; all the wealthy among the people plead for your favor,"[1] and so forth, up to the end of the psalm. For no city received the apostle, kept him and sent him on his way with greater kindness than Tyre. Finally, today the place is pointed out where they prayed together on the shore. COMMENTARY ON THE ACTS OF THE APOSTLES 21.5.[2]

---

[1]Ps 45:12 (44:13 LXX, Vg). [2]CS 117:165.

21:7-16 AGABUS PROPHESIES
PAUL'S IMPRISONMENT

⁷When we had finished the voyage from Tyre, we arrived at Ptolemais; and we greeted the brothers and stayed with them for one day. ⁸On the morrow we departed and came to Caesarea; and we entered the house of Philip the evangelist, who was one of the seven, and stayed with him. ⁹And he had four unmarried daughters, who prophesied. ¹⁰While we were staying for some days, a prophet named Agabus came down from Judea. ¹¹And coming to us he took Paul's girdle and bound his own feet and hands, and said, "Thus says the Holy Spirit, 'So shall the Jews at Jerusalem bind the man who owns this girdle and deliver him into the hands of the Gentiles.'" ¹²When we heard this, we and the people there begged him not to go up to Jerusalem. ¹³Then Paul answered, "What are you doing, weeping and breaking my heart? For I am ready not only to be imprisoned but even to die at Jerusalem for the name of the Lord Jesus." ¹⁴And when he would not be persuaded, we ceased and said, "The will of the Lord be done."

¹⁵After these days we made ready and went up to Jerusalem. ¹⁶And some of the disciples from Caesarea went with us, bringing us to the house of Mnason of Cyprus, an early disciple, with whom we should lodge.

OVERVIEW: Commentators often choose this passage to point to the resemblance between Paul's journey to Jerusalem and that of Jesus. Many remark that the RSV description of Philip's daughters does not adequately represent Luke's intention in using the Greek word *parthenoi* ("virgins") and which in his mind probably indicates a special call that includes prophecy. They also point to the hospitality of the early Christians and their esteem for Paul. Eusebius is fascinated by what historical information he can gather concerning Philip and his daughters. Chrysostom makes a moral application of the fact that Paul, ready for action, is girded with a belt; he also notes the hospitality of the Christians and extends it to the present. Origen, noting the similarity between Jesus' journey to Jerusalem and Paul's, goes on to show how Paul is an imitator of Jesus. Jerome remarks on the need to go beyond natural affection, and Bede notes the continuity in the action of God the Spirit who inspires prophecy in Israel and now in the church.

21:9 Four Unmarried Daughters, Who Prophesied

PHILIP. EUSEBIUS OF CAESAREA: In this epistle [to Victor, the bishop of Rome] he [Polycrates] mentions him [John] together with the apostle Philip and his daughters in the following words: "For in Asia also great lights have fallen asleep, which shall rise again on the last day, at the coming of the Lord, when he shall come with glory from heaven and shall seek out all the saints. Among these are Philip, one of the twelve apostles, who sleeps in Hierapolis, and his two aged virgin daughters, and another daughter who lived in the Holy Spirit and now rests at Ephesus; and moreover John, who was both a witness and a teacher, who reclined upon the bosom of the Lord, and being a priest wore the sacerdotal plate. He also sleeps at Ephesus." So much concerning their death. And in the Dialogue of Caius which we mentioned a little above,[1] Proclus . . . speaks thus concerning the death of Philip and his daughters: "After him there were four prophetesses, the daughters of Philip, at Hierapolis in Asia. Their tomb is there and the tomb of their father." Such is his statement. But Luke, in the Acts of the Apostles, mentions the daughters of Philip, who were at that time at Caesarea in Judea with their father and were honored with the gift of prophecy. ECCLESIASTICAL HISTORY 3.31.2-5.[2]

MORE ABOUT PHILIP. EUSEBIUS OF CAESAREA: That Philip the apostle dwelt at Hierapolis with his daughters has been already stated. But it must be noted here that Papias, their contemporary, says that he heard a wonderful tale from the daughters of Philip. For he relates that in his time one rose from the dead. ECCLESIASTICAL HISTORY 3.39.9.[3]

21:11 *Binding the Man Who Owns This Girdle*

BEING GIRDED FOR ACTION. CHRYSOSTOM: But why did [Agabus] use a belt with his cloak? This was the custom among people of ancient times, before men went on to dress in this soft and loose fashion. For instance, Peter[4] appears to have been so "belted," and Paul as well, for he says, "the man who owns this belt." And Elijah[5] too was dressed thus, and every one of the saints, since they were always in action, either traveling or working earnestly for some other necessity. But this was not the only reason: they did this also to trample on all display and observe every austerity. Indeed this is what Christ called the greatest praise of virtue, when he said, "What then did you go out to see? Someone dressed in soft robes? Look, those who wear soft robes are in royal palaces."[6] HOMILIES ON THE GOSPEL OF MATTHEW 10.4.[7]

THE DIVINE AUTHORITY OF THE HOLY SPIRIT. BEDE: Agabus is imitating the ancient

prophets who were accustomed to say, "The Lord God says this,"[8] because the Holy Spirit is Lord and God in the same way as the Father and the Son are, and it is impossible to separate the operation of those whose nature and will are one. Hence too we read above, "The Holy Spirit said, 'Set apart for me Barnabas and Saul for the work for which I have called them,'"[9] namely, the office of apostle. And Paul himself writes, "Paul, an apostle, sent not from people or by people but by Jesus Christ and God the Father."[10] We have said these things so that no one might believe, following Macedonius,[11] that the Holy Spirit is a creature or of less authority than the Father or the Son. COMMENTARY ON THE ACTS OF THE APOSTLES 21.11.[12]

PAUL THE IMITATOR OF CHRIST. ORIGEN: "When he was about to go up to Jerusalem, Jesus took the twelve aside and spoke to them on the road, 'Behold, we go up to Jerusalem, and the Son of man will be handed over to the chief priests and the scribes, and they shall sentence him to death, and they will hand him over to the Gentiles to be mocked and beaten and crucified, and on the third day he shall rise."[13] Paul both contemplated Christ, in the face of manifest dangers, proceeding and eagerly going up to Jerusalem with the foreknowledge that he would be handed over to the chief priests and scribes and sentenced to death, and he exhorted us to imitate him as he imitated Christ, as he says, "Be imitators of me as I am of Christ."[14] And he did something similar to what Christ did when he took his disciples aside. For Agabus, taking his belt and girding himself about the hands and feet, said, "These things the Holy Spirit says: they will bind in this way the man who owns this belt" when he goes off to Jerusalem. When Paul learned of this, in imitation of his teacher, he went up eagerly to

[1]*Ecclesiastical History* 2.25.6; 3.28.1. [2]NPNF 2 1:162-63. [3]NPNF 2 1:172. [4]Jn 21:7. [5]2 Kings 1:8. [6]Mt 11:8. [7]NPNF 1 10:65**. [8]Is 49:22; Jer 11:3, *et passim*. [9]Acts 13:2. [10]Gal 1:1. [11]4th century Arian bishop of Constantinople who denied the divinity of Christ. [12]CS 117:165-66*. [13]Mt 20:17-19. [14]1 Cor 11:1.

Jerusalem. Commentary on Matthew 16.1.[15]

21:13 Weeping and Breaking My Heart

No Room for Natural Affection. Jerome: The battering ram of natural affection, which so often shatters faith, must recoil powerless from the wall of the gospel. Letter 14.3.[16]

Paul's Concern for His Friends. Chrysostom: Others were crying, but [Paul] was exhorting them as he grieved for their tears. "What are you doing," he says, "crying and breaking my heart?" Nothing was dearer to him than these people. Because he saw them crying, he grieved, while he cared nothing for his own trials. "Let the Lord's will," he said, "be done." You wrong me by doing this, so stop making me grieve. They stopped when he said, "You're breaking my heart." "I weep for you," he says, "not for my sufferings, on behalf of which I am even willing to die." They said, "Don't go into the theatre," and he did not. Again and again they drew him away and he obeyed. He fled through the window,[17] but now, though myriads, so to speak, exhort him, and those in Tyre and Caesarea weep and foretell countless trials, he does not allow it. And yet they were foretelling terrible things for him, and, what is more, through the Holy Spirit. They were not holding him back through the Spirit, and they were not simply announcing terrible events to come his way. No, they were afraid for him because he had to go up to Jerusalem. Since they could not convince him not to go, they cried, and then they settled down. You see the love of wisdom, you see the affection. "The Lord," he says, "will do what is pleasing in his sight."[18] They realized it was God's will. Otherwise Paul, who was constantly having to snatch himself from dangers, would not have been so eager. Catena on the Acts of the Apostles 21.13-14.[19]

Paul's Weakness. Chrysostom: Tell me, what do you think about that adamant will of Paul?

Could weeping break it? "Yes," he says, "for I can hold out against anything except for love, since it is love that has overcome and rules me." In this he is like God, whom an abyss of waters would not break but teardrops could. Catena on the Acts of the Apostles 21.13-14.[20]

Paul's Courage. Didymus the Blind: To this sort of opposition, respond as follows: "Why are you trying to keep me from the way I have set out on by weeping at the mention of the chains and afflictions that await me when I arrive in Jerusalem? Let it be known that I will follow the Spirit that has made known to me what awaits me and that I am setting out on the road to the city. I do not go ignorant of what will happen there, for I have foreseen it, and I am not being checked from going.[21] So do not break my heart with your tears." Whoever has been nobly prepared to be courageous enough to have no thought for his own life does not succumb to fear even if someone tries to provoke it. Now among them such dread had come to grip their thinking, and so the apostle said that his heart was being broken. He was not saying that he was weak but that he had come to such a state because of their bitter weeping. One could also say that just as little sins, in their actual commission, seem great to a holy person, so do the initial movements toward them, and so here he says the breaking of his heart is great. Catena on the Acts of the Apostles 21.13-14.[22]

21:16 The House of Mnason of Cyprus

It Is in Our Power to Welcome Christ. Chrysostom: Paul was the guest he welcomed. Perhaps one of you will say, "If Paul was given to me as a guest to welcome, I would receive him

[15]GCS 40:461-63. [16]NPNF 2 6:15. [17]2 Cor 11:33. [18]Chrysostom appears simply to have rephrased "the Lord's will be done." [19]CGPNT 3:346. [20]CGPNT 3:346. [21]Didymus apparently means that Paul is saying, "I am not being checked *by the Spirit*," as he was in Acts 16:6, where the same word appears as Didymus uses here. [22]CGPNT 3:347.

readily and with great enthusiasm." But look, it is possible for you to welcome Paul's master as your guest, and you refuse. "For he who welcomes," says he, "the least among you welcomes me."[23] Inasmuch as the brother is "the least," so much the more is Christ present through him. For he who welcomes the mighty often does so for the sake of vainglory, but he who welcomes the lowly does so honestly, for the sake of Christ. It is even possible for you to welcome the father of Christ, and you refuse. "For I was a stranger, and you invited me in."[24] "Whatever you did for one of the least of these brothers who believe in me, you did for me."[25] Even if he is not Paul but a brother who believes and even if he is the least, Christ is present through him. Open your house, take him in. "Anyone who receives a prophet will receive a prophet's reward."[26] So likewise he who receives Christ will receive the reward due to one who welcomes Christ. HOMILIES ON THE ACTS OF THE APOSTLES 45.[27]

---

[23]Mt 18:5; Lk 9:48. [24]Mt 25:35. [25]Mt 25:40. [26]Mt 10:41. [27]NPNF 1 11:275-76.

21:17-26 PAUL COMES TO JERUSALEM AND PURIFIES HIMSELF

17When we had come to Jerusalem, the brothers received us gladly. 18On the following day Paul went in with us to James; and all the elders were present. 19After greeting them, he related one by one the things that God had done among the Gentiles through his ministry. 20And when they heard it, they glorified God. And they said to him, "You see, brother, how many thousands there are among the Jews of those who have believed; they are all zealous for the law, 21and they have been told about you that you teach all the Jews who are among the Gentiles to forsake Moses, telling them not to circumcise their children or observe the customs. 22What then is to be done? They will certainly hear that you have come. 23Do therefore what we tell you. We have four men who are under a vow; 24take these men and purify yourself along with them and pay their expenses, so that they may shave their heads. Thus all will know that there is nothing in what they have been told about you but that you yourself live in observance of the law. 25But as for the Gentiles who have believed, we have sent a letter with our judgment that they should abstain from what has been sacrificed to idols and from blood and from what is strangled^y and from unchastity." 26Then Paul took the men, and the next day he purified himself with them and went into the temple, to give notice when the days of purification would be fulfilled and the offering presented for every one of them.

y Other early authorities omit *and from what is strangled*

OVERVIEW: This text narrates the arrival of Paul and his companions to Jerusalem, thus ending Paul's third missionary journey. Various commentators point out that the description of Paul's account of the mission and all that God accomplished among the Gentiles echoes a similar wording in Acts 15:4 and is followed by the account of the reaction of some belonging to the "party of the Pharisees" (Acts 15:5). They also point to the ambiguity of James's role in the Jerusalem community. They are divided as to what the reference to the letter from the former Jerusalem meeting meant. Some argue it indicates that Paul was not there (unlikely) and is a Lukan way of linking the two Jerusalem encounters and recalling to the reader the first decision. Others argue that it is the Jerusalem community's manner of recalling it all to Paul. They also point out that it is not clear whether Paul should repeat a Nazarite vow (see Acts 18:18) or merely pay the expenses of the other four while he "purified" himself through another ceremony. Bede takes the time to tell us the tradition about James, and Chrysostom admires Paul's humility in ascribing all his success to God. Augustine, Chrysostom and Severus treat directly the problem of the continued practice of the law by Jewish Christians. They all advocate a gradual approach to the question, though they foresee a time when Jewish believers will cease practicing the law. This issue is being raised in our day, and their wisdom, if perhaps not their ultimate solution, is important to take into account. Severus notes how the apostles did not expect instant transformation but were patient and persevered in their teaching.

21:18 Paul Goes to James

PAUL WENT WITH US TO JAMES. BEDE: This James was "the brother of the Lord," that is, "the son of Mary, the sister of the Lord's mother, whom John" the Evangelist "mentions."[1] It was he who "was appointed bishop by the apostles immediately after the Lord's passion and ruled the church at Jerusalem for thirty years, that is, until Nero's seventh year."[2] Since the Jews were not able to kill Paul, though they very much sought to, soon afterwards, as Festus had died and Albinus had not yet come to the province, they turned their hand against James, who "was

buried next to the temple, where he had also been thrown down."[3] COMMENTARY ON THE ACTS OF THE APOSTLES 21.18.[4]

21:19 What God Had Done Among the Gentiles

WISHING TO SHOW GOD'S MERCY. CHRYSOSTOM: Again Paul describes to them in detail the things relating to the Gentiles. He does this not to indulge in vainglory, God forbid, but because he wishes to show the mercy of God and fill them with great joy.[5] Look at the result: "When they heard it, they glorified God." It was not upon Paul that they bestowed their praise and admiration. For he described everything in such a way as to refer it all to [God]. HOMILIES ON THE ACTS OF THE APOSTLES 46.[6]

21:20 Zealous for the Law

RESPECT FOR GOD-GIVEN ORDINANCES. AUGUSTINE: It is quite clear, I think, that James gave this advice in order to show the falsity of the views supposed to be Paul's, which certain Jews who had come to believe in Christ, but who were still "zealous for the law," had heard about him, namely, that through the teaching of Christ the commandments, written by the direction of God and transmitted by Moses to the fathers, were to be thought sacrilegious and worthy of rejection. These reports were not circulated about Paul by those who understood the spirit in which the Jewish converts felt bound to those observances, namely, because of their being prescribed by a divine authority and for the sake of the prophetic holiness of those ceremonies but not for the attaining of salvation, which has now been revealed in Christ and is conferred by the sacrament of baptism. Those who spread this rumor about Paul were the ones

---

[1]Jn 19:25. [2]Jerome On Illustrious Men 2. See FC 100 for a complete English translation. [3]Ibid. [4]CS 117:166. [5]See Acts 15:12. [6]NPNF 1 11:278.

who wished to make these observances as binding as if without them there could be no salvation in the gospel for believers. For they had experienced him as a most vigorous preacher of grace and as one who taught the exact opposite of their view, that one is not justified by these but by the grace of Jesus Christ and that all the ordinances of the law were foreshadowings meant to announce him. That was why they tried to stir up hatred and persecution against him, making him out to be an enemy of the law and of the divine commandments, and there was no more fitting way for him to repel the injustice of this false charge than by performing personally the ceremonies that he was supposed to condemn as sacrilegious. In this way [Paul] would prove two things: that the Jews were not to be prevented from observing these obligations as if they were wrong and that the Gentiles were not to be forced to observe them as if they were necessary. LETTER 82.[7]

SHADOWS OF THINGS TO COME. AUGUSTINE: I say, therefore, that circumcision and other ordinances of this sort were divinely revealed to the former people through the Testament which we call Old, as types of future things, which were to be fulfilled by Christ. When this fulfillment had come, those obligations remained for the instruction of Christians, to be read simply for the understanding of the previous prophecy, but not to be performed through necessity, as if people had still to await the coming revelation of the faith that was foreshadowed by these things. However, although they were not to be imposed on the Gentiles, they were not thereby to be removed from the customary life of the Jews, as if they were worthy of scorn and condemnation. Gradually, therefore, and by degrees, through the fervent preaching of the grace of Christ, by which alone believers were to know that they were justified and saved—not by those shadows of things, formerly future but now present and at hand—through the conversion of those Jews whom the presence of the Lord in the flesh and

the times of the apostles found living thus, all that activity of the shadows was to be ended. This was to be enough praise for it, that it was not to be avoided and despised as idolatry was, but was to have no further development and was not to be thought necessary, as if salvation either depended on it or could not be had without it. This is what some heretics thought, who wanted to be both Jews and Christians and could be neither Jews nor Christians. You [i.e., Jerome] were so kind as to warn me very earnestly against that opinion, although I have never held it. LETTER 82.[8]

21:21 Teaching Jews to Forsake Moses

THE PATIENCE AND PERSEVERANCE OF THE APOSTLES. SEVERUS OF ANTIOCH: Thus the apostles and the holy disciples of the Savior, in the beginning, allowed converts from Judaism to the life of the gospel to be circumcised according to the law of Moses in order that they would just believe in the Lord. Later, they themselves on their own, filled with worship in the Spirit and with evangelical perfection, rejected the small shadowy observances of the law. CATENA ON THE ACTS OF THE APOSTLES 21.21-22.[9]

21:26 Paul Purified Himself and Went into the Temple

PAUL CONDESCENDS TO THE JEW'S SENSIBILITIES. CHRYSOSTOM: Against this Paul defends himself and shows that he does this not of his choice. How did they persuade him? It was part of the divine plan and condescension on his part. So this was no hindrance to the preaching, since it was they themselves who decided such things. So he does not accuse Peter in any way. For what he himself did here is what Peter did on that occasion when he held his peace and established his doctrine.[10] And he did not say, "But why? It is not necessary to teach those

---

[7]FC 12:396-97. [8]FC 12:401-2. [9]CGPNT 3:349. [10]Gal 2:11-14.

among the Gentiles." It is not enough that he does not preach so there; he had to do something more to persuade them that you observe the law. Condescension is what it is. Do not be alarmed. HOMILIES ON THE ACTS OF THE APOSTLES 46.[11]

[11]NPNF 1 11:279-80**.

21:27-36 PAUL BROUGHT BEFORE THE TRIBUNE

[27]*When the seven days were almost completed, the Jews from Asia, who had seen him in the temple, stirred up all the crowd, and laid hands on him,* [28]*crying out, "Men of Israel, help! This is the man who is teaching men everywhere against the people and the law and this place; moreover he also brought Greeks into the temple, and he has defiled this holy place."*[29]*For they had previously seen Trophimus the Ephesian with him in the city, and they supposed that Paul had brought him into the temple.* [30]*Then all the city was aroused, and the people ran together; they seized Paul and dragged him out of the temple, and at once the gates were shut.* [31]*And as they were trying to kill him, word came to the tribune of the cohort that all Jerusalem was in confusion.* [32]*He at once took soldiers and centurions, and ran down to them; and when they saw the tribune and the soldiers, they stopped beating Paul.* [33]*Then the tribune came up and arrested him, and ordered him to be bound with two chains. He inquired who he was and what he had done.* [34]*Some in the crowd shouted one thing, some another; and as he could not learn the facts because of the uproar, he ordered him to be brought into the barracks.* [35]*And when he came to the steps, he was actually carried by the soldiers because of the violence of the crowd;* [36]*for the mob of the people followed, crying, "Away with him!"*

OVERVIEW: The tribulations prophesied now begin, significantly, at the temple. Modern commentators advert to the threefold accusation against Paul: he is teaching "against the people and the law and this place." A similar charge is laid against Stephen (Acts 6:11-14) and Jesus (Lk 23:2). Paul is further accused of bringing non-Jews within the temple precincts, whereas, as inscriptions from the balustrade from the former temple indicate, any non-Jew is liable to the death penalty (something the Jews could administer) for profaning the temple. Luke is not exaggerating the violence of the mob, as passages from the Jewish historian Josephus indicate. Now Paul is alone; no one is mentioned with him. Perhaps Luke means to evoke Jesus' passion. This is his last moment in the temple. The Fathers were spare in their comment. Bede argued that some Jews feared that the Romans would seize the temple and the land if they did not hold fast to their temple observance. Arator noted that the person can be bound, but the faith cannot be bound.

21:28 Teaching Everywhere Against the People

THE SURMISE OF PAUL'S ACCUSERS. BEDE: Because they saw that the followers of the new grace were less diligent about observing the rituals of the law and the rites of the temple, they became afraid, as we read in the Gospel, that the Romans would come and take away their place and their people.[1] COMMENTARY ON THE ACTS OF THE APOSTLES 21.28.[2]

21:33 The Tribune Arrested Paul

BOUND IN BODY, NOT IN MIND. ARATOR: Nevertheless the torments that lay harshly upon his constricted arms did not tie his mind, because Paul's epistle, full of light, proclaims that the servants can be bound [but] the faith cannot be bound, and the word is not allowed to be restrained by tortures.[3] ON THE ACTS OF THE APOSTLES 2.[4]

---

[1]Jn 11:48. [2]CS 117:168. [3]2 Tim 2:9. [4]OAA 85.

21:37-39 PAUL BEGS LEAVE TO SPEAK TO THE PEOPLE

[37]As Paul was about to be brought into the barracks, he said to the tribune, "May I say something to you?" And he said, "Do you know Greek? [38]Are you not the Egyptian, then, who recently stirred up a revolt and led the four thousand men of the Assassins out into the wilderness?" [39]Paul replied, "I am a Jew, from Tarsus in Cilicia, a citizen of no mean city; I beg you, let me speak to the people."

OVERVIEW: This narrative introduction is matched by a transitional narrative at the end of the speech (Acts 21:22-29). Luke records the remark about the Egyptian to clarify that Paul is not an agitator or insurrectionist; he also shows the impartiality of the representative of Rome. Chrysostom sees chiaroscuro in the conflict between good and evil, making good all the more brilliant.

21:38 Are You Not the Egyptian?

THE TRUTH SHINES EVEN THROUGH THE DEVIL'S EFFORTS. CHRYSOSTOM: This Egyptian was a deceiving sorcerer, and the devil expected to triumph through him and implicate Christ and his apostles in charges leveled at these sorcerers. But he did not succeed. The truth became still more brilliant, having suffered no

harm through the devil's machinations but shining all the brighter. . . . Therefore let us not grieve that heresies exist where false Christs wished to attack Christ, both before and after this, to throw him into obscurity. For we find the truth shining through on every occasion. This is also what happened with the prophets. There were false prophets, by contrast with whom the true prophets shone all the more. For sickness shows off health clearly, darkness light, and stormy weather calm. HOMILIES ON THE ACTS OF THE APOSTLES 46.[1]

21:39 A Citizen of Tarsus

PAUL AVAILS HIMSELF OF THE LAWS. CHRYSOSTOM: Look at him. When [Paul] argues with

---

[1]NPNF 1 11:280**.

those from the outside, he does not hesitate to use the help of the laws. Here he impresses the tribune by the name of his city. And likewise on another occasion he says, [he was accosted] "publicly without a trial, even though we are Roman citizens, and threw us into prison."[2] Homilies on the Acts of the Apostles 47.[3]

Paul's Background. Bede: The apostle was actually born[4] in Gischala, a town in Galilee. "When it was taken by the Romans he moved with his parents to Tarsus in Cilicia. They sent him to Jerusalem in order to study the law, and he was instructed by the very learned man Gamaliel," as he himself recalls below. Now he does not name himself a citizen but a burgher from [the word for] the municipality or the territory of the same city in which he grew up. A municipality was so-called because "it gave in return [for such status] great duties, that is, tribute that was owed, or services for legal factors that pertain to freemen and those factors that are most celebrated, as well as things that emanate from a prince, relate to the dignity of a city."[5] Nor should we be surprised if he calls himself a Tarsean and not a Giscalite, since the Lord himself, who was born in Bethlehem, was not given the name Bethlehemite but Nazarean. Commentary on the Acts of the Apostles 21.39.[6]

---

[2]Acts 16:37. [3]NPNF 1 11:282**. [4]Jerome *On Illustrious Men* 5. See FC 100 for a complete English translation. [5]Isidore of Seville *Etymologies* 15.2.10. [6]CS 117:169-70.

21:40—22:5 PAUL SPEAKS TO THE CROWD IN HEBREW

[40]*And when he had given him leave, Paul, standing on the steps, motioned with his hand to the people; and when there was a great hush, he spoke to them in the Hebrew language, saying:*

"Brothers and fathers, hear the defense which I now make before you."

22 [2]*And when they heard that he addressed them in the Hebrew language, they were the more quiet. And he said:*

[3]*"I am a Jew, born at Tarsus in Cilicia, but brought up in this city at the feet of Gamali-el, educated according to the strict manner of the law of our fathers, being zealous for God as you all are this day.* [4]*I persecuted this Way to the death, binding and delivering to prison both men and women,* [5]*as the high priest and the whole council of elders bear me witness. From them I received letters to the brothers, and I journeyed to Damascus to take those also who were there and bring them in bonds to Jerusalem to be punished."*

Overview: This is the first of Paul's speeches in his own defense and one of two in which he relates his conversion. This passage includes Paul's ingratiating introduction, the same as that of Stephen (Acts 7:2), and a brief summary of his career up to the moment of the journey to Damascus. The moderns point out that the high priest in office at this moment is not the same as the one who commissioned Paul. They surmise that he is speaking generally and that some of the council of elders would remember commissioning him. The point is to accent his "zeal for God," a rather common Old Testament phrase. Chrysostom provides the commentary from the Fathers. He gives close attention to Paul's self-description, to show how Paul makes himself agreeable to his audience and thus wins their goodwill from the beginning of his defense. Chrysostom shows that Paul's reverence for the law was demonstrable from the esteem he had for one of its leading teachers, Gamaliel. Chrysostom also sees in Paul's words, however, more than an attempt to secure a well-disposed audience; Paul stands before them as an accusation of their complacency. Perhaps, Chrysostom sees Paul implying, were you as zealous and devoted as I, you too would be a follower of Jesus.

22:3 Educated According to the Law

LED TO PREACH THE GOSPEL THROUGH A DIVINE POWER. CHRYSOSTOM: [Paul] shows that great was his zeal for the worship. His native city, great as it was, he left behind, so far away, and chose to be brought up here for the sake of the law. Look how from the beginning he heeded the law. He mentions these things not only to defend himself before them, but also to show that he was led to preach the gospel not by human intention but by divine power. For educated in the way that he was, he could not have changed all at once. For if he were one of the *hoi polloi*, it might have been possible to imagine this. But since he was one of those who were most bound by the law, it was not likely that he should change without strong necessity. HOMILIES ON THE ACTS OF THE APOSTLES 47.[1]

PAUL HONORS GAMALIEL. CHRYSOSTOM: He does not just say "in the school of Gamaliel" but "at the feet of Gamaliel." By these words, he

shows his patient endurance, his loving attentiveness, his eagerness to listen and his tremendous reverence for the man. CATENA ON THE ACTS OF THE APOSTLES 22.3.[2]

PAUL'S COMPLIMENTS. CHRYSOSTOM: He does not simply say "the law" but "the law of our fathers." This shows what type of person he had been, someone not ignorant of the law. Now this seems to be said for the benefit of his audience, but in fact, it is an accusation. For what if, with all his knowledge, he had been negligent? What if you have a thorough knowledge of the law but do not fulfill it? You do not love it, then, do you? [Paul] then states plainly that he was a zealot. So after he has delivered a great encomium about himself, he then extends this praise by adding, "just as all of you are today," and thus points out that what they are doing is not just for a human purpose but for their zeal for God. By bestowing this favor on them he also captures their understanding from the beginning. CATENA ON THE ACTS OF THE APOSTLES 22.3.[3]

22:4 I Persecuted the Believers

PAUL'S WITNESSES. CHRYSOSTOM: He brings forward as witnesses the high priest and the elders. On the one hand, [Paul] makes himself their equal when he says, "I being a zealot just as you," but then he shows through his deeds that he was a greater zealot than they. "I wasn't waiting around," he says, "to arrest them, but I was even stirring up the priests and being sent abroad. And I wasn't after just men, as you are, but I sought out women too, put them in chains and even threw them into prison." This is irrefutable testimony. His Jewish credentials could not be disputed. Count the witnesses he brings forward: the body of elders, the high priest, those in the city. Note how his defense is not fearful but instructive rather and educational. Had his audience not been stone,[4] they

---

[1]NPNF 1 11:283**. [2]CGPNT 3:357. [3]CGPNT 3:357. [4]See Ezek 11:19.

would have given heed to his words. CATENA ON THE ACTS OF THE APOSTLES 22.4-5.[5]

22:5 Journeyed to Damascus

GOD REWARDS THE BLIND YET EARNEST OF HEART. CHRYSOSTOM: Did you see how by his very experience in these things [Paul] has taught all of us that he deserved to be judged worthy of kindness from above and to be led to the path of truth? When God in his goodness sees a well-dis-

posed soul led astray through ignorance, he does not disregard that soul or give it up to its own great recklessness, but he shows it all the good things that come from him and fails in nothing that pertains to our salvation, if we make ourselves worthy to reap abundantly the benefit of grace from above, as did that blessed apostle. BAPTISMAL INSTRUCTIONS 4.8.[6]

---

[5]CGPNT 3:358. [6]ACW 31:69.

22:6-11 PAUL RELATES HIS CONVERSION

[6]"As I made my journey and drew near to Damascus, about noon a great light from heaven suddenly shone about me. [7]And I fell to the ground and heard a voice saying to me, 'Saul, Saul, why do you persecute me?' [8]And I answered, 'Who are you, Lord?' And he said to me, 'I am Jesus of Nazareth whom you are persecuting.' [9]Now those who were with me saw the light but did not hear the voice of the one who was speaking to me. [10]And I said, 'What shall I do, Lord?' And the Lord said to me, 'Rise, and go into Damascus, and there you will be told all that is appointed for you to do.' [11]And when I could not see because of the brightness of that light, I was led by the hand by those who were with me, and came into Damascus."

OVERVIEW: Both ancients and moderns note the divergences in this narrative from the descriptive narrative in Acts 9, though they explain them differently. The moderns look to Luke's intention in mentioning that, in contradistinction to Acts 9, Paul's companions see the light but do not hear the voice, and they ascribe it to Luke's different narrative goal, thus showing a sensitivity to the freedom employed by ancient narrators. It should be noted that in all three accounts Jesus' self-description is nearly identical. Bede, who is following Arator's hairsplitting, reconciles the two accounts by understanding the voice as incomprehensible and, therefore, they are said not to hear.

Origen, however, provides us with a reflection on how this event, or any event of Scripture, is to be understood as having direct application to the reader in the same way that every person's life, whether he or she is aware of it, has a direct bearing upon Christ.

22:8 Jesus of Nazareth

WE ACT OURSELVES INTO THE GOSPEL BY HOW WE LIVE. ORIGEN: It ought not to be forgotten that in such a Gospel as this[1] there is

---

[1]John.

embraced every good deed that was done to Jesus; as, for example, the story of the woman[2] who had been a prostitute and had repented, and who, having experienced a genuine recovery from her evil state, had grace to pour her ointment over Jesus so that every one in the house smelled the sweet savor. Hence, too, the words, "Wherever this gospel shall be preached among all the nations, there also this that she has done shall be spoken of, for a memorial of her."[3] And it is clear that whatever is done to the disciples of Jesus is done to him. Pointing to those of them who met with kind treatment, [Jesus] says to those who were kind to them: "What you did to these, you did to me."[4] So that every good deed we do to our neighbors is entered into the gospel, that gospel that is written on the heavenly tablets and read by all who are worthy of the knowledge of the whole of things. But on the other side, too, there is a part of the gospel that is for the condemnation of the doers of the evil deeds that have been done to Jesus. The treachery of Judas and the shouts of the wicked crowd when it said, "Away with such a one from the earth,"[5] and "Crucify him, crucify him,"[6] the mockings of those who crowned him with thorns, and everything of that kind, is included in all the Gospels. And as a consequence of this we see that everyone who betrays the disciples of Jesus is reckoned as betraying Jesus himself. To Saul, when still a persecutor it is said, "Saul, Saul, why are you persecuting me?"[7] and, "I am Jesus whom you are persecuting."[8] There are those who still have thorns with which they crown and dishonor Jesus, those, namely, who are choked by the cares and riches and pleasures of life, and though they have received the word of God, they do not bring it to perfection.[9] We must beware, therefore, lest we also, by crowning Jesus with thorns of our own, should be entered in the gospel and read of in this character by those who come to know how Jesus, who is in all and is present in all rational and holy lives, is anointed with ointment, is entertained, is glorified, or how, on the other side, he is dishonored and mocked and beaten. All this had to be

said; it is part of our demonstration that our good actions, and also the sins of those who stumble, are embodied in the gospel, either to everlasting life or to reproach and everlasting shame. COMMENTARY ON THE GOSPEL OF JOHN 1.12.[10]

22:9 *Those with Me Saw the Light*

WHAT PAUL'S COMPANIONS HEARD. BEDE: The earlier story of this vision relates that his companions stood "stunned, hearing indeed the voice but seeing no one."[11] Hence it can be inferred that they heard the sound of a garbled voice, but they did not hear the distinct words. COMMENTARY ON THE ACTS OF THE APOSTLES 22.9.[12]

HEARING THEY DID NOT HEAR. ARATOR: Paul, speaking of his deeds, says that his companions saw the light there some time ago, yet that they did not drink in the voice with their ears; but then, at the time when he fell blind, his companions are said also to have heard the voice.[13] Thus the work of the narrator varies. But there is no doubt that it is necessary for both [passages] to harmonize; for then [according to Luke] they are said to have heard, to have received the sound, now [in Paul's own words] undoubtedly *not* to have heard. This will be a simple way of explanation: the voice is justly denied to have spoken since it was indistinct, nor is a thing believed to be given by speech when a person receiving it does not store it up in his understanding. He is stimulated so little on account of his doubting ear, and ambiguous noise strikes only the air. They are said at the same time thus to have heard, thus not to have heard. The one standpoint is of noise, the other standpoint is of true speech, and a single circumstance bears and bears again a twofold meaning. ON THE ACTS OF THE APOSTLES 2.[14]

---

[2]Origen here combines Lk 7:36-50 (the sinful woman), Mk 14:3-9 (Jesus' words about the woman) and Jn 12:1-8. [3]Mk 14:9. [4]Mt 25:40. [5]Jn 19:6, 15. [6]Lk 23:21. [7]Acts 9:4. [8]Acts 9:5. [9]Mt 13:3-23. [10]ANF 9:303-4*. [11]Acts 9:7. [12]CS 117:173. [13]See Acts 9:7. [14]OAA 86-87*.

22:11 Led by the Hand

THE BLINDING LIGHT. EPHREM THE SYRIAN: Our Lord spoke humbly from above so that the leaders of his church would speak humbly. Now, if someone should ask, "How did our Lord speak humbly with Paul if Paul's eyes were seriously injured?" they should realize that this impairment did not [result] from our compassionate Lord, who spoke humbly there. Rather, [it was the result] of the intense light that shone radiantly there. This light was not a punishment that befell Paul on account of the things he had done. It injured him with the intensity of its rays, as he himself said, "When I arose, I could see nothing because of the brilliance of the light." HOMILY ON OUR LORD 26.1-2.[15]

---

[15]FC 91:301*.

22:12-16 PAUL'S BAPTISM RECOUNTED

[12]"And one Ananias, a devout man according to the law, well spoken of by all the Jews who lived there, [13]came to me, and standing by me said to me, 'Brother Saul, receive your sight.' And in that very hour I received my sight and saw him. [14]And he said, 'The God of our fathers appointed you to know his will, to see the Just One and to hear a voice from his mouth; [15]for you will be a witness for him to all men of what you have seen and heard. [16]And now why do you wait? Rise and be baptized, and wash away your sins, calling on his name.'"

OVERVIEW: Again, with sensitivity to Luke's narrative intentions, the moderns note the more abundant description of Ananias as law-abiding and well respected. They also point to the Old Testament phrases in Ananias's words to Paul, "the God of our fathers," "to see the Just One" (a designation of the awaited descendant of David in Jer 23:5-6; 33:15), "calling on his name." Also one may observe the clarity of Paul's commission and the description of baptism. Chrysostom's concerns are evidentiary, ethical and doctrinal. He notes how Paul's defense is plausible and how his description of baptism affirms the divinity of Jesus. Yet, while the strength of Paul's argument lies in his ability to call forth so many witnesses, for Chrysostom, as for Origen above (Acts 22:8), the primary witness to the truth of the gospel is not the demonstration of the trustworthiness of Paul but rather the integral connection between professed belief fulfilled in action.

22:15 A Witness to All People

OUR WITNESS IS TRUSTWORTHY IF WE LIVE ACCORDINGLY. CHRYSOSTOM: For [Paul] truly became a witness to [Jesus], and a witness as one should be, both by what he did and by what he said. We too must be such witnesses and not betray what we have been entrusted. I speak not only of doctrines, but also of our way of life. Look, what he knew, what he heard, he bore witness to this before all, and nothing hindered him. We too have heard that there is a resurrection and ten thousand good things; therefore, we ought to bear witness to this before all. "We do in fact bear witness," you say, "and believe." How,

271

since we do the opposite? Tell me, if someone should say he was a Christian but should then apostatize and act like a Jew, would his testimony be sufficient? No, not at all; for people would look for testimony through his actions. Likewise, if we say that that there is a resurrection and ten thousand good things but then look down upon them and prefer the things here, who will believe us? For all people pay attention not to what we say but to what we do. "You will be a witness," [Christ] says, "to all."[1] That is, not only to the friends, but also to the unbelievers. For this is what witnesses are for: they persuade not those who know but those who do not. Let us become trustworthy witnesses. How will we become trustworthy? By the life we lead. HOMILIES ON THE ACTS OF THE APOSTLES 47.[2]

22:16 Calling on Jesus' Name

THIS SHOWS CHRIST'S DIVINITY. CHRYSOSTOM: What he uttered here is important. For he did not say "baptized in his name" but "calling on the name of Christ." It shows that he is God; for it is not lawful to "call on" anyone else except God. HOMILIES ON THE ACTS OF THE APOSTLES 47.[3]

---

[1]See Acts 1:8. [2]NPNF 1 11:285**. [3]NPNF 1 11:285**.

22:17-24 PAUL TELLS OF HIS MISSION TO THE GENTILES

[17]"When I had returned to Jerusalem and was praying in the temple, I fell into a trance [18]and saw him saying to me, 'Make haste and get quickly out of Jerusalem, because they will not accept your testimony about me.' [19]And I said, 'Lord, they themselves know that in every synagogue I imprisoned and beat those who believed in thee. [20]And when the blood of Stephen thy witness was shed, I also was standing by and approving, and keeping the garments of those who killed him.' [21]And he said to me, 'Depart; for I will send you far away to the Gentiles.'"

[22]Up to this word they listened to him; then they lifted up their voices and said, "Away with such a fellow from the earth! For he ought not to live." [23]And as they cried out and waved their garments and threw dust into the air, [24]the tribune commanded him to be brought into the barracks, and ordered him to be examined by scourging, to find out why they shouted thus against him.

OVERVIEW: Omitted here is any mention of Paul's preaching in the area of Damascus and the account of his later return to Jerusalem. Instead, we are told of Paul's commissioning directly by Jesus to preach to the Gentiles and the fact that it took place in the temple. Commentators often point to Galatians 2:2, 7 as Paul's further account of this experience. Chrysostom continues to set out the contours of Paul's argument and its veracity, in contrast to the injustice he meets in being subjected to scourging. Bede sees in the clothing of the Jews a symbol of their refusal to believe.

22:18 Rejecting Your Testimony

PAUL'S TWOFOLD ARGUMENT. CHRYSOSTOM: Look how [Paul] thrusts himself into danger. Even after that vision, I came, he says, "to Jerusalem." This is again without witnesses. But look, the result provides the witness. He said, "They will not accept your testimony." They did not accept it. And yet, he says, if one had to make a reasonable guess, one would have guessed that they would certainly accept it. For I was the man who made war upon the Christians, and for this reason they ought to have accepted it. Here [Paul] constructs two arguments: one, they cannot defend their actions, for they persecute him against all likelihood and contrary to reason; and two, Christ was God, who gave prophecies contrary to expectation, not looking to things past but knowing beforehand things to come. HOMILIES ON THE ACTS OF THE APOSTLES 48.[1]

22:23 They Cried Out

DISROBED OF GLORY. BEDE: At the Lord's passion only the priest leaped from his throne and tore his garments,[2] because on that occasion the old priesthood was being changed to a new one. Now, however, since after the killing of the apostles the whole people together would be robbed of the glory of the kingdom, all of them flung off their apparel and raised up to the heavens an outcry mixed with dust, in accord with what the psalm says, "The pride of those who hate you ever rises."[3] COMMENTARY ON THE ACTS OF THE APOSTLES 22.23.[4]

22:24 Examined by Scourging

THE TRIBUNE WAS ALSO NEGLIGENT. CHRYSOSTOM: The tribune ought to have questioned more closely whether the things that Paul said were so—even if he had to question the Jews, and if these things were not so, and only then to order that he be scourged, "to find out why they shouted thus against him." Moreover, he ought to learn from those who were shouting and to ask if they had even heard anything that was said. Instead, he simply used his power and acted according to their pleasure. For he was not trying to do something just but only to stop their rage, unjust as it was. HOMILIES ON THE ACTS OF THE APOSTLES 48.[5]

---

[1]NPNF 1 11:287**. [2]Mt 26:65. [3]Ps 74:23 (73:23 LXX, Vg). [4]CS 117:173. [5]NPNF 1 11:287**.

22:25-29 PAUL APPEALS TO HIS ROMAN CITIZENSHIP

[25]*But when they had tied him up with the thongs, Paul said to the centurion who was standing by, "Is it lawful for you to scourge a man who is a Roman citizen, and uncondemned?"* [26]*When the centurion heard that, he went to the tribune and said to him, "What are you about to do? For this man is a Roman citizen."* [27]*So the tribune came and said to him, "Tell me, are you a Roman citizen?" And he said, "Yes."* [28]*The tribune answered, "I bought this citizenship for a large sum." Paul said, "But I was born a citizen."* [29]*So those who were about to examine him withdrew from him instantly; and the tribune also was afraid, for he realized that Paul was a Roman citizen and that he had bound him.*

OVERVIEW: Using the technique of the interrupted speech, Luke accomplishes two things. First, he once again establishes that Paul's vocation to preach the gospel to the Gentiles comes from a direct commission from Jesus. Second, he presents Paul's dignity as a freeborn citizen, superior in this regard to the tribune, Claudius Lysias, who had to pay for his citizenship rank—thus the name Claudius in recognition that he obtained his citizenship under the emperor of that name. Some commentators present a discussion of Roman citizenship, how it was obtained, why the notion of beating Paul would have been so grave an offense and the dignity that Paul has as a citizen rather than a foreign troublemaker. Augustine uses this event in order to explain the phrase in the Sermon on the Mount in Matthew, "If someone should slap you on the right cheek, offer the other."[1] Whereas Theodoret sees here a valid claim intended to secure Paul his rights, Augustine finds Paul making a stark contrast between the relative evaluations of heavenly and earthly honors, which highlights how the Christian must be ready to subordinate the latter to the former. Augustine notes the irony that Paul's detractors had despised the thing of most value to him, yet became most attentive to the thing that was of least value to him. Chrysostom draws his common distinction between ways human and divine to emphasize that God is at work in the former as well.

22:25 Lawful to Scourge a Roman Citizen?

TWO SIDES TO THE FACE OF DIGNITY. AUGUSTINE: However, the face cannot be designated as the right face and the left, but high rank can be either according to God or according to this world. Hence, it is as though the face were divided into the right cheek and the left, in order to signify that, whenever his becoming a Christian becomes an occasion of contempt in the case of any follower of Christ, he should be much more ready to be despised in his own person if he holds any of the honors of this world. Just as in the case of the apostle himself, when in his person people were persecuting the Christian denomination; if he then remained silent regarding the dignity which he held in the world, he would not have turned the other cheek to those who were striking him on the right cheek. But by saying, "I am a Roman citizen," he was not unprepared to have them despise in his person the thing that he deemed of least value, when in his person they had despised a name so precious and salutary. Did he thereby endure in any less degree the chains which it was not lawful to place on Roman citizens? Or did he blame anyone for this injustice? Even though some people spared him on account of the title of Roman citizen, he did not on that account fail to offer them something to strike, for he yearned to correct by his own patience the perversity of those whom he saw to be honoring in his person the left portion rather than the right. The one thing to be considered is the spirit of kindness and clemency with which he acted toward those from whom he was suffering the injuries. SERMON ON THE MOUNT 1.19.58.[2]

THE WAYS IN WHICH PAUL IDENTIFIES HIMSELF AND WHY. THEODORET OF CYR: For the divine command made what seems shameful honorable. Thus the apostle called himself at one time a Pharisee[3] and at another a Roman, not because he was afraid of death but because it was fair to do so in a fight. Likewise he appealed to Caesar upon learning of the Jews' plot against him.[4] He sent his sister's son to the tribune to report the plots being hatched against him, not because he clung to this present life but in obedience to the divine law. For our Master certainly does not wish us to throw ourselves into obvious peril. This [Jesus] taught us not only with words but also through action, for more than once he avoided the murderous violence of the Jews. LETTER 3.[5]

---

[1]Mt 5:39. [2]FC 11:83-84. [3]Acts 23:6. [4]Acts 25:11. [5]NPNF 2 3:251**.

22:29 *These Examiners Withdrew*

GOD WORKS THROUGH HUMAN WAYS. CHRYSOSTOM: He would have earned contempt had he been scourged. But as it is, [Paul] throws them into greater fear. If they had scourged him, they could have dismissed the matter or even killed him. But as it is, the result is not so. See how God permits many results to occur through human ways, both in the case of the apostles and with the rest of humankind. HOMILIES ON THE ACTS OF THE APOSTLES 48.[6]

---

[6]NPNF 1 11:288**.

22:30—23:5 PAUL IS STRUCK BY ORDER OF THE HIGH PRIEST

³⁰*But on the morrow, desiring to know the real reason why the Jews accused him, he unbound him, and commanded the chief priests and all the council to meet, and he brought Paul down and set him before them.*

23 And Paul, looking intently at the council, said, "Brothers, I have lived before God in all good conscience up to this day." ²And the high priest Ananias commanded those who stood by him to strike him on the mouth. ³Then Paul said to him, "God shall strike you, you whitewashed wall! Are you sitting to judge me according to the law, and yet contrary to the law you order me to be struck?" ⁴Those who stood by said, "Would you revile God's high priest?" ⁵And Paul said, "I did not know, brothers, that he was the high priest; for it is written, 'You shall not speak evil of a ruler of your people.'"

OVERVIEW: This incident, which evokes so much patristic comment, produces much less among the moderns, many of whom, while acknowledging the evidence of Lukan composition, doubt that the whole event is historically probable. Josephus's account of this high priest is consonant with his actions here, and the fact that Paul did not know him is explained by Paul's long absence in a primarily Gentile milieu. Paul's retraction establishes that whatever division eventually occurs is not due to him. For modern commentators, the significant fact of this second, and most important, of Paul's apologies is that the Pharisees declare Paul innocent. They see in Acts a primary goal of showing that Christianity is a logical development of Pharisaic Judaism, and it is here that this intention is most evident. For these five verses the attention of the Fathers is on three matters: Paul's ignorance about Ananias, his emotional state when he calls him a whitewashed wall and the intent of these words. Origen shows how Paul is but a type, one manifestation among many, of the one antitype, the true victim. Chrysostom's focus is more practical. Although he shares the concerns about Paul's apparent anger and duplicity, he focuses on how these actions and words affect the dispositions of the participants in the events. Physical punishment brought loss of honor and respect for the recipient,[1] and Chrysostom sees Paul's words as deflecting the high priest's attempt to shame him. He has an additional concern that his audience not take Paul's words as an instance and therefore an excuse for arrogance (Acts 23:3b). For Augustine and Bede, however, Paul's words are a prophecy. Augustine sees them as applying personally to Ananias; for Bede, Ananias is a symbol of the levitical priesthood that Christ has fulfilled. The most complex analysis of this exchange, however, comes from Augustine, who finds in Paul's declaration of ignorance an esoteric message that here the high priest is not Ananias but Christ, who by being in Paul is in truth being reviled.

23:2 The High Priest Ordered Them to Strike Paul

THE NATURE OF CHRISTIAN SUFFERING. ORIGEN: We read in the Acts of the Apostles that someone, ordered by Ananias the high priest, struck Paul because he said, "God will strike you, oh whitewashed wall." And even to this day, the Ebionites, under orders from their illegitimate high priest, strike the apostle of Jesus Christ with their calumnies,[2] and Paul says to such a high priest of the Word, "God will strike you," and such a high priest is beautiful from without and a whitewashed wall but "within full of dead bones and every filth."[3] But why do I speak about Paul . . . ? It is my Lord, Jesus Christ, himself who speaks: "I have given my back to scourgings, and my cheeks to slaps, and my face I did not turn from the shame of being spit upon."[4] The simple know of these things as happening at one particular time, when Pilate scourged him, when the Jews plotted against him. I, however, see Jesus daily giving his back to scourgings: go into synagogues of the Jews, and see Jesus scourged by their blasphemous speech. See those gathered from among the nations[5] plotting against the Christians, how they seize Christ, and he gives his back to scourgings. Consider the Word of God insulted, reviled, hated by unbelievers. See that he gave his cheeks to be slapped, and after he

taught "Should someone slap you on one cheek, offer him the other,"[6] that he himself did the same. HOMILIES ON JEREMIAH 19.12.[7]

23:3 You Whitewashed Wall

WORDS OF BOLDNESS, NOT ANGER. CHRYSOSTOM: Some say that he [Paul] did not know that he was the high priest. Then why does he defend himself as if there was an accusation and adds, "You shall not speak evil of a ruler of your people." For if he was not the ruler, was he then to be abused? Paul himself says, "When we are cursed we bless; when we are persecuted, we endure it."[8] But here he does the opposite. He not only reviles but also curses him. These are words of boldness rather than anger. He did not wish to appear contemptible to the tribune. For the tribune himself had refrained from scourging him, since he was about to be handed over to the Jews. Had he been struck by the servants, it would have rather emboldened the tribune. For this reason he directs his attack not at the servant but at the one who gave the order. The words "you whitewashed wall" and "you are sitting to judge me according to the law" stand for "you are responsible," as if he had said, "you deserve ten thousand lashes." See how they were thunderstruck by his boldness. The point was to undermine him completely, but they commended him instead. HOMILIES ON THE ACTS OF THE APOSTLES 48.[9]

A PROPHECY OF ANANIAS'S DOOM. AUGUSTINE: Of course, those who do not understand him think that [Paul] uttered a reproach when he had been slapped by order of the high priest, for, with seeming insolence, he then said, "God will strike you, you whitewashed wall." But those who

---

[1]Part of the culturally revolutionary effects of preaching a crucified man as divine was the subversion of the honorific status of the integral and impassive body. For a more explicit exposition of this, see Augustine's comments at Acts 23:4 below.   [2]On the Ebionites and what Origen here describes, see Irenaeus *Adversus Haereses* 1.26.2.   [3]Mt 23:27.   [4]Is 50:6.   [5]Ps 2:1-2.   [6]Mt 5:39.   [7]SC 238:222-24.   [8]1 Cor 4:12. [9]NPNF 1 11:288-89**.

understand him take this as a prophecy. The "whitewashed wall" stands for hypocrisy; it is pretense, veiled beneath the priestly dignity, and under this title—as though beneath a white covering—it conceals, as it were, an inner slimy filthiness. SERMON ON THE MOUNT 1.19.58.[10]

A PROPHECY OF THE END OF THE LEVITICAL PRIESTHOOD. BEDE: [Paul] did not say this because he was stirred by passion in his mind. Rather, he surely spoke by way of prophesying, for, as a figure, that high priesthood that had been compared to the likeness of a whitewashed wall was to be struck and destroyed, since the true priesthood of Christ had now come with the apostles' preaching of the gospel. And that is why he said, "God will strike you." He did not say, "May God strike you." In fact, he signified by the indicative mood that this thing was going to happen; he did not utter a curse by using the optative mood. COMMENTARY ON THE ACTS OF THE APOSTLES 23.3.[11]

CHRIST SPOKE SIMILARLY AND WAS NOT ABUSIVE. CHRYSOSTOM: This is well said. For to kill one who had done no wrong and moreover does not deserve punishment is a violation of the law. For his words could not be called abusive unless one also called Christ's words abusive, when he said, "Woe to you, teachers of the law and Pharisees! You are like whitewashed walls."[12] True, you will say. But since [Paul] spoke before he was struck, it was not out of anger but out of boldness. But I have mentioned the reason for this. Indeed, Christ often insulted the Jews, when he himself had been abused by them, as when he said, "Do not think I will accuse you before the Father."[13] But [Paul's words] are not abuse; God forbid. See with what gentleness he addresses these men: "I did not know that he was the high priest of God." And to show that he was not being ironic, he adds, "You shall not speak evil of a ruler of your people." [Paul] even acknowledges that he is still a ruler. Let us learn the gentleness as well as the boldness, so that we may be complete in both. For much exactness is needed to learn what each of them is.

Exactness, because these virtues have their attendant vices: near boldness stands audacity, near gentleness, cowardice. HOMILIES ON THE ACTS OF THE APOSTLES 48.[14]

23:4 Reviling God's High Priest?

A REVERSAL AND TRANSFERENCE. AUGUSTINE: But when [Paul] was asked, "Do you revile the high priest?" then he marvelously complied with the requirements of humility, for he replied, "Brothers, I did not know that he was the high priest; for it is written, 'You shall not speak evil of a ruler of your people.'"[15] The mildness of this prompt reply shows how calmly he had spoken what he seemed to have uttered in anger, for such a reply could not be given by those who are angered or perturbed. And in the reply, "I did not know that he was the high priest," he spoke the truth to those who understand him. It is as though he were saying, "I have come to know another high priest, for whose name's sake I am suffering these injuries—a high priest whom it is not lawful to revile but whom you are reviling, because in me you hate nothing else than his name." Thus, a man ought not to parade those prerogatives under a false pretense, but he should have his heart prepared for everything, so that he will be able to accord with that expression of the prophet, "My heart is ready, O God, my heart is ready."[16] SERMON ON THE MOUNT 1.19.58.[17]

23:5 I Did Not Know

I DID NOT KNOW. BEDE: Although [Paul] had actually recognized that this man was not the chief priest in the new covenant, nevertheless, in instructing others and advising them to conduct themselves more decorously toward those in power, he himself also decided to use moderation here. COMMENTARY ON THE ACTS OF THE APOSTLES 23.5.[18]

---

[10]FC 11:84. [11]CS 117:175. [12]Mt 23:27. [13]Jn 5:45. [14]NPNF 1 11:290**. [15]Ex 22:28. [16]Ps 57:7 (56:8 LXX, Vg). [17]FC 11:84-85*. [18]CS 117:175.

23:6-11 DISSENSION ARISES BETWEEN THE SADDUCEES AND PHARISEES

⁶*But when Paul perceived that one part were Sadducees and the other Pharisees, he cried out in the council, "Brothers, I am a Pharisee, a son of Pharisees; with respect to the hope and the resurrection of the dead I am on trial." ⁷And when he had said this, a dissension arose between the Pharisees and the Sadducees; and the assembly was divided. ⁸For the Sadducees say that there is no resurrection, nor angel, nor spirit; but the Pharisees acknowledge them all. ⁹Then a great clamor arose; and some of the scribes of the Pharisees' party stood up and contended, "We find nothing wrong in this man. What if a spirit or an angel spoke to him?" ¹⁰And when the dissension became violent, the tribune, afraid that Paul would be torn in pieces by them, commanded the soldiers to go down and take him by force from among them and bring him into the barracks.*

¹¹*The following night the Lord stood by him and said, "Take courage, for as you have testified about me at Jerusalem, so you must bear witness also at Rome."*

OVERVIEW: Moderns point to the way in which Paul divides his opponents, though they have difficulty with Luke's statement that the Sadducees "say that there is no resurrection, nor angel, nor spirit," since the latter two are mentioned in the Old Testament, which they hold to be authoritative. Some think that Luke intends "angels" and "spirits" to refer to anticipations of the resurrection. It is possible that Luke intends the Pharisees' statement that they find nothing wrong in Paul to be a Pharisaic defense of Paul, thus establishing Christianity as one legitimate expression of Judaism and so protected under the Roman category of a *religio licita*. The vision and words of Jesus mark the third of four such encounters of Paul with Jesus, not counting his conversion experience. Luke recounts them to insist that his story is really about God's activity, often through Jesus and the Holy Spirit in directing and empowering the church. Surprisingly, Israel's history is used as an explanatory model in two of the selections from the Fathers. Bede, always looking for some symbol or type beneath the events, connects Paul's strategy of defense with the parting of the Red Sea during the exodus. Origen consid-

ers it not a figural similarity of escape but rather one of immersion in the midst of worldly trials, the battle against Egypt: as God promised Israel a sojourn and then an escape from Egypt, so Christ promised Paul. Chrysostom views Paul as an example of how God consoles us in this life.

23:6 On Trial with Respect to the Hope and the Resurrection

BROTHERS, I AM A PHARISEE. BEDE: Just as agreement among good people is always beneficial, so agreement among evil people is always harmful to the good. Hence, the apostle attempted to cause dissension among his persecutors, so that they might in their division release the man whom in their agreement they had bound.[1] So it was that the Red Sea, which when it was whole had blocked the passage of the sons of Israel, freed them from Egypt when it was divided.[2] This is why [Paul] testified that he was "the son of Pharisees" (or, according to the Greek,

---

[1]Gregory the Great *Morals on the Book of Job* 34.4.8-9 (PL 76:722).
[2]Ex 14:9-10, 21-22.

"the son of a Pharisee"), which is what he gloried in above,[3] [and] that he learned the prophets and the law at the feet of Gamaliel, who, as we read, was a Pharisee.[4] COMMENTARY ON THE ACTS OF THE APOSTLES 23.6.[5]

23:8 The Sadducees Say There Is No Resurrection

THEY DO NOT BELIEVE IN THINGS INCORPO-REAL. CHRYSOSTOM: The Sadducees know of nothing incorporeal, perhaps not even God, so thick-headed are they. Consequently, they are also unwilling to believe that there is a resurrection. HOMILIES ON THE ACTS OF THE APOSTLES 49.[6]

23:9 Nothing Wrong in This Man

AN AMBIGUOUS PASSAGE. AMMONIUS: "What if a spirit or an angel has spoken to him?" These words are obscure or something is missing for the completion of the sentence, which would be, "If a spirit or an angel has told to him what to say in order to avoid dangers, he is being deceptive." Otherwise, what the Pharisees say must be understood in the sense, "Look! He's clearly talking about the resurrection, since he's been taught either this teaching on the resurrection by the Holy Spirit or an angel." CATENA ON THE ACTS OF THE APOSTLES 23.9.[7]

23:11 Bearing Witness Also at Rome

CONSOLATION GIVEN DURING AFFLICTIONS. CHRYSOSTOM: Notice how great is the consolation! First he praises him, "as you have testified about me at Jerusalem"; then, he does not leave him fearful of the uncertainty of his journey to Rome. For not only will you arrive there, he says, but you will also make use of this boldness of speech. From this it is revealed that not only will he be saved but that he will be saved in the great city, honored with great crowns. Why didn't [Jesus] appear to him before he fell into danger? Because, as always, it is in afflictions that God consoles. For then he appears more desirable, as he trains us even in the midst of dangers. HOMILIES ON THE ACTS OF THE APOSTLES 49.[8]

THE BATTLE AGAINST EGYPT. ORIGEN: Scripture says, "Fear not to go down into Egypt,"[9] which means, When you come against "the principalities and powers and rulers of the darkness of this world"[10]—those figuratively called Egypt—do not fear or recoil. If you wish to know why you should not fear, listen to my promise: "There, I will make of you a great nation, and I shall go down into Egypt with you, and I shall call you back from there in the end."[11] He is, therefore, not afraid to go down into Egypt. He fears neither the combats of this world nor the trials of demonic adversaries. Hear, then, what the apostle Paul says: "More than those others have I labored, yet not I, but the grace of God with me."[12] Even in Jerusalem, when a plot had been set in motion against him and he toiled in combat for the word and the preaching of the Lord, beside him the Lord stood and said these same things that are said to Israel: "Fear not, Paul, for just as you have been my witness in Jerusalem, so you must also be my witness in Rome." HOMILIES ON GENESIS 15.5.[13]

---

[3]Acts 22:3. [4]Acts 5:34. [5]CS 117:175-76. [6]NPNF 1 11:294**.
[7]CGPNT 3:369. [8]NPNF 1 11:294**. [9]Gen 46:3. [10]Eph 6:12.
[11]Gen 46:3-4. [12]1 Cor 15:10. [13]SC 7.2:364.

23:12-15 SOME BIND THEMSELVES BY OATH TO KILL PAUL

[12]When it was day, the Jews made a plot and bound themselves by an oath neither to eat nor drink till they had killed Paul. [13]There were more than forty who made this conspiracy. [14]And they went to the chief priests and elders, and said, "We have strictly bound ourselves by an oath to taste no food till we have killed Paul. [15]You therefore, along with the council, give notice now to the tribune to bring him down to you, as though you were going to determine his case more exactly. And we are ready to kill him before he comes near."

OVERVIEW: Modern commentators have little to say about this particular part of the narrative. Some are intrigued by the presence of Paul's married sister in Jerusalem (Acts 23:16), and some try to distinguish Luke's source for the whole incident from Luke's literary activity. Neither do the Fathers have much to contribute. Bede and Chrysostom both are drawn to the contrast between actions that on the surface resemble piety, and their true inner source.

23:12 Bound by Oath

THE DEVIL USES PRETEXTS OF PIETY. CHRYSOSTOM: Behold fasting, the mother of murder! Just as Herod imposed that necessity by oath upon himself,[1] likewise do these men. For these are the devil's ways. Under the pretext of piety itself he sets his traps. HOMILIES ON THE ACTS OF THE APOSTLES 49.[2]

BOUND UNDER A VOW. BEDE: While the Lord said, "Blessed are those who hunger and thirst for justice,"[3] these people on the contrary hungered for iniquity and thirsted as much for blood, so that they even gave up food for the body until they might be satiated by the death of a just man. But "there is no wisdom, there is no prudence, there is no counsel in opposition to the Lord."[4] For [as we have read] also above, although Paul offered sacrifices, shaved his head, "went barefoot and to the Jews became a Jew,"[5] nevertheless he could not escape the chains that had been foretold.[6] In this case too, although these men took counsel together, bound themselves under a vow and laid snares [for Paul], nevertheless the apostle was kept unharmed so that he could also give testimony to Christ in Rome, just as had also been said. COMMENTARY ON THE ACTS OF THE APOSTLES 23.12.[7]

---

[1]Mt 14:7. [2]NPNF 1 11:293*. [3]Mt 5:6. [4]Prov 21:30. [5]Acts 18:18; 21:23-26; 1 Cor 9:20; Jerome *Commentary on Galatians* 2.4.8-9 (PL 26:375). [6]Acts 21:11. [7]CS 117:176.

23:16-22 THE TRIBUNE INFORMED OF THE PLOT

¹⁶*Now the son of Paul's sister heard of their ambush; so he went and entered the barracks and told Paul.* ¹⁷*And Paul called one of the centurions and said, "Take this young man to the tribune; for he has something to tell him."* ¹⁸*So he took him and brought him to the tribune and said, "Paul the prisoner called me and asked me to bring this young man to you, as he has something to say to you."* ¹⁹*The tribune took him by the hand, and going aside asked him privately, "What is it that you have to tell me?"* ²⁰*And he said, "The Jews have agreed to ask you to bring Paul down to the council tomorrow, as though they were going to inquire somewhat more closely about him.* ²¹*But do not yield to them; for more than forty of their men lie in ambush for him, having bound themselves by an oath neither to eat nor drink till they have killed him; and now they are ready, waiting for the promise from you."* ²²*So the tribune dismissed the young man, charging him, "Tell no one that you have informed me of this."*

OVERVIEW: This part of the story could have been reduced, but its details give the impression that Luke had access to primary witnesses. Modern commentators usually ask how Paul's nephew could have had such easy access to a prisoner, especially at such a troubled moment, and they wonder, then, why Luke does not mention the Jerusalem community caring for Paul. The import of the passage, however, is that Jesus' words to Paul come to fulfillment through human circumstances. Chrysostom, our only witness from the Fathers here, is most keen, as usual, to make this sequence of events clear.

23:16 The Son of Paul's Sister Heard of Their Ambush

THE HUMAN NATURE OF THE EVENTS. CHRYSOSTOM: Again human forethought is saved. See, Paul allowed nobody to learn of this, not even the centurion, so that the matter might not be divulged. Instead, the centurion took him and brought him to the tribune. The tribune rightly ordered that he be hidden, so that the matter would remain secret. Then he told the centurions what had to be done. CATENA ON THE ACTS OF THE APOSTLES 23.17-21.[1]

23:17 Take This Young Man to the Tribune

PAUL DID NOT ABANDON ACTION BECAUSE HE BELIEVED. CHRYSOSTOM: Even after appearing to him, [Paul] again allows him to be saved by human means. And what happens? Paul was not thrown into confusion; he did not say, "So I have been deceived by Christ." Instead, he believed. Indeed, because he believed, he did not sleep and did not give up the abilities that human wisdom had given him. HOMILIES ON THE ACTS OF THE APOSTLES 49.[2]

---

[1]CGPNT 3:372. [2]NPNF 1 11:293**.

23:23-35 PAUL SENT TO THE GOVERNOR AT CAESAREA

²³Then he called two of the centurions and said, "At the third hour of the night get ready two hundred soldiers with seventy horsemen and two hundred spearmen to go as far as Caesarea. ²⁴Also provide mounts for Paul to ride, and bring him safely to Felix the governor." ²⁵And he wrote a letter to this effect:

²⁶"Claudius Lysias to his Excellency the governor Felix, greeting. ²⁷This man was seized by the Jews, and was about to be killed by them, when I came upon them with the soldiers and rescued him, having learned that he was a Roman citizen. ²⁸And desiring to know the charge on which they accused him, I brought him down to their council. ²⁹I found that he was accused about questions of their law, but charged with nothing deserving death or imprisonment. ³⁰And when it was disclosed to me that there would be a plot against the man, I sent him to you at once, ordering his accusers also to state before you what they have against him."

³¹So the soldiers, according to their instructions, took Paul and brought him by night to Antipatris. ³²And on the morrow they returned to the barracks, leaving the horsemen to go on with him. ³³When they came to Caesarea and delivered the letter to the governor, they presented Paul also before him. ³⁴On reading the letter, he asked to what province he belonged. When he learned that he was from Cilicia ³⁵he said, "I will hear you when your accusers arrive." And he commanded him to be guarded in Herod's praetorium.

OVERVIEW: Most modern commentators remark on the size of the force sent to accompany Paul, and they wonder how Luke could have access to the *litterae dimissoriae* which, according to Roman law, must be sent from an official to a superior when there is an appeal. They answer these questions variously. In regard to the first question they point to the danger because of the recent turmoil stirred up in connection with Paul; in regard to the second, most presume Luke is composing according to the model of such form letters. The point of the passage is to state clearly that Paul is considered innocent by the Roman authority. It also makes a subtle allusion to the irony of people who want to accuse Paul of infidelity to the law and are yet willing to contravene one of its most sacred commandments in murdering him. Chrysostom, our one patristic source

here, compares Paul's situation with Jesus' before Pilate. He then lays out the pattern of events: a handing over for condemnation that is subverted in the proclamation of the accused's innocence. Chrysostom's implications are clear: here we have the form of Christ's passion, with the exception that this time it is not through resurrection that vindication had to be known but rather through the proper application of imperial law.

23:30 Sent at Once

THE ROLE PLAYED BY OUTSIDERS. CHRYSOSTOM: See how Paul is reckoned innocent through the vote of the foreigners, like Christ with Pilate. See how their evil intentions are defeated: they handed him over, so that he might be killed and condemned, but the opposite happened, and he was saved and found innocent. If things did not go this way, [Paul] would have been torn into pieces, would have perished, would have been condemned. CAT-

ENA ON THE ACTS OF THE APOSTLES 23.28-30.[1]

---

[1]CGPNT 3:374.

24:1-8 TERTULLUS ACCUSES PAUL BEFORE FELIX

[1]*And after five days the high priest Ananias came down with some elders and a spokesman, one Tertullus. They laid before the governor their case against Paul;* [2]*and when he was called, Tertullus began to accuse him, saying:*

"Since through you we enjoy much peace, and since by your provision, most excellent Felix, reforms are introduced on behalf of this nation, [3]*in every way and everywhere we accept this with all gratitude.* [4]*But, to detain you no further, I beg you in your kindness to hear us briefly.* [5]*For we have found this man a pestilent fellow, an agitator among all the Jews throughout the world, and a ringleader of the sect of the Nazarenes.* [6]*He even tried to profane the temple, but we seized him.*[z] [8]*By examining him yourself you will be able to learn from him about everything of which we accuse him."*

z Other ancient authorities add *and we would have judged him according to our law.* [7]*But the chief captain Lysias came and with great violence took him out of our hands,* [8]*commanding his accusers to come before you.*

OVERVIEW: This singular instance of a debate in Acts reveals Luke's skill in composing discourse that suits the person he records as speaking. Tertullus uses ingratiating language and ties Paul to political rebellion—a charge not unlike that against Jesus, who also prophesied that just such legal proceedings would be brought against the disciples (Lk 21:12). Chrysostom, having been trained in rhetoric, is always attentive to the relationship that a speaker attempts to establish at the beginning of his speech.[1] A traditional and despised relationship to adopt was known as the flatterer, a stance Chrysostom sees Tertullus adopting.[2] As has been seen throughout this commentary, not only Chrysostom but many of the Fathers placed great value on what they call *parrēsia*, which is often translated as boldness

and entails speaking forthrightly.[3] Not only is

[1]See his varied comments above at Acts 22:3, especially the third. [2]For an ancient discussion of the flatterer, see Plutarch's *How to Tell a Flatterer from a Friend* in LCL 197. For a recent discussion that uncovers our difficulties with distinguishing between rhetoric and flattery, see William Ian Miller's *Faking It* (Cambridge: Cambridge University Press, 2003). [3]This word has a long history. It is used not only of speech among people in the New Testament, but also of how Christ's work has allowed the believer to approach God: see Paul's contrast between the worship of the Corinthian community and the synagogue (2 Cor 3:12-18). On the origin of the idea of *parrēsia* in classical Athenian democracy, a good and popular introduction can be found in Simon Goldhill's *Love, Sex and Tragedy* (Chicago: University of Chicago Press, 2004), part 3, "What Do You Think Should Happen?" Although the terms were different in Rome, Roland Mayer's introduction to his *Tacitus: Dialogus de Oratoribus* (Cambridge: Cambridge University Press, 2001) provides a useful and brief overview of how open debate became a great hazard in the empire. For a discussion of its place in late antiquity, see Peter Brown, *Power and Persuasion in Late Antiquity: Towards a Christian Empire* (Madison: University of Wisconsin Press, 1992).

Tertullus's approach fawning, but as Chrysostom shows, there are no witnesses other than the accusers themselves.

24:3 Accepted with Gratitude

TERTULLUS THE FLATTERER. CHRYSOSTOM: See how [Tertullus] approaches the judge with praises from the start and wants to hand Paul over as a revolutionary and a rebel. Then, notice how he hastens as if he has many things to say. CATENA ON THE ACTS OF THE APOSTLES 24.2-3.[4]

24:5 A Pestilent Fellow

THE NAZARENE SECT. BEDE: At that time Christians were called Nazarenes as an insult. Afterwards, however, a heretical sect arose among the Jews, which was called the Nazarenes. "They believed in Christ as the son of God, born of the virgin Mary, and they said that it was he who suffered under Pontius Pilate and rose from the grave. In him we also believe. But while they wanted to be both Jews and Christians, they were neither Jews nor Christians."[5] COMMENTARY ON THE ACTS OF THE APOSTLES 24.5.[6]

24:7 Lysias the Centurion[7]

THE WEAKNESS OF TERTULLUS'S CHARGE.

CHRYSOSTOM: Then comes the accusation against Lysias. "It was not right for him," he says, "to drag him away with great violence.". . . "He tried," he says, "to profane the temple," but [Tertullus] does not say how. He also magnified what concerned Paul, but see how he diminished what concerned him. "We seized him," he says, "and would have judged him according to our law." He claims that it was unpleasant to them to come to foreign courts and that they would have not given trouble to [Felix], if he had not forced them, and that it was not right for Lysias to take Paul away. "These," he says, "were in fact offenses against us, because the trial ought to have taken place among us." See now the rest as a confirmation that things were so, "with great violence," he says. That, indeed, was violence. "From him," he says, "you will be able to learn.". . . He puts Paul in the position to become his own accuser. "From him," he says, "you will be able to know by judging." And the very witnesses of the things that were said, they are the accusers—they are the witnesses and the accusers. CATENA ON THE ACTS OF THE APOSTLES 24.7-9.[8]

---

[4]CGPNT 3:375. [5]Jerome *Letter* 112.13 (CSEL 55:381-82). [6]CS 117:177. [7]Between verses 6 and 8, a small number of manuscripts introduce an explanation of how Paul was transferred to the Roman authorities. [8]CGPNT 3:376.

24:9-21 PAUL MAKES HIS DEFENSE

[9]*The Jews also joined in the charge, affirming that all this was so.*

[10]*And when the governor had motioned to him to speak, Paul replied:*

"Realizing that for many years you have been judge over this nation, I cheerfully make my defense. [11]*As you may ascertain, it is not more than twelve days since I went up to worship at Jerusalem;* [12]*and they did not find me disputing with any one or stirring up a crowd, either in the tem-*

ple or in the synagogues, or in the city. ¹³Neither can they prove to you what they now bring up against me. ¹⁴But this I admit to you, that according to the Way, which they call a sect, I worship the God of our fathers, believing everything laid down by the law or written in the prophets, ¹⁵having a hope in God which these themselves accept, that there will be a resurrection of both the just and the unjust. ¹⁶So I always take pains to have a clear conscience toward God and toward men. ¹⁷Now after some years I came to bring to my nation alms and offerings. ¹⁸As I was doing this, they found me purified in the temple, without any crowd or tumult. But some Jews from Asia—¹⁹they ought to be here before you and to make an accusation, if they have anything against me. ²⁰Or else let these men themselves say what wrongdoing they found when I stood before the council, ²¹except this one thing which I cried out while standing among them, 'With respect to the resurrection of the dead I am on trial before you this day.'"

OVERVIEW: Paul's third defense speech, on the contrary, is straightforward and summarizes his activity in Jerusalem and points to Tertullus's lack of proof. Felix postpones a decision, perhaps through weakness: moderns quote Tacitus, who describes Felix as someone who "with all cruelty and lust wielded the power of a king with the mentality of a slave."[1] This is the first time since Paul's arrival in Palestine that Luke makes mention of the collection made for the poor of Jerusalem. Jerome's comment (Acts 24:17) needs some explanation. This brief passage comes from a polemical work against Vigilantius, a former friend of Jerome. Vigilantius had lived with Jerome in Bethlehem but suddenly left without explanation and returned to Gaul. Years later, Jerome learned that he had begun to spread criticisms not only of lavish expenditures on reliquaries and vestments but also of the sending of alms to the Jerusalem church, which he thought should be kept for the poor in the local communities. Jerome's argument, as his own journey in life, reflects the cultural process of the sacralization of space, the creation of the sense, fully flourishing by his day, of Palestine as the Holy Land. Chrysostom takes up an analysis of Paul's character as portrayed in this speech, and, as usual, finds much to praise. Ammonius sees here an argument for the unity of the Father and the Son.

24:14 Everything Laid Down by the Law

IT IS PAUL WHO BELIEVES ALL. CHRYSOSTOM: He did not say that they believed "everything written in the prophets." For [Paul] was the one who believed everything, not they. To show how he believed in "everything" would take a long speech, and nowhere does he mention Christ. Here by the word *believing* [Paul] introduces the things relating to Christ. But for the present he dwells on the subject of resurrection, a doctrine shared by them, and so removes their suspicion of the whole sect. HOMILIES ON THE ACTS OF THE APOSTLES 50.[2]

WORSHIPING THE SAME GOD. AMMONIUS: [Paul] calls the faith or tradition "the Way." It must be noticed that the Nazarenes believe in their ancestral God, the precepts of the law, the prophets and the resurrection of the dead. Paul shows this from what he says: "I worship the God of our ancestors," that is, he believes in Christ and does not worship another God but him who is one with the Father, who was preached in the law and by the prophets. He shows also that all those believing in Christ, just as himself, accept the law of Moses and the prophets. CATENA ON THE ACTS OF THE APOSTLES 24.14.[3]

---

[1]*Histories* 5.9. Quoted by Fitzmyer, *Acts*, 727. [2]NPNF 1 11:299**. [3]CGPNT 3:377.

24:16 A Clear Conscience

THE PERFECTION OF VIRTUE. CHRYSOSTOM: "To have a clear conscience," he says, "toward God and toward people." This is the perfection of virtue, when we give no cause for grudge to people and strive to give no offense to God. HOMILIES ON THE ACTS OF THE APOSTLES 50.[4]

24:17 Alms and Offerings

THE POOR OF THE HOLY PLACES. JEROME: Could he not have distributed the gifts he had received from others in some other part of the world and in the infant churches he was training in his own faith? But [Paul] longed to give to the poor of the holy places, who abandoned their own meager possessions for the sake of Christ and turned with all their heart to the service of the Lord. AGAINST VIGILANTIUS 13.[5]

24:20 What Wrongdoing Did They Find?

PAUL KEEPS FROM SPEAKING EVIL. CHRYSOSTOM: Did you notice his gentleness in the midst of dangers? Did you notice how he kept his tongue from speaking evil? How he sought one thing only, to do away with charges against himself, and not to place charges against them, except in so far as he was forced to defend himself? HOMILIES ON THE ACTS OF THE APOSTLES 50.[6]

24:21 The Resurrection of the Dead

READINESS TO GIVE ACCOUNT TO ALL. CHRYSOSTOM: This is ample justification that [Paul] did not flee from his accusers but was ready to give account to all. "With respect to the resurrection of the dead I am on trial before you this day." And not a word did he say of what he could have said, that they conspired against him, detained him and imprisoned him. For these things can justly be said of the tribune, and yet they were not said by Paul, even though he was in danger. Instead, he is silent and only defends himself, when there was much he could have said. HOMILIES ON THE ACTS OF THE APOSTLES 50.[7]

---

[4]NPNF 1 11:299**. [5]NPNF 2 6:422. [6]NPNF 1 11:299**. [7]NPNF 1 11:298**.

24:22-27 FELIX SUMMONS PAUL AND HEARS HIM

[22]But Felix, having a rather accurate knowledge of the Way, put them off, saying, "When Lysias the tribune comes down, I will decide your case." [23]Then he gave orders to the centurion that he should be kept in custody but should have some liberty, and that none of his friends should be prevented from attending to his needs.

[24]After some days Felix came with his wife Drusilla, who was a Jewess; and he sent for Paul and heard him speak upon faith in Christ Jesus. [25]And as he argued about justice and self-control and future judgment, Felix was alarmed and said, "Go away for the present; when I have an opportunity I will summon you." [26]At the same time he hoped that money would be given him by Paul. So he sent for him often and conversed with him. [27]But when two years had elapsed, Felix was succeeded by Porcius Festus; and desiring to do the Jews a favor, Felix left Paul in prison.

OVERVIEW: Except for a few remarks about Felix's character as deftly portrayed by Luke, modern commentators find little to remark upon in this passage. The Fathers take interest in the characters: the source of Felix's knowledge of the faith, the type of woman Drusilla was, why Felix wanted her present. Chrysostom builds a picture of Felix as a man corrupted by greed.

24:22 Accurate Knowledge of the Way

FELIX'S FAITHLESS KNOWLEDGE. AMMONIUS: It must be noticed that Felix thoroughly knew the faith, as he had been taught the things concerning Christ from the Old Testament. Even so he did not dismiss Paul so that he might please men, as did his successor, as the following words indicate, "Wanting to please the Jews," and with the hope to get money from him. And still [Felix] knew the faith, thanks to having a Jewish spouse, from whom he often heard these things. CATENA ON THE ACTS OF THE APOSTLES 24.22.[1]

24:24 Felix and His Wife, Drusilla

DRUSILLA. AMMONIUS: She, being a Jew, was wed, contrary to the law, to a pagan. Although she was a Jew, perhaps on marrying she became a Gentile, and for this reason also revealed to him her faith. Or because she was Jewish, she also spoke in order to convert her husband. Or because she had transgressed the law, she transgressed it to this point. CATENA ON THE ACTS OF THE APOSTLES 24.24.[2]

THEY SHOW PAUL HONOR. CHRYSOSTOM: The wife also listens, along with the governor. This seems to me to show great honor. He would not have brought his wife to the hearing, unless he thought great things of Paul. It seems to me that she too longed for this. HOMILIES ON THE ACTS OF THE APOSTLES 51.[3]

24:26 Felix Hoped Paul Would Give Him Money

FELIX DID NOT WISH TO BELIEVE. CHRYSOSTOM: He sent for him frequently, not because he admired him, or because he praised his words or even because he wished to believe. Then why? "He hoped," it says, "that money would be given him." Look how [Luke] does not hide the mindset of the judge here. And yet if he had condemned him, he would not have done this or wished to listen to a condemned wretch. And look at Paul, although he is talking with a ruler, he says none of those things that are likely to amuse, but rather he speaks "about justice," it says, "and future judgment" and about the resurrection. And such was the force of his words that they even alarmed the governor. HOMILIES ON THE ACTS OF THE APOSTLES 51.[4]

24:27 Felix Left Paul in Prison

FELIX'S STUPIDITY. CHRYSOSTOM: See his stupidity: after hearing these things, [Felix] expected that money would have been obtained from [Paul]; and not only this, but as he was at the end of his tenure, he left him in chains, in order to please the Jews, so that he did not only desire money but fame too. How can you, scoundrel, look for money from a man who preaches the opposite? It is clear that he left him in chains because of what he did not gain, whereas he would have freed him, if he gained it. CATENA ON THE ACTS OF THE APOSTLES 24.25-26.[5]

---

[1]CGPNT 3:380. [2]CGPNT 3:380. [3]NPNF 1 11:304*. [4]NPNF 1 11:303**. [5]CGPNT 3:381.

25:1-5 FESTUS IS ASKED TO HAVE PAUL
SENT TO JERUSALEM

¹*Now when Festus had come into his province, after three days he went up to Jerusalem from Caesarea. ²And the chief priests and the principal men of the Jews informed him against Paul; and they urged him, ³asking as a favor to have the man sent to Jerusalem, planning an ambush to kill him on the way. ⁴Festus replied that Paul was being kept at Caesarea, and that he himself intended to go there shortly. ⁵"So," said he, "let the men of authority among you go down with me, and if there is anything wrong about the man, let them accuse him."*

Overview: In Luke's plan this chapter, having four episodes, prepares for Paul's climactic defense speech in the next chapter. These verses set the stage for Paul's appeal to Caesar that begins the fulfillment of Jesus' words to him, "Take courage, for as you have testified about me at Jerusalem, so you must bear witness also at Rome."

25:6-12 PAUL APPEALS TO CAESAR

⁶*When he had stayed among them not more than eight or ten days, he went down to Caesarea; and the next day he took his seat on the tribunal and ordered Paul to be brought. ⁷And when he had come, the Jews who had gone down from Jerusalem stood about him, bringing against him many serious charges which they could not prove. ⁸Paul said in his defense, "Neither against the law of the Jews, nor against the temple, nor against Caesar have I offended at all." ⁹But Festus, wishing to do the Jews a favor, said to Paul, "Do you wish to go up to Jerusalem, and there be tried on these charges before me?" ¹⁰But Paul said, "I am standing before Caesar's tribunal, where I ought to be tried; to the Jews I have done no wrong, as you know very well. ¹¹If then I am a wrongdoer, and have committed anything for which I deserve to die, I do not seek to escape death; but if there is nothing in their charges against me, no one can give me up to them. I appeal to Caesar." ¹²Then Festus, when he had conferred with his council, answered, "You have appealed to Caesar; to Caesar you shall go."*

Overview: This is Paul's fourth and penultimate defense speech in Acts. Most of it repeats what has been said before. The difference is that Paul is now in the situation of an official Roman hearing (Festus "took his seat on the tribunal"). Festus appears as one who is learning the advantages of yielding where possible to Jewish wishes. Paul's rejoinder to his question about being tried in Jerusalem reminds Festus that [Paul] is already standing before the emperor's agent and then adds pointedly that he has done no wrong as Festus "knows very well." Finally, Paul makes the momentous move of appealing to Caesar. Commentators are divided at this point as to whether Festus and his council were obliged to send Paul to Rome, since there has been no verdict on the basis of which an appeal could be made. Paul's appeal, however, is granted and opens the way to Rome. Both Bede and Chrysostom investigate Paul's intention in appealing to Caesar. Chrysostom does not want his audience to interpret Paul's initiative as a lack of faith in Christ's prophecy. Paul did not tempt God by taking futile or unnecessary risks but used available means to protect life (CHRYSOSTOM). Both Fathers find Paul's intention to be a matter of publicity: trials provide a means of spreading a message, and so Paul, by taking charge, forces the imperial justice system to become the space not where Paul fights for his life but where the gospel becomes known.

25:11 I Appeal to Caesar

PAUL DOES NOT TEMPT GOD. CHRYSOSTOM: Someone might ask, "Why is it that when [Paul] heard 'You must testify about me in Rome,' he did this, as if he did not believe?" God forbid! He did this not because he did not believe but because he believed very strongly, for it would have been the action of one who is tempting God to be bold on account of that declaration, to plunge himself into ten thousand dangers and to say, "Let's see if God can deliver me even so." Paul did not do this

but made use of all that was in himself, entrusting everything to God. HOMILIES ON THE ACTS OF THE APOSTLES 51.[1]

TO ROME. BEDE: [Paul] appealed to Caesar and hastened to Rome so that he could pursue [his] preaching longer, and from there, with many believers and crowned by all,[2] he might go to Christ. COMMENTARY ON THE ACTS OF THE APOSTLES 25.11.[3]

25:12 To Caesar You Shall Go

FOR THE SAKE OF THE PREACHING. CHRYSOSTOM: [Paul] did not say, "I am not worthy of death," or "I am worthy to be acquitted," but "I am ready to stand trial before Caesar." At the same time, remembering the dream, he was all the more confident to appeal. . . . "When he had conferred with his council," it says, "[Festus] answered, 'You have appealed to Caesar; to Caesar you shall go.'" Notice again how his trial is extended, how the plot against him becomes an occasion for preaching, so that with ease and security he is conveyed to Salem,[4] with no plot against him. For it is one thing to simply be there and another to be there for this reason. For this is what made the Jews gather there. Again, [Festus] stays at Jerusalem for some time, to teach us that although time has passed, in no way do the plottings against him succeed, since God does not permit it. HOMILIES ON THE ACTS OF THE APOSTLES 51.[5]

---

[1]NPNF 1 11:303**. [2]Phil 4:1. [3]CS 117:181. [4] Following *Catena in Acts*, CGPNT 3:384, line 11. NPNF reads "Rome." [5]NPNF 1 11:305**.

25:13-21 FESTUS EXPLAINS PAUL'S CASE
TO KING AGRIPPA

¹³*Now when some days had passed, Agrippa the king and Bernice arrived at Caesarea to welcome Festus.* ¹⁴*And as they stayed there many days, Festus laid Paul's case before the king, saying, "There is a man left prisoner by Felix;* ¹⁵*and when I was at Jerusalem, the chief priests and the elders of the Jews gave information about him, asking for sentence against him.* ¹⁶*I answered them that it was not the custom of the Romans to give up any one before the accused met the accusers face to face, and had opportunity to make his defense concerning the charge laid against him.* ¹⁷*When therefore they came together here, I made no delay, but on the next day took my seat on the tribunal and ordered the man to be brought in.* ¹⁸*When the accusers stood up, they brought no charge in his case of such evils as I supposed;* ¹⁹*but they had certain points of dispute with him about their own superstition and about one Jesus, who was dead, but whom Paul asserted to be alive.* ²⁰*Being at a loss how to investigate these questions, I asked whether he wished to go to Jerusalem and be tried there regarding them.* ²¹*But when Paul had appealed to be kept in custody for the decision of the emperor, I commanded him to be held until I could send him to Caesar."*

OVERVIEW: Commentators point out that once again Luke stresses Paul's innocence in a legal process. Luke's skill at fitting the words to the speaker is apparent in Festus's self-laudatory description of his actions.[1] The moderns also provide a useful identification of Agrippa and his sister Bernice. Some also remark that Paul has now appeared before a "synagogue" and a "governor" and will soon appear before a king (Lk 12:11-12; see also Acts 9:15-16). Chrysostom reads Festus's testimony not only as a condemnation of the petulant persistence of Paul's Jewish opponents but in some way as a proxy of God's vengeance.

creating a large audience. Even Agrippa himself falls into a desire for a hearing—and not only does he listen, but he does so with intensity. And then, look at [his] defense. As Festus presents it, he exposes the cruelty of the Jewish leaders. Because when the governor says these things, he is beyond suspicion, resulting in the Jewish leaders being convicted by him. For, after he has exposed the truth about all these things, then God metes out punishment. Felix condemns them, Festus condemns them and, even though he was favorably inclined, Agrippa condemns them too. HOMILIES ON THE ACTS OF THE APOSTLES 51.[2]

25:14 Paul's Case Set Before Agrippa

THE WITNESS OF FESTUS. CHRYSOSTOM: See [Paul's] enemies who unwittingly conspired in

---

[1]In regard to this passages see Jacques Dupont, "Aequitas Romana: Notes sur Actes 25:16," *Recherches de Science Religieuse* 49 (1961): 354-85. [2]CGPNT 3:386.

25:22-27 PAUL BROUGHT BEFORE AGRIPPA

²²And Agrippa said to Festus, "I should like to hear the man myself." "Tomorrow," said he, "you shall hear him."

²³So on the morrow Agrippa and Bernice came with great pomp, and they entered the audience hall with the military tribunes and the prominent men of the city. Then by command of Festus Paul was brought in. ²⁴And Festus said, "King Agrippa and all who are present with us, you see this man about whom the whole Jewish people petitioned me, both at Jerusalem and here, shouting that he ought not to live any longer. ²⁵But I found that he had done nothing deserving death; and as he himself appealed to the emperor, I decided to send him. ²⁶But I have nothing definite to write to my lord about him. Therefore I have brought him before you, and, especially before you, King Agrippa, that, after we have examined him, I may have something to write. ²⁷For it seems to me unreasonable, in sending a prisoner, not to indicate the charges against him."

OVERVIEW: These verses set the stage for Paul's final and most complete defense of his life and his call by Jesus Christ which then becomes a preaching of the gospel. And it is at this final point that Luke uses the speech to present the christological climax of his work, speaking of faith in the suffering Messiah. Chrysostom again points out how the Roman legal system provided Paul a voice, how the event is quite grand and even grants Paul greater prestige. But he moves on from Paul's situation to make a more theological point that true harm comes to the Christian only through the harm he does to himself.

25:22 I Should Like to Hear Him

NOTHING CAN HARM A CHRISTIAN, UNLESS HE INJURE HIMSELF. CHRYSOSTOM: Do you hear the appeal? Do you hear the plotting of the Jews? Do you hear the strife? All this spurred him on in his desire to hear Paul. Festus pleases him, and so Paul becomes more renowned. For such, as I said, were their designs. If it were not so, none of the rulers would have agreed to listen to him or to have listened with such peace and quiet. He seems to be teaching and defending himself; in fact, he is making a public speech in good order. Therefore let us not consider plots as something difficult to bear, as long as we are not plotting against ourselves. For no one will be able to plot against us; or rather, they will plot, but they will do no harm but instead help us greatly. For it is within our power both to suffer and not to suffer evil. Look, I testify and affirm with a loud voice, more piercing than even the trumpet—and if it were possible, I would not hesitate to ascend on high and shout it out, that none of the human beings who inhabit the earth can harm a Christian. But why do I say "humans"? Not even the demon himself, not the tyrant, not the devil could do this, unless the Christian were to wrong himself. Indeed, whatever anyone does to us, he does it in vain. HOMILIES ON THE ACTS OF THE APOSTLES 51.[1]

25:23 Agrippa and Bernice

A GRAND EVENT. CHRYSOSTOM: See what a great audience is gathered around Paul, "With the prominent men," he says, "of the city." The governor brought all the bodyguards, and the king and the tribunes were present. CATENA ON

---

[1]NPNF 1 11:306**.

25:25 Nothing Deserving Death

JUSTICE PROVIDENTIALLY DELAYED. AMMO-NIUS: The judge himself bears witness to him that he is innocent, and even so he did not free him, since the Lord had so arranged things that he made an appeal, and as a consequence of his appeal he was sent to Rome. In this way, what he had predicted, "I must see Rome,"[3] might be fulfilled. CATENA ON THE ACTS OF THE APOSTLES 25.25.[4]

---

[2]CGPNT 3:386. [3]Acts 19:21. [4]CGPNT 3:387.

26:1-8 PAUL ADDRESSES AGRIPPA

[1]Agrippa said to Paul, "You have permission to speak for yourself." Then Paul stretched out his hand and made his defense:

[2]"I think myself fortunate that it is before you, King Agrippa, I am to make my defense today against all the accusations of the Jews, [3]because you are especially familiar with all customs and controversies of the Jews; therefore I beg you to listen to me patiently.

[4]"My manner of life from my youth, spent from the beginning among my own nation and at Jerusalem, is known by all the Jews. [5]They have known for a long time, if they are willing to testify, that according to the strictest party of our religion I have lived as a Pharisee. [6]And now I stand here on trial for hope in the promise made by God to our fathers, [7]to which our twelve tribes hope to attain, as they earnestly worship night and day. And for this hope I am accused by Jews, O king! [8]Why is it thought incredible by any of you that God raises the dead?"

OVERVIEW: This fifth and final defense speech serves as the finale of Luke's theological presentation. It is probably based on notes from the occasion and shows Paul as a martyr (witness) and a prophet (in Acts 9 he was "the chosen instrument," and in Acts 22 he was "the witness"). The analysis of the speech given here combines the remarks of several modern commentators. In this section, after making the gesture of an orator by stretching out his hand and giving a well-thought-out *captatio benevolentiae* ("winning of good will"), Paul gives a brief account of his early life as a Pharisee and then goes on to state the principal point of disagreement between himself and his Jewish accusers: the resurrection of the dead, Jesus' resurrection and what follows from this fact. Chrysostom, in his analysis of Paul's introduction, sees two things: Paul's innocence in his boldness and the possibility that Paul be seen as a flatterer, which he denies by using Agrippa's words. Agrippa's knowledge of Jewish customs is not intimidating but reassuring to an honest defendant with a clear conscience. Bede, although not defending Paul against flattery, draws on an introduction from one of Jerome's epistles to praise Paul's own introduction. Chrysostom's third comment notes that the charge against Paul is senseless and without merit.

26:2 I Think Myself Fortunate

A MARK OF PAUL'S INNOCENCE. CHRYSOSTOM:
Paul speaks clearly with boldness. He calls himself fortunate, not to flatter Agrippa but because
Agrippa knew everything.... And yet, if [Paul]
had a guilty conscience, he ought to have been
afraid to stand trial before one who knew everything. Instead, it is indicative of a clear conscience that he does not ask to be excused from a
judge who has an accurate knowledge of everything. On the contrary, he rejoices and calls
himself fortunate. HOMILIES ON THE ACTS OF
THE APOSTLES 52.[1]

THE WISDOM OF PAUL. BEDE: Another text
translates this verse as follows: "I consider
myself fortunate before you, commencing to give
a reckoning today." It is put as follows by Saint
Jerome in a certain place, along with his explanation: "'I consider myself fortunate, O King
Agrippa, since before you today I am to be
defended concerning all those things of which I
am accused by the Jews, especially since you are
acquainted with all the Jewish customs and controversies.' For he had read that saying of Ben
Sira, 'Fortunate is he who speaks in the ears of
those who will hear,'[2] and he recognized that the
words of a speech will only be successful to the
extent that the wisdom of the judge has come to
acknowledge the facts of the case."[3] COMMENTARY ON THE ACTS OF THE APOSTLES 26.2.[4]

PAUL NOT A FLATTERER. CHRYSOSTOM: He did
not say those words in order to adulate him—
God forbid—but because he wanted to profit
from gentleness; and to some extent, he did
profit, since he, assumed to be guilty, won over
even the judge. The judge, upon being defeated,
confessed the victory with his preeminent words
to all those present: "You persuade me in so short
a time to become a Christian." CATENA ON THE
ACTS OF THE APOSTLES 26.2.[5]

26:8 Why Is It Thought Incredible?

AN ARGUMENT FOR THE RESURRECTION.
CHRYSOSTOM: Paul lays down two arguments for
the resurrection. One of them comes from the
prophets. He does not bring forward any prophet
in particular but the doctrine itself as held by the
Jews. The other argument, the stronger because it
comes from facts, is that Christ conversed with
him. He further prepares the ground for this with
other arguments, describing his former madness
accurately. Then, along with a praise of the Jews,
"as they worship night and day," he says, expecting "to attain." "So even if I had not led an
unblemished life, King Agrippa, I should not be
tried for the belief that God raises the dead."
HOMILIES ON THE ACTS OF THE APOSTLES 52.[6]

---

[1]NPNF 1 11:308**. [2]Sir 25:9. [3]Jerome *Letter* 57.1 (CSEL 54:504).
[4]CS 117:183. [5]CGPNT 3:388. [6]NPNF 1 11:308-9**.

26:9-18 PAUL RECOUNTS HIS CONVERSION

[9]"I myself was convinced that I ought to do many things in opposing the name of Jesus of Nazareth. [10]And I did so in Jerusalem; I not only shut up many of the saints in prison, by authority from
the chief priests, but when they were put to death I cast my vote against them. [11]And I punished
them often in all the synagogues and tried to make them blaspheme; and in raging fury against

them, I persecuted them even to foreign cities.

¹²"Thus I journeyed to Damascus with the authority and commission of the chief priests. ¹³At midday, O king, I saw on the way a light from heaven, brighter than the sun, shining round me and those who journeyed with me. ¹⁴And when we had all fallen to the ground, I heard a voice saying to me in the Hebrew language, 'Saul, Saul, why do you persecute me? It hurts you to kick against the goads.' ¹⁵And I said, 'Who are you, Lord?' And the Lord said, 'I am Jesus whom you are persecuting. ¹⁶But rise and stand upon your feet; for I have appeared to you for this purpose, to appoint you to serve and bear witness to the things in which you have seen me and to those in which I will appear to you, ¹⁷delivering you from the people and from the Gentiles—to whom I send you ¹⁸to open their eyes, that they may turn from darkness to light and from the power of Satan to God, that they may receive forgiveness of sins and a place among those who are sanctified by faith in me.'"

OVERVIEW: This third telling of Paul's actions "opposing the name of Jesus of Nazareth" and his meeting with Jesus goes into more detail in regard to the nature of the persecution. Again Jesus' first words, Paul's question and Jesus' response are given in almost the exact words as the other two accounts with the addition of a popular Greek proverb applied to the fruitlessness of resisting Jesus and his action in Paul's life. Jesus' commission, reported in his own words, is retold by Paul in the mode of a prophet. Here [Paul] is described as "servant and witness" of what he has seen and will see, thus fulfilling the words of Isaiah 42:7 (LXX) and opening the eyes of the people and the Gentiles so that they may turn from darkness to light (Is 42:16). Those who so turn are described as gaining "a place among those who are sanctified by faith in me."

The treatment of Chrysostom here is cursory. He runs through the sequence of events and adds brief asides that one wishes he had expanded upon. For example, Chrysostom remarks that the appearance of the persecuted one himself to Paul is in itself an expression of God's mercy. Ephrem allows us to open up a different reception of this event in his attempt to grasp what Paul's experience might have entailed. In the final comment on this passage, we find Chrysostom, again being quite brief, examining Paul's narrative of the events and how they are designed, for the pur-

pose of persuasion, to lay out God's plan and avoid any assignation of guilt to his audience.

26:9 Convinced That I Ought to Do Many Things

PAUL'S CREDIBILITY. CHRYSOSTOM: He shows how he persecuted and how he was made fit for this, for which he calls the high priests to testify and "the cities outside" Jerusalem. [Paul] tells of how he heard the voice of someone saying to him, "It hurts to kick against the goad." Then he shows God's clemency, because it was the persecuted one who appeared to him. "He not only benefited me but sent me as a teacher for others." And he shows the prophecy, which came and said to him, "I will choose you from among your people and the Gentiles." "I thought to myself," that is, "I made the decision 'to work steadfastly against' the name of Jesus of Nazareth. I was not one of the disciples of Christ; I was with those who fought him." Thus he is a witness worthy of belief, because after doing countless things, fighting and killing the faithful, persuading them to blaspheme and bringing so many people, cities and rulers along, and after undertaking all this on his own initiative, he was so suddenly changed. And there are again witnesses present for this. Then [Paul] shows he had been rightly persuaded and not deceived by the light, by the prophets, by the facts, by the events that were unfolding at that very moment. In order that he may not appear to be an innovator, even though he could speak of such great things, he takes refuge once more in the prophets, and he puts them forth for public scrutiny. This is more trustworthy, as it happens in the present; but since he alone had seen, again he is confirmed by the prophets. CATENA ON THE ACTS OF THE APOSTLES 26.9-11.[1]

26:13 A Light from Heaven

THE UNCREATED LIGHT. EPHREM THE SYRIAN: Now if the sun here below, of the same nature as our eyes here below, can do harm to them with its intensity, not with its anger, and with its brilliance, not with its rage, how much more can a light from above, of the same nature as the things from above, do harm with its intensity to one who is below, who is not of its nature and who looks at it suddenly? Now if this sun to which Paul was accustomed could cause injury from its intensity when he looked at it in an uncustomary way, how much more harmful would the brilliance of that light be for one whose eyes had never been accustomed to it. HOMILY ON OUR LORD 27.2-3.[2]

26:18 Turn from Darkness to Light

TO MAKE APOSTLES OF THE GENTILES. CHRYSOSTOM: And notice how [Paul] does not speak in court as he did in the assembly. There he said, "You killed him."[3] Here, nothing of the kind, so that he might not kindle their anger more. Nevertheless, he shows the same thing by saying "if the Christ must suffer." Thus he frees them from accusations. For "even the prophets," he says, said this. Therefore, accept the rest as well. Since he mentioned the vision, without fear he goes on to speak of its successes as well. "That they may turn from darkness to light and from the power of Satan to God." "For I have appeared to you for this purpose," not to punish you but to make you an apostle. Then he points out the evils encompassing the unbelievers, Satan, darkness, and the good surrounding the believers, light, God, the inheritance of the saints. He exhorts them not only to repent but also to exhibit a life worthy of admiration. And look, everywhere the Gentiles embraced the Word. For those present were Gentiles. HOMILIES ON THE ACTS OF THE APOSTLES 52.[4]

---

[1]CGPNT 3:390-91. [2]FC 91:302. [3]Paul does not, in fact, do this. These are the words of Peter at Acts 3:15. Paul is careful to note the role of Pilate (see Acts 13:28) and to state in Acts 26:23 that Christ had to suffer, as in Acts 17:3. [4]NPNF 1 11:311**.

26:19-23 PAUL DEFENDS HIS PREACHING

[19]"Wherefore, O King Agrippa, I was not disobedient to the heavenly vision, [20]but declared first to those at Damascus, then at Jerusalem and throughout all the country of Judea, and also to the Gentiles, that they should repent and turn to God and perform deeds worthy of their repentance. [21]For this reason the Jews seized me in the temple and tried to kill me. [22]To this day I have had the help that comes from God, and so I stand here testifying both to small and great, saying nothing but what the prophets and Moses said would come to pass: [23]that the Christ must suffer, and that, by being the first to rise from the dead, he would proclaim light both to the people and to the Gentiles."

OVERVIEW: These words give a Lukan summary of Paul's gospel. The statement that Paul is "saying nothing but what the prophets and Moses said would come to pass" indicates one of the New Testament texts that grounds the "spiritual sense" of the Fathers of the church, while the notion that "the Christ must suffer" is found in Luke 24:7, 26, 46 as formulated by Jesus as he explains "Moses and all the prophets" in the light of his suffering and resurrection. The last words of this section mention once again both "the people and the Gentiles" and explicitly say that *Jesus* would proclaim light to them.

The passages here from Ammonius and Didymus are not well structured, and yet there is a common anthropological element to both that can be summarized in the symbol of the mirror. Paul has the quality of being a reflector of the Light that he has seen. Ammonius's passage is quite clear: there is an inaccessible quality to what we must know, and so human models leading communities are requisite for the continuation of this message. Didymus's passage is not so straightforward. He has several concerns, but here we will only point out the commonality with Ammonius. As the context of Didymus's passage, Romans 15:7-13, makes clear, Paul not only became light but also encouraged it in others.[1] There must be visible effects of the revelation in the lives of believers; otherwise the revelation ceases to refract in them. In other words, the locus of revelation becomes the community, and those who are graced with experiences such as Paul's receive them for the community.

26:19 Not Disobedient

A CALL TO IMITATION. AMMONIUS: After Paul announced the faith of those by whom he is judged, near the end of his speech he speaks to the people and to the Gentiles, so that he may convert Agrippa and the Gentiles, who were with him, and all the Jews, who were present. And then he says, "King Agrippa, I was not disobedient to the heavenly vision: just as I believed, so must he, who listens to me, believe me. I do not proclaim what I have heard from others but what I heard and saw from heaven. Through the vision comes the pure view, which is beyond humankind: one, who is in the flesh, is unable to see what is not revealed to bodily eyes." CATENA ON THE ACTS OF THE APOSTLES 26.19-20.[2]

26:22 Help That Comes from God

SHOWING CHRIST. DIDYMUS THE BLIND: Since he wanted to show that Moses knew the passion and resurrection of Christ and that he enlightened the people and the Gentiles, [Paul] made use of the praise addressed to Judah and transferred completely to Christ, which is in part, "Judah is a lion's whelp; from the prey, my son, you have gone up. He crouches down, he stretches out like a lion's whelp: who raises him up?"[3] . . . And [Christ] is the expectation of the nations: among them death is called sleep, and resurrection is called a rising. After this resurrection, he sent his disciples to "teach all the nations."[4] Many have thought that other words said by Moses are about the cross: "You will see your life suspended on the tree before your eyes,"[5] but you may also use, "Rejoice nations with his people,"[6] which are reported in Deuteronomy. By proclaiming Christ, Paul has shown the light not only to the nations but also to the people of Israel. CATENA ON THE ACTS OF THE APOSTLES 26.23.[7]

---

[1]Rom 15:7-13: "Receive one another as Christ received you for the glory of God. Indeed, I say, Christ became a servant of the circumcised to reveal God's truth, to confirm the promises to the patriarchs, and so that the nations would glorify God for his mercy, as is written: 'Therefore I will praise you among the nations and sing to your name' (Ps 18:49 [17:50 LXX]; 2 Sam 22:50), and again it says, 'Rejoice, nations, with his people' (Deut 32:43), and again, 'Praise the Lord, all nations, and let all the peoples praise him' (Ps 117:1 [116:1 LXX]), and also Isaiah says, 'The root of Jesse shall be, and he will rise up to rule the nations, and in him the nations shall hope' (Is 11:10 LXX). The God of hope fill you with all joy and peace in your believing that you may abound in hope in the power of the Holy Spirit." [2]CGPNT 3:392-93. [3]Gen 49:9. [4]Mt 28:19. [5]Deut 28:66 (LXX). [6]Deut 32:43. [7]CGPNT 3:394.

26:24-32 PAUL DESIRES AGRIPPA'S CONVERSION

[24]*And as he thus made his defense, Festus said with a loud voice, "Paul, you are mad; your great learning is turning you mad." [25]But Paul said, "I am not mad, most excellent Festus, but I am speaking the sober truth. [26]For the king knows about these things, and to him I speak freely; for I am persuaded that none of these things has escaped his notice, for this was not done in a corner. [27]King Agrippa, do you believe the prophets? I know that you believe." [28]And Agrippa said to Paul, "In a short time you think to make me a Christian!" [29]And Paul said, "Whether short or long, I would to God that not only you but also all who hear me this day might become such as I am—except for these chains."*

[30]*Then the king rose, and the governor and Bernice and those who were sitting with them; [31]and when they had withdrawn, they said to one another, "This man is doing nothing to deserve death or imprisonment." [32]And Agrippa said to Festus, "This man could have been set free if he had not appealed to Caesar."*

OVERVIEW: Once again we have the device of the interrupted speech and then the contrasting reactions of Festus, who seems frightened by these words that speak of matters he has never considered, and Agrippa, who is avoiding their consequences by a clever deflection. The passage ends with the Roman authorities agreeing on Paul's innocence. Bede reads the accusation that Paul is mad in light of Paul's words in 2 Corinthians 5:13, and thus he sees in Agrippa's words an unintended affirmation of the truth of Paul's testimony. Chrysostom, again fearing that Paul's words might become a bad example to his audience, is quick to comment on the significance of Paul's apparent disparagement of his chains that make him so resemble Christ.

26:24 Paul, You Are Mad

TRUE MADNESS. BEDE: [Festus] reckoned it insanity that a man in chains, put in the position of defending himself, would deliver a discourse not about the false charges with which he was assailed from without but rather about private knowledge that he interiorly gloried in; and that he would review all the wonders of the revelation by which he had been changed from a persecutor into an apostle; moreover that in the style and vigor of public address he would discuss the resurrection of the dead revealed by our Redeemer's will. Truly, however, just as it was foolish madness for the prodigal son to forsake his father and feed the pigs,[1] so also it was "spiritual, that is, true madness, of which the apostle spoke [when he said], 'For if we were out of our mind, it was for God; if we are sane, it is for you.'"[2] And, in agreement with this the psalmist sang, "Happy the one whose hope is the name of the Lord and who has no regard for vanities and false insanities."[3] COMMENTARY ON THE ACTS OF THE APOSTLES 26.24.[4]

26:27 Do You Believe the Prophets?

I KNOW THAT YOU DO BELIEVE. BEDE: He did not say this in flattery, as some think, but he made a true statement. Agrippa, inasmuch as he was imbued with the ritual and laws of the Jews, believed that the prophets spoke the truth; but,

---

[1]Lk 15:11-15. [2]Jerome *Commentary on Psalm* 39.5 (CCL 72:207); 2 Cor 5:13. [3]Ps 40:4 (39:5 LXX, Vg). [4]CS 117:183-84.

as one lacking faith, he did not know to whom this truth pertained, that is, the Lord Christ. COMMENTARY ON THE ACTS OF THE APOSTLES 26.27.[5]

26:29 Except for These Chains

PAUL DEPRECATES THE GLORY OF HIS BONDS FOR THEIR SAKE. CHRYSOSTOM: Notice how his speech is devoid of flattery. "I pray," [Paul] says, "that this day all might become such as I am— except for these chains." This man, who glories in his bonds, who displays them as if they were a gold chain, deprecates them for these men. For they were still too weak, and he had spoken rather in condescension. For what is better than those chains, which often appear in his epistles, as in "Paul, a prisoner of Jesus Christ,"[6] and, "On this account I am bound with this chain,"[7] "but the word of God is not bound," and, "Even to the point of being chained like a criminal."[8] Not only chains, but even "like a criminal." The punishment is twofold. For if he were so chained for some good, the matter would carry some consolation. As it is, [Paul] is chained "like a criminal," and for terrible purposes too. But he takes none of this into consideration. HOMILIES ON THE ACTS OF THE APOSTLES 52.[9]

CHAINS ARE A GLORY. CHRYSOSTOM: It was not out of distress or fear that Paul acted thus but from an abundance of wisdom and spiritual understanding. He was addressing a Gentile, an unbeliever who knew nothing of us. Naturally he was unwilling to introduce him by way of disagreeable things. He acted in the present instance in accordance with his own words, "To those outside the law I became as one outside the law."[10] This is what he meant: "If the Gentile hears of chains and tribulations, he will immediately take flight. He does not know the power of chains. Let him first become a believer, let him taste of the word preached, and then he will, of his own accord even, run toward these chains." HOMILIES CONCERNING THE STATUES 16.9.[11]

LEAD PEOPLE TO THE CROSS SLOWLY. CHRYSOSTOM: Indeed, up to this time they have heard false reports of our doctrine and are hostile to the cross. If I should then add chains as well, their hatred becomes greater. This is why I removed these, so as to make that more acceptable. For they consider it disgraceful to be chained, because they have not yet tasted the glory that is with us. We must therefore condescend. For once they learn of the true life, they will also know the beauty of this iron and the distinction that comes from these chains. . . . In the meantime, one must be content that the listeners are not ashamed of the cross. For this reason he proceeds methodically, like a guide who is introducing someone to a palace: he does not force him, before he has seen the vestibules and while he is still standing outside, to survey what is within; for unless he enters and observes everything closely, it will not appear marvelous to him. HOMILIES ON 1 CORINTHIANS 33.7.[12]

26:32 If He Had Not Appealed

RECKONED AMONG THE TRANSGRESSORS. CHRYSOSTOM: Look, once again they pass a sentence in his favor. After saying "you are mad," they release him not only from the death sentence but also from his chains. Indeed, they would have released him altogether had [Paul] not appealed to Caesar. But this happens providentially, likewise his departure in chains. "Even to the point of being chained like a criminal."[13] For if his Lord "was counted with the lawless ones,"[14] all the more so ought he (Paul) to be. But just as the Lord had nothing in common with the character of those men, neither did Paul. For the wonder is then apparent: although he was mixed up with these men, in no way was he harmed by them. HOMILIES ON THE ACTS OF THE APOSTLES 53.[15]

---

[5]CS 117:184. [6]Eph 3:1. [7]Acts 28:20. [8]2 Tim 2:9. [9]NPNF 1 11:312**. [10]1 Cor 9:21. [11]NPNF 1 9:448**. [12]NPNF 1 12:200**. [13]1 Tim 2:9. [14]Mk 15:28. [15]NPNF 1 11:314**.

27:1-8 PAUL EMBARKS FOR ITALY

^{1}And when it was decided that we should sail for Italy, they delivered Paul and some other prisoners to a centurion of the Augustan Cohort, named Julius. ^{2}And embarking in a ship of Adramyttium, which was about to sail to the ports along the coast of Asia, we put to sea, accompanied by Aristarchus, a Macedonian from Thessalonica. ^{3}The next day we put in at Sidon; and Julius treated Paul kindly, and gave him leave to go to his friends and be cared for. ^{4}And putting to sea from there we sailed under the lee of Cyprus, because the winds were against us. ^{5}And when we had sailed across the sea which is off Cilicia and Pamphylia, we came to Myra in Lycia. ^{6}There the centurion found a ship of Alexandria sailing for Italy, and put us on board. ^{7}We sailed slowly for a number of days, and arrived with difficulty off Cnidus, and as the wind did not allow us to go on, we sailed under the lee of Crete off Salmone. ^{8}Coasting along it with difficulty, we came to a place called Fair Havens, near which was the city of Lasea.

OVERVIEW: The general remarks of the moderns usually concern the tale of a shipwreck, a common theme in antiquity most often portraying how an evil person is destroyed by the forces of the sea. Luke's story of Paul's single-handed triumph over these forces for his own sake and the sake of all his companions is a counterpoint to this, easily understood by his contemporaries. The dangers of the sea also provide tales of great adventure in which the sea is often the primary tool of a vengeful deity's opposition to the hero's accomplishment of a desired or fated end.[1] Luke makes use of this genre to call attention to Paul the prophet as well as to his faith and the role he plays in bringing about the saving of all who travel with him. Luke thus portrays the role of the Christian in the world. They also ask questions about Luke's sources of information, usually answered by pointing to the "we sections" of the narrative and to Luke's memory even after the most probable loss of his notes. The present passage begins the note of foreboding since the winter winds have begun. It also begins a most detailed account of the events on this journey. In contrast to all the lessons derived from this chapter by the ancients, the moderns are quite matter of fact, concentrating on Luke's portrayal of the role of Paul. Here,

our best commentator at this point is Chrysostom. His attention is on the spreading of the gospel in the very situation and circumstances that Paul finds himself. Although Chrysostom never directly notes that now the narrative of Acts has shifted from "the things concerning Jesus the Christ" to "the things concerning Paul," his own attention is clearly on how Paul is, as it were, a node in an ever-expanding web of connections spreading across the Mediterranean precisely because those who encounter Paul tell *Paul's* story. Throughout this chapter it becomes clear that, for Chrysostom at least, the telling of a saint's life is the telling of the work of Christ's in the world. Eusebius recounts the martyrdom of James as an event that occurred in consequence. In this first section, we have a passage from Eusebius who gives, as it were, a footnote to the events of Acts 27. Chrysostom will constantly be drawing our attention to some of the minor characters of this chapter, and here, the first is Aristarchus, who will become for Paul what Paul has become for Christ. For Chrysostom, all of this incident of the voyage serves to spread the gospel; he further points out that the ordinary course is the most

---

[1]Most famous are the epic poems of the *Odyssey* and the *Aeneid*.

usual not just for humans but for God as well, as even Paul's tumultuous journey demonstrates.

27:1 Paul and Other Prisoners Delivered to a Centurion

BACK IN JERUSALEM. EUSEBIUS OF CAESAREA: But after Paul, in consequence of his appeal to Caesar, had been sent to Rome by Festus, the Jews, being frustrated in their hope of entrapping him by the snares that they had laid for him, turned against James, the brother of the Lord, to whom the episcopal seat at Jerusalem had been entrusted by the apostles. The following daring measures were undertaken by them against him. Leading him into their midst they demanded of him that he should renounce faith in Christ in the presence of all the people. But, contrary to the opinion of all, with a clear voice and with greater boldness than they had anticipated, [James] spoke out before the whole multitude and confessed that our Savior and Lord Jesus is the Son of God. But they were unable to bear longer the testimony of the man who, on account of the excellence of ascetic virtue and of piety that he exhibited in his life, was esteemed by all as the most just of people, and consequently they killed him. Opportunity for this deed of violence was furnished by the prevailing anarchy, which was caused by the fact that Festus had died just at this time in Judea and that the province was thus without a governor and head. The manner of James' death has been already indicated by the above-quoted words of Clement, who records that he was thrown from the pinnacle of the temple and was beaten to death with a club. ECCLESIASTICAL HISTORY 2.23.1-3.[2]

27:3 Julius Treated Paul Kindly

THE SPREAD OF THE MESSAGE. CHRYSOSTOM: Aristarchus accompanies Paul for a while. He is fittingly and usefully present with the intention of reporting everything concerning him in Macedonia. CATENA ON THE ACTS OF THE APOSTLES 27.1-3.[3]

27:4 The Winds Were Against Us

GOD LETS NATURE TAKE ITS COURSE. CHRYSOSTOM: See how God does not alter or change the order of nature but allows him to sail into unfavorable winds. But even so the miracle happens. To ensure that they sail safely, he did not allow them to go out to the open sea; they always sailed along the coast. HOMILIES ON THE ACTS OF THE APOSTLES 53.[4]

27:5 To Myra in Lycia

PAUL AN EXAMPLE. CHRYSOSTOM: Again trials, again contrary winds. See how the life of the saints is so composed of all these things: he escaped the court, and they fall into a shipwreck and a storm. CATENA ON THE ACTS OF THE APOSTLES 27.4-5.[5]

---

[2]NPNF 2 1:125*. [3]CGPNT 3:397. [4]NPNF 1 11:315**. [5]CGPNT 3:397.

27:9-12 PAUL PREDICTS A SHIPWRECK

[9]As much time had been lost, and the voyage was already dangerous because the fast had already gone by, Paul advised them, [10]saying, "Sirs, I perceive that the voyage will be with injury and much

*loss, not only of the cargo and the ship, but also of our lives." ¹¹But the centurion paid more atten-
tion to the captain and to the owner of the ship than to what Paul said. ¹²And because the harbor
was not suitable to winter in, the majority advised to put to sea from there, on the chance that
somehow they could reach Phoenix, a harbor of Crete, looking northeast and southeast,ᵃ and winter there.*

a Or *southwest and northwest*

OVERVIEW: Paul's first prophetic message is set
aside under pressure from those who have most
to gain financially from a continued voyage.
Chrysostom's remarks begin to focus on three
things. First he is attentive to the circumstances,
that Paul being a prisoner will not be trusted immediately and that he must little by little earn
their trust. Second, he pays attention to the
course of events as laying a foundation for the
trust of Julius the centurion. Third, he sees God
working through the authorities in control,
namely, Julius, who must be won over to Paul in
order for the events to fall out properly. Here,
Ammonius enters with a matter that was of no
small concern to early Christian teachers by
countering the idea that our lives are determined
by fate and that there is no such thing as free will.

27:10 A Voyage with Injury

**THEY WOULD NOT HAVE BELIEVED A PRIS-
ONER.** CHRYSOSTOM: See [Paul's] modesty: in
order that he may not appear to prophesy but to
speak as if from supposition, he says "I see." They
would have not received his words if he had pronounced them at once. In the first place he prophesies and says, "God, whom I worship," thus
leading them. How would have it happened without a loss of lives? There surely would be such a
loss if God did not save them. CATENA ON THE
ACTS OF THE APOSTLES 27.10.[1]

27:12 The Majority Advised to Put to Sea

NOT FATE BUT FREE WILL LED THEM. AMMO-
NIUS: Since Paul was a prophet, he announced
the danger, which would have threatened them
on the ship. But he was not able to convince them
to spend the winter in Crete, so that it was not
fate that dragged them into danger but their will.
CATENA ON THE ACTS OF THE APOSTLES 27.10.[2]

---

[1]CGPNT 3:398. [2]CGPNT 3:398.

27:13-20 THE SHIP CAUGHT IN A STORM

*¹³And when the south wind blew gently, supposing that they had obtained their purpose, they
weighed anchor and sailed along Crete, close inshore. ¹⁴But soon a tempestuous wind, called the
northeaster, struck down from the land; ¹⁵and when the ship was caught and could not face the
wind, we gave way to it and were driven. ¹⁶And running under the lee of a small island called
Cauda,ᵇ we managed with difficulty to secure the boat; ¹⁷after hoisting it up, they took measuresᶜ to*

undergird the ship; then, fearing that they should run on the Syrtis, they lowered the gear, and so were driven. [18]As we were violently storm-tossed, they began next day to throw the cargo overboard; [19]and the third day they cast out with their own hands the tackle of the ship. [20]And when neither sun nor stars appeared for many a day, and no small tempest lay on us, all hope of our being saved was at last abandoned.

b Other ancient authorities read *Clauda*   **c** Greek *helps*

OVERVIEW: After a detailed and nautically exact account of the storm, Luke notes that "all hope of our being saved was at last abandoned," thereby seemingly including himself. This remark is meant to set the stage for Paul's words which follow. The banks of Syrtis were notoriously dangerous. Hence Bede attempts to explain how an anchor could prevent a ship from capsizing in a storm at sea. Chrysostom brings us back to the course of the narrative, the role the events play in turning the minds of Paul's fellow passengers.

27:15 We Gave Way to It

THE SYRTIS BANKS. BEDE: Another version puts this more clearly,[1] "And the ship was caught when they could not oppose the wind; with the ship at the mercy of the gale, they began to furl the sails. Then we sailed past an island which is called Cauda, which they could not reach; but having lowered the skiff, they began to strengthen the ship, girding her [with ropes]. Also they dragged anchors, being afraid to encounter the Syrtis banks." From this it is shown that they lowered ropes from the middle of both sides of the ship and around its foremost parts, and to these they attached anchors which were dragged along, just as in our, that is, the British sea, they customarily tie millstone-sized

stones behind the stern, so as to hold a ship back. They did these things to restrain the vessel, lest by a misdirected rush of waves she might run aground on the Syrtis banks, which are "terrifying even when they are only heard of, because they seize all things to themselves."[2] Hence Sallust says that their name was derived from the word for a dragging away.[3] COMMENTARY ON THE ACTS OF THE APOSTLES 27.15.[4]

27:19 They Cast Out the Tackle

SO THAT PAUL MIGHT OBTAIN A HEARING. CHRYSOSTOM: Fierce was the storm then, and thick the darkness. Even the ship breaks up, so that they should not forget. The grain is thrown overboard along with everything else to prevent them from being able to behave shamelessly after this.[5] For this is why the ship breaks up and their lives are in danger: in no small way did the storm and the darkness contribute to [Paul] getting the hearing that he did. HOMILIES ON THE ACTS OF THE APOSTLES 53.[6]

---

[1]This is the WT. [2]Josephus/Hegesippus *Jewish Wars* 2.9.1 (CSEL 66:153). [3]Isidore of Seville *Etymologies* 13.18. 6; Sallust *The War Against Jugurtha* 78.3. The Greek for "to draw" or "to suck" is *syrō*. [4]CS 117:187-88**. [5]I.e., eat and drink too much. [6]NPNF 1 11:317**.

27:21-26 PAUL COMFORTS THOSE ON BOARD

[21] *As they had been long without food, Paul then came forward among them and said, "Men, you should have listened to me, and should not have set sail from Crete and incurred this injury and loss.* [22] *I now bid you take heart; for there will be no loss of life among you, but only of the ship.* [23] *For this very night there stood by me an angel of the God to whom I belong and whom I worship,* [24] *and he said, 'Do not be afraid, Paul; you must stand before Caesar; and lo, God has granted you all those who sail with you.' * [25] *So take heart, men, for I have faith in God that it will be exactly as I have been told.* [26] *But we shall have to run on some island."*

OVERVIEW: Paul the prophet now speaks quoting the words of an angel who refers to Paul's commission from Jesus, which will not be set aside (note the "must") and states the fact that all who sail with Paul have been given to him, that is, put under his spiritual protection. Paul concludes with his declaration of faith and a final detail of his prophecy. Here the Fathers speak of how God uses the instrumentality of creatures to establish Christ's grace in the world. Bede sees the noisy waters of the sea as signifying the grace that is in Paul. Origen's comment, somewhat tangential, nonetheless draws our attention to those above humans, the angels, whose ordering corresponds to the ordering of human souls "according to the dispensation of Christ." Jerome, Chrysostom and Ammonius all bring out a similar concern, but they also give closer attention to the events of the narrative. Jerome points to the unequal merit of those saved as analogous to the difference between Lot and Zoar, reminding us that God hears the prayers of a righteous person. Chrysostom turns Jerome's external perspective to an internal one. Chrysostom is aware of Paul's certainty as portrayed in the text, and so he reflects on the course of events through Paul's awareness of his responsibility to his fellow travelers, as a realization that he has a duty not just to appear in Rome but also to bring them to trust in him for their own safety and salvation. Ammonius's comments bear resemblance to those of Chrysostom and Jerome. They begin with a quotation and refutation of a line from Homer's *Iliad*. His refutation focuses, somewhat like Jerome, on how the impious are spared for the sake of the just one. By the end, however, Ammonius has given a hint that the events of Acts 27 can be read as a type of the holy man's role who, like the father of the possessed boy in Mark, as mother/midwife brings nonbelievers to a new birth, through the stormy waters (of baptism) in Christ. He does this in the last lines that allude to the words of the distraught father in Mark 9 and to Elizabeth's words to Mary that blessed is the one who believed that what had been foretold would come to pass. Ammonius suggests that merit is the burden of being pregnant with faith that must bear fruit in the transformed lives of others, a merit lost should faith be betrayed by not being passed on. So what Chrysostom portrays as being the consciousness of Paul, Ammonius suggests is to be the consciousness of all Christians.

27:23 An Angel of God

AN ANGEL OF GOD STOOD BY ME. BEDE: He was not building himself up in saying this but was summoning them to faith. For this reason the sea was permitted to be stirred up, that both through that which was not heard and through that which was heard, the spiritual grace in Paul might be revealed. Commentary on the Acts of the Apostles 27.23.[1]

The Work of the Angels. Origen: Both good and bad angels are among people. Not by chance or without reason was that angel, for example, allotted to be the guardian of Peter[2] or that other one for Paul or those of the children of the church, those that always "behold the face of their Father, who is in heaven."[3] Concerning these things there can be no doubt that, by the judgment of God, who clearly sees their ranking and the quality of our souls, these angels are allotted to the guardianship of each one of us by a certain mystical allotment according to the dispensation of Christ. Homilies on Joshua 23.3.[4]

27:24 Do Not Be Afraid, Paul

A Question of Merit. Jerome: You cannot deny that the prisoner and the jailers were of unequal merit. And what were the circumstances of that shipwreck involving the apostle and the soldiers? The apostle Paul described a vision afterwards and said that those who were on the ship had been given to him by the Lord. Are we to suppose that he to whom they were given and they who were given to him were of the same merit? Ten righteous people can save a sinful city. Lot together with his daughters was delivered from the fire. His son-in-laws would also have been saved, had they been willing to leave the city. Now, there was surely a great difference between Lot and his son-in-laws. One city out of the five was saved—Zoar, a place that lay under the same sentence as Sodom, Gomorrah, Admah and Zeboiim, but was preserved by the prayers of a holy man.[5] Lot and Zoar were of different merit, but both of them escaped the fire. Against Jovinianus 2.24.[6]

Paul Seizes the Moment. Chrysostom: See how, after such a storm, [Paul] does not speak to them by insulting them but desiring that later

they will believe him. Therefore he takes the things he had said as a testimony of the truth of those things he will say. And he predicts two events: first, that they will land on an island, lose the ship, but be safe (and this was a prophecy and not a supposition), and second, that "he had to stand before Caesar." Catena on the Acts of the Apostles 27.21-24.[7]

A Birth to New Life Through Raging Waters. Ammonius: "God has granted safety to all," so that what Homer says appears to be false:

"I say that no one can avoid his fate, neither good man nor bad, even though he be noble."[8] And this means that it is impossible to escape the death that Fate establishes at the moment of birth. Therefore, without Paul, all would have died, if God had not granted life to them out of respect for the righteous. So if it had been sanctioned that all would have died, as it surely appears, he would have died, he that had not eaten for fourteen days and then had been shipwrecked: indeed those false words say, "neither good man nor bad," so that it was necessary that both the good and the bad died together, being liable together to the evident danger of death. On the contrary, however, Scripture says that the righteous was saved from the evident danger, even though anyone else would have died in that circumstance. God thought it opportune that he go to Rome; God could have placed him in Rome, after taking him from Jerusalem through an angel, as he had put Habakkuk, after he took him from Judea, in Babylon, by the den of lions where Daniel was.[9] But he did not do so, and, nevertheless, showed a miraculous event by saving Paul and his companions. He granted their souls to him, so that he might have benevolence for his

---

[1]CS 117:188. [2]Acts 12:7-10. [3]Mt 18:10. [4]SC 71:460. [5]Gen 19:18-21. [6]NPNF 2 6:407. [7]CGPNT 3:400. [8]*Iliad* 6.488-89. Hector's words to his wife, Andromache. Ammonius does not complete the thought, which continues, "none can escape . . . once he has been born." This is not just death for Hector but a definite lot that has been appointed and cannot be changed. [9]*Bel* 1:33-39 (Dan 14:33-39 Vg).

brothers, but not the ship and its cargo, because the pious has no consideration for earthly things, nor is grieved by their loss. Here the impious live thanks to the pious; but sometimes the opposite happens, so that the impious dies before his time because of his iniquity, according to the command of God, as Ecclesiastes says, "Be not wicked, and be not stubborn, lest you die before your time."[10] I think that, thanks to God, these things happen in this way. Everything is possible for the one who believes,[11] but he did not obtain salvation for his companions through faith or prayers but because he believed that what had been said to him would be.[12] CATENA ON THE ACTS OF THE APOSTLES 27.25-26.[13]

---

[10]Eccles 7:17 (LXX). [11]Mk 9:23. [12]Lk 1:45. [13]CGPNT 3:401-2.

27:27-32 THEY NEAR LAND

[27]*When the fourteenth night had come, as we were drifting across the sea of Adria, about midnight the sailors suspected that they were nearing land.* [28]*So they sounded and found twenty fathoms; a little farther on they sounded again and found fifteen fathoms.* [29]*And fearing that we might run on the rocks, they let out four anchors from the stern, and prayed for day to come.* [30]*And as the sailors were seeking to escape from the ship, and had lowered the boat into the sea, under pretense of laying out anchors from the bow,* [31]*Paul said to the centurion and the soldiers, "Unless these men stay in the ship, you cannot be saved."* [32]*Then the soldiers cut away the ropes of the boat, and let it go.*

OVERVIEW: Paul learns of the sailors' treachery and once again, in his prophetic authority, he warns the centurion of the consequences of letting the sailors abandon the ship. His authority has grown so that now the centurion listens to him. The Fathers here are concerned to explain the differing motives of the various characters in this episode. Bede sees in the soldiers' obedience a sign of division on the ship: the sailors with more experience than the soldiers can see no way out of the predicament. Chrysostom sees the differing actions as evidence of belief or disbelief in what Paul has said. As will become clear later,[1] this disbelief is taken as evidence of diabolical action, and so Paul's efforts to prevent their attempted escape are in fact a battle against the devil's attempts to foil Paul's prophecy and thus his credibility. Ammonius continues with his argument against fate; his interpretation of how the soldiers acted, which is almost that of Chrysostom's, sees their motive as flowing from the realization that their predicament was their own responsibility and that Paul's words, which the outcome confirmed, had made this evident to them.

27:31 People Must Stay in the Ship

THE MOTIVES OF THE SOLDIERS. BEDE: Since when there was danger of shipwreck, the knowledge of the sailors, who are familiar with the sea, was more helpful than the arms of the soldiers,

---

[1]See Chrysostom's comment at Acts 27:43 below.

they more willingly endured the loss of the skiff than the sailors. COMMENTARY ON THE ACTS OF THE APOSTLES 27.31.[2]

27:32 The Soldiers Cut Away the Ropes

TAUGHT THE LOVE OF WISDOM. CHRYSOSTOM: Here the text shows that the sailors would have fled, as they did not believe [Paul's] words; but the centurion believed together with the soldiers. Therefore Paul said, "Unless these men stay in the ship, you cannot be saved." Not that their escape would have doomed the rest. He said this to stop them, so that the prophecy would not be broken. See how they, as if they were in a church, are taught the love of wisdom by Paul, who pulls them away from dangers. They did not believe Paul through providence, so that they might believe him after the experience of the facts, as happened. HOMILIES ON

THE ACTS OF THE APOSTLES 53.2.[3]

PAUL'S AUTHORITY BRINGS THEIR CONVERSION. AMMONIUS: After they realized that their bad will had caused them to fall into dangers, they began to believe Paul by thinking that the appropriate words of the righteous were more effective for their salvation than the fate in danger, which has no name. In fact, if they had believed in fate, like the Gentiles, after despising the words of that pious man, they would have allowed the sailors to escape by saying, "Let them go. This has nothing to do with our salvation." But they did not speak nor act so foolishly, neither were they deceived or enticed by ignorance. Therefore, based on these facts, many must reject their opinion about fate and fortune. CATENA ON THE ACTS OF THE APOSTLES 27.31-32.[4]

---

[2]CS 117:188-89. [3]PG 60:369. [4]CGPNT 3:403.

27:33-38 PAUL ENCOURAGES ALL TO EAT

[33]As day was about to dawn, Paul urged them all to take some food, saying, "Today is the fourteenth day that you have continued in suspense and without food, having taken nothing. [34]Therefore I urge you to take some food; it will give you strength, since not a hair is to perish from the head of any of you." [35]And when he had said this, he took bread, and giving thanks to God in the presence of all he broke it and began to eat. [36]Then they all were encouraged and ate some food themselves. [37](We were in all two hundred and seventy-six[d] persons in the ship.) [38]And when they had eaten enough, they lightened the ship, throwing out the wheat into the sea.

d Other ancient authorities read seventy-six or about seventy-six

---

OVERVIEW: Another prophetic message and gesture was Paul's effort to take care of those who were "given to" him. Because of certain terms in the account of the meal, some commentators wonder if Luke intends this to be a eucharistic

sharing. This is most unlikely. As one commentator says, this is not a meal of thanksgiving but one of hope. For the Fathers, however, the ecclesial parallel is in some ways inevitable. First, because some of these comments emerge within the church, in homilies or in commentaries designed to aid in the preparation of homilies. Second, Ammonius has already hinted at the baptismal nature of their journey, which was the doorway to full participation in the communion of the body of Christ.[1] Chrysostom does not go so far as to see the meal as a Eucharist, and yet he is explicit that Paul's role mirrors the lessons of the church, where we enter to be taught, through participation in Christ, true knowledge of the world around us as a hopeful place of passing and beneficial hardship. This knowledge comes through the testing even of the one who bestows it. The irony is that the centurion who was free needed his prisoner who was in chains, and the pilot needed one who was not a pilot. Bede draws the parallel that no one escapes the tempests of this world except those nourished by the bread of life.

Arator makes an explicit connection between the Passover of Exodus, celebrated on the fourteenth day of the first month of the Jewish calendar, Christ's final meal and crucifixion and Paul's meal here. Ammonius, however, keeps the event narrated a simple meal that Paul uses to initiate his companions into piety but that opens up to what is done in church.

27:33 Paul Urged People to Eat

THE TRUE KNOWLEDGE OF THIS WORLD.
CHRYSOSTOM: Look, just as in a church, they are instructed by Paul's true knowledge. He saved them from the midst of danger. It is part of the divine plan that Paul is disbelieved; he is to be believed only after he is tried in action. So this is what happened: he urges them to partake of nourishment again and persuades them. He himself is the first to partake, thus persuading them not only by word but also by action that the storm in no way harmed them but rather benefited their souls. HOMILIES ON THE ACTS OF THE APOSTLES 53.[2]

THE WORK OF THE CONDEMNED JUST MAN.
CHRYSOSTOM: With the ship in danger and ship-wreck awaiting, the prisoners were saved through Paul. Imagine what it would be like to have a holy man in a house. For many are the storms that assail us, even more fierce than those storms of nature. But God is able to forgive us, if only we obey the holy men as those in the ship did, if we do what they command. For they are not only saved but also carry the faith with them. Even if the holy man is a prisoner, he does greater things than those who are free. The centurion who was free needed his prisoner who was in chains, the skillful pilot needed him who was not a pilot, or rather, who was the true pilot. For it is not a vessel such as this that he steers but the church of the whole world (for he had learned from him who was also the master of the sea), and [Paul] does this not by the art of humankind but by the wisdom of the Spirit. In this vessel are many shipwrecks, many waves and spirits of wickedness, "conflicts on the outside, fears within."[3] That is why [Paul] is the true pilot. HOMILIES ON THE ACTS OF THE APOSTLES 53.[4]

AN ALLEGORY OF THE SPIRITUAL LIFE. BEDE: A most beautiful allegorical sense is evident in this passage, when Paul persuaded the men he had promised would be saved from shipwreck to take food; also in the fact that in the middle of the night they were kept from going wrong by four anchors in the violence of the waves; and that with the coming of day they climbed out onto a point of land. No one escapes the tempests of this world except those who are nourished by the bread of life, and one who in the night of present tribulations depends for all his strength on wisdom, fortitude, temperance and justice will soon, with the shining forth of divine help, reach the port of salvation which he had sought, provided that, unencumbered by things of the world, he seeks only the flame of

---

[1]See also Ambrose of Milan *On the Mysteries*, Cyril of Jerusalem *Catechetical Lectures* and John Chrysostom *Baptismal Instructions*. [2]NPNF 1 11:316**. [3]2 Cor 7:5. [4]NPNF 1 11:318**.

love with which he may warm his heart. COM-MENTARY ON THE ACTS OF THE APOSTLES 27.33.[5]

BREAD FOR THE JOURNEY. ARATOR: Let us examine by what formula the memorable mysteries of the godly figure have significance: the multitude was ordered to be fed from the flesh of a lamb at that time when the lights of the first month shone forth, on the day proceeding from this number [fourteen]; when the protection of this [flesh] had been tasted, the free [multitude] deserved to avoid the darkness of the Nile.[6] Paul at a similar interval persuades those whom he wishes to take out of the sea of the world to feast with him and to taste sacred food. He is following the esteemed footsteps of Moses. The actions of Moses and Paul, if looked at intently, are different in their locations but alike in their causes, and the repeated deliverance is raised out of one font: in it Christ is the Lamb, [and] Christ too is considered the Bread from heaven, which he himself also teaches.[7] One who will have consumed Jesus in his body is free from the Enemy, nor do Pharaoh and Egypt now keep their powers. Immediately all the weapons of the demon are sunk in these waters, from which he who had been a captive is reborn as a child. The surge of the salty depths is also left behind, and the marshes of the foul serpent are overcome. Christ lavishes pastures upon his rescued flock, in their own names,[8] as true Shepherd to one who now eats. ON THE ACTS OF THE APOSTLES 2.[9]

27:36 All Were Encouraged

GIVING THANKS BEFORE EATING. AMMONIUS: "He took bread, and giving thanks to God in the presence of all, he broke it and began to eat." Since Paul saw that they had believed out of necessity and that the time was not opportune to announce Christ to them, as they were broken in spirit and uncertain, he teaches them some piety, namely, not to break bread before giving thanks to the one God, and then to eat. And he teaches us the same, and the way of celebrating Eucharist appears to be this: "We give thanks to you, God, because you deigned to allow us to live until now, without eating bread. Therefore giving glory to you, we break bread for sustenance." CATENA ON THE ACTS OF THE APOSTLES 27.35-36.[10]

---

[5]CS 117:189. [6]Ex 12:1-13. [7]Jn 6:35. [8]Jn 10:3. [9]OAA 91*. [10]CGPNT 3:404.

27:39-44 THE SHIP IS LOST

[39]*Now when it was day, they did not recognize the land, but they noticed a bay with a beach, on which they planned if possible to bring the ship ashore.* [40]*So they cast off the anchors and left them in the sea, at the same time loosening the ropes that tied the rudders; then hoisting the foresail to the wind they made for the beach.* [41]*But striking a shoal[e] they ran the vessel aground; the bow stuck and remained immovable, and the stern was broken up by the surf.* [42]*The soldiers' plan was to kill the prisoners, lest any should swim away and escape;* [43]*but the centurion, wishing to save Paul, kept them from carrying out their purpose. He ordered those who could swim to throw themselves*

overboard first and make for the land, ⁴⁴and the rest on planks or on pieces of the ship. And so it was that all escaped to land.

e Greek *place of two seas*

OVERVIEW: The last act in the shipwreck drama is here recorded. Julius, the centurion, now wishes to save Paul and stops the soldiers, who wish to protect themselves from the charge of losing the prisoners, from killing them. The last line of the passage points out the fulfillment of Paul's prophetic words. In this final event of Acts 27, Bede carries on his concern to illustrate truths of the life of the soul in its struggle here against the trials and temptations of the world. Chrysostom, as usual, respects the course of the narrative and completes his analysis of the transformation of Paul from condemned prisoner to savior of the group of travelers. Chrysostom frames this transformation in terms of revelation, a coming to knowledge of the identity of Paul.

27:41 They Ran the Ship Aground

A SHIPWRECK OF THE MIND. BEDE: This ship perished because it did not glide over the waves with a smooth movement. Rather it became violently stuck upon the sea floor, part [of the ship] held fast, while part was broken up by the smashing waves. Such, without a doubt, is the fate of a mind attached to this world. When such a one has made no effort to trample mundane desires underfoot, he fixes the prow of his intention radically upon the earth, and therefore with the waves of cares he dashes to pieces the whole structure of works that follow [from that intention.] However, those who escaped on the pieces of this ship made for the land, because, affected by the example of those who are perishing, others conduct themselves with greater care. COMMENTARY ON THE ACTS OF THE APOSTLES 27.41B.[1]

27:43 The Centurion Wished to Save Paul

THE CENTURION'S DEFENSE. CHRYSOSTOM: Again the devil tries to impede the prophecy: the soldiers wanted to kill the prisoners, but the centurion prevented them in order to save Paul. The centurion had become a very dear friend. CATENA ON THE ACTS OF THE APOSTLES 27.41-43.[2]

27:44 All Escaped to Land

THEY LEARN WHO PAUL IS. CHRYSOSTOM: The ship breaks up in the daytime in order that they should see the prophecy in action and not be paralyzed with fear. Do you see that in this as well [the prisoners] were given by grace to Paul? For because of him the centurion did not allow them to be killed. Those men seem to me so patently bad that they would choose to kill them. But some jumped into the sea, and others were borne on planks. All were thus saved, and the prophecy was fulfilled, even though time had not yet endowed it with solemnity. . . . And through their own deliverance they learned who Paul was. HOMILIES ON THE ACTS OF THE APOSTLES 53.[3]

---

[1]CS 117:190. [2]CGPNT 3:405. [3]NPNF 1 11:318**.

28:1-6 PAUL IS BITTEN
BY A VIPER AND DOES NOT DIE

¹After we had escaped, we then learned that the island was called Malta. ²And the natives showed us unusual kindness, for they kindled a fire and welcomed us all, because it had begun to rain and was cold. ³Paul had gathered a bundle of sticks and put them on the fire, when a viper came out because of the heat and fastened on his hand. ⁴When the natives saw the creature hanging from his hand, they said to one another, "No doubt this man is a murderer. Though he has escaped from the sea, justice has not allowed him to live." ⁵He, however, shook off the creature into the fire and suffered no harm. ⁶They waited, expecting him to swell up or suddenly fall down dead; but when they had waited a long time and saw no misfortune come to him, they changed their minds and said that he was a god.

OVERVIEW: This passage and the following one, which describe the sojourn of the company at Malta, are once again centered on Paul and the works the Lord does through him. The inhabitants of the island welcome them warmly, but when Paul is bitten by a viper they conclude that Justice (*dikē*), who somehow failed in her mission to destroy this evil man in the shipwreck, is now killing him through a snake. When nothing unfortunate happens to him they conclude he is a god. This incident may be alluding to the saying of Jesus found at Mark 16:18. Eusebius sees in Paul's time on Malta the fulfillment of a prophecy from Isaiah, and he provides a master narrative of the steady spread of the gospel. Other Fathers offer more detailed comments. Chrysostom tries to locate the change of perspective in the Maltese from compassion to condemnation to belief. Paul's humanity is at first evident from his subjugation to both the elements and other people: his guilt then seems apparent from the snake bite, and his immunity to harm reverses these prior judgments. Bede and Arator interpret the events allegorically. Bede reads the narrative as an outward manifestation of inner virtues or of general principles of how the devil (the snake) attacks. Arator has an intriguing interpretation. For him, too, the snake is the devil, and this event is a sign

that the devil never learns but continues to try his same tactics. Wisdom of Solomon 2 seems to be lurking behind some commentators' interpretations (BEDE, THEODORET, BASIL) and specifically Wisdom of Solomon 2:23-24: "God created man for incorruption and made him in the image of his own eternity, but through the devil's envy death entered the world, and those who belong to his party experience it." Bede makes explicit mention of how the envy of the impious is the motivation for their attacks against the good. Basil and Theodoret see the impotence of the serpent's venom as the effect of faith that brings incorruption not just to the soul but in its fullness to the body as well. Ammonius manages to sum up all these thoughts quite succinctly: we are called to be as God, and no matter the schemes that the envious plot who have no idea what God is up to. The only thing that is truly to be feared is infidelity to God. The divinization of humanity is even grasped, though inaccurately, in the way that the pagans developed their pantheon by exalting exceptional humans to the status of divinities.

28:1 *The Island Was Called Malta*

HOW THE GOSPEL TAKES PASSAGE THROUGH THE SEA. EUSEBIUS OF CAESAREA: "And they shall be scattered on the merchant ships of foreigners and together plunder the sea."[1] For they, in their wanderings among the nations, had to make use of the passage through the sea, just as though they were flying on it, they made a swift course through the sea so that they might proclaim the gospel to most nations in a short time. Sometimes they went by foot, sometimes through the sea, but instead of employing Jewish ship captains, they hired those who had received the message of Christ. At the same time, they plundered the sea, that is the islands, through which they passed and made known to their inhabitants the salvific teaching. So you may understand this passage, here is one example. The apostle Paul, being one of those whom this passage prophesies, took a course through the sea on his way to Rome, and when he was shipwrecked on the island called Malta he worked a miracle of great astonishment to the inhabitants, and by healing the physically ill, he so amazed the onlookers that he plundered many and drew them to the salvific teaching. COMMENTARY ON ISAIAH 1.63.[2]

28:2 Unusual Kindness

THE KINDNESS OF THE BARBARIANS. CHRYSOSTOM: The Jews, who saw so many miracles, persecuted and harassed Paul. The barbarians, on the other hand, saw none and were kind to him solely because of his misfortune. "No doubt," they said, "this man is a murderer." They did not simply pronounce their judgment but added, "No doubt," as if this was clear for anyone to see. "Justice," they say, "has not allowed him to live." So they too had an account of providence. These barbarians were far closer to truth than the philosophers. The latter did not allow providence to extend to the sphere below the moon. The former believed that God was present everywhere and that, even if one should escape many dangers, he would not escape in the end. Still, they do not make it their business to bring him to this end but respect him for now on account of his misfor-

tune. They do not broadcast their judgment but only speak to each other. For the chains led them to suspect this. And yet they were prisoners. Let those be ashamed who say, "Do not do good to those in prison." Let us feel shame before the barbarians. For they did not know who those men were, only that they were human beings from their misfortune. HOMILIES ON THE ACTS OF THE APOSTLES 54.[3]

28:3 A Bundle of Sticks and a Viper

ANOTHER DISPLAY OF HIS HUMAN NATURE. CHRYSOSTOM: See how active [Paul] is, how he never works miracles simply for the sake of it but only in time of need. In the storm, when there was a reason, he prophesied, and it was not simply for the sake of prophesying. Here too, he puts sticks on the fire, not for vain display but to save them and to enjoy some warmth. HOMILIES ON THE ACTS OF THE APOSTLES 54.[4]

THE FIRE OF CHARITY. BEDE: When the apostle came out of the sea, he kindled a fire on account of the cold, for with the heat of love he warmed the hearts of those whom by his teaching he had saved from the waves of the tempests. For the sticks are any things said in his exhortations which, having the power to enkindle charity, are plucked from the fullness of the Scriptures as though they were cut from sprigs of foliage. COMMENTARY ON THE ACTS OF THE APOSTLES 28.3A.[5]

DEMONS ATTACK THE TEACHERS OF TRUTH. BEDE: Because an unclean spirit is driven out of the hearts of the faithful by the flame of the virtues, it strives to pour out the venom of its persecutions on teachers of the truth, so that it can in this way wound their hand, that is, hinder the work of spiritual teaching. COMMENTARY ON THE ACTS OF THE APOSTLES 28.3B.[6]

---

[1]Is 11:13 (LXX). [2]GCS 66:88. [3]NPNF 1 11:320-21. [4]NPNF 1 11:319**. [5]CS 117:193. [6]CS 117:193.

THE DEVIL'S WAYS NOT CHANGED. ARATOR:
You wickedly hurtful serpent, why do you still
wish to call [us] back from the Lord and contrive
your old pillaging on the newness of the law?
O lover of death, whose very parent you are, why
do you renew your warfare upon the redeemed?
You come as a plunderer, but you lie there as
plunder, and, bringing death [from a tree],[7] you
are destroyed by the branches of a second tree,
O evil one, and since the cross of Christ, death is
your portion of the wood. ON THE ACTS OF THE
APOSTLES 2.[8]

THE FULL ARMOR OF VIRTUE. THEODORET OF
CYR: And so the viper, which drove its teeth into
the apostle's hand, since it did not find any entry of
sin in him, immediately released him and threw
itself into the fire by inflicting on itself a punishment, because it had made an attack against an
impenetrable body. Therefore let us fear the beasts,
if we do not possess the full armor of virtue. CAT-
ENA ON THE ACTS OF THE APOSTLES 28.3.[9]

**FEAR LESS THE BEASTS THAN FAITHLESS-
NESS.** BASIL THE GREAT: The beasts prove your
faith. Do you believe in the Lord? "You will tread
upon the asp and the adder, you trample down
the lion and the serpent."[10] And you have the
power to walk over snakes and scorpions. Don't
you see that the snake that bit Paul as he gathered
sticks did him no harm, since the holy man was
found to be full of faith. If you have no faith, fear
less the beast than your own faithlessness
through which you make yourself susceptible to
every type of corruption. HOMILIES ON THE
HEXAEMERON 9.6.[11]

28:4 Paul Thought to Be a Murderer

CONDEMNATION PAVES THE WAY FOR TRUTH.
CHRYSOSTOM: "No doubt this man is a murderer. Though he has escaped from the sea, justice has not allowed him to live." This was
permitted for a good reason. They were to see the
thing and utter the thought, so that when it took

place, the miracle would not be disbelieved. See
how respectfully they speak among themselves,
how natural judgment is clearly expressed even
among barbarians, and how they did not condemn without giving a reason. HOMILIES ON
THE ACTS OF THE APOSTLES 54.[12]

28:5 Paul Suffered No Harm

THE DEVIL'S ENVY. BEDE: He burned up the
beast in the same fire by which he provides them
[his companions] with warmth. The saints
advance by the same virtues that are the downfall
of the impious and their instigator because of
their envy.[13] As the prophet says, "Zeal lays hold
on an uneducated people, and now fire consumes
enemies."[14] COMMENTARY ON THE ACTS OF THE
APOSTLES 28.5.[15]

28:6 They Changed Their Minds

WHY THEY THOUGHT PAUL DIVINE. AMMO-
NIUS: "He, however, shook off the creature into
the fire." The faithful are superior to any scheme,
either if it is planned by people or beasts, and
they are similar to gods, as Scripture says: "I say,
'You are gods; nevertheless, you shall die,'
because of infidelity, 'like mortals.'"[16] So the barbarians, seeing that [Paul] did not die but
escaped from certain death, considered him to be
a god, as they used to consider anyone that performed miracles to be a god. And in this manner
they named their ancient gods, either because of
the excellence of their strength, which they saw
to be superior to theirs, as in the case of Hercules,
son of Semele,[17] or because of their magical arts,
which raised the admiration of the spectators, as
in the case of Simon in Samaria.[18] CATENA ON
THE ACTS OF THE APOSTLES 28.5.[19]

---

[7]See Gen 3:1. [8]*OAA* 91-92. [9]CGPNT 3:408. [10]Ps 91:13 (90:13
LXX). [11]PG 29:204. [12]NPNF 1 11:320**. [13]See Wis 2:24. [14]Is 26:11
in the version of Jerome *Commentary on Isaiah* 3.26.11 (CCL 73:335).
[15]CS 117:193. [16]Ps 82:6-7 (81:6-7 LXX). [17]Ammonius has confused
Hercules with Dionysos, whose mother was Semele. The mother of
Hercules was Alcmene. [18]Acts 8:9. [19]CGPNT 3:409.

28:7-10 PAUL HEALS THE SICK OF MALTA

⁷Now in the neighborhood of that place were lands belonging to the chief man of the island, named Publius, who received us and entertained us hospitably for three days. ⁸It happened that the father of Publius lay sick with fever and dysentery; and Paul visited him and prayed, and putting his hands on him healed him. ⁹And when this had taken place, the rest of the people on the island who had diseases also came and were cured. ¹⁰They presented many gifts to us;ᶠ and when we sailed, they put on board whatever we needed.

f Or honored us with many honors

OVERVIEW: This account of the hospitality offered by Publius (probably the leading Roman authority on the island) intrigues moderns, who wonder how he provided for 276 people for three days. Luke's accent is rather on Paul's healing activity as part of preaching the gospel (Lk 10:9-10) and the generosity of the people when their visitors left them, which would have been after winter's end (probably after March 10 of 61). Logically, the notice of this generosity should have followed the mention of the securing of the ship for Rome, but it is a characteristic of Luke's style to finish one story before starting another. Chrysostom notes the hospitality of Publius as providing the ground for Paul's continued work of evangelization, which profited his host more than the cost of any of his goods. Bede and Ammonius examine the role of miracles in the life of faith, both concluding that they are initiatory and not something needed for those who already believe.

28:7 Publius Entertained Hospitably

RIGHT JUDGMENTS. CHRYSOSTOM: Look, even after they were rid of the storm, they did not become negligent, and what a lavish welcome they received because of Paul. For three days they stayed there and everyone of them was well-provided with sustenance.... It was for Paul's sake that all this took place, so that the prisoners, as well as the soldiers and the centurion, should believe. For even if they were made of stone, from the counsel they heard him give, from the predictions they heard him make, from the miracles they saw him accomplish and from the nourishment they enjoyed because of him, they would have thought him great. See how quickly sound judgment, when it is not overtaken by some emotion, delivers right decisions and discerning verdicts. HOMILIES ON THE ACTS OF THE APOSTLES 54.[1]

THE PROFIT OF GENEROSITY. CHRYSOSTOM: Behold, again another hospitable man, the rich and wealthy Publius, who had seen nothing but had mercy on them because of their calamity. He received and took care of them.... It is certainly an act of great benevolence to give hospitality to 270 people. Meditate on what a great profit is hospitality: not because there was necessity or because he acted against his will, but because [Publius] considered it a profit, did he give hospitality to them for three days. CATENA ON THE ACTS OF THE APOSTLES 28.7.[2]

28:8 Healing Publius's Father

INNER AND OUTER HEALTH. BEDE: Why did [Paul] heal a sick unbeliever by prayer, when he

---

[1]NPNF 1 11:320**. [2]CGPNT 3:409.

restored Timothy, one of the sick believers, by the art of medicine,[3] and Trophimus, another sick believer, he left entirely?[4] Was it not because this outsider had to be healed by a miracle since he was not inwardly alive, while those who were living with inner health had no need [of healing]? COMMENTARY ON THE ACTS OF THE APOSTLES 28.8.[5]

28:9 Others Also Cured

FAITH MAKES MIRACLES SUPERFLUOUS. AMMONIUS: Dysentery is a difficult disease to cure. He, who received healing from Paul, led many to faith. Therefore miracles are mostly performed among and for unbelievers. CATENA ON THE ACTS OF THE APOSTLES 28.9.[6]

28:10 Presenting Many Gifts

RECEIVING PAUL, THEY MUST ALSO HAVE RECEIVED THE FAITH. CHRYSOSTOM: "They presented," it says, "many gifts to us." Not that [Paul] received wages, God forbid, but as it is written, "The worker is worth his keep."[7] "When we sailed, they put on board whatever we needed." It is clear that their hosts, who afforded them such hospitality, also received the word of the preaching. For they would not have been treated so kindly for three days had their hosts not believed strongly and shown the fruits of conversion. HOMILIES ON THE ACTS OF THE APOSTLES 54.[8]

---

[3]1 Tim 5:23. [4]2 Tim 4:20. [5]CS 117:193-94. [6]CGPNT 3:410. [7]Mt 10:10. [8]NPNF 1 11:321**.

28:11-16 THEY ARRIVE AT ROME

[11]*After three months we set sail in a ship which had wintered in the island, a ship of Alexandria, with the Twin Brothers as figurehead.* [12]*Putting in at Syracuse, we stayed there for three days.* [13]*And from there we made a circuit and arrived at Rhegium; and after one day a south wind sprang up, and on the second day we came to Puteoli.* [14]*There we found brothers, and were invited to stay with them for seven days. And so we came to Rome.* [15]*And the brothers there, when they heard of us, came as far as the Forum of Appius and Three Taverns to meet us. On seeing them Paul thanked God and took courage.* [16]*And when we came into Rome, Paul was allowed to stay by himself, with the soldier that guarded him.*

OVERVIEW: The final stage of the journey is described undramatically; no mention is given of how the brothers knew Paul was coming. Laconically, Luke announces the fulfillment of Jesus' words to Paul and indeed his prediction that the mission would reach "to the ends of the earth" (Acts 1:8) by simply stating, "And so we came to Rome." The notice of the terms of Paul's captivity prepare for the final scene, the meeting with the Jewish leaders in Rome. The two comments from Chrysostom focus on the effects of the spread of the gospel, in that it creates an extended family bonded together in affection that strengthens its members. Here is the visible effect of the gospel message that spreads peace in society among its members even when they do not know one another. Our worldly status, whether imprisoned or free,[1] is not the basis of our relations but our bond in Christ.

28:13 We Came to Puteoli

THE MESSAGE HAD PRECEDED HIM. CHRYSOSTOM: The preaching had already reached Sicily. See how it ran: in Puteoli they found some brothers and met them and others. The affection of the brothers was such that they were not troubled by the fact that Paul was in chains. CATENA ON THE ACTS OF THE APOSTLES 28.11-13.[2]

28:15 Paul Thanked God and Took Courage

PAUL RECEIVES COMFORT AS OTHER PEOPLE DO. CHRYSOSTOM: Observe, if you please, how Paul himself was affected in a human way. "On seeing them," it says, "he took courage." In spite of all the miracles he had worked, the sight of the brothers still afforded him assistance. From this we learn that he received comfort and its opposite as other people do. HOMILIES ON THE ACTS OF THE APOSTLES 54.[3]

---

[1]See Gal. 3:26-28. [2]CGPNT 3:411. [3]NPNF 1 11:320**.

28:17-22 PAUL CALLS TOGETHER THE JEWS OF ROME

[17]*After three days he called together the local leaders of the Jews; and when they had gathered, he said to them, "Brothers, though I had done nothing against the people or the customs of our fathers, yet I was delivered prisoner from Jerusalem into the hands of the Romans. [18]When they had examined me, they wished to set me at liberty, because there was no reason for the death penalty in my case. [19]But when the Jews objected, I was compelled to appeal to Caesar—though I had no charge to bring against my nation. [20]For this reason therefore I have asked to see you and speak with you, since it is because of the hope of Israel that I am bound with this chain." [21]And they said to him, "We have received no letters from Judea about you, and none of the brothers coming here has reported or spoken any evil about you. [22]But we desire to hear from you what your views are; for with regard to this sect we know that everywhere it is spoken against."*

OVERVIEW: This passage and the following are enclosed within two mentions of the conditions of Paul's imprisonment (Acts 28:16, 30-31). Commentators wonder why Luke makes no mention of Paul's meetings with the believers but instead chooses to recount his contact with the Jewish leaders. This surely indicates that contrary to Paul's own repeated statements, the fact that the gospel is destined for Gentiles as well and despite the conclusion of this meeting, neither Paul nor Luke consider that the offer made by God to Israel has been withdrawn. Paul makes a brief defense establishing his legal innocence and speaking of the "hope of Israel." The leaders' reference to "this sect" (*hairesis*) may mean here little more than a school of thought which nevertheless is "everywhere spoken against." The matter at the center of the Fathers' comments is the structuring of society in relation to God's work of salvation. Ammonius, perhaps aware of the irony of his interpretation, turns the tables on the perceived accusation of Christianity being heresy by using this title to name a foreordained process of exalting the truth. For Chrysostom, however, the structures of society in the history of salvation produce the outcast with whom God stands in order to condemn the supposed self-sufficiency of the "world" that needs its victims. God's "resourcefulness," according to Chrysostom, lets evil do its worst and thus shows forth the greatness of God's chosen ones. For Chrysostom, it is those who are cast out that show forth the judgment of God.

28:17 The Local Leaders of the Jews

THE UNDOING OF EVIL IN EVIL. CHRYSOSTOM: [Paul] called together the leaders of the Jews and argued with them. They left in disagreement. They were taunted by him, yet they dared not say anything. For the matter concerning Paul had not been turned over to their authority. It is wonderful how all things come about on our behalf not through what seems to be for our safety but rather through the opposite. I give the following example for your edification. "The Pharaoh ordered the infants to be thrown into the Nile."[1] Had the infants not been thrown into the Nile, Moses would not have been saved, nor would he have been raised in the palace. It was not when [Moses] was saved that he was in honor but when he was exposed. This was done by God to show his ingenuity and resourcefulness. The Jew threatened him, saying, "Are you thinking of killing me?" This helped him. It was part of the divine plan to ensure that he would see that vision in the desert, that the proper time would be fulfilled and that he would learn philosophy in the desert and live in safety. The same thing happens in all the plots of the Jews against him. He becomes more renowned, as was the case with Aaron. They rose up against him and thereby made him so renowned[2] that his ordination was unquestionable and he was subsequently held in admiration because of the bronze tablets. Of course you know the story, so I will leave out the narrative. If you wish, let us go back to the beginning for other such examples. . . . The three children were thrown into the furnace, and through this they became more renowned. Daniel was cast into the pit and was thus made more illustrious.[3] You see, in every case, trials bring forth great good even in this life, not to mention in the life to come. For with evil the same thing happens as when one is fighting fire with a reed: it seems to beat the fire but is in fact making it brighter and consuming itself. Evil becomes the fuel and the foundation of brightness for virtue. For with God turning unrighteousness to good account, our character shines forth all the more. Again, when the devil contrives anything of this kind, he is making those who endure more renowned. HOMILIES ON THE ACTS OF THE APOSTLES 54.[4]

28:22 This Sect Is Spoken Against

THE NECESSITY OF HERESIES. AMMONIUS: The Jews call the faith in Christ a heresy,[5] because "everywhere it is spoken against." You see, the Jews themselves testify that Christ is preached everywhere, even though not all receive this preaching, as the text says, but some of the Jews or the Gentiles speak against it, while the heretics, in a different way, do not conform to the true faith. In fact, it was necessary that there be heresies, so that the elected might appear, and all might fulfill what had been predicted by the prophet Simeon about Christ: "This child is destined for the falling and the rising of many in Israel, and to be a sign that will be opposed."[6] CATENA ON THE ACTS OF THE APOSTLES 28.21-22.[7]

---

[1]Ex 1:22. [2]See Num 16. [3]Dan 3, 6. [4]NPNF 1 11:321-22**. [5]The word *hairesis* had long meant "heresy" by Ammonius's day. [6]Lk 2:34. [7]CGPNT 3:415-16.

28:23-31 PAUL PREACHES ABOUT JESUS

²³*When they had appointed a day for him, they came to him at his lodging in great numbers. And he expounded the matter to them from morning till evening, testifying to the kingdom of God and trying to convince them about Jesus both from the law of Moses and from the prophets.* ²⁴*And some were convinced by what he said, while others disbelieved.* ²⁵*So, as they disagreed among themselves, they departed, after Paul had made one statement: "The Holy Spirit was right in saying to your fathers through Isaiah the prophet:*

²⁶*'Go to this people, and say,*
You shall indeed hear but never understand,
and you shall indeed see but never perceive.
²⁷*For this people's heart has grown dull,*
and their ears are heavy of hearing,
and their eyes they have closed;
lest they should perceive with their eyes,
and hear with their ears,
and understand with their heart,
and turn for me to heal them.'
²⁸*Let it be known to you then that this salvation of God has been sent to the Gentiles; they will listen."*ᵍ

³⁰*And he lived there two whole years at his own expense,*ʰ *and welcomed all who came to him,* ³¹*preaching the kingdom of God and teaching about the Lord Jesus Christ quite openly and unhindered.*

g Other ancient authorities add verse 29, *And when he had said these words, the Jews departed, holding much dispute among themselves*   h Or *in his own hired dwelling*

OVERVIEW: In this meeting with the Jewish leaders Paul explains himself by preaching the gospel, "testifying to the kingdom of God and trying to convince them about Jesus both from the law of Moses and from the prophets." The Jewish reaction is divided, and the leaders decide to withdraw. This merits Paul's blame as he cites a text often used in the New Testament in regard to Jewish resistance to the gospel. This can hardly be an expression of God's complete rejection of Israel: Paul had already described Jesus' activity now risen from the dead: He "would proclaim light both to the people and to the Gentiles"

(Acts 26:23). The work ends with another description of the conditions of Paul's captivity and his freedom in preaching the Lord Jesus Christ here "at the ends of the earth." Modern commentators go on to ask about the way in which the book of Acts ends. Was a third volume of Luke's lost? Did Luke die and leave his work unfinished? Perhaps the best answer is that Luke, like Mark, with his enigmatic ending wishes to indicate that the narrative ends here but that the story is meant to continue in each generation and in each believer. Paul's preaching in Rome is, according to Chrysostom, without reference to miracles, so as to underscore faith. For Chrysostom, simply to preach from the law and the prophets is a great miracle, especially in the center of the pagan world offering Paul a platform for the message that would conquer it. His preaching, while it calls to belief, also points to the fulfillment of prophesied rejection. Bede is concerned to show that the rejection of the gospel is not determined but a matter of free will. Two final passages: one by Chrysostom that hints at what happens beyond the end of Acts; another from Eusebius that aims at giving a summary of Paul's end. Chrysostom's is an encomium of one who is triumphant. Successful generals, during the republic and under the emperors, would celebrate their military accomplishments with a triumph, a parade of their spoils through Rome. Chrysostom praises Paul as a victor who has made a circuit of the world, ended in Rome and was crowned. Eusebius offers a more subdued account that tries to give a sequence to Paul's activity between this imprisonment in Rome and his martyrdom there under Nero.

28:23 Paul Expounded from Morning Till Evening

No Miracles in Order to Underscore Faith. Chrysostom: Look, again it is not by miracles but with the law and the prophets that he silences them, and this is what he does on every occasion. And yet [Paul] had the power to perform miracles, but then it would no longer be a matter of faith. For this was a great miracle, to discourse from the law and the prophets. Homilies on the Acts of the Apostles 55.[1]

28:25 The Holy Spirit

It Is Not Paul That They Disbelieve. Chrysostom: The expression "the Spirit said" is unremarkable, for angels too are said to say what the Lord says. "The Holy Spirit," he says, "was right in saying." This is no longer unremarkable.

When someone describes the speech of the angels, he does not say, "The angel was right in saying" but "The Lord was right in saying" or "The Spirit was right in saying." That is, it is not me that you disbelieve, but God has known this from the beginning. Homilies on the Acts of the Apostles 55.[2]

28:27 Hearts Grown Dull

Their Dullness Is a Matter of Will. Bede: Lest we think that their hardness of heart and their being hard of hearing are attributable to their nature and not to their will, he added a fault, their free will, saying, "And they have closed their eyes." Commentary on the Acts of the Apostles 28.27ab.[3]

28:31 Teaching Openly and Unhindered

Rome Receives Its Conqueror. Chrysostom: Do you see God's providence? . . . "He spoke about the kingdom," it says. Not about anything tangible, not about the present, but with hopes he feeds them. . . . "I am in haste to go to Spain, and I hope," he says, "to see you in my journey."[4] This is in part directed toward you. Do you see how everything was foreseen by that sacred and divine head, the man who is higher than the heavens, whose soul is able to grasp all things at once, Paul, who holds the first place, whose very name, to those who know, is sufficient to awaken the soul to soberness, to shake off all sleep? Concerning this [Paul] says, "I will come and rest together with you in the fullness of the blessing of the gospel,"[5] and again, "I am going to Jerusalem to minister."[6] This is also what he says here, "I came to bring to my nation alms and offerings." He was nearer now to heaven. Rome received him in chains and saw him crowned and proclaimed.[7] "I will rest together with you," he says. It was the beginning of the course. He added

---

[1]NPNF 1 11:326**. [2]NPNF 1 11:326**. [3]CS 117:196. [4]Rom 15:24. [5]Rom 15:29. [6]Rom 15:25. [7]With martyrdom.

trophies to trophies, invincible as he was. Corinth held him for two years, Asia three, and this city two. Then for a second time he enters this city, when he has reached perfection. Thus he escaped and having filled the whole world brought his life to a close. Why did you want to know what happened after this? There followed such things as before: chains, tortures, battles, imprisonments, treacherous plots, false accusations, deaths day by day. You saw a small part of it. Whatever you saw is what the rest is like. Homilies on the Acts of the Apostles 55.[8]

After Acts. Eusebius of Caesarea: And Luke, who wrote the Acts of the Apostles, brought his history to a close at this point, after stating that Paul spent two whole years at Rome as a prisoner at large and preached the word of God without restraint. Thus after he had made his defense it is said that the apostle was sent again upon the ministry of preaching and that upon coming to the same city a second time he suffered martyrdom. In this imprisonment [Paul] wrote his second epistle to Timothy, in which he mentions his first defense and his impending death. But hear his testimony on these matters. "At my first answer," he says, "no one stood with me, but all forsook me: I pray God that it may not be laid to their charge. Notwithstanding the Lord stood with me and strengthened me, that by me the preaching might be fully known and that all the Gentiles might hear; and I was delivered out of the mouth of the lion."[9] He plainly indicates in these words that on the former occasion, in order that the preaching might be fulfilled by him, he was rescued from the mouth of the lion, referring, in this expression, to Nero, as is probable on account of the latter's cruelty. He did not therefore afterward add the similar statement, "He will rescue me from the mouth of the lion"; for he saw in the Spirit that his end would not be long delayed. Wherefore he adds to the words "and he delivered me from the mouth of the lion" this sentence, "The Lord shall deliver me from every evil work and will preserve me to his heavenly kingdom,"[10] indicating his speedy martyrdom; which he also foretells still more clearly in the same epistle, when he writes, "For I am now ready to be offered, and the time of my departure is at hand."[11] In his second epistle to Timothy, moreover, he indicates that Luke was with him when he wrote[12] that at his first defense not even Luke was there.[13] So it is probable that Luke wrote the Acts of the Apostles at that time, continuing his history down to the period when he was with Paul. But these things have been adduced by us to show that Paul's martyrdom did not take place at the time of that Roman sojourn that Luke records. It is probable indeed that as Nero was more disposed to mildness in the beginning, Paul's defense of his doctrine was more easily received; but that when he [Nero] had advanced to the commission of lawless deeds of daring, he made the apostles as well as others the subjects of his attacks. Ecclesiastical History 2.22.1-8.[14]

---

[8]NPNF 1 11:326-27**. [9]2 Tim 4:16-17. [10]2 Tim 4:18. [11]2 Tim 4:6. [12]See 2 Tim 4:11. [13]See 2 Tim 4:16. [14]NPNF 2 1:124*.

APPENDIX

Early Christian Writers and the Documents Cited

The following table lists all the early Christian documents cited in this volume by author, if known, or by the title of the work. The English title used in this commentary is followed in parentheses with the Latin designation and, where available, the Thesaurus Linguae Graecae (=TLG) digital references or Cetedoc Clavis numbers. Printed sources of original language version may be found in the bibliography of work in original languages.

Ambrose

Concerning Repentance (*De paenitentia*)	Cetedoc 0156
Joseph (*De Joseph*)	Cetedoc 0131
Letters (*Epistulae*)	Cetedoc 0160
On His Brother Satyrus (*De excessu fratris Satyri*)	Cetedoc 0157
On the Christian Faith (*De fide*)	Cetedoc 0150
On the Holy Spirit (*De Spiritu Sancto*)	Cetedoc 0151
On the Patriarchs (*De patriarchis*)	Cetedoc 0132

Ammonius

Catena on the Acts of the Apostles (*Catena in Acta*)	TLG 4102.008

Anonymous

Catena on the Acts of the Apostles (*Catena in Acta*)	TLG 4102.008

Arator

On the Acts of the Apostles (*Historia apostolica = De actibus apostolorum*)	Cetedoc 1504

Athanasius

Festal Letters (*Epistulae festales*)

Augustine

Against Two Letters of the Pelagians (*Contra duas epistulas Pelagianorum*)	Cetedoc 0346
Christian Instruction (*De doctrina Christiana*)	Cetedoc 0263
Explanations of the Psalms (*Enarrationes in Psalmos*)	Cetedoc 0283
Harmony of the Gospels (*De consensu evangelistarum libri iv*)	Cetedoc 0273
Homilies on 1 John (*In Johannis epistulam ad Parthos tractatus*)	Cetedoc 0279
Letters (*Epistulae*)	Cetedoc 0262
On Original Sin (*De gratia Christi et de peccato originali*)	Cetedoc 0349

On the Merits and Forgiveness of Sins and on Infant Baptism (*De peccatorum meritis et*
    remissione et de baptismo paruulorum)   Cetedoc 0342

On the Spirit and the Letter (*De Spiritu et littera*)   Cetedoc 0343

On the Trinity (*De Trinitate*)   Cetedoc 0329

Predestination of the Saints (*De praedestinatione sanctorum*)   Cetedoc 0354

Sermon on the Mount (*De sermone Domini in monte*)   Cetedoc 0274

Sermons (*Sermones*)   Cetedoc 0284

Tractates on the Gospel of John (*In Johannis evangelium tractatus*)   Cetedoc 0278

Basil the Great

Homilies on the Hexaemeron (*Homiliae in hexaemeron*)   TLG 2040.001

Homilies on the Psalms (*Homiliae super Psalmos*)   TLG 2040.018

Letters (*Epistulae*)   TLG 2040.004

The Long Rules (*Asceticon magnum sive Quaestiones [regulae fusius tractatae]*)   TLG 2040.048

The Morals (*Regulae morales*)   TLG 2040.051

On the Spirit (*De spiritu sancto*)   TLG 2040.003

The Short Rules (*Asceticon magnum sive Quaestiones [regulae brevius tractatae]*)   TLG 2040.050

Bede

Commentary on the Acts of the Apostles (*Expositio Actuum apostolorum*)   Cetedoc 1357

Cassian, John

Conferences (*Collationes*)   Cetedoc 0512

Institutes (*De institutis coenobiorum et de octo principalium vitiorum remedies*)   Cetedoc 0513

On the Incarnation of the Lord Against Nestorius (*De incarnatione Domini contra Nestorium*)   Cetedoc 0514

Cassiodorus

Exposition of the Psalms (*Expositio Psalmorum*)   Cetedoc 0900

Clement of Alexandria

Stromateis (*Stromata*)   TLG 0555.004

Cyprian

Letters (*Epistulae*)   Cetedoc 0050

Works and Almsgiving (*De opere et eleemosynis*)   Cetedoc 0047

Cyril of Alexandria

Against Julian (*Contra Julianum*)

Catena on the Acts of the Apostles (*Catena in Acta*)   TLG 4102.008

Cyril of Jerusalem

Catechetical Lectures (*Catecheses ad illuminandos*)   TLG 2110.003

Didymus the Blind

Catena on the Acts of the Apostles (*Catena in Acta*)   TLG 4102.008

(See also *Fragmenta expositionis in Actus apostolorum ex Wolfii Anecdotis*)   TLG 2102.x07

Ephrem the Syrian
Commentary on Tatian's Diatessaron (*In Tatiani Diatessaron*)
Homily on Our Lord (*Sermo de Domino nostro*)
Hymns on Paradise (*Hymni de paradiso*)

Eusebius of Caesaria
Commentary on Isaiah (*Commentarius in Isaiam*)   TLG 2018.019
Ecclesiastical History (*Historia ecclesiastica*)   TLG 2018.002
Proof of the Gospel (*Demonstratio evangelica*)   TLG 2018.005

Fulgentius of Ruspe
Letters (*Epistulae*)   Cetedoc 0817

Gregory of Nazianzus
On the Holy Spirit, Theological Oration 5 (31) (*De Spiritu Sancto*)   TLG 2022.011

Gregory of Nyssa
Against Apollinaris (*Antirrheticus adversus Apollinarium*)   TLG 2017.008
Against Eunomius (*Contra Eunomium*)   TLG 2017.030
Homilies on the Song of Songs (*In Canticum canticorum*)   TLG 2017.032
Homily 2 on St. Stephen (*Encomium in sanctum Stephanum protomartyrem ii*)   TLG 2017.064
Life of Moses (*De vita Mosis*)   TLG 2017.042
On Not Three Gods (*Ablabium quod non sint tres dei*)   TLG 2017.003
On Perfection (*De perfectione Christiana ad Olympium monachum*)   TLG 2017.026
On the Holy Trinity (*Ad Eustathium de Sancta Trinitate*)   TLG 2017.001
Refutation of Eunomius's "Confession of Faith" (*Refutatio confessionis Eunomii*)   TLG 2017.031

Gregory the Great
Letters (*Registrum epistularum*)   Cetedoc 1714
Pastoral Care (Quoted by Bede in *Expositio Actuum apostolorum*)   Cetedoc 1357

Hilary of Poitiers
On the Trinity (*De Trinitate*)   Cetedoc 0433

Irenaeus
Against Heresies (*Adversus haereses*)   Cetedoc 1154
Catena on the Acts of the Apostles (*Catena in Acta*)   TLG 4102.008

Isidore of Pelusium
Catena on the Acts of the Apostles (*Catena in Acta*)   TLG 4102.008

Jerome
Against Jovinianus (*Adversus Jovinianum*)   Cetedoc 0610

Against Vigilantius (*Contra Vigilantium*)   Cetedoc 0611
Homilies on the Psalms (*Tractatus lix in Psalmos*)   Cetedoc 0592
Letters (*Epistulae*)   Cetedoc 0620
On Illustrious Men (*De viris inlustribus*)   Cetedoc 0616

John Chrysostom

Against the Anomoeans (*Contra Anomoeos*)
  2 (*De incomprehensibili dei natura*)   TLG 2062.012
  12 (*De Christi divinitate*)   TLG 4201.020
Baptismal Instructions (*Catecheses ad illuminandos*)   TLG 2062.382
Catena on the Acts of the Apostles (*Catena in Acta*)   TLG 4102.008
Homilies Concerning the Statues (*Ad populam Antiochenum homiliae [de statuis]*)   TLG 2062.024
Homilies on 1 Corinthians (*In epistulam i ad Corinthios [homiliae 1-44]*)   TLG 2062.156
Homilies on 2 Corinthians (*In epistulam ii ad Corinthios [homiliae 1-30]*)   TLG 2062.157
Homilies on Genesis (*In Genesim [homiliae 1-67]*)   TLG 2062.112
Homilies on Romans (*In epistulam ad Romanos*)   TLG 2062.155
Homilies on the Acts of the Apostles (*In Acta apostolorum*)   TLG 2062.154
Homilies on the Gospel of John (*In Joannem [homiliae 1-88]*)   TLG 2062.153
Homilies on the Gospel of Matthew (*In Matthaeum [homiliae 1-90]*)   TLG 2062.152
On the Epistle to the Hebrews (*In epistulam ad Hebraeos*)   TLG 2062.168

Justin Martyr

First Apology (*Apologia*)   TLG 0645.001

Leo the Great

Sermons (*Tractatus septem et nonaginta*)   Cetedoc 1657

Letter to Diognetus (*Epistula ad Diognetum*)   TLG 1350.001

Origen

Against Celsus (*Contra Celsum*)   TLG 2042.001
Commentary on 1 Corinthians (*Fragmenta ex commentariis in epistulam i ad Corinthios*)   TLG 2042.034
Commentary on Matthew (*Commentarium in evangelium Matthaei [lib. 12-17]*)   TLG 2042.030
Commentary on the Epistle to the Romans (*Commentariorum in Epistolam
  B. Pauli ad Romanos*)
Commentary on the Gospel of John (*Commentarii in evangelium Joannis*)   TLG 2042.005
Homilies on Exodus (*Homiliae in Exodum*)   TLG 2042.023
Homilies on Genesis (*Homiliae in Genesim*)   TLG 2042.022
Homilies on Jeremiah (*In Jeremiam [homiliae 12-20]*)   TLG 2042.021
Homilies on Joshua (*In Jesu nave homiliae xxvi*)   TLG 2042.025
Homilies on Leviticus (*Homiliae in Leviticum*)   TLG 2042.024
Homilies on Numbers (*In Numeros homiliae*)   Cetedoc 0198 0
Homilies on the Gospel of Luke (*Homiliae in Lucam*)   TLG 2042.016
On First Principles (*De principiis*)   TLG 2042.002
Palestinian Catena on Psalm 118 (*Catena Palestinensis*)   TLG 4142.001

Paulus Orosius
Defense Against the Pelagians *(Liber apologeticus contra Pelagianos)*   Cetedoc 0572

Polycarp of Smyrna
Letter to the Philippians *(Epistula ad Philippenses)*   TLG 1622.001

Pseudo-Basil
Against Eunomius *(Adversus Eunomium)*   TLG 2040.019

Pseudo-Justin
Fragments of the Lost Work of Justin on the Resurrection *(De resurrectione)*   TLG 0646.005

Severus of Antioch
Catena on the Acts of the Apostles *(Catena in Acta)*   TLG 4102.008

Tertullian
On Baptism *(De baptismo)*   Cetedoc 0008

Theodoret of Cyr
Catena on the Acts of the Apostles *(Catena in Acta)*   TLG 4102.008
Dialogues *(Eranistes)*   TLG 4089.002
Letters *(Epistulae: Collectio Sirmondiana [1-95])*   TLG 4089.006
  (Epistulae: Collectio Sirmondiana [96-147])   TLG 4089.007

This bibliography refers readers to original language sources and supplies Thesaurus Linguae Graecae (=TLG) or Cetedoc Clavis (=Cl.) numbers where available. The edition listed in this bibliography may in some cases differ from the edition found in TLG or Cetedoc databases.

Ambrose. "De excessu fratris Satyri." In *Sancti Ambrosii opera*. Edited by Otto Faller. CSEL 73, pp. 207-325. Vienna, Austria: Hoelder-Pichler-Tempsky, 1895. Cl. 0157.

———. "De fide libri v." In *Sancti Ambrosii opera*. Edited by Otto Faller. CSEL 78. Vienna, Austria: Hoelder-Pichler-Tempsky, 1962. Cl. 0150.

———. "De Joseph." In *Sancti Ambrosii opera*. Edited by Karl Schenkl. CSEL 32, pt. 2, pp. 71-122. Vienna, Austria: F. Tempsky; Leipzig, Germany: G. Freytag, 1897. Cl. 0131.

———. *De paenitentia*. Edited by Roger Gryson. SC 179. Paris: Éditions du Cerf, 1971. Cl. 0156.

———. "De patriarchis." In *Sancti Ambrosii opera*. Edited by Karl Schenkl. CSEL 32, pt. 2, pp. 123-60. Vienna, Austria: F. Tempsky; Leipzig, Germany: G. Freytag, 1897. Cl. 0132.

———. "De spiritu sancto." In *Sancti Ambrosii opera*. Edited by Otto Faller. CSEL 79, pp. 5-222. Vienna, Austria: Hoelder-Pichler-Tempsky, 1964. Cl. 0151.

———. "Epistulae; Epistulae extra collectionem traditae." In *Sancti Ambrosii opera*. Edited by Otto Faller and M. Zelzer. CSEL 82. Vienna, Austria: F. Tempsky; Leipzig, Germany: G. Freytag, 1968-1990. Cl. 0160.

Ammonius. "Catena in Acta (catena Andreae) (e cod. Oxon. coll. nov. 58)." In *Catenae Graecorum patrum in Novum Testamentum*, vol. 3. Edited by J. A. Cramer. Oxford: Oxford University Press, 1838; reprinted, Hildesheim: Olms, 1967. TLG 4102.008.

Arator. *Historia apostolica = Aratoris subdiaconi: De Actibus apostolorum*. Edited by Arthur Patch McKinlay. CSEL 72. Vienna, Austria: Hoelder-Pichler-Tempsky, 1951. Cl. 1504.

Aratoris Subdiaconi Historia apostolica. Edited by A. P. Orbán. CCL 130 and 130A. 2 vols. Turnhout, Belgium: Brepols, 2006. Cl. 1504.

Athanasius. "Epistulae festales." In *Sancti Athanasii: Syriace et Latine*. Edited by Leonis Allatii. Nova Patrum Bibliothecae 6. Rome: Typis Sacri Consilii Propagando Christiano Nomini, 1853.

Augustine. "Contra duas epistulas pelagianorum." Edited by Karl Franz Urba and Joseph Zycha. CSEL 60, pp. 423-570. Vienna, Austria: F. Tempsky; Leipzig, Germany: G. Freytag, 1913. Cl. 0346.

———. *De consensu evangelistarum libri iv*. In *Sancti Aurelii Augustini*. Edited by Francis Weihrich. CSEL 43. Vienna, Austria: F. Tempsky; Leipzig, Germany: G. Freytag, 1904. Cl. 0273.

———. "De doctrina christiana." In *Aurelii Augustini opera*. Edited by Joseph Martin. CCL 32, pp. 1-167. Turnhout, Belgium: Brepols, 1962. Cl. 0263.

———. "De gratia Christi et de peccato originali." In *Sancti Aureli Augustini*. Edited by Karl Franze Urba and Joseph Zycha. CSEL 42, pp. 125-206. Vienna, Austria: F. Tempsky; Leipzig, Germany: G. Freytag, 1902. Cl. 0349.

———. "De peccatorum meritis et remissione et de baptismo parvulorum." In *Sancti Aureli Augustini op-*

era. Edited by Karl Franz Urba and Joseph Zycha. CSEL 60, pp. 3-151. Vienna, Austria: F. Tempsky, 1913. Cl. 0342.

———. "De praedestinatione sanctorum." In *Opera omnia*. PL 44, cols. 959-92. Edited by J.-P. Migne. Paris: Migne, 1861. Cl. 0354.

———. "De sermone Domini in monte." In *Aurelii Augustini opera*. Edited by Almut Mutzenbecher. CCL 35. Turnhout, Belgium: Brepols, 1967. Cl. 0274.

———. "De spiritu et littera." In *Sancti Aurelii Augustini De peccatorum meritis et remissione et de baptismo parvulorum ad Marcellinum libri tres, De spiritu et littera liber unus, De natura et gratia liber unus, De natura et origine animae libri quattuor*. Edited by Karl Franz Urba and Joseph Zycha. CSEL 60, pp. 155-229. Vienna, Austria: F. Tempsky; Leipzig, Germany: G. Freytag, 1913. Cl. 0343.

———. "De Trinitate." In *Aurelii Augustini opera*. Edited by William John Mountain. CCL 50-50A. Turnhout, Belgium: Brepols, 1968. Cl. 0329.

———. "Enarrationes in Psalmos." In *Aurelii Augustini opera*. Edited by Eligius Dekkers and John Fraipont. CCL 38, 39, 40. Turnhout, Belgium: Brepols, 1956. Cl. 0283.

———. "Enarrationes in Psalmos." In *Opera omnia*. PL 36-37. Edited by J.-P. Migne. Paris: Migne, 1865. Cl. 0283.

———. *Epistulae 185-270*. Edited by A. Goldbacher. CSEL 57. Vienna, Austria: F. Tempsky; Leipzig, Germany: G. Freytag, 1911. Cl. 0262.

———. "In Johannis epistulam ad Parthos tractatus." In *Opera omnia*. PL 35, cols. 1379-2062. Edited by J.-P. Migne. Paris: Migne, 1841. Cl. 0279.

———. "In Johannis evangelium tractatus." In *Aurelii Augustini opera*. Edited by R. Willems. CCL 36. Turnhout, Belgium: Brepols, 1954. Cl. 0278.

———. "Sermones." In *Augustini opera omnia*. PL 38 and 39. Edited by J.-P. Migne. Paris: Migne, 1844-1865. Cl. 0284.

Basil the Great. "Asceticon magnum" *sive* "Quaestiones" [regulae brevius tractatae]. In *Opera omnia*. PG 31, cols. 1052-305. Edited by J.-P. Migne. Paris: Migne, 1885. TLG 2040.050.

———. "Asceticon magnum" *sive* "Quaestiones" [regulae fusius tractatae]. In *Opera omnia*. PG 31, cols. 905-1052. Edited by J.-P. Migne. Paris: Migne, 1857. TLG 2040.048.

———. "Homiliae in hexaemeron." In *Opera omnia*. PG 29, cols. 3-208. Edited by J.-P. Migne. Paris: Migne, 1857. TLG 2040.001.

———. "Homiliae super Psalmos." In *Opera omnia*. PG 29, cols. 209-494. Edited by J.-P. Migne. Paris: Migne, 1857. TLG 2040.018.

———. "Epistulae." In *Saint Basil: Lettres*. Edited by Yves Courtonne. Vol. 2, pp. 101-218; vol. 3, pp. 1-229. Paris: Les Belles Lettres, 1961-1966. TLG 2040.004.

———. *De spiritu sancto*. In *Basile de Césarée: Sur le Saint-Esprit*. Edited by Benoit Pruche. SC 17. Paris: Éditions du Cerf, 2002. TLG 2040.003.

———. "Regulae moralis." In *Opera Omnia*. PG 31, cols. 692-869. Edited by J.-P. Migne. Paris: Migne, 1885. TLG 2040.051.

Bede. "Expositio Actuum apostolorum." In *Bedae opera*. Edited M. L. W. Laistner. CCL 121, pp. 3-99. Turnhout, Belgium: Brepols, 1983. Cl. 1357.

Cassian, John. *Collationes xxiv*. Edited by Michael Petschenig. CSEL 13. Vienna, Austria: F. Tempsky; Leipzig, Germany: G. Freytag, 1886. Cl. 0512.

———. "De institutis coenobiorum et de octo principalium vitiorum remediis." In *Johannis Cassiani*. Edited by Michael Petschenig. CSEL 17, pp. 1-231. Vienna, Austria: F. Tempsky; Leipzig, Germany: G. Freytag, 1888. Cl. 0513.

———. "De incarnatione Domini contra Nestorium." In *Johannis Cassiani*. Edited by Michael Petschenig.

CSEL 17, pp. 233-391. Vienna, Austria: F. Tempsky; Leipzig, Germany: G. Freytag, 1888. Cl. 0514.

Cassiodorus. *Expositio Psalmorum*. Edited by Marcus Adriaen. CCL 97, 98. Turnhout: Brepols, 1958. Cl. 0900.

"Catena in Acta." See *Catenae Graecorum patrum in Novum Testamentum*, vol. 3. Edited by J. A. Cramer. Oxford: Oxford University Press, 1838; reprinted, Hildesheim: Olms, 1967. TLG 4102.008.

Clement of Alexandria. "Stromata." In *Clemens Alexandrinus*. Vol. 2, 3rd ed., and vol. 3, 2nd ed. Edited by Otto Stählin, Ludwig Früchtel and Ursula Treu. GCS 15, pp. 3-518 and GCS 17, pp. 1-102. Berlin: Akademie-Verlag, 1960-1970. TLG 0555.004.

Cyprian. "De opera et eleemosynis." In *Sancti Cypriani episcopi opera*. Edited by Manlio Simonetti. CCL 3A, pp. 53-72. Turnhout, Belgium: Brepols, 1976. Cl. 0047.

———. *Epistulae*. Edited by G. F. Diercks. CCL 3B, 3C. Turnhout, Belgium: Brepols, 1994-1996. Cl. 0050.

Cyril of Alexandria. "Catena in Acta (catena Andreae) (e cod. Oxon. coll. nov. 58)." In *Catenae Graecorum patrum in Novum Testamentum*, vol. 3, pp. 1-424. Edited by J. A. Cramer. Oxford: Oxford University Press, 1838; reprinted, Hildesheim: Olms, 1967. TLG 4102.008.

———. "Contra Julianum." In *S. P. N. Cyrilii: Opera quae reperiri patuerunt omnia*. PG 76, cols. 489-1058. Edited by J.-P. Migne. Paris: Migne, 1863.

Cyril of Jeruslaem. "Catecheses ad illuminandos 1-18." In *Cyrilli Hierosolymorum archiepiscopi opera quae supersunt omnia*, 1:28-320; 2:2-342. 2 vols. Edited by W. C. Reischl and J. Rupp. Munich: Lentner, 1860 (repr. Hildesheim: Olms, 1967). TLG 2110.003.

Didymus the Blind. "Catena in Acta (catena Andreae) (e cod. Oxon. coll. nov. 58)." In *Catenae Graecorum patrum in Novum Testamentum*, vol. 3, pp. 1-424. Edited by J. A. Cramer. Oxford: Oxford University Press, 1838; reprinted, Hildesheim: Olms, 1967. TLG 4102.008.

———. "Fragmenta expositionis in Actus apostolorum ex Wolfii Anecdotis." In *Opera omnia*. PG 39, cols. 1653-78. Edited by J.-P. Migne. Paris: Migne, 1863. TLG 2102.x07.

Ephrem the Syrian. "Hymni de Paradiso." In *Des Heiligen Ephraem des Syrers Hymnen de Paradiso und Contra Julianum*. Edited by Edmund Beck. CSCO 174 (Scriptores Syri 78), pp. 1-66. Louvain: Imprimerie Orientaliste L. Durbecq, 1957.

———. *In Tatiani Diatessaron*. In *Saint Éphrem: Commentaire de l'Évangile Concordant—Text Syriaque (Ms Chester-Beatty 709)*, vol. 2. Edited by Louis Leloir. Leuven and Paris: Peeters Press, 1990.

———. "Sermo de Domino nostro." In *Des Heiligen Ephraem des Syrers Sermo de Domino Nostro*. Edited by Edmund Beck. CSCO 270 (Scriptores Syri 116). Louvain: Imprimerie Orientaliste L. Durbecq, 1966.

Epistula ad Diognetum = A Diognète. Edited by Henri Irénée Marrou. 2nd ed. SC 33. Paris: Éditions du Cerf, 1965. TLG 1350.001.

Eusebius of Caesarea. "Commentarius in Isaiam." In *Eusebius Werke, Band 9: Der Jesajakommentar*. Edited by Joseph Ziegler. GCS 66. Berlin: Akademie-Verlag, 1975. TLG 2018.019.

———. "Demonstratio evangelica." In *Eusebius Werke, Band 6: Die Demonstratio evangelica*. Edited by Ivar A. Heikel. GCS 23. Leipzig: Hinrichs, 1913. TLG 2018.005.

———. "Historia ecclesiastica." In *Eusèbe de Césarée. Histoire ecclésiastique*, 3 vols. Edited by G. Bardy. SC 31, pp. 3-215; SC 41, pp. 4-231; SC 51, pp. 3-120. Paris: Éditions du Cerf, 1952, 1955, 1958. TLG 2018.002.

Fulgentius of Ruspe. *Epistulae XVIII*. In *Sancti Fulgentii episcopi Ruspensis Opera*. Edited by John Fraipont. CCL 91, pp. 189-280, 311-12, 359-444; and CCL 91A, 447-57, 551-629. Turnhout, Belgium: Brepols, 1968. Cl. 0817.

Gregory of Nazianzus. "De spiritu sancto (orat. 31)." In *Gregor von Nazianz. Die fünf theologischen Reden*, pp. 218-76. Edited by J. Barbel. Düsseldorf, Germany: Patmos-Verlag, 1963. TLG 2022.011.

Gregory of Nyssa. "Ablabium quod non sint tres dei." In *Gregorii Nysseni opera*, vol. 3.1, pp. 37-57. Edited by F. Mueller. Leiden: Brill, 1958. TLG 2017.003.

———. "Ad Eustathium de Sancta Trinitate." In *Gregorii Nysseni opera*, vol. 3.1, pp. 3-16. Edited by F. Mueller. Leiden: Brill, 1958. TLG 2017.001.

———. "Antirrheticus adversus Apollinarium." In *Gregorii Nysseni opera*, vol. 3.1, pp. 131-233. Edited by F. Mueller. Leiden: Brill, 1958. TLG 2017.008.

———. "Contra Eunomium." In *Gregorii Nysseni opera*, 2 vols. Edited by W. Jaeger. Vol. 1.1, pp. 3-409; vol. 2.2, pp. 3-311. Leiden: Brill, 1960. TLG 2017.030.

———. "De perfectione Christiana ad Olympium monachum." In *Gregorii Nysseni opera*. Edited by W. Jaeger. Vol. 8.1, pp. 173-214. Leiden: Brill, 1963. TLG 2017.026.

———. "De vita Mosis." In *Grégoire de Nysse. La vie de Moïse*. Edited by J. Daniélou. 3rd ed. SC 1, pp. 44-326. Paris: Éditions du Cerf, 1968. TLG 2017.042.

———. "Encomium in sanctum Stephanum protomartyrem ii: sermons 2" In *GNO*, Vol 10.1, pp. 75-94. Edited by O. Lendle. Leiden: Brill, 1990. TLG 2017.064.

———. "In Canticum canticorum (homiliae 15)." In *Gregorii Nysseni opera*. Vol. 6, pp. 3-469. Edited by H. Langerbeck. Leiden: Brill, 1960. TLG 2017.032.

———. "Refutatio confessionis Eunomii." In *Gregorii Nysseni opera*, vol. 2.2, pp. 312-410. Edited by W. Jaeger. Leiden: Brill, 1960. TLG 2017.031.

Gregory the Great. *Registrum epistularum*. 2 vols. Edited by Dag Norberg. CCL 140, 140A. Turnhout, Belgium: Brepols, 1982. Cl. 0714.

———. *Regula pastoralis*. Quoted by Bede in "Expositio Actuum apostolorum" in *Bedae opera*. Edited M. L. W. Laistner. CCL 121, pp. 3-99. Turnhout, Belgium: Brepols, 1983. Cl. 1357.

Hilary of Poitiers. *De Trinitate*. Edited by P. Smulders. CCL 62 and 62A. Turnhout, Belgium: Brepols, 1979-1980. Cl. 0433.

Irenaeus. "Adversus haereses [liber 3]." In *Irénée de Lyon. Contre les heresies, livre 3*, vol. 2. Edited by Adelin. Rousseau and Louis Doutreleau. SC 211. Paris: Éditions du Cerf, 1974. Cl. 1154.

———. "Catena in Acta (catena Andreae) (e cod. Oxon. coll. nov. 58)." Pages 1-424 in *Catenae Graecorum patrum in Novum Testamentum*, vol. 3. Edited by J. A. Cramer. Oxford: Oxford University Press, 1838; reprinted, Hildesheim: Olms, 1967. TLG 4102.008.

Isidore of Pelusium. "Catena in Acta (catena Andreae) (e cod. Oxon. coll. nov. 58)." In *Catenae Graecorum patrum in Novum Testamentum*, vol. 3, pp. 1-424. Edited by J. A. Cramer. Oxford: Oxford University Press, 1838; reprinted, Hildesheim: Olms, 1967. TLG 4102.008.

Jerome. "Adversus Jovinianum." In *Opera omnia*. PL 23, cols. 211-338. Edited by J.-P. Migne. Paris: Migne, 1845. Cl. 0610.

———. "Contra Vigilantium." In *Opera omnia*. PL 23, cols. 339-52. Edited by J.-P. Migne. Paris: Migne, 1845. Cl. 0611.

———. "De viris inlustribus." In *Texte und Untersuchungen zur Geschichte der Altchristlichen Literatur*, 14, 1a, pp. 1-56. Edited by Ernest Cushing Richardson. Leipzig: J. C. Hinrichs, 1896. Cl. 0616.

———. *Epistulae*. Edited by I. Hilberg. CSEL 54, 55, 56. Vienna, Austria: F. Tempsky; Leipzig, Germany: G. F. Freytag, 1910-1918. Cl. 0620.

———. "Tractatus lix in psalmos." In *S. Hieronymi Presbyteri opera*. Edited by Germain Morin. CCL 78, pp. 3-352. Turnhout, Belgium: Brepols, 1958. Cl. 0592.

John Chrysostom. "Ad populam Antiochenum homiliae (de statuis)." In *Opera omnia*. Edited by J.-P. Migne. PG 49, cols. 15-222. Paris: Migne, 1862. TLG 2062.024.

———. "Catecheses ad illuminandos 1-8 (series tertia)." In *Jean Chrysostome: Huit catéchèses baptismales*,

2nd edition. Edited by Antoine Wenger. SC 50, pp. Paris: Éditions du Cerf, 1970. TLG 2062.382.

———. "Catena in Acta (catena Andreae) (e cod. Oxon. coll. nov. 58)." In *Catenae Graecorum patrum in Novum Testamentum*, vol. 3, pp. 1-424. Edited by J. A. Cramer. Oxford: Oxford University Press, 1838; reprinted, Hildesheim: Olms, 1967. TLG 4102.008.

———. "Contra Anomoeos (homiliae 11): De incomprehensibili dei natura." In *Opera omnia*. Edited by J.-P. Migne. PG 48, cols. 795-802. Paris: Migne, 1862. TLG 2062.012.

———. "Contra Anomoeos [homilia 12]: De Christi divinitate." In *Opera omnia*. PG 48, cols. 801-12. Edited by J.-P. Migne. Paris: Migne, 1859. TLG 2062.020.

———. "In Acta apostolorum (homiliae 1-55)." In *Opera omnia*. Edited by J.-P. Migne. PG 60, cols. 13-384. Paris: Migne, 1862. TLG 2062.154.

———. "In epistulam ad Hebraeos (homiliae 1-34)." In *Opera omnia*. Edited by J.-P. Migne. PG 63, cols. 9-236. Paris: Migne, 1862. TLG 2062.168.

———. "In epistulam ad Romanos." In *Opera omnia*. Edited by J.-P. Migne. PG 60, cols. 391-682. Paris: Migne, 1862. TLG 2062.155.

———. "In epistulam i ad Corinthios (homiliae 1-44)." In *Opera omnia*. Edited by J.-P. Migne. PG 61, cols. 9-382. Paris: Migne, 1862. TLG 2062.156.

———. "In epistulam ii ad Corinthios (homiliae 1-30)." In *Opera omnia*. Edited by J.-P. Migne. PG 61, cols. 381-610. Paris: Migne, 1862. TLG 2062.157.

———. "In Genesim (homiliae 1-67)." In *Opera omnia*. Edited by J.-P. Migne. PG 53, 54, cols. 385-580. Paris: Migne, 1859-1862. TLG 2062.112.

———. "In Joannem (homiliae 1-88)." In *Opera omnia*. Edited by J.-P. Migne. PG 59, cols. 23-482. Paris: Migne, 1862. TLG 2062.153.

———. "In Matthaeum (homiliae 1-90)." In *Opera omnia*. Edited by J.-P. Migne. PG 57-58. Paris: Migne, 1862. TLG 2062.152.

Justin Martyr. "Apologia." In *Die ältesten Apologeten*, pp. 26-77. Edited by E. J. Goodspeed. Göttingen, Germany: Vandenhoeck & Ruprecht, 1915. TLG 0645.001.

Leo the Great. *Tractatus septem et nonaginta*. In *Léon le Grand: Sermons 3*. Edited by René Dolle. 2nd ed. SC 74. Paris: Éditions du Cerf, 1976. Cl. 1657.

Origen. *Catena Palestinensis*. In *La chaîne Palestinienne sur le Psaume 118*, passim. Edited by Marguerite Harl with the collaboration of Gilles Dorival. SC 189. Paris: Éditions du Cerf, 1972. TLG 4142.001.

———. *Commentarii in evangelium Joannis (lib. 1, 2, 4, 5, 6, 10, 13)*. In *Origenes Werke*, vol. 4. Edited by Erwin Preuschen. GCS 10. Leipzig: H. C. Hinrichs, 1903. TLG 2042.005.

———. "Commentariorum in Epistolam B. Pauli ad Romanos." In *Origenis: Opera omnia*. PG 14, cols. 837-1292. Edited by J.-P. Migne. Paris: Migne, 1862.

———. "Commentarium in evangelium Matthaei [lib. 12-17]." In *Origenes Werke*, 2 vols. Vols 10.1 and 10.2. Edited by E. Klostermann. GCS 40.1, pp. 69-304; GCS 40.2, pp. 305-703. Leipzig: Teubner, 1935-1937. TLG 2042.030.

———. "Contra Celsum." In *Origène Contre Celse*. Edited by M. Borret. SC 132, 136, 147 and 150. Paris: Éditions du Cerf, 1967-1969. TLG 2042.001.

———. "De principiis." In *Origenes vier Bücher von den Prinzipien*, pp. 462-560, 668-764. Edited by Herwig Görgemanns and Heinrich Karpp. Darmstadt, Germany: Wissenschaftliche Buchgesellschaft, 1976. TLG 2042.002.

———. *Fragmenta ex commentariis in epistulam i ad Corinthios (in catenis)*. See "Documents: Origen on 1 Corinthians." Edited by Claude Jenkins. JTS 9, pp. 232-47, 353-72, 500-514; JTS 10, pp. 29-51. Oxford: Clarendon Press, 1908-1909. TLG 2042.034.

———. "Homiliae in Exodum." In *Origenes Werke*, vol. 6. Edited by W. A. Baehrens. GCS 29, pp. 217-

30. Leipzig: Teubner, 1920. Cl. 0198/TLG 2042.023.

———. "Homiliae in Genesim." In *Origène: Homélies sur la Genèse*. Edited by Henri de Lubac and Louis Doutreleau. 2nd ed. SC 7. Paris: Éditions du Cerf, 2003. Cl. 0198/TLG 2042.022.

———. "Homiliae in Leviticum." In *Origenes Werke*, vol. 6. Edited by W. A. Baehrens. GCS 29, pp. 332-34, 395, 402-7, 409-16. Leipzig: Teubner, 1920. TLG 2042.024.

———. "Homiliae in Lucam." In *Opera omnia*. PG 13, cols. 1799-1902. Edited by J.-P. Migne. Paris: Migne, 1862. TLG 2042.016.

———. "In Jeremiam [homiliae 12-20]." In *Origène: Homélies sur Jérémie et Homélies latines*. Edited by Pierre Husson and Pierre Nautin. SC 238, pp. 10-298. Paris: Éditions du Cerf, 1977. TLG 2042.021.

———. "In Jesu nave." In *Homélies sur Josué*. Edited by Annie Jaubert. SC 71. Paris: Éditions du Cerf, 1960. TLG 2042.025.

———. "In Numeros homiliea." See *Origène: Homélies sur les Nombres*, vols. 2-3. Edited by Louis Dourtreleau. SC 442, 461. Paris: Éditions du Cerf, 1999-2001. Cl. 0198.

Paulus Orosius. "Liber apologeticus contra Pelagianos." In *Sancti Paulus orosius. Opera*. Edited by C. Zangemeister. CSEL 5, pp. 603-64. Vienna: F. Tempsky, 1882. Cl. 0572.

Polycarp of Smyrna. "Epistula ad Philippenses." Pages 114-20 in *Die apostolischen Väter*. Edited by K. Bihlmeyer and W. Schneemelcher. 3rd ed. Tübingen: Mohr, 1970. TLG 1622.001.

Pseudo-Basil. "Adversus Eunomium (libri 5)." Lib. 4-5 [Sp.] are col. 672-768 in MPG 29. TLG 2040.019.

Pseudo-Justin. "De resurrectione." Pages 210-248 in *Corpus apologetarum Christianorum saeculi secundi*, vol. 3. Edited by J. C. T. Otto. 3rd ed. Jena: Mauke, 1879; reprint: Wiesbaden: Sändig, 1971. TLG 0646.005.

Severus of Antioch. "Catena in Acta (catena Andreae) (e cod. Oxon. coll. nov. 58)." In *Catenae Graecorum patrum in Novum Testamentum*, vol. 3, pp. 1-424. Edited by J. A. Cramer. Oxford: Oxford University Press, 1838; reprinted, Hildesheim: Olms, 1967. TLG 4102.008.

Tertullian. "De baptismo." In *Tertulliani opera*. Edited by J. G. P. H. Borleffs. CCL 1, pp. 277-95. Turnhout, Belgium: Brepols, 1954. Cl. 0008.

Theodoret of Cyr. "Catena in Acta (catena Andreae) (e cod. Oxon. coll. nov. 58)." In *Catenae Graecorum patrum in Novum Testamentum*, vol. 3, pp. 1-424. Edited by J. A. Cramer. Oxford: Oxford University Press, 1838; reprinted, Hildesheim: Olms, 1967. TLG 4102.008.

———. "Epistulae: Collectio Sirmondiana (epistulae 1-95)." In *Théodoret de Cyr: Correspondance II*. SC 98, pp. 20-248. Edited by Y. Azéma. Paris: Éditions du Cerf, 1964. TLG 4089.006.

———. "Epistulae: Collectio Sirmondiana (epistulae 96-147)." In *Théodoret de Cyr: Correspondance III*. SC 111, pp. 10-232. Edited by Y. Azéma. Paris: Éditions du Cerf, 1965. TLG 4089.007.

———. "Eranistes." Pages 61-266 In *Theodoret of Cyrus: Eranistes*. Edited by G. H. Ettlinger. Oxford: Clarendon Press, 1975. TLG 4089.002.

Bibliography of Works
in English Translation

Ambrose. *Letters*. Translated by Mary Melchior Beyenka. FC 26. Washington, D.C.: The Catholic University of America Press, 1954.

———. "On His Brother Satyrus." In *Funeral Orations by Saint Gregory Nazianzen and Saint Ambrose*, pp. 157-259. Translated by John J. Sullivan and Martin R. P. McGuire. FC 22. Washington, D.C.: The Catholic University of America Press, 1953.

———. *Select Works and Letters*. Translated by H. De Romestin. NPNF 10. Series 2. Edited by Philip Schaff and Henry Wace. 14 vols. 1886-1900. Reprint, Peabody, Mass.: Hendrickson, 1994.

———. *Seven Exegetical Works*. Translated by Michael P. McHugh. FC 65. Washington, D.C.: The Catholic University of America Press, 1972.

[Arator]. *Arator's On the Acts of the Apostles*. Edited and translated by Richard J. Schrader. Cotranslated by Joseph L. Roberts III and John F. Makowski. Classics in Religious Studies 6. Atlanta: Scholars Press, 1987.

Athanasius. "Festal Letters." In *Selected Works and Letters*, pp. 500-553. Translated by Archibald Robertson. NPNF 4. Series 2. Edited by Philip Schaff and Henry Wace. 14 vols. 1886-1900. Reprint, Peabody, Mass.: Hendrickson, 1994.

Augustine. "Answer to the Two Letters of the Pelagians." In *Answer to the Pelagians*, vol. 2, pp. 97-219. Translated by Roland J. Teske. *WSA* 24. Part 1. Edited by John E. Rotelle. New York: New City Press, 1998.

———. *Anti-Pelagian Writings*. Translated by Peter Holmes and Robert Ernest Wallis. NPNF 5. Series 1. Edited by Philip Schaff. 14 vols. 1886-1889. Reprint, Peabody, Mass.: Hendrickson, 1994.

———. *Augustine: Later Works*. Translated by John Burnaby. LCC 8. London: SCM Press, 1955.

———. "Christian Instruction." In *City of God, Christian Doctrine*, pp. 513-97. Translated by Marcus Dods and J. F. Shaw. NPNF 2. Series 1. Edited by Philip Schaff. 14 vols. 1886-1889. Reprint, Peabody, Mass.: Hendrickson, 1994.

———. *Expositions of the Psalms, 73-98*. Translated by Maria Boulding. *WSA* 18. Part 3. Edited by John E. Rotelle. New York: New City Press, 2002.

———. *Homilies on the Gospel of John, Homilies on the First Epistle of John, Soliloquies*. Translated by John Gibb et al. NPNF 7. Series 1. Edited by Philip Schaff. 14 vols. 1886-1889. Reprint, Peabody, Mass.: Hendrickson, 1994.

———. *Letters*. Translated by Sister Wilfrid Parsons. FC 12, 18, 20, 30 and 32. Washington, D.C.: The Catholic University of America Press, 1951-1955.

———. "On the Merits and Forgiveness of Sins and on Infant Baptism." In *Answer to the Pelagians*, vol. 1, pp. 17-137. Translated by Roland J. Teske. *WSA* 23. Part 1. Edited by John E. Rotelle. New York: New City Press, 1997.

———. "Sermon on the Mount." In *Saint Augustine: Commentary on the Lord's Sermon on the Mount with Seventeen Related Sermons*, pp. 17-199. Translated by Denis J. Kavanagh. FC 11. Washington, D.C.: The Catholic University of America Press, 1951.

———. "The Letters of St. Augustine." In *Prolegomena, Confessions, Letters*, pp. 219-593. Translated by J. G. Cunningham. NPNF 1. Series 1. Edited by Philip Schaff. 14 vols. 1886-1889. Reprint, Peabody,

Mass.: Hendrickson, 1994.

———. *Tractates on the Gospel of John, 1-124*, 4 vols. Translated by John W. Rettig. FC 78, 88, 90 and 92. Washington, D.C.: The Catholic University of America Press, 1988-1995.

———. *Sermon on the Mount, Harmony of the Gospels, Homilies on the Gospels.* Translated by William Findlay, S. D. F. Salmond and R. G. MacMullen. NPNF 6. Series 1. Edited by Philip Schaff. 14 vols. 1886-1889. Reprint, Peabody, Mass.: Hendrickson, 1994.

———. *Sermons (51-147a).* Translated by Edmund Hill. WSA 3, 4. Part 3. Edited by John E. Rotelle. New York: New City Press, 1991-1992

———. *Sermons on the Liturgical Seasons.* Translated by Mary Sarah Muldowney. FC 38. Washington, D.C.: The Catholic University of America Press, 1959.

Basil the Great. *Letters and Select Works.* Translated by Blomfield Jackson. NPNF 8. Series 2. Edited by Philip Schaff. 14 vols. 1886-1889. Reprint, Peabody, Mass.: Hendrickson, 1994.

———. *Letters (1-185).* Translated by Agnes C. Way. FC 13. Washington, D.C.: The Catholic University of America Press, 1951.

———. *On the Holy Spirit.* Translated by D. Anderson, Crestwood, N.Y. : St. Vladimir's Press, 1980.

Bede. *Commentary on the Acts of the Apostles.* Translated, with an Introduction and Notes by Lawrence T. Martin. CS 117. Kalamazoo, Mich.: Cistercian Publications, 1989.

Cassian, John. "On the Incarnation of the Lord Against Nestorius." *Sulpicius Severus, Vincent of Lerins, John Cassian*, pp. 547-621. Translated by Edgar C. S. Gibson. NPNF 11. Series 2. Edited by Philip Schaff and Henry Wace. 14 vols. 1886-1900. Reprint, Peabody, Mass.: Hendrickson, 1994.

———. *The Conferences.* Translated and annotated by Boniface Ramsey. ACW 57. New York: Paulist Press, 1997.

———. *The Institutes.* Translated and annotated by Boniface Ramsey. ACW 58. New York: Paulist Press, 2000.

Cassiodorus. *Explanation of the Psalms.* Translated by P. G. Walsh. ACW 51 and 52. New York: Paulist Press, 1990-1991.

Clement of Alexandria. "Stromateis." In *Fathers of the Second Century: Hermas, Tatian, Athenagoras, Theophilus, and Clement of Alexandria*, pp. 299-568. Translated by F. Crombie et al. ANF 2. Edited by Alexander Roberts and James Donaldson. 10 vols. 1885-1887. Reprint, Peabody, Mass.: Hendrickson, 1994.

———. *Stromateis: Books 1-3.* Translated by John Ferguson. FC 85. Washington, D.C.: The Catholic University of America Press, 1991.

Cyprian. "Letters." In *Early Latin Theology*, pp. 143-72. Translated and edited by S. L. Greenslade. LCC 5. Philadelphia: Westminster Press, 1956.

———. "Works and Almsgiving." In *Treatises*, pp. 223-53. Translated and edited by Roy J. Deferrari. FC 36. Washington, D.C.: The Catholic University of America Press, 1958.

Cyril of Jerusalem. "Catechetical Lectures." In *S. Cyril of Jerusalem, S. Gregory Nazianzen*, pp. 1-202. Translated by Edward Hamilton Gifford et al. NPNF 7. Series 2. Edited by Philip Schaff and Henry Wace. 14 vols. 1886-1900. Reprint, Peabody, Mass.: Hendrickson, 1994.

———. *The Works of Saint Cyril of Jerusalem.* Translated by Leo P. McCauley and Anthony A. Stephenson. FC 61 and 64. Washington, D.C.: The Catholic University of America Press, 1969-1970.

Ephrem the Syrian. "Homily on Our Lord." In *St. Ephrem the Syrian: Selected Prose Works*, pp. 267-332. Translated by Edward G. Mathews, Jr. and Joseph P. Amar. FC 91. Edited by Kathleen McVey. Washington, D.C.: The Catholic University of America, 1994.

———. *Hymns on Paradise.* Translated by S. Brock. Crestwood, N.Y.: St. Vladimir's Seminary Press, 1990.

———. *Saint Ephrem's Commentary on Tatian's Diatessaron: An English Translation of Chester Beatty Syriac MS 709*. Translated and edited by C. McCarthy. Journal of Semitic Studies Supplement 2. Oxford: Oxford University Press for the University of Manchester, 1993.

Eusebius of Caesarea. "Church History." In *Eusebius: Church History, Life of Constantine the Great, and Oration in Praise of Constantine*, pp. 73-403. Translated by Arthur Cushman McGiffert. NPNF 1. Series 2. Edited by Philip Schaff and Henry Wace. 14 vols. 1886-1900. Reprint, Peabody, Mass.: Hendrickson, 1994.

———. *Ecclesiastical History: Books 1-5*. Translated by Roy J. Deferrari. FC 19. Washington D.C.: The Catholic University of America Press, 1953.

———. *Proof of the Gospel*. 2 vols. Translated by W. J. Ferrar. London: SPCK, 1920. Reprint, Grand Rapids, Mich.: Baker, 1981.

Fulgentius of Ruspe. "Letters." In *Selected Works*, pp. 277-565. Translated by Robert B. Eno. FC 95. Washington, D.C.: The Catholic University of America Press, 1997.

Gregory of Nazianzus. "On the Holy Spirit, Theological Oration 5 (31)." In *Cyril of Jerusalem, Gregory Nazianzen*, pp. 318-28. Translated by Charles Gordon Browne and James Edward Swallow. NPNF 7. Series 2. Edited by Philip Schaff and Henry Wace. 14 vols. 1886-1900. Reprint, Peabody, Mass.: Hendrickson, 1994.

Gregory of Nyssa. *Gregory of Nyssa: The Life of Moses*. Translated by A. J. Malherbe and E. Ferguson. Classics of Western Spirituality. New York: Paulist Press, 1978.

———. "On Perfection." In *Ascetical Works*, pp. 91-122. Translated by Virginia Woods Callahan. FC 58. Washington D.C.: The Catholic University of America Press, 1967.

———. *Select Writings and Letters of Gregory, Bishop of Nyssa*. Translated by William Moore and Henry Austin Wilson. NPNF 5. Series 2. Edited by Philip Schaff and Henry Wace. 14 vols. 1886-1900. Reprint, Peabody, Mass.: Hendrickson, 1994.

Gregory the Great. "Letters." In *Gregory the Great, Ephraim Syrus, Aphrahat*, pp. 1-111. Translated by James Barmby. NPNF 13. Series 2. Edited by Philip Schaff and Henry Wace. 14 vols. 1886-1900. Reprint, Peabody, Mass.: Hendrickson, 1994.

———. "Pastoral Care." Quoted by Bede in *Commentary on the Acts of the Apostles*, p. 162.. Translated, with an Introduction and Notes by Lawrence T. Martin. CS 117. Kalamazoo, Mich.: Cistercian Publications, 1989.

Hilary of Poitiers. *The Trinity*. Translated by Stephen McKenna. FC 25. Washington, D.C.: The Catholic University of America Press, 1954.

Irenaeus. "Against Heresies." In *The Apostolic Fathers with Justin Martyr and Irenaeus*, pp. 309-567. Translated by A. Cleveland Coxe. ANF 1. Edited by Alexander Roberts and James Donaldson. 10 vols. 1885-1887. Reprint, Peabody, Mass.: Hendrickson, 1994.

Jerome. *Letters and Select Works*. Translated by W. H. Fremantle. NPNF 6. Series 2. Edited by Philip Schaff and Henry Wace. 14 vols. 1886-1900. Reprint, Peabody, Mass.: Hendrickson, 1994.

———. "Letter 75." In *Saint Augustine: Letters (1-82)*, vol. 1, pp.342-67. Translated by Wilfrid Parsons. FC 12. Washington, D.C.: The Catholic University of America Press, 1951.

———. *Saint Jerome: On Illustrious Men*. Translated by Thomas P. Halton. FC 100. Washington, D.C.: The Catholic University of America Press, 1999.

———. *The Homilies of Saint Jerome (1-59 on the Psalms)*. Translated by Marie Liguori Ewald. FC 48. Washington, D.C.: The Catholic University of America Press, 1964.

John Chrysostom. "Against the Anomoeans." In *On the Incomprehensible Nature of God*. Translated by Paul W. Harkins. FC 72. Washington, D.C.: The Catholic University of America Press, 1984.

———. *Baptismal Instructions*. Translated by Paul W. Harkins. ACW 31. New York: Newman Press,

1963.

————. *Chrysostom: Homilies on the Gospel of Saint John and the Epistle to the Hebrew.* Translated by Philip Schaff and Frederic Gardiner. NPNF 14. Series 1. Edited by Philip Schaff. 14 vols. 1886-1889. Reprint, Peabody, Mass.: Hendrickson, 1994.

————. "Homilies Concerning the Statues." In *On the Priesthood, Ascetic Treatises, Select Homilies and Letters, Homilies on the Statues,* pp. 331-489. Translated by W. R. W. Stephens et al. NPNF 9. Series 1. Edited by Philip Schaff. 14 vols. 1886-1889. Reprint, Peabody, Mass.: Hendrickson, 1994.

————. *Homilies on Genesis 18-45.* Translated by Robert C. Hill. FC 82. Washington, D.C.: The Catholic University of America Press, 1990.

————. *Homilies on the Acts of the Apostles and the Epistle to the Romans.* Translated by J. Walker et al. NPNF 11. Series 1. Edited by Philip Schaff. 14 vols. 1886-1889. Reprint, Peabody, Mass.: Hendrickson, 1994.

————. *Homilies on the Epistles of Paul to the Corinthians.* Translated by Talbot W. Chambers. NPNF 12. Series 1. Edited by Philip Schaff. 14 vols. 1886-1889. Reprint, Peabody, Mass.: Hendrickson, 1994.

————. *Homilies on the Gospel of Saint Matthew.* The Oxford translation. NPNF 10. Series 1. Edited by Philip Schaff. 14 vols. 1886-1889. Reprint, Peabody, Mass.: Hendrickson, 1994.

————. *Saint John Chrysostom: Commentary on Saint John the Apostle and Evangelist.* Translated by Thomas Aquinas Goggin. FC 33 and 41. Washington, D.C.: The Catholic University of America Press, 1957-1959.

Justin Martyr. "First Apology." In *The Apostolic Fathers with Justin Martyr and Irenaeus,* pp. 163-87. Arranged by A. Cleveland Coxe. ANF 1. Edited by Alexander Roberts and James Donaldson. 10 vols. 1885-1887. Reprint, Peabody, Mass.: Hendrickson, 1994.

Leo the Great. *Sermons.* Translated by Jane Freeland et al. FC 93. Washington, D.C.: The Catholic University of America Press, 1996.

Origen. "Against Celsus." In *Tertullian (IV); Minucius Felix; Commodian; Origen (I and III),* pp. 395-669. Translated by Frederick Combie. ANF 4. Edited by Alexander Roberts and James Donaldson. 10 vols. 1885-1887. Reprint, Peabody, Mass.: Hendrickson, 1994.

————. *Contra Celsum.* Translated with an Introduction and Notes by Henry Chadwick. Cambridge: Cambridge University Press, 1953.

————. "Commentary on the Epistle to the Romans." In *Origen: Spirit and Fire, A Thematic Anthology of His Writings,* passim. Edited by Hans Urs von Balthasar. Translated by Robert J. Daly. Washington, D.C.: Catholic University Press of America, 1984.

————. *Commentary on the Gospel According to John Books 13-32.* Translated by Ronald E. Heine. FC 89. Washington, D.C.: The Catholic University of America Press, 1993.

————. "Commentary on the Gospel of John." In *The Gospel of Peter, The Diatessaron of Tatian, The Apocalypse of Peter, The Vision of Paul, The Apocalypse of the Virgin and Sedrach, The Testament of Abraham, The Acts of Xanthippe and Polyxena, The Narrative of Zosimus, The Apology of Aristides, The Epistles of Clement, Origen's Commentary on John (Books 1-10), and Commentary on Matthew (Books 1, 2, and 10-14),"* pp. 297-408. Translated by Allan Menzies. ANF 9. Edited by Alexander Roberts and James Donaldson. 10 vols. 1885-1887. Reprint, Peabody, Mass.: Hendrickson, 1994.

————. *Homilies on Genesis and Exodus.* Translated by Ronald E. Heine. FC 71. Washington, D.C.: The Catholic University of America Press, 1982.

————. *Homilies on Leviticus: 1-16.* Translated by Gary Wayne Barkley. FC 83. Washington, D.C.: The Catholic University of America Press, 1990.

————. *Homilies on Luke; Fragments on Luke.* Translated by Joseph T. Lienhard. FC 94. Washington, D.C.: The Catholic University of America Press, 1996.

————. *On First Principles*. Translated by G. W. Butterworth. London: SPCK, 1936. Reprint, Gloucester, Mass.: Peter Smith, 1973.

Orosius. "Defense Against the Pelagians." In *Iberian Fathers: Pacian of Barcelona, Orosius of Braga*, pp. 115-67. FC 99. Translated by Craig L. Hanson. Washington, D.C.: The Catholic University of America Press, 1999.

Polycarp of Smyrna. "Letter to the Philippians." In *The Apostolic Fathers with Justin Martyr and Irenaeus*, pp. 31-36. Translated by A. Cleveland Coxe. ANF 1. Edited by Alexander Roberts and James Donaldson. 10 vols. 1885-1887. Reprint, Peabody, Mass.: Hendrickson, 1994.

Pseudo-Justin. "Fragments of the Lost Work of Justin on the Resurrection." In *The Apostolic Fathers with Justin Martyr and Irenaeus*, pp. 294-99. Translated by Marcus Dods. ANF 1. Edited by Alexander Roberts and James Donaldson. 10 vols. 1885-1887. Reprint, Peabody, Mass.: Hendrickson, 1994.

Theodoret of Cyr. "Theodoret." In *Theodoret, Jerome, Gennadius, Rufinus: Historical Writings, etc.*, pp. 1-348. Translated by Blomfield Jackson. NPNF 3. Series 2. Edited by Philip Schaff and Henry Wace. 14 vols. 1886-1900. Reprint, Peabody, Mass.: Hendrickson, 1994.

See the volume *Commentary Index and Resources* for a collection of supplemental ACCS material, including a comprehensive Scripture index and authors/writings index.

Subject Index